A Guide to Fiction Set in Vermont

A Guide to Fiction Set in Vermont

Ann McKinstry Micou

VERMONT
Humanities
COUNCIL

Montpelier, Vermont

2005

Vermont Humanities Council

11 Loomis Street, Montpelier, Vermont 05602-3021

802.262.2626

info@vermonthumanities.org

www.vermonthumanities.org

The Vermont Humanities Council thanks the Vermont Department of Libraries for assistance in the publication of this book.

The Vermont Humanities Council, Montpelier, 05602

Published 2005

Cover and book design by The Laughing Bear Associates, Montpelier, Vermont

Artwork by Joy Huckins-Noss, Adamant, Vermont

Printed in the United States of America

ISBN 0-9768355-0-9

Contents

Preface

The Vermont Humanities Council is pleased to present *A Guide to Fiction Set in Vermont*. After moving to Vermont in 1999, Ann McKinstry Micou decided to read her way through the state's literary incarnations as a way of learning about the character of the state. What started for her as a hobby quickly became, she freely acknowledges, "a passion." This guide is the result of that wonderfully productive passion; her thorough review of Vermont fiction enables us to examine overarching themes and impressions of the state through fiction set here.

Lovers of literature, students of Vermont and New England history and culture, librarians, educators, scholars, and curiosity seekers will all find this guide absorbing, comprehensive, and unlike anything else in print today. The guide's descriptions are neither analyses nor reviews; they are detailed, but concise synopses of the fictional works. The works reach as far back as 1835 and as far forward as 2005. Numerous genres — literary fiction, mysteries, historical novels, gothic tales, and more — are represented. Their common thread is that they are wholly or partially set in Vermont.

Some of the authors are Vermonters, some are transplants, and some never set foot in the Green Mountain State. But for one reason or another, all chose Vermont as the setting for their stories. Why? For some authors, undoubtedly, one of a number of popular, if stereotypical, images of Vermont fit well with their plot and themes. For other authors, writing about Vermont may have offered the chance to craft a new, more complex image of the state as a challenge to shallow and clichéd characterizations. In any case, the way that Vermont has been presented in literature over time enables us to trace the history of thought about the state. Fiction offers readers not only an escape into an imagined world, but also a window on that world. Literature both comments on, and re-imagines, the place and time it seeks to capture.

Some ambitious souls may read this guide cover to cover, but it is meant primarily as an encyclopedia, a reference tool that one will reach for again and again. Bibliography, appendixes, and indexes facilitate using the guide in various ways. One may be interested to learn, for example, about fiction set in certain towns. We hope that this guide will encourage people to read and enjoy the books referenced here, and to think about our state in new ways.

As inclusive as this guide is, it is surely not wholly complete. Moreover, fiction set in Vermont continues to be published. Plans call for publishing revised and updated versions of this guide every few years. If you know of a novel, short story, or author that should be included in a new edition, please contact us. Or just let us know how you like the guide, how you use it, and how it might be improved.

The Vermont Humanities Council is most grateful to Ann McKinstry Micou for her work and her desire to share this resource with the public. Heartfelt thanks also to State Librarian Sybil Brigham McShane for the Vermont Department of Libraries' generous financial support of this project, to Amy Howlett, Southeast regional coordinator of the Vermont Department of Libraries for supporting this effort from day one, to VHC's Larissa Vigue Picard and Sylvia Plumb for their editorial and project supervision, and to Mason Singer of The Laughing Bear Associates for design and production.

Peter A. Gilbert, Executive Director
Vermont Humanities Council

Vermont Humanities Council
Sharing Our Past — Shaping Our Future

The Vermont Humanities Council is dedicated to creating a state in which every individual reads, participates in public affairs, and continues to learn throughout life. VHC helps strengthen Vermont communities with programs for people of all ages and backgrounds — from reading and discussion programs for adults in libraries and hospitals to weeklong summer camps for middle-school kids. Founded in 1974, the Council is a statewide nonprofit organization and an affiliate of the National Endowment for the Humanities.

Introduction

Reading fiction is a way to absorb a new culture. When I moved to Vermont, I turned to novels with Vermont settings to grasp its essence and ethos. I found bookshop sections devoted to Vermont authors like Chris Bohjalian, Dorothy Canfield Fisher, Castle Freeman, Jr., Archer Mayor, and Howard Frank Mosher. I encountered writers of fiction set in Vermont previously unknown to me, like Sarah N. Cleghorn, Zephine Humphrey, Daniel Pierce Thompson, and Frederic F. Van de Water. I was surprised to discover that familiar authors like Pearl Buck, William Dean Howells, Sinclair Lewis, John O'Hara, Harriet Beecher Stowe, Hendrik van Loon, William Carlos Williams, and Owen Wister had written fiction set in Vermont.

I sought every available resource. I consulted *Vermont Prose: A Miscellany*, edited by Arthur Wallace Peach and Harold Goddard Rugg (Brattleboro: Stephen Daye Press, 1932). I searched databases like NoveList, Contemporary Authors, the Vermont Automated Libraries System, the Library of Congress, Latter-day Saints FamilySearch, and abebooks.com. As the list grew to unanticipated lengths, I had to make difficult choices. I included all adult fiction set in Vermont: in publisher's parlance, literary, mid-list, and popular fiction. I omitted young adult fiction with regret (using criteria from sources like the University of Vermont Bailey/Howe Library Special Collections and NoveList), given talented writers of this genre like Karen Hesse (*Witness*, 2001), Jessie Haas (*Westminster West*, 1997), and Leon W. Dean (*Green Mountain Boy: Seth Warner*, 1941). I included short stories published in collections, not those in periodicals. Self-published books are excluded. Also omitted are narrative poems of writers like Walter R. Hard

(*A Mountain Township*, 1933). Because the topic is Vermont settings, not Vermont authors, writers who lived in Vermont but did not write novels about it, like Robert Penn Warren, are not included (although many of Warren's poems in, for example, "A North Point," *Rumor Verified*, 1981, depict Vermont).

I acknowledge with gratitude the assistance of Peter Gilbert, Larissa Vigue Picard, and Sylvia Plumb of the Vermont Humanities Council; Amy Howlett of the Vermont Department of Libraries; the in-house and interlibrary loan services of Brooks Memorial, Dover Free, Marlboro College Rice-Aron, and Moore Free Libraries; writers Don Bredes, Castle Freeman, Jr., and Abby Frucht; Mary Hill, Olde & New England Books, and Beth and Dave Kanell, Kingdom Books; Michael Sherman, co-author of *Vermont History* (2002), and Paul A. Eschholz, co-editor of *The Literature of Vermont: A Sampler* (1973); Mary E. Wilkins Freeman scholar Marjorie Pryse and Kipling scholar Jaysinh Birjepatil; John Burt, Robert Penn Warren's Literary Executor, and Robert Penn Warren scholar James A. Grimshaw; Nathanael West biographer Jay Martin, Dorothy Thompson biographer Peter Kurth, and Henry James biographer Sheldon M. Novick; the University of Vermont Bailey/Howe Library Special Collections; Bethel, Ferrisburgh, and Vermont Historical Societies; Bennington Museum; and reference departments of Fletcher, Greensboro, and Rutland Free Libraries, and the St. Johnsbury Athenaeum. I am solely responsible for the contents of this publication.

This reference provides summary descriptions of 484 titles by 334 authors of fiction set in Vermont. These synopses are neither jacket blurbs nor book reviews but informal discussions of venue, plot, and character, with occasional examples of imagery. The cumulative effect of reading many and varied accounts of life in Vermont through the centuries, and multiple titles by some authors, is rich, comprehensive, enticing, and revealing.

To facilitate use of material so extensive and so varied, I have analyzed its component parts in eight categories. First, a bibliography gives the author, title, city and publisher, date, Vermont milieu (real and fictitious), and the author's residence (with dates if deceased) and connection with Vermont. The first of three appendixes classifies the titles by genre (campus, comic, and coming-of-age fiction, dramatic and tragic fiction, fantasy and magic realism fiction, historical and horror fiction, mystery, political, and romance fiction, and plays and short stories). The second appendix presents titles, with authors, chronologically by date of publication. The third appendix lists authors who live or lived part-time or full-time in Vermont. Four indexes refer the reader to the page numbers for real places, for fictitious places, for titles alphabetically, and for subjects (from Abenakis to World War II).

These works with Vermont settings exhibit for the most part a profound sense of place. Speaking broadly, there are four approaches to context. One approach creates a setting that is an integral part of the story. Another makes a political or social point that is largely dependent upon the setting. A third sets the novel only partially in the state but imbues the story with a Vermont sensibility. The fourth tells a story without emphasizing the local color.

Two main and interdependent themes emerge (as well as many sub-themes found in the Subjects Index). These recurring themes relate to, first, the individual's place in Vermont life and, second, the role and use of land in Vermont. In the first, a tension between Here and Away makes characters feel they do not belong because their ancestors have not lived in Vermont for generations or because forces within the community oppose or reject them. The second is the dilemma between Then and Now, which looks at land, lifestyle, and their loss, the challenges of new development, and the effects of progress on status quo and tradition.

Whether the essence and ethos of Vermont can be captured through an immersion in fiction is impossible to answer: every reader's sense of Vermont is different. Many aspects of the culture and character of Vermont, a state distinctive in its landscape and distinguished in its history, are revealed through the fiction written about it. High-quality fiction set in Vermont contends with human issues that are universal: if these are regional novels, then so are Mark Twain's. This fiction also evokes a breathtaking part of the world: as Holden Caulfield says to Sally Hayes when he invites her to drive to Vermont with him, "It's beautiful as hell up there. It really is."

Ann McKinstry Micou

Ann McKinstry Micou holds a bachelor's degree from Mills College and a master's from The New School. She spent roughly a third of her forty-six-year career as an English teacher, a third working as an editor and director of communications in international nonprofit organizations, and a third directing the Southern African Information Exchange at the Institute of International Education in New York. In the last position she traveled frequently to southern Africa and produced more than thirty-five directories on resources for anti-apartheid groups. In the late sixties, she lived with her family and worked in Ankara, Turkey, for three years and in Tehran, Iran, for two years. She retired in 1999 and moved to South Newfane, Vermont, where she lives with her husband, Paul, a retired United Nations officer.

Summary Descriptions

These descriptions are presented alphabetically
by author. Titles marked with an asterisk indicate
works set partially in Vermont; titles of novels
are in bold italic type; and short stories are in
bold roman type, framed by quotation marks.
Years within parentheses are publication dates.

A

Peter Abrahams

In *Hard Rain* (1988), Jessie Shapiro marries musician Pat Rodney and has a little girl, Kate. After their divorce, Jessie is living with Kate in California when her daughter and Pat disappear together. She traces them to Bennington, where Pat once lived in a commune called Spacious Skies. There she meets Pat's sister, Blue, and the used car salesman who sold a van to Pat. Jessie describes the countryside: "rocky meadows, a piebald herd of Holstein cows in the lee of a spruce grove, a big Rockwell-red barn." Locales switch from Bennington to Washington, D.C., to Morgantown, Massachusetts, and back to Bethel. Blue, punished for helping Jessie, is murdered and disposed of in the trunk of a car sunk in Little Pond near Bennington. The key to the action is an identity switch during the Vietnam War in the sixties. By the time all is revealed, the expert plot has drawn in a Vermont Senator and his wife as well as a new CIA suitor for Jessie and new grandparents for Kate. (The title is from Bob Dylan's 1963 song, "A Hard Rain's A-Gonna Fall.")

Glenda Adams

The Tempest of Clemenza (1996), about Abel Chase and her thirteen-year-old daughter, Clemenza, begins in a cottage that belonged to Abel's mother on Lake Rescue in Ludlow and moves back and forth between Ludlow and Sydney, Australia, where Abel is married to James Joyce-scholar Vickers Chase. Blended into the narrative are passages from the *Memoirs of Cornelia Benn*, which has many similarities to Abel's own life. Abel found the document in a box of old books in Cuttingsville, twenty minutes away. When Vick Chase was her professor, Abel married him and assumed the care of his two sons. During their marriage, he continued to seduce other women students. Clemenza is dying of an unnamed disease, and Abel must tell her daughter an ugly secret about the past.

Dean Albarelli

Three of the nine stories in *Cheaters and Other Stories* (1996), "Passengers," "O Sole Mio," and "Cheaters," offer deft vignettes of fragile family relationships in Burlington. Michael, the twenty-three-year-old narrator of **"Passengers,"** works as captain of *Ethan Allen,* a ferryboat plying Lake Champlain between Burlington and New York. When he was seventeen, after the death by automobile accident of his parents and sister, he began sleeping with his girlfriend, Nell: her pregnancy compelled their teenage marriage. Ethan, now five, loves to hear about the Lake Champlain monster. Feeling that he has missed out on "life," Michael drifts toward an affair with Margaret, who is fourteen years older than he is. He discovers by chance that his father-in-law, Jack, has been having an affair with Clair Coleman but is breaking it off. The two men go to pick up Clair's furniture before she leaves for Minnesota. They understand each other; they have behaved "stupidly." In **"O Sole Mio,"** a university professor father is consumed with the aggressive behavior of his sixteen-year-old, Nick, and his contentious relationship with his wife, Maggie. They bicker as they try to organize a trip to Chittenden's Cider Mill in South Burlington with Nick, their daughter, and the baby. Maggie is defensive about her weight gain since the birth of the baby. At the last minute, Nick refuses to accompany them: he says he doesn't want to be trapped in the car with them to hear the same anecdotes and the same quarrels. The father muses wryly on the fact that some day his grown son will hear the same "little narrative boredoms" in his own life. Brendan Kellogg, thirty-seven, a former detective now private investigator in **"Cheaters,"** is hired by a man named Sam Truax for surveillance of his wife, Liz. Brendan remembers him from high school baseball games, when Truax played on the Winooski team and once graciously lent Brendan his mitt. Brendan also knows something about adultery, having left his wife Rachel, briefly, three years previously, for a woman named Poppie

Hansen (who left town after their affair), and feels guilty about following Liz. He checks out her schedule and tails her to an art history class at the University of Vermont, to a swim at the YWCA, and to other meetings. One day, driving with his two daughters, Beth and Addie, he is astounded to recognize Liz Truax in her car with Poppie. That night, he cases Poppie's apartment and discovers the two women in an amorous pose. He reports to Truax that his wife is not having an affair with another man; he doesn't call Poppie, although he still loves her. He is going to concentrate on his wife and daughters — "his three women."

Laurie Alberts

"Dealing" (1995) is from *Goodnight Silky Sullivan*. This nostalgic story, which appears in somewhat different form as a chapter in *The Price of Land in Shelby*, focuses on Mitchell Chartrain, who has a wife and two children and is famous in the town of Shelby for never holding down a job. Now he is dealing cocaine. If only he could get off this cursed land, he thinks. Jerry Rawley in Brattleboro is selling "executive lots" in what was once a hay meadow; Mitchell knows that "agricultural land is a goner." Lenny Garber was a rich kid whose parents built a weekend mansion up in the orchards above Gramps Chartrain's land; now Lenny is a cocaine addict in New York and a client of Mitchell's. Mitchell thinks about the times his father beat him and about their poverty and the food stamps. He goes fishing with his cousin, Jamie, who is four years older; Jamie has the coke habit now. Mitchell imagines the land before Gramp's time, when it was a "farmer's dream." He had seen a picture of Shelby in 1800 — "nothing but bald hills, fields sliding down to the river." When Mitchell finds his children playing with some coke, he almost becomes his abusive father.

In the skillful *The Price of Land in Shelby* (1996), the Chartrain family came down from Quebec and settled in Windsor County in southern Vermont. Grandfather (not a Chartrain but a Yankee from the other side of the family) owned one hundred acres, which he is forced to sell off in parcels to pay the taxes. The five Chartrain grandchildren and their cousin, Jamie Milligan, live a very different life from the "flatlanders" who come up from New York or Connecticut "to buy pretty historic clapboard houses and grow perennials." They are exposed to poverty, disease, abuse, humiliating jobs, adultery, and ramshackle unfinished houses surrounded by trash and rusting cars. "There was ruination in the dark seeping mulch under the ferns, the bones of deer dragged home by dogs, baby rabbits run over with a lawn mower, crowded saplings, relentless brush, tangles of scratching blackberry vines, mosquitoes whizzing past his ears." Lowell Chartrain is an alcoholic who abuses his daughter, Nancy, sexually, and his son, Mitchell, spiritually. Nancy endures her life by being a good housekeeper and tenderly caring for her spastic daughter, Michelle. Mitchell is full of energy and enthusiasm but finds it difficult to see a job through. Marsha dies when her careless husband, Eddie Wells, has a fatal automobile accident while drunk. Donna falls in love with a high school sweetheart and undergoes a traumatic abortion but survives to marry Claude and become successful in terms of material possessions. Sally and Gary are divorced, after two children, but she finds Mel, also divorced with children, and they accommodate themselves to a new life. Jamie starts out working the property with his grandfather, but feels he has to get away. He tries other jobs but finally comes back to the land. Despite the suffering, each member of the family tries to make something of him or herself and some succeed: there is hope as well as hardship.

Clifford Lindsey Alderman

In *The Arch of the Stars* (1950), Jared French sets off in 1770 from Millbrook, Connecticut, for Arlington in the New Hampshire Grants to join his sister and her husband. Jared works hard in this "wild, silent region." He falls in love with Ruth Prentice, daughter of a Tory, and makes a friend of Eli Burroughs. Arabella Druce, daughter of a tavern owner in Millbrook, runs away to New York and begins speculating on land "in the wilderness."

A

Jared and Eli are at Fay's Tavern in Bennington to hear Ethan Allen exhort the Grants farmers to raise an army against the Yorkers' proposition that farmers buy back the land they already own. The following year the Act of Outlawry is passed; the leaders of the Green Mountain Boys are marked men. In New York, Arabella persuades Mr. Prentice to allow Ruth to be Arabella's companion. Jared and Eli travel to New York to look for Ruth and find that the Friends of Liberty dominate the town. Arabella has escaped with Ruth. After the Battle of Lexington in 1775, Jared is uneasy that the patriots' opposition to the Yorkers over land is leading to war with Britain. In Bennington, Ethan Allen reveals his plan to capture Fort Ticonderoga. After its capture, Seth Warner is chosen commander of the Green Mountain Boys. Allen takes a position as scout with Philip Schuyler's offensive on Montreal; Jared goes north with Seth Warner and the Green Mountain Boys. At St. John's, Jared and Eli run into Ethan Allen, who plans to attack Montreal with Major John Brown of Massachusetts. Brown misses the rendezvous and the British capture Allen. Jared and Eli rejoin Warner's forces; Montreal falls. Jared and Eli stay in Quebec with Ira Allen, under Montgomery and Arnold. The American assault on Quebec is repulsed. Jared retreats from Quebec with the Green Mountain Boys. He is captured by the British but escapes and rejoins Seth Warner, whose regiment is beaten at Hubbardton. Vermont is now a free, sovereign, and independent state. Eli and Jared, pretending to seek the protection of the Crown, sign the oath and Colonel Skene sends them as scouts to Burgoyne's headquarters where Arabella identifies them as spies. In the shoot-out, Eli is killed but Jared escapes. The Battle of Bennington is won after the suspenseful wait for Sam Safford and the Green Mountain Boys. The Americans' greatest hatred is not for the British or the mercenaries but for the Tories. Burgoyne realizes his mistake was using Indians against the farmers and sending mercenaries into Vermont to seize the stock and farms. Ethan Allen is still in prison in New York. Jared knows their side is right: he has a vision of what Vermont

will become. (The title is from Carl Sandburg's poem, "Always the Mob:" "One more arch of stars,/In the night of our mist.")

Charlotte Vale Allen

The backdrop of *Promises* (1979) is the 1930s Depression. Jess, eighteen, and her sister, Tillie, twelve, are destitute orphans in New York; Jess, unable to find work, decides to sell herself on the street. A well-known photographer, Jamieson Land, happens by and hires her to sit for him. When he departs for his summer home at Echo Lake near Ludlow, he takes along Jess, with whom he has fallen in love, and a reluctant and resentful Tillie. Jamieson Land grew up in a big, white-clapboard, black-shuttered house with a lopsided barn he now uses as his studio. The Vermont setting acts as an introduction to the rest of the story: the girls run away to Canada and spend their lives in Toronto.

In *Grace Notes* (2002), Grace Loring, the victim of an abusive husband, flees with her daughter, Nicky, to Brattleboro to stay with her brother, Gus, who lives in a three-story Victorian house on High Street, a fifteen-minute walk from Main Street. She writes a memoir of her experiences called *Hit or Miss*, an immediate bestseller, and starts writing full-time. Her brother is a professor at a local college (like Marlboro), until he is stricken with rheumatoid arthritis, requiring Grace to hire several women to help take care of him. Gus tries to break off his relationship with his lover, Jerry, a state trooper, to free Jerry to find another partner. Grace's daughter, Nicky, has turned into an attractive, bright young woman, who is attending the local college and looking forward to leaving "Appalachia north" upon graduation. Grace has been involved for some years with Vinnie, an amusing and talented artist who lives in Manhattan but spends time in neighboring Maple Valley. Grace has given advice to battered women over the years and is not surprised when she receives e-mail from someone named Stephanie Baine. Stephanie describes her trauma after being raped sixteen years earlier and her sadistic husband and his hateful parents, who will not allow her to forget her anguished experience. Grace is touched by Stephanie's plight and responds sympathetically. Soon, they are exchanging daily e-mails and Grace is offering advice based on her twenty years' experience. Suddenly, Grace receives an e-mail message from a friend of Stephanie's reporting a violent event that plunges Grace into a nightmare of guilt and responsibility.

Marguerite Allis

Not Without Peril (1941) is based on the life of Jemima Sartwell, who dwells in 1741 in a forthouse (later Vernon) west of the Connecticut River below Fort Dummer with a sister, Hepzibah, a brother, Jebediah, and their father. William Phipps, who is settling farther north at Great Meadows (later Putney), wants Jemima to help him with chores and to bear children. She is hustled off with a brusque and unkind man whom she doesn't know or love. She has two babies, Mary and Submit. The housework is overwhelming for Jemima, feeding and clothing five or six men so they can girdle trees and grow corn. Nehemiah and Margaret Howe arrive with their sons. Jemima feels an instant sympathy for Caleb Howe. Abenakis attack their forthouse and scalp and kill William. Caleb and Jemima marry and head north to Fort Number Four (later Charlestown, New Hampshire). Jemima and Caleb have five sons over the next few years. Sister Hepzibah runs off with an Indian raiding party; Jebediah tries to betray the settlers but is captured. When the men leave the fort to gather food, an Abenaki raiding party captures Jemima and her family. They are marched over the Green Mountains to Saint Francis, where they find many white captives and a Catholic priest teaching the children. Jemima's only hope is for ransom. The children quickly accommodate to Abenaki ways. Jemima's daughter, Mary, falls in love with the Grand Sachem's son. The Abenakis sell Jemima in Montreal to a French couple. She escapes and appeals for help from the French Governor of Montreal (who is calls her "Fair Captive"). Colonel Peter Schuyler of New Jersey, another captive, buys Jemima's freedom. Israel Putnam has the influence to free three of her boys and

agrees to accompany her and her children home. She learns that Caleb has been dead for three years. Her sons are incorrigible. Jemima marries Amos Tute, an honest, hard-working man, and they have one son who dies of small pox. The political climate is heating up: some in the Grants are Yorkers; others are Yankees. Two of Jemima's sons become Tories. Ethan Allen asks: "Why should the Grants be governed by *either* New York or New Hampshire? Why shouldn't they have their *own* Commonwealth?" Jemima joins the cause; two of her sons and one son-in-law fight in the Battle of Bennington. Their territory is recognized as a free and independent state named "Vermont," though not without some threats about merging with Canada. Jemima knows these "lean, tight-mouthed, hard-headed, keen-eyed men of mountain and river would never voluntarily put themselves back under British rule!" Amos Tute dies of lung fever, but Jemima lives to be eighty years old. (The chapter headings, such as "In Perils in the Wilderness" and "In Perils by the Heathen," are from one of St. Paul's letters to the Corinthians.)

Lisa Alther

In *Kinflicks* (1976), Virginia ("Ginny") Hull Babcock, twenty-seven, of Stark's Bog, has two sides to her character. One is a combat-booted, lesbian, counter-cultural hippie who lives with her lover, Edna ("Eddie") Holzer, in a cabin on a lake north of St. Johnsbury and shocks the residents of Stark's Bog with her frizzy Anglo-Afro hair and her family-planning clinic. The other is the serene, conformist, loyal, and loving housekeeper and wife of Ira Braithwaite Bliss IV, living in his stone colonial homestead with their little girl, Wendy, scrubbing toilets, and attending surprise showers and Tupperware teas. (Despite his heritage, Ira is building an Authentic Vermont Village next door called "Pots o' Gold." Villagers want to knock down the early colonial houses their families have lived in for centuries and "throw up a prefab ranch house.") The narrative shifts back and forth from Stark's Bog to Hullsport, Tennessee, where Ginny's mother is hospitalized with clotting disease. While there,

Ginny thinks back to her Southern past, her life with Eddie in Cambridge, and their moving to Stark's Bog to live at Free Farm with three other women. Eddie initially sees the commune in Vermont as a "rural rest-home for fucked over radicals," but agrees to try it. They are leaving behind the "American capitalist-imperialist economy" (they are actually living on Ginny's trust fund from her father's munitions factory). "They will grow their food, their clothes, their fuel." Ginny is smart and funny. The descriptions of life at Free Farm and their attempts to form a Third World Commune are hilarious. They find they have not "befriended or instructed" any Stark Boggers in the ways of the Revolution. Tragically, Eddie is killed in a snowmobile accident. Ira marries Ginny and takes her away from the Free Farm; Ginny tries to live his life and fails. She can't help the fact that "her standard reaction to any unfamiliar concept is burlesque." While Ira is away at National Guard camp, an interesting young man appears in Ginny's yard. He is Will Hawk, a Vietnam deserter, and his presence is misinterpreted by Ira, who assumes Ginny is having an affair with Hawk. The concluding chapters contain separation, death, and decisions for Ginny about how and where to live her life.

In *Bedrock* (1990), Clea Shawn has it all—a handsome, rich husband; a son at prep school and daughter at Smith College; a divine house in New York; fabulous taste; a riveting job as a photographer; endless travel; numerous lovers. What she doesn't have is a house in rural Vermont. Roches Ridge "sat on a granite outcropping that plunged down into the marshes of Mink Creek, which flows into Lake Champlain." After a skiing trip to Alpine Glen, Clea buys Calvin Roche's house on a whim and settles into village life. Clea is certain she has found "a race endowed with droll good humor and rock-solid integrity," although slightly shaken when the bathtub falls into the cellar. She observes that talking of her new house to Darius Drum, descended from a dynasty of Vermont carpenters, is "like reading a telegram: Bad news. Dry rot." Once the snow melts she begins to notice trash and rusted cars. The rickety tenement next door has a sign saying, "This house

insured by Smith and Wesson." Waneeta Marsh's family owned all of the property thereabouts until her grandfather sold out for groceries during the '92-and-Froze-to-Death. Her son, Dacron, thinks flatlanders should be "restricted to ski areas, like wildlife reserves." Clea is inspired to do one of her photo-journalistic studies of Roches Ridge and even visualizes the title—*The Town That Time Forgot*, in which she plans to illustrate that "the past is still flourishing in rural Vermont." As a city slicker, a "flatlander," she has no idea what is going on in the minds of the townspeople, who are revealed in quick sketches. A commune of lesbian hippies, called The Boudiccas and led by Starshine the guru, lives down at Mink Creek. Born-again Daryl Perkins is in charge of a harem of veiled women living at Granite Gap. Astrid Starr at the IGA expresses her public service by controlling the flow of rumors through town. The corporate families attached to the Xerox facility live in Colonial Manor Estates. Zeno Racine, the exterminator from the cemetery, is a pathological killer. The local minister of the Church of the Holy Deliverance has had an affair and an illegitimate child with his housekeeper. By the end of the novel, after Clea has helped to organize a bicentennial celebration (it is hard to schedule meetings because everyone watches TV in the evening), she has a change of heart and perception; other characters change as well.

Harriette Ashbrook

In *The Murder of Sigurd Sharon* (1933), serial investigator and Manhattanite Philip ("Spike") Tracy finds himself embroiled in a murder case in Colville, several hours north of Burlington. His car breaks down near the "rugged sandstone Victorian" house of Dr. Sigurd Hallsberg Sharon, who lives with an eccentric group: his trained nurse, Miss Wilson; twin wards, Mary and Jill Jeffrey; Jerome W. Featherstone, family friend; and the hired man, Henry Yonson, whose wife is the cook. The night Spike arrives, Dr. Sharon is stabbed. After the local constable, Ephraim Silcox, is summoned, he and Spike undertake the solution of the case. The young Jeffrey women are very different: Jill is pert, irreverent, and flirtatious; Mary is solemn, shy, and nervous, requiring the constant attention of suave Dr. Carmack from Burlington. Silcox's son, Beverly, is an admirer of Jill's: she teases him, confessing she "loathes" his "lovely state" of Vermont. Ephraim and Spike learn that Jill has been corresponding romantically with Jerome via an anonymous post office box in Burlington and that she hates Dr. Sharon. Spike unlocks the key to an important secret as well as to the identity of the killer, who, in his arrogance, overlooked one small detail.

Paul Auster

In *The Book of Illusions* (2002), David Zimmer is a professor of comparative literature at Hampton College in Hampton and author of *The Silent World of Hector Mann*, a study of the silent film actor and director's two-reel films. Everyone assumes that Mann, who disappeared in 1928, is dead. Three years previously, just before Christmas, Zimmer drives his wife and two sons to the airport in Boston—he doesn't want them to take off from Burlington in a small, dangerous craft and then have to change planes. Zimmer himself stays behind to correct papers and hand in final grades for the semester. His entire family is killed in a plane crash. He takes a leave of absence from Hampton College and finally resigns, but after the book about Mann is published he returns to Vermont and buys a house in West T_____, about twenty-five miles south of Hampton. It is without charm, a prefab ski chalet with wall-to-wall carpeting, but "to inhabit these bland depersonalized interiors was to understand that the world was an illusion that had to be reinvented every day." He is halfway up a mountain on a dirt road, surrounded by thick stands of birch, spruce, and maple. An old friend offers him a job translating Chateaubriand's memoirs. He shops in Brattleboro once a week—twenty miles away—and tries to get on with his life by immersing himself in his work. Zimmer receives a letter from Mann's wife, Frieda Spelling, informing him that Mann is still alive. He finds

this hard to believe, but Alma Grund, the daughter of Mann's cameraman, appears on his doorstep to demand that he fly to Albuquerque to meet Hector before the latter's imminent death. She fills in Zimmer on Mann's past, his marriage to Frieda, and his move to Albuquerque. Alma and Zimmer arrive in time for Zimmer to see Mann once before his death. The aftermath is tense and unanticipated.

Phil Austin

In *On Bethel Ridge* (1998), Bella and Giorgi Orlovsky's Russian accents linger, although they have lived on a small hilltop in Bethel Ridge in central Vermont for forty-five years. Their one daughter, Anna Orlovsky-Brenner, is married to Jerry, lives in Brookline, and has twin children, Mathilde and Nicholas. It is Christmas Eve and the Orlovskys are disappointed: Anna has telephoned that she and her family will not spend Christmas in Vermont again this year. Nevertheless, Giorgi goes out into the snow to cut down a traditional tree. He has a heart attack and falls onto the snowy ground. While he is hovering between consciousness and unconsciousness, a woman (his "snow angel") appears and speaks comfortingly to him. He is taken to the Hanover hospital. Bella sends word to Anna who, after an argument with her husband who refuses to accompany them, starts out with her children by car for Hanover. In the snowstorm, Anna's car goes off the road. Mathilde wanders away; a kind woman in a white scarf driving a sleigh gives her some presents. A neighbor of the Orlovskys happens upon Anna and her children and drives them to the hospital. Giorgi is allowed to come home for Christmas and Jerry arrives at the last minute. Mathilde gives her grandfather the strange woman's presents, a coin and a Christmas tree ornament. He explains that, when he was a little boy in St. Petersburg in 1927, his grandfather was arrested, his parents went off seeking food, and he was left alone— until a woman in a white scarf, driving a troika, came to him with those same two presents.

B

Irving Bacheller

Eben Holden: A Tale of the North Country (1900) concerns a Vermonter, one of many, who left Vermont early in the 1800s. "They were survivors of a ruined home in the north of Vermont, and were traveling far into the valley of the St. Lawrence, but with no particular destination." Many "hardy wood-choppers" came out of Vermont and founded their homes in the Adirondack wilderness, imbuing the environment with their Vermont values and their experience with "toil in a rigorous climate." Leaving Vergennes, Uncle Eben, a "jolly old man," takes Willie, six, whose parents have drowned, and Willie's dog, Fred, to the Valley of the St. Lawrence River, where they find David and Elizabeth Brower, who have recently lost a son and are interested in adopting Willie. They have another child, Gerald, who dies of consumption, and a daughter, Hope, with whom Willie falls in love as they grow from childhood to young adulthood. As teenagers, Hope and Willie are sent away to boarding school at Hillsborough Academy. A rich woman named Mrs. Fuller adopts Hope, who is very musical, and takes her out of Willie's range to Europe. He attends college and then goes to New York and is hired by Horace Greeley on the *Tribune*. In 1861, he joins the army and goes to the Battle of Bull Run, where he performs heroically and is seriously wounded. After his recovery, he is one of the soldiers taken to Washington to be thanked personally by President Lincoln. He and Hope finally marry; he works for Greeley again for a while and then enters politics. The last words of Uncle Eben, a voice of Vermont, are engraved upon his tombstone by his loving nephew: "I'm not afraid or ashamed of anything I ever did. I always kept my harness traces tight, never swore unless it was necessary, never caught a fish bigger than it was or lied in a horse trade or shed a tear I didn't have

to. I never cheated anybody but Eben Holden. I'm going off somewhere—I don't know the way either—I don't know if it is east or west or north or south, or road or trail, but I'm not afraid."

Abbey Pen Baker

The basis of *In the Dead of Winter* (1994) is the discovery of an unknown manuscript in a locked bureau drawer describing the meeting at Smith College—and first mystery case solved by the duo—of Faye Martin Tullis and Myrl Adler Norton. The story, told by Faye and based on notes she took during the case, begins at Smith College in 1918, where Myrl teaches logic and Faye is her teaching assistant. Their discovery of the body of the actress, Alyssa Dansen, in a boarding house in Northampton—a body that has been stuffed and mounted like an animal trophy and later shot through the head—takes them to Brattleboro, where the actress summered and belonged to a theatrical troupe. Myrl and Faye stay with a famous soprano, Mary Howe, at her Victorian house, Hayes Tavern, on Western Avenue. Through her, they meet all the members of the troupe at Wheel House, an elegant bicycling club on Elliot Street in West Brattleboro, across from the Brattleboro Opera House (they take one of the new trolleys). Any one of them is a suspect: Henry Mitchell, a KKK sympathizer, or Frances Hall, or Marion French, or Hollister McClean, a taxidermist. The only member not present and therefore not suspicious is Giles Wilcox, Alyssa's fiancé, who is off on one of his periodic safaris. Giles returns, and they are summoned to Putney—in those days a forty-minute drive over a dirt road—to his "pristine" farm, The Willows. He has found that a pistol has been stolen. Continuing to seek evidence and examine clues, they are all invited to Rankomana, Frances's estate, with lakes, apple orchard, and sugar maples on Black Mountain. While they are shooting clay pigeons (Faye is a crack shot), Frances is poisoned, though not fatally. Myrl quickly grasps the crux of this crime—diamonds and blackmail. She and Faye travel to Northampton where they find letters hidden in Alyssa's room but return to Brattleboro for the

Winter Carnival on the Island (with boardwalks on the Connecticut River). On the train to Brattleboro are two men, clearly British, who look vaguely familiar. The pièce de résistance of the Carnival is Giles's Carousel, with exquisitely carved horses and pipe organs made by Brattleboro's Estey Organ Company. Myrl fears for Marion's safety (she is privy to the information that Marion and Alyssa were lovers) and, in trying to warn her, is lured onto the ice, falls through, and almost drowns. She and Faye soon set out to find Marion, who has also been lured by a mysterious note to the Retreat Meadows. There, as a masked man tries to kill Marion, Faye draws her gun and he surrenders. The killer is unmasked, the identities of the two British men are revealed (clues in Faye's introduction have laid the groundwork), and Myrl explains to the astounded onlookers the entire plot.

Harry Barba

In *For the Grape Season* (1960), Armenian migrant workers from northwest Iran arrive in Barstowe near St. Albans to tend wild grapes for the Gadsons' grape juice concern. Eugene ("Gene") D. Gadson, Jr., the son of the deceased local minister, has been studying theology but is considering dropping out of school. He doesn't know what he wants to do with his life. His uncle, Aaron ("A.D."), Dunston, is head of the family grape juice industry, a godsend to the little community of Barstowe that has lost its milk market to producers of condensed and powdered milk. The migrant workers are staying at the parsonage, Gene's former residence, at the invitation of Gene's mother, Elizabeth Gadson. The community is not pleased ("They *act* so foreign"), but Elizabeth (whose brother is first selectman Enos Morrill) persuades the congregation to invite the workers to join the church community and to participate in the Easter service with Sloecum, the twin village over the hill. The Armenians experienced hostile treatment at the hands of the Kurds; now they are subjected to the antipathies of an upright New England community. The Armenians bring hard work, spirited music, and vibrant life to Barstowe. Armenian

Bachelor Bedros falls in love with widow (and putative witch) Sarah Belmountain (whose deceased husband, Joel, was referred to as a "Canuck" in the community). Lalice, the young Armenian girl who is betrothed to Sonny Zar, her third cousin, falls in love with Gene. He takes her to Secret Lake, where the remains of two log cabins and a connecting barn can be discerned beneath the water. Suddenly, a flood overruns the valley. The Armenians throw themselves into the rescue effort. Mootik, the brave black horse belonging to Bedros, pulls a sleigh, rescuing villagers in danger of drowning, and afterward drops dead from heart strain. The flood has destroyed the grapevines, but it has also drained Secret Lake, leaving very fertile soil for farming—perfect, in fact, for wine grapes. Gene and Lalice want to marry (she is pregnant), but the village is indignant at this "mixing of blood." Enos announces the secret of the lake: Barstowe-founder Hiram Newton's second wife, great-grandmother of Barstowe residents, was a Pequot. Bedros stays in the village with his new wife, Sarah; the rest of the Armenians feel unwelcome and leave, as do Gene and Lalice.

Elaine Barbieri

In "**Winter Moon**" (1995), Holly Collins, an orphan schoolteacher in 1892 Benton Falls, meets widower Judd McBain, uncle of one of her students, Daniel. Although Holly and Judd resist their mutual attraction (she wants to be independent; he doesn't think he can forget his wife), by the end of the story they are in love.

Philip E. Baruth

In *The Dream of the White Village: A Novel in Stories* (1998), the characters are linked through their relationship to the city of Burlington. On the outside, "Burlington was the dream of the white village. White people moved through the streets in small, pale groupings, families and day-tourists from Montreal and knots of children who knew one another from school. Everyone was clean. Everyone seemed to wear glasses and neat khaki pants, pressed skirts." The characters in these stories, however, are not the privileged students or the wealthy tourists. Maurice Masseau, whose father is Chris Masseau, a corrupt policeman, and whose older brother, Reuben, is in prison, feeds on younger people like hippies or young stonecutters from Barre whom he tries to mold into a gang to support him when he runs for mayor. Alison, whose activism is dating activists, works at the bar at the Metronome, sharing shifts with Cheever, who is gay. Her mother, Monica Reed, the second-best woman poet in Vermont, fantasizes about a schizophrenic, Leon Charlesbois, in one of her classes. James Craig, a shy, divorced carpenter whose relatives live in South Hero, moves to Burlington to make friends. He is beaten up by Maurice but finds a friend in Alison. Cheryl-Lin is a lesbian and diabetic who works the bar at Pearl's and lives at a halfway house, where Leon also stays. Her Taiwanese mother can't abide Burlington and returns to Taiwan. Racist men in the neighborhood break raw eggs each night over the car of her father, Deng-Xin Lin, who works for IBM, and force him to leave town. Suzanne Masseau almost has an affair while her husband, Chris, is away one Saturday; she is sidetracked by taking Cheryl-Lin's side on a charge of shoplifting. The police, looking for an arsonist, suspect Leon because he is sick and lives in a halfway house. After the real arsonist is arrested, Alison observes: "I grew up in this town, and it's flat-out amazing. I mean the rest of the world has changed, it's *gone* somewhere. People have learned to live together, you know? All kinds of people. But here it's just blah, it's just like, *white*. I don't know. There's this conservativeness that goes way beyond politics."

Tricia Bauer

Three episodes set in northern Vermont shape *Hollywood & Hardwood* (1999). Renata, an actress, and Lou, a playwright, meet at the White Birch Lodge in Greene while in summer stock doing *Our Town*. They fall in love and marry in a matter of days. Renata has a great affection for Vermont: "Just by the smell I could distinguish Vermont from all the New England states;" "The smell of fresh-cut wood hung strong as peeled fruit." Returning to Greene for the summer stock production of *Peer Gynt*, they stay for a year in an apartment with shutters that are "slate blue; boxes for pansies and nasturtiums punctuated the windows." Lou is writing a play called *Woods We Know*; Renata writes obituaries for a newspaper in Burlington. When they run out of money and are unable to afford heating oil, Lou cuts and burns hardwood in the fireplace. Her body "betrays" her: she has an abortion. They move to New York, where they struggle and Lou finally attracts some attention: his play, *Blue Corners*, is made into a movie. They buy a house in Connecticut before moving to Hollywood. Old friends think success has changed them; some are scornful that Lou is writing a movie-of-the-week and Renata is doing a voice-over for a TV commercial. They return to Vermont to see the fall leaves and visit old friends, Doug and Leah Jackson, who in the old days ran an apple stand. Doug now works for Green Mountain Power Corporation; Leah is defensive about not working and jealous of Lou, who has a new film project, and Renata, who is about to go into rehearsal for *Look Back in Anger*. Leah wonders if they are still as much in love as they used to be and is envious when she finds after they leave that they have crowded into a single bed. Circumstances pall for Renata and Lou: he hasn't written an original play in a year; he runs out of money and takes a job in a liquor store. They head to the Madison Inn in Vermont for a long weekend, after which they are able to make important decisions about their future.

Ann Beattie

Two of the stories in *Distortions* (1976), "Vermont" and "Wally Whistles Dixie," take place in Vermont. **"Vermont"** begins in Manhattan, where David and the narrator live in an apartment building with their daughter, Beth. Noel and Susan also live in the building, as do John Stillerman and his wife. When John's wife leaves him, Susan moves in with John and David finds another place to live. After Noel moves in with the narrator, they and Beth go to visit Noel's friends, Charles and Sol, in Vermont. After a long stay, they return to Manhattan but soon buy a house in Vermont near their friends. When David and his new girlfriend, Patty, come to visit, the narrator notices that they don't have proper boots for walking in the woods. Noel is happy in Vermont: "Being in Vermont means that he can do what he wants to do. Freedom, you know." Although Noel starts to read novels so that he can understand the narrator's witty remarks and is lovely with her daughter, she continues to love David. When David drives away with Patty, he "backs down cautiously—the way someone pulls a zipper after it's been caught." In **"Wally Whistles Dixie,"** David, a youthful prodigy, marries Sheila, an older ballerina, and they move to Vermont to open a restaurant. David writes a cookbook. The restaurant is a success, "sushi being very hard to find in that part of Vermont." Living the hippie life, Sheila dances, David sews his own shirts from material bought in Hong Kong, and they produce a baby prodigy, Wally. Wally expresses his giftedness by repeating only what others say to him, running away often, wishing to marry at age thirteen, and moving out of his family's house and into a tent with his girlfriend, Diana Leigh. The restaurant receives a glowing recommendation from the AAA.

In **"Summer People,"** from *Where You'll Find Me* (1986), Tom and Jo are at their summer place in southern Vermont with Byron, Tom's son by his first wife. This is the second summer Tom and Jo have come there. Tom works hard in the garden setting out vegetables and marigolds; Byron goes fishing; Jo, a teacher, sits by the pool and reads eighteenth-century novels. Once in a while they go to a roadside café and drink Rolling Rock. One day an odd-looking man comes by to ask about the property, saying he had been interested in buying it. Tom is disturbed enough about this visit to mention it to the police. The police officer taking down his complaint looks at him, Tom feels, with the expression, *"summer people."* Tom loves Vermont—"it was the sky he loved in the country—the sky more than the house," but something is missing this year. What have they done this summer? They have fished, rafted, attended a spareribs dinner outside the Town Hall

on the Fourth, and watched the fireworks. Perhaps Jo has been more interested in her books than in being in this setting. Perhaps she is pregnant, even though they had agreed before they married that he doesn't want another child. As they drive down to Connecticut to visit Jo's sister, the mountains gradually slope down, and the car is suddenly on flat highway. He realizes that in New York he will be "remembering Vermont—the garden, the neon green of new peas, the lumpy lawn, the pine trees and the smell of them at night."

In *Love Always* (1985), Lucy Spenser is smart and shrewd, except about relationships. She moves to Lake Venue near Burlington because the man she loves, Les Whitehall, is already teaching at a college there. He takes off, but she stays to work with her friend (and occasionally lover) of fifteen years, Hildon, who has assembled a group of young, educated New Yorkers to work for *Country Daze*, a magazine that satirizes country life. Myra DeVane, a local reporter, is writing a piece about the magazine (and admiring the male employees). Hildon, the editor of the magazine, is married to Maureen but has been in love on and off with Lucy, who writes the lonely-hearts column as Cindy Coeur. Her sister Jane, in Los Angeles, sends her fourteen-year-old daughter, Nicole, to spend the summer with her Aunt Lucy. (Lucy responds to Jane: "She'd be bored to death. You know what happens here? In the late afternoon the cows walk on the field.") Nicole is the star of a soap opera called *Passionate Intensity* (Nicole's publicity man, Piggy Proctor, is surprised and infuriated to learn the title of the series comes from a Yeats poem). Andrew Steinborn, who has taken one class in creative writing, is chosen by mistake to make a novel of the TV show. Maureen leaves Hildon to work with Davina Cole in a commune run by women. The conclusion relates what happens to Nicole, to her mother, Jane, and to Lucy. Lucy forges some plans but still does not understand the people who live in Vermont: "From where Lucy sat, she couldn't see the trickle of muddy river below. The farmhouse with the blue roof she had always loved was visible on the hillside, and peo-

B

ple hardly larger than dots were moving around it—people and cows—more of those mysterious people who thought something and felt some way Lucy couldn't fathom. People who lived in a house in the valley."

Geoffrey Becker

Bluestown (1996) is narrated by Spencer Markus, whose insolvent guitarist father, Daniel ("Spider") Markus, takes Spencer out of his Brooklyn high school and on a road trip with him. Claiming an audition in Montreal, Spider stops at the Traveler's Inn just over the border in Vermont. Spencer and Spider drink whiskey and sit in with a band. They head to Denton, south of St. Johnsbury, because Spider wants to show Spencer a typical New England town: "one of those picture-postcards of a town, with tree-lined streets, big old houses with well-kept yards, two neat white-steepled churches only a couple of blocks apart." Spencer wonders what people do for a living. When he gets out of the car to pick up some snacks, his father drives off and leaves him. "There was no audition, just an idea of them starting over again some place else." Seven years later, Spencer's life is a dead-end job in a music company, troubles with a union, and failed relationships with women. After a death that affects him deeply, Spencer takes his girlfriend back to the same inn in Vermont to try to summon up the interlude with his father, who once told him that "Bluestown" is at the North Pole, where all the great guitarists are alive and still playing.

Madison Smartt Bell

Anything Goes (2002), told in the idiomatic, sympathetic voice of Jesse, twenty-five, concerns one year in his life. He is a young musician who was beaten as a child by his alcoholic father (who called him a "Melungeon"—not pure white) and has joined a band called "Anything Goes." The leader is Perry, who sings and strums the acoustic guitar; Jesse plays bass but is also seriously fooling around with the guitar; Allston, who is a black man, is on drums; and Chris McKendrick is lead guitar. No matter the name of the club where they are playing, Perry calls it

"The Black Cat." In Ocean City, Jesse spends the night with a young woman he likes named Susan. The band heads south; in Tennessee, Jesse's father, Wendell, reappears in his life and introduces him to a black woman named Estelle Cheatham, a great singer. She is so good that Perry hires her; the caravan now includes Estelle, her sister, Rose-Lee, and her little boy, James Culla. In the course of the travels, Jesse learns that Estelle is Rose-Lee's mother and that Wendell is the father of her little boy. They play gigs and Jesse practices his guitar in private. The last two chapters take place in Vermont. In "Seven Songs inside Your Head," the band is playing in Vergennes, about half an hour from Lake Champlain, and has rented a summer home on the lakeshore. The local Black Cat draws "old grey-beard hippies in holey jeans and Birkenstocks, and college students on summer adventures, and New Agers who lived up there year-round, plus Deadheads and Pfishophiles and other packs of pilgrims." From the yacht club are "men dressed in stiff jeans and polo shirts, their wives Bean-catalogue refugees, homely in an expensive way." Willard and Perry are both arrested for charges ranging from statutory rape to drug possession, so it is up to Jesse to play lead guitar—and he can finally do it. In the last chapter, "Feeling," the band goes to Burlington, at Perry's suggestion, to cut a tape at the studio of Doug Lumera, "typical Vermont hold-out, hide-out hippie," in Perry's words. The band then moves to a Black Cat in Johnson, near the Canadian border, and down the eastern side of the state, stopping in St. Johnsbury, Montpelier, Springfield, and Brattleboro, where the band stays three or four weeks. Jesse moves on to experience some modest success and some happiness.

Jason Berger

Eric Ballard, the thirteen-year-old protagonist in *Forested Moments* (2002), lives with his grandfather, Eli, in a small town on Route 4A in a part of Vermont that has been heavily mined for slate. The seasons of one year pass. Eric goes to Fall Hill High School on the Vermont-New York border, which caters to a "divided population" of middle-class and impoverished-family children. Eric, whose mother is dead (the first scene shows her suicide), is hoping his father, whom he does not remember, will return to claim him; his relations with his grandfather are rocky and tense. Eli, tortured by something, spends much of his time drinking at the Dog. Other characters include Ralph Mahar, a science teacher who loves to teach and appreciates Eric; Joe Perry, a lonely eighty-five-year-old widower, who communes with the trees in the forest; and Peggy Lock, who hates living in a trailer and drives the school bus. Eric has grown up with Mary Harris, the daughter of the owners of the general store. He is unhappy because she has abandoned him for a set of football-playing, cheerleading youngsters. At the end of the year, when Eli finally blurts out his secret, the news is liberating for Eric. Knowing the truth, he can grow up. In the last scene, he drives off to town in Eli's pick-up, waving to his grandfather in the mirror.

Ambrose Bierce

"At Old Man Eckert's" (1971) tells of the disappearance without a trace of Philip Eckert, a farmer living alone in Marion. When neighbors fail to find him, the house is considered haunted. Five years later, to put an end to tales of the supernatural, three respected citizens decide to hold a vigil in Eckert's house to investigate the scene. After two of the men have waited for an hour, the third, Andrus C. Palmer, appears, walks through the room, and goes out into the darkness. In the morning, no tracks in the snow can be seen where he passed out of the house. No one ever sees or hears of Palmer again. The editor of the local paper claims that Eckert "reached out and pulled him [Palmer] in."

Robert Bingham

"Marriage is Murder" is the one story in *Pure Slaughter Value* (1997) set in Vermont, in which a couple from Los Angeles (he rewrites murder mysteries for a living) spends their honeymoon skiing at the resort in Killington. The first-person narrator, who is introduced in the

general store buying a pocketknife, is immediately unlikable. His take on Killington: "The snow is terrible, the people rude and insular, the food fattening." A skier at the resort (they name him Mr. Wang because he works at that company in Boston) makes a pass at the narrator's wife, Shelly, and he and Shelly plan his murder. They decide that she will seduce Mr. Wang on the mountaintop where the narrator, waiting in the trees, will emerge and kill him with his new knife. Shelly and Mr. Wang actually culminate the act before the narrator plunges the knife into Mr. Wang (not fatally), leading to the dissolution of their marriage. She becomes pregnant, and her husband can think of nothing but a baby looking just like Mr. Wang.

Chris Bohjalian

Hangman (1991) is situated in the small town of Deering, halfway between Burlington, where Brian Middleton, thirty-one, works at IBM, and Middlebury, where Marcia Middleton, twenty-nine, is with an ad agency. ("To be local in these little hill towns, your family has to stick around a good seven generations. And stick around on the same piece of land. You cross the street or move 'round the bend, you got to start all over again.") Coming from New York, the Middletons are inspired by the old Finch house and the friendly team, led by head selectman John Nash, which is doing the modest renovations. The real estate woman feels fortunate to have unloaded the ninety-year-old house where, it is said, a turn-of-the-century railroad baron, Everett Barrington, murdered his daughter, Thistle Peep Barrington, and walled her up in the basement. Helping John Nash are David Dunbar and Simon Burrows, the retarded younger brother of Detective J.P. Burrows, thirty-two. Brian and Marcia are trying to repair their marriage, which has been marred by his affair with Joyce Renders while in New York. David and Carrie Dunbar invite the newcomers for supper, during which the Dunbars tell them that there is a noose in their attic. Marcia, who begins to believe the house has some bewitching power, is proved right when a tragedy occurs.

In *Past the Bleachers* (1992), Bill and Harper Parrish, who live south of Burlington in Havington, are struggling with an unbearable tragedy: their lovely, cheerful, ten-year-old son, Nathaniel, died of leukemia. The Parrishes, self-professed flatlanders, work in the community: Bill is director of development at Sedgebury College; Harper is a third-grade teacher. They get on with their lives, loving each other but numb with grief. While Bill himself was not a good Little Leaguer, his son, Nathaniel, was a wonderful athlete. Bill decides to coach a Little League team—the one his son would have joined; his older friend, Hilton Burberry, Commissioner of the Sedgebury County Little League, encourages him. The members of the team are Nathaniel's classmates; some have visited Bill's house. A newcomer, a mute boy named Lucky Diamond, is a superb hitter. Some of the children are mean to him, the girls on the team avoid him, but Bill is drawn to the boy. Trying to find out about his family, Bill learns only that Lucky's mother is dead and his father is a logger. One day Bill drives Lucky home, past the bleachers, off the logging road, and finds that Lucky lives in a trailer. One of the team contracts a mysterious heart ailment, and Bill, worried about Lyme disease, fusses with the children about deer tick checks and keeping their socks pulled over their pants. A wet bat slips out of a batter's hand and almost hits another player. The Parrishes' cats have an insane fight over Lucky's wristband, left at the house. Bill is obsessed with the boy, but also uneasy; something is wrong with Lucky. He and Harper drive up to the trailer, look in the window, and see three of the same books Nathaniel owned. It is a mark of Harper's gentle, loving nature that she does not resent a new boy in Bill's life, but embraces the idea of Lucky. The Parrishes decide they want another baby; soon Harper is pregnant. One of the team hides Lucky's mitt; Bill gives him Nathaniel's. Bill learns about Lucky's past from Hilton: the harmonious conclusion stems from that secret.

Water Witches, *Midwives*, *The Law of Similars*, and *The Trans-Sister Radio* address alternative lifestyles that are feared or scorned by the establish-

ment—dowsing, midwifery, homeopathy, and gender dysphoria or transsexuality respectively. The setting for *Water Witches* (1995) is Landaff, between Montpelier and St. Johnsbury, where many of the inhabitants are related and everyone turns out every March for the town meeting. The narrator is Scottie Winston, a corporate lawyer in Montpelier, who plays baseball every Wednesday evening and whose nice sense of humor creates lively dialogue. He and his wife, Laura Avery ("among the maelstrom, a gentle tidal pool"), have a daughter named Miranda. The Avery women — Laura, her sister Patience, and Miranda — have a pronounced talent for dowsing. Patience, a practicing, well-paid dowser, has a history of finding other items as well, lost property or missing persons. She is respected among dowsers and a member of the American Society of Dowsers, whose motto is *Indago Felix* ("fruitful search"). Scottie's client, Schuss International, is developing Powder Peak ski resort, which requires water from the Chittenden River, now dangerously low in this summer of drought. Roger Noonan, editor of the *Montpelier Sentinel*, expresses concern about the drought's effect on crops. State Senator Reedy McClure, who is engaged to Patience, is thoroughly opposed to the resort development plans and forms a group called COPPER — Citizens Opposed to Powder Peak Environmental Rape. Scottie faces a dilemma: his family is with the opposition, but his law firm needs Schuss International as a client and he believes the resort provides jobs in the state. He muses: "When I went to law school, I never said to myself, 'I hope someday I get to represent ski resorts.' I never set out to help developers build condominiums and vacation homes in Vermont's older towns, or to assist the state's Agency of Economic Development recruit new factories, new plants, new manufacturers. It just worked out that way. I grew up as something native Vermonters refer to as a flatlander, a person from New York or New Jersey who visits the state to ski, to hike, to watch the leaves turn in the fall. And then goes home." An important hearing in Montpelier considers Powder Peak's proposal to tap the river for water and to cut down trees for trails. Then something happens to make Scottie feel ambivalent about the project. The resolution of this engrossing story emerges from the new stand Scottie takes. He is not popular ("They suddenly saw in me the sort of self-righteous, smug, and moneyed liberalism that comes from Manhattan and vacations once or twice a year in his mountains. His hills. His woods. The fact that I had lived in Landaff for close to twenty years, married to one of the local Avery girls, held no weight. I was, abruptly, an outsider"), but he finds a satisfactory solution to all the problems that have arisen.

Midwives (1998) is narrated by a forty-four-year-old woman, now an obstetrician, who was fourteen when the action takes place in Reddington in northern Vermont. Connie is the daughter of Sibyl and Rand Danforth, who were counter-culture hippies, many of whose contemporaries went to Vietnam. Each chapter begins with an excerpt from Sibyl's journal. Sibyl, a midwife for many years, is called out with her assistant, Anne Austin, to the bedside of Reverend Bedford's wife, Charlotte, near Newport. The labor is long and hard; Sibyl decides that it is time to take Charlotte to the hospital, but an ice storm has developed, the telephone lines are out, and her car cannot navigate the slippery roads. When Charlotte appears to have a stroke and die, Sibyl tries cardiopulmonary resuscitation to no avail. Making the desperate decision to save the baby, she performs an emergency cesarean section on the dead woman. The child, Veil, survives. Sibyl is arrested and charged with voluntary manslaughter. Her assistant testifies that she saw the body flinch when Sibyl punctured its flesh with the knife. Connie learns that her mother keeps a journal and reads some of the pages, in which her mother begins to question her actions. The gripping and complex plot culminates in the trial and its ramifications for all parties.

The framework for *The Law of Similars* (1999) is quotations from the *Organon of Medicine* (1842), by Dr. Samuel Hahnemann, founder of homeopathy. Leland Fowler, chief deputy state's attorney, has charge of his little girl, Abby, after

his wife, Elizabeth, is killed in an automobile accident. He lives in East Bartlett about twenty miles from Middlebury ("If East Bartlett had been known for anything in recent memory, it had been known for dairy farming. As recently as 1946, the hill town of barely eight hundred people had forty-five dairy farms. By the time Elizabeth and I had moved there—a half-decade after the federal government's attempt to stabilize the price of milk by buying whole dairy herds from small farmers—there were five, and by the time Elizabeth died, there were none"). Two years after his wife's death he develops disagreeable cold symptoms that he is unable to shake. Whitney, a young woman in the local health store, recommends that he make an appointment with her aunt, Carissa Lake, a homeopath with an office in Bartlett. Leland, who has not been on a date for two years, is immediately attracted to Carissa. She explains to him that homeopathy is akin to immunization: "like cures like" or, the Law of Similars. It is an alternative approach that the medical establishment distrusts. Carissa gives Leland arsenic in highly diluted form and tells him to stop drinking coffee before he begins his treatment. Almost instantly he feels better and is soon sleeping well. Against Carissa's better judgment, they go out together; on the next date, Christmas Eve, they spend the night together. Another patient of Carissa's, Richard Emmons, seeks her help because the drugs with which he is being treated for serious asthma have given him painful and disfiguring dermatitis. Carissa prescribes a remedy derived from poison ivy. On Christmas Eve, he has a bad asthma attack, goes downstairs, eats a cashew nut to which he is violently allergic, and, when his wife, Jennifer, finds him, has crashed to the floor unconscious. On Christmas morning, Leland learns from his boss that Richard is in a coma and that his wife believes his homeopath is responsible. Leland finds himself in a compromising situation, and the decisions he makes affect in a stimulating and challenging fashion a number of lives. When Leland visits Richard in the ICU, he is reminded of his mother's death: "Bags of blood and nutrition dripped into his veins through the sorts of tubes I saw every spring linking maple trees in the woods."

The structure for the expertly told *Trans-Sister Radio* (2000), which also takes place in Bartlett, is a transcript of a two-day segment on gender dysphoria from *All Things Considered*. There are four main characters. Will Banks is the president of Vermont Public Radio (VPR). His ex-wife, Allison, is an elementary schoolteacher. His daughter, Carly, is a freshman at Bennington. Alison's lover is Dana Stevens, a professor at Middlebury College, who teaches a course in fiction and film in which Allison is enrolled. Although Will and Allison are divorced, and Will has remarried a woman lawyer named Patricia, he and Allison remain close friends and parents committed to Carly. The story unfolds through the eyes of each of these four characters. Allison is attracted to Dana while taking his course, and they soon become lovers. Shortly thereafter, Dana reveals to Allison that he is receiving hormone treatment and psychotherapy before undergoing a sexual reassignment operation. Allison at first feels horror and betrayal but is soon persuaded that she actually loves Dana the person rather than Dana the man, and, after seeking her daughter's approval, invites Dana to move in with her. Dana starts appearing in dresses, and, after the operation, becomes more and more feminine and attractive. She is ecstatically happy with her gender choice, but cannot enjoy her new state because of what her relationship with Allison has done to the latter's career and general reputation. The town is up in arms; petitions are circulated; Allison is accused of perversion and immorality; she receives hate mail; her house is vandalized; children are removed from her classroom; parents urge her to move to another town. The conception of the VPR show is a splendid device to reveal what happens to these appealing, intelligent characters.

Each chapter of *The Buffalo Soldier* (2002) begins with an excerpt from letters by Sergeant George Rowe, who was a black member of the Tenth Regiment United States Cavalry during and after the Civil War, and from WPA-conducted interviews with his widow during the thir-

ties. These former slaves were called "Buffalo Soldiers," a name coined by the Indians presumably because the soldiers' hair looked like the animals' coats. Laura, who works in an animal shelter, and Terry Sheldon, a sergeant in the state police, live in Cornish, thirty miles from Middlebury. Their nine-year-old twin daughters drowned in a flash flood, and they are paralyzed with grief. Two years later they take on a foster child, a ten-year-old black boy, Alfred, with the option to adopt him. Neighbors Paul and Emily Hebert give Alfred a cap with a buffalo on it and a book about the Buffalo Soldiers. Just before the second anniversary of the girls' death, Terry is deer hunting at his camp in Lunenburg and casually and unexpectedly spends the night with Phoebe Danvers, with whom he finds himself talking easily in a bar. Alfred has a hard time adjusting to his new life. He assumes it is impermanent like the rest of his home stays; he makes no friends at school and is considered "different;" and he has trouble talking to Laura and Terry, who are so unhappy that they treat each other with caution and solicitude like strangers. If only they would talk to him about what happened to their daughters, he believes it would clear things up. Fortunately, their neighbor, Paul Hebert, knows exactly how to talk to children (he is a retired professor of many years). He buys a Morgan horse, Mesa, and asks Alfred to help him take care of her. Mesa's body is auburn—"the color of the hills on the day the leaves have just started to turn." Soon Alfred has a regular job with the Heberts and is learning to ride. He reads the book about the Buffalo Soldiers and sees parallels between George Rowe's life and his. Rowe, born a slave, was "disciplined and sharp. He didn't care that he was an outsider. He'd won a medal." Suddenly Phoebe gets in touch with Terry to tell him she is pregnant with his child. He likes this woman: she is attractive and amusing and he wants another child. Laura had her tubes tied when the twins were young. Terry and Laura's relationship is at low ebb; guilty and sorrowful, he becomes vengeful in his trooper's job and hateful to Alfred. Finally Laura asks him to move out. He stays at a friend's house on Lake Champlain where Phoebe often visits him. The culmination of all this unhappiness comes on a stormy day in which, paralleling the harrowing day on which the twins were drowned, the river overflows its banks. The ending is noble and moving.

In *Before You Know Kindness* (2004), there are three venues: New Hampshire, Manhattan, and Vermont. The vacation planned by hyperactive Nan Seton, seventy, for her family at the Sugar Hill ancestral home in New Hampshire is supposed to be fun. Her granddaughters, Charlotte McCullough, twelve, and Willow Seton, ten, are already in her care for the summer, and the two sets of parents are expected. Catherine Seton McCullough, thirty-eight, an English teacher at the Brearley School in Manhattan, is contemplating telling her husband, Spencer, that their marriage is not working; Spencer, a vegan, heads communications for FERAL, an organization devoted to rights for animals. Catherine's brother, John Seton, forty, a public defender who lives in Hinesburg, his wife, Sara, a therapist, and their six-month-old baby, Patrick, arrive, exhausted from the pressures of their jobs and the demanding schedule of a new baby. John, who has taken up hunting but doesn't want his rather extreme brother-in-law to know, tosses his brand-new Adirondack rifle in the trunk of his car. A bullet is still stuck in the chamber after the magazine was unloaded. Unable to dislodge it, he plans to drop the rifle off at a gunsmith's in Essex Junction on the way back to Burlington. Spencer is enormously disappointed to discover, on arrival, that deer have eaten up or destroyed all of the vegetables he had planted to enjoy on his vacation. Catherine, a flirt and a snob, sees in her sister-in-law an "upcountry lack of refinement." The second night, after dinner at the local country club, the two girls are allowed to attend a bonfire for teenagers. Charlotte, who is precocious and a flirt like her mother, sneaks a couple of beers and a joint for her and Willow to share. They giggle their way back to the car, half stoned. Later that night, the girls are outside when John asks Willow to bring him some diapers from the

trunk of the car. Charlotte sees the rifle and grabs it. Willow tells her not to touch it and goes off to deliver the diapers. The rest of this wholly absorbing story describes the incalculable consequences of a tragic accident.

Jon Boorstin

The scenes in *Pay or Play* (1997) alternate between Hollywood and Mucklinburg. In Hollywood, sharks like Annette Foray, head of Studio Pictures, producer Jason Fo, and actor Klaus Fotner zero in on an excellent script, *The Agonizer*, written by Elmo Waltz. In Vermont, Homer Dooley is fired from Mucklinburg State Junior College. Dean Planck, who is committing his meager resources to a new Department of Media-Meteorology, does not consider Homer's film course current enough. Planck finds Vermont a "godforsaken frozen hellhole" with nothing but "rocks, ice, and sap." While Hollywood fights over Waltz's script (Flaherty has been hired to rewrite it), Homer rethinks his career. He lives with his mother, Frances, and grandfather, Ham (a sixth generation Vermonter); Frances and Abby, Homer's deceased father, started a commune in Vermont during the Vietnam years. The house is "a living catalogue of cost-effective building materials familiar to slum dwellers from Soweto to Rio." Homer likes winter, finding it relaxing to study the "implacable geometry" of the snowy scene. His tracks in the snow "looked like a series of small explosions, boot prints through a mine field." Silas Grant, head of Granite Plywood, hires Homer to do a film about the company for the next stockholders' meeting. Fortune smiles on Homer while he is shooting his film. He gets great shots of the log stripper—the central image of his film—peeling the veneer into sheets and a confrontation between Silas Grant and Trent Lockwood, head of the tree huggers, sabotaging the factory by tree-spiking to break the machines. Without his knowledge, Homer's mother sends his film to the Academy of Motion Pictures, Arts, and Sciences Nominating Committee for Documentary Features. Annoyed and tired by the time *Granite Plywood* is finally screened, the committee sits up and pays attention. According to accompanying publicity (also from Homer's mother), the film had won the Gold Medal at the Mucklinburg Festival of the Arts. Someone on the committee reports it is the premier arts festival in Vermont; someone else says he once did *Measure for Measure* there with Burt Reynolds and Loni Anderson. Homer's film about making plywood, "told straight, is acerbic, insightful, and funny." One committee member considers it a brilliant view of commerce and the environment "head-to-head." The film is nominated for Best Feature Documentary; Homer and Frances are at the awards presentation in Los Angeles, leading to Homer's being hired to direct *The Agonizer*, a multimillion-dollar film (*Variety* headline: "*Agonizer* Homers."). The resounding finale takes place on location in Papua New Guinea. Because Homer is honest, modest, and smart, the cast and crew think he is a genius: all these losers are now radiating competence and following his suggestions. Despite a tragic death on location, the movie is a success, but Homer returns to Vermont. The press pronouncements about Homer Dooley: "He did not go the tabloid route;" "He could not be bought;" and "He was too good for the business."

Miriam Borgenicht

Booked for Death (1987), clever and literary, begins at a university near Boston when administrator Celia Sommerville, in her thirties, tells her fiancé, George Theroux, in his fifties, that she cannot go through with their marriage, which was to take place in ten days' time. She suddenly realizes that she cannot live with his uptight, rigid behavior for the rest of her life; his vindictive response to her announcement corroborates her intuition. When he is found dead in Cedar Springs the next day, presumed a suicide because of his broken betrothal, everyone in the university community turns against Celia. Knowing in her heart that someone of George's temperament couldn't commit suicide, Celia decides to go to Vermont to investigate the circumstances surrounding his death. Her heart-

throb friend in the English department, Jason Bailey, finds her the perfect guise: his elderly, nearly blind colleague, Professor Eric Ellsworth, is looking for someone to record and transcribe his dictations and look up references for his new book. This is an apt opportunity for Celia to play sleuth, because Professor Ellsworth is the father of deceased Roy, who was George Theroux's best friend at the Cedar Springs Preparatory School and the reason George headed for Vermont. When Celia arrives in Cedar Springs, she finds a hostile and unattractive Ellsworth family. Madeleine, the widow of Roy, her four children, Jill, Marcia, Jerry, and Cindy, and Marcia's husband, Bernie Lenox, are all staying at the same hotel. So is the charming and literate Professor Ellsworth, whose lectures, Celia begins to figure out, have something to do with the mystery she is trying to unravel. The device for discussing and solving the mystery is Celia's nightly telephone call to Jason, often playing him one of the day's tapes, since English literature is his field. The book Professor Ellsworth is writing concerns children in nineteenth-century fiction. "What makes them act the way they do? How much can you blame on parents? How much can parents blame on the mandates of their time? How much would have happened anyhow?" The professor discusses these questions in relation to novels like *Oliver Twist*, *David Copperfield*, *Dombey and Son*, *Jane Eyre*, *The Mill on the Floss*, and *The Turn of the Screw*. Celia talks to the police chief, to an old teacher from George and Roy's school, to members of the family, and to Mattie Haines, the old family retainer. She forms various theories, focusing on her thesis that the family murdered George because he had discovered their plan to murder their father for his money. Abruptly, Madeleine and Jerry deny Celia access to Ellsworth and keep him a virtual prisoner. Just as Celia despairs of making any progress in the investigation, a male nurse arrives to take charge of the case, an ambulance is called, and the professor is spirited away to the local hospital where he can confer with his lawyer. The dénouement is smooth and satisfactory.

Gerald Warner Brace

In *The Wayward Pilgrims* (1938), Lawrence Minot, who teaches freshmen at Harvard, is presented with a summer fellowship in the field of American dialects and sets forth to travel by train, and then by foot, to study language in Vermont. On the train he meets a young Vermonter, Mary Butterfield, from a farm in Rockington in Windham County. Her father went to Dartmouth, but her grandfather was injured, so her father had to come home to run the farm. Mary's sister, Helen, is doing most of the work. Lawrence alights at the station where he meets Margot Anton, who has lost her purse and has no money. Capriciously, she starts walking alongside him, telling him that she has run away from her painter husband in Peru. He is the sort, she says, who thinks "everyone in the mountains is incestuous or half-witted or both." She has been married to two other men as well. Their pilgrimage covers three days, in which they walk and talk at length and spend the three nights in the sugarhouse of a real Vermonter, in a modest house they stumble upon, and in the comfortable guesthouse of a happy elderly couple. During that interlude, Lawrence climbs alone into the Green Mountains and has a religious experience: "The world was vaster than he had ever seen it." "The windy hills and sky had become the sum of all reality." He feels he has taken "a great voyage through Vermont, the tour of earth and sky, solitude and exaltation." They are both well educated, well adjusted, sporting, honest, humorous, and, at the end, in love. Older and more experienced, Margot knows that she cannot stay with Lawrence and leaves while he is out foraging for food. He follows her to Peru, where he learns that her husband has killed himself; she has left, leaving no word of her destination. He is heartbroken but regenerated by his three days with Margot, who has made him "see life plain."

The Gaunt farm in *Light on a Mountain* (1941) has clung to Stafford Mountain for three generations. John Gaunt sells three hundred acres of giant spruce for timber in order to support his family: his wife, Carrie Haven; his son, Morton, a tireless worker who "delighted in his virtues;"

his beautiful daughter, Sylvia, with a dreamy, artistic temperament; and his second son, Henry, a poet and thinker who is away at college. The nearest train station is Rutland, where they shop. From their mountain, the village of Stafford "lay like a scatter of white chips in a green bowl." When Henry comes home from college for the summer, he sees his mother "half dead from the burden of life," yet always showing "certainty and a shrewd humor." He knows that the early Vermont farmers walled in the wild but promising pastureland, which they worked with labor and patience. Now, the land is a "makeshift sort of place where you grubbed out a living year-by-year." Sylvia has several beaux. One is John Scarci, the son of a laid-off marble cutter who is scorned as a "foreigner;" her father calls John a "damn wop agitator." Sylvia realizes that Vermonters feel that only those born in Vermont are normal. Henry, too, sees Vermonters as "convinced of their own virtues." One night Henry has an insight on the mountain that he barely understands: "One light on a mountain meant life; many lights in the valley meant war—or the beginning of war." Unexpectedly, Morton brings home a wife, Marjie Howe, who is superficial, lazy, spoiled, and hates farming; the family is never the same after she moves in and, in time, has a baby, Beverly, for whom she is unable to care. Henry returns with a professor friend, Lincoln McGann, thirty-eight, who falls deeply in love with Sylvia. When she learns he is married, she is "silent as a moth." She is aware of the "strong current flowing between them" but does not encourage him. Carrie has a stroke and dies from overwork; Henry goes to New York to get his master's degree; and Sylvia decides, with certainty and optimism if not romantic love, to marry Tommy Drew, a fine young local, and to help her father through this difficult time.

Ned and Yanna Brandt

In *Land Kills* (1991), Mitchell Stevens, who teaches journalism at a university in New York, is asked by an ailing friend, Ham Johnson, to come to Southborough to run Ham's newspaper, the *Courier,* while Ham recovers from an operation.

The timing is good: it is Mitch's summer vacation, Mitch's son is grown, and his wife, Val, an actress, has a summer job in Williamstown. Southborough, in the southeast corner of Vermont, was founded before the Revolution. It shares many of Brattleboro's characteristics: a bus station housed in a trailer on the outskirts of town; Hill Street, with a tangle of traffic; Southborough College; Mount Vert Music Festival; sixties hippies (first outsiders, then assimilated); "cosmopolitan flatlanders;" and development. A ski resort, SkiLand, has been voted in, in addition to a proposed mall with outlet store and a surveyor who is not pleased with "New Yorkers coming here and sending land values sky high." It occurs to Mitch that while in Vermont he might look at some property upon which to build a retirement home. He stumbles upon the dead body of a real estate woman, Vera Holvey, shot in a hunting accident. Mitch settles in with temporary staff to run the daily paper. Soon there is another death—an economics professor, Telford Eagleston, who helped push the zoning ordinance through for SkiLand. The publisher of the *Courier*, John Haye, forces Mitch to accompany him to a dinner for supporters of the development. He meets Brad Cummings, a selectman and store owner whose wife, Jesse, works at the *Courier*; Bert Lester, the bank president; William Handler, a retired New York police officer; and Harvey Troupe, head of SkiLand. Much to Mitch's discomfort, Haye pledges the *Courier*'s support for the effort to permit Britfair to build the outlet and warehouse next to SkiLand. There is a third death, this time the musician Putzgarov, whose car plows into a telephone pole. Mitch happens to be nearby and hurries to the scene. The car smells of alcohol, but Mitch learns from one of his reporters that the dead musician was a member of Alcoholics Anonymous. The selectmen call an emergency town meeting to vote through the proposal for Britfair. Although they give only one day's notice to the newspaper, the meetinghouse is jammed. Gaps in state regulations allow developers to buy many acres of undeveloped land and divide them up for sale as building lots without state review.

The townsfolk are not going to allow these greedy developers to get away with murder; the town meeting is dissolved, and John Haye is furious with Mitch. Ham's house is burned to the ground by an unknown arsonist, and Mitch barely escapes with his life. Mitch tries to explain all of these coincidences to the publisher, who thinks that Mitch is a grandstanding New Yorker trying to take over the paper. Mitch cleverly solves the crimes, putting himself in some danger, and he and Val decide not to build a house in Vermont.

Don Bredes

Cold Comfort (2001) begins with the return of Hector Bellevance to his mother's house in Tipton in northern Vermont to start his life over. Tipton is between Mt. Joseph and Ferdinand Grove near Arrow Lake. When Hector was ten, Tipton stopped being a successful and promising town: the railway service ended; the station house was dismantled for stone; the fashionable girls' camp went bankrupt; the last of the saw logs was cut; and family farms went under. A Harvard graduate, former Boston homicide detective, and deserted by his wife, Hector killed his partner in an accidental shooting. Exonerated from any responsibility for the shooting, Hector resigns from the force and assigns his pension to his partner's widow and children. Back in Vermont, he earns his living as a truck farmer and town constable and has simplified his housekeeping arrangements. Spud, Hector's half-brother and a dairy farmer, lives nearby and next door to an A-frame house owned by Otto and Gaea Morganthau. When Spud finds the couple murdered—and fails to report it for two days—he becomes the sheriff's prime suspect. Hector dedicates himself to solving the mystery, with no help from the local police but lots of help from Wilma Strong-Parkhurst, an attractive reporter for the local paper. Hector moves around the community talking to old friends, including a man who runs Mt. Joe Militia, a paramilitary organization. This cult turns out to be involved in smuggling marijuana in the form of reefer bricks to Canada by water. The Morganthaus were ferrying the consortium's ill-gotten greenbacks to offshore accounts in Curaçao, whence the money might be invested in the acquisition of land and the profits taken by the players. Spud was sleeping with Gaea, but he did not kill her. Hector and Wilma manage to tie all the threads together, with some bodily harm, and also to fall in love. They may stay together; there are hints Hector still loves his divorced wife, Naomi. Here is an evocative image of the couple's first kiss: "Then, little by little, like a sawn tree just beginning to fall, she leaned toward me." (The title is from Shakespeare's *King John*: "I do not ask you much,/I beg cold comfort.")

The Fifth Season (2002), intricate and fascinating, opens in April the following year. Constable Hector Bellevance is still seeing reporter Wilma Strong, nurturing his market produce, and working part-time for his half-brother, Spud. Hector, sympathetic and stoical, has grown up in Tipton and knows everyone. Marcel Boisvert, the current road commissioner, is a direct descendant of the first Abenaki landholders in the valley. In 1759, after the fall of Quebec City to the British, Sam Boisvert fled south, married Mary Gill, a St. Francis Abenaki, and settled on the land now known as the ash plain. By the time Hector's grandfather, Norman, bought his farm, most of the denizens of the ash plain had left. Although Marcel's father, Philo, and Reg Bellevance played baseball with the Tipton Catamounts for many summers, Marcel has always been curt with Hector. Marcel's wife, Shirley, is unhinged and drug-dependent; his little boy, Philo, was "sent away" and died thirty-five years ago; and his daughter, Kathy, "Tipton's princess," was killed in a hang-gliding accident. Marcel, bitter about her death, refuses to plow the road to Greenwood Hollow, inhabited by Kathy's widower, Vaughn Higgins, an urbane outsider and professor at Allenburg State College, and their five-year-old son, Marc. Hector has to serve a relief-from-abuse order on Marcel from Shirley, who is at the house of Ella McPhetres, the town clerk. Marcel refuses to obey the court order and Hector finds Ella shot dead. He sees Marcel, wearing a red hat, drive by in a police cruiser. Hector hurries to the Boisvert farm

where Pete Mueller, Montcalm County sheriff, who went to high school and played football with Hector, is lying dead in the driveway. The state police, hostile to Hector's "lone ranger" modus operandi and "haughty" demeanor, arrive at his house with a search warrant. They believe Marcel is dead: his septic tank is full of his rare blood type. When Hector learns from Vaughn that he cancelled his Monday morning classes, that the warranty deed for the transfer of property from Philo Boisvert to Kathy is missing from Ella's office, and that Vaughn has a red cap, he begins to wonder if he was mistaken about Marcel. Hector finds another dead body and turns for help to Hugh Gebbie, once an English teacher at Mount Joseph Academy and Hector's mother's partner for twenty years. A balloonist and dowser, Hugh takes Hector over the lake to look for Marcel's tracks and accompanies Hector and Wilma to the Boisvert farm to dowse for "emanations." Shirley and Marc, whom Hector has put in Shirley's protection against his father's wishes, disappear. The resolution is wrenching and believable. Wilma and Hector's future is unclear. The imagery is arresting: "eight white wood-frame houses along the west side of the common, their east-facing windows like scraps of gold foil in the sun," "The cliffs, a sinewy façade of shifting colors, were bearded this morning with columns of pale blue ice," and "Fresh snow in the yard looked crisp as a bed sheet."

Thomas Brennan

In *The Debt* (2005), Steve Burnett, a young police officer in Manhattan, goes out on a routine patrol with his partner, taking with them at their boss's request a writer named Carl Shaw, who is from Eastham, between Enosburg Falls and Sheldon, close to the Canadian border. Carl says he is carrying neither controlled substances nor a firearm. Ambushed as they check out a deli, Steve and his partner are both wounded; while Steve is lying on the pavement he sees Carl draw a weapon from an ankle holster and kill the robber, Tyrone Cursell. Carl has saved their lives: they owe him a debt. Carl tells the police he grabbed the robber's gun. When Steve learns that Carl's gun was used in a killing in Eastham the previous year, he says nothing in response to Detective Mendez's questions because he is wrestling with his obligation to Carl. Instead, Steve heads for Vermont to investigate the murder of Sarah Westlake, a postgraduate in psychology at the University of Vermont, found dead in her car on Lake Champlain. During his investigations, he talks to Fran Dutroux, editor and owner of the *Eastham Courier,* and Elaine Shaw, Carl's expensively dressed and seductive wife. He meets Shirley at the diner and her waitress, Patti, who worked for the Shaws. He visits Alex Crosby, Sarah's professor at the University of Vermont, Ed Petchey, who found Sarah's body, Police Chief Peterson, and Louise and Derek in Cardford Springs (a stop on the Underground Railroad), where the murder occurred. Sarah was living with the Shaws to study alcoholism and drug dependency; Leon Mathers, whose car was seen at the crime site, also lived at the Shaws for a while. Steve's car is sabotaged and his hotel room trashed; as Peterson says, "Small town like this, strangers stand out." The body of private investigator Harry Braid, who was hired by Sarah's parents, is fished out of Lake Champlain. At the Shaws, Steve sees a newspaper clipping about him and his partner, giving details of their regular early morning trips to the deli. Mendez tells Steve that Cursell received a large amount of money from a bank in Eastham. Evidence against Carl is piling up. Steve finally finds Sarah's laptop (at Louise and Derek's, on the waterfront), which contains the key to the mystery—but some files are missing. Steve perseveres in his quest and survives a final violent confrontation with the killer. He is ready to tell Mendez the truth in order to stay on the force.

Howard Breslin

In *The Tamarack Tree* (1947), the year is 1840; the place, Stratton; the issue, the presidential race between Martin Van Buren and William Henry Harrison. The great Daniel Webster is coming to Stratton to speak at the Whig Convention. Van Buren has already beaten Harrison in the 1836 election; the Panic of 1837

has caused a depression. Most of the residents of Stratton feel hostile toward Van Buren for his "New York connections." There is a classical unity of time and place: a prologue, the three days of the Convention on the clearing at Glastenbury Pass on Stratton Mountain, and an epilogue. The prologue introduces some of the residents of Stratton and sets up the human drama that plays out against the Convention. Reverend Chester is there with his wife, son Putnam, and daughters, especially Lovina, who is loved by Charles Chittenden. Innkeeper David Tarbox comes with his family. Abner Reed, the blacksmith, greets folks who congregate to chat around his fire. Lem Brayton beats his son, Asa, and knows his wife is unfaithful to him. Nathan Patch, son of the sawmill owner, also loves Lovina. Lot Purdy is the stage driver and only Democrat in town. The wagons begin to arrive. Soon thousands of people are in the clearing, getting ready to camp out or to sleep under their wagons. An impromptu village springs up. A platform is built under the tamarack tree that stands in the clearing. A huge log cabin is erected in honor of "Tippecanoe and Tyler too," and an armed guard sits by the supply of hard cider. Thomas Jefferson Dunbar, a young gentleman from Virginia, and his Negro slave, Hoc, arrive by horse and seek refuge in the Inn. Doc Merrifield comes with his adopted daughter, Mercy, aged fourteen, and his Elixir medicine for sale to the crowds. Jabez Tute and his gang of ruffians from Bondville assemble to rob the participants and disrupt the Convention. Webster, who has spent the night before the Convention nearby, speaks for two hours to some applause and some criticism. The attempted departure of the wagons becomes a rout, confused and violent, choking the narrow turnpike. The human toll in Stratton is significant. Dunbar makes insulting remarks about a young woman; Charles, thinking he is referring to Lovina, challenges him to a duel. Both survive, but Dunbar loses an arm. Purdy loses control of his stage horses, which run down Put Chester, who is seriously injured. Lem Brayton shoots dead his wife's lover, axes his wife to death, and flees only to be eaten by a bear.

T. Alan Broughton

Julie Cobb, the first-person narrator in *Hob's Daughter* (1984), lives in Charlotte just south of Burlington with her lover, Michael Gardener, a Special Collections librarian at the University of Vermont, his daughter, Melissa, a graduate of UVM, and his blind father, Sheldon. Julie is seven years younger than Melissa. Much of the narrative deals with Julie's unhappy childhood in Burlington: her mother, Jane, killed herself when Julie was thirteen; her brother, Tim, nine years older, ran away from home. Her father, J. Howard ("Hob") Cobb, is a famous writer. When fifteen-year-old Julie first meets Michael, he is trying to buy Hob's papers for the university. She does a stint as an apprentice woodworker for Art, who beats his wife, and, after college, she becomes a sculptor. In 1969, after Julie and Michael have lived together for five years, a terrible tragedy occurs in which Julie is forced to play a role. Afterward, she must make decisions about her future. (The epigraph is the first and last lines of Robert Frost's poem: "I have been one acquainted with the night.")

Two stories from *Suicidal Tendencies* (2003) are set in Vermont. In **"Bill's Women,"** Bill Tonson lived in northern Vermont in Orleans County. After his first wife killed herself, he married Sheila, who was twenty years younger than he was. Their marriage was quiet, "reticent," not passionate. He was stubbornly independent. He went out to try to fix the power line without calling for help from the electricity department and electrocuted himself. Now Sheila, forty, childless, is a widow. She quit her job before their four-year marriage and has nothing to do. Bill's taciturn identical twins, Harry and Harvey, whom she has never met, come to see her. She lashes out at them, blaming them for leaving their parents, for driving their mother to suicide. They turn their backs on her verbal assault and vanish. "Only her own body seemed to hang still in the bright air." Hannah, the narrator in **"My Other Life,"** is from Burlington. She meets Polly Brent at Swarthmore College during the early seventies and is swept into the crowd of Polly's admirers. Polly is mainline Philadelphia,

the glamorous center of attention, who makes jokes about Vermont ("Didn't I read recently that in the past census there are more cows than people there?"). The following year, Hannah, finding Polly sick in the bathroom, skips a quiz to comfort her and discovers that she is a drinker, a liar, and prone to fantasy. They room together the following year. Then Polly marries Dave Warnock, and Hannah leaves Swarthmore to study at the University of Vermont. Hannah student-teaches at Burlington High School and has a beau named Don Mahoney. Dave accepts a position at UVM, but almost immediately Polly decides to divorce him. She persuades Hannah to accompany her to Mexico for a divorce. As she listens to Polly talk about her life, Hannah clings to her mantra: "I am Hannah of Burlington. I am a teacher. I live as best I can." She thinks about that time in Swarthmore: if she had gone to her quiz she never would have become involved in Polly's life. That night, Polly commits suicide and Hannah wonders: "What can we do about the lives of others when we so insufficiently understand our own?"

Joseph Bruchac

This haunting, genuine trilogy about Abenaki life set in prehistoric times consists of *Dawn Land, Long River*, and *The Waters Between*. They are filled with lyrical descriptions of animals and birds. Each of the chapters has a story within the story, describing Abenaki lore and culture. The tribe called Only People lives in Dawn Land, which is made up of thirteen villages on Lake Champlain (*Petonbowk*) near Otter Creek. *Dawn Land* (1993) introduces the hero, Young Hunter (whose parents were killed by a falling tree), the girl he has chosen to marry, Willow Girl, and his grandparents, Sweetgrass Woman and Rabbit Stick. Other characters are Bear Talker, a deep-seer (*mteowlin*), and his wife, Medicine Plant; Young Hunter's uncle, Fire Keeper, and his son, Raccoon; his best friend, Sparrow; Muskrat, the oldest person in the village, and Uncle Fish Hawk and his twin sons, Red Hawk and Blue Hawk. Young Hunter goes as a "pure hunter" (no weapon) to catch a deer for his people to eat. In the process, a poisonous snake bites him, but he falls into some cold mud that helps heal his wound. He is successful in his hunt and appointed by Bear Talker to represent his people on another quest to meet an unknown enemy. Young Hunter sets out in the company of his three dogs, Agwedjiman, Pabetcimar, and Danowa. Before he leaves, his uncle, Fire Keeper, shows him some new wrestling moves, his grandfather gives him a new stone knife, and Bear Talker gives him the Long Thrower, a bow. One of his tasks is to find the small spears to use as arrows. He goes to the Salmon People, where Uncle Fish Hawk has taught him to catch salmon and where he finds his twin cousins, Red Hawk and Blue Hawk. Medicine Plant, who was taught by Oldest Talker, is a far-seer and midwife. It is she who gives him the small spears; he spends several days practicing with the bow. He knows that something burning with anger is waiting for him somewhere. That presence is Weasel Tail, who has grown up twisted after the deaths of his parents. He is working for the Ancient Ones, bringing them human sacrifices to satisfy their cannibalistic hungers. One of his women victims escapes, after striking him with a huge branch, and is found by Young Hunter, who escorts her to her village. He has traveled to the other side of Lake Champlain; she is one of the People of the Long Lodges (Iroquois) and, after they have made him run the gauntlet, they welcome and adopt him. He comes upon Weasel Tail, who helps Young Hunter's dogs kill the black hunter and, in the process of the sacrifice, becomes human again and renames himself Holds the Stone. Pabetcimar is killed. Young Hunter and Holds the Stone join forces in killing the Ancient Ones and Holds the Stone dies, going over the cliff while struggling with One-Eye. At last, Young Hunter has freed his people and can return home.

Long River (1995) finds Young Hunter's people in their spring village on the eastern side of Vermont on the Connecticut River (*Kwanitewk*). He is married to Willow Woman, has his two dogs, Agwedjiman and Danowa, and a puppy, Pabesis, which Young Hunter believes is a reincarnated Pabetcimar. This story traces the paths

of many creatures that converge in the dramatic ending at the Great Falls. Walking Hill is a lonely mammoth, with a huge trunk and vast teeth, whose family has been killed and who is wandering the countryside crushing small, soft humans. He has been struck in one tooth with a spear and is in great pain. The last of the Ancient Ones, a grey giant, is lurking mournfully in his cave. Angry Face, who fell into a fire and was burned when she was a child, has escaped the village of the Bear People, destroyed by Walking Hill, and is looking for revenge. Sparrow, Young Hunter's friend, is looking for a woman who will make him as happy as Willow Woman makes Young Hunter. Mikumwesu, one of the Little People, has been separated from his family and is searching for it. It is he who has wedged his weapon between the tooth and jaw of Walking Hill. As these actors are drawn together, Young Hunter's life continues. Willow Woman tames a black crow. Medicine Plant and Bear Talker have a baby, with Sweetgrass Woman as the midwife for a breech birth. Young Hunter rescues Yellow Stick from a fall over a cliff while escaping the Ancient One. And all the time Young Hunter knows that danger is stalking his people. In the resolution, the Ancient One attacks Walking Hill with a huge spear and, from now on, will watch over the Only People. The body of Walking Hill is covered with huge rocks; his salvaged broken tooth is the size of a man. Sparrow and Angry Face, who changes her name to River Woman, fall in love. Pabesis, who hurled himself at Walking Hill, is healing. And Young Hunter will take Mikumwesu to Lake Champlain to look for the other Little People.

In *The Waters Between* (1998) Young Hunter's wife, Willow Woman, is pregnant. The familiar characters are back with a few additions. His nephew, Raccoon, and his best friends, the twins Red Hawk and Blue Hawk, participate, as well as Medicine Plant, a healer, and her husband, Bear Talker. Also involved in the story are Fire Keeper, Young Hunter's uncle and the sagaman of the village ("No man can lead the people unless the women have first agreed upon the direction in which he will go"), Grey Otter and his twin daughters, and Carries Snakes, Young Hunter's other grandfather. Young Hunter is training to become a deep-seer or shaman. From the shore, Young Hunter sees the snake-being-bigger-than-big (*padoskoks*) in the lake; he also has a vision of a deep-seer with a twisted mind. This is Watches Darkness, an albino who was abused as a child and now travels around with his pet, a large white bear, killing and eating the hearts of all the deep-seers he can find. Young Hunter sets off to warn the villagers of these dangers. Watches Darkness arrives at Gray Otter's (a cousin of Medicine Plant's) to kill him, but he has vanished through a hole in the floor of his wigwam, taking the bones of his parents with him. The twins, Red Hawk and Blue Hawk, come to Gray Otter's, where they are fated to fall in love with his twin daughters. When Young Hunter reaches Carries Snakes, the latter gives him his snake, Black Friend. Willow Woman searches for Young Hunter at the lakeshore and bravely fights off the bear (who is innately good and can be healed by Bear Talker). Young Hunter takes his dugout (designed to move across the water "like a froth blown by the wind") into the lake, attached to a rope made by his wife and grandmother. He meets Padoskoks, whose head is as big as a bear's body. Young Hunter and the sea serpent stare meaningfully at each other; Black Friend rises out of his bag and hisses. The people on the shore start pulling the dugout back to shore, while the monster follows the boat. The sea creature snatches Watches Darkness in its jaws and drags him to the bottom of the lake. The people on the shore sing and pray that if the monster does not trouble them, they will always respect it. Young Hunter's last act is to return Black Friend to the lake. When a storm approaches, a character "saw already how the waves would come across the lake, like great herds of animals running through the tall grass."

Frank Bryan and Bill Mares

In *Out! The Vermont Secession Book* (1987), the year is 1991. Alexander Haig is President of the United States. Vermont has seceded from the Union. After all, in 1777 Vermont set up its own form of government, wrote its own constitution,

and existed for fourteen years as an independent commonwealth. Its values were and are "self-reliance, thrift, liberalism, industry, and self-respect." The Revolutionary Council of the Republic of Vermont is headquartered in The Stone House in Brownington. Lt. Col. Bentley Bentley, USMC, takes some Special Forces to The Stone House to arrest the revolutionaries, only to find that his men are defecting to Vermont. The Council disbands, after deciding to run the country on a Town Meeting of the Republic format. Any Vermonter who wishes to show up can vote. "In Vermont, everyone is equal." The place of the town meeting alternates, as does the moderator. When Bentley finally believes he has captured the Government of Vermont (they are meeting in Strafford), he finds that those particular people aren't the government anymore: "In Vermont, the government is everyone."

Perdita Buchan

Called Away (1980) introduces Clover and Jared, two romantic young people who want to start over in a new, simpler life. They drive north across the Massachusetts border into Vermont and settle in a tiny hamlet called Circe (based on Marlboro). Clover and Jared meet the rich summer folks, and the more stolid all year-round people, and the Jesus Freaks who camp out at the fairground. Are they all trying to recreate the past? Clover and Jared take their new situation seriously: they buy animals, plant seeds, and build pens. Before the snow comes, Clover explores the surrounding landscape and finds evidence of former inhabitants—old cellars and older apple trees. When winter comes, they struggle with the elements. She is attracted to an itinerant peddler, Surt Mudspell, who spirits her away to Circe in 1815. It is important to suspend disbelief in this time-warp story because it is a charming tale about a young woman who wants desperately to learn about the past and is given a chance to live in it. In old Circe, she meets the forebears of people she knows in twentieth-century Circe. She becomes a schoolteacher. She falls in love with Justin, the father of two of her students, a widower who reminds her of Jared.

They marry and "the homesteading zeal with which Clover had attacked the camp when she and Jared had first come to Circe returned to her now. She planted the dooryard with flower seeds: phlox, pinks, nasturtiums. She scoured the house from cellar to attic. She worked in the barn and in the cowshed, where the milk cow and her heifer were sheltered. The work was hard, and it was constant, and it was the only way of life. Living on the land was no longer an aesthetic and moral choice; it had no overtones of craft, art, or rediscovery." After a winter that doesn't end, when Justin leaves his family to go out West to find a new life for them, she understands why the old Vermont towns faded away, why people abandoned their homes and farms, why there are empty cellar holes, and what it takes to change old ways to survive. Finally, when the natives blame her for the cold weather and the drought, Surt Mudspell spirits her back to Jared and the present. She realizes that she and Jared have over-romanticized their Vermont experience.

Pearl S. Buck

The Winsten mansion in Manchester in *Voices in the House* (1953) was built in the early nineteenth century. William Asher married Elinor Winsten twenty-five years previously and changed the house's name to "Asher," but it is still referred to as the "Winsten house." All the other Winsten children went out West, but Elinor stays in Vermont. The other surviving Winsten, Cousin Emma, lives in New York. William is a successful lawyer with offices in Manchester and New York. Their son, Winsten, is married with children; Edwin and Susan are still at college. The Ashers are "gentry," belong to the country club, and keep servants—a couple called Bertha and Heinrich, their daughter, Jessica, a maid, and Herbert Morris, a chauffeur. Jessica, twenty-five, is engaged to marry Herbert. William considers his own marriage "successful and therefore safe." From time to time, he notices the maid, Jessica, in the East Parlor acting like the mistress of the house. He ignores this behavior. At Christmastime, all the children are home, including Vera Bates, "a silver birch of a girl" and daughter of a local banker, whom Edwin wishes to marry. William, a snob, believes in the "station" of a servant and is fond of his "own kind." When Susan brings home rough-mannered Peter Boggs, accompanied by his large black dog, Pirate, William finds it hard to be polite to Peter. When the dog misbehaves, Jessica, the maid, offers to take him home with her. William's work is going badly, and at home all is not well either. A "corruption" has appeared in his well-ordered house. Jessica and Herbert are unhappy; the dog has bitten a child, who is in the hospital; Susan is engaged to Peter. William finds it hard to discuss these matters with Elinor, who is evasive about the "depths" between them: it was "the Vermont in her." Suddenly, Jessica accuses Edwin of having spent a day with her in a hotel in New York. She also claims that William has been forcing her to have sexual relations with him since she was seventeen, just back from the convent. She suffers a psychotic break and is taken to the hospital. William continues to dislike Peter: he had come into their lives because "all classes were churned together by war." Susan despairs of her parents' understanding and elopes with Peter. After three years, Jessica is released from the hospital. Someone kills Cousin Emma, poking knitting needles through her eyes into her brain. Jessica is found guilty and returned to an asylum. Elinor thinks there is something wrong in the house; William agrees that there are "strange voices, disturbing, corrupting, cutting across the human grain of their common life." To atone, the Ashers welcome back Peter by opening their hearts and their house to him.

Letters from Peking (1957) is a poignant, lyrical story about a bicultural marriage and a coming home. Elizabeth Duane Kirke MacLeod, educated at Radcliffe, lives in Raleigh (near Manchester) in a mountain valley in her grandfather's house. Elizabeth was forced to leave her half-Chinese husband, Gerald, when the Communists entered Peking in 1949. She lives in a half-stone, half-timbered house with her seventeen-year-old son, Rennie. She is often offered a fortune for her house and always refuses. Matt

Greene, the hired man, helps with the cows, the sugaring, and the ploughing. Gerald requests permission to marry a "Chinese wife." She does not tell her son but continues with her chores, pruning apple trees. "And I have learned to prune severely. A close, clean cut heals soon—that I have learned. But I know that too deep a cut will never heal. The branch will bear no fruit." She understands that "My grandfather did not belong to the valley and my parents were summer people first, and I cannot expect in one generation to be considered a valley woman." She is putting the land into permanent hay, because she believes grass farming is the only answer to their short season in the mountains. "A hundred years ago men made fields among the rocks and tried to grow grain and their fields have returned to wilderness. Eighteen thousand-fold...once gathered on the side of Mount Stratton to hear Daniel Webster speak. I doubt eighteen hundred could gather now...They have gone away, those folk, and their children and children's children are living their lives in strange and distant places. They went away in search of home, even as I have returned to find my home." Rennie falls for a local girl and is ashamed to tell her he is a quarter Chinese (Buck coined the term "Amerasian"). She and Rennie bring Gerald's American father from the Midwest to Vermont. When he has a stroke, she calls the local doctor, Bruce Spaulden. His is the calm, sensible voice of Vermont, and also the face, "lean" and "controlled." Gerald's Chinese wife smuggles letters to her about Gerald and their son. Elizabeth contrasts Peking with Vermont: "How still the Vermont mountains are, how empty of human life! The forest, as night falls, grows sinister in darkness. Sometimes the sun shines through the trees upon the brakes and ferns and that underworld appears all innocence and tender beauty. But the suns sets early in the valley and the shadows descend." At her father-in-law's funeral, she is able to laugh with Rennie and Bruce. "I belong here, I kept thinking. It is here I was born, and if I were not so lonely, I could forget Peking and at last perhaps I could even forget Gerald. I have not laughed for a long time...I felt a tenderness, amused, unspecified, but valid." In Peking, Gerald is shot, as his grandmother was shot.

David Budbill

A Pulp Cutter's Nativity (1981), a tragicomic and devout drama, is set in Judevine, a poor and struggling town in northern Vermont, in which characters from Judevine act out a modern adaptation of *The Second Shepherds' Play*, a medieval miracle play. Three Judevine woodcutters, Antoine, Doug, and Tommy, take the place of the fifteenth century shepherds; Judevine's Arnie steals a chainsaw instead of a lamb; and his cantankerous and conniving wife, Gil, plays the original Gil. In this version the Announcing and Attending Angel is a waitress at the local diner. The play follows the structure of the original English play, diverging from it only at the end when Vietnam vet Tommy Stames sees in the Baby Jesus a vision of Gandhi, Martin Luther King, and himself.

Judevine (1992), a play narrated by David, a poet, presents a parade of twenty-four characters again in Judevine, a rural mountain town that combines great physical beauty and profound suffering and hardship with a tenacious and indomitable will to survive. The lives of the characters are seen singly and in relation to others. Raymond and Ann have in their fifty years together become a symbol of love, warmth, and cooperation. Grace's tortured and lonely life explodes into bitterness, violence, jealousy, and finally madness. Teenager Carol Hopper, middle-aged Conrad, and Tommy withdraw in their isolation into themselves. Lucy has lost her mind and Jerry loves and protects her. Alice is "half man, half woman" and "embraces other people's lives." Laura and Edgar pass ordered, proper, and restrained days while bursting with repressed passion for each other. Antoine is the irrepressible, effusive, and ebullient lover of women and all the rest of life. These portraits of ordinary people reveal the survival strength of the oppressed and hurt.

B

Frederick Buechner

In *The Entrance to Porlock* (1970), Peter Ringkoping lives on Tinmouth Mountain with his almost-blind wife, Sarah (she refuses to have cataract operations). Son Nels is a bachelor and Dean of Students in a nearby boys' school, Putnam; son Tommy, his wife, Alice, and their nineteen-year-old son, Thomas, Jr. ("Tip"), live in the town of Langdon. Peter, after celebrating his eightieth birthday, announces that he is thinking of giving away his not inconsiderable acreage to Hans Stasser, the owner of an insane asylum called Pilgrim's Village. The bulk of the story — a spiritual journey — takes place as the characters drive to Pilgrim's Village, spend the day there, and drive home. They are all concerned with their own lives and their own problems. Peter sees ghosts in the used bookshop he runs in his barn. Alice is maintaining her family's old home and wondering why her son doesn't live in it. Nels is dealing with a problem boy at the school whom he is threatening to expel. Tommy is trying not to play the fool. Tip is seeking his identity and writing a letter in his head to the young woman he loves in Langdon. A taste of the appealing and eloquent prose: "What with rocky soil, steep grades, and the preponderance of rock maple, ironwood, thorn apple that were lovely to look at but valueless, the property was scarcely destined to make the family fortune, except that in a slow, underground way, over the years it had come to seem so to them. There would always be the land. It was big enough to get lost in. It was crisscrossed with bumbled stone walls and marked with overgrown cellar holes where here and there a clump of lupine or an apple tree rearing up among the tall weeds witnessed to families who, in the years before the opening of the West, had once worked that unyielding soil. Deer grazed the edges of its fields or shot up impossible slopes with their white rumps flashing. There was a beaver dam. There were picnic places, fire ponds for swimming, unmistakable traces, Peter had told his children, of a lost civilization buried under the hills."

Pamela Burford

Is Dr. Noah Stewart in *His Secret Side* (1996) a split personality or is he a reincarnation? Kathleen ("Kit") Roarke asks herself these questions when she comes to Pratte ("a quaint little tourist trap") between Montpelier and Burlington to investigate the murder by curare poisoning of her best friend, Jo Merino. Kit is attracted to Noah, but he sometimes thinks he is Dr. Ray Whittaker, who died thirty-two years earlier after killing Anita David with curare. Or did he? The answer to the riddle lies in the book Jo was writing on the Whittaker murder, *Poisoned Love*, which has disappeared along with her computer, but a back-up disk exists. Henry David, the editor of the *Pratte Citizen*, Jo's boss and Anita's husband, is now married to well-toned, youthful-looking Bettina. Also in the mix is hippie Brian Carlisle, Whittaker's grandson, who is certain his grandfather was innocent. So it is proved, when the murderer tries to kill Kit to obtain the disk implicating the killer in both murders.

Herbert Burkholz

Sister Bear (1969) describes the incestuous love of Steven and Anna Matthias who, after the deaths of their parents, are raised by their Aunt Esther in Burlington in the Vermont winters and by their father's best friend, Professor Axel Peterson, in New York in the summers. As they grow old enough to be on their own, they spend all their time skiing at Copperjack Mountain near Stowe. When Steve marries Claire Sullivan, one of the best racers in the country, Anna, often wearing the mask of a bear, begins her jealous descent into promiscuity and decadence. They and their dissolute, hedonistic friends pass months skiing in Europe. Anna returns to the United States and marries Axel, who is dying of cancer. She joins Claire and Steve and their hangers-on in Vermont and announces to the assembled crowd that she and her brother are lovers. She and Steve acknowledge their guilty love and live together for the rest of the winter; when spring — and facing up to reality and responsibility — comes, Anna kills herself in a reckless skiing stunt.

Michael Burns

In *Gemini* (2001), Jack Scanlon's wife, Katie, leaves him, taking their daughter, Lucy. Burdened with a heavy drinking problem and fired from his job at Consolidated, Scanlon decides to return to Groveton in the Northeast Kingdom, where he grew up, to start life over as a science teacher at Fairfield High School during the 1968-1969 academic year. Short of funds because of alimony and child support payments, he boards with his Aunt Alice and Uncle Ira. They live on River Road, which "merged with Route 5, the busy thoroughfare to Canada." Before Scanlon left Groveton at age eleven, eighteen years ago, his name was Johnny Labalm; he does not want his past known. He soon befriends an attractive colleague couple at the school, Josh and Rachel Patterson. Other colleagues, such as "mean-minded" Lyle Higgins and draft-resister Douglas Stambaugh, are less friendly. Jack immediately raises the hackles of the "jelly-fish" principal, Daryl Winship, who, perhaps jealous of Jack's popularity with the students, finds fault with his meeting them three evenings a week to give them extra help in chemistry. When Scanlon insists upon including the theory of evolution in one of his classes, Winship warns him that the parochial community may take offense. Scanlon plays basketball in the gym one night with the students he is supposed to be tutoring and arouses the hostility of the coach, Ron Sorenson, who complains to Winship. To deal with his past, Scanlon seeks the weekly help of a therapist, Bob Kennedy. He wants to ask his Aunt Alice about his "unknown father," but can't find the opportunity. He continues to drink compulsively at family parties and faculty get-togethers, to turn back the students' papers and tests late, and to lust after Samantha Burnham, who reads paperback Hermann Hesse novels in his eighth-period study hall. Scanlon is belligerent and sarcastic, but he is honest with himself and he refrains from seducing Samantha, who is a more-than-willing accomplice. At the end, he learns the secret of his birth. Although he is invited back, he decides not to teach the following year.

C

Carl M. Chapin

In *Three Died beside the Marble Pool* (1936), Tremont Valley, the "summer-resort" section of East Tremont in southern Vermont, is where the advantaged, educated social crowd lives, swapping partners and drinking heavily. Paul Ruggdale, at thirty one of the younger members, is a strong, tall, former college football-player who has been deaf for ten years. (He hears with the help of a small microphone attached to his collar and a hand-held ear phone; he communicates with friends by teletype.) He chronicles the events of six dreadful days in the summer of 1934 after the pregnant body of Doris Brown is found in the Marble Pool, a huge basin of spring water in an abandoned quarry. She was a siren who had been involved with Paul, with the married Bill Moore, with young Ernest Gardner, and with federal investigator Pike Anderson. Who could have killed her? Not Ernie Gardner, because his body is found shortly thereafter. Not Bill Moore, who was jealous of Ernie, but is killed the next day. Not Lydia Moore, who was going to divorce Bill to marry New York-millionaire Boylston Ames, but is found dead the day after. Was it Diane Ogden, a forty-year-old beauty who has been the lover of both Ames and Kenelm Rankinson, the novelist? Or was it Ames or Rankinson? Ames tries to throw suspicion on Pike Anderson, the county detective. Helping Paul think through the series of crimes is Clemency ("Clem") Moore, the beautiful petite daughter of Bill and Lydia. Paul is in love with her, but thinks she would not want to marry a deaf man; Clem is in love with Paul, but can't make him propose to her. Finally, the killer, also a hoarder of large quantities of gold bars, is exposed.

Joan Chase

Laura, the first-person narrator in **"The Harrier"** (1991), lives with her writer husband in a small town near Lincoln in central Vermont.

She feels aimless, as though she is just treading water, and pines for a baby though her husband says he is not ready for one. A group of hippies moves to town and forms a commune. Laura sees the girls barefoot in their long calico skirts and the boys on their motorcycles on Main Street. After they drift on, a man named Jace stays. Laura is fixated upon him. "In that winter of cold and driving spikes of ice he seemed to slam against my bedroom window all night like some night bird wanting in." As she becomes acquainted with him—he comes into the thrift shop where she volunteers; she takes her old car to him for repairs—the imagery becomes thick with allusions to Indians and captivity. "It was as though I followed him with a bundle banded to my forehead over a forest path, my feet in deerskin." She thinks of him as a "wolf-boy." When she goes to his place one rainy day and finds a young woman there, she quickly leaves; he follows her to her house. When he tells her to come with him, she lets him drive her car, "as if to convince myself I had been abducted by force, carried captive across a wasteland." In the background is Vietnam—the locals think the hippies are all draft dodgers—and development. "The hasty exit of the developer had left Mountain Vista another dependent on the town, the water giving out and the old town road unsuited to school bus travel. Not a tree was left standing." And, finally, Jace is gone. "A drifter who gave only the appearance of drifting, he had come with unerring aim, a harrier drawn to prey upon the end of things."

Ruth Chatterton

Homeward Borne (1950) addresses anti-Semitism in America in the mid-1940s. The scene is the town of Mapleton, twenty-five miles from Burlington and site of a college where the widowed president, Edmund Gifford, has always lived with his daughter, Pax, and Negro cook, Pansy. Pax was born in 1920; the year is now 1946 and her husband, Robert Lyttleton, is serving in the occupying army in Germany. Pax loved a young man named Jake Felder, who was Jewish, but the night of the senior prom she failed a test: she felt ashamed of his immigrant

parents. Jake realized that he could not ask her to face a life with him and went away; she married his best friend, Robert. Jake is killed in the Pacific. Pax decides to adopt a refugee child, an eleven-year-old named Jan ben Rozov, who was raised in a concentration camp. It is only at the end of the book that she realizes she adopted Jan to make up for failing Jake. Jan faces appalling anti-Semitism, especially at the private school where Pax places him to fill some of his educational gaps (he has never been to school and, upon arrival, speaks no English). Robert returns home racist, anti-Semitic, and anti-Communist ("We were fighting the wrong people over there.") Pax divorces him and dedicates herself to raising Jan. (The title is from William Wordsworth's poem, "Guilt and Sorrow:" "but now along heaven's darkening cope / The crows rushed by in eddies, homeward borne.")

Steve Chontos

The Death of Dover, Vermont (1974) is a treatise, in the form of a novel, on the practice of local government in southern Vermont. It uses the experiences of a young couple, Mark and Lee Terrick, who move from New York to Dover seeking the good life, to illustrate how state and local regulations and individuals' needs and greed intersect. Mark first builds and runs a ski shop and later builds and runs a gas station. All of his spare time is spent studying government and state regulations and serving as selectman. Every kind of planning and development concern is examined through Mark's or his friends' experiences. One of the laws discussed in detail is Act 250, which pits the state and environmental protection against individual property rights. The State Environment Agency comes to a town meeting to expound on the notion that "Sometimes we must give up certain rights in order to achieve a better quality of life." Mark is not so sure. Another confrontation is over the improvement of the Seaton Road, which is a public road. Mark and the board of selectmen want to improve the road; the inhabitants, summer people, are against improving it—and they are not even voters. Mark finally becomes fed up with the paradox that he perceives in the state's philosophy. "On the one hand, they tell us that they want Vermont to remain rural with all its old traditions, but at the same time they are adopting all the latest developments and discoveries that have resulted directly from urban life." The stand-off between perspectives kills the town; Mark and Lee move back to New York.

Joseph A. Citro

The five following novels are steeped in research about Celtic ruins, Abenaki legends, Lake Champlain monster tales, and other local lore that lends authenticity to the narratives. In *Deus-X: The Reality Conspiracy* (1994), Dr. Karen Bradley is a clinical psychologist practicing in Burlington. Young, inexperienced, and faced with the case of Lucy Washburn, twelve, who is suffering from Multiple Personality Disorder, Karen seeks the guidance of Dr. Stan Gudhausen in Boston and discovers that he has a patient, Herbert Gold, who shares with Lucy Washburn an identical persona called "Splitfoot." While in Boston, Karen meets Dr. Jeff Chandler, who has recently taken a job with the Massachusetts Technology Academy under Ian ("Skip") McCurdy; Jeff's specialty is investigating UFOs. After Lucy's father (who calls new residents "born-again Vermonters") is suddenly possessed and murders her mother and brother, Lucy disappears, meets Herbert Gold, who is on his way back from Washington where he murdered his therapist, and hitchhikes with Herbert to Canada. They go to Montreal to see Father Mosely, who has been in a vegetative state after participating in an exorcism in Hobston ten years earlier. Alton Barnes seeks professional help from Karen. He was deer hunting with Stuart Dubois in Hobston near Stattler Mountain when a UFO abducted Stuart. Fugitives Lucy and Herbert take Father Mosely to the farm of widow Daisy Dubois in Hobston. At the Academy, McCurdy begins acting strangely. Jeff Chandler is so alarmed by events there that he leaves Boston and heads for Karen's with his wheelchair-bound six-teen-year-old daughter, Casey. He believes the Academy is collecting and experimenting with

magical data. The Academy instructs McCurdy to assassinate Jeff. The police interview Father William Sullivan, who has taken over Father Mosely's former church in Hobston after Mosely's disappearance. Jeff explains to Karen that Hobston has always been associated with "windows" to unknown worlds, going back to Indian tales involving spirits and monsters. Karen hypnotizes Alton Barnes so that he can tell them about his UFO experience—or was it a "porthole" to another reality?" The thrilling climax takes place on the mountain near Hobston.

Shadow Child (1998) is set in Antrim north of Chester on the Connecticut River. Eric Nolan was raised in Vermont. (Eric's grandfather thought the "railroad was responsible for the downfall of Vermont farming. Trains brought rich folks from the city. They liked the looks of the land and purchased greedily. Land prices soared beyond the means of the locals. The ski develop-ers weren't far behind. It was the train that brought the money, and the money separated Vermonters from acres and traditions the like of which could never be recovered.") After a series of losses (Eric's older brother, Brian, disappears; his grandparents die; his parents die), Eric moves to New York for marriage and career. Now that his wife, Karen, has died in a car crash, he returns to Vermont to seek solace with his cousin and childhood friend, Pamela, in the family home-stead in Antrim. Pamela, her husband, Clint Whitcombe, a native Vermonter of many genera-tions who works for the highway department, and their small son, Luke, live a contented rural life. (For Clint, a true Vermonter was something that took generations to build. Just because someone's son was born in Vermont, he would never be a real Vermonter. "Just because a cat has kittens in the oven don't make 'em biscuits.") Shortly after Eric arrives, weird happenings occur: an Antrim policeman disappears; Clint and Eric find Luke's dog tied to a tree, dead; an archeologist comes to look at the stone cellar on Clint's property as a possible Celtic site and dis-appears. Clint goes after him, finds his hanged and mutilated body, then disappears himself. There is talk of "little people." Billy Newton, owner of the local garage and the gathering place for swapping gossip, is killed. Clint returns, shocked by what he has experienced at the hands of the little people. Eric is a contributing force to these "happenings" because his brother, Brian, is out there in the woods. Eric and the Whitcombes decide to consult Mrs. McKensie, who has done a lot of research on this topic (the Abenaki, for example, have a tradition of little people going back thousands of years). While they are huddled in the Whitcombes' house, the little people (there are always eight of them in a coven) stage a terrifying and bloody scene. When Chief Bates arrives the next morning, he arrests the person he believes to be the murderer and puts him in the state mental institution.

In *Guardian Angels* (1999), a sequel to the previous story, fifteen-year-old William Crockett moves to Antrim with his mother, Sheila, and his stepfather, Dan Wilder. They buy an old, abandoned house and do it up in "colonial modern" (Sheila can afford this because she has published three successful novels for young adults). The realtor neglects to tell them that a terrible triple murder took place in the house four years before. Their only neighbor is Mona Grant, not yet fourteen, who lives near them in a trailer with her drunken, abusive father (there are suggestions of incest and abortion). Chief Bates of the local police force knows about the triple murder, having investigated it, and has intimations of further problems. One is that Eric Nolan, the suspect in the murders, has escaped from the local mental hospital. He turns up at the Crockett's house and persuades them that not only is he not guilty, or insane, but that there is a phenomenon on Pinnacle Mountain that they are going to find very hard to believe: a coven of lost children is hiding there. "It may sound fatuous," Eric explains, "but what we're fighting isn't human. It's something...supernatural." These little people, known as the Gentry, abduct Sheila, who is pregnant, because they have a use for her baby. The culmination of the drama is a scene of horror on Pinnacle Mountain.

The setting for *The Gore* (2000) is Eureka in the Northeast Kingdom. Roger Nelson, a former

reporter, runs a bar in Eureka called The Newsroom. Laura Drew, his lover, works at the bar, is separated from her violent and abusive husband, Dalton ("Hank") Drew, a state trooper, and has a son, Stacy. Stacy's best friend is Jarvis Lavigne, whose father, Lunker Lavigne, "has seen something out there" in the gore (land that lies outside the borders of official townships). Lunker commits suicide. Harley Spooner has found some mysterious stones in the gore, which he shows to a scientist, David Potter, in Burlington. Potter sends one of his team, a stunning blonde named Leslie Winthrop, to take a look at the site, which he imagines is Indian. Her guide is elderly Cooly Hawks, the only black person in Eureka. His father, a slave, had come into the state on the Underground Railroad. In the 1880s there was a hotel up in the gore that catered to loggers and prostitutes. "It was clear from the house's size and design that it had once been the prize of its occupants. Now the complex of buildings was like a mammoth relic of vanishing Vermont, a forgotten monument where ancient vehicles crawled to die, their rusted carcasses littering the unmowed lawns and grounds." Leslie, about to return to Burlington where she has an assignation with the married Potter, is attacked by something awful and falls into a coma. Potter comes back to Eureka to find out what is going on. After Lunker's funeral, Stacy and Jarvis persuade Cooly to take them into the gore to find out what Jarvis's father had seen. When coydogs attack them, Cooly urges the boys to climb a tree, while he fends off the terrifying animals with his walking stick. Cooly disappears, then Harley Spooner, then the boys, and finally Roger Newton. Laura sends for the police; unfortunately, her abusive husband answers the call. The final episode provides a fascinating historical explanation for the mysterious circumstances.

In *Lake Monsters* (2001), Harrison ("Harry") Allen is thirty-five years old and has just been found redundant by his Boston employer. He is not involved in any serious relationship, he has no other ties, and he has six months' unemployment insurance. He decides to spend his free time on Friar's Island on Lake Champlain near St. Albans

Bay, at the vacation home of his friends Mark and Judy Chittenden, who live in Burlington. Harry has not been to Vermont for fifteen years, since he went to the University of Vermont. He decides he wants to investigate the Lake Champlain monster: evidence that the beast exists dates back to Samuel de Champlain in 1609. Harry hears a woman sobbing in his attic, is followed as he walks home, and finds naked footprints outside that aren't quite human. The Islanders do not want to talk about their secrets. Harry falls in love with Nancy Wells, the local schoolteacher. They meet a witch, Abigail Snowden, the descendant of a spiritist's cult, and her weird son, Jabez. They learn that Professor Hathaway, an outwardly amiable man, is actually after the papers of turn-of-the-century spiritualist Cortney Dare, hidden in Harry's attic. A drunken, loutish man, Cliff Ransom, who saw the Lake Champlain monster as a child, lusts after Nancy. Cortney mated Abigail with a satanic creature; this union produced her idiot son and her horrifying daughter, Jenny, sixty, who is infatuated with Harry. This narrative, starting benignly, builds to a shocking climax.

Eleanor Clark

Gloria Mundi (1979) is set in Boonton, thirty miles from Compton, known as "the gateway to the Green Mountains." Louise and Brit Horton and Ellis Horton (Brit's brother) live at Horton Hill, built by their grandfather. Jim Pace (former lumberman, thrice married) of New England Land Company (Nelco), looking for property for his ski-resort development, has started felling trees on the Horton property. They are distraught by this literal uprooting of their lives. Lem and Hannah Palz, musician and former Trotskyite respectively, have lived there for thirty years and accommodate hippies in cabins on their property. The Nelco boss makes vile remarks about immigrants like Lem Palz and the hippies, "latter day immigrants," and almost wipes out their "domestic colony" with "only one or two weirdos left." Chip Holloway is a handsome young resident in one of the cabins. Margo Philipson arrives after learning that her husband,

John, a former minister presumed dead, is living as Philip Johnson in one of the Palz cabins with a young woman named Penny (who works at Nelco). Walt Hodge, who worked at the Banks farm until it was sold to Nelco, starts to drink. Jeff Smith, who stole the minister's typewriter in Michigan and ran over his dog, hopes to blackmail the minister into helping him rob Pace's office. Gossip flourishes about drugs at the local high school, mysterious fires, break-ins, and vandalism. There are references to tourists who come to look at the leaves and are either too early or too late, never satisfied. Brit feels sorry for entrepreneur Pace, a poor, hard-working boy who supported his sick mother and sisters, but it is this same Jim Pace who falsifies a deed so that he can get right-of-way through Brit's sugarbush. There is a final scene of rage and violence. At the end, Pace is once more flying over the scars that he has created in the landscape. Here are two sharp images: "A perfect afternoon, top of the mountain gleaming in sun and its shadow cutting down at their right, like carpentry work, black as the swamp water," and "Here and there an extra-stubborn leaf, already brown, nothing to drive from anywhere for, tugs and blows and at last falls like an unpaid bill, disreputably, in the dark." (The title is from "*sic transit gloria mundi*," Thomas à Kempis, "Imitation of Christ.")

In *Camping Out* (1986), two women in their mid-thirties, who have known each other in the past, are thrown together by a chance meeting at a funeral. Denise Hensley, who is married to a foreign-service officer named Carter, has come home from Europe for her mother's funeral in New Hampshire. A school acquaintance, Marilyn Groves, a poet and lesbian, meets Denise there and persuades her to go on an overnight camping trip with her and her little terrier, Corky. The place in Vermont is unspecified, but from the clues they probably crossed the Connecticut River at Claremont and camped at Ascutney State Park. The summer season is not yet upon them, and their camping site is deserted except for the wildlife and the insects. It turns out that the site is not quite deserted, however; a lurking escaped convict starts to terrorize them. During this tense situation Dennie muses, in flashbacks, upon her past, her unhappy marriage, and her incestuous relationship with her twin brother, Rick.

Felicia Buttz Clark

In *Hester of Pepper Tree Ranch* (1931), the Bell Inn in Stanton, twelve miles from Burlington, has catered to summer boarders since proprietor John Dodd's great-great-grandfather's day. Dodd hopes that his son, Jack, now twenty-four and a graduate of Harvard, will continue the family tradition; he also hopes Jack will marry Virginia Lawrence, daughter of a wealthy Burlington lawyer, whose son, Gray, is also a friend of Jack's. Dodd fears he will have to foreclose on the house of Widow Dufour, whose handsome, rather insolent son, Jacques, a violinist, is home after a two-year odyssey. Working as a waitress at the inn this summer is charming Smith College graduate (class of 1923) Hester Euwer, an orphan whose father was a major in the Canadian Light Horse. Although the Dodds are kind, Hester is slightly jealous of Virginia's advantages and discontented with her own life. She would like escape this place, "so stagnant, so formal, its atmosphere of New England Puritanism, the narrow long street of Stanton, the old houses, stained and weather beaten." She, and Jack and Jacques as well, cannot stand the "cast-iron determined fanaticism of those who worshiped in the white church." Out of the blue, her opportunity arises: her Cousin Leonard Euwer writes from New Mexico, urging her to live with him and sending her the money to do so. Jack also leaves Vermont for Boston to work as a civil engineer. Madame Dufour dies. Hester leaves without telling the Dodds that she is the grandniece of Hugh Euwer, a baronet. En route, Hester stays in New York with her Smith roommate, Constance; among the dinner guests one night are Mr. Beetham, an archeologist, and Virginia and Gray. Three years pass. Hester, now twenty-five, is contented living with her Cousin Leonard and a familiar figure around the ranch with her horse and dog. Guests arrive: Mr. Beetham with his pilot, Jacques Dufour, and Virginia and Gray. Gray is in love with Hester;

Virginia has become interested in law enforcement and prohibition. Leonard presides over family prayers every night, including all the workers on the ranch. The sheriff thinks a still is operating somewhere on the property. Jacques's presence makes Hester nervous: he too is clearly in love with her. He persuades her to go flying with him; they encounter a storm and crash. Hester is not seriously hurt; Jacques is in a coma but recovers. Virginia decides to marry Beetham. Cousin Leonard sells the Beethams his ranch and moves to Burlington with Hester, where she takes a course in library training. Hester has just begun a romance with Jack when they learn that Leonard has succeeded to the Euwer title. Hester and Leonard go to England, but Jack follows her there and proposes. After their marriage, they will live at the Dufour house in Stanton. Through the composition of "The Wings of God," Jacques has become religious and travels the world performing the piece on his violin.

Mary Higgins Clark
and
Carol Higgins Clark

Three groups of characters collide in Stowe in *The Christmas Thief* (2004): Packy Noonan and his accomplices, the not-too-bright twins, Jo-Jo and Benny Como; Alvirah and Willy Meehan and their friend, Opal Fogarty; and two Vermont farmers, Lemuel Abner Pickens and Wayne Covel. First, Packy, just out of jail after serving twelve years for cheating investors out of eighty million dollars, converted his loot to diamonds before his arrest and hid them in a tree in Stowe, where he had spent time as a troubled youngster working on Lemuel's farm. Hiring a van in New York, they head for a farmhouse with a big barn in Stowe. Waiting there with a rented flatbed truck is Milo Brosky, a poet (he feels a bit like Solzhenitsyn). Second, Alvirah, a cleaning woman, and Willy, a plumber, members of the Lottery Winners' Support Group in New York, are heading to Stowe to stay at the Trapp Family Lodge with Opal, one of the women investors cheated by Packy. Third, Lemuel and Vidya, who live in an eighteenth century farmhouse, planted a blue spruce on their wedding day fifty years previously. Rockefeller Center has chosen this eighty-foot, three-ton beauty as its Christmas tree. Neighbor Wayne, wildly jealous that his best tree was not chosen, climbs into Lemuel's tree to mar its symmetry with his machete. He finds the flask full of diamonds and takes it home to hide. Meanwhile, the Rockefeller Center crew has left its flatbed and crane by the tree, awaiting the cutting ceremony with press in attendance. Packy's gang steals the tree, only to find when they get it to the barn that the diamonds are missing. When Lemuel sees that his tree has been cut down, he is certain Wayne is the culprit. Opal goes off on her snowshoes and is captured by Packy's gang. The various strands of the novel are knitted together humorously and satisfactorily.

Sarah N. Cleghorn

A Turnpike Lady (1907), touching and noble, is set in a valley between Red and Bald Mountains, in the turnpike hamlet of Beartown, where it looks "no bigger than a child's necklace of beans or spools, lost in the mountain hollow." The heroine is Naomi Polke, one of eleven children of Richard Polke; her mother and four of the children are dead and three are married and moved away. Those at home are Titus, fifteen, Eliza, eleven, Naomi, nine, and Saul ("Budsey"), about five. Marm Partridge, their great-aunt, takes care of them and the house. Richard Polkes's brother-in-law, James Darby, is the tollkeeper. On the other side of the mountain, trouble is brewing in Westminster; the locals do not want the King's Court to sit. William French, the fiancé of Pleiades Darby, is killed in the Westminster Massacre; she never recovers from the shock. Titus Polke announces to his father, a confirmed Tory (as is all of Beartown), that he is joining the Liberty party. In the summer of 1777, the Beartown Whig-Biters, of which Polke and Darby are members, receive orders to march on Bennington with Captain Hawley. They come back, beaten by Peleg Sunderland and the rebels, who had been informed of the troop movement by Pleiades Darby. The Whigs walk into an ambush of Green Mountain Boys; Richard Polke

is jailed in Manchester (but later escapes) and Titus is dead on the field of Bennington. In 1781, a Tory family named Lucy comes along the turnpike having been banished from Charlotte county; Flavia Lucy becomes a great friend of Naomi's. The war is a backdrop for the social activities and marital aspirations of the Polke family. Eliza becomes a belle of the neighborhood and, at a corn-husking bee in Jamaica, falls in love with the fiddler, Frederick Dukes. Because he is the son of a rebel, a nephew of Sunderland, and not steadily employed, Eliza's father is not in favor of the match; she elopes in 1783. Two years pass, and Naomi, now seventeen, loves music and poetry and is a dreamer. Flavia's mother is determined to have Flavia marry before Cassandra, the younger Lucy daughter, an alluring, though shallow, creature. Since Flavia receives no offers, Mrs. Lucy proposes Mr. Snodgrass. To her distress, Naomi perceives that Flavia does not love him, and yet she marries him and seems content. More years pass and, although Naomi attends sugarings, barn warmings, and huskings, she hasn't learned to flirt and does not have a beau. Cassandra Lucy is now the star of the county and courted by Budsey. Henry Tibbald, the schoolmaster, begins to call on Naomi, who likes the attention but has a "warning" in her heart: she does not love him. The war ends and every window in Beartown is hung with black. Marm, Mrs. Lucy, and others pressure Naomi to accept Henry and bemoan the fate of spinsters. Mr. Polke suffers several strokes and dies. "The mountains began to show the winter afterglow, maroon and purple lakes in their hollows." Budsey and Cassandra are about to announce their engagement. Naomi turns to her brother for help, begging him to allow her to live with him and his wife. He urges her to accept Henry—and her fate. Unexpectedly, Eliza, who has led a traveling life for eight years but has been happy with her husband and eight children, returns to Westminster. Naomi confides in Eliza, asking if she would change her life in any way. Eliza persuades Naomi to wait until she finds someone she really loves. Henry proposes and she painfully rejects him, explaining that she is "like a tree with not a leaf stirring." Her nephew, Sim, hurries to Naomi to tell her that Eliza is very ill. After Eliza's death and at her request, Naomi adopts Alfred, four, a wizened, retarded albino (the doctor, noting his blue complexion, knows Alfred will not live long). Selfish and spoiled Cassandra refuses to have them in the house, so Marm, Naomi, and Alfred go up to her mother's saltbox house on the north turnpike. Marm dies and Naomi lavishes all her love and attention on Alfred, teaching him his letters and how to catch fish—and throw them back. She finally finds a man she loves—John Michaelfergus, her brother's indentured Irish farmhand. She is not glamorous, but she is deep and good, and "they walked hand in hand, like very young lovers."

The Spinster (1916), moving and intelligent, begins in 1892 in Tory Hill, twenty miles north of Bennington, with the arrival of Ellen Graham, nine, and her brother, Jim, seven, who are to be raised after their mother's death by her single sisters, Frances and Sarah Mowbray. Their father will stay at his job in the Midwest and visit them on holidays. Aunt Fran and Aunt Sally dwell in their ancestral home, Wakerobin, on Old Street, the "porticoed, shuttered, wide-clapboarded, elmed, and lawny part." Ellen's best friend is Julia Oldenbury, an orphan, who lives in Tewkesbury and shares her love of poetry and ideas. Ellen at eleven is earnest, humorless, and an avid reader. At thirteen, she is ready for the Seminary, which she attends with Julia, where they adore their first year, especially Latin, taught by an "ambrosial" young man fresh from Middlebury College. In their second year, discontent creeps in. Other girls have boys with crushes on them; Ellen still admires the Latin teacher, Mr. Scott, who is "tenderly reproachful" with girls who cannot grasp the ablative absolute. Finally, Jennie Willets's cousin, Webster, sees her home from a Lyceum debate night. Ellen wins the pro-vivisection debate, then changes her mind on the issue and returns her medal. When Carrie, a French-Canadian "colored girl," comes to their house as a maid, Ellen is distraught at the thought that Carrie eats thousands of meals alone in the kitchen. While they are in New York with the aunts, Jim falls seriously, almost fatally, ill with pneumonia. Ellen broods on the disparities between care available for the "sick poor" and the "sick rich." Tory Hill turns into a "summer cottage" place. Ellen goes to parties with the summer people, but finds their conversation superficial and boring. In 1902, the family dips into Ellen's mother's savings to send her to Radcliffe for a year, where she chooses to study three courses in English and one in philosophy. Her writing teacher finds her poetry "pallid and weak." (One of her classmates is reading *The Virginian*.) Ellen becomes a suffragist and meets the charismatic Susan Redmond, who develops into another intimate friend. They talk in her boarding-house room, where Ellen "loved a dusky light indoors; it seemed Vermontish and summer-like, like the dark blue-green bloom of maple shade." Ellen learns that Sue has relatives in Tewkesbury and knew Julia as a child. Julia now has a beau, the same Webster Willets; her intellectual family is distressed by this alliance. Ellen receives a visitor, Frank Tallman, who spends a week walking with her in the mountains. Ellen falls passionately and hopelessly in love with him. While he is there, she takes him to Tewkesbury in the hope that when Julia meets him she will recognize from the comparison Webster's inadequacies. Alas, Julia is not there but Sue is, with her beau David Micantoni, and in one lightning flash Frank falls in love with Sue. He can never act on this love; neither can he marry Ellen. It takes her four years of "brooding remembrances" before she can recover from her disappointment and throw herself into the "world's work." She returns to her "sunbonnet verses," trying to embody them with a "covert gospel of gentleness and brotherly love." Sue and David, an economist, now married with a baby, move to Tewkesbury. Sue is writing a novel on social issues; Ellen wants to imbue her poetry with problems like infant death rate and occupational diseases, but can only seem to beg for more kindness in the world. When her father dies, he leaves her and Jim, now a doctor, a little money. She frets about the lack of social conscience of the companies in which her money is invested. She gets in touch with a local socialist, William Horn, who suggests books for her to read. She is engrossed in *Christianity and the Social Crisis*, which makes her verses seem "wistful and quaint." Visiting Jim at his hospital in New York, she happens upon a May Day Parade and finds herself, suddenly, marching with the workers. She is overcome with a passion she has not felt since Frank touched her hand in that "vanished, enchanted time" six years ago, and joins the Socialist Party. Sue and David have a little girl, whom they name "Ellen." After the march in New York, she writes a poem called "Alias Jesus," which is published in *The Proletariat*. A few weeks later she receives a letter ("Dear comrade") from four workers for the revolution, who tell her that they have memorized her poem. When she goes to sleep that night, she puts the letter on her heart, where she used to keep Frank's picture.

Judith Beth Cohen

The twenty-nine-year-old narrator in *Seasons* (1984) and her husband, Sam, buy a farm with seventy acres and a ramshackle house ("weary of protesting, we sought a simpler life") on Leech Pond near Hardwick in 1972. Vietnam is the context. The couple, who are no longer close (they act as if they were "allergic" to each other), consider Vermont a "well-composed pastoral idyll." The population of this community, once thriving with dairy farmers and granite workers, had declined until city people started buying property here (the owner of their farm moved to a mobile home with wall-to-wall carpeting). They start redoing the house (the cellar is an "unspeakable place...worthy of Poe"), with many of Sam's former students as helpers (with whom he is more "responsive and available" than he is with her). She observes that "Sam tries to become a native here, heating with wood, mimicking our poor Yankee neighbors who live as their ancestors did, from necessity not choice." Another couple builds a cabin on their property; the helpers sleep in the shack the former owner used as a hunting camp. They are perceived as a hippie commune. Marijuana is common. They get

to know the storeowners. A college graduate hippie acquaintance, Sarah, flaunts her affair with "a local, a worker" (Roy, the Esso station man). On top of the hill is Ainsley's working farm, one of the last remaining (when he started there were seventy-three farms in the neighborhood shipping milk; now there are eight or ten). Ruth, a feminist, leaves her husband and child for the commune to write a book; she is remodeling the old schoolhouse and organizing a woman's group. The hills around them are dotted with ashrams, whose gurus run retreats and meditation centers. Sam doesn't want any children. He believes that "dissecting everything, by questioning and conflict" has destroyed much of what they had between them. Developers are threatening to turn Pine Mountain into a summer campsite. Ruth's husband, Stephen, a former SDS chairman, comes to Vermont to advise the Democratic governor-elect ("Vermont needs another Ethan Allen"); FBI agents question them about their past and arrest Sam briefly. "Vermont was a good place before all you hippies got here and started ruining things," opines the former owner of their house. Winter is oppressive; roofs have to be shoveled. At the town meeting in March, the new Vermonters stand out, "marked by youth and long hair." Out-of-state landowners are also noticeable. The World War II Honor Roll lists names of people who still live there—owning family land and struggling to pay the taxes. Whether Sam and the narrator stay together is inconclusive.

Merle Estes Colby

In *All Ye People* (1931), hardly a day goes by that a party moving out West does not pass the Bray family farm north of St. Johnsbury in Billymead township. "West!" shouts a mover. "A word like any other...but in our day a heavy-rolling word, with a shove behind it." The year is 1810; James Madison is president; Ohio is since 1802 one of the seventeen states. John Bray, son of Nathan, has been ordained to go out to Ohio as a missionary. There is talk around the Bray table of calling the United States "Fredonia" (a utopian concept). Matthew Putnam, a schoolteacher, decides to accompany John. The first section of the novel is a detailed account of their trip by horseback the length and breadth of the state of Vermont—the conveyances that pass them, the people with whom they talk. They ride with the Passumpsic River on their left, pass through the turnpike tollgate behind a Conestoga wagon. They have dinner in Barnet and follow the Connecticut River south. They see a post rider, cavalry officers, Knights Templars, farmers, a fellow from Dartmouth College. On one straightaway John counts thirty vehicles. They spend the night in Newbury with its sulfurous spring and bathing houses and arrive in Putney just before sunset the next day. Matthew, a facile orator, decides to stay in Putney to assist the ailing Congregational minister; John continues alone. In Brattleboro, he turns west, spends the night in Wilmington, and enters New York State. He starts keeping a journal of his trip. The people moving out West are as numerous as an army; he joins a caravan and helps them with their wagons. They reach the Ohio River and John discovers that a young "man" standing near him is a runaway girl named Clarissa Danforth, whose family has placed a reward on her head. She turns up later at a wedding at the Griswolds and Howlands, who own the biggest cornfield in Ohio. Someone recognizes her, so she and John steal away north where they find a deserted cabin. Johnny Appleseed stops by and shows them land for sale with salt in the ground. John is too late to procure the land; Clarissa has already left the cabin to find her brother. Following her, John works briefly for a group of Rangers headed by, unbeknownst to John, Clarissa's brother, Lieutenant Rounsevil Danforth. Clarissa has by this time returned to Philadelphia. John, staying at Fort Recovery on the Wabash River digging up cannon, realizes that he has come out West for the wrong reason—he is not a preacher—and wants to go home to Vermont, one thousand miles away. He thinks about what they are doing in Billymead and arrives home in time for Thanksgiving, sorely ill from being caught in a snowstorm. He takes his journal to a printer (who names it "The New Emigrant's Guide to the Western Countries"), and then departs to find Clarissa, who has turned twenty-one and accepted her inheritance. They set their course Westward in a new Conestoga.

Linda Collins

Going to See the Leaves (1986) is a collection of seven stylish short stories, two of which take place in Vermont. The couple in **"When the Pipes Froze"** are professional people who leave their college-age children at home to go skiing at their country place in Ashfield. They find to their dismay that the electricity has gone off and the pipes have frozen. Everything will be ruined when the ice finally melts. They are forced to seek shelter in a motel, where the narrator, who is the wife, reviews their life together—their friends and their analysts, their "work" (which was everything to them), and their experiments in living. She had tried to write but wasn't so sophisticated and European as some of their friends were. She remembers how they bought this house in the country two years ago and redid everything. They were involved together in "choosing workmen, building a center chimney, putting down new pine floors, replacing the asphalt roof with cedar shingles, and buying the new kitchen appliances, the new tiles and faucets for the bathroom, and the new gleaming pink copper pipes to replace the plumbing in the whole house." This weekend signifies the end of their marriage. In **"Going to See the Leaves,"** Thomas and Elizabeth invite their son, Luke, and his wife, Sarah, to drive up to southern Vermont with them to see the leaves, have a picnic, and go to a concert at the Congregationalist Church in the village. The action is seen from Elizabeth's point of view. The atmosphere is uncomfortable at first. She is critical of the daughter-in-law, who brings black-and-white film in her camera instead of color; of the son, who is evidently not "doing anything" at the moment and smokes a marijuana cigarette during their picnic; of the way Thomas drives, passing trucks and other cars. The colors of the leaves are wonderful— "apricot" and "dark mustard." The concert is perfect, until Elizabeth notices birds nesting up near the ceiling. As they come out of the concert, Luke says something that reminds her of his childhood and their nature walks together. Luke drives carefully on the way home. Everyone else sleeps. The tension is dissipated.

Peter Collinson

The town of Gilchrist in *The Northeast Kingdom* (2002) is facing economic collapse. The fortunes of the town have seriously declined in a recession: the railroad, the millworks, and the asbestos mining have all failed and young families are migrating to other towns. The solution, according to Tom Duggan, town administrator-cum-undertaker, is a federal correctional facility. Marshall Polk, who opposes the prison bailout plan, takes to the hills to live as a recluse. The town wins the bid, an Administrative Maximum Unit Prison (ADX) is built in Gilchrist, and huge financial benefits begin to pour in. Thriller-writer Rebecca Loden, divorced, moves from Manhattan to rural Vermont to write a sequel to her popular *Last Words*, whose anti-hero is modeled after a sadistic killer named Jasper Grue. She visits ADX Gilchrist to interview another killer, Luther Trait, an African-American who heads a brotherhood of revolutionaries. The day after her interview, cons and ex-cons take over the prison and the town in a brilliantly coordinated effort. About forty of them force the citizens to evacuate the town, murder the two hundred and sixty other prisoners, and threaten the U.S. government with destroying two American communities with Ricin if they are not left alone to live in Gilchrist. Everybody is evacuated except Rebecca and about ten others who are staying at the Gilchrist Inn. They are on their own against the terrifying Luther and make their way through the woods from hiding place to hiding place with the aim of destroying the convicts. The suspense is palpable.

B. Comfort

In *The Vermont Village Murder* (1982), Elizabeth ("Liz") Bell, in her thirties, breaks off with her partner and, packing her possessions, painting materials, and three animals into a car and trailer, takes off for Bellsville on the Battenkill River. It is not chance that has brought Liz to Bellsville: her great-great-great-grandmother, Elodie Bell, founded the village (contemporary population, forty) in 1780, which is why Liz feels she belongs in Vermont. Her painter's eye notes that "the moon was drawn with the finest sable brush." Elodie bequeathed her house in Bellsville to the first female descendant, which turns out to be a Liz. Liz soon learns that developers are seeking to mine uranium and that the epicenter of the uranium is at Harriet Lane's (Elodie Bell's) house. She meets almost immediately a number of residents, many of whom have a reason to want Harriet's house. She starts an affair with Evan Fairchild, a charming environmentalist, though she is not certain she trusts him. Harriet is found dead of a heart attack. Did someone withhold her pills from her? Her will provides that the house cannot be sold until her dog, Agatha, dies. Liz is appointed to stay in the house with Agatha until Harriet's niece arrives. When Agatha is abducted, there is an array of suspects and much confusion. Bob Quimby, a lawyer, straightens out the mystery, stops the digging on Harriet's property, and invites Liz to marry him and move into Harriet's house.

Green Mountain Murder (1984) establishes that Liz did not marry Bob but instead bought property in Lofton, went back to live in New York for three years while her house was being built, and has now returned to stay. She can illustrate her children's books from afar. She learns, to her dismay, that Inger Maas Swenson, head of the Lofty Mountain Corporation, is rapidly buying up property to build condominiums and tourist attractions on the mountain; worse, he wants to buy her house. She goes to visit her Aunt Amy, who lives at the Amber Trees Rest Home. A young man has come by, claiming to be her nephew. This young man is Dana Danner, who has taken a job with the Lofty Mountain Corporation, but claims he is really working underground for an environmental group. Liz, dazzled by his movie star looks, is soon having an affair with him. Other residents of Lofton have reason to be angry with Swenson because his corporation's plans impinge on their property. They jokingly form a Killers' Club, which includes Norine, the wife of Liz's hired hand; Martha, Liz's best friend at the country store; Harry and Bea Oats, managers of the Lofton Inn; Violet Vollard, in charge of the rest home; and Barney Broadbent, an elderly, wealthy gentleman. Norine is murdered, making one of the other club members a murderer.

Letitia ("Tish") Bray McWhinney, about sixty-five when this gentle, amusing series begins, is an attractive, energetic, widowed painter who lives in Lofton (five miles from Bennington to the north and eight miles from Weston to the east) in Clement County. She enjoys the company of her next-door neighbor, a widower and gourmet cook named Hilary Oats about ten years older than she, who formerly ran Alpha Press in Rutland, and with whom she shares drinks and meals—and adventures. Her constant companion is a pug called Lulu. Also starring is Sophie Beaumont, stepdaughter of Tish's niece, Susan. *Phoebe's Knee* (1986) introduces Tish, her best woman friend, Kay Anderson, who owns an art gallery, and Hilary. Others in their circle are Walter, a handsome condominium and ski-resort developer, and Terry, who runs the local inn. Lofton has been rocked by the recent invasion of a cult called the Ring of the Right, which, led by its "marshal" Alan Smith, has moved in and begun buying up valuable property on the main street of the village. Tish happens to fall into conversation with a young man, Lew Weber, who says he is a reporter investigating the cult. The next thing she knows, Lew has disappeared. Since no one else saw or talked to him, and thus no one really believes in his existence, she sets out to find him herself. She solves the secret of the Ringers.

Grave Consequences (1989) takes place in Weston, as well as Lofton, where Tish and Hilary are helping at a museum show when Arlene Motley is murdered and all the irreplaceable artifacts are stolen. That is, Tish saw Arlene's body, but it has disappeared by the time the police arrive. Tish is against development in Vermont ("I'm a selfish old retread to want the

landscape to remain the same") and immediately suspects Whitney Diamond, who is planning to open Wonderworld Body Works spas and condos all over the state. Whitney is the wife of handsome Duncan Diamond, who is running for governor of Vermont. Arlene's last words to Tish had concerned a picture in the museum: in the back of the frame she finds a pornographic photograph of Arlene and a naked man with his back—and tattoo—to the camera. She is certain the man is Duncan Diamond. Sophie Beaumont arrives just as Tish is receiving mysterious threats; she is almost run over and her house is set on fire. Teddy Baker, a state trooper, becomes involved—and takes a fancy to Sophie. Tish learns that Harry Motley, Arlene's husband, is Whitney Diamond's partner. As usual, the first isn't always the best suspect.

In *The Cashmere Kid* (1993), Sophie, twenty-five, has now bought property near Tish in Clement County and is raising goats, including a handsome Australian cashmere buck named William the Conqueror. Her boarder, Mike Flynn, has left the vicinity, but her brother, Sandy Beaumont, just out of rehab, has arrived to help her. Suddenly their neighbor, Stu Simpson, is murdered, William the Conqueror is stolen, and Sandy has disappeared. Tish ("Twenty-five years in residence made me an old-timer but certainly not a native") and Hilary become involved in the intrigue. Into the mix comes handsome Peter Colwell (brother of Lenny Colwell, first husband of new widow Grace Simpson), and Sophie instantly falls for him. Tish is suspicious of two men in a white truck whom she has seen driving near the goat farms, but the police are unable to trace them. Peter is organizing a goat exchange for developing countries. Sophie and Tish discover that there is a huge, deep ravine between her property and the Andersons and that Libby Lupin, goat-raiser and friend, has had William the Conqueror all this time. Tish decides that the van must have something to do with illegal dumping. Mike, just arrived back on the scene, is murdered. At goat-lift day, Sandy and Tish spot the suspicious truck and climb in back just before it pulls away (on the ride, Tish observes a "sculptural heap of farm machinery"). Tish handily serves up the culprits.

In *Elusive Quarry* (1995), Sophie, now twenty-seven, is still tending her cashmere goats. She has a new beau, Sid Colt, who owns the Ethan Allen Slate Company in nearby Poultney. Hilary invites Tish, Sophie, and Sid to dinner to meet Graham Gray, an attractive, young, recently divorced man who wants to buy Hilary's property; this is the same property that the local ski group is also interested in buying. Someone blows up Sophie's house with dynamite used at the slate quarry. The Treasury Department sends an agent to investigate. Then someone tries to kill Hilary, first by fiddling with his car and then attempting to detonate dynamite connected to his house. Sid is murdered in Hilary's house and someone places a rattlesnake in his sofa upon which Tish sits. The local police suspect Sophie because Hilary has just given her his property. The other obvious suspect is the foreman at the quarry, whose brother-in-law rented a car like the one Tish saw just before the explosion. Jake and Wanda Miller, the proprietors of the country store, disappear mysteriously. Tish sorts out the murderer.

A Pair for the Queen (1998) finds Tish, now seventy-seven, still in Lofton, painting, seeing Hilary frequently and sleeping with him occasionally. She still has her pug dog, Lulu. Hilary's godson, Bruce Hemphill, has arrived in Lofton in time for the local dog show in Bennington. He is engaged in a new business venture as concessionaire at the show. He asks Tish to restore an old dog painting for him to hang at his concession. Sophie is building herself a new house nearby and has two house guests—Kim, Bruce's daughter, and George Rouse, who is doing a paper for his Harvard MBA on Vermont's first millionaire. Tish is on the committee to hire a new couple to run the village store. She votes to approve the application of Jeremy and Lily Blount but senses something mysterious about them. The group converges at the dog show where Tish finds, to her horror, that Bruce has forged the painting as a Landseer. During the show, Bruce is murdered and the painting disap-

pears; it has not been stolen, however, but taken by his daughter, Kim. Kim's mother, who is now Jean Connors and married to Texan Jack, brings her dogs to show. Is Jeremy Blount a pornographer? Does he abuse his childlike wife, Lily? Is Jack Connors in the hot car business? Is Jean having an affair with Tish's old beau, Ian? Who abducts Tish? Who is George? Is the dog painting really a Landseer? Tish finds another dog painting in Hilary's attic, which, after she cleans it, is also by an old master. In the end, all turns out well (except for Bruce's death). Hilary continues to cook gourmet meals for his friends, and the pair of dog paintings may be sold to the Queen for a huge sum of money.

Richard S. Conde

In *Shelburne, Vermont* (1998), Angel Bartholmew visits the town on July 4, 1975, on a special mission—to give selected residents of the town magic watches that allow them to relive, through time-travel, certain periods of their lives. The main characters affected by this unusual compensation are Farnham and Gillian Smith, happily married; Conroy Compton, married to Tracy, an invalid; Buddy and Allison Bates, who were happy until an automobile accident blinded him; and Jerry Candella, unmarried, who takes care of his dead sister's boy, Tim.

Edward J. Connolly

In *Deer Run* (1971), after Josh and Pat are both wounded in Vietnam, they meet at the base hospital in Honolulu and decide to start a commune with other young friends looking for a new way of life. Josh rents an abandoned farm on a mountain road in Heartwell from an old man named Ritter, who has lived in Vermont for fifty years, whose children grew up in Heartwell and left, and whose wife is dead. He gives Josh the farm rent-free plus the use of his equipment and some weekly cash in return for fixing up the farmhouse, planting vegetables, and helping later in the year with the apple harvest. Josh is joined by a group of friends that includes Pat, Maureen and Mike, Jerry and Alice, Peter and Mary, Cyndee, and a run-away from a local college called Christine, who becomes Josh's girl. The others arrive, to the horror and contempt of the residents of the town, in a hearse. They paint the house and learn how to plow the fields, but local young men start to drive by to harass them. Ritter is receiving nonstop telephone calls complaining about the "hippies." After Josh puts a salt lick in the orchard, deer begin to congregate there. The young people all want to mind their own business except for Pat, unbalanced and uncensored, who acts in a provocative and often obscene way. The townspeople gather to decide how to get rid of the hippies. The state police and the county sheriff raid their house one night, hoping to find drugs (these are buried in a small wooden chest in the cornfield). Josh and Christine spend time with Ritter in the evenings. Crusty and embittered, he warms to them and tells them stories about the past, such as using horses pulling giant cylinders to pack the snow instead of plowing it. The villagers place an embargo on the communards, refusing to sell them any goods or services. Josh is trying not to fight back; Pat is infuriated and frustrated by Josh's pacifism. When a drive-by shooting injures Jerry, Josh has a difficult time convincing the local doctor to treat him. Pat departs in disgust. Ritter tells Josh he wants to leave him his house, the orchards, the land, everything. Peter is beaten up by a group of young men and refuses to defend himself. That night, he is keeping watch when someone sneaks behind the house, empties a can of kerosene on the kitchen floor, and throws in a lighted rag. The house burns to the ground; the volunteer fire department arrives after the fire is out. Everyone leaves the commune but Josh and Christine, who move into Ritter's cabin; then she, too, takes off. When the deer season starts, Josh takes final, fatal steps.

Joan Connor

The title story of **Here on Old Route 7** (1997) consists of vignettes about people whose undernourished lives turn tragic after the building of new Route 7, when many small businesses on old Route 7 were left to die. Anna, whose father ran the dump, and her husband, Paulie, built some tourist cabins on old Route 7; when their business dries up, they have to sell off some of their cabins. Siege (whose real name is Timothy Taylor) rents one of the cabins long-term and runs the Wayside Inn, lodged in a Quonset Hut; he becomes an alcoholic after his business falls off. Anna has an affair with Red Switchel, and Paulie kills himself. Red, who comes from a lumber family in Vermont, allows his charm to get him into trouble: he is responsible for Meg's pregnancy, they marry, and his father sets them up with a gas station, a Mom & Pop store, and a trailer. Drunk, Red sets fire to the trailer by mistake, killing his wife and baby. Dave's story is told in the first person, because he is a spectator, "a champion watcher of people wasting their lives." He built a drive-in theater on old Route 7 and has spent time in prison. Maria lives in one of the cabins with her four boys. Her husband stayed home in Latin America. She dreams—in Spanish—of escape. The epilogue shows a man in a fancy car taking old Route 7 by mistake, and another man, a developer, who has plans to buy out all the old businesses. Three other stories in the collection are set in Vermont. In **"Camp,"** the heroine, divorced twice, with a son, Toby, is staying with her mother in Healdville, "my bottomland." On the lake she meets a divorced man and his daughter. She thinks of her childhood with her brother on this very lake. In **"The Attic,"** Siobhan tells of coming with her brother, Patrick, and his wife, Janice, to a farmhouse in a small town in Vermont to celebrate Thanksgiving with their father, who has cancer and is also a drunk. The visit is not a success. In **"Aaron's Rod,"** Wayne Aaron Dooley, who has lived in Vermont "forever," is invited by some summer people ("they don't belong") to dowse for water on their property. He is made to feel stupid, inferior, and a loser; he has too much to drink.

"We Who Live Apart," the title story in *We Who Live Apart* (2000), is about childlessness. Katie, the narrator, grew up in Taylorsville, where she lived with her mother, father, and brother, Gary. There, Edna Bone was childless and Aunt Esther was childless. Katie, now forty-two, is childless. After she and Wade split up, she moves to Barre to teach high school English. She has a dog, Flossie: "People who do not have children simply need something that will rise like water to fill the volume of their lives." In **"October,"** Sherry meets Foster at an Alcoholics Anonymous meeting. After a drunken accident in which Sherry sideswiped a child ("He didn't die, but he might have"), her husband Rory's parents took custody of her son, Tim. Sherry works in a shopping mall in Rutland and lives in a trailer camp with Donna, divorced. They cheer each other through their tough lives. Sherry sleeps with Foster and doesn't think she will see him again, but she meets him later and fixes his automobile engine. They look at each other more directly, and she is able to tell him about the accident: after Tim left, she felt "hollow, rotten, like the burnt orange flesh of a jack-a-lantern, soul gone up in smoke." Foster gives her a ride to the mall. In **"And I, Isolde,"** Isolde works in traveling carnivals as a diviner. She meets Tristan, a chain-saw artist, when he gets on the bus: "We were both midway people doing the Vermont crafts circuit." He "lugged a chain saw and dropped into place as solidly as a felled tree." At the Tannerville fairgound, Isolde falls in love with Tristan; he tells her he is married. A year later, she sees him again: "her life to that point was a pen waiting to write his name." He goes back to his wife. Isolde grows old, blind, toothless, telling herself the story of her life until death emends it: "Death is a painstaking editor." **"Ursa Major in Vermont"** is also about a childless woman, Anna Mansfield, and her husband, Forrest. A bear appears and ambles through the woods near the Mansfield place. "The bear's footprints froze, tatting ice doilies in the hollows." Forrest sees the bear; then, "its hulky darkness haunched off." Anna sees it next and, because winter is coming, begins leaving out pots of strawberry jam or pie filling for it, but she doesn't tell her husband: "Their silence had a respectable weight to it." Others see the bear, too. It sits and stares at

the family cemetery (where "the family headstones in the pasture glint like mica in the lightless night"). When the town committee decides to shoot the bear, Forrest sets up a watch to protect the bear if he can. He feels sad for Anna's sake. The bear shambles off, unharmed. In **"Second Nature,"** the two oldest families in town are the Chassures and the Lacroys. Seth Lacroy, the ten-year-old narrator, describes the Chassures as hunters, trappers, and loggers; the Lacroys are carpenters and farmers. Seth idolizes Wayne Chassure, whose arm was cut off in a chain-saw accident and has a reputation around town. The first time Wayne takes Seth hunting, he says, "There's nothing to do around here so you have to raise your own hell or heaven." Wayne's camp is so covered with racks "it quilled like a porcupine." Seth's father sold the farm and, after keeping lots for the family, sold the rest to people from away. Wayne says the town is changing because of "out-of-staters"— there are no more summer people; just a lot of tourists coming through to look at "a bunch of hicks." He thinks that flatlanders are running the state. Wayne complains about gossip in the town: he explains to Seth that there are two kinds—public-domain gossip and behind-doors gossip. In the old mill, tourist shops have sprung up where natives never go. Ms. Schwarz owns a shop in which she hangs a sign saying, "Keep Vermont Safe: Support Gun Control." Wayne takes Seth bird hunting on a "perfect day crisp as a Macintosh." Ms. Schwarz is collecting signatures for gun control; someone trashes her store. At a town meeting, there is a shouting match between the transplants and the natives. Wayne tells Seth that hunting isn't second nature to him, but first nature: "It's the way I am, not the way I fit myself in." Later, Seth wishes he had thought more about this idea; instead, he starts avoiding Wayne. One day, Wayne shoots Ms. Schwarz dead and goes to prison. He gives his dogs, Frank and Jessie, to Seth. As Seth grows older, he feels the woods closing in. He's going to move to the hills and live like Wayne.

C

Robin Cook

To escape urban crime and poverty, Doctors Angela (pathologist) and David (internal medicine) Wilson leave a Boston university medical center in *Fatal Cure* (1994) for "idyllic" Bartlet Community Hospital near Rutland with their ten-year-old daughter, Nikki, who has cystic fibrosis. They buy a stately home (despite a strange smell in the basement) that belonged to Dr. Dennis Hodges, a doctor who has disappeared under mysterious circumstances. Bartlet Community Hospital has been taken over by a managed care company, Comprehensive Medical Vermont (CMV). The unpleasant management team is headed by Dr. Traynor, who is married but having an affair with the woman president of the hospital. CMV is running the hospital on the "capitation system:" Barlet Community Hospital has negotiated to be paid a certain amount of money per potential patient; if fewer than the decided number are admitted, the hospital does well financially. David Wilson inherits a number of patients who, critically ill, have been treated for cancer. When they come back to him with seemingly insignificant symptoms, he tends to hospitalize them to ensure their wellbeing. One by one, they start to die. He always calls in consults toward the end, but the patients are beyond help. CMV management becomes highly critical of David's ordering consults and tests; he receives very low scores from the utilization board. Whenever a relatively healthy patient is assigned room 204 (which has an orthopedic bed), it is not long before he or she develops cramps, diarrhea, pneumonia, and rapidly dies. At board meetings Traynor et al try to figure out incentives for lowest yearly hospitalization. Meanwhile, Angela complains about sexual harassment by her pathology mentor. When Angela and David find the body of Dr. Dennis Hodges buried in their basement, they are ready to return to Boston — were it not for a huge debt incurred from buying their house. The local police don't seem very interested in "big-shot city people" who went to "Harvard or some place like that." Angela hires a private investigator, Phil Calhoun, to help solve the murder. Meanwhile, nurses are developing flu-like symptoms. The misanthropic caretaker, Van Slyke, becomes more psychotic. David and Angela are fired but continue their investigation. At first they think it is "misguided euthanasia," but, in a clever conclusion, they learn the truth.

Ellen Hodges Cooley

In *Boom of a Western City* (1897), the climate in Blankridge in northern Vermont has a "salubrious reputation," drawing inhabitants from throughout the state during the malarial summer months. In the spring of 1878, a different sort of fever comes to Blankridge—the Westward movement to Fargo, Dakota, hailed in newspapers as "a very Eldorado." Jonathan Bullard, who lives on a farm held by three previous Bullard generations, is infected with the travel bug, as is his daughter, Almira, eighteen. His son, Jonathan, fourteen, who lives on the adjoining property with Grannie Bullard, wants to stay in Vermont. Mrs. Bullard is undecided, because she knows that Jonathan will inherit Grannie's farm and hopes that Almira will marry young Alonzo Peters, whose parents are prosperous. The Blankridge grocery store, a self-constituted court that meets evenings, watches the proceedings with interest. When Alonzo asks Almira to marry him, she says she wants to explore the West; he then offers to buy Bullard's farm. In late December, three of the Bullards take the Northern Pacific Railroad express-train to Fargo and go straight to a hotel. It is very cold. Mr. Bullard becomes a real estate agent and begins buying and selling; the two women join a number of charitable societies. Mr. Bullard finds them a cottage to rent, and Mrs. Bullard holds a reception for their new friends. In Vermont, she and Almira would have prepared the food themselves; here, they hire an expensive caterer. Their social whirl is extreme: every minute is taken up with sewing parties, tea drinking, and shopping expeditions to procure the appropriate clothes for all their events. Exhausted, their spirits cry out for "the peace, the haven" of their Vermont home. Mr. Bullard offers to build them the grandest house in Fargo; Almira thanks him, but says, "I *love* Vermont." Even though Almira receives many proposals of marriage, she wonders why they ever left Blankridge. In the spring, Mr. Bullard squares every bill he owes, and they return to Vermont. Almira and Alonzo declare their love for each other. All the neighbors and friends want to hear about Fargo. Mrs. Bullard has only one secret worry—her tasteless Fargo gowns ("all sham") that she doesn't want anyone to see, but luckily she trades the dresses to a peddler on his way to Boston.

Arnaldo Correa

In *Spy's Fate* (2002), a Cuban Intelligence Officer, Carlos Manuel Armas, has earned the eternal hatred of Timothy Sidney King, head of CIA's Cuban Section, whom Carlos Manuel nearly assassinated years before. It is now 1994: Carlos Manuel's wife is dead by her own hand; his three estranged children plan to emigrate from Cuba to Florida. When he sees the raft they plan to use, he hijacks a yacht to pursue them. He saves their lives but is forced to murder a man who is trying to drown them. Once in the United States, Carlos Manuel eludes the CIA through a variety of disguises and reaches Burlington, where he rents a room near the University of Vermont. He has assumed the identity of John Wilkinson, a man whose license he stole. He befriends the landlady, Janice, and her son, Michael. He spends his days at the UVM library, researching historical records of Vermont settlers as well as surveying maps of the area between Burlington and Canada. A contact in Cuba is sending Carlos Manuel's old Swiss passport by DHL to Montreal. Carlos Manuel takes Janice and Michael sailing on Lake Champlain, where, unfortunately, they are seen by Janice's abusive former boyfriend, Milton Lafayette. When Milton comes to Janice's house to beat her up, Michael attacks him brutally, sending him to the hospital. The John Wilkinson identity leads the CIA to Burlington, but Carlos Manuel has already escaped through Mexico to Cuba. He is arrested and interrogated by officials at the Ministry of the Interior, who are trying to decide whether to charge him with treason. The events that follow involve the way Carlos Manuel arranges for the safety of his children,

for his own escape, and for a future in Burlington with Janice. (A "spy's fate" is "the price we all have to pay for what we do.")

Art Corriveau

The exquisite *Housewrights* (2002) describes the delicate web that envelops identical twins and the difficulty on the part of outsiders to perceive and penetrate that web. The action begins in 1907 when Lily Willard is eight. She lives in Cabot Fields within view of Mount Mansfield at a time when Vermont's eight cities had electricity and some people were getting telephones. The Pritchards, a father with his twin sons, Ian and Oren, arrive in a caravan to build the Willard family's new house. Because Oren and Ian, part Abenaki, are identical, Lily knits them colored bracelets to tell them apart. All summer Lily and the Pritchard boys play together; she teaches them to ride her pony and to read. By 1917, Lily is the town librarian. Oren returns to Cabot Fields to ask her to marry him. He and Ian have been separated by the war, which has taken the latter to the trenches of France. The Willards are delighted with the match and give Lily a piece of property next door so that her husband can build the couple a new house, The Knoll. When Ian returns from the war shell-shocked and speechless, shortly after their marriage, his brother and Lily move him into their house. The Pritchards start building houses together, as they did growing up, and the trio leads an almost idyllic life. Ian's health improves. He is also in love with Lily, even though she does not know it. Cabot Fields is a small town, and village tongues begin to wag about the unconventional living arrangements at The Knoll, especially after Oren, Lily, and Ian perform a rather tipsy dance, all three clasped together, at a Grange party. Villagers begin to treat Lily with hostility and to discourage her patronage. She confides her difficulties to her mother who provides the solution: Lily begins inviting her recently divorced childhood friend, Hallie Burke, to supper with Oren and Ian. After their wedding trip, Hallie and Ian move in with Oren and Lily at The Knoll with unfortunate consequences.

Gail Crease

In *The Dream Spinner* (2000), although her father owns half of New York City, Kate Pedigrew, thirty-two, has chosen to make a life for herself in Barre, where she is a stained-glass artist living in a restored stone church. Her brother, Matthew, thirty-seven, his wife, Meg, and their ailing baby, Christian, live nearby. Kate is suddenly overwhelmed with the desire to own an antique spinning wheel and finds one in a fancy shop in Springfield. At a party and exhibition at the house of Madeleine Carstairs, the head of the local craft association (crafts are a big part of the area's tourist industry), Kate meets attractive Englishman Cole Beresford. An expert in antiques, with offices in New York and London, Cole wonders why Kate has decided to "chuck it all and move to the country." At the party, Cole meets a Professor Morris, who tells him that the Lockton spinning wheel is at large and that Jeremy Davenport, an unscrupulous art collector, is on its track. Cole learns that the spinning wheel has been sold—but to whom? This is a case of black magic: he must find the buyer before something happens to her. While idly spinning the wheel, Kate begins to communicate with a woman, Eleya, who was spiritually trapped in the spinning wheel five hundred years before. Kate's estranged father appears from New York. Events escalate, but after some dangerous occurrences all ends happily and symmetrically.

Jay Cronley

To achieve the widely touted simple life, Andrew and Elizabeth Farmer in *Funny Farm* (1985) buy twenty-five acres with a seventy-five-year-old house and pond on Dog Creek Road near Redbud in northern Vermont: "The sky was big. The land was cheap. There were no yellow cabs." Andy has quit his job at *The New York Times* in order to write a serious novel. The catastrophes pile up in quick succession. The movers get lost. Their possessions are ruined. The drunken mailman does not deliver their mail. They buy a dog, which runs away. The phone does not work (the phone man leaves a note saying, "The lemon pie needs sugar"). There is a coffin in the flowerbed.

Their little MG is destroyed when pranksters remove the road signs. What concerns Elizabeth, as she increasingly hates the "stark" landscape, is that Andrew now loads the slovenly dog into the back of the banged-up truck and goes shopping with a beer can in one hand and a ball cap turned around backward, looking "exactly like a native." Finally, at a town meeting, Andy announces that they want to sell their house and will pay the residents of Redbud to help them make the place attractive to potential buyers. The locals overplay their parts, and the plan fails miserably. To pay off their exponential debts, the Farmers rent the house for a month to a film company for a horror feature. They are going to persevere in Vermont.

Willis T. Crossman

The stories in *Told in Vermont* (1938) and *Heard in Vermont* (1939), collected in *Willis T. Crossman's Vermont* (2005), are wryly humorous, gentle, insightful, peopled with villagers and farmers, loners and busybodies, ministers and storekeepers. In the first collection, Barzilli Butson of Braintree in **"Bad Company"** strenuously prefers his horse, Jerry, to the automobile. Zadbiel Morton in **"Fulfillment,"** who runs the general store in Worcester, is a strictly fair man, but hard; no one is sorry when he dies. Cephas Colby in **"Instructed"** has a sugar orchard, which one of his summer boarders insists upon calling a "sugarbush;" he ignores her, having called it a sugar orchard for sixty-five years. Julana Jeffords in **"Colder"** is pleased when an international commission decides that her land near the Canadian border is in Vermont: the winters in Canada are very cold. Wahela Walbridge in **"Interested"** lives alone on her farm between Morgan and Charleston, with only the hired man, Wouldbe Wright, to keep her company. When she seems ill and listless, Wouldbe tells her friend, Undecemilla Urquhart, who summons a doctor. She is pronounced physically sound, but the isolation has proved too much for her. She is moved to Undecemilla's front room on Main Street, where the activity outside the window (arranged by the doctor) restores her to good health. She feels well enough to go home, but plans more trips to town.

In "**Logic**," all the organizations in North Montpelier are trying to raise money through events like plays, dances, and oyster suppers. Finally Freegrace Fessenden puts a stop to selling refreshments: the lemon pie that his wife, Enola, made cost him $1.47 (lots of eggs and butter) and the whole "shindig" netted the organization $2.14. After her husband dies, Penelope Peelor in "**Solvent**" runs her farm with the help of a hired man. She spends all she earns, acting as an aunt to everyone in the village. When urged to save her money, she asks why: she has no heirs and no debts. In the second volume, Zabzeel Kingsley of Barnard in "**Prepared**," who runs a productive farm, marries Keturah, a termagant who makes his life miserable. He loses weight. After she dies, a typographical error on the part of the chiseler puts on her tombstone: "She has gone to her eternal roast." Frumentius Furber in "**Impossible**" is not a handsome or personable man. He takes care of his farm, despite the "mountainous and untillable" land in Hanksville in the center of the Green Mountains. He never marries, because he would not be the choice of the person he would choose, and vice versa. In "**Deliberate**," Stanstill Shackshober of Eden is a slow-moving, slow-thinking man, while his wife, Sybil, is a hustler, doing her housework with lightning speed. A villager asks him if a married man lives longer than a single man. After ten minutes: "No, it only *seems* longer." In "**Installment**," Carabus Crabtree is a good ordinary man who lives near Newfane. After many years his wife, Caraway, dies. The minister extends his condolences, but Carabus is philosophical: "You can hardly expect one wife to last a whole lifetime." Jehu Jordan, who lives near Bristol in "**Educated**," has not had many advantages, but acquired the necessary education to get along. He is touchy, though, and, when he receives a typewritten letter from a company about a farm implement, writes back: "You don't have to print your letters to me. I can read writing." Innocent Ingersoll, a farmer near Belvidere Center in "**Dependent**," relies so heavily on his wife, Impulsia, that when the dentist asks him which is the aching tooth he replies he will have to go home and ask Impulsia.

Janet Dailey

Green Mountain Man (1979) describes the return after ten years of Jonas Concannon to Randolph. He is still in love with Bridget Harrison O'Shea, twenty-eight, who married another man soon after Jonas left Vermont. Bridget continues to be attracted to Jonas but believes that he abandoned her. She has a nine-year-old daughter, Molly, a job managing a craft show, and an interfering mother, Martha Harrison. Little Molly is instantly hostile to Jonas, until he makes an effort to gain her favor. During his absence from Randolph, he trained to become a doctor and, now back for good, buys the old Hansom farm that abuts Bridget's property. An important and surprising revelation allows the couple to reunite.

Gloria Dank

In *As the Sparks Fly Upward* (1992), Bernard Woodruff, in his thirties, a corporate lawyer and author of children's books, is married to Maya, a magazine journalist, whose brother, Snooky Randolph, is a handsome young man-about-town. The Woodruffs, who live in Connecticut, are invited to visit Snooky at his cabin in the woods of Lyle. He introduces them to his new girlfriend, Sarah Tucker. She is staying with widow Irma Ditmar, her sister-in-law, Gertrude Ditmar, her brother, Roger Halberstam, and his stepson, Dwayne, in a mammoth Victorian mansion called "Hugo's Folly." A trio of deaths occurs. First, young Bobby Fuller, to whom the elderly Irma has just become engaged, is shot fatally in the woods. Then Irma dies from an overdose of her heart pills followed by Gertrude, who succumbs from a heart attack in the woods. Since Irma is extremely wealthy, someone stands to gain from her death, but why the other deaths? The Woodruffs discover the answer. Afterwards, the village turns out enthusiastically for Irma's funeral, but more reluctantly for Gertrude's: two deaths in one family are considered in bad taste. (The title is from Job: "Man is born unto trouble as the sparks fly upward.")

Jeff Danziger

Teed Stories (1988) chronicles the Teeds, who have worked the family farm outside Plainfield ever since Hieronymous Teed first settled on the land during the period of the New Hampshire Grants. These amusing stories record events in the daily life of Pa and Ma Teed (William and Ida), and the Teed heir apparent, Hiram, twenty-six, and illustrate the importance of land to hardworking families, even though they are unable to make much money from farming. The Teeds live on potatoes, chicken, and their own cheese and vegetables, with maple sugar and hay as cash crops. In one of the stories, Arnold Kraznitz, a presidential advance man seeking a suitable campaign stop in New Hampshire, comes upon the Teed farm and pronounces it a "goddam Norman Rockwell theme park!" William struggles to run a town meeting and fiddles endlessly with the "unnecessary parts" of his tractor. He figures out his taxes, postpones haying, and shows off in front of Hiram and his girlfriend, Julie, recreating his childhood by jumping off a high cliff into the water ("The water falls like an albino mare's tail into a shimmering misty rainbow"). William is often stuck in a traffic jam clogged with representatives of the "nonindigenous population." The Teeds, like all farmers, spend the summer—the great weather—doing backbreaking work; when they are through working, suddenly winter has arrived.

Deane C. Davis

The brief stories in *Justice in the Mountains: Stories and Tales by a Vermont Country Lawyer* (1980) succeed because, although the author is dealing in "country humor," he never condescends to his subjects and his characters are alive and real. Davis describes for the most part events that took place during his early years as a lawyer, which coincide with the Prohibition years (the "uninhabited terrain at the Vermont-Canadian border made it a natural corridor for rum running"). He sets up each incident by carefully explaining the legal precedent (all of which are contained in the one-volume *Vermont General Laws*) and ends each with an example of "the capacity of cryptic retort, which is a characteristic of Vermont humor." He tells several stories of horse traders, or "horse jockeys" as they are known in Vermont, and several about the right to refuse to give evidence against oneself. His expressed theory is that, even if the witnesses cannot articulate this right, the judge should lean over backward to grant it. In a case about a bastardy claim, he says, facetiously, "in Republican primaries and bastardy cases, nomination is equivalent to election." He gives examples of the frequent use of justices of the peace, explaining that often sessions—"lawing"—before a justice of the peace are the only entertainment in remote areas. He reiterates cases of the power of suggestion in persuading witnesses to remember events that they actually could not have remembered. In the issue of a new schoolhouse, a witness is asked how long he has lived in Vermont. "Thirty years." How long in Stowe? "Thirty years." The lawyer turns to the judge, exclaiming, "Your honor, I don't think we need to be told our business by any goddam tourist!" He cites occasions when his father, also a lawyer, gives him some very useful advice. Once when, in his father's absence, he assures a man that the town will be liable for an accident involving a hole in the road, his father says, "Some lawyers succeed through thorough knowledge of the law; some by fitting the facts to what little law they know." In the heyday of the family farm, farmers constituted the large majority of the members of the legislature. The themes that come through these stories are the common sense of the juries and the humor tinged with compassion of the judges and justices.

Eugene N. Davis

In *The Axe with Three Nicks* (1929), Edgar Mason, thirty, of Plymouth, is robbed of a valuable gold necklace and his faithful axe with three nicks. This theft launches him into a melodrama that nets him a dangerous enemy, Earle Parkhurst, a best friend, Frank Van Loon, and the woman he loves, Ethel Kingsley, twenty-five. Parkhurst steals the necklace, marries Ethel, and flees with her. Edgar and Frank pursue them, buy a Siberian bloodhound, "Spot," and return to Bridgewater in southern Vermont where they find work in a lumber camp. Starting as "swampers," their sterling qualities are soon appreciated by the boss, Mr. Daniels, who hires Edgar as superintendent with Frank as his assistant. The domain is fifteen thousand acres of lumber, a sawmill, fifteen trucks, fifty teams, mostly oxen, and three hundred men. Edgar's first challenge is a cut of ash trees high upon a treacherous ledge; he fashions a chute to bring the logs down. Daniels goes off on other business, leaving Edgar in charge of the lumber camp, "teeming and pulsing with the activities of its very essence—the lumber jack." With Prohibition in force, bootleggers are rampant; Edgar fires some men who drink and misbehave. He moves into the camp to learn to know his men and enjoys the music and card playing after supper; many are immigrant Swedes, Irish, Italians, and Frenchmen. Spot kills first a lynx and then a black bear. The camp books show a good profit. Spot leads Edgar to the place where Parkhurst and Ethel are staying; Edgar learns Parkhurst is head of the biggest gang of thieves, bootleggers, and murderers in Vermont. When the fishing season opens, Edgar and Frank spend time trout fishing. Summer working hours are adjusted so the men can play baseball on the grounds of the Baseball Benefit Association of Bridgewater. Having pitched at college, Edgar becomes the team pitcher, with Frank as catcher. They are challenged to a game by Parkhurst's team, the Dawson Dabblers; naturally, his side cheats and many umpires are members of his gang. Edgar and Frank visit his birthplace, Plymouth, and stay at the Woodstock Inn. Back in Bridgewater, they attend husking bees, sociables, and sleigh rides, in which the Parkhursts participate. Ethel is revealed to be the daughter of Mr. Daniels; Edgar overhears Ethel telling her father that she only married Parkhurst to retrieve Edgar's necklace. The final confrontation with

Parkhurst occurs during a huge log drive—two million feet of lumber—organized by Edgar, who has total faith in his "rough-and-ready, stalwart, hard, iron-fisted men." Parkhurst refuses permission to trespass on his land. When Frank starts to break the boom, Parkhurst's men fire upon him. Edgar's men, all armed, overcome Parkhurst's gang. Parkhurst and Ethel are stranded on an island. She throws Edgar the necklace, which Spot carries to shore. Edgar manages to save Ethel, but his conscientious efforts to rescue Parkhurst are in vain. Edgar and Ethel are free to marry.

Thomas C. Davis

The Duval Conspiracy (1995) recounts the events leading up to the campaign of Vermont Congressman Alan Duval from St. Albans for the U.S. Senate against former Governor Brad Meacham. With his robust good looks and commitment to the environment, Duval is a certain victor, according to his staff, led by Jack Marston, a widower in his early fifties, who runs the office in Burlington and lives in nearby Underhill. Duval is in Burlington to receive the Vermont Leadership Award from the prestigious Vermont Way Council. In the background, intimations of dirty tricks surface. A recently retired CIA agent named Ben Willey, learning of a plan that will discredit Duval, makes copies of the incriminating documents and photographs and takes them with him in a padded envelope to Maine. One set he gives to a friend; if he should disappear after three days, the friend is to send the material to Duval's office. The CIA officer who is responsible for this smear, Edgar Steele, hires a young travel writer, Lila Maret, to procure the padded envelope. Lila, who lives at Jay's Peak, does not suspect her duplicitous role; it is only when she and Jack fall in love that she realizes she has been duped. When the slanderous information is aired on TV—stories of Duval's meeting with a drug overlord in Colombia and other compromising activities, Duval believes his only course is to resign. The conclusion resolves his future and implies that a fascist group persists, which can be traced to the highest levels of government.

Nicholas Delbanco

The Sherbrookes Trilogy consists of *Possession*, *Sherbrookes*, and *Stillness*. Daniel "Peacock" Sherbrooke, the first settler by that name in North Bennington, built Sherbrookes in 1869. Dubbed Peacock's Palace, the Big House is four stories high, with a cupola on top, fourteen fireplaces, and a replica called the Toy House, all on one thousand acres. (The Big House is loosely based on the Park-McCullough House in North Bennington.) The farm was a theater of the Revolutionary War. *Possession* (1977) portrays one day in the life of Judah Porteous Sherbrooke, seventy-six, who lives with his spinster sister, Harriet ("Hattie"), eighty-one, in Sherbrookes. He has ordered forty cords of wood split and stacked. He has instructed his lawyer, Samson Finney, to inform his wife, Maggie, in New York that Judah is dying. Judah has made a will leaving everything to Maggie (except for Hattie's fixed portion and certain charities). Maggie writes that she will come at once. Judah reminisces about Maggie, their first son, Ian Daniel Sherbrooke, whom Maggie took away when he was thirteen from the "prison" of Sherbrookes, and their little son, Seth, who was born two years after Ian and died of "crib death." Judah first met Margaret Cutler when he was thirty-eight and she was thirteen; ten years later, he married her. Throughout the novel, the writings of Peacock Sherbrooke (Judah's grandfather) are quoted; he moved to California and ordained the building of the Big House from there. "Vermont is the repose of the soul," he announced, and, in 1869, he came home to die in his house. The point of view shifts back and forth from Peacock to Judah to Maggie to Hattie. The last three deem Seth's death the turning point when relationships soured. Hattie believes the death was divine vengeance; Maggie anguishes over whether she might have heard the baby whimpering and failed to check on him. Judah remembers his first wife, Lisbeth McPherson, who died after two years of marriage. He recalls obsessively the time, after Seth's death, when Maggie began traveling and bringing her lovers to the house. Then, he was mad with jealousy: she was his possession. Now, he fears real estate development and state highway extension: Sherbrookes is his possession. Maggie thinks of Ian, who knew "the Sherbrooke knots around him would tighten not loosen with time." Hattie, who has been caring for and then nursing Judah all these years, feels displaced by Maggie. All during the time Maggie lived there, Hattie had to endure the sounds of their lovemaking. Judah remembers painful scenes with Ian, who wasn't the son he wanted. Why, he asks himself now, had he never visited Ian at college?

In *Sherbrookes* (1978), Ian Sherbrooke returns to Sherbrookes after almost fifteen years. His father is dead and his mother is living there with his Aunt Hattie. Ian, an Exeter and Harvard graduate, has been a political activist and an actor. On his return to the homestead, he immediately feels a change in the house (which he finds useless), in his mother (who has a problem she has not revealed even to herself), and in himself (who used to be treated like a little prince). Ian knows that this world is not his world. He seems uninterested in any social life, although he finally goes to a party at Sally Conover's, where he meets Miles and Jeanne Fisk and Samson Finney, the family lawyer. The point of view often switches to Hattie, who is jealous of the rapport between Ian and Maggie, which makes her feel like an outsider, and who suspects that Maggie is pregnant. Hattie tries to figure out if the child could be Judah's or — here her suspicions turn to incest. Samson Finney has told Maggie that Judah's will prohibits her remarrying. Maggie reveals to Ian that she is pregnant (but does not tell him that the father is Andrew Kincannon, a lover in Manhattan "of her social class.") All three feel, for different reasons, that the Big House is a trap. Hattie finds her solution by drowning herself in the pond. Maggie has lost her chance to go back to New York, which would have been "leaving, not going home." Interspersed in the narrative is Anna-Marie Sherbrooke's diary from her missionary trip, which helps to explain the past. After Hattie's suicide, Maggie goes into labor. It appears the household will just be Maggie, Ian, and the baby after all.

Stillness (1979) begins in Manhattan at the apartment of Andrew Kincannon, the successful head of a management company for artists. He has never married but known many women, including Maggie Sherbrooke. Out of the blue, Ian Sherbrooke telephones from Vermont to say that Maggie's three-year-old daughter, Jane, is Andrew's daughter and Maggie is depressed. Andrew agrees to come to Vermont; the scene shifts there. Ian recalls Hattie's suicide, believing she killed herself because the baby was not Judah's. Meanwhile, Ian has been trying to register Sherbrookes as a historic tourist museum to keep the state from pushing Route 7 through his property. The issue is whether the selectmen will endorse the bypass and a mall or oppose them. The town is facing a number of problems, such as polluted water. "Vermont is a place," says Vito, the barber, "where everything becomes a problem lately of worse after bad." The local theater group wants to use the Sherbrookes carriage barn for one of their plays. Through this cooperation, Ian begins an affair with Jeanne Fisk, a married mother of twin girls. He finds and reads Judah's father's day book, selections of which are quoted throughout the novel. Inspired by this material, Ian begins a play about Judah and Maggie called *The Green Mantle*. When Andrew arrives from New York, Ian complains to him about farming: "It's a losing proposition, and you get burned in the bargain. You wake up one morning and find yourself dead; you find out the cows have mastitis and the feed's run out and prices have been raised for everything but milk. You go downtown to wrangle with the Agway man, and while you're gone the vet shoots the herd and says it's for the taxpayers' safety." Ian agonizes over his affair with Jeanne, whom he genuinely loves. Maggie and Jane finally go with Andrew to New York; Ian gives Andrew a copy of his play; he is alone. An example of a pleasing image: "Yew trees as conical as igloos with new snow."

In *Old Scores* (1997), thirty-six-year-old Paul Ballard is a child prodigy who, after a marriage and a divorce in his early thirties, goes to teach at Catamount College in southern Vermont. He

lives in North Catamount: "The village of North Catamount conveyed the feel of rural life but none of its harsh exigency; the poverty he noticed was, when authentic, picturesque." Elizabeth ("Beth") Sieverdsen, just twenty-one, is one of a few students with "real flair," he observes. He is attractive and sought after, but stays aloof. She is the seducer: once approached, he is lost. Their love affair is at first secret, but this is 1969 — the year of the Vietnam War, Richard Nixon, and protests — and soon they are one of a number of acknowledged faculty-student couples. They live openly in his old farmhouse and are happy. He believes they can get away with this happiness with "no price to pay." He asks her to marry him after her graduation; she refuses. Thinking back she realizes that "We thought time and the river had altered things irrevocably and nothing would ever be the same again and all that Puritan repressiveness was finished, over, done." Then Paul is struck in a hit-and-run accident and left for dead. A couple who had been parking nearby drive him to the back entrance of the local hospital, but do not take him inside because of some irregularity in their relationship. Badly hurt, limbs broken, pelvis shattered, he closes in upon himself and is unable to talk to Beth about what has happened. She leaves college; he slowly recovers and, retired from teaching, leads a monk-like existence in his farmhouse, doing research on the Newcomb family, which came to Catamount in 1720. In leaving Paul, Beth takes away a secret that belonged to him: she is pregnant. Her shocked family persuades her to give up the baby for adoption. Four years later she marries an adman named Michael Vire and moves to Italy. She has a son, William, and a daughter, Serena, before Michael leaves her for Rome and his lover, Giovanni. Beth receives a letter from the daughter whom she gave up: Sally Axelrod works in Rutland and lives in Sandgate, twenty miles from Catamount. Beth returns to Catamount to tell Paul about his daughter. The adoptive father, Sam Axelrod, a journalist, is the man who anonymously saved Paul's life twenty-five years earlier. "There were debits and credits; things fit," muses

Paul. "In the room of his reclusiveness there was no distraction, no generations scrabbling at the edges of composure like June bugs at the screens." After a quiet and moving ending, Beth's children assume she will return to their summer place in Michigan, but she wants to stay in Vermont "where I belong."

Barbara Delinsky

In *An Irresistible Impulse* (1983), Abby Barnes, beautiful, slim, and impeccably dressed, is thrown together with Ben Wyeth, virile and graceful, as part of a sequestered jury locked up in a mansion near Woodstock. Nurse-practitioner Abby is pleased to be chosen because she is trying to escape the advances of her boss, Dr. Sean Hennessey; political-scientist Ben, who teaches at Dartmouth, is eager to serve because he plans to write a book about the experience. The defendant is accused of kidnapping and assaulting his former lover, Greta Robinson. His lawyer presents the irresistible impulse defense: his client was temporarily insane. The devastating sexual attraction Abby and Ben feel toward each other, which leads them to bed, is another kind of irresistible impulse.

The main character of *Suddenly* (1993), Dr. Paige Pfeiffer, thirty-nine, has been practicing pediatrics in Tucker (near Hanover) for about ten years. She chose that place because her grandmother, born in Vermont, now lives forty minutes away in West Winter. Three doctors practice with Paige: Angie Bigelow, Peter Grace, and Mara O'Neill, who has just been found dead in her car, presumably of carbon monoxide poisoning. At the time of Mara's death, an adoption agency arrives with an East Indian baby, Sameera, for Mara; Paige agrees to be temporary guardian of the baby. The agency assures Paige that "the older she gets, the more Americanized she becomes. Vermonters like that." Paige, a volunteer coach for the Mount Court Academy girls' track team, meets the new Head of School, good-looking Noah Perrine. He has come to this "godforsaken" town to inject a little discipline into the school. His daughter, Sara, is on Paige's track team. The students think "the town is the

pits — there's nothing here." Angie is perceived as "domineering" by her husband, Ben, a cartoonist who has carried on an eight-year affair with the local librarian, and "smothering" by her teenager, Dougie. Peter, a third generation Vermonter, had an affair with Mara and dabbles in pornographic photography. Mara worked hard to clean up certain parts of Tucker, including the ancient movie theater; this foretells the collapse of the balcony, crushing hundreds. The strands of the plot are gathered up in an interesting and fulfilling way.

Three Wishes (1997) is set in Panama in northern Vermont, just off the truck route running from Concord to Montreal. The truck route is important, because the critical center of Panama is the diner, Flash 'n the Pan, where Bree Miller works. Bree is radiant and much loved; people in Panama are happy, employed, supportive, and sensitive to each other's needs. Bree lives in the house she inherited from her father; her mother left when Bree was a baby. Walking home from the diner, Bree is hit by a car rebounding from a collision with a pick-up truck. The driver of the car feels responsible, remains by her bedside in the hospital, and, when she is able to return home, stays through the nights with her. The other members of the community are not happy about this flatlander's appropriating Bree, especially when they find out he is celebrity author and lawyer, Thomas Gates. Bree and Tom fall in love. Bree tells Tom that in a near-death experience on the operating table a "kind being" appeared and gave her permission to return to life if she would promise to employ three wishes. Bree's internal injuries prevent her from having children, but she exercises one of her wishes to become pregnant. What happens next gives Tom a chance to rethink his values, start practicing pro bono law, and reconcile with his entire family.

Barbara Dimmick

In *Heart-Side Up* (2002), Professor Zoe Muir was living in Rhode Island teaching young people with learning disabilities when one of her students, Adam, slashed her with a knife. Despite psychiatric counseling, she is slow to recover from the attack. In a letter from a friend of her mother's, Zoe learns that the father of her first love, Dayton Deming Reed, has died in Pennsylvania. She drives to Pennsylvania to renew her friendship with Dayton. At his house, she is told that Dayton is a Catholic monk somewhere in Vermont. She takes a leave of absence from work, informs her psychiatrist, and sets out to find Dayton. With the help of a Catholic priest in southern Vermont, she finds out that Dayton is at Shroveton Skete, a controversial commune run without an abbot by five Catholics. She heads for Montpelier and northwest through Benton to Shroveton. She identifies the Skete's location, but, finding the inhabitants in retreat, she impulsively buys five hundred acres and an unfinished house on Morning Hill Road (she has received a great deal of money from her assailant's wealthy parents). She buys her supplies at the General Store, which is known as Gossip Central and Radio-Free Shroveton. She meets Hal Westerbrook, a state senator in Montpelier, and Spark Everett, the town constable. The Everett family has lived in Shroveton "forever." Other people, including developers, are interested in her property and bets are on over how long she will stick it out. She addresses all the chores herself, reading manuals carefully to find solutions, cleaning the chimney, using a chain saw to cut up deadfall, and enjoys the physical exhaustion and gratification. "Skills and patterns...that's all life should be." She attends the town meeting in early March and sees the monks there, including Dayton. She hears constant criticism of the people "from away:" "It's the people from away who change things;" "you people from away." She begins to be harassed by garbage left on her land, then a jacked deer on her porch. Alan, her assailant, is apprehended on her property; she feels sorry for his ruined life. Zoe and Dayton eventually spend a night together and decide what to do with their lives. (The title is from Dayton on carpentry. "You are looking for the center...the heartwood. Because it's the strongest, you always turn it to face the weather, up or out.")

Edwin Asa Dix

Deacon Bradbury (1900), a moving account of family life in the 1870s in the village of Felton near Montpelier, features an inspiring figure, Deacon Nathan Bradbury. A small farmer, he lives with his wife, Martha Streeter Bradbury, and his three children, Charles, Martha, and Emmeline, in a house built by his grandfather. People on the main street keep the slats of their shutters slightly open to "peer out" at the comings and goings. Nathan had to mortgage his farm and wishes to keep this a secret, but, as his wife says, "People will talk so." He is loath to borrow money, but "his land is gradually becoming exhausted and his surplus produce is selling for less and less." His girls stay at home with their mother, but Charlie works at the post office. He had a very good job at the pharmacy—his interest is chemistry, but he lost his job because he came home apparently drunk one night, helped by his friend, Enos Reed. Although Enos promised not to tell, word got out and Charlie was fired. Nathan borrows one thousand dollars to send Charlie to a technical college to study chemistry, but "after the reserved, often secretive way of New England folk," he has not told Charlie. Both Charlie and Enos Reed are interested in Mattie Pickering, who clearly favors the former. Although not formally educated, Nathan is a profound thinker. He is as devoted to his past as his Puritan ancestors were, yet he finds he values his current physical existence more than the spiritual existence to follow. He admires the virile New Englanders who preceded him. "However much they might seek to subdue the flesh through the spirit—and they did wonderfully succeed—the very conditions of their life, the struggle for life's existence, the hearty, hardy, brave, and always noble mode of living, had inevitably bred in the best of them a high, true perception of the value of that life and living, a certain just pride in their having conquered existence, wrested it from adverse nature, without lowering or brutalizing their own nature, without ever descending from their lofty, inborn ideals of character and conduct." People are polite to Charlie at the post office, but "the village ban was evidently upon him in part."

He hates "Felton humanity and its artificial code." At Mr. Leavitt's request, Charlie stays late one night to put away the day's cash receipts, over seven hundred dollars. That evening, Mr. Leavitt and Mr. Pickering come to the Bradbury house to announce that the money is missing. The father, unwisely, looks at Charlie with anger and accusation. Much to the astonishment of the three men, Charlie admits he took the money. His heartbroken father removes from his cache the appropriate amount (saved for Charlie's education) and gives it to the protesting Mr. Leavitt. Charlie leaves the house that night and "on the morrow there were evil whispers in town." Nathan is obdurate: his son's behavior and flight prove his guilt. Charlie's mother, sisters, and Mattie proclaim his innocence. Nathan is suffering in a world of sorrow and perceived punishment. Not understanding how Providence could treat his family this way, he decides to leave the church. He has tried to live a godly life; at least he has never led an "ungodly life," but he realizes he "never did believe those lines about our all being miserable sinners and vile worms." The Reverend Mr. Marshall calls on Miss Jewett for help in dissuading Nathan. Forthright, understanding, and a voice of Vermont, she asks good questions and respects Nathan's right to follow his conscience. "Rumor flies fast," and the Felton Congregational Church is packed the morning Nathan leaves the church. He becomes perceptibly more "tender and universe-embracing." He is now a better family man. He is less irritable about minor matters and more sympathetic with his wife and daughters. He is a kinder neighbor and every poor family in Felton knows him. He cannot give money, because his own family is in need, "but he gave of his strength in aiding to make the weather side of some poorer neighbor's house tight against the winter wind; in helping with his advice or his team some smaller farm-holder in more urgent difficulties; in sitting up with a sick neighbor whose family were feeling the strain of watchdog." While Nathan and Martha are out one day in the cutter, Nathan steps down to gather boughs in the woods for the girls' wreaths; two tramps attack Martha, who is almost overcome before a traveler saves her. Nathan and the stranger bind up the felons and carry them off to jail. The man is Mr. Lee, a member of a chemical business hired to test the water Mr. Reed is proposing to sell the town. At the meeting to discuss the findings, Mr. Lee tells the assembly that his chemist (Charlie, who has been working for two years in Burlington) finds the water polluted. Mr. Reed explodes with anger, refusing to accept the word of a drunk and a thief; Nathan explodes right back, saying Charlie never stole anything in his life. And so saying the father knows it is true. "The news of the afternoon's event flew swiftly in all directions." Daughter Martha inveigles Enos Reed into confessing that on both occasions he did not tell the whole truth. In the first instance, Charlie inhaled a poisonous substance and quaffed the medicinal brandy to keep from choking to death. In the second, he carried the box of money home with him for safekeeping because he had noticed one of the windows did not close properly. Reunited with his family, Charlie goes up the hill to see Mattie.

Old Bowen's Legacy (1901) takes place in Felton in the same period as *Deacon Bradbury*. Old Simeon Bowen, on his deathbed, summons lawyer Sam Clark lawyer to make his will. When Sam hears that Simeon is dying, he is sad. In a town like Felton, "People come to interlock so closely into one another's lives and associations, their personalities are so near and vivid and constantly present, that anything affecting one sends a thrill through all." Simeon tells Sam he does not see any point to life or any good in mankind; Sam replies that the reason Simeon thinks men are "despicable" is that he has "practiced despising" all his life. Simeon wants to leave his money (five thousand dollars from selling his house plus his savings) to three trustees, Sam, Nathan Bradbury, and Mr. Pickering, a quarry owner. They are to distribute the money in a lump sum to any person or group of their choice (with the exception of the church) within a year. Miss Lorinda Park, the town gossip, spreads the word and groups begin applying for the legacy. The trustees, not wanting to foment local jealousies, ask Miss Jewitt's advice. She suggests they wait as long as possible because circumstances have a way of unfolding. Garrett Coe, forty-five, is a harsh, angry, bullying farmer who lives a hard-scrabble life with his wife, Sally Mitchell, his grown daughter, 'Vinie, and two little boys, Garrie and Bruce. Sally is exhausted and nervous from overwork and listening to her husband's continuous grievances. 'Vinie has a beau, Burt Way, to whom she is half-engaged, but she is dispirited by the example of her parents' marriage, "like being sold into bondage." Mr. Reed, owner with Mr. Kemble of the local store, holds a small mortgage on the Coe farm; Coe hates Reed and starts a fight at the post office. In fact, Coe hates the world in general and directs his anger toward his poor wife. Just before Reed & Kemble's store catches fire, Burt Way and Cheever Hayes see Coe slinking down the alley next to the store. The entire town assembles to fight the fire; the rumor that Coe purposely set the fire spreads as rapidly as the flames. Everyone is convinced Coe is guilty, but they do not go after him: "Sober Vermonters are not in the habit of going lynching." Coe, unaware of the gossip about him, pushes his wife, both figuratively and literally, so far that she suddenly breaks down and tells him what she thinks of being his slave for twenty-one years. He has never done anything but grumble and complain and she is leaving him and taking Garrie with her. Now the main topic in town is whether a wife has the right to leave her husband (the weight of opinion is against Sally). Because Garrett refuses to hire anyone to help 'Vinie, she accepts the invitation of Mr. and Mrs. Wheeler to bring Bruce to live with the kindly old couple in their big house. Coe rapidly goes down hill: his hired man leaves; his cows die; a landslide denudes his one fertile slope; he is near penury; and he is ill. Hiram Wheeler is so uncomfortable with the way the town has abandoned Coe that he goes to see him. Coe tells Hiram he wants to "get right with the world;" Hiram explains that Coe has hated people all these years. With Hiram's intervention, 'Vinie and Bruce begin to visit their father again. Taking produce to Hingham one day, Coe runs into a tricks-and-

juggling performer, a Frenchman named Franco, who persuades Coe to arrange a performance in Felton. On the way back to Felton, Coe picks up a run-away named Julie B. Joline, who has been beaten by her father. Feeling protective and gentle, Coe takes her home to 'Vinie's care. Franco turns out to be a disgruntled former employee of Coe's who tries to kill Coe during the performance. Julie (whose middle name is Bowen) is Simeon's grandniece. The trustees unanimously choose to give Simeon's legacy to the Coe family to start over in the warmer Kentucky climate where a relative of Sam's will sell them a nice, sunny farm. The neighbors come up the hill to congratulate them. Ironically, benefactor and legatee once shared the same negative view of life.

Susan M. Dodd

"What I Remember Now" (1999), striking and intense, is told from the point of view of June, thirty-six, a free-lance illustrator who has recently moved to the Burlington area from Illinois. She is something of a loner ("Solitude suits me"), whose only acquaintances are Ham and Gladys, the couple running the diner on the reservoir road. June becomes aware that, as she is driving somewhere, she often passes a man in a pickup who "lifts two fingers from the steering wheel" in greeting. Once, in the diner, he says, "Hey," as he sits down six stools away. She is aware of him now, interested, even though she did not think she was looking for someone. She gets her hair cut and buys a new down jacket. They meet, unexpectedly, in a bookstore in Montpelier. His name is Barter Cunningham and he is "beautiful." They spend the afternoon, the evening, the night together. He follows her car: "his headlights, in my rearview mirror, doted on me all the long way home." He starts coming to her house regularly at night, letting himself in a side door. They are strangers. She is mad about him. He disappears for awhile and returns, shaven and shorn, having attended his son John's graduation. This turns out to be their last night together. He suddenly begins talking about his older brother, who committed suicide; about

D

his mother, who disappeared after Kennedy was killed; about his wife, who left him and whom he still loves. What she remembers now is passing him on the road and seeing the "scant" lift of two fingers from the steering wheel. They remain strangers.

Julia Dorr

Farmingdale (1854) celebrates the stalwart character of fifteen-year-old Mary Lester. After her mother dies, she and her little brother, Tommy, are sent to their mother's sister, Aunt Betsy Graham, and her farmer husband in Farmingdale, a village in a valley that "nestles so lovingly in the embrace of the Green Mountains." Affectionate little Mary is grieved by the harsh welcome she receives from Aunt Betsy. Mary hopes to go to school, but instead her aunt dismisses the hired girl and assigns all her tasks to Mary. Mary is a willing worker, but the load is cruel. Her cousin John, eighteen, who left school to help his father, is friendly but not so awakened to intellectual stimulation as she. Mary makes friends with Amy Thompson, who goes to school but stops by when possible. (Using the village telegraph system, the girls hang a piece of white material out an upper window when they want to communicate.) A year passes. Mary has become tall and womanly; Aunt Betsy is as "hard and forbidding" as ever. Mary's "gentleness, thirst for knowledge, the perfect purity of thought and deed" have had a salutary influence on John; he enrolls in Carrolton Academy much to his mother's annoyance. A family named Vaun buys the Sherwood property: the advent of newcomers in Farmingdale is a real event. Aunt Betsy takes offense because the Vauns have a library and a "pianer." In fact, the Vauns are not fancy and snobbish: Mrs. Vaun is graceful and loveable and Mr. Vaun works in the fields with his men. Their daughter, Alice, and Mary form a special bond. The Vaun house is charming and comfortable inside; outside, they plant shade trees. The Grahams continue to be harsh and unpleasant. Some of the children in the village fall ill with scarlet fever: little Ellen Vaun dies; Alice recovers but is blind. Tommy is not strong, but Aunt Betsy

makes him pick wool in the stifling attic for hours; when he falls asleep, she strikes him. When Aunt Betsy finally goes too far with her sarcasm and sadism, Mary complains of their treatment, and Aunt Betsy turns them out of her house. They seek refuge with Mrs. Thompson, where Mary earns her keep spinning and weaving while eager to "take a school" to earn her own living and save enough to send Tommy to college. Mr. Huntington, husband of a friend of Aunt Betsy's, is on the school committee; Aunt Betsy has told everyone that ungrateful Mary left of her own accord. Mr. Huntington does not hire Mary, but Mr. Vaun examines her and finds her a position in the Hemlock schoolhouse, where she boards. Her "air of quiet unassuming dignity, gentleness, and kindness of manner" win the love of the children. In the summer, Mrs. Vaun engages Mary as companion to Alice and tutor for little Ralph; Tommy, now twelve, stays with them, too. Alice, though blind, can help tend baby Willie, knit, and play the piano. In the fall, Mary and Tommy move to Carrolton, where they board with Miss Skinner. Soon Mary has enough pupils, although some of the girls are scornful of her because she works for her living. Cousin John has returned home after five years out West, after his father apologizes for treating him unfairly all these years. Mary is happy as her school flourishes, but something changes in Miss Skinner's demeanor, and Mary notices coldness in other quarters: mothers take their daughters from her school, and Miss Skinner asks her and Tommy to leave. Gossip (Amy calls it "Scandalania") spread by Aunt Betsy reports that John went out West because Mary was importuning him to marry her. John has never thought of Mary in this way, but now he asks her to be his wife. She refuses. Aunt Betsy falls ill, and Mary is forced to take care of her aunt and uncle. After John and Amy marry, Mary is free to take the post of principal at the Carrolton Seminary. Her uncle dies, leaving the farm to John and enough money to Mary to render her independent and able to educate Tommy. A lovely image of Indian summer: "A soft haze hung over the landscape; and although the fields were robbed of their summer glory, and the meadows were brown and bare, the scene was surpassingly beautiful. The mountains — those in the distance — lay like misty clouds against the deep blue sky."

In *Sybil Huntington* (1869), devoted sisters Ruth, twenty-one, and Sybil Huntington, sixteen, live in the village of Valleythorpe, with towering mountains on one side and Lake Champlain on the other: "the sparkling Otter wound like a thread of silver through emerald velvet." Their father, Ralph Huntington, is a "noble specimen of the old-fashioned New England farmer;" his wife is helpless and indolent. Ruth, engaged to farmer John Gardiner, has a thirst for knowledge but decides that Sybil, five years younger, should go away to school (Oakwood is thirty miles away), since they cannot both be spared from home. Sybil, the first-person narrator, has "vague dreams of a loftier and more beautiful life," although she does not want Ruth to make this sacrifice. Ruth presents the case to their parents: the father agrees it is a fine opportunity for Sybil; her mother is sarcastic and mean. John drives Sybil to Oakwood, through views of mountainsides, snug farmhouses, scattered villages, busy farmers, and flashing mill wheels. Miss Raymond, the headmistress, is tall and majestic. Sybil loves her school days but readily enters into home life upon her return: her mother is surprised that Sybil is not too spoiled to do housework. At the end of several years, Sybil is valedictorian of her class and offered a position as governess by a widow, Mary Gordon, who lives in northern Virginia. Her children, Edith, fourteen, Arthur, ten, and Fanny, eight, are charming, and Sybil, though nervous about living among "haughty aristocrats," is easily integrated into the household. She is dazzled by the attentions of Mary Gordon's suave younger brother, Guy Tremaine, but finds the racist attitudes in Virginia antipathetic. Sybil befriends a young slave, Violet, and tries to help her before Violet's death. Word comes that Ruth has had a serious fall. When Sybil arrives home, Ruth is bedridden, and their father is dead. Ruth is so ill that her wedding to John is postponed indefinitely. In the meantime, Sybil, struggling with family finances,

is helped by Mark Halsey, an attractive, sympathetic lawyer who is ten years older than Sybil and has known her all her life. Unscrupulous Lysander Moore, who is after the family farm, proposes to Sybil. When she rejects him, he vows to punish her. At this difficult juncture, Mrs. Huntington decides to marry Squire Mason and sell her portion of the farm. Sybil counts on Mark's sage advice. Lysander Moore's revenge is to claim that the Huntingtons owe him a large sum of money. In the midst of this situation, Guy appears on the scene. Sybil is attracted to him but does not want to marry him. Just in time, she finds the legal, signed note that negates Moore's claim and a doctor who can help Ruth with an operation. John and Ruth finally marry. Sybil finds that it is Mark she has always loved and they marry and have two boys.

Expiation (1872) begins in 1851 when John Armstrong buys the old Elliot place (the Elliot quarry failed) in Altona, bringing with him sons Kenneth and Clyde. The narrator, Margaret Rossiter, is a friend of Patsy, the neighbor who is getting the house ready. Altona is a picturesque village high up in the hills with mountains above and below it and broad stretches of meadowland in the valley. "The mountains towered peak on peak, their summits wrapped in rose and purple, amber and amethyst." Rumors swell about why the Armstrongs are returning to Greyholt (as the house is called). Patsy thinks there is some mystery about the second wife, Clyde's mother, whose name is never mentioned. Five years pass to find Armstrong on his deathbed. Kenneth has been away at college and medical school. The night that Armstrong dies, Margaret sees Kenneth putting a document in the safe. Margaret, now forty, has a boarder at her house (named Cozytoft) — Elsie Meredith, niece and ward of Dr. Howard Bellinger of New York, who grew up in Altona. Elise, unconsciously enchanting, and Clyde, now twenty, form a spontaneous, childlike affection for each other; Kenneth, now twenty-three, is more reticent, but Margaret can see that he is in love with Elsie. The weather is lovely — "dreamy, misty, Indian summer-like." Elsie spends her time in this "mountain fastness" practicing philanthropy—books to worthy children, sisterly counsel to bewildered young women—and thinks Kenneth is idling away his time in repose. When Elsie and Clyde ride out on horseback to deliver clothes to a new baby and are caught in a fierce storm, Kenneth rescues them. Five days pass, and neither young man calls at Cozytoft. Finally, both men visit; Margaret realizes that Clyde loves Elsie, too. Kenneth is ever gentlemanly but attempts to keep Elsie and Clyde apart. Patsy confides to Margaret that trouble is brewing with Tom Bradshaw, a local worker who has held a grudge ever since John Armstrong dismissed him. Bradshaw is fanning the flames of the rumor that, because Armstrong's money comes from his second wife, Clyde will inherit the entire estate. Clyde proposes to Elsie, who rejects him; Clyde wants to follow her to New York, but Kenneth will not allow it. After Clyde develops a brain seizure, Dr. Bellinger is summoned from New York, bringing with him a nurse, Sister Agnes. Clyde dies; at the simple, tender funeral, Kenneth, though heartbroken, seems relieved. Only then is the mystery revealed: Clyde's mother did not die but abandoned her husband and child: in expiation, she became a nurse, Sister Agnes. Kenneth had feared all those years that Clyde had hereditary insanity and murdered his mother. Kenneth and Elsie marry and have a little Clyde; "Aunt" Margaret and Patsy live with them at Greyholt.

Basil S. Douros

The first part of *The Roots of the Blackthorn Tree* (2002) provides background about the oppression of Irish-Catholic families who fled to America; the second part begins when Irish-Catholic immigrants arrive in Underhill in 1856. Michael Barrett and Elizabeth Breen, engaged, come with their big families, carrying a shillelagh (made of blackthorn wood) that is a significant symbol for the family. Michael's first job is selling potash. His son, Luke, has the ability to design, engineer, and direct the construction of wooden bridges. This talent leads to his building and maintaining a fleet of steamships to haul freight and passengers on

Lake Champlain, the beginning of an avocation for all the Barrett men at Shelburne Harbor. When Luke dies in 1925, he passes on the family shillelagh to his son, Fred, who serves in World War I and comes home to marry Ellen Kidder from Middlebury and go to work at Shelburne Harbor. Another family in this Irish-Catholic community is the Welches, whose daughter Mary marries Daniel O'Sullivan. Their daughter, Mame, marries William Provost, son of Antoine Provost, a Canadian, and Ascah Ball. Antoine, whose mother was an Abenaki, fought in the Third Vermont Regiment during the Civil War. The last steamship built at the shipyard at Shelburne Harbor is the *Ticonderoga*, built in 1906. The Irish were driven out of their homes in Ireland by the wealthy landowners but welcomed in Vermont.

Anne Miller Downes

Jessie Perkins, who is twenty at the start of *So Stands the Rock* (1939), descends from Moses Perkins, one of the Hampshire Grantees of the town of Winston near Bennington. Her grandfather built a large wooden house; his four sons went off to the Civil War; only one, Sam, came back. His wife died in childbirth with Jessie. Will Nicholls, son of neighboring farmers, is Jessie's steady beau. At Fanny Brown's wedding, Jessie meets and falls in love with Angus Shawn, also twenty; they decide to marry at once. Jessie and Angus are sadly and irreparably unsuited. She, though not unintelligent, is stolid, entrepreneurial, and single-minded. Her school attendance was spotty; she never reads a book. She is happy to cook, clean, and do chores; she has no idea what goes through Angus's mind. Angus is intellectual, poetic, and light-hearted, with Irish charm and a questing soul. He wants to improve himself, to read, write, and create. He fits poorly into the role of farmer and woodworker. A rich woman from New York, Lucy Malverne, buys the Haskell place in Winston. She hires Jessie to cook a daily meal for herself, her younger sister, Patricia, and her brother, Dr. Charles. Patricia starts hanging around Angus's shop, which causes gossip in the village. Tilly

Lawrence, his former girlfriend, returns to Winston to run the library. She is lovely, thoughtful, and literate; she and Angus have everything to say to each other and he realizes his mistake in judgment. Jessie, now pregnant, is hateful to Angus, refusing, for example, to hire someone to do the night chores so that he can study. The midwife, Sarah Palmer, spends every afternoon with Jessie. Angus goes off one afternoon with Tilly in her carriage and, when they are caught in a fearful storm, breaks his leg. Jessie has her baby, Matthew, the same day as the accident. Tilly appreciates Angus's aspirations and arranges for him to have a printing press so that he can edit a paper. He starts *The Winston Chronicle* and befriends the local doctor, John Ayres, who is courting Tilly. Tilly realizes that Angus is in love with her and tries to spend less time at the printing press. In a surprise move, Jessie buys out the stockholders of the paper so that she is sole publisher. Jessie has a little girl, Fay; Jessie and Angus realize that they are not only incompatible personally but on different sides politically. Out with Matthew one day, Angus drowns trying to save the little boy, who has fallen into a river and also perishes. Shortly after this, Jessie has twin boys, sells the paper for a large fortune to Angus's political enemy, Si Benson, and turns their barn—The Long Barn—into a successful tearoom. As she always says, "things seem to turn out for the best."

In *Heartwood* (1945), Sammy Crocker, whose face shows "strength and endurance," returns from war in 1919 to the village on the "northern bleakness" of Matlin Mountain near Burlington. He goes at once to his Aunt Seba Burton, who lives in the finest house in the village. His widowed father has left his second wife, "Mom" Turnbull, who lives with her son and his family in the old Crocker farmhouse built by Sammy's great-grandfather. Sammy's oldest brother, Walt, ran away, and the middle boy, Edgar, drowned himself. Sammy, a "mountain boy," went to the village school as a teenager and "learned the first day the solidarity of village snobbery." Sammy's best friends on the mountain are the Wicks family, Sate, and her younger sis-

ters, Lin and Jess. Sate helped raise Sammy after his mother's death; though poor and denigrated in the village, Sate and her sisters are warm, happy, and play the piano and sing. Lin has loved Sammy all her life. John White, the minister, appreciates Sammy's qualities, as does his daughter, Dorothy, who goes to Vassar. Dorothy's wealthy aunt has lavished social opportunities on Dorothy. When Ralph, a rich boy in the same set as Dorothy, talks about skiing in Europe, Sammy feels "awkward, silent, an outsider." People on the mountain are considered "backward." When Dorothy and Sammy walk down the main street together, "Mary Bunting was peeking though her lace curtains watching everything that was going on." Sammy meets painter Robert Culver, who has bought an old house on the mountain. He is concerned that people are not conserving their forests, "their very life-blood." Sammy explains they are forced to sell lumber because the land is too highly taxed. Sammy works at Pete Carter's store. After a robbery, Sammy is accused of stealing, but Carter realizes Sammy couldn't have robbed him. After Carter dies, for "many days women walked quietly through the snow with odd-shaped bundles in their arms or balanced carefully in their hands; pails of soup, roast, hot biscuit, cakes, cookies." Sammy and Dorothy acknowledge their love and the social "chasm" between them. "He knows the unforgivable sin of being different." Miss Quimby and others gossip about Sammy's relationship with the Wicks family. The village seems pleased when Dorothy and Sammy break up because Sammy will not relinquish his friendship with Lin. Dorothy goes abroad as a nurse. Sammy tries to rehabilitate the Crocker farm. Lin visits Pap Crocker and his mistress, Carrie Palmer, every day. When Carrie dies, she leaves her valuable property on the other side of the mountain to Sammy. After Sate's younger sister, Jess, becomes pregnant, Sate takes her away, abandoning Lin. Sammy realizes the only way he can suitably take care of Lin is to marry her. Word comes that Dorothy has found Walt in a hospital in France and is bringing him home. Lin is killed in a skiing accident, leaving Sammy free to marry Dorothy.

Elizabeth Doyle

In *A Country Christmas* (2002), the Bass family, father (a salesman) and mother, daughter Charlotte Lynn, seventeen, and son Peter, twenty, live comfortably in 1831 Peacham. This Christmas, Peter brings home a Harvard friend, Shaun Jackson Matheson, who is, from his manner and clothes, a wealthy Bostonian. Charlotte falls madly in love with him and takes pleasure in parading him as her beau in front of her jealous village friends. Shaun's enraged father arrives to drag Shaun home to Boston. Shaun doesn't answer Charlotte's letters. For some reason, Mr. Matheson accepts Margaret Bass's invitation to spend the following Christmas in Peacham. Charlotte, piqued, pretends to be engaged to Giles Williams. Caught in a snowstorm together, Shaun and Charlotte overcome their petty differences.

David Drake

The battle for the New Hampshire Grants and the capture of Fort Ticonderoga are recast in *Patriots* (1996) in the year 2349, when human settlements are spreading to habitable planets as interstellar travel becomes easier. The universe is split between an Atlantic Alliance (Great Britain) and an East Asian Sphere. The Alliance administers newly discovered worlds through Protectors of established colonies. Harvard-educated Mark "Lucius-son" Maxwell, twenty-two, finds himself on the frontier when he visits the colony called Greenwood (Vermont). Greenwood is informally headed by a huge, powerful, red-haired, heavy-drinking, pragmatic man named Yerby Bannock (Ethan Allen), who lives in a compound with his slightly older and assertive wife, Désirée (Mary Allen), and his sister, Amy. The Protector of Greenwood has sold settlement grants to a planet that was under the jurisdiction of the Protector of Zenith (New York). Surveyors from Zenith arrive to claim their grants in order to build planned communities of fifty thousand people each. Amy and Mark are concerned with the environmental impact of so many inhabitants. Investors arrive with plans to raise a militia. Yerby is chosen the leader of the militia,

which he names the Woodsrunners (Green Mountain Boys). Blaney's Tavern (Fay's) is the unofficial headquarters. There is talk of self-government, which would mean rebellion against the Alliance. Zenith mounts an invasion of Greenwood, but the invaders are outsmarted. Yerby likes to play the "simple frontiersman" but is an excellent strategist. The Alliance summons them for negotiations; Greenwood's delegation is headed by Dagmar Wately, a neighbor of Yerby's, and Mark. The offerings of the Counselor are not satisfactory, but Mark counters with a deal: if Zenith will make Greenwood free and self-governing, Greenwood will provide Zenith with the arms it needs to free it from Alliance tyranny. The weapons are stored at the fort named Minor at Dittersdorf (Fort Ticonderoga). Mark's lawyer father arrives to solicit their participation in an open rebellion against the Alliance. If they do not succeed, the Alliance will ship millions of Earth citizens to every settled planet. As the Woodsrunners are preparing to attack the fort, Berkeley Finch (Benedict Arnold), wearing the uniform of the Zenith Protective Association, proposes himself to lead the expedition but is rejected. The patriots are successful, capturing the officer-in-charge, a dreamy horticulturist named Captain Easton (Captain William Delaplace). Yerby takes the fort "in the name of Almighty God and the Assembly of Self-Governing Worlds" (the Continental Congress). Mark is elected to the Committee of Governance; he and Amy affectionately join forces.

Robert Luther Duffus

The Chapin family in *Roads Going South* (1921) has lived in Middleton for generations. The first Chapins came up from Connecticut after the Revolutionary War into the newly named state of Vermont. Almost immediately a steady drain of migration out West began. In 1883, Dr. Josiah Chapin and his wife, Emily Snow (Jennie Hilmer, who loved Josiah, committed suicide when he did not choose her), have a baby called Joe. From Joe's childhood, the roads going south from Middleton—the road to the village, the railroad to Norton, the highway to New York—have stood for adventure and release. (He is depressed that in Middleton "there was an almost heroic desire never to forget death.") He grows up playing with and admiring Ethel Holloway; the town expects they will marry. An only child, he feels pressures from different directions: his father wants him to be a doctor; his mother wants him to be a musician. Horace Brewster writes the scandal sheet for the *Middletown Gazette*: the town loves gossip. A new, younger doctor, George Harris, arrives in town from the University of Vermont. To Dr. Chapin, now sixty, "life was primarily work to do, hardship to endure, and danger to face." Joe delivers the class oration in 1900 and believes himself in love with Nancy Claire, a glamorous visitor from Richmond, Virginia. Joe takes his friend, Ethel, to several parties before going to Wilmington College. While he is away, his mother dies. His friend, Sam Allen, invites Joe to go to New York City, where Nancy Claire is studying music; Joe tells her he loves her. When Joe's father falls ill, Joe goes home to visit him. Joe's friends are planning their lives: Ethel tells him she will marry Dr. Harris; Sam leaves college to marry Harriet; Walter, too, is engaged to marry. Joe ships out to sea, taking a road going south to discover the world and his place in it. Perhaps Nancy will be waiting when he returns.

In *That Was Alderbury* (1941), fourteen-year-old Phil Burns witnesses the lives of this close-knit community near Williamstown in 1897. His father is a self-educated immigrant working in the granite sheds. Their landlord is George Gainsby, a newspaper reporter and town gossip. His brother, Alfred, runs the local drugstore. Phil founds the Seers Club with his friends. The Caswell store is an evening hangout for Scotch and Italian stonecutters and farmers. A new schoolteacher, Sylvia Hale, and a new minister, Arthur Thorpe, with his slightly older wife, Anne, arrive. Phil, who is in Sylvia's class, admires her beauty and friendly manner. At Christmastime, Arthur decides to put on a temperance play to raise money to paint the church. The George Gainsby faction does not approve.

After the play, Phil notices that Arthur walks Sylvia home. George sees them, too, and tells everyone. George also criticizes Abner Brand for not attending church: Abner is working himself to death taking care of his wife and his farm. Mr. Thorpe challenges George, saying that some Christian people have a good reason for staying away from church. The Seers Club buries thirty-three cents in a cave. When Alfred happens on them, they make him an honorary member. Phil, sensitive to everyone's feelings and expressions, often notices how "lonesome" people look. When a poor man drowns trying to save his son, Arthur preaches a sermon on the theme of "Judge not, that ye be not judged." Some George Gainsby adherents squirm. Arthur also annoys George by saying that he does not believe in Original Sin. In April 1898, the United States goes to war against Spain. Phil's club establishes the Junior Volunteers, writes President McKinley offering to fight Spain, and performs at the Decoration Day ceremony. The villagers are jubilant because Admiral Dewey, victorious at Manila Bay, is a Vermont boy. Alfred warns Phil that Alderbury is a "man trap." Abner Bland continues to work seven days a week. When he finally has a stroke, the village rallies to help, but George feels that his God has triumphed. Sylvia decides not to come back, claiming her ailing mother in Boston needs her. George does not renew the minister's contract. The boys find that Alfred has left each of them money for their college education. Alfred, found dead of poison, has also left one thousand dollars to the minister, "as a slight recognition of his courageous attempt to introduce Christianity among the heathen of Alderbury." Inadvertently, Phil witnesses a farewell scene between Sylvia and Arthur: they love each other deeply but must part. Phil's mother begs him never to be ashamed of his town or his people.

Victory on West Hill (1942) also takes place in Alderbury. It is the ninety-fifth birthday of old Washington Hendricks at West Hill, which has been in the family for one hundred and fifty years and before that was an Indian hunting ground. Four generations of his family are coming to West Hill to celebrate this occasion. The narrator is the young village doctor, Rowland Hastings, who is giving Hendricks an experimental drug that is harmless physically but restores long-term memory. It works so effectively that Hendricks remembers his own experiences in the Civil War as well as what his grandfather told him of his exploits in the Revolutionary War. Hendricks is disappointed in his grandson, Bryan, who has focused on getting rich, and worries about his great-grandson, Pershing, who is in need of a cause. Hendricks is eager that his other great-grandson, Washington Hendricks Seidler (whose German-born father, Karl, is presumed dead in the war), join him at West Hill to learn about Vermont life. During the reunion, Hendricks expresses to the family what it means to belong to a tradition that stretches far back into American history. He says that when they came to Vermont, their side of the mountain was all woods, "beeches and birches and maples and oaks, pine and spruce and hemlock. There wasn't any underbrush to speak of. You could walk easily in those woods, and everywhere you looked it was like the aisles of a church, only bigger than any church you ever saw. There was all the game you wanted—deer and bear and sometimes moose, and partridge till you were tired shooting them, and trout in the brooks that would pretty nearly take a bare hook, they were so glad to have somebody come around and try to catch them. There were strawberries and raspberries and blackberries and blueberries bigger than they ever grow wild now. A man wouldn't starve in the woods in those days if he had powder and shot, and maybe, if he liked to live high, a bit of salt. We came up here with a mare and a stallion and a cow and some chickens." He describes their equipment, axes and spades and rifles, but no plough at first. They broke the land by girdling the trees and digging in among them with a spade so they could plant the first corn. They got sheep after a while so that his wife, Sarah, could weave and make clothes for the family. He tells of all her chores, curing and salting the meat, putting up fruit and vegetables, and making soap in a big kettle in the yard. "It's around here somewhere yet." Karl escapes from Europe, returns to West

Hill, and, despite anti-German attitudes on the part of some, finds he is welcomed home by Hendricks. Hendricks's "victory" is to show the family what it once stood for and to hope that his great-grandson, Washington, will restore the family strength. West Hill is left to Washington, with his father as trustee until he comes of age.

E

Dikkon Eberhart

In *On The Verge* (1979), Noah Carmichael, twenty-eight, is living in a house near New Haven (in the "austere embrace of this countryside"), about fifty miles from Nash's Water, where his parents live and his father runs a museum. Noah's best friends are Vermont natives Will and Virginia North. When Noah's friend, Robert Thomas Dugan III, and his wife, Jill Meriwether Kincaid, ask Noah to build them a stone house, Will, an expert stone mason, trains Noah. Through Robert and Jill, Noah meets their friends, Calvin, a university professor, and Lauren Donovan, a painter, and their daughter, Kate, who come up weekends to help with the house. Jill is scatterbrained and flirtatious; Robert is simpler and quieter. They are desperate to have a child and embroil Noah in continuous discussions of procedures. The house is progressing, with insulation and roof installed. (Noah lovingly describes the stone-building process, choosing and hefting the perfect shapes and sizes.) Taking off his hot shoes, Noah walks into the kitchen: "The tile floor was a dappled, cool trout stream to wade in." He realizes he is in love with Lauren. They all help Will with the haying. "Now was the hay-time, sweet, hot, hay-time: scythe-sharp slither through white, dry hay." Noah visits his parents and fields the usual questions about when he is going to decide what he wants to do with his life. He wonders if his tenure in Vermont is over. He is tired of the coming-and-going of the seasons: "We grow tight and bitter before it." He feels "his childhood is gone." Once, when Jill and Noah are alone, she tries to seduce him. Robert and Jill fight because he has "dragged her up here to these stupid mountains." Waiting for the crane operator to come to move the support beams into place, Noah stops for breakfast with the Norths and watches them in the kitchen perform tasks "with the spare choreography of the years." As Noah leaves to help with the beams, Will says, "Don't be careless," foreshadowing impending disaster. A terrible accident occurs. Lauren thinks Noah is selfish and "hiding in the hills." The stone house attracts some attention and an architectural journal asks Noah to write a piece; soon he is publishing other articles. He recognizes that "the magic the hills offer does not suffice." He is ready to leave; the implication is that Laura is waiting for him in Boston.

Bret Easton Ellis

The Rules of Attraction (1987), a stream-of-consciousness outpouring from four hedonistic, self-indulgent, self-absorbed characters in the "Reagan eighties," is about sex, drugs, and rock 'n' roll at Camden College (identified as in New Hampshire but modeled on Bennington College). Sean Bateman, a bisexual financial-aid student dealing drugs, is attracted to Paul Denton but in love with Lauren. His sarcastic advisor informs him that he is flunking three of his four courses; he retorts, equally sarcastically, "Not sculpting workshop?" Paul is a drama major in love first with Mitchell and then with Sean. Lauren Hynde, who is unable to decide whether to specialize in poetry, is in love with Victor Johnson but sleeps with Sean and others as well, leading to a pregnancy and an abortion. Victor is in Europe for most of the novel but returns to Camden to claim Lauren, if she is the one he thinks she is. The conversation at The Pub or the dining hall is full of pseudo-intellectual jargon: "oily Lit majors all dressed in black and exhibiting dry yet caustic wit." Sean attends one class on "Kafka/Kundera: The Hidden Connection." Lauren shows up at a "post-modern condition" tutorial to find her tutor drunk and stoned. Lauren says, "I don't care. It's all so boring." Paul muses, "No one ever likes the right person."

Margaret Erhart

In *Old Love* (1996), the Haas family in New Jersey is fraught with sexual ambiguity and inarticulate grief. At college, Frank Haas is aware of erotic tension between himself and a fellow crewman, who kills himself when Frank marries Margaret Fair ("Tommie") Thomas. Their first child, Faith, dies. Tommie takes a lover named Jeanne Ann Love. Hal, the gay man next door, is Tommie's best friend. Tommie's daughter, Helen, has a crush on Hal; she comes into his house while he is engaged with Dennis. Brighton, Tommie's son, is seeing a psychiatrist because no one will talk about Faith. Helen goes to college and, attracted to her anthropology professor, beds the latter's husband. Brighton goes to college. In the midst of this dysfunctional behavior, Tommie abandons her family and goes to Vermont to live in an A-frame house on a small farm with five women friends and a dog, Penelope. As Hal scornfully puts it, "Back to the land, that's our squaw Tommie. This time it's a farm near Barre. I call it the lesbian theme park. No men allowed unless they're schlepping something."

Earl Faine

In *Green Mountain Man: The Odyssey of Ethan Allen* (1996), after the capture of Fort Ticonderoga, Ethan Allen and John Brown try to take Montreal with their small complement of men; Brown betrays Ethan by deserting the field and Ethan is captured with thirty-three of his men. The British, who are delighted to seize Ethan, manacle, shackle, and imprison him in the stinking hold of the *Gaspé*. Ethan and his men are then put aboard the *Adamant* and taken in hideous conditions for over two months to England, where they are informed they will be executed as traitors. Landing at Falmouth, they are marched in shackles to Pendennis Castle.

Governor Jonathan Trumbull, George Washington, John Hancock, and General Schuyler all write to the British Prime Minister, Lord Frederick North, arguing against the execution of the captives and proposing an exchange with the British officers held by the Americans. Edmund Burke, who has been against the war, seeks conciliation. Queen Charlotte, receiving a moving letter from Ethan's wife, Mary, attempts to change the mind of King George, who wants the men to hang. The British propose releasing the Americans if they will perform certain "services" for the Crown; the Americans refuse. The debate continues in Parliament over the fate of the captives. Ethan and his men are put aboard the *Solebay* on a trip to America that takes three months and causes great suffering. They make Cape Fear, North Carolina—it is now May 1776—and are transferred to the *Mercury* to head for Nova Scotia. All the men are ill with scurvy. When they arrive in Halifax, five escape and five die in jail. Ethan is sent to New York on the *Lark*, arriving as General Howe is defeating Washington's troops. British jails are so full that Ethan is released on parole. In December, Howe suspends military operations until spring and throws away his advantage. Ethan, helped with funds from his brother, Ira, meets daily with other paroled officers in a local pub in Lower Manhattan. Sir William Howe again asks Ethan to switch sides. Deciding to break parole and go home to Bennington, Ethan is offered aid by Lieutenant Walter Dunbar, who turns out to be a British spy. By January of 1777, Ethan and the other American officers are still in New York. General Burgoyne is defeated at Saratoga. The next spring Ethan, released, goes directly to Washington at Valley Forge to apply for a commission and is made a Colonel in the Continental Army Reserve, a great disappointment to him. Riding directly to Fay's Tavern, he learns that the Grants are the free and independent Republic of Vermont. Tom Chittenden is President; an assembly is held at the Bennington meetinghouse. Ethan works on the Board of Confiscation, selling Loyalist property to raise money for the Republic, and on the Banishment Act, to rid the Republic of Tories. Ethan is never summoned back to the army and returns to Bennington with his wife and daughters (his precious son died of small pox in Ethan's absence).

John Farris

In *Son of the Endless Night* (1985), journalist Richard Devon, twenty-two, and child psychologist Karyn Vale, both graduate students at Yale, head for Chadbury on the Connecticut River half an hour south of Londonderry. They plan to ski and to check up on a teenaged friend, Polly Windross, who left a frightened message on Richard's answering machine. Richard never finds the "real" Polly, but her evil persona possesses him. In the guise of a demon, Richard bludgeons Karyn to death. Richard's brother, Conor, a former priest, meets with Richard at the prison and immediately realizes that he is not himself; in fact, Richard tells his astonished visitors that he is Zarach' Bal-Tagh, brother of Lucifer. The narrative, which has multiple characters and numerous gruesome scenes, tests the Vermont legal system: in *Vermont v. Devon*, the defense does not plead not guilty by reason of insanity, but by reason of "demonic possession." Through a former classmate at seminary, now a Monsignor, Conor uncovers an exorcist, a black man named Father Merlo. The black exorcist, seeing the look of surprise on his client's face, remarks: "Who were you expecting—Max van Sydow?" Father Merlo, experiencing one of Richard's horrifying exhibitions as Zarach,' knows that only one person can help: Edith Leighton, a British lawyer who now lives at an isolated place called Sundial with a group of people who have powers against "the son of the endless night." The trial pulls out all the stops, setting a Vermont legal precedent followed by a happy ending.

Sebastian Faulks

In *A Fool's Alphabet* (1992), Raymond Russell meets Francesca in Anzio in 1944; their baby, Pietro Thomas Russell, is born in Backley, England, in 1950; the novel ends in Zanica, where Pietro visits the hotel in which he was conceived. In between is the rest of Pietro's geographical A-Z journey through life: the time jumps forward and backward effortlessly; the Vermont strand is Pietro's friendship with Laura Heasman. By 1964, his mother is dead and he is attending the U.S. Collegiate School in Fulham near London, where one of his classmates is electrifying Laura from Vermont. The young people ski together in France and, a few years later, Pietro visits Laura in Lyndonville. The family enjoys a large Christmas meal. "It seemed that almost everything they ate had been grown or killed by the family. No wild goose ventured unmolested over the neighboring woods; no square inch of the vegetable garden was not silently toiling, even as they ate, to yield up more knotty tubers or fibrous greenery." He and Laura go to a lake with friends who suggest they catch some fish for their lunch: "No day in Vermont, it seemed, was complete without taking a life." Pietro returns to Lyndonville the next summer for another visit, and this time he and Laura become lovers. The hired man, Jack, has only been out of the country once—to Vietnam.

Frederick Fenn

Journey to Common Ground (2002) begins in 1770 in Connecticut with Joshua Caleb Brown's marriage to Sarah Anne Hopkins before starting out for the Hampshire Grants. On the way, they meet an escaped slave, Umbarro, who is heading for Canada. The three find common ground and become friends and allies. Umbarro helps them establish their farm above Fort Number Four on the Connecticut River. They sow their fields, some of their babies die, their grant is challenged, but they prevail.

Dorothy Canfield Fisher

Three collections of short stories, *Hillsboro People*, *Four-Square*, and *Raw Material*, are discussed, followed by descriptions of six novels. In *Hillsboro People* (1915), **"Nothing Ever Happens"** is emblematic of many of Fisher's stories, showing the difference in perception between people who live in the "pleasant, long valley in Vermont" and people who "come in

from the high-speed, modern world outside." **"Petunias—That's for Remembrance"** portrays Virginia, a member of the summer colony, who returns at age twenty-three to visit Hillsboro after college, European tours, and an absorbing social life. From her point of view, the tasks of the Pritchards with whom she is staying are "stupefying and monotonous," and their lives are "embittering and imprisoning." One day, she is exploring an abandoned house and, from the interior, overhears a conversation in which Grandma Pritchard is criticizing her. The family thinks that Virginia has nothing to say about the advantages she has enjoyed. Then Virginia learns that Grandma Pritchard ran the farm alone for four years, both while her husband was in the Civil War and after, when she heard that he was killed at Gettysburg. He survives and returns home to find her doing the haying by herself. He comes up quietly alongside her and says, "Here, you drive and I'll pitch." In **"The Heyday of the Blood,"** old Professor Mallory tells young Farrar about his great-grandfather's taking him to a fair. It is against all the rules of his parents, but they have a wonderful time, spending all six of the dollars the old man has saved. He is so worn out when he returns that Joey is afraid the experience may have done him in, but he learns his grandfather's motto: "Live while you live and then die and be done with it!" In **"As a Bird Out of the Snare,"** sexton Jehiel Hawthorn has just sold his woodland and now has enough money to travel, as he has always wanted to do. He planned to join the navy when he was a lad, but he had to stay on the farm to support his mother and then his sister-in-law; they are now dead and he is free. Then his nephew, Nat, finds himself in the same predicament as Jehiel had been. Nat wants to join the navy, but he has to stay home to support his stepmother and the baby she is expecting. Jehiel persuades Nat to invite his stepmother and baby to come to live with Jehiel, so that Nat can be free to live his own life. Aunt Mehetabel Elwell in **"The Bedquilt"** is a perfect example of the unmarried woman who passes from young spinster to old servant in the household. No one pays any attention to her, except to give her the least interesting tasks to do, until she begins making an intricate quilt. Soon people are coming from all over town to admire it. She becomes something of a personage in the household and her niece actually says things like, "Don't bother Aunt Mehetabel, she is working on the quilt." Aunt Mehetabel's quilt is entered in the local fair and wins first prize. She misses its being nearby to look at — having worked on it for four years, but she is given an opportunity to see it at the fair. That is all she wants to look at, much to the surprise of her family. In **"Portrait of a Philosopher,"** Professor Gridley dies, leaving his Gino Sprague Fallères portrait to Middletown College. Aunt Amelia destroys the painting because she thinks it makes him look like a "bad man." In **"Flint and Fire,"** sardonic Cousin Horace comes up from the city to stay with the narrator and her husband, Paul. He is even more caustic than usual about the "barrenness and sterility" of the lives of country people. Adoniram Purdon, a handsome young man with "austere self-control," is plowing the fields: "The ineffable odor of newly turned earth steamed up about him like incense." His predicament is that he loves Ev'leen Ann, the servant at the narrator's house, but cannot marry her because he has to take care of "Aunt Emeline" Purdon who raised him and is now an invalid. He shows a "refusal to be melodramatic." Ev'leen Ann's "Aunt Emma" is Emeline's twin; the two haven't spoken for thirty years because they fought over the same man (Mr. Purdon). Ev'leen Ann, heart breaking, tries but fails to drown herself. Emeline, who has always been totally independent, asks her twin to take care of her so that the young people can get married. Cousin Horace, who appears so unobservant and bored, is actually the one who told Emeline Purdon that Ev'leen Ann had tried to kill herself. **"In Memory of L.H.W."** relates the distressing life of Lem Warren, whose mother, a poor washerwoman, is always criticizing him. He was apparently a slack-jawed, slow youth who was fourteen when she was stricken with paralysis, leaving him to take care of her, do all the chores, and raise sheep. When Charlotte, a local girl, gets pregnant by a drummer and tries to kill

herself, Lem offers to marry her. After Susie is born, Lem raises the little girl. As a child she loves him, but, when she becomes a teenager, she is ashamed of his sagging mouth and stammering speech. She wants to marry Bronson Perkins but does not want to take care of Bronson's lunatic father, so Lem takes the crazy old man into his own home and cares for him as well as for his own mother. When one of his grandchildren needs an expensive operation, he sells everything so that the child can get well. After fulfilling every one of his responsibilities, he takes to his bed and dies exhausted. **"In New New England"** is set in 1762. Hanna Sherwin, sixteen, does all the work in her motherless family; Ann Mary, nineteen, is the "beauty." When Ann Mary falls into a "decline" (because she has nothing to do all day), Hannah takes her on a perilous journey across the mountains to Heath Falls on the Connecticut River, where there is reputed to be an Indian healer named Necronsett. His prescription is for Ann Mary to live alone in a little hut and cultivate a garden of herbs. The outdoor exercise soon puts a bloom in her cheeks and she sleeps and eats well. She also meets the local minister's young cousin, Captain Winthrop, and they fall in love. Young Winthrop teaches Hannah to read and write, and she returns to Hillsboro to teach, marry, and have children. She treats all the young women who go into a decline and the town, in gratitude, names the river after the Indian healer. Winthrop becomes a general under Washington, and Ann Mary becomes a great lady, comely yet illiterate. **"The Deliverer,"** set in 1756, is about a community of Puritans. Reverend Everett is constantly harassing his son, Nathaniel, who fears that he is damned because he loves the sights and sounds of spring: he wants to be a painter. He is unhappy because he cannot share his father's faith. In the woods one day he meets Colonel Gideon Hall, a famous solider on the French and Indian side, who is traveling with the French painter LeMaury. As Colonel Hall lies dying, Nathaniel goes to see him and witnesses his rejection of Nathaniel's father's belief in damnation. Hall tells Nathaniel he is not afraid of death: "It is a part of life." After his death, the townsfolk and the minister refuse him a coffin or burial. On his way to join LeMaury to go to France to become a painter, Nathaniel pays his respects to the body, draped in a flag. Hillsboro has always had a small private library run by volunteers, but **"Hillsboro's Good Luck"** describes the decision of Josiah Camden of Chicago to build the town an elaborate library and to endow it with thirty thousand books and a trained librarian, Miss Martin. The villagers are unhappy with the way the library is run—they can't get their old favorites any more—so it is not considered a tragedy when the building burns down and Miss Martin marries a bibliographer from Albany. In **"Avunculus,"** J.M. (Jereboam Mordecai) Atterworthy has been the librarian at Middletown College for forty years. With no life of his own, he yearns for a nephew to teach and nurture. He finally returns to the home of his birth, Woodville, which, to his unbelieving eyes, has become a dirty, crowded factory town. He visits his old house, where three families now live, is hit accidentally by a baseball, and finds himself recuperating in his old room and called "Uncle Jerry." It happens that he resembles the uncle of the Italian woman who is nursing him. He has a wonderful time with the three families and brings Ivan Petrofsky back to Middletown to attend the college and board with him in his tower rooms above the library. In **"Finis,"** old Matilda Prentiss and her husband, Nathaniel, are being forced for health reasons to live in the city with their son Hiram, his German wife, and his children. The doctor says Mrs. Prentiss cannot stand another winter. She thinks mournfully of the "continuity of human life," of all her ancestors who have lived in this house. She purposely goes outside in the cold so that she will become sick and die; die she does but not before realizing that her husband does not value life without her. In **"A Village Munchausen,"** Jebediah Chillingworth is known for his exaggerated tales. One of them is about a sailor (himself) who kills a bull moose. The narrator, then a little boy, laughs with everybody else in the village over this story. Years later he discovers the story was true and hurries to Jebediah's deathbed to apologize for not believ-

ing him. The look ("You didn't believe me all these years?") in the dying man's eyes fills the narrator with lifelong remorse. Later, his granddaughter finds out the story was false but hasn't the heart to tell the old man. In **"The Artist,"** Mme. Olga Orloff, the surgeon, and Vieyro, the picture dealer, are in Europe talking about the dealer's traveling to Vermont to seek out a painter whose work resembles Vermeer. A foreigner looking at Vermont, Vieyro finds it "a parched place in the wilderness." He sees only a "lean, tall, sullenly silent race who live in preposterously ugly little wooden houses of the most naked cleanliness."Then he finds the painter he is looking for—a man who had gone to Europe to paint but was compelled to return to raise his nephews and nieces and run the farm. The picture dealer does not actually approach the uncle, but sees him in the "crimson wood" under the spell of a "vision" as he looks about him at the beauty of the mountain and the trees. When the painter dies, he says, "I have had a happy life," and the dealer understands that he does not need the decorations, the palms, of the French government. **"A Drop in the Bucket"** is about Cousin Tryphena, the only person in Hillsboro who seems to visitors as picturesque as a "Mary Wilkins character." Next door to her moves an old cobbler named Jombatiste, a socialist who fills Cousin Tryphena's head with socialist teaching. Cousin Tryphena has always believed that poverty comes from shiftlessness. Until recently, her creed had two important aspects: keep your starch clear and never be late for church. Now, information about human destitution and desperation begins to inflame her soul and she sells her precious Sheraton desk to the antique dealer, goes to the city, and brings back a poor family—an ill woman, her son, and her baby. The woman dies, and Cousin Tryphena brings up the children as her own. She realizes it is only a drop in the bucket, but, as the narrator says, "we do nothing at all." In **"Adeste Fideles!"** poor old Miss Abigail is suffering because everyone is leaving Greenford and moving to Jacksonville where the factory and the jobs are. "The well-kept old village still preserved its outer shell of quaintness and had a constantly increasing charm for strangers who rejoiced with a shameless egotism in the deathlike quiet of the moribund place, and pointed out to visiting friends from the city the tufts of grass beginning to grow in the main street as delightful proofs of the tranquility of their summer retreat." Miss Abigail conceives of the idea of offering the waterpower from her property to the owner of the print mill in Johnsonville whose waterpower has failed. Now people will come back to Greenford and the school and the church will be used again. Typically, the last word is from an outsider who comments ironically: "That bespeaks the materialistic Yankee, doesn't it—to want to spoil a quiet little Paradise like this village with a lot of greasy millhands?"

In *Four-Square* (1949), **"Ann Story"** presents the life of a famous Vermont heroine. Ann Story's husband, Amos, goes up to Salisbury from Connecticut with his fourteen-year-old son to build a house for the family. While chopping trees for the log cabin, a giant tree falls on the father and kills him. After the son sees to his father's burial, he walks one hundred and fifty miles back to Connecticut. The young widow, thirty-three, three sons (Samuel, Ephraim, and Solomon), and two daughters (Hannah and Susanna) embark to carry out what they had planned. In late 1775, she moves into the log cabin her husband had built. She is a model mother and homemaker, and she is also a citizen and a patriot. She wants her children to own their own land and not be forced into "semi-feudal subservience to rich folks." She becomes an aid and advisor to the Green Mountain Boys: "Give me a place among you, and see if I am the first to desert my post." When Indians come to the area, she takes the children by boat to hide in the reeds of Otter Creek; they watch while their home is burned down. They rebuild. She and the children collect information to pass to the Green Rangers. They dig a passageway into the bank and make a cave where they hide every night. One day they rescue a pregnant white woman, a captive left behind by the Indians; Ann delivers her baby. Many Vermont Royalists are on their way to Canada to inform on

Vermont settlers. One such traveling Tory wakes the baby, who cries. A Story son alerts the Green Mountain Rangers, who capture the whole lot of Royalists. Self-respect and self-control keep them from killing the Tory fugitives, whom they turn in at Fort Ticonderoga. In **"The Old Soldier,"** all the Revolutionary War veterans of the town of Sunmore have died. Two little boys remember an old man living in the hills, and he is brought down, deaf, bent, and carrying a gun, to be honored in the July Fourth celebration. Someone notices that his gun belonged to a Hessian enemy. The audience is hushed, until one of the little boys stands up and makes an impassioned speech: after seventy-five years, he says, it is time to forget about taking sides. A mother in **"As Ye Sow"** teaches her children to carry a tune and, more importantly, to listen. A little girl in **"The Apprentice"** learns the love and terror of owning a dog. Pauline, the schoolteacher with three children in **"Uncle By's Schoolteacher's Wife,"** feels humiliated and leaves town when her husband falls in love with a younger woman. After the second wife bears three children and dies and the husband breaks his leg, Pauline moves back into the household to take care of everyone. Soon she and By remarry and the family is reunited. In **"Grand Opera,"** the businesses of Alonzo King, the barber, and Henry Deming, the grocer, are bypassed by modern stores and automobiles, but they content themselves with listening to opera on their radio and then on a record-player. A summer resident, who considers them "ignorant old rustics," invites Alonzo and his wife to attend the opera in New York. Shocked by the overweight singers, the make-up and costumes, and the bright lights, Alonzo finds attending the opera not nearly so satisfying as listening to it with Henry in the back of their store. Fragile Miss Philanda in **"The Bradlock Chest"** lives up the hollow (the sheep pasture was "draped like a green velvet scarf over the shoulder of the mountain") and loses her savings when the bank closes. Well-meaning friends discover that she has a handsome antique chest and send an antique dealer to assess its value, thinking she would like to sell it and move into the rest home. The antique dealer tells her it is a fake. She is outraged: her grandfather brought this chest to Vermont and it is authentic. He insists it is an imitation. Miss Philanda is so distraught that another dealer is brought in, who opines that the chest is authentic and valuable; he offers her a great deal of money on the spot. She draws herself up. The chest is not for sale; that "Yorker" called her a liar. Tigger is at camp in **"Sunset at Sixteen,"** dreaming about a boy she has met. An old couple is staying at the same place. She is disgusted by old people, remembering the fearful smell of her dying grandmother. Then she sees them sitting together, watching the sunset; he is quoting poetry to her, and this image illuminates for Tigger what their life together must have been. Stina, in **"One Day Late,"** makes a mess of painting her spare room and takes out her frustrations on everyone she meets. Aunt Minnie, in **"Sex Education,"** confesses that a story she told about a teacher's attacking her was actually about her approaching the teacher in an inappropriate way. In **"The Biologist and His Son,"** a mother and father observe with fascination what their baby is able to accomplish. In **"Henry and His Aunt Anna,"** Henry Boardman works hard on the orderly family farm and the family does well. The Lindseys are unsuccessful and shiftless, and the Boardmans try to help them out, as does the town. When the mother goes out to clean, ten-year-old Phil is left in charge of Maggie and three-year-old Bess. When Bess disappears, the whole town turns out to look for her and, three days later, she is found alive. Henry's Aunt Anna, a nurse, breaks down in sobs because the town made this effort to look for the baby, but it will not vote a cent to help the mother who has to go outside the home to work. It is 1859 when Reverend Ellsworth in **"Deep Channel"** is taking the night boat up the Hudson to his Vermont home. He works in a rich New York City parish, which he has shocked by telling he is going to officiate at the funeral of John Brown. The story skips to the present day, when Ellsworth's great-grandnephew finds documents about the case and learns that Ellsworth lost his job and was then

killed in the Civil War. In **"The Moran Scandal,"** George Moran was a reformer for social justice who left his first wife for a younger woman (the narrator's Cousin Nell). Moran was a great man who was criticized because of this one moral slip. During World War I, the narrator while in France comes upon Rachel Moran (the first Mrs. George Moran) living and doing social work with the second wife, Nell Moran. After his death, their friendship developed through serving their social-justice ideal together. They were persecuted with "unsavory gossip about free love" and fled to France, where they continue to carry out their work helping disadvantaged people. **"Americans Must Be Told"** is about Emily Hancock, the daughter of Norwegian immigrants, who lives in Clifford Center but is preoccupied with German-occupied Norway. An old friend from Norway passes through on his way to Canada to join his RAF comrades. He urges her to tell Americans the real story of what is happening in Europe. Emily tries to speak of the atrocities, but no one wants to hear her. One neighbor even says she is disgusted by Emily's talk: "decent people" don't speak of such things.

In *Raw Material* (1923), the main character in **"Uncle Giles"** thinks of himself as a "gentleman." He never bothers to earn a living but tells people he is preparing for the ministry. He considers his family "commonplace." It becomes a point of honor for his family not to believe in anything he does. He is a coward, a fake, and a hypochondriac, and his memory makes the family "stand up to life and come to grips with reality." In **"Old Man Warner,"** the eponymous hero inherits a farm in Arnold Hollow, settles, marries, has sons, and fights in the Civil War, losing a son in the Battle of the Wilderness. He comes home, though many of the younger soldiers move out West. The settlement becomes smaller and smaller. His wife dies and his sons invite him to move to Iowa. The townsfolk begin to plan what they will buy at auction, while the selectmen decide to cut out service to the road up into Arnold Hollow. He does not leave. Twenty-two years pass. He refuses to move down to the settlement; the town has to maintain his road. There

F

is no law in Vermont to turn a man off his own farm, he says in a voice of Vermont, "s'long's he paid his taxes and didn't owe any debts that he knew of." He keeps himself and his animals well and clean and, over ninety, dies in front of a "well-blacked stove" on a kitchen floor "you could have et off of, 'twas so clean." He becomes the town hero. "**Angela Hawley Canfield**" was Fisher's great-grandmother, about whom Fisher tells many anecdotes. Angela's last act before she dies is to put her finger to her lips to warn the family not to wake the baby. "**Fairfax Hunter**" is an ailing Virginia Negro whom a relative brings to Arlington to sleep in the barn and work around the place for his board. "There is very little caste feeling in the valley and not a bit of color prejudice." He regains his health and becomes cook, gardener, and useful hired man. He is invited to the church supper and, although he dresses up, he never goes inside. The narrator cannot guess what brutal discrimination he has suffered. He reads their whole set of Thomas Hardy novels. He visits with neighbors but will never go indoors. After the family moves to France, Fairfax drinks himself to death within six months. In "**While All the Gods**," some little boys feed angleworms to the chickens and cannot understand why they all attack the one that finally picks up a worm to eat. Maria Pearl Manley is poised between two evils in "**Scylla and Charybdis**." Losing her mother when she is a baby, she spends her time between the Purdon side of the family, which calls her "Maria," and the Manley side, which calls her "Pearl." The Purdons are strict church folk who worship thrift and force her to clean from morning until night. The Manley household is cheerful and affectionate, but carefree and feckless. They do not keep house or serve regular meals. Maria Pearl is always behind in her lessons because the house is so noisy. She escapes from the two households as quickly as possible by marrying a young man she meets at a high school dance. There is not a happier household anywhere: she has merged the best parts of her old ways into her new life. "**Colonel Shays**" begins after Shays's Rebellion (1786-87) in Massachusetts. Shays, in hiding, comes through

the Beartown notch over the mountains and makes camp. One day, seeing a child, Shays asks him for some seed corn and salt. The boy's father, an illiterate trapper, has no idea of Shays's identity. Shays begins to cultivate his ground. He lives this way for many years and is considered, by those who know he is there, a harmless old man. Unbeknownst to him, he is no longer a dramatic and hunted fugitive. In fact, a year earlier he was pardoned. He finally goes across the border into the town of Cambridge in New York. There, he hears someone looking for him (to tell him about the pardon); he runs off and stays in hiding for another ten years. In "**A Great Love**," Flossie loves Peter Carr, who reveres singer Eleanor Arling. Because Eleanor Arling leaves town ("personal happiness must be sacrificed for her art," she says), Peter marries Flossie. Flossie is the perfect wife and mother; Peter becomes bald and stout. Then Flossie reads in the paper that Miss Arling, on a tour of the states, is coming back to their town. Flossie hurries to her hotel to beg Miss Arling not to stir up Peter's dormant passions. Miss Arling is old and lame and cannot even remember Peter's name. "**The Old New England Stock**" describes two branches of a family that moved to Vermont after the end of the French and Indian Wars. Both men spend their boyhood on family farms. One leaves, becomes a preacher, buys books, lives comfortably, travels widely, and retires to Vermont. The other courts hardship, goes out West in 1849, and marries a Vermont girl who follows him into the wilds. He dies, leaving a penniless thirty-five-year-old widow with five helpless girls.

The following are descriptions of six novels —*The Bent Twig*, *The Brimming Cup*, *The Home-Maker*, *Her Son's Wife*, *Bonfire*, and *Seasoned Timber*. **The Bent Twig** (1915) begins in the Midwest university town of La Chance, where Professor Elliott Marshall and his wife, Barbara, are raising their three children, Sylvia, Judith, and Lawrence. They live in the "wrong" part of town in a ramshackle house where Barbara tends a vegetable garden and does her own housework. Professor Marshall, a musician as well as a scholar, plays with a string quartet every Sunday evening; the rest of the week the house is filled with "unfashionable" people who come and go as they please. Elliott's elegant and wealthy sister, Victoria Marshall-Smith, and her stepson, Arnold, visit; the Marshalls and Barbara are all Vermonters. The Marshalls were rich summer people in Lydford, thirty miles south of Rutland. Barbara lived there year-round on a farm. The Marshalls lost their money when Elliott was twenty-five and Victoria, twenty. He married Barbara and became an academic; Victoria married a rich man for whom she cared nothing. Sylvia greatly admires her ornamental and soignée aunt. After Sylvia has graduated in five years with a master's degree and begun to give piano lessons, Aunt Victoria reappears in Sylvia's life to invite her to spend some time with her in Lydford. There she is reacquainted with her step cousin, Arnold Smith, and meets some of Aunt Victoria's rich neighbors, notably, the Sommerfields, and their houseguest, famous art critic Felix Morrison. Initially indifferent to Felix, Sylvia begins to spend afternoons in the library with him and soon finds that they are mutually attracted; in fact, she comes to love him and believes he loves her. Molly Montgomery Sommerfield intervenes in this idyll by confiding to Sylvia that she, Molly, loves Felix and is determined to marry him. Sylvia, idealistic and true to female sisterhood, steps aside and within ten days Molly, of the Montgomery millions, and Felix, intellectual and poor, are engaged to be married. Sylvia and Molly are swept up in fighting a terrifying forest fire. Doughty Molly ferries men in her little automobile from a local factory up to the fire site where they are able to extinguish the fire before it has done too much damage. Into this scene appears Molly's cousin, Austin Page, a millionaire owner of a coal mine in Colorado, who is spending the summer at his nearby property, Austin Farm (his ancestors came to Vermont in 1762). He is immediately taken with Sylvia. They walk home from the fire site over the mountains. Sylvia, having spent her days in Aunt Victoria's drawing room and in her gladiola-appointed garden, appreciates the natural beauty of Vermont for the first time. "They passed from the tempered green light of the wood and emerged upon a great windy plateau, carpeted thickly with deep green moss, flanked right and left with two mountain peaks and roofed over with an expanse of brilliant summer sky. Before them the plateau stretched a mile or more, wind-swept, sun-drenched, with an indescribable bold look of great altitude, but close to them at one side ran a parapet-like line of tumbled rock and beyond this a sheer descent. The eye leapt down abrupt slopes of forest of the valley they had left, now a thousand feet below them, jewel-like with mystic blues and greens, tremulous with heat. On the noble height where they stood, the wind blew cool from the sea of mist-blue peaks beyond the valley." She spends a great deal of time with Austin Page and when, after the wedding of Molly and Felix, Aunt Victoria takes Sylvia to Paris with her, Austin suggests that he meet them from time to time. While they are abroad, Molly is killed in an automobile accident, and Felix joins his friends in Paris. It is clear that Felix still loves Sylvia. Sylvia is ambivalent, and Austin is his usual imperturbable self, though he does declare his love to Sylvia before he returns to America and asks her to answer when she has had time to think about his proposal. She has already told him how difficult it is for a poor young woman to respond to a millionaire's proposal. While abroad, they read in the newspapers that Austin has turned over his coal mine to the state and is engaging in social and economic programs to uplift the miners and their families. Sylvia indifferently agrees when her Aunt and Felix propose Naples; it is while they are getting ready to go to Italy that she hears of her mother's death. She hurries home to find her father undone with grief. While Sylvia is dealing with her sorrow and with family matters, she realizes that it is Austin whom she loves. At Lydford, she climbs their mountain and finds him waiting for her. One image at a concert describes the "brimming cup" of the next novel: "The cup of that vast building suddenly brimmed with a magical flood of pure tone, coming from everywhere." Another eloquent image: "On their edge, overhanging the water, stood a single sumac, a standard-bearer with a thousand little down-drooping flags of crimson." (The title comes from Alexander Pope's "Moral Essays:" "As the twig is bent, so grows the tree.")

In *The Brimming Cup* (1921), Marise and Neale Crittenden, who meet and fall in love in Italy in 1909, move back to America to live in the small town of Ashley. Here generations of Crittendens have lived and a suburb of Ashley is called Crittenden's; here Marise visited her Cousin Hetty regularly as a girl. She concedes that a small town in Vermont may not be "wide," but it is very "deep." The war is just over. Neale starts a lumber mill to provide jobs and stimulate the economy of the area; Marise organizes and leads a community choir. Their three children, Paul, Elly, and Mark, grow up in a loving, small-town atmosphere with old Cousin Hetty living nearby (her great-grandmother came to Ashley in 1776, carrying a willow switch that she stuck into the ground; both she and Marise have a connection to Ethan Allen). Outsiders arrive to observe this Vermont community: Mr. Welles, a retired businessman who moves next door to Marise; Vincent Marsh, a vibrant and handsome young millionaire and Mr. Welles's houseguest; and Eugenia Mills, Marise's friend from Europe, who is a petite, manicured, big-city girl. Mr. Welles, old, tired, but sensitive, appreciates everything about Marise and her Vermont life. Vincent falls in love with Marise and wants to take her away (to a "civilized world") from what he believes to be a waste of her life and talents. He perceives all Vermonters as insensitive clods. Eugenia is not interested in small-town life or children, but she is in love with Neale and hopes that Marise's interest in the fiery-eyed Vincent will leave the field free for her. All the descriptions of various aspects of Vermont — the sawmill, the countryside, the square dance, the neighbors, and "the local wireless information bureau"—are appealing and realistic. Touclé, the Indian woman who lives with them and helps out, is a powerful local force. There are four passionate threads to the novel. The first relates to the desire Marise had in Europe "to be filled with

some emotion, something great and fine, that I would be an urn too full, gushing up in a great flooding rush." Vincent overwhelms her with a physical passion that she can hardly understand. He criticizes her mundane existence and tempts her with a new life "brimming over." The second is about Neale, his work with the sawmill (helping the economy by filling many of the empty houses in Ashley) and his relationship with his employees (he was an officer in the war and has hired one of his men out of a hospital to be his stenographer). He attempts to right the wrongs against the Powers family (to get their wood lot back in their hands) and is eager to free Marise to live the life that she wants ("what is deepest and most living in *you*"). The third is Mr. Welles's realization that he has never served anyone but only made profits for people he didn't like in a job he hated. He determines to go to Georgia to work on behalf of oppressed Negroes. The fourth is the love triangle of Nelly and Gene Powers and Frank Warner, the death of Frank, and the tragic killing of Nelly and Gene in the felling of the giant pine. Marise and Neale's relationship becomes stronger than ever, and she no longer believes she is living only through her children.

The name of the town in *The Home-Maker* (1924) is not specified: it is a traditional place, with potluck suppers in a Congregational Church basement, a population of farmers who come into town to shop at the stores, and a village to the north, Brandville, where the parents of the heroine live. Maine is "way up there" and New York is accessible by train. Evangeline (Eva) and Lester Knapp live near the railroad tracks (the wrong side of the town for Eva) with their three children, Helen, thirteen, Henry, ten, and Stephen, five. Lester toils unhappily and unsuccessfully in the accounting office at the Willing Department Store, making very little money. Evangeline toils unhappily and successfully (by certain standards) in the home, scrubbing the floors by hand and constantly harping at the children to sit up straight or pick up their rooms. She has made Helen into an introvert, given Henry a nervous stomach, and bullied Stephen into becoming a sullen tyrant. Her perfection as a housekeeper has overwhelmed every other emotion and instinct. Lester is a poet and dreamer by nature; Eva is an organizer and manager. When Lester loses his job, he feels himself a complete failure and, believing that his insurance and the price of their house will save the family, tries to kill himself by throwing himself from the roof of a neighbor's house. He does not succeed in his intention, but ends up crippled in a wheelchair. Once the danger to his life is over, Eva presents herself to young Mr. Willing for any sort of a job to pay the family bills. Mr. Willing, who feels guilty about having fired Lester, hires her as a stock-girl. Lester devotes himself to the household and his children blossom under his care. Several service people who worked at the department store—the delivery boy and the cleaning woman—appreciate Lester's goodness and kindness to them at the store and return his favors by daily seeing to his furnace and his household washing. Aunt Mattie Farnham, who has been away, returns home and rushes over to see how Lester is getting along, expecting the worst. She can't believe he is taking care of the household, cooking, entertaining the children. She is shocked by some of his innovations, such as putting down newspapers to keep the floors clean (which are whisked away when Eva comes home from work). When he gets out his darning needle to do Stephen's little stockings, she cries: "Oh, *Lester*, let me do that! The idea of your darning stockings! It's dreadful enough your having to do the housework!" "Eva darned them a good many years," he said, with some warmth, "and did the housework. Why shouldn't I?" He looked at her hard and went on, "Do you know what you are saying to me, Mattie Farnham? You are telling me that you really think that home-making is a poor, mean, cheap job beneath the dignity of anybody who can do anything else." Knowing that Lester's spinal cord is not paralyzed, the doctor suspects that there are psychological reasons for Lester's inability to use his legs. Eva guesses the truth when she looks at Lester asleep one night and sees him draw up his legs quite normally. Instead of being happy, she is horrified that his getting well will return her to the slavery of housekeep-

ing when she is so happy in her job. She feels guilty and conflicted. Lester himself learns the truth when Stephen's curtains catch fire and Lester finds himself running to put out the fire. He realizes that if it were discovered he could walk, he would have to return to work and Eva would have to stay home. He acknowledges that tradition is too strong to fight: people would never understand their exchanged roles, so he keeps his secret to himself. When the doctor comes to do some tests, Lester takes the doctor into his confidence. The doctor's report to the family: Lester will never walk again.

Mary Bascomb, forty-three, the mother in *Her Son's Wife* (1926), is a long-time teacher in Gilmanville and the possessive, dominating mother of Ralph, twenty-one. She has "given her life to him" and feels worn out before her time. Ralph writes that he has married Charlotte (Lottie) Hicks and will leave law school in order to support her. Ralph is clearly infatuated with his seductive young wife. Mary can hardly bear their presence: she is "resentfully wrathful" over their selfish behavior. Mary, who has to give up her bedroom of twenty-two years, considers Lottie "cheap, ignorant, and vulgar." Gossip in the town reaches a crescendo when it is obvious that Lottie is pregnant; she delivers a little girl, Dids, five months after the hasty marriage. Ralph finds a job in a printing establishment where the management is brutally indifferent to him; he and Lottie are living off his mother who has "shut herself up in a self-contained fury of silent martyrdom and hard work." Lottie is an indolent young mother, a sloppy housekeeper, and useless with babies; Mary often finds herself in an "orgy of her rightness" or "an ecstasy of self-approval." Little Dids, Mary discovers, has inherited her husband John's eyes; Mary takes over all the chores to which Lottie is too lazy to attend. Lottie starts entertaining a gentleman caller in the afternoons and, soon, runs off with him. She returns and Ralph, gluttonous for her flesh, forgives her. Mary cannot endure the tension in the house and takes a teaching job in Harristown; to her dismay, Ralph seems relieved to have her go. She does well, makes friends, joins committees, and saves money, but she is constantly aware the couple is living in her house. Three years pass and, visiting Gilmanville, she sees Dids with some school chums. To Mary's alarm, Dids is learning her mother's vulgar ways and is looking ill and thin. Mary humbles herself and moves back into her house; Lottie is delighted to turn over the work to Mary; Ralph is only interested in sports. Lottie's mundane conversation ruins every mealtime for Mary. Most of Lottie's complaints are about her feet, which she crams into very tight, high-heeled shoes. A quack, taking advantage of Lottie, persuades her, for high fees Mary pays, that she must have complete bed-rest to cure her back. Mary knows the doctor is dishonest but, to her shame, she goes along with the charade and assists willingly in Lottie's becoming an invalid (and ensures that Ralph moves into the guest room). Mary fills the patient with fattening food and her room with fresh flowers, and concentrates on Dids, who becomes a lovely, intelligent girl with ambitions to attend university. Ralph is hired as a sportswriter, a more congenial job. Mary tries to leave the household to a nurse, but Lottie says she will refuse permission for Dids to go to university unless Mary stays with her. Mary is sentenced to spending the rest of her life taking care of her son's wife.

Bonfire (1933) is set in Clifford, seventeen miles from Ashley in Necronsett Valley in Windward County. Anna Craft, the district nurse, has returned from work abroad. Although barely older than her half-brother, Anson, Anna took care of him after the death of their mother and has invested heart, soul, and savings in his medical education. In his practice, he is often saturnine and sarcastic, especially with Anna, although he is respected as an excellent doctor. Clifford is divided into social strata. On The Street the well-to-do old families reside in their neat, white houses. Churchman's Row is for more modest families. Clifford Four Corners is where the "back-roads" Canadian and Polish inhabitants live. The Other Side is the place of the more prosperous farmers. Searles Shelf, home to those with the no education and no opportunity, is a hotbed of abuse, incest, and alcoholism.

Intolerance is deep-seated against the people living on Searles Shelf: "I never let one of 'them' inside the house." Miss Bessie has already turned down Anna's request to help a boy who has been in prison: "Who'd put fertilizer around weeds in a garden? You hoe 'em up!" Anna takes an interest in orphan Lixlee Burdrick, who lives on the Shelf, and persuades the Misses Bessie and Gussie to welcome Lixlee into their home to "civilize" her. Isabel Foote, a student at the Academy, falls in love with Anson and helps him in his laboratory in her spare time. Anson, however, becomes enamored of Lixlee and, under the pretense of tending to Miss Bessie's angina, starts an affair with Lixlee. Henry Twombley, a rough thug from Searles Shelf who loves Lixlee, shoots Anson and Lixlee in her bed. They survive their wounds and Anson insists that they marry while at the hospital. Though devoured by his longing for Lixlee, Anson awakens from his lust to realize that she is stupid and manipulative. She finally runs off with Lawrence Stewart, one of the aristocratic old-timers on The Street. Anna, disappointed, had banked on the theory that "the only difference between ignorant and dirty people in small weather-blackened shacks, and comfortable well-washed people in large white houses with clean window-panes, is a difference of opportunity." Anson begins drinking and is rapidly going downhill when Isabel Foote returns from her nursing course to marry him and help with his work. Anna, releasing her grip on Anson, falls in love with Fred Kirby, the local clergyman whom she has known all her life. She has been seeking support for a cooperative residence to enable young people who live out of town to attend Clifford Academy. The moment for the vote comes at the yearly town meeting, at which Sherwin Dewey officiates. After his invalid wife, whom he has been taking care of for years, dies, he donates part of his house for the residence. Dewey, who can be counted upon to be tolerant, says of Anson's marriage, "I think more of him than if he'd married a rich summer woman." After a year that contains a shooting, marriage, new jobs, and myriad other happenings, the summer people return and tell each other that "it was a comfort to have one old hole-in-the-ground where nothing ever happened." The summer people are not "exactly to Clifford taste." The professional families who did some of their own housework, wore old clothes to go berrying in, "hated cordial back-slapping as much as you did, and knew how to recognize a dry joke" were soon considered part of life in the Valley. Many of the city-bred families with money fit in well, staying all year round and getting "quite country and plain." There is no patience with "those butter-smooth, middle-aged summer ladies with white gloves and liveried chauffeurs! The more ingratiatingly they smiled on you, the glummer you felt. They were like good coffee spoiled by too much cream and sugar. They took you up at a word in such a hurry, did to your feelings with their wordy cordiality what with their excellent manners they never dreamed of doing physically—stood too close to you, breathed too warmly in your face. Invisibility was really the only way to cope with them." The language is rich with images: "A deer floated like thistledown across a newly plowed field and up a wood-road," "The Wall stretched its long bulk, clad as in velvet by the mauve bloom of early spring," and "The white houses were cubes of snow."

Seasoned Timber (1939) concerns forty-five-year-old widower Timothy Coulter Hulme, who lives with his Aunt Lavinia in the town of Clifford and has been at Clifford Academy for twenty years, first as teacher and then as principal. The three who serve as trustees of the Academy are Mr. Wheaton, a rich man from the Midwest and New York City; Mr. Randall, a former Clifford boy and a local clergyman; and Sherwin Dewey, the conscience of the piece. In his Vermont voice he uses expressions like, "Take a deep breath—you aim better," and "What's the use of saying things the meanest way there is?" Unexpectedly, Tim falls in love with twenty-four-year-old Susan Barney, a third-grade teacher who was raised at Crandall Pitch by her grandfather. Timothy, trying to ingratiate himself with Susan, buys her grandfather's house from the bank and recovers some of the original furniture. The backdrop of the novel is the rumbling

of unrest in Germany and the Nazi savagery against the Jews. Timothy goes to New York to meet with Mr. Wheaton and to interview prospective parents. While in New York he is aware of the isolation and privacy of the city as compared to the "crowded closeness of the country." He finds Mr. Wheaton as unsympathetic as ever; he interviews a domineering Jewish woman and agrees to accept her son, an appealing adolescent who misses his dead father and is being stifled by his mother. In the spring, Canby Hunter, Tim's nephew, arrives back in Clifford, and Mr. Wheaton dies, leaving a million dollars to the school if it will agree to exclude Jews and change to a preparatory school bearing Wheaton's name. Tim and Sherwin lead the fight against this bequest, complicated by the fact that the school is partially owned and funded by the town: they will need to win over the votes of all the townspeople in order to elect a new trustee who will vote against the bequest. Tim, who is overwhelmed by his passion for Susan Barney, watches her and Canby fall in love. The centerpiece of the novel is not the unrequited love of an older man for a desirable young woman but the campaign to educate the townspeople about prejudice and principle. They understand the issues, but they have never faced the fact that what happens to four Jewish students at Clifford Academy transcends their own community and is connected to events unfolding in Europe, the outcome of which will have everlasting effects on humanity. Tim and Sherwin talk through the issues with the community. Their campaign is a model of the democratic process on a small scale; the fight is successful. Canby and Susan marry and have a baby, which they name after Tim. He gives them the house on Crandall Pitch. Canby supports his family by remodeling old houses into summer places for flatlanders, and Tim goes on as before, though inspired by the recent campaign to concentrate on training country boys who have had no athletic experience and who are never chosen for teams. He is in his element once again, siding with the underdog. (The title is from George Herbert's poem, "Virtue:" "Only a sweet and virtuous soul,/Like seasoned timber, never gives.")

Tourists Accommodated (1932) is a play in six acts reminiscent of Æsop's fable of the city mouse and the country mouse. The Vermont family is the Lymans, consisting of Sophia, forty, and her husband, Hiram, a farmer; their children, Lucy, eighteen, Philip, twelve, Roger, seven, and Blossom, five; Great Aunt Jane, who is stone deaf, and Great Aunt Nancy Ann, who is practical and entrepreneurial. The other characters are the hired man, six groups of tourists, and an artist. Hiram is unable to send Lucy, who yearns for an education, to Normal School because of the high tuition and the rise in taxes. Aunt Nancy Ann proposes they take in tourists during the summer. Group One includes a woman who is surprised they don't boil their water since they live "in the wilderness." Group Two makes comments like, "You must find it terribly lonesome in the winters, with everyone gone back to the city." The Lymans sell several pieces of furniture to these tourists. The next group contains the Pretentious Tourist, who remarks, "I suppose we should make more of an effort to talk to these rustics…bring a civilized influence into their narrow lives…how sad it must be when the summer people go away and leave them to their sordid, penny-pinching existence." The Silly Tourist wonders why they don't grow sweet potatoes. The next group, however, is a father, mother, and little boy who are appreciative and generous, paying more than they are asked. This nice family suggests sending their boy to Vermont next summer to learn to farm and inviting the Lyman boys visit them in New York City. The wife wants to donate some books and magazines to the local library. A couple of French-Canadians arrive, producing a farcical scene in which no one can understand anyone else. Then an aggressive tourist, with a wife and two children, arrives, asking, "What makes Vermont people so backward? There's no sense to their being as poor as they are." He wants to know why Hiram doesn't use a tractor instead of a horse on his hill farm. And why he doesn't have an electric stove. And why not sugar all year round. An artist comes, but the house is full, so they give him bedding to sleep with the boys in the barn. Philip has swallowed the tourists' assertion that it

is better to travel than to stay in one place. In a moving speech, the artist kindly enumerates for him all the good points about living in the country and knowing everyone in the community. "Caring about what happens is what makes life interesting," says the artist. In the last scene, the Lymans have made enough money for school fees and taxes and are happy to put the sign away in the attic.

Ian Fleming

In *For Your Eyes Only* (1960), the title story of this collection of five novellas, James Bond is summoned to M's office to be told that M's great friends, the Havelocks, who have lived at a hacienda in Jamaica for three generations, have been murdered. They leave a twenty-five-year-old daughter, Judy. Hoodlums based in Cuba have killed the Havelocks because they refused to sell their property. M has learned with the help of Canadian police that the villains have fled to Vermont to a place called Echo Lake (a fictitious one) just south of the Canadian border near Enosburg Falls. There they have rented a millionaire's estate in the mountains with a pool on the grounds. M wants Bond to go to Vermont to neutralize them. The head killer is a German named Von Hammerstein; his lieutenant is named Gonzales. Bond flies to Montreal and drives to Ottawa for a briefing. The Mounties have taken aerial photographs of the estate. Bond approaches the border for a certain distance by car and then walks through the woods: "Among the spruce and silver birch there was an occasional oak and beech and sycamore and, here and there, the blazing Bengal fire of a maple in autumn dress." In the woods he meets the Havelock's daughter, Judy, who flew to Burlington and walked for four days through mountains and woods to wreak, with a bow and arrow, her own revenge for her parents' death. After some sparring, Bond and Judy join forces and manage to wipe out Von Hammerstein, Gonzales, and their minions around the pool. With an arrow, Judy pierces Von Hammerstein in mid-dive. Exhilarated by their success, Bond and Judy plan to spend some time together.

Edith Forbes

In *Nowle's Passing* (1996), the newspaper article states that Vernon Nowle, sixty-seven, of Worthing, committed suicide, despondent after the auction of his dairy herd and farm equipment. His wife, Phoebe, predeceased him, killed in a tractor accident. His three children, Vernice ("Vincie"), Chad, and Darrell, gather in the Owen's River Valley house for the funeral. The novel is about the three children's relationships with their father (and mother), their childhood, their loyalties, and their difficulties growing up. Vincie is accompanied by her professor husband, Gifford, who is glib, handsome, and fashionable; Darrell lives nearby with his wife, Georgianne, and their two children; Chad, the incandescent, charming salesman, comes up from his home in New Jersey. When Vincie arrives, she looks with affection at her childhood home. "On the right stood the house, a white clapboard structure in the farmhouse style, which began as a simple two-story box with a steeply pitched roof, and then, over a span of one or two centuries, sprouted ells, dormers, chimneys, shed, and porches in response to each new inhabitant's desire for more space, light, or heat. Such farmhouses were as common yet distinct as so many wild-growing trees, all of which had begun life as a neat single shoot, but after a century had grown into a multitude of shapes according to the vagaries of wind, sunlight, rainfall, and whatever unseen impulse it is that decides to send out a branch here rather than there." As Vincie studies the clipping about her father's suicide, she realizes he could not have killed himself: his body was not found for two days; the two dogs in the kitchen with him had no food or water and had soiled the floor. Vincie knows that her father would never have subjected his dogs to this treatment, no matter how desperate he was. She goes to the police with her theory and finds an old high school friend, Sergeant Bret LeRoux. The result of her revelation is that the entire family is now under suspicion of murder. Vincie has several insights during these few days of the funeral and the investigation, not the least of which is that she will divorce Gifford and try to find a purpose to

her life. The novel ends before she decides whether to get to know Bret better and/or to try to run the farm herself. The writing is crisp and poetic. Vincie describes her husband: "Gifford's defenses were his sarcasm, his command of language, and most of all, the enveloping, squid's ink cloud of indifference with which he surrounded himself."

Frederick Forsyth

The plot of *The Negotiator* (1989) is to bring down the U.S. presidency on the eve of a major disarmament pact. The final confrontation between the hero, Quinn, and the villains, Moss and McCrae, takes place in the Northeast Kingdom. "In winter a cold descends on the Northeast Kingdom so terrible it is as if the land had been subjected to a state of freeze-frame—literally. The lakes become ice, the trees rigid with frost; the ground crackles beneath the feet. In winter nothing lives up there, save in hibernation, apart from the occasional lonely elk moving through the creaking forest. Wits from the South say there are only two seasons in the kingdom—August and Winter." Quinn drives his Jeep from Burlington to Montpelier and from there past Plainfield and Marshfield to West Danville. He is seeking a remote place in which to hide out to write his report. The locale is described in detail: "They headed back toward Danville, then branched north up an even smaller road. At North Danville the agent guided Quinn west into the wilderness. Ahead the Kittredge Hills reared up to the sky, impenetrable. The track led to the right of the range, toward Bear Mountain. On the slopes of the mountain the agent gestured to a snow-choked track. Quinn needed all the power of the engine, the four-wheel drive, and the chains to get there." The outcome is almost fatal for Quinn and Sam, his girlfriend, who has unwittingly led him into a trap. Fortunately, just as Quinn is about to have his head shot off, a Russian friend, who had dropped him off at the airport and then followed him, picks off the villains from a distant mountain peak. Sam is also saved in the nick of time from an assault, and she and Quinn leave Vermont together.

Catherine Ann Fought

In *Rabble's Curse* (1980), Lisa Sanderson, a thirty-two-year-old practicing attorney in Boston, hastens to Rowe, just over the Vermont border, to assist her aunt and uncle, Chloe and Simon Sanderson, and her younger brother, Tim, who are concerned about affairs in their village. Known as the Rowe Boys, a gang of young men is terrorizing this small milltown. Uncle Simon is attacked; the retarded boy next door is abused; the police chief, Clyde Oldham, is a drunk and a coward; the police in the next town are uninterested; and a local lawyer represents the hoodlums' "rights." A strike at the mill is brewing and soon the strikers are pitted against the hoodlums. Lisa arranges for a Circuit Judge to hear the town's complaints; he dismisses them. Lisa tries to enlist the aid of the state police and is again rebuffed; she fears that the townspeople may resort to taking violence into their own hands, particularly after a murder occurs. Dr. George Almquist, divorced with a daughter and on the staff at Mass General part-time, is an involved participant; he and Lisa fall in love during these stressful days. A scene of appalling violence follows. When the police arrive, it is too late. (The title is from Shakespeare's *Macbeth*: "And to be baited with the rabble's curse.")

Castle Freeman, Jr.

Ambrose, twenty-five miles north of Brattleboro, is the small-village domain of one collection of short stories and two novels. *The Bride of Ambrose* (1987) is a wistful, spare, thoughtful collection of terse, often ambiguous, stories about a small village without much to do, about dead-end lives and lives that are just beginning, and a past that is long gone. The narrators are almost invariably male, often young. In "Seven Prophecies of Egypt," Norman Pettibone is a man who sees himself as a visionary about tourism in Ambrose. He starts up a tourist camp, but will not invest in the liability insurance ordered by the selectmen. Norman believes that the selectmen resent him because he is trying something new. His ten tourist cabins are hauled away. The narrator currently uses one as his tool-shed. The farms are gone. And Egypt Road, the route by which the cabins were removed, is gone, too. In "The Ride," Toby works at a gas station. He has no sense of where he lives: "He didn't pay any attention to the old farming life." He drops in at his girlfriend Rowena's; her brother, Woody, is there. Toby is crazy about cars; he and Woody discuss various deals. He hitchhikes back and is robbed by the driver of the car. As he arrives home, he decides he will marry Rowena and stay in the village. Maybe it will be all right. In "Not Everyone Can Be a Soldier," Rob, the narrator's father, is overseas during World War II. Willard Kent, who is helping out with chores, and Rob are painting the house. Rob compares his father's slap-dash approach to Willard's careful scraping and preparation. "Vermont bored my father to death," Rob thinks. The house in Ambrose belonged to his mother's family, and Rob's father constantly mocked the village: "They speak English up there?" "Even the white houses with black shutters look like cows." Once he and his father rescue a young woman whose car has broken down. The scene is full of sexual innuendo. Rob wonders if Willard is in love with his mother. Willard falls from the ladder, but is not badly hurt. In "That Is No Country for Old Men," nineteen-year-old Erskine, who is working at Clark Johnson's farm, is asked to bury the farmer's big horse, Gentleman Jack. Huey, an old hand in his nineties, goes along to sit in the sun and watch the procedure. It is a complicated task, digging in and around the big, heavy carcass. Erskine doesn't really understand what Huey is saying to him: "You can dig, but can you walk?" In "The Song of Roland," Roland Bailey goes to Alan Weatherhead's funeral, although he resented Alan for trying to steal the affections of his son, Dorr. Dorr had worked for Alan, who had offered to send him to college. Roland remembers that Alan gave a speech on Memorial Day ("Memorial Day in Vermont is like Christmas in Jerusalem," observes Roland) that was not well received by the spectators. Roland was born in Ambrose, married, and had children. He bought a place with an orchard to run, but he could not make a success of it and his wife divorced him.

He now works at Clifford's grocery store. With very little warning, his son's girlfriend — and dog — stop by to stay with him. The provocative girl swims nude in his presence and says that she doesn't like to sleep alone. He remembers that Alan Weatherhead once said there was nothing up above Roland's orchards, and Roland told him there was once a whole town there called "the mills." In the store, Roland hears young Clifford tell some hunters not to waste their time "up there." Roland's frustrations with his life—and the girl—burst out: "You don't know a god-damned thing. There were a hundred people living up there!" In **"Before He Went Out West,"** Ben, the narrator, finds "there was nothing to do in Ambrose," so he joins the Dead River Rescue squad. One night he and another member are called halfway up Round Mountain. They have to break into the house where they find, upstairs, a dead man, Harvey, and a woman whom they discover is blind. She begins to scream and a neighbor, Bean, comes over to help. The two young men load the corpse into their ambulance and head for the hospital in Brattleboro. They hit a bump and the man sits up, fully alive. "The rescue broke up. There was nothing to do in Ambrose. I moved to Wyoming." He couldn't deal with all the things he didn't know. **"Dreaming of Africa"** tells of Leet and his delinquent son, Wayne, who come to fix the narrator's stone wall. The narrator's redheaded wife, Amy, is away in Boston, and he is home alone with his son, Neddy. He and his family used to live in Dar es Salaam, where Neddy had many friends, but the father developed a heart condition and had to come home to Ambrose. Neddy is very lonely, because there are few kids, even in the village. Wayne will not play with Neddy, except to hurl rocks at him from the top of a tree. Leet is a firm defender of Ambrose as a place to live; his son is out of control. **"My Life on the Snowplow"** is about Andrew, who begins his story by telling what he has learned about growing up: "I don't care who you are or from where, what your condition of life. It's with you as it is with the first wildflowers that come out on our brown hillsides after the snow has gone: you have to push up

through trash and hard thorns and a weight of old dead wood from other years, before you can feel the sun on your head." He is expelled from Middlebury College, and, with the help of his ambitious father who is a county prosecutor, gets a job with Arthur Tavistock on the road crew. He does well and works harder than he ever has before in his life. The men go without sleep and eat at headquarters and "were dogged and silent as oppressed miners mining snow." He learns during that winter that his parents are unhappy with each other. He has a strange experience one night when he is driving the snowplow and sees a blond, hatless man standing in the road. He stops as soon as he can and comes upon the driver of a car who thinks he has hit a man. They drive back together to look for a body, but the blond man has disappeared. Andrew goes back to college in the fall. "Ambrose was quiet, empty. It was just far enough back in the hills that nobody wanted to go anywhere, except for those who already had and wouldn't return. It had been that kind of town for a hundred years." Clark Johnson, the farmer, reappears in **"Crime of the Century."** The narrator, who worked on Johnson's farm twenty years ago, is driving to White River to visit the retired sheriff, Orson Bland, who is in the Veteran's Administration Hospital there. As he is traveling north, he notices, too late, a hitchhiker carrying a sign. He recognizes the hitchhiker as a man named Kevin, with whom he worked at Johnson's, but by the time the driver turns around, the hitchhiker has already been picked up. He recalls that Johnson thought Kevin had stolen his new hunting jacket and had insisted that the sheriff do something about it. When the narrator gets to the hospital, he and Bland share a laugh about the old days. In **"The Exile, the Housekeeper, and Flora, the Beauty of Rome,"** Anne and Harold Tavistock are a married couple twenty years apart in age: "The difference in their ages was like a long ladder they carried, one at each end. It kept them together, and it kept them apart." Anne works for their neighbor, Bruno Tyzack, a Berliner confined to a wheel-chair. Anne's brother, Hugh, owns the house and rents it to Tyzack. Hugh and Anne's husband,

F

Harold, do not get along and do not speak. Working around the foundation of the house tying up daylilies, Anne notes that "Today, fortunate people lived in what had been ordinary peoples' houses, and ordinary people lived somewhere else." In **"The Bride of Ambrose,"** the narrator, who is from Ambrose, is with his wife in Mexico where they meet a formerly famous movie star called "Stash." Stash tells them that thirty-five years ago in Manhattan he met a woman named Brenda Yarbrough, also from Ambrose. The narrator concedes that he knew her. Stash, the movie star, recalls that Brenda spoke of Ambrose as beautiful but "there's nothing to do." On a whim, she took him to Ambrose for the weekend to visit her sister and brother-in-law. Stash also observes that "there's nothing to do" in Ambrose. "Everybody sits around." Some unhappiness about Brenda's life there is alluded to, though obscurely. When the narrator's wife comments on the coincidence of his knowing Brenda, he says, "You have to understand. It's such a little place."

The dominant character in *Judgment Hill* (1997) is Garrett Benteen, whose family has lived in Ambrose for at least three generations. A rich farmer, he owns almost everything around these parts, land, buildings, and people, for whom he provides jobs and whose debts he pays. He sent Cordelia Blankenship's son, Hugh, to Dartmouth, but Hugh left and is working temporarily for Benteen. Hugh does not plan on staying in Ambrose forever: "Towns like this is like having the same job all your life." "There's nothing to do." Mario Condosta and a crew are logging and building a house on Judgment Hill. Benteen has tried to buy the property, but Condosta has refused. Benteen, watching the activities through binoculars, obsesses about them. Sheriff Buddy Rackstraw finds a girl who claims she is fleeing an abusive relationship with an Indian Satanist and takes her to Hugh's mother, who finds employment for abused women in her residence, also owned by Benteen. Hugh is immediately attracted to the girl, Tyler McClellan, but she becomes fascinated with Benteen, who invites her to live at his house.

Benteen's past relationships with people in the town are ambiguous. What, for example, was the nature of Benteen's relationship with Cordelia's father, Clay, who was going to write a history of the town but gave it up because "nothing ever happened here. The history of the town is that the town has no history." Hugh goes into business with a private dealer and con man named Townsend Guest. Hugh steals Benteen's antique pony cart and is about to replace his antique golden-ram weather vane with a phony one when he is arrested by the sheriff. He makes a deal with the law to join the marines instead of going to jail. Tyler is sympathetic to Hugh's wanting to get away from Benteen, who, she says, makes everyone his servant. At the end, Benteen explains his two recurring mantras: *"Here they come. This is no drill"* and *"a country in transition."* He is talking about developers, builders, and construction taking over the land and waves of tourists coming to Vermont. He wants to stop them, but he doesn't think he can. "It wasn't their life he wanted to hold, to know, and it wasn't the past, not quite, but an image that partook vainly of both: men, women, and children, working, busy right here, now gone. He cares for them and for their fading signs, a country where men had labored and then for whatever reason had quit their labor and gone away, a country in transition." He realizes that he was wrong to think that if one held onto the old land and the old ways one could hold onto the old life. "It don't work. If you got to buy it it don't count." Among the felicitous images: "The bales were weightless by now. The air took their weight. They rose up from the field like trout from a brook, they hung in the air, they settled down into place on the load, feathers dropping onto the still surface of a pool, so softly, so easily that way;" "Behind her three sets of underwear hung in a row by their long sleeves, stirring uneasily in the air like ghosts who are giving up, who are trying to say, *Don't shoot.*"

My Life and Adventures (2002) is a tragi-comic tale told by Mark Noon thirty years after the events. Noon's life has been changed by a surprising bequest from an unknown person named Hugo Usher, who has left him a house on Bible

Hill in Ambrose. The period is the late age of President Carter, early Reagan. Mark is tall, young, with a college degree and some work experience in college teaching (from which he was fired) and with a mysterious foundation in Latin America. At first, Mark reveals very little of himself. If someone asks the ethnic origin of his name—for example, "Is it German?" he will answer "Sioux" or "Abenaki" or "Choctaw." He has a dry sense of humor about himself: a recurring line is "We Noons are the kind of people…" filled in by phrases like "…nothing is lost on." "We Noons operate from a certain diffidence." He is humorously vague, ending sentences with "whatever you please" or "whenever you please," as in, "He went to Harvard, Yale, or wherever you please." The story is told in layers. The first is the contemporary Vermont setting, in which he fixes up his house, gets "dumb end" jobs, and falls in love with Amanda Applegate. The second is slivers of his experiences with Hitchcock in Latin America. The third is the diary of the original owner of the house, through which Mark "relives" Mr. Littlejohn's life. The fourth is his conversations with Orlando Applegate, a lawyer and father of Amanda, whose son dies tragically in a hunting accident. The fifth is factual, thoughtful essays on aspects of Vermont life, geography, place names, population, mice, culture, and so forth, accompanied by charts. There are fitting epigraphs for the chapters, like Job's "Hast thou entered into the treasures of the snow?" People in Vermont spend a lot of time thinking about who is a "real Vermonter." Mark learns that there is a huge gap between "born here and not born here," affecting every choice, every discussion. Amanda says to Mark, "You don't belong here. You never will. But you don't seem to care. I like that." It is only at the end of this lovely and profound book, after Orlando has died and Amanda has left to go out West, that Mark tells us something of himself, his family, his father's serving in the Navy with Hugo Usher, Usher's turning up at Hitchcock's office. Mark's significant discoveries about himself and his life emerge from reading Littlejohn's diary, "The Bible of Bible Hill." It becomes "a manual for liv-

ing, a primer, a document full of hope, a book of life." From Littlejohn's terse daily entries (a voice of Vermont), Mark gleans lessons he needs to learn: "Keep it low. Keep it simple. Keep it exact. Trust not to gear. Avoid self-satisfaction. Believe little. Be alert. Above all, take your time."

Mary E. Wilkins Freeman

A number of Freeman's stories are set in Vermont; three from *A Humble Romance and Other Stories* (1887) are described here. When a woman boarder in **"A Symphony in Lavender"** stays with Mrs. Leonard in Ware, she is enchanted by the gracious house and lilac-filled yard across the street and learns that the owner is a maiden lady, Caroline Munson. The boarder and Mrs. Leonard are invited to tea with her and go across the street with their sewing at three o'clock—"That's the way people go out to take tea in Ware." Miss Munson is a gentle, nice person, with a rare sweetness rather like a lilac—"that same dull bloom about her, and a shy, antiquated grace." The boarder and Miss Munson like each other, and before the boarder leaves Miss Munson tells her a personal story she has never revealed to anyone. When she was young, she dreamt of meeting an appealing young man. She was carrying a basket of lilies and roses, and he asked her to give him one of her flowers. She wanted to give him a flower more than anything in the world, but when she gazed up at him, his face was both attractive and repulsive: she felt a "horror of something." A year from that time, walking in her lilac gown and holding a sprig of lilac, she actually met that same young man with the handsome, dark face (she doesn't give his name, because today he is a well-known artist). They began to see each other regularly and to care for each other a great deal. He asked her to marry him and, when she looked up into his face to accept, she saw kindness and love and something else, "evil—and the same horror came over me." She wonders if her dream was sent to her as a warning or if she "dulled the happiness of my whole life for a nervous whim." Inez Morse promises her mother **"A Taste of Honey"** as soon as Inez has paid off the mortgage on the farm, a pledge she made to her father before he died. In the meantime, she sells her produce—eggs, cream, and honey—to customers in the large market town of Bolton. Inez has never had a beau, never really had a young girlhood, until Willy Linfield begins calling. When Willy asks Inez to marry him, she accepts on the condition that he wait three years until she has paid off her mortgage. She makes her last payment and hurries to Willy's house, where she learns he has lost patience and married another girl in Sharon. That night, Inez and her mother eat their biscuit and honey: her mother is sorely saddened by her daughter's disappointment. "The pleasant patience in Inez's face was more pathetic than tears." In "**A Modern Dragon**," David Ayres is one of the singers in church when Almira King steps down the aisle in her new, pink silk dress. He is amazed at how sweet she looks; she doesn't have a beau because the villagers think her mother is odd in her ways—and a spiritualist who does not attend church. Her husband dead, Mrs. King manages the farm herself, toiling in a man's hat and boots and old cotton dress to her ankles. When David begins calling on Almira, the village of Dover assumes they will marry. Mrs. Ayres announces to David that if he marries Almira King it will kill his own mother. After a week of brooding, David accedes to his mother's wishes and stops seeing Almira. After Almira goes into a decline, Mrs. King, putting on a long black dress and a bonnet, goes to church. David doesn't come to the King house. Mrs. King humbles herself to Mrs. Ayres. David doesn't come. Finally, Mrs. King, exhausted with anxiety and sorrow, falls fatally ill. When the doctor arrives, Mrs. King sends for David. Now that she will be out of the way, she wants him to swear his fealty to Almira. As Almira throws herself weeping on her mother's bed, David is "beside himself with pity and shame."

The next two stories are from *A New England Nun and Other Stories* (1891). In "**A Village Singer**," influential members of the Derby congregation, having decided to ask Candace Whitcomb to step down from her office as leading soprano after forty years, fête her with a party and present her with a photograph album

and the notice of their decision. The new soprano, Alma Way from the adjoining village of East Derby, is singing on her first Sunday when Candace, who lives next door, starts to play her organ and sing another hymn simultaneously, drowning out the young woman. The congregation is half-amused, half-annoyed. Candace repeats this performance at the afternoon service. The minister, Mr. Pollard, calls upon Candace to ask her not to compete with Alma; Candace says she has a perfect right to play her own organ and sing whenever she wants. Her nephew, Wilson Ford, who has been engaged to Alma for ten years, tells his aunt he is angry at her behavior. Candace counters that she had planned to leave him her house but would change her will. Wilson storms out of the house. Later that evening, Candace begins to feel weak and feverish. She is able to crawl to the door to cry for help. When the minister calls, she apologizes for being rude and she asks to see Wilson and Alma. They are disconsolate that she is dying. She confirms that she wants them to inherit her house and her possessions and asks Alma to sing "Jesus, Lover of my Soul." At first, Alma's voice quavers, but she is soon singing sweetly and clearly. Candace looks up and speaks, and "it was like a secondary glimpse of the old shape of a forest tree through the smoke and flame of transfiguring fire the instant before it falls. 'You flatted a little on—soul,' said Candace." In "**A Wayfaring Couple**," Araminta and David May are the most devoted young couple in Saundersville. He works in the Saunders Cotton Mills and she cares for their little home. When he is fired ("turned off") from his job, they have no savings upon which to rely. Their only recourse is to pack up a few possessions and walk one hundred miles to White River in search of another job for David. Weary and hungry, they reach their destination to find "the shops are full." They come upon an abandoned house where they seek shelter. In the great old barn, there is the "very phantom of an old sulky." They sup off sweet apples and crackers and fall asleep on a heap of hay. Each day David walks off to find work, but there is nothing in Waterbury or Bassets. One morning, David is so sick he cannot sit; in a few days he is very ill. In the evenings, Araminta goes into the broad meadows and milks one or another cow to keep him alive. "She brushed through the sweet fern, knee deep, with the tall jar half-poised on her right hip, carrying her strong, beautiful figure like an Eastern woman." She knows she must go for a doctor, but David begs her not to leave him. She realizes what she has to do: she takes hold of the shafts of the old sulky and drags it to the front door. She helps David into the sulky, in which she has fixed up a bed of hay, and covers him with her shawl. She places herself between the shafts and pulls him the three miles to Bassets. She knocks at the door of the first house she sees. The old man and woman who live there—and then the town of Bassets ("the story of the journey in the sulky spread fast")—are full of emotion and pity for this simple couple. The old man and woman care for them at their house; when David is well, they find him a job at the tub factory. "They seem jest as happy as the day is long, now."

Madelon (1896), passionate and powerful, is about undeclared love and self-sacrifice. In Ware Center, a village in northern Vermont that suffers severe winters, lives a family named Hautville, descended from a French nobleman and an Iroquois maiden: the widower father David, his four sons, Abner, Eugene, Louis, and Francis, and his daughter, Madelon, who cooks and keeps house for them. The family is considered musical and bohemian, although "anything of alien race was looked upon with a mixture of fear and aversion in this village of people whose blood had flowed in one course for generations." Madelon, ravishing with black hair and dark skin, is strong, tireless, independent-minded, and can handle a horse like a man. Burr Gordon, handsome and dashing, lives with his mother across the street from his cousin, Lot Gordon, who is pale, sickly, and suffers from a terrible cough. Burr, who owes his cousin money on his property, may have to forfeit his land to him. People in Ware Center are unable to communicate openly, but gossip is widespread. Burr loves Madelon but pays court to Dorothy Fair, the blonde and blue-eyed daughter of the parson. Lot has always loved Madelon,

but knows he repels her. Madelon loves Burr. Eugene loves Dorothy but says nothing because he believes she loves Burr. "Those soft blue glances of Dorothy's came back to him [Eugene] so vividly that he seemed to see them anew whenever his eyes fell upon the way-side bushes, or the cloud-shadowed slopes of white fields, or the dark gaps of solitude between the forest pines." When a local dance is held and the fiddler cannot come, Burr asks Madelon to "lilt" for the dancers. She is forced to stand on the stage and watch Burr dance with Dorothy. When Jim Otis arrives and offers to fiddle, she slips away. Her youngest brother, Richard, urges her to take his knife, because of the danger of walking home alone. The footpath she takes is "in its way a little humble track of history of simple village life." In the darkness, a man approaches and tries to kiss her. Thinking it is Burr, who has broken her heart, she plunges the knife into his side. When she cradles his head in her arms, she realizes it is Lot. Just at that moment, Burr arrives on the scene. Urging her to go home, he says he will take care of Lot, who is still alive. The next morning, no one comes to arrest Madelon. A town gossip announces that Burr has been arrested and taken to the New Salem jail. Madelon tells everyone that she stabbed Lot, but no one believes her. Richard refuses to admit that he gave her his knife. Burr continues to insist the assailant was he. She goes to Lot's house, but he will say nothing. She takes Dorothy to the jail to make Burr proclaim his innocence, but he will not. Finally, since the family thinks she has gone crazy because Burr has jilted her, she walks ten miles to Jim Otis's house, because he saw her take her brother's knife. He denies this. In the landscape through which she walks the numerous habitations cease until there are only isolated farmhouses, "with long, sloping reaches of woods and pasturelands between. The pasturelands were hummocked with ice-coated rocks and hooped with frozen vines; they seemed to flow down in glittering waves, like glaciers, over the hillside. The woods stood white and petrified, as woods might have done in a glacial era. There was no sound in them except now and then the crack of

F

a bough under the weight of ice, and slow, painful responses, like the twangs of rusty harp-strings, to the harder gusts of wind." She returns to Lot's house (where he is looked after by the village's most pernicious gossip, Margaret Bean) and begs him to tell the truth. Lot will do so on one condition: she must marry him. Turned to stone, she agrees. The sheriff and Parson Fair are summoned to take his statement. He announces that Burr did not stab him. Who did? "I stabbed myself." Madelon, bound to marry the man she most despises, begins to sew her wedding gown and replenish linen supplies for her family. She seems normal, but her heart is breaking. Madelon "felt in greater measure than the gently staid female descendant of the Puritan stock around her the fire of savage or primitive passions." "There is no village in this world so sheltered in situation that it is not exposed to the full brunt of the great forces of human passion, when they lash themselves at times into the fury of the storm." While she sews, there is another snowstorm, the last of the season: "Snow fell upon snow, and the bare ground was never seen. This time the storm lasted two days. In the morning of the third the sun came out and the wind blew. There was a northern gale all day. The new snow arose like a white spirit from its downfall, and was again all abroad in the air. It moved across the fields in great diamond-glittering shafts; it crested itself over the brows of hills in flashing waves; it lengthened its sharp slant of white light from hour to hour against the windward sides of the fences and houses." Shortly after Madelon's wedding date is set, Burr and Dorothy announce their engagement. Lot tries to woo Madelon with trinkets and dress lengths and newly furnished apartments, but she will accept none of his gifts. Finally, he releases her from her bond. She senses the good in this tragic man and feels miraculously liberated. The gossips think she has been dropped again. The day of Burr's wedding arrives. The guests wait an hour, an hour and a half. Finally, Dorothy announces that she cannot go through with the wedding because Burr will not proclaim his innocence to her (in fact, she returns Eugene's love). Madelon sings in the choir after Burr has been jilted. "For the time she stood before and led all the actors in that small drama of human life which was on the village stage, and in which she took involuntary part; and the audience saw and heard nobody but her." Finally, winter is over: "That year spring seemed to break over the village in a day, like a green flood. All at once people's thoughts were interrupted, and their eyes turned from selfish joys or pains by the emerald flash of fields and hill-sides in the morning sun, and the white flutter of flowering boughs past their windows like the festal garments of unexpected guests." The townsfolk announce that if Lot dies they will charge Madelon and Burr with his murder, so Lot commits suicide—leaving all his property and his gifts to Madelon.

Frances Frost

This Innocent Summer (1936) consists of fragments describing the struggling lives of young people in a northern Vermont valley. Paul Hagar is the fifteen-year-old son of Bart Hagar, a drunken farmer who beats his children regularly. Paul and his six siblings have never owned a pair of shoes. His older half-brother, Amos, has left the farm to work in a gas station in town. Ten-year-old Mart O'Brien's father abuses her and often strikes her mother. Donald Moffatt, thirteen, is infected with the tuberculosis that killed his parents. Fern Denoyier, twelve, shyly loves Donald, but her mother hints to her about the "facts of life" in a "vile and insidious" way. Dorothy Burke, five, is too unstrung for her anxious parents. Sam Evans, fourteen, son of Wilfred, who frequently beats him, hates the "sordid stratum" into which he has been born; he has a "hankering for knowledge" that is a "fever" within him. His father may not allow him to return to school. Paul and Sam have summer jobs: Paul works at the Burnham farm; Sam mows lawns. Paul's best friend is Indian Johnny, part French-Canadian, who seems to understand life. Sam mows the lawn of Mrs. Horton, a prostitute whose daughter, Nina, finishes high school and becomes pregnant by the town sheriff, Ben O'Connell. Colonel Cutler, the town aristocrat, invites Sam to look at the library in his mansion. Sam, starved for his mother's love, touches little Dorothy in a dream of longing. When she inarticulately tells her parents, Sam loses his lawn jobs, but Doctor MacFarland offers him a driving job. Sam's mother tells him that his real father is Rob Burnham, whom she loved when they were young before a tree fell and crippled him. Dr. MacFarland, who knows the truth, takes Sam up to the Burnhams' farm to meet Rob. Paul falls in love with Farmer Burnham's granddaughter. Paul, dreaming of owning a catalogue suit, gives all his haying and ferning money to his father but asks to keep four dollars for a suit. Paul's father hits his mother and forces Paul to turn over all his money. Paul goes to Indian's Johnny's, steals his pistol, and commits suicide. The sheriff dismisses the Burnhams and the Hagars: "These poverty-stricken hicks up here are a shiftless bunch." Dr. MacFarland disagrees: he knows how hard they work and how difficult their lives are. At the end, Sam and Fern go walking together; perhaps they will have a chance at life. The narrative is structured around four summer months. In June, "the sun swung up quickly...the summits softened into blue and green." In July, "the long rows of corn stood motionless, the long ribbed leaves silent and drooping over the crumbly loam." In August, "on several nights the northern lights shot beams of cold fire up the sky." In September, "the air smoked from the leaf fires, blue fog brushed the coral of hawthorn and rose-haws, lifted to bathe the boughs in the acrid fragrance of disaster."

Yoke of Stars (1939) is divided into seven sections seven years apart in Judy York's life. She lives in central Vermont with Hannah and Orrin York, her genial, hard-working father and her angry, punitive mother. When Judy is seven, her father buys her a piano. Mrs. Easton from next door spends a great deal of time gossiping with Hannah. If Judy is naughty, Hannah beats her. At fourteen, her mother doesn't allow Judy to practice because it makes so much noise; when Judy's piano teacher intervenes, Hannah strikes Judy across the face with her exercise book and tears up her music. Her mother is always asking her where she has been, if she has seen any boys,

whether she is lying. At school, Thomas Newton begins to notice her; she goes on a straw ride with him and holds his hand. At twenty-one, Judy is about to graduate from college. She is dazzled by Nicholas O'Neil, a handsome, aristocratic tennis star, and goes to the senior ball with him. She sees Tommy Newton again, who tells her he loves her. She remains interested in music and is almost expelled for sneaking into the music room at night to practice the concerto she has written. Seven years later, a well-known composer, she has married Nick and had three children—Nick, Sally, Orrin—and is going home to Vermont because her mother is dying. Nick, who abused the children, has abandoned the family. After her mother dies, Judy's children come to Vermont to live there with her. Tommy, now a doctor, and Judy acknowledge their love for each other; Judy begins divorce proceedings against Nick, who has been gone for three years. At thirty-five, she is still working with a famous composer in New York; Tommy has died of peritonitis. By the time Judy reaches forty-two, Nick is married to Kit Gregory, and Orrin, a musical genius, wants to be a composer. She decides to relinquish the memory of Tommy and marry architect Kendall Hewes, fifty. The family, which has always been close and loving, is even more united by this happy event. Then her son, Orrin, is killed in an automobile accident. Judy, anguished, is composing more fluently than ever. Nick and Kit and their two children are coming for Christmas. Sally, twenty-six, unmarried, is absorbed in her work at a newspaper and is contented living with another woman, Elizabeth, after years of unhappiness caused by Orrin's death. Judy and Ken build a new house in Vermont. In New York the famous conductor, Neumeister, conducts Orrin's posthumous work, "Nocturne for Violins."

The eponymous heroine of *Kate Trimingham* (1940), seventy-three, lives in view of Weather-Glass Mountain in northern Vermont in the big, white corner house left to her by her parents, who blighted her life by not permitting her marriage to Nathan Rogers, whom she had met at the Conservatory. Kate has very little money and supports herself and her cat by giving music lessons to local children. Among them are Gladys ("Gaddy") Glaston, whose parents fight so noisily that she can barely study, and Mike Murraty, whose mother is a virulent gossip. Despite her financial straits, Kate always makes a cake to give her students. Her high-spirited and freethinking contemporary, Sara Drew, who always had beaux as a girl, has just had a great-grandchild. Clifford Cooper, who mows Kate's lawn, is in love with Gaddy. Tim and Christine Dugan, who live next door, are expecting their first child; Tim is nervous because his mother died in childbirth. He has unhappy memories of an abusive father and stepmother. Sara, who can't abide living with her conformist son and querulous daughter-in-law, buys a little white saltbox next the cemetery where she can commune more conveniently with her deceased husband, Homer. Tim and Christine have a little boy, Michael. Gaddy, who can no longer stand her drunken father's beating up her mother, drowns herself in the pond; she leaves a note saying that her life is impossible and that she loves only her music and her teacher, Kate Trimingham. The village gossips descend upon Kate, denouncing her as a corrupter of youth and demanding her arrest. The parents of her students forbid them to take lessons with her. She will have no way to support herself and her cat. The day of Gaddy's funeral, Sara accompanies Kate to the church. The villagers mutter vile things about her. Kate puts a lilac bloom on the coffin, smiles encouragingly at the brokenhearted Clifford, and walks home. Sara briefly addresses those at the gravesite, asking them to look within themselves for blame related to Gaddy's suicide. When Sara hurries back to Kate's house, she finds her dead of a heart attack.

Village of Glass (1942) was written in 1937, almost five years before the attack on Pearl Harbor in 1941. The village of Young-Water lies in a small valley at the foot of Young-Water Mountain in northern Vermont. It is a close-knit community in which neighbors look out for each other, an important factor given that the country is on the brink of war. Robin Thorn, twenty-four, a glassmaker and native of the village, is a lieu-

tenant in the airforce reserve. After his mother died, when Robin was fifteen, his father hanged himself. Laurel O'Hare, twenty-two, who keeps house for her father and makes crocheted bedspreads to sell to tourists, is in love with Robin. She walks up the mountain and looks down at the "infant farmhouses and the lucid puddles of lakes." The Marriners live next door; Jeff works at the quarry, as does Laurel's father. Lugena Smith takes care of the house for her brother, Brud, twenty-four. When the enemy attacks the village from aircraft carriers, everyone is affected. All the young men go off to their units. The enemy repeatedly bombs the village, with many casualties resulting. Evacuees straggle through the village, heading away from the coast. Laurel, working late hours in the hospital, knows the residents will never leave their village. Robin and she are now exchanging love letters. Everyone is helping everyone else. They double up in houses when some are destroyed and work long hours cooperatively, with the exception of one person. There is a fifth columnist in their midst, signaling enemy airplanes from the top of the mountain and committing other acts of sabotage, including blowing up the train bringing an anti-aircraft gun and gun crew. The town manages to have a happy Christmas despite its travails. Robin is wounded and comes home on leave. The saboteur is revealed to be Jeremiah Edwards's son who, while trying to escape capture, inadvertently kills himself before they can send him to prison. Lugena and Aaron, the shopkeeper, are married after a twenty-year courtship, and Jeremiah and Granny, the town character and honorary mayor, both in their seventies, become engaged. No matter what the enemy does, it cannot annihilate the beauty of the valley and its people.

Len Fulton

The hero of *Dark Other Adam Dreaming* (1975) is Quentin August Jensen, born on his grandparents' dairy farm near Essexville on the Lamoille River in northern Vermont. In 1948, now a sophomore in high school, he lives with his hard, brutish father, Big Sam; his small, kind mother, Laura Knolls, from Windsor Locks; his self-centered, cruel brother, Sam'l; his older sister, Liz; and younger sister, Olna. The young men and their father do backbreaking chores on the farm, herding and milking cows, getting in oats from the fields, using heavy equipment and horses. Quentin keeps a book of poems under his pillow, including Emerson's "The Mountain and the Squirrel." Out riding on his father's property one day, he comes across an attractive girl his age, also riding. Named Nina Van Tyne, she grew up in New York City; Quentin has never been to a city. The action is framed by the seasons. Summer is over and, with fall, school starts. At a family dinner, Quentin learns that Nina is staying with her uncle, Ike Crowley; Big Sam curses Crowley as a "Jew." In the last ten years, he claims, Crowley has "maneuvered a half dozen sheriff's auctions over grain sales." Jed Elston hanged himself after he lost his farm. Quentin sees his brother lauded as a basketball star, but knows that Sam'l brutally beat up a younger boy and tried to rape a girl at school. Quentin thinks constantly of Nina, with whom he formed a bond when they were out riding. Sam'l and two other young men from the basketball team rape Nina. In defense, Sam'l claims that his father urged him to have sex with Nina because she was a Jew and therefore "knew all about it." The sheriff and Ike Crowley bring the three young men to Big Sam's barn for a showdown, with Quentin eavesdropping in the beams. Ike Crowley will not bring charges, because he doesn't want Nina hurt any more. He says, "Just let a man say 'Jew,' and the roof is off, the floor out. And three boys are ruined for life — and one damned sweet girl. 'Jew.' Funny." In the last chapter in spring, the Jensens are doing the sugaring. Quentin almost falls off a cliff through an ice floe. He sees Sam'l coming with the sledge and horses and doesn't warn him. Sam'l sees the danger just in time. The gentle mother is not able to stem the feuding, the violence, and the hatred in the family. Poor Liz, with her thick legs, gets pregnant, and the new, handsome teacher has to marry her. Quentin comes of age. (The title is from Lorca's poem, "Adam:" "But a dark other Adam dreaming yearned/for a stone neuter moon, where no seeds bud.")

G

John Gardner

James L. Page is an irascible old widower in *October Light* (1976) who lives on a farm on Prospect Mountain near Bennington. His widowed sister, Sally Page Abbott, eighty, lives in his house. James's daughter, Ginny, lives in nearby Arlington with her husband, Lewis Hicks, and her son, Dickey. The plot involves the protracted, spiteful feud between James and Sally. The circumstances of the deaths of James's sons — one fell from a roof; the other, Richard, committed suicide — are revealed. James learns by inference that Richard killed himself because he believed himself responsible for his Uncle Ira's heart attack out of shock at a Halloween trick. The leaves turn. "Now, in October, the farmwork was slackening, the drudgery had paid off: the last of the corn went flying into the silo with a clackety roar and a smell as sweet as honey; the beans were harvested in half a day, like an afterthought; on the porch and out by the roadsides stood mountains of pumpkins. The trees turned — those along the paved roads first, dying from the salt put down in winter — sugar maples orange, pink, and yellow on one branch, elm trees pale yellow, birch trees speckled with a lemony yellow, still other trees carmine and vermilion and ochre, red maples as red as fresh blood. Soon — anytime from mid-October to the end of November — it would be locking time." One day a blast from James L. Page's twelve-gauge shotgun tears a hole in Sally Page Abbott's television set, and he proceeds to chase her upstairs, brandishing a piece of firewood and locking her in her room. Sally subsists on a diet of green apples and reads a trashy novel she finds in her room, a fantasy of illicit drugs, violence, and casual sex, paralleling in some way her feud with her brother. It is nearing "locking time" — death — for them both.

David Gates

Doug Willis, musician, wordsmith, and smart aleck, is experiencing a life crisis in *Preston Falls* (1998). Taking a leave of absence from his job in New York writing advertising copy for a sports-drink manufacturer, Doug heads for the family's summerhouse in rural Preston Falls, New York, on the Vermont border. His wife, Jean, and the children, Melanie, twelve, and Roger, seven, drive up for a visit. The atmosphere bristles with hostility between both the parents and the children, and Doug's behavior deteriorates rapidly. Jean finally takes off with the children (divorce proceedings are in the air) for a night's camping before going home; Doug decides to join them and enters into an altercation with the campground's attendant. Before the children's eyes, a sheriff is called and Doug is taken to jail. Panicked, Jean calls Calvin Castleton, an unfriendly neighbor in Preston Falls, to ask for the name of a lawyer. Calvin recommends Philip Reed, who lives in Rutland. Philip plays in a band in Brandon and invites Doug to sit in. Insidiously, Philip takes hold of Doug's life and blackmails him into running drugs from Preston Falls to Vermont and returning to the contact (whose identity is a surprise) in Preston Falls with a check. Philip's irresponsible behavior sets in train a series of events with irreparable effects.

Rebecca Gilman

Spinning into Butter (2000), an engrossing and provocative play, takes place at Belmont College, a small liberal arts college "near a ski slope." Sarah Daniels, Dean of Students, previously worked at a small college with a majority African-American population and no funds to support them. Eager to help the minority students at Belmont, Sarah persuades Patrick Chibas, a Hispanic student, to declare his ethnicity on an application for a scholarship. She has been having an affair with Dr. Ross Collins, an art history professor who reveals he is living with someone else. The Dean of the College, Catherine Kenney, and Burton Strauss, Chair of the Humanities Department, had a sexual relationship and now depend on each other for political support in college affairs. They, Sarah, and Ross are in Sarah's office when the campus security guard, Mr. Meyers, reports that Simon Brick, an African-American student (a "student of color," as Patrick Chibas corrects Sarah) has had two racist notes left on his door (one calls him "Little Black Sambo"). Both Ross and Burton quickly understand that they may be able to benefit personally from this scandal and call a meeting of the students to discuss racism on campus. The students boycott Burton because of his racist attitudes. White student Greg Sullivan, very much "the Belmont man," senses that he, too, can work this issue to his advantage, since his law school application is "a little thin," and proposes to Sarah that he form a student committee to discuss tolerance on campus. Patrick tells Sarah that he wants to leave Belmont, which he hates, and go to NYU. Sarah realizes she has failed him while trying to help him. She confesses to Ross that she perceived racist feelings in herself when she was at her former place of employment; at least, she found herself getting drunk at a faculty party and announcing that she hated Toni Morrison's books. She didn't believe that remark made her a racist, but she thought she was unburdening herself of something smacking of racism and she ran away—to Vermont: "I was afraid of the kind of thought that popped into my head. I was afraid of what I might say. I began to fear for my soul. Belmont, Vermont. Beautiful mountain, green mountain. I knew it would be quiet and clean and white. It wasn't a noble way to save myself, or a brave way, but it was the only way I could think of. But now I'm back where I started." The faculty discusses the case, unable to understand what motivated the letter-writer. It is Burton who remembers the way the person referred to the recipient in one of the notes: "Little Black Sambo." He reminds them of the story (also explaining the title), in which the tigers take Little Black Sambo's clothes, argue among themselves about who is grander, and start chasing each other around a tree until they spin themselves into butter. Little Black Sambo scoops up the butter, puts it on his pancakes, and eats up the tigers. The outcome of the case affects Sarah's future and shows hopeful signs about the student body.

Gerald Jay Goldberg

In *The Lynching of Orin Newfield* (1970), Orin Newfield is a successful dairy farmer in Farnum near East Corinth and Route 5 on the Connecticut River. The period is the forties. The first person narrative takes place in Newfield's head; he often refers to himself in the third-person singular. A big ox of a man, he is arrogant, hardworking, and rich, surpassing his "resigned," unsuccessful ancestors who lived in this town for generations. He is particularly pleased that a "poor local boy" has done so well, "Doubly so when you stop to consider that practically everyone else my age had run off to the cities. Looking for the quick buck. Afraid to stick it out in a town grimly marking time like a patient with some incurable disease." In his drive to make his dairy farm pay, he has developed an aggressive demeanor and snarls meanly at the various townsfolk who cross his path courteously during a shopping day in Farnum. He believes he can go it alone: he threatens the storekeeper about losing his liquor license; he is cruel to Roy Carter, his hired hand; he tells the local former senator that the latter had no more chance of being reelected than a "Jew-black Mongoloid idiot." His mousy wife, Alma, wants to be liked by the neighbors and suffers from her husband's nasty ways. She has no children and is very lonely. Orin is rude to her brother, Ben Barlet. Carter drunkenly spills two big containers of milk. After Orin, infuriated, throws Carter out of his barn and hurts the latter badly, he knows the gossips will go to work: "Thinking on my way out that now there'd be a new horror story. Featuring the Villain vs. Carter. Like the others they told about me among themselves. Black and bloody tales of crime and passion muddling history with spite. Ah, the Farnum imagination! It must have something to do with the long winters." Newfield was ashamed of his father, who could never hold a job, and was responsible for his father's death, although he never admitted it, even to himself. He has

alienated everyone: "If there was only a way to do it all yourself." He once went to New York, where he hired a Latino named Jesus to work for him. Orin liked him, but the man only stayed six days: Orin told his brother-in-law that "Farnum didn't care to have any dark-skinned stranger taking jobs away from them." Orin is arrested for assault and battery on Carter. When Orin is asked to take an oath on the Bible, he announces to the courtroom that he does not believe in God. The audience is shocked. Called to the witness stand, his wife perjures herself, saying that she was present for the entire scene: Carter fell, drunkenly, and hurt himself. Orin is acquitted, but the town—and his wife and brother-in-law—retaliate by acting as if he were dead. Orin Newfield achieves his own strange revenge.

Christopher Golden

The Gathering Dark (2003), part of a series called "The Shadow Saga," again features Peter Octavian, born in the fifteenth century and turned into a vampire who, though he chose in the twenty-first century to be a human, remains a sorcerer as well. Keomany Shaw, twenty-three, runs Sweet Somethings Candy Shoppe in Wickham, one hour south of the Canadian border. Keomany, half-English and half-Cambodian, is an earthwitch, dabbling in earth magic since college. Nikki Wydra, a singer with a band, is an old friend of Keomany's and a former lover of Peter's. At this point in the century, the Roman Catholic Church has collapsed, the Church of the Resurrection has emerged, and a horrific vampire jihad has taken place. Father Jack Devlin, who keeps a tiny demon in a jar (with a perforated top), is trying to recreate the ancient *Gospel of Shadows*, which contained spells for destroying demons. After a demon manifestation in Texas, Devlin summons the "mage" (Peter) to help dispel the demons. Keomany drives south to a Druidic festival in Brattleboro; when she returns to Wickham, the picture-perfect village has been occupied by hissing creatures with deadly rapier tongues; the air is fetid and the sky putrid and orange. She uses her earthwitch powers to tap into Gaea, combats the demons, and makes her

G

bloodied way to Nikki in Los Angeles; through Nikki's offices, Peter and Devlin assemble, and the four return to Wickham to confront the evil there. Peter is able to pull part of Wickham back into their dimension but doesn't have the strength to combat the storm everywhere. They retreat to Brattleboro to seek out Keomany's earthwitch colleagues and a means of finding the source of the evil. Tori Osborne and her wife (Vermont has legalized gay marriage), Cat Hein, run the commune at Summerfields together. From the map of open wounds that have appeared on Cat's body, Peter is able to identify the next spot where the Whispers will invade—a small town in Spain. The confrontation with the evil forces occurs there and the lives of all the characters change.

Lee Dana Goodman

Dunster Revealed: Echoes from a Vermont Town (1997) is a collection of vignettes about a small town called Dunster, with a population of about ten thousand, of which ninety-eight percent is white (five black families descended from a fugitive slave). Whipple Mills closed in 1938 and the town is remote from the economic benefits of interstate highways 89 and 91. Dunster began in the sixties to enjoy a "creeping prosperity," due only partly to "outsiders" (the way Dunster natives refer to residents born elsewhere). Attorney George Rutledge ably defends Sam Parsons, a genial and "beloved" bootlegger. The town spinster, Emily Jenkins, always leaves her front door open, summer or winter. After her death it is disclosed, but only to her doctor and lawyer, that as a young woman she left her husband, Dr. Carl Curtis, whom she loved deeply, because his divorce was a few weeks short of final. When their baby died of influenza forty years ago, Emily wrote to her husband that she would keep the door open in case he came back. The letter was never delivered. He returns all these years later, too late to see her. Lydia Whipple, heir of the Whipple Mills fortune and resident of "The Castle," is forced to take in bed-and-breakfast guests. Fred Haskell's Dodge won't make it up the hill in the snow, so he rides his horse, Clyde, to town. His wife, Maud, is a vira-

go; he loves Joyce, who is too honorable to love him back. The Lundgrens, immigrants, buy the Rutledge place, still known as the "Rutledge place." The Lundgrens welcome young people to their land, teach them skills, and offer them solace and friendship. When they cannot meet their mortgage payments, the neighbors raise twelve thousand dollars to keep them from losing their property at auction and succeed in getting their patently inflated interest rates lowered.

James Gordon

Escape from Vermont (1948) gives a bleak picture of a town south of Manchester in the early 1930s. The story is dominated by the patriarch of a large, unnamed family consisting of the grandfather and grandmother (who haven't spoken to each other in ten years), five aunts, occasional uncles, and two boys, Micah and the narrator. Grandfather is a rich, unforgiving skinflint who runs the mill and the lumberyard and owns mortgages on all the farms in the vicinity. The example he sets his family is to hate and disparage the Finnish mill workers ("They were strange and terrifying people," says the narrator, "because they were foreigners"). When the Roudenko family buys the old farm near Grandfather, he doesn't lift a finger to help them, calling them "Hunkies" and "goddamn foreigners." The narrator, fourteen when his story begins, is hardworking, rising early to do the milking, taking the milk to the creamery before school, and getting a job with Mr. Rambeau to take in oats. The family does all the grueling work in the summer picking berries and boiling them down to make jam and jellies, which gives the women tremendous satisfaction. They work all day "at a million jobs that never needed doing." The narrator notes that "when Vermonters find themselves with a day off, they remember that it is a sin to enjoy it." Grandfather is a deacon in the local church, but "his religion was like that of the rest of New England, a quiet, deep-seated, fundamentalist atheism." In fact, says the narrator, "Thrift is his grandfather's religion." Summer boarders from Manchester come through town frequently. "Summer people always called us 'natives' and it made us feel like naked blacks in a jungle." The worst summer people are "the kind who buy a farmhouse and pretend they are Vermonters." Everyone gossips; his Aunt Holly has "the longest nose for gossip in town." At twenty-eight, she finally marries Stanley, "the Polack." The narrator thinks that the town "killed people by undermining them with meanness and gossip." One day he goes deer hunting with Henry Waters, a broken-down prizefighter. When Henry's wife, Beryl Hall, walks "her hips moved like the walking beams on the Albany night boat." Henry kills a big buck; the carcass makes the narrator feel sick and sad. When they get home they find Moses from the creamery has been with Beryl. Grandfather is envious of his neighbor, Volney, and tricks him out of his fast horse. Garrit Hallock is the first in town to be "seduced by tourist cash" and starts selling old farmhouses. The narrator realizes that "Vermonters might never have known their barren farms were picturesque" if tourists hadn't admired them. Grandfather refuses to sell any of his land to Garrit. By the end, the narrator is learning a trade plastering and painting a house for some summer people. City guests come to visit the house and exclaim, "It's so rural, so honest-to-God, down-to-earth, real American!" Grandfather dies; the narrator has become a man.

Peter Gould

Burnt Toast (1971) is a stream-of-consciousness narrative by a young man named Silent, who is in search of words to describe his "power vision" of burnt toast. "This world that was born in silence is returning there, I know, and that's my story, and it too would be perfectly silent (and it will be, there's time), but that I thought it would be fun to tell it." This fable is about Silent's coming of age, the disappearance of his best friend, Sam, and the death of his incomparable father, whose presence he continues to feel "riding his shoulder like a bird." The ethos of Silent's existence symbolizes an era: a farm commune in southern Vermont up Old Country Road near Adam's Ear. Over the Mountain is Spirit Lake, where the people live who used to be part of this community when Two were One. Silent lives

amidst serene, loving, hardworking people: in addition to his father, there are his mother; his sister, Margot; Lila, who lives at Spirit Lake and takes part in his initiation before his quest; and Kathy, the most beautiful woman in the world. He looks across the field, "warm and vigilant," to the hardwood and the sugarbush. He sits in the vegetable garden and eats radishes with his father. He visits with the chickens, and Rosemary, the goat, and King Something, the horse. Kamoo, the Holy One (who also runs the auto-body shop), officiates at the initiation in a tent with music. On his quest, Silent meets a milkmaid who lets him choose words (free) from her box, after which he has the "clearest semblance yet" of his power vision: "knowing what is and isn't" and "gaining power over words by visiting their source." Silent describes an old farmer, "the kind who's lived through so many hard winters and lean summers you could slice into his arm and read his story in the annual rings."

Anna Katharine Green

A Strange Disappearance (1879) begins in New York with a gathering of experts to discuss unusual mystery cases. Q, a detective who works with the famous Mr. Gryce, relates the strange disappearance of a seamstress named Emily from the household of a wealthy former congressman, Holman Blake. Mrs. Daniels, the housekeeper, summons the police when the young woman disappears but is curiously unable to provide any information about Emily, other than what she looks like; Mr. Blake doesn't remember having seen the young woman in his house. Mr. Gryce puts Q on the case, implying that Gryce has already noticed a clue that will solve the mystery. Q, who is adept at disguise, begins a surveillance of Mr. Blake, following him first to a society ball where Blake has an emotional exchange with his cousin, Evelyn Blake, now the Countess de Mirac. Q then follows Blake to the railroad station, where Blake buys a ticket on the Hudson River Railroad for Panton. Blake makes his way to an old abandoned inn, where he knocks on the door but finds no one home. Q recognizes the house as the hide-away of the Schoenmakers, robbers of the Rutland Bank, who have escaped from jail. After Blake leaves, Q climbs onto the roof and drops into the house, where he finds a *Rutland Herald* bearing a date two days' old and a piece of red chalk, which he pockets. Q admires the view. "Hills on hills piled about a verdant basin in whose depths nestled a scanty collection of houses, in number so small they could be told upon the fingers of the right hand, but which notwithstanding lent an indescribable aspect of comfort to this remote region of hill and forest." When confronted by Mr. Gryce and Q with the evidence against him, Blake is compelled to tell his story. He was madly in love with his cousin Evelyn, whom his father did not want him to marry. He was at Lake George, trying to forget her, when a friend invited him to visit Vermont, "where trout streams abounded and, what is not so often the case under the circumstances, fishers were few." He was on his way to Panton, but the night was stormy and he took refuge in an old inn, where the dreadful Schoenmakers, father and son, were living with Luttra, their daughter and sister. Luttra, who had lustrous red-gold hair, helped Blake escape from the felonious clutches of her father and brother, who had planned to rob and murder him. As a reward, he funded her education. His father insisted that he choose a wife or be disinherited. Blake decided to marry Luttra, but she discovered his motive and, as he was introducing her to his dying father, disappeared. She is Emily, the seamstress, in a black wig (Mr. Gryce had noticed the red-blond hair in the comb of the black-haired seamstress). Luttra and Blake are happily reconciled with the Countess de Mirac's blessing.

Michael Green

In *Dry Skull Dreams* (1995), Molly Coughlin of Brattleboro works in Francophone Africa where she runs the Mamadou Mothers and Infants Center, financed by World Vision. Sibatia, the village lunatic, attacks Molly the night before she is to return to Brattleboro. Sibatia has murdered the shaman and eaten six black seeds from his skull. These seeds he vomits into Molly's mouth, and she arrives home feeling strange. The seeds drive Molly crazy: she tries to kill her parents and endangers a van full of young people by driving them to her parents' cabin on a pond near St. Johnsbury. Her father, Charlie, stops her before she can create any more havoc.

Jennifer Greene

In *Wild in the Moment* (2004), Daisy Campbell, divorced, returns home to White Hills in the middle of a blizzard. She is forced to abandon her house and seek shelter at her neighbors. There she finds Teague Larson, who is remodeling the Cunninghams' house. A new resident of Vermont, he is a loner; Daisy does not plan to stay any longer than necessary. Despite resolutions to the contrary, they fall in love.

Thomas Christopher Greene

In *Mirror Lake* (2003), Nathan Carter, who descends from an old Boston family, moves to northern Vermont after his father's death. About ten years out of college, he has had a series of brief affairs with women to whom he was unable to make a commitment. He decides to simplify his life, finds a small cabin in the town of Eden near Montpelier, and gets a job as a mailman. He tries to deliver mail to a crusty old neighbor named Wallace Fiske on Mirror Lake, who refuses to accept the mail, but, after Nathan has an accident in Wallace's driveway and Wallace rescues him and takes him to his own house, the two become friends. Nathan meets a young woman in the village named Kate Linger, with whom he begins an affair. As Nathan spends time with Wallace, he begins to learn something about Wallace's wife, Nora, and the hired man, Guy LaRoche, a Canadian, who helped with the farm chores. The narrative becomes two separate but interrelated and moving stories. After Nathan learns the truth about Wallace's life, he feels he can take a chance on loving another person.

T. Greenwood

Breathing Water (1999) begins in 1991 with the drowning death of a young African-American girl, Kiesha, who is a Fresh Air Kid hosted by one of the families on Lake Gormlaith near the town of Gumby in northern Vermont. There are hints of malfeasance on the part of Effie Greer's boyfriend, Max. Effie returns in 1994 to her grandparents' camp on the lake. The plot swings from the present to 1991 and back, revealing that Effie was badly battered and abused by Max, who has died of a heroin overdose since the incident on the lake. Her grandmother, Gussy, and her best friend, Tess, are very supportive; her parents and her sister, Colette, are not. Maggie, a local waitress who is also an abused woman, and her mute daughter, Alice, are appealing acquaintances. Devin Jackson, an African-American summertime neighbor and artist, starts leaving little gifts on Effie's front porch. The resolution of the story is a gratifying surprise.

H

Jane Haddam

Since 1934 the town of Bethlehem in *A Stillness in Bethlehem* (1993) has held a Christmas pageant. The celebration has become more elaborate and more popular with tourists and now nets for the town about three hundred thousand dollars a year. The natives are delighted with the income, although they "didn't much like flatlanders in spite of the money they spent" and "Flatlanders had very strange ideas about Real Vermont." Peter Calisher was born and raised in Bethlehem and, after some years away at school and college, has returned to serve as editor of the *Bethlehem News and Mail*, as his father did before him. Despite his credentials, he is considered "away" by the town (the gossiping women who do good works in the basement of the Congregational Church). Peter lives above the store with glamorous Amanda Ballard, thirty-six, whose slim good looks are slightly flawed by a deformed ear lobe. He has just run a piece on the famous Armenian detective, Gregor Demarkian, who by coincidence is in Bethlehem with two friends to attend the festival. Gregor

soon meets other town characters. Tisha Verek, forty, who is researching crimes committed by children, lives with her drunken, stoned artist husband, Jan Mark. Mark is having an affair with Gemma Bury, a woman minister. Franklin Morrison, seventy-two, is the chief of police, assisted by his deputy, Lee Greenwood, thirty-two. Stuart Ketchum lives with his mother, Dinah, in a house built in 1687. Timmy Hall is a retarded man from a local institution whom Amanda has hired to work for the newspaper. Teenager Candy George lives with her abusive husband, Reggie. Just as the town is girding its loins for the influx of tourists, Tisha, who had threatened to file an injunction against the religious celebration, is murdered. Then Dinah is killed with one of Stuart's guns. Franklin seeks Gregor's advice. At an evening performance of the Nativity play (with Candy as Mary), Gemma, sitting next to Gregor, is killed by a sniper who escapes unseen. Gregor sifts to the bottom of the mystery with the help of an exhibit from Tisha's research.

Sue Halpern

The chapters in *The Book of Hard Things* (2003) are named for "hard things" like granite, agate, schist, and copper. The place names, Poverty, Stover, Halcyon Falls, Whisper Notch, exist in an unnamed state, but signs of Vermont are everywhere—a bleak northern setting (mountain lions have been sighted), mountains, dumb-end jobs, deer hunting, leaf peepers, woodchucks and flatlanders, and Rolling Rock beer. Cuzzy Gage's life is in ruins. His father is in a mental institution; his mother is dead; his cousin Hank, with whom he lived for a while, takes into his house and impregnates a string of teenaged girls; and his young male friends are ill educated and aimless because they have no place to go. They live in poverty. Cuzzy has a son named Harry with Crystal, but she won't let him see the boy. He is unemployed and homeless. When Michael ("Tracy") Edwards arrives in town in his Porsche, Cuzzy is envious. When Tracy befriends him, Cuzzy is nervous and suspicious, thinking Tracy is probably gay. In fact, the local minister, Jason Trimble, asked Tracy to be a "Good Samaritan" to Cuzzy, which explains why Tracy invites Cuzzy to his fancy estate, The Larches, up past Whisper Notch. Cuzzy learns that Tracy has inherited a share in this house and the car from his best friend, Algie Black, who is dead. Tracy offers Cuzzy a job organizing Algie's papers. These two men, unimaginably different, have a great deal to offer each other: Cuzzy knows about birds, animals, and trees; Tracy, who is a teacher, about music and literature. Tracy quotes frequently from poets like Wallace Stevens and Robert Frost ("I dwell with a strangely aching heart"). Leo Gage, Cuzzy's father, invites Jason to visit him at the hospital. Leo is making notes for a book, *The Book of Hard Things*. The question he is researching: "Why is everyday life so *goddamned* hard?" Tracy receives word that he has been awarded a Fulbright to teach in New Zealand. The climax of the plot is a party he gives to celebrate his departure. The suspense leading up to the end is excruciating. The imagery is unusual and intelligent. People passing through Poverty look different, "cleaner and softer, as if they had a higher thread count." There are signs of lost civilizations, old chimneys, and "tin cans that had rusted to filigree."

Robert P. Hansen

The solution to the murders in *Back to the Wall* (1957) lies somewhere in the old Parrish property. Dr. Daniel Bedford, a marine veteran of the Korean War and veterinarian like his father, lives in Waynesbury (off Route 7, near Manchester) with his sister, Roxa; Newt, the handyman for over thirty years, stays in the carriage house. Someone shoots at Daniel, narrowly missing him; shortly thereafter, Miss Mindwell Parrish is found murdered. Daniel seeks the help of Ed Bacon of the state police. A few days before, Daniel bought the Parrish house to enable Miss Parrish to stay there until her death. Now someone desperately wants that house. Is it glad-hander George Casey, who appears in town with his alluring wife, Jessica? Is it Pepe Smith, here to shoot photographs of glamorous model Kate Breen in front of antique exteriors?

Is it arrogant Professor Slocum, who comes with sensitive treasure-seeking equipment? Is it the uncouth Alten brothers, who have camped up beyond the Parrish house? Is it Homer Dade, the slimy lawyer? The next victim is George; then Daniel's dogs are killed. Papers turn up revealing that John Parrish discovered gold in the gold rush. Is it buried on the Parrish property? Meanwhile, Daniel and Kate have started dining together. A sampler embroidered with "half a rod from his own door" leads Daniel, Newt, and Kate to the fifty thousand dollars in gold. After the murderer is disclosed and the excitement over, Kate decides not to go to Hollywood.

Rosemary Harris

At the start of *Three Candles for the Dark* (1976), Candida Goodman, twenty-five, has been recently released from a California hospital after a trial in which she was found guilty of arson (resulting in the death of Mrs. Olsen) and mentally incompetent. Innocent but doubted by her husband, Peter Caravel, she cut and badly scarred her face. She is being divorced by her husband, is deep in Jungian analysis in Manhattan, and is looking for a job. Through a meeting of analysands, Candida accepts an invitation from Martlett Holbetter, twenty-nine, to spend Christmas vacation at his family home near Cabb Town as companion to his appealing orphaned nephew, Joss. The big stone mansion, reached through locked gates, houses Martlett's hostile mother, his gregarious Aunt Bea, his mentally backward sister, Tally (the result of a fall), a stone-deaf, senile great-uncle, and an angry black servant named Mary. Joss is charmed by Candida and refers with distaste to the young woman who was his former companion. The plot turns on the suspicion that someone is planning to murder the owner of the house, burn it, implicate Candida, who has a similar crime already on her record, and collect a large sum in insurance money. Having been warned to stay away from the boundaries of the estate, Candida disobeys and meets attractive Cary, who reveals the secret underlying the plot.

Richard Warren Hatch

This Bright Summer (1933) evokes the town of Lobe's End in southeastern Vermont (ten miles from the Connecticut River near Bellows Falls), which is cursed with a feud lasting one hundred years between the Carver (timber) and Hallowell (horse-breeding) families. Lake Carver, twenty, the youngest of three sons of widow Carver, is brooding and suffering—"the mark on those who wanted to leave the place and could not." When his older brother and protector, Frank, dies, Lake is left to his brutal, bullying brother, Matt. Sarah Wales, eighteen, is a delicate young woman whose drunken father, Enoch, lusts after her and her younger sister, Lizzie, and plays her two suitors, Matt Carver and Sam Hallowell, against each other; her mother, Annie, who does washing out, has been stupefied by abuse into silence. Sarah and Lake discover that they love each other; they begin to meet in the meadow at the bottom of Lobe's Cliff. It is "a bright summer, with little rain," yet underneath the scene is dark and ugly. Sarah hates and fears Sam, who "creeps," and Matt, who "crushes." Sam has impregnated Ella Smart, who marries Sam's unknowing younger brother, Joshua. Lake innocently asks Enoch for Sarah's hand; Enoch threatens Sarah that, if she does not promise to marry Sam (who has offered Enoch a prime piece of property free), he will tell Sam about Lake. Intent upon helping Sarah, who is locked in the house, Annie takes the laundry to John Briggs, justice of the peace, to propose a solution. Matt hears about Sarah's wedding and goes to Lobe's End to kill Sam. They fight violently while people are arriving for the wedding. Annie (who has brought a gun) takes Sarah into the back room where Briggs quietly marries her to Lake. During a fierce thunderstorm, Annie's gun attracts lightning and she dies, leaving Lizzie to the incestuous passions of her father, Enoch. Lake and Sarah go to his house, where Mrs. Carver is dying; she begs them to leave town, but they refuse. While Lake is out farming, Matt comes home wounded from his fight and rapes Sarah. Sarah becomes pregnant: whose baby is it? Meanwhile, Lizzie is pregnant with her father's baby. Enoch, drunk, comes into town to preach: a crowd falls upon and kills him. Briggs gives Mrs. Carver enough "powders" to finish her, so that the young couple can escape. Before leaving, Lake goes to town to kill Sam and end the feud. When he returns, he finds that Sarah has shot herself. He and Sarah lived their entire life together in one bright summer. After accomplishing all his chores slowly and carefully, Lake throws himself over Lobe's Cliff.

Nathaniel Hawthorne

"The Ambitious Guest" (1837) pictures a happy family that lives in a primitive tavern at the stage-coach stop in the Notch of the White Hills of New Hampshire, with Maine on one side and Vermont on the other. One evening, a young wayfarer stops to spend the night. The family greets him with delight. "Then you are going towards Vermont?" asks the host. "Yes; to Burlington, and far enough beyond," replies the young man. "I meant to have been at Ethan Crawford's tonight; but a pedestrian lingers along such a road as this. It is no matter; for, when I saw this good fire, and all your cheerful faces, I felt as if you had kindled it on purpose for me, and were waiting my arrival. So I shall sit down among you, and make myself at home." They enjoy a meal together and the young guest feels he is among his own people. In fact, he feels so at home that he pours out the contents of his heart—his ambition, his desire for recognition. He has done nothing notable yet in life. "Were I to vanish from the earth tomorrow, none would know so much of me as you...Not a soul would ask, "Who was he? Whither did the wanderer go? But I cannot die till I have achieved my destiny. Then, let Death come! I shall have built my monument!" Suddenly, there is an awful sound outside and they know a slide is coming. They rush outside and are covered by one whole side of the mountain. Ironically, the house remains untouched. The story of the Willey family (for such was their name) and their five children is forever a legend in these mountains. But who remembers the dreamy youth? Hawthorne describes Burlington, the ambitious guest's destination, in his essay, "An Inland Port" (written in 1835 and collected in *Outsiders in Vermont*, edited

by T.D. Seymour Bassett, 1967). Hawthorne was struck by the handsome and busy square. The tin roofs on some of the edifices "glitter in the sun with a cheerful splendor." He watches the pleasant mixture of people, Canadian, British, Irish, and Scotsmen, and a "great throng of Green Mountain boys, with their horse-wagons and ox-teams, true Yankees in aspect, and looking more superlatively so, by contrast with such a variety of foreigners."

Joseph Hayes

Lucinda Durand, a French-Canadian student at Melville College near Burlington, is camping out in the woods in *The Ways of Darkness* (1985) with her boyfriend, Matt Horgan, when they are terrorized by two strangers. Matt tries to fend them off while urging Lucinda to run. One man follows her; the other throws Matt off a cliff. Matt survives the fall into a marsh, finds his car, and drives to the police station in Shepperton to report the crime. He is arrested and jailed as a material witness and for marijuana possession (but is really a homicide suspect). The police trace his father, Andrew Horgan, who does not know of his son's existence, having left his wife before he knew she was pregnant. Matt's mother, Julia Craven, an actress, arrives from New York with her famous lawyer, Gerald Usher Lewis. Tracy Larkin, a local TV broadcaster, becomes involved in helping Andrew discover the identities of the two men whom Matt saw. A mafia gang dumps dioxin into Lake Echo and puts pressure on the state's attorney to close the case. A dishonest lawyer wants young Matt to plead guilty to manslaughter. The distraught father of the victim will do anything to avenge his daughter. A terrified coroner changes his report then commits suicide. Savage murders along the way lead up to the final exciting chase.

Emory James Haynes

A Farmhouse Cobweb (1895), a tale of passion, property, and parentage, centers around four sympathetic young people and one charismatic villain. The four live in the northern Vermont village of Northbrook ("stony hillsides and vales") on the eve of the Civil War. Sensible

Elisha Stone, the narrator, is a farmer whose best friend, handsome Horace (Hod) Parkridge, was once a Naval Academy man but now is also a farmer. Elisha has always loved pretty Mary Holyoke, who is ten years younger, while Hob worships raven-haired Cynthia Littlewood, adopted daughter of the deacon. Into the community bursts the irresistible new singing master, Arthur Alfred Felton, a Dartmouth graduate who is studying law. Felton's black curls and winning ways impress both young women. Elisha, Mary, Hod, and Cynthia attend the country singing-school at the Congregational Church: "The two rows of windows were blazing with the warm light that was laying itself out in rosy tints on the snowy earth of the village green." Cynthia is rumored to be in love with Felton, and "a girl's first love was likely to burn long, like smoldering fire in spring turf." When the young people emerge, a wild storm is raging. The men are reluctant to set out, but Cynthia says: "Let us drive on. We girls are Vermonters." They and their horses almost perish in the deep snow; Hod risks his life to save Felton, who overturns his carriage on the frozen pond. Elisha owns a fine house that once belonged to Senator Bosworth. The hired man, Peleg Rumney, who believes the house to be haunted, and a housekeeper named Polly Cark assist Elisha on his farm. It is soon apparent that Felton has designs not only on Cynthia, but also on Elisha's house, and begins spreading rumors about her birth. Elisha travels with his lawyer to Nashua, New Hampshire, where they learn that Cynthia is Senator Bosworth's daughter; everyone in the village believes that Elisha acted in collusion with Bosworth's brother, who had illegally inherited the house: now the Littlewoods want Elisha's property. Elisha helps Hod to kill wolves that are attacking the local sheep; Hod saves Elisha's life. While Elisha is recovering for two months, nursed by Mary, they learn that Hod's mother raised Elisha from infancy. War is declared and Felton buys himself a colonelcy; the men elect Hod captain of Company C of _____ Regiment of Vermont Volunteers. Great excitement fills the villagers: "These men of the fields are phlegmatic until a great excitement seizes on them. Then they are wilder, more irresistible, than any other people, as runaway oxen are more destructive when they get started than runaway horses." Elisha, who by this time has been ejected from his house by Deacon Littlewood, senses that Mrs. Parkridge and Mrs. Cark know something about his parentage. Cynthia confides in Mary that she still loves Hod, wants to break off with Felton, and is not Bosworth's daughter. Just as she is about to reveal the truth about her mother and Elisha's, Felton reappears, announcing that Hod has been cashiered for drunkenness. Pulling a gun, Felton is restrained by Elisha; Mrs. Cark sets fire to the house ("a burning farmhouse is helpless"), but fortunately the brick wing is saved. With Mary's teaching wages to pay for the trip, Elisha hurries to New York to find Hod; there he learns that Hod lost an arm in battle and was breveted major for bravery. Among the concluding disclosures: Cynthia is Mrs. Cark's daughter; Elisha is Bosworth's son; Felton forged the deed and goes to prison. Both couples marry. Elisha is elected representative to Montpelier in Felton's place and eventually lieutenant governor. Hod becomes a brigadier general and then a representative in Washington. Elisha and Mary are happy at Bosworth House, reflecting the season: "What a soft frame of mind Nature seems to fall into in a Vermont Indian summer of the late autumn!"

Mary Hays

The invisible entity in *Learning to Drive* (2003) is "the Porter," standing guard at the door of thought in the Christian Science religion. Charlotte McGuffey, the enormously appealing heroine, was raised as a Christian Scientist. Living in Syracuse in 1952 and married to Melvin, with two little boys, Baird and Hoskins (the latter is not developing "normally"), she cannot sleep and feels miserable in her marriage. The day before her husband leaves on a trip to Vermont, she tells him she wants a separation. Several days later he is dead, hit by an automobile on a snowy day in St. Johnsbury. Charlotte has two sisters: Kitty Clatter, a Christian Science healer, is married to paranoid Harry and has two young children, Norman and Roberta, a precocious teenager; Rosey is unmarried and an hysterical worrier. After Mel's death, they converge on Charlotte for a family Christmas. The McGuffey family owns a house in Beede (a fictional Waits River), once belonging to Mel's parents, where they have summered every year. Feeling responsible for Mel's death, Charlotte takes her little boys back to the house in Vermont to spend the summer together and to look for any clues to Mel's state of mind before his accident. She hires Paul Bellini from the Nest (a bohemian outpost) to help her around the place and Rita to do the housework. The Porter visits her regularly. Hoskins won't talk and has tantrums. Baird falls ill with a high fever but recovers. Francis Roux, a sculptor from the Nest, comes to call. He has a reputation as a Lothario; Charlotte, grudgingly and suspiciously, finds Francis attractive. Charlotte's troubles escalate, but she also begins to find joy in her blossoming relationships and in the unreliable and sometimes painful human realm, which her Christian Science training had taught her to discount. She starts asking questions about troubling family matters, such as the circumstances of her mother's death. With Francis's help, she learns about diabetes and its symptoms, which she believes she sees in her sister, Kitty. Her new willingness to look at problems leads her to seek help for Hoskins as well, who is diagnosed as autistic by a flamboyant but kindly woman doctor. Charlotte takes this in her stride and forges ahead to seek help for him, thus charting new territory for herself and her children. (The metaphor in the title is gratifyingly applicable to all the problematic situations in this splendid novel.)

Daniel Hecht

In *Skull Session* (1998), Paul Skoglund is thirty-eight, divorced, unemployed, and suffering from Tourette's Syndrome; his son, Mark, eight, also has neurological problems. Paul lives in Norwich with his girlfriend, Lia McLean, who teaches at Dartmouth. The first third of the novel takes place in Vermont as Paul thinks about his childhood, his father who committed suicide, and his experiments with lowering his dose of haloperidol. When his Aunt Vivien Hoffman offers him a job restoring Highwood Lodge, her estate in Westchester County, he accepts; he is aghast when he views the damage that has been wreaked on the house by psychopathic vandals. Meanwhile police officer Mo Ford is investigating a case of missing adolescents that soon meshes with the terrifying incidents at Highwood. Paul learns that his cousin, Royce Hoffman, inherited Highwood when his parents divorced and that Vivien had another child, Erik, who was institutionalized and has escaped. Paul returns to Vermont periodically to see his son in Hartland but spends most of his time in biomedical research trying to figure out what kind of creature is at large. There are many suspects: the identity of the berserk person is unexpected.

William Heffernan

Blood Rose (1991) takes place in the "remote and insular" town of Blake in the Northeast Kingdom. Thirty-two-year-old Paul Devlin, a former New York police officer who left the force after accidentally killing his partner, is the police chief. Widowed, he is the father of Phillipa, seven. Devlin is still considered an outsider by the town. Leslie Adams moves to Blake with her brother, Robbie, eleven, to hide from her estranged and abusive husband, Jack Chambers. A series of brutal murders of attractive young women takes place, each body mutilated in the same way and each corpse left with a pressed red rose. The town is full of suspects. The newspaper editor, Jim McCloud, is a drunk. Louis Ferris, the schoolteacher, may have molested a student years ago. Gunter Kline is an urbane restaurant owner. Pop Duval is a woodsman, whose Vietnam vet Section Eight son, Jubal, lives in a cave up the mountain. Electa Litchfield is a taxidermist. Ray Perot, who is the richest man in town and a sexual predator, has a son, Billy. The narrative is laced with asides from the point of view of the psychotic killer who evidently killed his or her own mother twenty years earlier. In a faux finale, Electa kills Ray, who molested her when she was a girl, and commits suicide, thus leading everyone to assume she is the killer. It is actually someone else.

In *Beulah Hill* (2000), the era is the Great Depression in 1933; the setting is northwestern Vermont, south of Burlington near Lake Champlain, in the "splendor" and "serenity" of the woods in the foothills of the Green Mountains. Above Jerusalem's Landing, on a hill called Beulah Hill by its inhabitants (and "Nigger Hill" by the locals), live the descendants of Negro slaves who came to the state by Underground Railroad or with slave owners who moved their families there. Under Vermont law, an owner did not have to free a slave until he or she was sixteen. The crux of the novel is the murder of a white youth, Royal Firman, on Beulah Hill; the youth's father, Preserved, and most of the racist townsfolk, immediately assume the Negroes on the Hill killed Royal. The constable, twenty-eight-year-old Samuel Barber, is a third-generation "bleached" white (his great-grandmother, Isabel Stewart, was a Negro slave owned by one of the white landowners, Amos Firman), who is deeply conflicted about his own identity. Samuel's father, classified "colored," was the constable before he had a stroke; the deputy sheriff, Frenchy LeMay, an old friend of Samuel's father, takes over the murder case. An Abenaki, Johnny, helps them as a tracker. There are a number of standoffs, racial epithets, and threats before the final confrontation on the Hill. The explanation is dramatic.

Ursula Hegi

In *Salt Dancers* (1995), the traumatized heroine, Julia Ives, dips and swoops into her past, plumbing and revealing forgotten layers. Julia, who lives in Proctor, decides, after more than twenty years, to visit her father, who still lives in Spokane, Washington. She was an abused child: her drunken father beat her, threatened her sexually, and alienated her from her brother, Travis. When she was nine, her mother vanished (pregnant with her Greek lover's child), leaving Julia even more vulnerable to her father's rages and intimidation. When she finally escapes from her father, she moves to Vermont. As she walks near Otter Creek, she describes the "spider pattern of frost on the flat rocks." Skiing one day at a winter carnival in Killington, she meets an Austrian member of the ski patrol named Andreas, with whom she falls in love. She has a good job in Rutland with an architect's firm and, after her divorce from Andreas, buys a rundown farm with an 1820 hip-roofed federal house together with her friends, Claudia and Matt, who are both dentists. She announces to Claudia that she plans to sleep with a lot of men. "Not here in Vermont," responds her friend. At her doctor's office in Rutland, Julia meets Coop when he draws her blood, and she begins an affair with him. When she decides to confront her father, she is forty-one, pregnant, and unmarried. She wants to force an apology from him. When she does challenge him, he denies that he ever drank or touched her. While she is visiting her father, she feels a longing for her bedroom in Vermont, with its sloping ceiling, and the lake where she swims. She discovers her mother's whereabouts in Oregon and visits her. As she is driving there, she thinks of Coop in his cabin in Vermont. Her meeting with her mother is key to developing her plans for the future.

Mark Helprin

"A Vermont Tale" (1976) is an exquisite tale within a tale. The outer tale is of a young boy (the narrator) and his younger sister, Julie, who are sent to Vermont to spend the month of January (perhaps longer) with their grandparents because their parents are fighting in a divorce court. The children travel by the steam-driven train, The Star of the North, to White River Junction, where they are met by their grandparents and taken to their isolated cottage in Addison County. There the children learn to do chores (the boy outside, the girl inside) and to ride on horseback when the weather allows. There is a slow-motion quality about the prose when the weather turns glacial: "We were possessed by the flawless isolation and the numbing cold." The boy recalls that "Later, when I was wounded in war, they shot me full of morphine. The slow bodiless breathing was just like the way time passed in that crystalline January." One night they hear the cries of the Arctic loons returning to their lake. Grandfather tells them the inner tale of the loons, a love story of loss and redemption. The loons are inseparable

and in love. Then they have a misunderstanding and are separated for two years, even though the male tries to find her. Finally, he looks up and sees her coming back, "pointing like an arrow to the lake." "He trembled from expectation and fear. But he knew her flight. He knew the courage she had always had, despite her frailty, in coursing the clouds. And on that last run, as she came closer and closer, she became an emblem of herself. He sped to the middle of the lake with all the energy he had unwittingly saved. The blood was rushing through him as if he had been flying for a day, and she swooped over his head, turned in the air like an eagle, and landed by him in a crest of white water." The children have been inside for a long time. "It snowed so hard that the air was like tightly loomed cloth." They are spellbound by the story. Julie falls into a deep sleep; the boy puts on his gear and goes outside to the lake to look at the loons. His grandmother finds him there. When he cries, she takes him in her arms. Her eyes are "as cold as ice."

George V. Higgins

The backdrop to *Victories* (1990) is the Vietnam War. It is 1968: Eugene McCarthy is running against Lyndon B. Johnson. Robert Wainwright, Jr., is a third-generation Vermonter: his family has lived in Canterbury near Charlotte since before the Civil War. Wainwright, who started his career as a banker, has served in the U.S. Congress from Vermont's Sixth District for almost thirty years. Andrew Prior, Wainwright's chief of staff, describes his boss's habits: he leaves the office at six in the evening, cooks his own dinner, makes his own breakfast, and is back in the office by six in the morning. He does not travel around the country or make long weekend trips home but once a session. He hates to spend money. He is annoyed with outsiders coming into the state with their dollars, thinking they can run things. Henry Briggs, a former Big-League pitcher turned game warden, is from Occident ("a weekending place with city folks who like to ski and pose as squires" on Route 7, north of Vergennnes). Ed Cobb, the speaker of the Vermont House, persuades Henry to run as a

Democrat for Wainwright's seat. Henry may have been a womanizer in his ball-playing days, but he is honest, straightforward, and kind. His wife, Shirley, is overweight and querulous; his wastrel son, Ted, spends Henry's money on booze and drugs; only his daughter, Sally, a student at Marlboro College, seems sane and calm. Cobb interests Caroline Cooke, a wealthy, no-nonsense Democrat from New York, and a hired gun, Tom Calley, in Henry's candidacy. Whipple, the owner of the IGA store, has known Henry all his life. He doesn't like Wainwright—thinks there's "something wrong"—but votes for him because "the Wainwrights asked us to." Andy concocts a way to blacken Henry's name, but when he proposes this ploy to Wainwright, saying it could "mean his career," the latter rejects it: "I have no career. My name is Wainwright. Robert Wainwright. 'S what it's always been. I don't, and I never have, thought about much else. I am who I am. Do what I do. And I've told you before, and I'll tell you again. I just will not do that." Tony French, a local boy once involved in manslaughter, is killed in Vietnam and being returned with four buddies as military escort. Andy seizes upon this event as a way to dramatize Wainwright's position in the community. Russ Wixton, a newspaper reporter for the *Valley News* in Burlington, is an old friend of Henry's and enemy of Wainwright's (whose bank foreclosed on all the farmers' mortgages and put the land into timber). When he hears of Henry's candidacy and the French funeral, he hires two cub reporters to dig up the unpleasant, suppressed facts. The result of the 1968 election is a surprise. Henry sums up, "So who knows what victories really are, then. What they mean, if they mean anything? The only thing that matters is that we were all there when it happened, and now when we look back at it, it seems like it was probably worth the try."

Grace Livingston Hill

The Prodigal Girl (1929) of the title is Betty Thornton, who is a disrespectful and wild young woman. Her father, Chester, decides to move the family to a farm and a simpler life in Briardale. To escape what she considers a boring life in Vermont, Betty elopes with rich Dudley Weston. After almost dying in an automobile accident, Betty, like the Prodigal Son upon whose character she is based, returns home. She also finds love with a handsome stranger whom she meets in a snowstorm.

Gerald A. Hinckley

The Great Green Mountain Horn Hunt (1988) looks at what happens when "traditional Vermont collides with the modern world." Flat Henderson, who lives in Dunbar near Sudbury and Castleton, reads in the local paper that the original carved horn cup with the state seal (motto: "Freedom & Unity") is missing along with other state symbols. Since the secretary of state is in charge of such artifacts, Flat decides to run for the office himself, which means challenging the incumbent, Upton Yourse. Flat's slogan is that "Vermont is a shrine in the minds of people all over the world" and should therefore revere its symbols. First, Flat talks to Veronica Illness, an expert in gourds, who is the source for the newspaper story about the horn cup; next, Flat hires a private eye named Nero Leptic (also known as Mona Newman, girl gumshoe, when he dresses in drag) to find the cup. Flat addresses the local Rotary Club, stressing his theme that native Vermonters are disappearing, newcomers are trying to change everything, and state symbols are important to the identity of Vermont. Absentee landlords, mercantile outlets for foreign manufacturers, and ski trails and condominiums characterize his "Vanishing Vermont." Nero's first move is to visit Johnny Itchyfoot, the last of the Neshobe, who has claimed Neshobe Island as tribal land. Johnny communicates in shaman-speak, but Nero interprets his instructions: "Look for the cup in Montreal" and "Follow the green." While Flat, Nero, and Moonbeam, Flat's hippie girlfriend, are driving to Montreal, Upton, anxious about his seat as secretary of state, consults Veronica, who, in Upton's mind, is the instigator of his problems. She explains that Vermonters are having a hard time deciding who they are: "They want to keep their scenery and their farms, but they are caught up in a larger scheme that's turning them [the farms] into ski lifts and power lines." She recommends that Upton visit a medium, Philura Colorme Brown, at the Church of the Amber Aura, the local commune. He has to join the commune and follow the members' rules before Philura will attempt a seance to locate the cup. Upton organizes a state event for the dramatic finish of the campaign; he is a changed man after his sessions at the Amber Aura. Flat speaks with passion about the importance of new symbols and a new motto, but the crowd is tiring of his rhetoric.

Tami Hoag

Mismatch (1989) teams Bronwyn Prescott Pierson, jet setter, model, liberal, and heiress to the Pierson Chewing Gum fortune, with good-looking Wade Grayson, a conservative Indiana politician, in her ramshackle Victorian house in the backwoods of Vermont. She has just left a groom at the altar. She and Wade hate each other on sight. The question is whether they can bridge their differences.

Douglas Hobbie

In *This Time Last Year* (1997), Henry Ash, a professor at the New School for Social Research in Manhattan, comes to Speedwell in southern Vermont (Brattleboro is a forty-minute drive) to spend the summer alone in a house owned by his widowed sister-in-law, Mary. His beloved daughter died several years ago, and, grief-stricken, he is not getting along with his second wife, Elizabeth (not the mother of his daughter). Elizabeth, thinking a short separation a good idea, goes on a tour of England. Henry's son, David, is also in Europe. Mary and her two children, Kelly and Adam, have not used the house since Mary's second husband, Fitz (her children's stepfather) dropped dead the previous summer. Henry meets the next-door neighbor, Helen, a summer resident who has not heard of Fitz's death. A cancer survivor, she seems inconsolable at the news. Henry is determined not to get involved in any social life while he tries to begin a book on "those three misfits," Whitman,

Dickinson, and Melville, which he plans to call *The Loners*. He is unable to work. He is compelled to call his former wife, Sally, to talk about their daughter. He is attracted to Helen, the temptress next door. And he is fascinated with Fitz—his house; his garden; his stone wall; his mistress. Is that what Helen was? Inevitably, he is drawn to Fitz's study and to Fitz's computer, which has a folder called "Vermont." In this journal Henry finds that Fitz was gay, his marriage to Mary was an accommodation, and he was obsessed with Helen. Henry throws away his own manuscript and begins an essay on Vermont, incorporating Fitz's journal as part of his narrative. Kelly and Adam appear unannounced with their friend, Jane, to stay for a few days. They and Helen seem close and sympathetic; Henry feels alienated and jealous. The last night of Helen's summer stay, she is invited for supper at Henry's. He shops neurotically. This may be the night they sleep together. When she doesn't appear, he hikes off to look for her, suddenly afraid she has killed herself. The final narration by one of the younger people gives the tender and fitting ending. (The title is from Emily Dickinson: "'Twas just this time, last year, I died.")

Emma Holly

In the novella, *The Night Owl* (2005), Mariann O'Faolain, late thirties, divorced, lives in a nineteenth century clapboard farmhouse inherited from her grandparents, located in Maple Notch on the "southern tail of the Green Mountain spine." She also took over their bakery, which is in a building attached to the Night Owl Inn, owned by newcomers Bastien and Emile Luce. The Luces are *upyr* (immortal vampires, part-wolf, and blood drinkers). Mariann becomes involved sexually with Bastien and competitively with her former bakery partner, Arabella Armand, who is passing off as her own the O'Faolains' family recipes on a television show. Arabella runs over Mariann, who is on her bicycle, and leaves her for dead. An unusual transformation follows.

Ann Hood

In *Three-Legged Horse* (1989), classically trained violinist Abby Nash plays in a band, Three-Legged Horse, with Sean and Doug. Because her husband, failed artist Zach Plummer, is rarely around, she takes her twelve-year-old daughter, Hannah, with her on their gigs. Home for Abby and Hannah is Vermont (somewhere on Route 7 between Mount Snow and Bennington), to which they retreat when they are not on the road. There are interludes when Hannah is in New York with her grandmother, a soap-opera actress, and Abby, abandoned by the band, plays with an orchestra in the Berkshires. Back in Vermont, Abby feels new confidence in her life. When Zach turns up again with more baseless promises of a life together, will she be able to let him go?

Lester Eugene Hood

You Must Love the Enemy (1974) salutes the pioneer spirit of George Morgan and his pregnant wife, Fannie, who move to Bradford in central Vermont in 1790, bringing animals, provisions, seeds, and small bushes to plant for apple orchards. Neighbors Jim and Florence Hardy take them in while they and other neighbors help build their house, culminating in a raising bee with potluck supper. The years pass. The Morgans have worked hard: "A workman is known by his chips." The bushes have become a flourishing orchard. Frank Olin Morgan is now twenty-one and engaged to the Jamesons' daughter. Fannie, forty-four, is expecting another baby. Frank is clawed and crushed to death by a bear the day Fannie gives birth to Lewis Frederick Morgan. Lewis grows up to run the farm, marry Mary Owen from Concord, New Hampshire, and have a son, David Benjamin Morgan. Community members have been conducting religious meetings until about 1832, when Dr. Baker, a physician and minister, moves there. A schoolhouse is built; Nellie Saunders, a schoolteacher, is imported. Logging is an important industry; the lumberjacks are rough and tough: "To hell with the man—save the cant hook." Railroads are built and a clothing store opens. When the Civil War starts, David, trained as a surgeon, joins the Fourth Vermont Regiment. He experiences the horrors of war and is wounded gravely in the arm. Others have noticed his exact resemblance to a Confederate patient, Captain William Randolph, who dies in captivity. Since David cannot operate, he is sent on a mission to impersonate Randolph and pick up valuable information. During the course of this risky undertaking, he falls in love with Randolph's widow, Elizabeth, who sees through his disguise but does not give him away. They are married after the war.

William Dean Howells

At the start of *The Rise of Silas Lapham* (1885), Bartley Hubbard (the protagonist in *A Modern Instance*) interviews Silas Lapham for his newspaper's "Solid Men of Boston" series, eliciting details of Silas's birth and early life. Silas was born on a farm in Vermont, "pretty well up under the Canada line." His father and mother worked hard—there were six boys—and, although the father discovered the mineral-paint mine, he did not exploit it before his death. It is Silas, while working in Lumbertown, who has the paint analyzed and, finding all the best ingredients, soon puts "Lapham's Mineral Paint" advertising on every barn and rock surface. In gratitude for Silas's success, the town names itself after him. This paint business makes Silas a millionaire many times over, and soon he is building an ostentatious house for his wife, Persis, and daughters, Penelope and Irene, on Beacon Hill. Only one sour note is struck: he had a business partner, William K. Rogers, who put some money into the business at a crucial time; later, Silas forced him out of the business. Into their lives comes Boston mandarin Tom Corey, who is attracted to the entrepreneurial side of Silas's business and asks to be taken on as international representative. Perhaps he is also attracted to Irene, the younger daughter. Everyone assumes so, and, after Tom has become established as a contributing member of Lapham's firm, the Coreys invite the Laphams to dinner. The dinner is not a success: Silas, who is not accustomed to wine with dinner, drinks—and talks—too much.

The Coreys are quite snobbish, especially Tom's mother. The Laphams, on the other hand, are good, decent people. Silas has depths even his wife hasn't plumbed: for years he has been supporting the mother and daughter of John Millon, a man with whom he fought in the Civil War and who gave his life for Silas's. The embarrassment of the Corey dinner is surpassed by a more serious problem: Tom, whom everyone thinks has been courting Irene, tells the older sister, Penelope, that he loves and wants to marry her. She loves him but, out of solidarity with Irene, refuses him. Rogers returns and asks Silas to lend him some money, giving him stock as security. Guilty over his past behavior, Silas agrees. When Silas loses all his money, Rogers offers him a way out that Silas feels is dishonorable—again showing his fine character. Irene departs for the town of Lapham, leaving the field clear for Penelope, who finally accepts Tom. Silas returns to where he began—"the hills at Lapham."

The site for *The Landlord at Lion's Head* (1897) is a plateau in northern Vermont whose prospect is the mountain called *le lion couchant* by French pioneers and Camel's Hump by their Yankee successors. The novel presents two men who are diametrically opposed: Jere Westover, a painter, is effete, dispassionate, judgmental, and conventional; Thomas Jefferson ("Jeff") Durgin, son of a farmer, is handsome, satirical, good-natured, and seductive. The farmhouse where Westover rents a room is run by farmer James Monroe Durgin and his wife, whose father, Mason, kept the tavern to the west of the mountain and almost joined the raid on St. Albans. Many of the Durgin children died of tuberculosis; two escaped by going out West; her other son, Andrew Jackson Durgin, has contracted the disease. From Westover's room, as the afternoon deepened, "The Lion's Head stood out against the intense clearness of the west, which began to be flushed with exquisite suggestions of violet and crimson." In the wooden house at the end of the road live a widower, Mr. Whitwell, his two children, Cynthia and Franky, and Jombateeste, a "Canuck" hired man. Whitwell is clearing his land for timber: "The ground was paved with broad,

clean chips." After her husband dies and she can no longer farm, Mrs. Durgin decides to take in boarders. Five years later, Westover returns after a sojourn in Europe. He looks out at Lion's Head in the moonlight: "It slumbered as if with the sleep of centuries, austere, august." Cynthia and Franky are now working at the hotel; their father takes the lady guests for nature tramps. (There is a lovely picture here of the hotel waitresses resting outside in a shady angle of the hotel while one reads aloud from a novel.) At a picnic for the guests in Whitwell's Clearing, Jeff is treated like a servant by one of the guests. Mrs. Durgin evicts from her room the woman who makes the social blunder. Jeff, a "young Hercules" at nineteen, finishes Lovewell Academy and goes to Harvard, where he is considered a "jay." Westover finds Jeff "quite at odds with his environment" but doesn't help him out. Jeff gets off on the wrong foot and is suspended. When Westover goes to Lion's Head the following summer, Jeff is away, having worked his way to London. When Jeff returns, he finds two guests at the hotel, Mrs. Medora Vostrand, and her daughter, Genevieve, who were on the same boat returning from Europe (he in second class; they in first). They find him gentlemanly, even though he is a hotelkeeper. The Vostrands winter in Boston and Jeff, smitten with Genevieve, proposes; she turns him down. In the two years until Jeff's graduation, the hotel grows "like a living thing." Jackson is helping his mother run the hotel. They do not consult Jeff because they expect him to graduate from Harvard and become a lawyer; his ambition, however, is to be landlord at Lion's Head. When he tells his mother the way hotels are run in Europe, she calls him "conceited and unpatriotic." Cynthia and Jeff make a natural couple, having grown up together, and he asks her to marry him. Cynthia's father is unresponsive to her news: "The New England training is not such as to fit people for the expression of strong emotion." Mrs. Durgin is disappointed, wanting him to marry a Boston girl; he tries to explain to her that Boston girls marry their own kind. Jeff wants to leave Harvard, but Cynthia persuades him to finish his last year. Excluded and neglected for three years at Harvard, Jeff is now indifferent to social success. The hostess at a sumptuous tea party introduces him to Bessie Lynde, an unconventional and irreverent flirt. Bessie's brother, Alan, is annoyed at her going about with "a jay and a cad." Alan is a drunk and, at a party, Jeff encourages his drinking, sees him home, and is observed alone with Bessie at three in the morning. Westover, sanctimonious, is disgusted by Jeff's behavior and considers him "malevolent." Westover goes to Lion's Head to paint during the winter for the first time: "The burnished brown of the hardwood trees, the dull carbon shadows of the evergreens, seem to wither to one black as the red strengthened in the sky." Cynthia is pure and fine, mothering the household with her little services. She senses that she and Mrs. Durgin should not go to Class Day at Harvard: "It would be better for us to leave that part of his life alone." Bessie is seriously interested in Jeff, even though people in her set do not flirt with people outside of it, especially with "a man like that, so wholly alien in origin, in tradition." Jeff's flirtation with Bessie comes to a head: he kisses her but doesn't love her. He breaks off their relationship and hastens to Lion's Head to tell Cynthia what has taken place. Cynthia breaks their engagement. Mrs. Durgin is stricken with paralysis and dies; Jeff covers the hotel to the maximum with insurance policies and takes off for Europe. When the hotel burns to the ground, Whitwell fears the law will think Jeff paid him to do it. He consults with Westover, who calls Jeff a "blackguard;" his belief is that people cannot change. Jeff meets Genevieve again in Florence; her husband is dead and she and Jeff still love each other. He, his new wife, and mother-in-law return to Vermont to rebuild Lion's Head as a European inn. The Whitwells move to Boston where Cynthia accepts Westover's marriage proposal.

Barbara Howes

"The Road Commissioner" (1983) is a study of Marion Alston, who has been staying near Bennington for the summer with her husband, John, two children, and Pancho, their beloved black cat. She sees Anson Wilcox, the road commissioner, and his motorcycle-riding brother, Jo, while they work on the road below Marion's house. She admires Anson Wilcox's type ("so independent and solid...no nonsense, no affectation") and develops an infatuation with him. When she sees him in the village she feels awkward. The Alstons suffer a brief crisis when their cat, Pancho, disappears for three days. Fortunately he returns unharmed. Shortly before the Alstons leave, Marion has a conversation with Anson. She explains to him that "Already we feel at home. I've always heard that one is looked on as a foreigner in New England if one wasn't born and bred here, but honestly we haven't run into that attitude at all. I almost feel I have lived here all my life...One must put down roots quickly." She hopes she hasn't expressed too complicated a thought. She feels he knows what he wants from life and is willing to work for it. She is certain he isn't married; he would surely look for someone more sophisticated than one of the farm girls. He hears she is looking for a keeper for Pancho over the winter and offers his mother — "She's crazy about cats." At the last possible moment, Marion takes Pancho over to Mrs. Wilcox. She is a large and sensible woman, "kind and capable," and Marion feels strongly that she is leaving behind "a sense of participation in simple yet timeless country values." When the family returns in May, Marion goes to retrieve her cat. She learns from Mrs. Wilcox that her son, Jo, has taken off and that Anson's wife is pregnant. Then Mrs. Wilcox gives her the wrong cat. Marion lurches out of the house and into her car: "Was everything she had thought about them false? The New England mind, so neatly charted by her last summer, now frightened her with its convolutions, its duplicity. Some edifice of rectitude had crashed to the ground. Eyes blurring for her lost innocence, cheeks flushed with a sensation she was loath to examine, she bumped on over the dirt road, of whose twistings and turnings she was now almost entirely oblivious."

David Huddle

The first four stories discussed are from *The High Spirits* (1989). Braxton in **"The Gorge"** is a musician and music teacher who lives in Burlington with his wife and twelve-year-old daughter. His trumpet student, Monica, tells him she has a lesbian lover. He finds that she is both a wonderful musician and an unhappy young woman. She talks often of suicide; he hopes that she will respond positively to his teaching. He realizes that he has "shut down a part of himself and is capable of only minor achievement," but Monica has "great forces within her." Is he jealous of her talent? Is she trying to seduce him? One afternoon, she persuades him to cancel his office hours to go to Pennington Gorge with her. She frightens him by driving too fast and, once there, walking too close to the steep edge. He is extremely uneasy with her. That night, he brings her home for supper with his wife and daughter; he is cooking because his wife works late. He behaves foolishly, showing off at supper, and drives Monica away by his behavior. He comes to the horrifying conclusion that Monica's death would keep him and his wife safe. **"In the Mean Mud Season"** is a sympathetic portrayal of a middle-aged English professor's relationship with his eighth-grade daughter, Victoria. He and his wife moved to Vermont from Virginia sixteen years earlier; he insists that he is still nostalgic for its weather and its manners. It is March ("The stars glisten meanly") and the northern season, he believes, is helping him to understand his daughter's personality. "Abrasion was the Yankee way." Victoria spends all her time speaking on the telephone with someone named Prescott Rochester. In a northern climate, the father says to himself, a daughter will make a northern choice—such as picking the one boy her father can't stand. The snow falls another foot. He determines to leave Vermont to teach somewhere in the South. He trudges out to shovel snow and finds Prescott has come over to help, bringing his own shovel. "He had the face of an altar boy." The father grumpily takes a nap. Later, the sun comes out and Victoria calls him upstairs to his studio. Squeezed together, they peer out of the little

alcove. It is warmer outside: "With no leaves on the trees now, we could see the hillside sweep of the city of Burlington down to the waterfront and Lake Champlain and the Adirondack Mountains on the New York side. The sun was huge and red-gold. The lake was molten. The sky was so clear that I saw a gull flying high over Plattsburgh, thirty miles to the northwest." The narrator understands that this is where his daughter comes from, that what they are seeing is hers. "Victoria was grinning as if the city below us were a boy she was flirting with at recess." They are happy there together, "bumping shoulders." In **"The Crossing,"** the narrator travels to Virginia to pick up his recently widowed mother to bring her back to his home and family in Burlington. They are companionable on the ride. He mentions his wife, Marie, and daughters, Victoria and Sally. It is a long trip and his mother becomes exhausted, her brow tight with headache. She wonders if she should have come. They just make the last ferry from Essex across Lake Champlain to Charlotte. She finally smiles at her son. "'I wonder if I'm entitled to all this.' The gesture she made with her hand was up ahead, where the water took the reflection of the Vermont shore and held it like a treasure. 'You're entitled,' I heard myself saying. I was surprised it was mine to give. 'It's all yours,' I told her." **"The Beautiful Gesture"** is also about an English professor in Burlington, Frank Berry, married to Marie, with two sons, Steve, fourteen, and Charles, eight. Frank, invited by a former student, Susan Larrick, to give a paper at Portland State where she is now teaching, thinks back sixteen years to the days when he and Scott Puckett were the only two writing Masters of Fine Arts on the staff. They often played squash and talked about their students, Susan Larrick and Candace Winters. In recalling these days of the end of the Vietnam War and the resignation of Nixon, Frank gives the impression that it was acceptable to flirt with women students. He has let Susan know how talented she is, which makes her spend even more time in his office. Susan and Candace invite Frank and Scott to a Halloween Party in their dorm; it was perhaps not judicious to accept. Candace and Scott start an affair and are soon seen together frequently in public. When Susan is in need and calls Frank, he goes to her apartment. There he is shocked to realize from her books and artifacts the influence he has had on her life. He has the painful insight that he assigned her the wrong kinds of poems to read and wishes he had the experience to do over. They spend a chaste and uncomfortable night on her bed. Today, Susan is married and the mother of a son, Michael. Frank has prepared his talk for the conference and imagines giving it to an audience in which she and her son are present.

The next two stories are from *Intimates* (1993). "**The Hearing**" is a riveting, first-person account of the testimony Frank Riggins plans to give in his own defense before Dean Poulin's "informal" hearing. Riggins, professor of English, teaches at a Burlington campus (his view is of Lake Champlain and the Adirondacks). He has been teaching for forty years; he has tenure; he has nothing to worry about. After all, he only spent a couple of hours alone in the company of his student, Honorée Evans. He considers himself unusually sensitive to issues of student-faculty relationships and to maintaining their "integrity." It is not that he is unaware of the charms, youth, and beauty of his students. He was particularly struck by the "radiant presence" of Jennifer Talley in his Modern Short Fiction classroom, but, when he ran into her on campus later, she did not seem to recognize him. The business with Honorée begins during a conference in his office. When she reveals that she is unhappy, he naturally responds with a comforting hug. She writes him a thank-you letter. She follows up that gesture by coming to his office over the weekend with a bottle of wine. He has settled himself down with some reading and music. When she enters his office, he closes the door (as he always does when he is listening to music). Before Riggins knows what is happening, Honorée is undressing; soon she is lying across his desk, naked. He does not say, "Stop." When the custodian hears noises and unlocks the door, they are flagrante delicto. In his monotone and chilling voice, Riggins confides that he feels no remorse;

rather, he felt, during that time with Honorée, "*immortal*." "**Henry Lagoon**" is told in the pitch-perfect voice of a fourteen-year-old boy, Henry Larue, whose grandfather came from Québec City to work in the granite quarry. In the sixth grade, the other children had started calling Henry "Lagoon," and, although he didn't know what it meant, he rather liked the sound. He finds himself spending time with Lisa Yancey, another freshman, who has just had braces removed from her teeth and is much in demand. She seems to be his girlfriend. They have quite daring (though chaste) adventures together, like hitchhiking to Montpelier to look into the legalities of changing his name. She invites him to her house to "make a video." They mug for the camera, roughhouse, and exchange a kiss before Lisa's father sends them downstairs. Mr. Yancey calls him "Henry Larue." When Henry leaves Lisa's house, after another more considered kiss, he is a different person. He knows he is going to leave Barre when he graduates; he doesn't know exactly what his future holds, but he has lots of time to decide.

Not: A Trio (2000) consists of two fluid, stylish stories and a novella, set in Bennington, about three interrelated characters: Danny Marlowe, Ben McClelland, and Claire McClelland. In "**The Village**," Danny is a small-business computer person with a bad reputation in the village regarding women. He goes to the office of Claire, "the best shrink in southern Vermont," once a week for what is ostensibly a therapy session but is, in fact, a sexual encounter on the rug of her office floor. Though she craves sex with him, she doesn't really like him and fears having the village know about their relationship. In "**Wherever I am Not**," Ben, a political science professor at Bennington turned administrator, is Claire's second husband; he too has been married before. He finds himself uttering little prayers to himself; he believes "some kind of pattern-maker is or was 'out there,' *anywhere I am not*." He is obsessing about where he went wrong with Julie, his first wife, and succumbs to a compulsion to telephone her while Claire is sleeping. Although he hasn't spoken to her in over a year, Julie knows all about him from small-town gossip around

Bennington. On his way to Robert Hargreaves's grocery store, he meets Danny, who appears to recognize him. He wonders what Robert has been telling Danny about him in the market. At that instant Margaret Allen, who really should not be driving, crashes her car up over the curb and kills Ben. In **"Not,"** Claire owns the deed to land once owned by her grandfather in Lincoln. She decides to leave town, her clients, and her lover, and escape to Lincoln. She remembers a smell like "a plowed field on a rainy night…It is to that fragrance I mean to return." She has saved medication given to her when Ben died; she proposes to kill herself. She believes that she has never been able to help any of her patients or herself. When the moment comes, she is unable to achieve her goal; instead, she looks forward to a "life sentence."

La Tour Dreams of the Wolf Girl (2002) takes place both in contemporary Burlington, where Suzanne, thirty-eight, and Jack Nelson live, and in Suzanne's imagination in seventeenth-century Lunéville, France, where the artist, Georges de La Tour, resides. Suzanne is a professor of art history at the University of Vermont; Jack is a public relations whiz-kid "townie." Perhaps because of his skill at "spin," he is unable to tell the truth to himself, to his wife, or to his lover, Elly, who teaches studio art also at UVM. Suzanne grew up in the sticks of Virginia and sat every day on the school bus next to a mute boy, Elijah, who both attracted her sympathy and revolted her. She often thinks with shame of the way she treated him. Jack was raised in a privileged household, went to Choate, and took a job as counselor at a camp in Vermont where he discovered that a little girl, Colleen, who seemed to be acting out, actually had a tumor on her brain. Jack is a loud mouth (his awful parents whispered at meals) and Suzanne just wants to be left alone to do her research on Georges de La Tour. The scenes switch rapidly from Suzanne and Jack, to Suzanne, to Jack and Elly, to La Tour, and back again. La Tour is a gross and unpleasant old man who invites fifteen-year-old Vivienne Lavalette, the daughter of the village shoemaker, to sit for him. She assumes that he wants to sleep with her,

but he only wants to look at her. Once she has disrobed, he discovers that she has a thick, coarse patch of hair on her shoulder and back. Her parents have kept this secret from her. Elly joins Halvorsen's String Quartet, named for the downtown restaurant where Mac Delgado, the first violin, is a waiter. Suzanne is temporary head of the Art Department; Elly's performance review is up to Suzanne. Suzanne knows that UVM is Elly's platform to a better university; Suzanne suspects that Elly is sleeping with Jack. As Vivienne sits in La Tour's studio, the old master asks her questions about her life. She spins tales out of her head to entertain him. One day, after looking at his painting and seeing the hair on her back, she leaves his studio in a fury. She feels that La Tour has turned her into a liar. She informs her parents that the "thatch" on her back is beginning to fall out. Several years later, she decides she wants the painting. She goes to the studio, but La Tour has already sold it; he is blind and dying. He sends for her, wanting to see her again. "You've seen me already, old man!" she thinks. Jack and Suzanne divorce, and Jack and Elly move to California. While Elly is out, Jack calls Suzanne in the middle of the night. La Tour wants Vivienne, who hates his meddling in her life. Suzanne develops a friendship with Mac Delgado in which they talk endlessly. Vivienne returns to La Tour's studio where he is dying and answers his questions about her life. She tells him that her father and mother are dead. The two stories—contemporary and time past—merge.

Richard E. Hughes

In *Unholy Communion* (1982), Pineville north of Montpelier is the site of an elaborate new ski resort called Jordan's Crossing after its designer and owner, Walter Jordan, who has ambitious expansionist plans. It is soon clear to observers ("New York people bored with Bromley") that Jordan's theme is religious: the ski runs have names like "Walls of Jericho" and "Jacob's Ladder" and the big lodge has many aspects of a cathedral. The resort has brought prosperity to Pineville. One of the skiers at Jordan's Crossing, Joe Connors, runs a guest lodge in Pineville and is trying to recover from the death of his wife, Greta. He teaches classics at St. Benedict's, a local college, and was once in training for the priesthood. When a young ski instructor turns up dead on the lift, the local police chief, Sam McChesney, is almost certain that Joe is the murderer. Glimpses are given of the murderer carrying out his foul deeds in a liturgical manner. A second murder, this time of the ski-slope siren, Marilyn Schaeffer, causes Sam to close the place down. Joe has a wild snowmobile confrontation with the killer on the stormy mountain. Joe survives to win the hand of Karen, a photojournalist staying at his guesthouse.

Maria Hummel

In *Wilderness Run* (2002), wealthy railroad-magnate Daniel Lindsey and his wife, Faustina Gale Lindsey, have a daughter, Isabel ("Bel"); Daniel's brother, co-owner George, and his wife, Pattie, have several children, one of whom is Isabel's cousin and great friend, Laurence, five years older than she. In 1847, the year of Isabel's birth, the railroad connects with Allenton, a city on Lake Champlain where the Lindseys have lived for generations. In 1859, Laurence and Bel help a runaway slave named Nathan (the Underground Railroad password: "I am the friend of a friend"). Bel's father discovers the slave's hiding place and orders the hired man, Johnny Mulcane, to shoot him in the leg and return him to his Georgia master. Laurence joins the Second Vermont Regiment; his baptism by fire is the Battle of Bull Run, along with his handsome, natural-leader friend, John Addison. Other horrifying battles follow. One of his friends, Loomis, talks about going out West after the war. "No more Vermont winters," he says. "No more waiting for a brief four months of summer, when everything had to be sown and reaped in rapid succession." The scenes switch back and forth between the war and Allenton. Bel stays at home in her elegant surroundings, with her silly twin cousins, Anne and Lucy, dances, and lessons. Her mother hires a Canadian named Louis Pacquette to tutor her in French; Bel and Louis fall in love but do not speak of their love before he leaves for

the army. Laurence is badly wounded and taken to the hospital in Washington and, afterward, to the Convalescent Camp, where the conditions are abysmal. For a brief period he is sent to a hospital in Brattleboro before reporting back to the front. He is in love with his cousin, Bel. He later meets Louis Pacquette on a battlefield when John Addison, now a sergeant, is forced to have two deserters shot. Observing the execution, Louis's face is "as distant and expressionless as a winter pasture." Laurence barely survives the inferno of the Battle of the Wilderness, saved by Nathan, the former slave now contraband, and by Louis, although Laurence has lost a leg, a hand, and an eye. Bel and her Aunt Pattie come to Washington to nurse him, but gangrene sets in and he dies. Louis, also wounded, is serving as a nurse in the hospital; he and Bel have a chance to reveal their love. Laurence's father pays the army to keep Louis in the hospital to save his life. Written in eloquent, poetic prose, this novel effortlessly evokes the period and the people. Despite their money and advantages, the Lindseys are not able to evade the sorrows and disappointments that befall less fortunate people. (As children, one of Bel and Laurence's favorite places was a creek Laurence named "Wilderness Run.")

Zephine Humphrey

In *The Homestead* (1919), the Marshalls have lived in the big old house in Marshall Hollow ever since John Marshall built it as a young man and died in it at age ninety-three. The family was governed by one tradition—the Marshall tradition. John's son, Thomas, married an unsuitable girl who died. The next child, Prudence, married Barnaby Rogers, a sea captain. Their son, Marshall Rogers, was killed falling from the roof. His sister, Hester, married her third cousin, Henry Marshall, from Dakota, who made great improvements on the farm. Their daughter, Barbara, is twenty when the story begins, and Reuben, her brother, is eighteen. William Sloan, thirty-two, is a neighboring farmer who has been Barbara's best friend all her life. He lives with his spiteful mother, Martha, and is in love with Barbara but unable to tell her.

When Hester dies suddenly, Barbara is thrust into the role of head of the household. She, her father, and her brother are brought closer together in the "brave intimacy of that pensive winter," the first since Hester's death. Barbara's spirit feels "fettered" by her many new responsibilities. She shares the "fatalistic passivity" of other Vermont women and believes the homestead claims her; she feels "smothered and oppressed." Dick Marshall, one of her Dakota cousins, comes East to ask her to marry him, but she rejects him almost rudely, much to her father's dismay. He wants to leave her, his older child, the homestead when he dies; Reuben marries Jenny Slocum and becomes master of her farm. When the traveling lecturer, Daniel Pritchard, blond and handsome, comes to town to talk about Italy, it is as though a fresh wind has blown into the village. He, too, was born on a Vermont farm but managed to get away. He and Barbara are greatly drawn to each other, even though she is torn between "roots and wings." William watches the friendship develop and believes unselfishly that Daniel provides the vehicle for Barbara to escape her ancestral acres; at the same time his mother's spirits and mental capacity are deteriorating. Daniel asks Barbara to marry him, but she realizes, just in time, that it is William she loves. Martha manages to burn down the homestead before dying: Barbara and William are free.

Over Against Green Peak (1908) charmingly describes a family unit of three ladies, the narrator, her sister Kate, and their Aunt Sophie, as they settle into an old white house with an orchard at the back just outside the village of Dorset. They fall in love with their domicile, a tavern in pre-Revolutionary days, and, when their possessions arrive, easily "settle house" with the help of taciturn James Rose ("Speech was a commodity for which the family had small use"), who was "stately and calm," and his brother. Every article fits perfectly: they were destined to live in the house. The narrator has a lovely time arranging and classifying her scholar-uncle's books in the library: Would Ruskin be happier with the essayists or the art books? Because they live in a rural community, they must have a horse

and carriage; Lorna, a delightfully humorous horse, who is procured by next-door neighbor Cousin Joseph Carter, serves them well. One of the three will often arise in the night to go to the barn to offer Lorna treats. They struggle with the challenges of housekeeping, including finding a meat peddler, until they turn over the job to Bridgit. Aunt Susan takes on the garden, with Peter to dig the beds. Suddenly there are automobiles in Manchester, where they do the shopping. Summer people drive by their house, "gazing with languid interest at our primitive ways." Their two cash crops will be apples and hay. They decide to sell their apples in New York (not the Dorset way), the agent waits too long, and their apples arrive in New York frozen and useless. They had known the community people for years, ever since they were summer boarders, but "it makes all the difference in the world whether one boards or lives in a place." Before, the people had been "characters, oddities, types;" now, they are "our people." They are, by necessity, versatile: one might see the man furnishing one's eggs also acting as church organist and local photographer. In her last chapters, the narrator gently describes their beast neighbors and the excitement of the passage of the seasons.

The trilogy consisting of *Mountain Verities*, *Winterwise*, and *Chrysalis* describes the return to Vermont of a landscape painter and a writer who have been in France. Each story concerns a marriage, a house, and a way of life. *Mountain Verities* (1923) introduces the couple, in which the writer explains that she and Christopher, "from some deep-lying need for re-self possession and self-orientation," return to Vermont to their dear old house. It isn't from a wish to escape life but to rediscover life as it really is. They have always had cooks (to whom she refers generically as "Bridgits"), but now she wants to do the housework herself. She finds the process of simplification even more pleasurable than she thought it could be and is delighted with "the joys of cooking." She believes that it is in kitchens, orchards, and gardens that "human history works itself out." She begins ordering items from catalogues that she has heretofore spurned. She and

Christopher that summer "celebrate the lowly and commonplace." Soon the kitchen has absorbed all of her energy and interest. Now that she is doing her own housework, the neighbors are much friendlier. She considers country gossip flattering not offensive. The "city people" and "summer cottagers" are not so interested in her culinary endeavors. She and Christopher begin gardening seriously. They realize they are assuming many other roles—farmer, carpenter, and plumber. More and more, they are practicing "vegetarianism" as part of their new rule of simplicity. As winter nears, warnings and preparations proliferate. When it becomes quite cold and the wind rises, it is apparent that there are "several weak places in the armor of our home." They apply weather-stripping. It snows and the hills have domes of "chiseled silver." They find they don't miss the music, exhibitions, and plays of the city: "Green Peak and West Mountain were perfectly capable of being opera, drama, gallery." All kinds of "sociables," grange suppers, and other gatherings answer the question, "What do you ever find to do with yourselves?" City people come to visit, who "dress up for the country;" they play at country life rather than live it. A country funeral, for which Christopher is a pallbearer, makes them feel even more a part of the community. They discover shopping in Rutland and are touched by how friendly and interested the salespeople are. They enjoy the summer bounty of their garden and nutting in the fall. "Woodchucks drowsed thoughtfully at the mouths of their holes." They have come through a year and begin receiving mail from family members remonstrating with them for "living apart from the world." They decide it is not selfish to live happily, to mind their own business, and to share their life experience with their books and paintings.

Winterwise (1927) takes the form of a journal kept in middle age by the writer, who continues to live with her husband in Dorset. They have no children, but friends and neighbors foist animals upon them. She finds that a rural environment — the garden, housekeeping — makes "insistent demands" upon them, and the summer cottagers and boarders complicate their lives. Grizel and Tommy are appealing, loyal cats; Tommy, sadly, dies of pneumonia at the vet's despite the humans' heroic efforts. While canvassing for the Red Cross, she encounters a range of characteristics in her neighbors —"humor, shrewdness, skepticism, serene independence, and persnicketiness." Miraculously, the vet returns Tommy to them: he has survived his illness. The couple spends a great deal of time reading and discussing books sent from New York. She realizes that there are two sides to living in an old house during winter storms, but it does have a great deal of atmosphere. They go on snowshoes to get their milk and are laughed at, pleasantly, by the saleswoman. "To native Vermonters, particularly women, winter sports seems rather absurd." One cat, Tippet, they give away, perfidiously, and she finds her way back to have scores of kittens. In March, the town meeting is where they see all their acquaintances, "real country people met on their own merits with no contamination of city people influence that, in the summer, tarnishes them." "Goodwill prevailed, a special Vermont brand, spicily mixed with skeptical humor and raillery, with local prejudice." Spring comes; farmers begin tapping out; she and Christopher make out their seed orders. Native Vermonters believe winter is a hardship; she and Christopher, transplanted city people, consider the last four months among the happiest of their married life. Now the season of activity is starting and the summer residents begin to arrive.

Chrysalis (1929) continues the story of the painter and the writer. They have lived in their wonderful old house in Dorset with family members and servants for twenty-five years. The one-hundred-and-fifty-year-old house, formerly a tavern, was built close to the road. Tourists begin to arrive; automobiles create traffic problems; the people who had helped them with house and garden are busy with other activities. They decide to move to a smaller house and simplify their lives. A friend offers them a meadow in a hollow away from the village with an "acquiescent" mountain and a "reassuring" brook. "Vermont is at its best in the autumn—serene, triumphant, exhilarating, mystical with the on-coming pres-ence of winter, strong and confident." They don't want to take on another old house but to start afresh with a smaller house. Plans are drawn and construction progresses, accompanied by much rain, interruptions, and postponements. Lumber is delivered. The beloved old house remains unsold. They find they have to "keep after" the builder, who has other jobs as well. They do not want to offend him: "Native Vermonters have no idea what pain and what pleasure they can bestow on a citybred supplicant by a mere look or tone." The workmen on the new house were "typical Yankees...genuine Vermonters: humorous, self-reliant, alert, invested with a native dignity which lent them a certain impressiveness as they moved about their work, yet free and easy too." The cou-ple's decisions about items like plaster and shin-gles were made on the principles of "harmony and convenience." Their former house is full of the hampers and trunks of other generations. They make a bonfire of the objects they can't give to the rummage sale or to friends and neighbors. They enter into a kind of "delirium" as they won-der what they are doing with their lives. The old house is sold to suitable people. The neighbors bring the couple all sorts of housewarming comestibles. "The tenderest loving-kindness and the most thoughtful, painstaking generosity seem to us to characterize the typical Vermonter." They call the new house "Chrysalis," the "home of two spirits waiting to be born again."

Siri Hustvedt

What I Loved (2003) examines the inter-twined lives of two couples living in Manhattan. Leo Hertzberg is a professor of art history; his wife, Erica, is a professor of English. Above them live a painter, Bill Wechsler, and his wife, Lucille. Both women have sons at the same time, Matthew and Mark. Bill and Lucille divorce; she stays in the apartment and Bill moves to a loft with his new lover, and later wife, Violet Blom, a model for some of his most famous paintings. The Vermont episodes come in mid-stream: for four successive summers the two families share a big, one-hundred-and-fifty-year-old farmhouse near

Newfane. They live on a hill called a "mountain" by the natives. They shop for vegetables at Dutton's on Route 30. They swim in the pond. The boys go to a day camp in Weston, twenty minutes away. Bill is working on fairy-tale boxes (he has moved from one-dimensional paintings); Violet on a book on eating disorders; Erica on a book on Henry James; and Leo on medieval and early Renaissance art. The summer after the last one in Vermont, the two boys go to camp in Pennsylvania where a tragic accident occurs. The lives of the remaining characters are transformed as they deal with loss, grief, change, rehabilita-tion, loneliness, and death.

Elisabeth Hyde

Her Native Colors (1986) explores whether a close friendship between two young women who grew up together in Vermont can survive two diametrically opposed life styles—one in northern California and one in northern Vermont. Phoebe Martin, a litigator, now twen-ty-nine, divorced with a five-year old son, Andrew, left Winslow in the Northeast Kingdom to go to Wellesley and Boalt Law School in California. Molly Adams received a degree in geology from the University of Vermont and returned to Winslow to teach at the Barrington Union School, which she and Phoebe attended, and to weave, quilt, and knit. When Molly and her beau, Nick (who has a master's degree in American literature but is currently chopping wood for his livelihood), accelerate the date of their wedding because they are expecting a baby, Molly asks Phoebe to be matron of honor. Phoebe is in the midst of a difficult case at her prestigious corporate firm, working killing hours, but wants to return home, not only to see Molly, but to see her mother, Louise, and her brother, Jack, and his wife. The reunion between the two childhood friends is disastrous. Phoebe is hypercritical, insensitive, and condescending, accusing Molly of "wasting her life." Molly, hurt to her core, responds defensively. Phoebe even suggests that Molly is jealous of Phoebe's life, because Molly has never lived anywhere but Vermont. Phoebe thinks that she is "smarter, more ambitious, stronger, more capable" because she broke away from Winslow, which she considers a "narrow-minded WASPy community of bigots." The visit is ruined for the two young women, because they are unable to mend the damage that is done in their first vituperative clashes, but they have given each other a lot to think about. Molly wonders what it would be like to be free from the demanding Yankee culture, like not waiting until after Thanksgiving to put on the flannel sheets. Phoebe, in turn, begins to feel a growing sense of inferiority toward Molly and the latter's inner confidence. Phoebe realizes that she misses "the comfort, the security" of the late November afternoon "gloom." The questions raised in the novel are thoughtful and interesting, as is the resolution.

Elizabeth Inness-Brown

The initial point of view in *Burning Marguerite* (2002) is James Jack Wright's, who lives on Grain Island on Lake Champlain. At the outset, he finds his aged guardian, Marguerite Anne Bernadette-Marie Deo, dead in the woods. He sets out to report the death to the sheriff, but then changes his mind when he realizes that "Tante," as he calls her, would not want to be taken to the morgue; he will bury her himself. He visits Faith, the woman he loves. She lives in the trailer of her father, Doc Milton, who is "different from other summer people; he never had pretensions, always liked the island for what it was, never wanted to change things." Faith understands how James Jack feels about Marguerite. The perspective changes to Marguerite, who tells her story. Her father, Marcel Deo, found marble on his property and became rich. When she was a teenager, she had an affair with an Indian farmhand, Daniel, and became pregnant. Her mother, claiming she was taking her for an examination, had her sterilized; her father murdered her lover

and buried his body on the property. Marguerite left Vermont and went to New Orleans, where she married William. He divorced her because she could not have children and moved in with Judith, the quilt-maker. Marguerite returns to Vermont in 1955 when she is in her early fifties. At first, she does not make much effort to fit into island life but is soon asked to take care of the boy, James Jack, while his parents are at work, though most of the islanders view her with suspicion. She accepts the "island pragmatism." Her grandfather dies and his brother, Homer, courts Caroline, her grandfather's wife. (Homer gets odd jobs with the summer people, although they "weren't his friends. They pretended to be— waving in summer when they drove by in their air-conditioned cars, slapping him on the back in the hardware store or in the market, joking with him while they paid for their birdseed or light bulbs or toilet paper or beer. But their smiles said, 'You're lucky to have been born here, just too dumb to know why,' and their friendship was as superficial as their needs.") Marguerite is an accomplished artist, specializing in horticultural subjects. After James Jack's parents die in a fishing shanty accident on the lake, Marguerite becomes his official guardian, even though the deputy sheriff and his wife want to adopt him. "As a little boy, he'd clung to her, but growing up he'd pulled away, like a box elder leaning to get out of her shade and into the sunlight." The final events on the day of Marguerite's death are beautifully and touchingly shown. Examples of the supple imagery: "One day the hickory buds were tight, glossy fists; the next day they were open palms," and "Cattails stuck up out of the ice like quenched torches."

J

Samuel Alexander Jackson

Among the Maples (1908) starts with a sugaring-off party given by Hugh MacLean and his wife, Martha, in the Scottish community of Renwicktown in Caledonia County in 1891. Malcolm MacGregor, patient and humorous, is there with his girl, Mary Ferguson. Luke Burney, gloomy and irascible, is jealous of Malcolm. In this town, business and scholarly activities are under the influence of the Presbyterian Church. Renwicktown High School is established and Emma MacLaren engaged to be the teacher. Twice Malcolm happens to save Emma from drowning on the river. Andrew Melville, the new preacher, arrives; Hugh MacLean tells Andrew stories about the early Canadian settlers who "chopped and dug" their way to transform "the savage wilderness into a fruitful plain." Malcolm and Luke work with other young men in the stone sheds cutting granite. In an attempt to woo Mary away from Malcolm, Luke gossips to people that Malcolm does not love her. Traveling in his buggy, Malcolm picks up a drunken Jonah Grubb and is seen by Luke throwing Jonah's bottle into the river; Luke spreads the rumor that Malcolm helped Jonah finish his flask of rum. Malcolm's faith is sorely tried when he is told it is "blessed" to be slandered and to forgive. Luke has belittled the growing union of granite men and is making enemies in the quarry. One evening at the smithy's, Wullie, Malcolm's "little" brother, spars with Luke and hurts him badly (Wullie swears never to fight again and goes to Seminary). Mary visits Betsy Cameron, a sensible old lady, and shows her an upsetting anonymous letter she has received. Soon the gossips are saying that sinful Saphira Blackthorn has sent the letter; Saphira quarrels with her husband and kills herself. Malcolm, on his way to college in Burlington, visits Mary to repair their friendship. Later that night, Luke falls unconscious from his

horse; Malcolm takes him home and nurses him back to health. They, too, are reconciled. Betsy's house catches fire and all her possessions are destroyed. Renwicktown comes together to supply lumber, haul it, and find three carpenters to rebuild the house. Malcolm is away at college for three years before the Spanish War starts in 1898. He volunteers for the First Vermont Regiment and goes to Chickamauga, Georgia, where the soldiers are greeted with cheers for the Green Mountain Boys. He becomes very ill but survives and returns home to find that Mary is dead. He continues his studies, earning a degree from the University of Vermont and doing postgraduate work in chemistry and mathematics. He is proposed as an instructor at the Academy in Mt. Joy (based on St. Johnsbury), and the vote is seconded by his former teacher, Emma, now Mrs. MacDonald. On the train, he meets a young woman who looks wonderfully familiar: she is Mary's cousin from Springfield, and she and Malcolm fall in love.

Shirley Jackson

"The Lottery" (1948) is a brief, matter-of-fact tale that begins in a festive mood with a gathering of townspeople for a ceremony near Bennington. It is an ordinary village affair, much like a Halloween party or a square dance, with references to the antiquity of the gathering ("the original paraphernalia for the lottery had been lost long ago"). At first, the crowd is seen to stand a bit removed "from the pile of stones in the corner." People chatting in the crowd say that other nearby towns are no longer holding the lottery. The drawing begins by head of family, and the Hutchinsons win. Each holds a blank piece of paper, save Tessie, the mother, who has been complaining about the draw. She has drawn the paper with the "black spot." "The children had stones already, and someone gave little Davy Hutchinson a few pebbles. Tessie Hutchinson was in the center of a cleared space by now, and she held her hands out desperately as the villagers moved in on her. 'It isn't fair,' she said. A stone hit her on the side of the head. Old Man Warner was saying, 'Come on, come on, everyone.' Steve

Adams was in the front of the crowd of villagers, with Mrs. Graves beside him. 'It isn't fair, it isn't right,' Mrs. Hutchinson screamed, and then they were upon her."

Life among the Savages (1953) describes Jackson's own experience: a woman writer and her writer husband, with two children and five thousand books, evicted from their city apartment rent a house in North Bennington. They have heard from friends who had bought a house there "glowing accounts of mountains, and children playing in their own gardens, and clean snow, and homegrown carrots." They rent the "Fielding house," and soon fill it with toys, children, books, some of their city furniture, and lots of old pieces left in the house or procured from secondhand stores. The husband commutes to New York from the nearby train station. The narrator, with a witty and allusive voice, talks about every-day life with children and a rather absent-minded husband and father. She is immediately attracted to Vermont. "Oh, those first fall days, with the sad sharpness in the air and the leaves bright so that our road is a line of color, and the feeling of storing against the winter, and the pumpkins." The narrator is natural, accepting, and affectionate toward her new venue. All the seemingly mundane phases of family life are keen-sighted and amusing, kindergarten for Laurie, making lists, shopping with children, and "day help," but the most delightful is her experience having her third baby (Sarah). While she is in labor, a woman in a blue bathrobe visits her. Later, as the narrator is being wheeled to the operating room, she sees the same woman standing in the doorway to her room. "She loved me for the dangers I had passed," quoting *Othello* to her doctor, "and I loved her that she did pity them." By the end, she has had her fourth baby — Barry — and there is no talk of moving back to the city.

Raising Demons (1957), the warm, witty sequel to *Life among the Savages*, begins with the narrator's realization that the family needs a larger house; simultaneously, the grocer, the postman, and the gas station attendant all suggest that the Wilbur House on Main Street would be a good buy. The Fieldings want to reclaim their family house. The move is chaotic; the spacious new house hardly holds all the possessions of a family of six. The narrator needs a break; a friend invites her for a weekend. Her delightful, wry husband assures her he is perfectly capable of taking care of the children and the household. She leaves a lengthy, chronological outline of detailed instructions ("jar in refrigerator labeled 'mayonnaise' is extra coffee to heat up"). She is away just one night. When she returns Sunday evening, she finds no one home, but her husband has left her a note. He writes that the dog ate up the instructions; they are all out for supper and the movies, which the baby had also enjoyed when they went to the movies the day before; and the jar in the refrigerator labeled "mayonnaise" was mayonnaise. The narrator has all the children in the car when a speeding driver hits her car, planning to make an insurance claim. No one is hurt, but the children are funny and grown-up with the police officer. The new house is convenient to everything — the gym, the library, and the school — and the children are changing: "They belonged to the town now." They tap off the four maple trees in their yard, figuring a pint of syrup cost them about seventy-five dollars. She has another near accident with a parked car "from some state where land is not so jealously parceled out as it is here in Vermont." She is mournful when Barry, the youngest, goes to nursery school and muses about taking courses in "endocrinology or advanced French." Her husband takes a job at Bennington College; she becomes an unsuccessful faculty wife. As a "prominent educator," he is invited to Burlington to judge a beauty contest for Miss Vermont. They watch Laurie pitch a baseball game, and her husband, "who was not a lively man," shouts at and applauds for his son. She becomes overwhelmed with housework and grouchy when he is expecting an old girlfriend to visit. They all go for a weekend in New York, where the children express their high spirits ("In Vermont, we do not have revolving doors").

In *The Haunting of Hill House* (1959), the point of view is that of Eleanor Vance, thirty-two, just released from a ten-year ordeal taking care of a difficult, ailing mother. Dr. John Montague, a doctor of philosophy interested in supernatural manifestations, wants to spend a week doing experiments at Hill House, an old Victorian monstrosity in Hillsdale near Ashton (modeled on Jennings Hall at Bennington College). Out of a number of potential candidates who have had some sort of paranormal experience, he accepts Eleanor, and a theatrical young woman named Theodora, who runs a shop. He also invites Luke Sanderson, the attractive nephew of the owner of Hill House who wants a family representative present. Mr. and Mrs. Dudley, the gatekeeper and cook at the establishment, make it a point never to stay after dark. The first night, Dr. Montague explains to the participants that he wants the experiment to be as scientific as possible, testing certain theories regarding psychic phenomena, and asks them to take notes of anything unusual they experience. He also tells them about the background of the house, over which there is wild speculation in the village ("Gossip is always a bad enemy"), involving two sisters who fought over the property. The older, unmarried sister lived in the house with a companion; when the older sister died, the companion inherited the house and then killed herself. The four explore the many rooms: in the library "over the mantel a deer head looked down upon them in patent embarrassment." The house is disorienting because the walls are not square and everything is off-center. The second night something happens; it is not anyone's imagination because everyone feels it. Then, chalk writing is discovered on the wall: "help eleanor come home." Eleanor begins to feel that the group is turning against her—that they think she wrote the note. On the third morning, they try to measure the "cold spot" on the floor of the upstairs hall. Theodora discovers that her room and clothes are covered with blood. Theo moves into Eleanor's room; Eleanor begins to hate Theo. That night they again hear something in the hall. The next day bossy Mrs. Montague and her driver, Arthur Parker, arrive with Mrs. Montague's planchette, which, under the right circumstances, spells out supernatural messages. Eleanor finds her "impossible, vulgar,

possessive;" Eleanor is also entertaining murderous thoughts about Theo. Mrs. Montague's first session with the planchette records a voice asking for "Eleanor." Eleanor becomes increasingly paranoid, sure that they are all singling her out. That night, they all huddle in the doctor's room while something pounds and whines at the door. It feels to Eleanor as though the terrible knocking is inside her own head. The house is about to crash down around her. Guilt-ridden, depressed, and terrified, Eleanor believes that she is responsible for her mother's death. Eleanor begins to hear a little girl singing, although no one else does. She climbs to the top of the tower and has to be rescued by Luke. When Dr. Montague insists that she leave she confesses that she has no home to return to and that she has stolen her sister's car. The ending is as frightening as the rest of the story.

Four of the stories collected in *Just an Ordinary Day* (1996) are set in Vermont, two of which are told from Jackson's point of view and are in the same vein as those described above. In **"Maybe It Was the Car,"** Jackson feels so imposed upon by the fact that her mothering and housekeeping have eclipsed her life as a writer that she simply gets in the car one day and drives off. She heads east from North Bennington, passing through a dozen small towns. She goes about forty miles to a little town with a sign saying, "Settled 1684." It is just what she is looking for: "There was a broad village green and a handsome old colonial building called The Colonial Inn, and all around there were split-level ranch houses and glass-brick stores." The Colonial Inn boasts a dining room called The Old Cow Shed and a bar named The Trough. The receptionist recognizes her, but she insists she is a tourist and signs the register, "Mrs. Pancho Villa." She has a lovely evening, reading a mystery story and drinking a couple of daiquiris. The next day she looks at a house for sale. The owner describes its advantages. She says it is "too big." "Too big for what?" "Too big for me. I'm a writer." Then she drives home. The family does not comment on her departure, except to describe what domestic crises have occurred in her absence. **"Fame"** takes place just as Jackson, who is publishing her first book, is on her way to New York. She receives a telephone call from the woman who writes the "North Village Notes" column for the local paper. Jackson tries to tell her about her new book, but the woman is only interested in who was the previous owner of her house and whether she has any little items of local news. Jackson explains where they have lived—for three years—and, despite interruptions, tries to describe her book, the price, the publisher, and other aspects of her impending fame. The column is published in the paper and, after three or four other items of illness, visitors, or birthdays, the piece about Jackson appears: "Mrs. Stanley Hyman has moved into the old Thacher place on Prospect Street. She and her family are visiting Mr. and Mrs. Farrar-straus of New York City this week." Two short horror stories based in Vermont are also in the collection. In **"Home,"** Ethel Sloane and her husband move into the Sanderson house to find that it is haunted. In **"The Possibility of Evil,"** Miss Adela Strange Worth, whose grandfather built the first house on Pleasant Street, takes it upon herself to chastise people by sending anonymous notes for perceived malfeasance. She has not recovered from the fact that the town wishes to put up a statue of Ethan Allen rather than one of her grandfather.

William Jaspersohn

Peter Boone is a literate, sympathetic, and wise-cracking private investigator born and raised in Montpelier, who graduated from Dartmouth with a degree in comparative literature and was a pitcher for the Boston Red Sox. After his wife is murdered in Burlington ten years earlier, he captures her killer, gives up baseball, and moves to a house on a hillside near Earlsville on Route 15 near Underhill. In *Native Angels* (1995), Floyd and Myrtle Brand, a disagreeable couple living in Regis, hire Boone to find their missing fifteen-year-old daughter, Holly. He checks out the school first, finding that no one has any idea where she is or that she has missed thirty of the last hundred days of school. Only the English teacher, Mr. Kittredge,

seems to be interested in her disappearance. Boone checks with the hopeless guidance counselors, who finally give him the name of a former employee, Nan Holland, who might know something. Nan is an attractive young divorcée who shares Boone's passion for fishing and is indeed interested in helping to find Holly—and in getting to know Boone, as well. He finds Holly at the airport, takes her home, and begins an affair with Nan. He receives word that Holly is dead—"accident or suicide"—at the bottom of Regis Falls. He interviews the staff at the sordid Maple Spa and Restaurant, where Holly worked. He checks the license plate for the Porsche belonging to a man whom Boone saw picking up Holly at a fair. He even goes to the Northwest Correctional Facility to consult with Warren Fryar (the man who murdered Boone's wife) about teenagers and drug-dealers in northern Vermont. Warren gets him an appointment with the local drug lord, Lorch ("the Vole"). At Holly's funeral, her only friend, Tina, tells Boone she has something to give him related to Holly's murder. When he goes to see Tina, he finds her dead, clutching a key to a bungalow at the Maple Spa. What Boone finds in her room tells him who killed both "native angels."

In *Lake Effect* (1996), Boone and Nan have decided live apart; Nan is in Connecticut finishing a novel, taking care of her mother, and starting an affair with another man. Arthur Cole, who lives on Gatwick Lake up toward the Northeast Kingdom, hires Boone to find his wife, Chelly, who has bipolar disease and has been missing for three days. She is the daughter of wealthy Claire and Win Killbridge, who live nearby on the lake. Leaving the Coles, Boone is badly beaten up by two cops and warned to stay away. He goes to his friends, Anny (a black woman) and John (Nan's psychologist) McArrigal, for stitches in his head and friendly succor. Then he heads for Professor Kenneth Hewlitt at Dartmouth, who has been discussing with Chelly her interest in Beat poet Armen Karillian, who ran a commune on Gatwick Lake and has been missing for some years. Hewlitt is of little help, but his research assistant, Taylor

Swimm, gives Boone a lead on three members of the Karillian Poetry Group who are now successful businessmen in and around Burlington. Boone meets Chelly's parents and traces Shondra Maine to her house in Groton, Connecticut, where he finds pornographic pictures of her and Chelly. Shondra is murdered and her house burned. Files, a friend from the state police, learns that Karillian and company were involved in the drug-overdose death of a retarded youngster while fifteen-year-old Chelly was staying at Karillian's house and that Karillian's son, Mikah, was arrested for arson in the burning of Kenneth Hewlitt's house on Gatwick Lake. Boone seeks the help of another good friend, Ernie Bellino, a special investigator, Buddhist practitioner, and catcher on Boone's high school baseball team. Boone finds Taylor's body in Hewlitt's brook. Documents on her body show that she is Willow Goltz, the daughter of Karillian, who went undercover to discover who murdered her mother. Boone and Bellini tape Alden Clapp, the police chief, collecting laundered money from one of the Poetry Group and follow him toward the Northeast Kingdom, where they rescue Chelly and leave the police chief handcuffed and promising to resign. Boone learns that, although Hewlitt and Cora Goltz (Karillian's wife) were lovers and Hewlitt's wife and Karillian were lovers, Hewlitt didn't kill anybody. Meanwhile, Boone and Bellino have taken Chelly to John and Anny's, where she is reunited with her husband, Arnold. John helps Chelly recollect what happened to her as a teenager. The final confrontation with her mother, Claire Killbridge, at the Guggenheim Museum in New York, has stunning consequences. ("Lake effect" is the effect of any lake in modifying the weather in nearby areas.)

Sarah Orne Jewett

*"Fame's Little Day" (1895) is a glimpse into the life of Abel Pinkham and his wife, Mary Ann, who live in Wetherford, where Abel runs a maple-sugar concern. They are plain folks, comfortable in their home and family, who are in New York on affairs connected with the maple-sugar industry. In fact, feeling lonely and out of place, they rather wish they hadn't come, even though "the maple sugar was all made and shipped, and it was still too early for spring work on the land." They missed "their good bed at home," and the food in the New York Ethan Allen Hotel was inferior to that of someone "whose cooking was the triumph of parish fairs at home." In the lobby of their hotel, a young reporter with a sense of fun and himself a country boy, takes note of something "honestly rustic and pleasing" in Abel's behavior. From observation and a few questions to the desk clerk, he puts together a story about Mr. and Mrs. Pinkham's visit to New York for the morning papers. Imagine the surprise of this simple couple when they come across the article about Abel. Their entire perspective changes: they are now eager to enjoy their visit, to see the sights, and to go to the circus in the evening. Abel settles satisfactorily with his correspondents for the spring consignment of maple sugar. One of the partners of the firm, in fact, is a Wetherford boy. It was he who, when there was a renewed interest in maple sugar, "remembered that there never was any sugar made in Wetherford of such melting and delicious flavor as from the trees on the old Pinkham farm." The Pinkhams have a lovely happy day, relaxed and ready to enjoy their visit to New York. They feel their hard work has been rewarded. "They were both thinking of their gray farm-house high on a long western slope, with the afternoon sun full in its face, the old red barn, the pasture, the shaggy wood that stretched far up the mountainside." As they return to the hotel, a young man bows to them. They don't remember him, but he recognizes them, because he is the young reporter who wrote the story about them. "Their look of seriousness and self-consciousness appealed to him unexpectedly." He wonders what effect his article would have on their life. He thinks he might send marked copies of his paper to some of the weeklies in the Pinkhams' part of Vermont to enhance their reputation.

Arthur F. Joy

In *Vermont Adventure* (1985), the narrator and his wife and his brother-in-law and his wife buy in 1935 for three hundred dollars an abandoned dairy farm in central Vermont near East Wallingford (chartered 1761). This flight from the city for summers and weekends is intended to be an idyll, living without plumbing or electricity, enjoying the abundant scenery and sports. Relations with the owner of the general store never become cordial; they find his prices high and bring their own supplies. They are perplexed by the relationship between neighbor Francis Dubois's wife, Yvette, and the young retarded cripple named Peter Lars. On a hunting expedition with houseguests, one of them shoots and kills another by mistake. The forays to auctions and occasional picnics on the nearby lake are enjoyable, but four events in their last summer persuade the narrator to sell his forty acres. His brother-in-law pulls out (his wife has never really liked being so far away). He makes covers for the cows to alleviate the torture they suffer from flies, but the farmer never uses them. He is arrested and taken to court for not holding a legal hunting license (he attributes this to the hostile storeowner). Finally, a double murder occurs next door (Francis Dubois kills his wife and her lover).

Margaret H. Judd

In *Murder is a Best Seller* (1959), Jeannie Hartley Wells is the librarian at Loomis Memorial Library in Loomisville in northern Vermont. She unexpectedly publishes to resounding reviews ("worthy of a Frederick Van de Water or a Kenneth Roberts") a historical novel about early days in Vermont featuring Robert Rogers of the Rangers. Her two best friends, St. Helena's Academy librarian Ann Halsey, and bookshop owner Norah Leighton, are surprised and pleased. Ann has a pleasant boyfriend, Jim Hagen, but Norah has broken up with her beau, Vincent Farrell, out of jealousy over glamorous New York actress Claudia Carlton. When Claudia is murdered, there are several suspects: Norah, for one, and old Joshua Loomis, who hates Claudia because his son, George, loves her and Old Josh wants him to marry Norah. While Ann is cataloguing old historical volumes at her school library, someone tampers with the boxes. A student who had been looking at the books with Ann is run over and almost killed; then Norah's next door neighbor, Ella Mitchell, is strangled. The explanation for the murders is clever and entertaining.

Ward Just

Two stories in *Twenty-One Selected Stories* (1990) are set in Vermont. **"A Guide to the Geography of Vermont"** (1980) is about the aftermath of Vietnam and its victims. John, the narrator, was an undergraduate at Yale when Hank Beers was in the School of Architecture. Hank, an intelligence officer in Vietnam, was dropped into a mountain village and transfixed by way the houses were built into the forest. "He had dreamed of working in rural Vermont, feral terrain, and now saw his ecstatic dream declare itself." "Unnerved and terribly afraid," he shoots himself in the foot and is sent home. It is 1966. He purchases three hundred acres on a mountain slope in the Northeast Kingdom: "impoverished but not yet exhausted, redneck country: dirty white clapboard farmhouses with television aerials that resembled radar apparatus, ancient barns and tractors, mutts, tomcats, snowmobiles and abandoned sedans rusting in the front yard, windows broken and the interiors filled with snow." Hank invites five architects to Vermont to build a "homestead." He finds that "the seasons in Vermont are more oppressive than any ruling class," but, by the 1980s, there are seven houses on his property. John comes and stays for a year. Charlotte, who built a house there, has been with Beers nine years and is "thirty-four and restless." For Beers, this mountain in Vermont constitutes the world; Charlotte sees the Vermont experience as "maintenance. That was what it was in Vermont: one maintained in order not to break down. She understood suddenly that it was a pessimist's state—perseverance, patience, and fatalism. The region was littered with false beginnings, buildings abandoned or burned, mills empty, fields lying fallow, the deer dying for lack of forage." Charlotte leaves, as does the narrator, but he returns ten years later, when his nephew graduates from Middlebury College, and drives up to the Northeast Kingdom to find that Hank is living with a preacher's daughter. Hank is not there, but John speaks with the girl—a young, Vermont girl working in her garden. John thinks: "The geography of Vermont is different from New Hampshire. The mountains of Vermont are less majestic, and the valleys narrower and more self-contained. In the Northeast Kingdom the mountains are known as the Granite Hills and are gentle in contour, giving no hint of the hardness and density beneath. Of course Vermont is land-locked; it is an island state in all respects. There is more forest now than at the turn of the century, owing to the lack of profitability in lumbering the high country. Walking away, I thought about that." John passes Hank's car as he drives away but doesn't want to go back to visit. He is leaving Hank's utopia. John imagines Hank Beers at work alone on his mountain, "a feature of the geography of Vermont."

"**Maintenance**" (1982) is also set in the Northeast Kingdom. The narrator takes an interest in Burns, the meteorologist on Channel 8, whom he considers totally unreliable, even though Burns has a "special affinity for winter, recognizing the immense effect it had on all our lives, and he reported it as a foreign correspondent would report a losing war." The narrator spends time with Burns at the local bar (Burns has a drinking problem; so does the narrator) in Lyndonville and finds out that Burns "was obsessed by the weather in Vermont, being a connoisseur of bad news." Burns's philosophy is that people are more interested in what the weather has been like than what it is going to be: "We have to describe exactly the flow of the thing now because tomorrow's always another day, and different. And you can't do anything about it. Maintenance, that's the essence of the north country. 'Use it up, wear it out, make it do, or do without.' Tomorrow depends on today and yesterday." As they drink more and more, and learn that each of their marriages has dissolved, the

narrator picks up Burns's language: "It's hard on some people, they don't understand the drill. You expect one thing, you get another thing. We're so remote here, and they don't get it. You don't advance. There's no such thing as an advance. You *maintain*." The narrator now spends four or five nights a week in the bar with Burns. "Vermont is not the rustic paradise it's cracked up to be, and we all felt the pressure." His wife leaves him; he stays drunk with Burns.

The venue for *The American Blues* (1984) is once again the Northeast Kingdom against the backdrop of the Vietnam War. At the time of the fall of Saigon, the narrator, his wife, and son, now eight, fled Washington, D.C. for the "natural environment, clean air, safe schools, wood stoves, and preindustrial economy" of the north country of Vermont. It is back-to-basics time. In the north country, they waited impatiently for weather forecasts, how much snow had fallen, how it compared to last year. "We depended on statistics." The narrator, in his forties, obsessed by the war, is writing its history and cannot complete the last chapter. A helicopter is flying over his home, a banker inspecting building sites. "Condominiums are spoiling the wilderness of the north country; people are replacing bears." "Two-hundred-year-old towns nestle close to small seedy rivers; here and there are red-brick mills, sturdy as fortresses, vacant now. The mills always seemed to be located at a pretty part of the river, a bend or a rapids; the marriage of aesthetics and convenience. They manufactured essentials: shoes, bobbins, woolens, lumber. All that was gone, and had been gone for many years." The narrator is moody, pessimistic, drinking. "Hard drinking in the north country was a part of the scenery, beauty accomplice… Hard drinking was as necessary as wearing sunglasses on a bright day." He decides to visit his best friend, Quinn, who lives in London part of the year but spends October, November, and December at a clapboard-and-fieldstone house with pool in the Northeast Kingdom, built as a summer retreat for a lumber baron. Quinn is a blues piano player and a novelist who has invented a popular spy character named Tom Plumb.

J

The narrator finds Tessa Dane with Quinn and a roomful of partying people. There wasn't a Vermonter in the room, the narrator noted. He finds the crowd "unreliable, as exiles generally were unreliable." Quinn decides that the way to shock the narrator out of his writer's block is to introduce him to Marty Neher, an accomplished skier in her twenties. Quinn has hopes for an encounter between "a man who came from the fundamentals and a woman who was looking for them." The narrator falls for Marty instantly and tells her about his north-country life, the forests, the western range, "rising in seven different shades of blue." Their affair, ardent at first, slowly dissolves. Saying goodbye to her, to Quinn and Tessa, and to his wife and his son, he returns to Vietnam to find the ending for his book.

K

Garrison Keillor

When Jim, a nearsighted lad in **"Christmas in Vermont"** (1993), runs away for eleven hours with his dog, Tony, his mother doesn't even miss him. Jim's parents, Jack (who smells of cilantro aftershave lotion) and Sara (size eight), own a palatial "traditional-style home" on Hickey Avenue in Redford, which "twinkled with handmade Christmas lights she [his mother] had purchased from native Vermont crafts people." The narrator interrupts his story to comment upon Bert and Willy, dope-crazed hippies who came to Vermont and started an ice cream business, selling it for three dollars a quart to tourists, "which is the effect Vermont can have on people." Jack runs away because he hates Vermont—"the dark green shutters, picket fences, maple trees, wood piles, white spires of the Congregational church, the cemetery, snow, lantern jaws, and flinty blue eyes." When his father points out that there is a McDonald's in Redford, Jim retorts that "the one here looks like a Quaker meetinghouse." The narrator mar-

ries Sharon and moves into an eighteen-room redwood cabin in Plainfield on the edge of a ten-thousand-acre wildlife preserve. He intersperses his text with advertisements from his Vermont Christmas Catalogue for artifacts like Vermont woodsmen's sweaters and handcrafted tiles.

Judith Kelman

Only one person in the neighborhood in *The House on the Hill* (1992) knows that someone is living in the old house on the hill in Dove's Landing near Wilmington. That person is Quinn Gallagher, the parole officer for the new resident, the unspeakable psychopath, child murderer, and mutilator, Eldon Weir, who was released from prison on a technicality and accommodated in this house with full electronic surveillance. Quinn has moved to Rutland with her younger brother, Brenden, after their parents' fiery death in an automobile accident. Red-haired and stubborn, Quinn is not pleased to meet handsome FBI agent Bernie Levitsky, who has come from Washington to interview Weir as part of a study on violent criminals. Bernie and Quinn fight constantly; he is wonderful with Brenden, teaching him how to hit a baseball; he and Quinn fall in love at the end. Nora Eakins moves with her new husband, Charles Brill, and her daughter, Abigail, eleven, to the inn in Dove's Landing that has been operated by the Brill family for six generations (the first owners, Irish immigrants, were participants in the Underground Railroad). Abigail runs away, leaving a note describing her unhappiness, but Quinn fears that Eldon has something to do with Abigail's departure. Quinn and Bernie are soon deeply involved in the case, which involves a creepy and dishonest mayor, magic tricks, and Houdini disappearances. The final scenes are filled with suspense and menace.

Clarence Budington Kelland

Scattergood Baines, the eponymous hero of *Scattergood Baines* (1921), in his late twenties and of ample proportions, arrives in Coldriver (population four hundred, it is based on Wilmington) with aspirations to develop the Coldriver Valley; his aim is not "pursuing money for himself—his objective was achievement." Although he appears placid and guileless, Scattergood is a shrewd planner and developer and a gifted visionary. He begins business with a hardware store and, in ten years, in addition to acquiring his bride, Amanda Randle, whose business talents almost match his, he owns a dam and boom company, a provision company, a railroad, a mill, a bank, and one hundred thousand acres of timber. Local businessmen Keith and Crane entirely underestimate Scattergood, thinking he is just a "fat, backwoods rube." In fact, he is astute, many-faceted, and full of business-related aphorisms; for example, he is not a man "to shingle his roof before he built his foundation." No deal is too small to receive Scattergood's "best and most skillful attention." Once he has created his place in the community, he can begin to serve as arbiter and problem-solver; he becomes the "undisputed political dictator" of his state, where he works for progress and the public good. Although Scattergood looks to some like a "tricky businessman," he has another side: he is a good neighbor and fellow townsman and a tender philanthropist. He loves to "meddle"—doing most of his thinking sitting on the piazza of his hardware store—and is able to make many villagers happy, especially with his matchmaking skills. He is a master of indirection and seemingly "purposeless discussion." Scattergood is a voice of Vermont: "You kin find more kindness and charity and long-sufferin' and tenderness and goodness right here amongst the cantankerous-seemin' of Coldriver 'n you kin find anywheres else on earth."

When the reader is reunited with the irresistible hero in *Scattergood Baines Returns* (1939), the old hardware-store man has been "livin' and observin' and dickerin'" in Coldriver for fifty years and has watched several generations grow up. Johnny Bones, his lawyer, is now a respected U.S. senator; Pliny Pickett still brings him news from the railroad; Mandy is his matchless partner for life. Scattergood, decent, sympathetic, perceptive, humorous, is dealing with the ordinary problems of the village and the state as well as the extraordinary challenges of the

Depression era. He tinkers with aspects of peoples' lives ("Remember never to kick the wrong fella's dog") to create better outcomes. He arranges jobs for two young men who have engineering degrees but no prospects. He figures out a way for two lonely old people to marry and support themselves. He manages to solve the moral outrage of Deacon Pettibone and Elder Hooper when the new minister, Reverend Wilbur Jepson, starts—and plays on—a baseball team. Bub Hooper, the Elder's grandson, helps Scattergood with this last case: Scattergood tells the boy he's "the kind of a fella a body could ride the river with." The son of his old enemy, Crane, tries to outsmart Scattergood: Scattergood bests him but gives him his money back. While he is away, Scattergood's assistant buys many plastic replicas of famous statues: Scattergood is able to persuade "majestic" Mrs. Minturn to found and fund an art gallery, for which she purchases his statues ("I like a deal where everybody comes out ahead"). Some summer people on Handle Road ask Scattergood and Mandy for a weekend: Scattergood knows there is an ulterior motive here and, sure enough, someone is murdered during the house party and Scattergood is sworn in as deputy sheriff to solve the crime. When Simeon Bolster, another resident on Handle Road, decides to move out West, people assume Bolster will hire the new auctioneer in town, Dynamite Dan, which would mean cutting old Pazzy Oakes out of the job. Scattergood solves this problem, too. Scattergood's biggest worry is the young men who are planning to migrate. He persuades a group of them to go into business together as a cooperative, renting them the Red Mill to turn out small wooden objects like clothespins and wooden handles for carrying parcels. Inspired by this model, the young women enter the cooking business—apple jelly and butter, maple cream and sugar—and form Coldriver Products. All the farmer's wives and housewives become involved, selling their products in "dandy jars" in New York and Boston. The whole town becomes one big factory and the young men can stay in Coldriver and marry their sweethearts.

K

Victor J. Kelly

In *MacIntosh Mountain* (1983), Ira and Bea MacIntosh and Jerome and Jael Springer live in Croughton's Corners, about an hour north of Burlington, where Ira has taken over the failing farm of his dead father and Jerome is the ambitious minister. Jerome takes a more prestigious post in Shelterport, New Hampshire, but the couples' lives intersect when teenager Tammi Springer turns up pregnant at the MacIntosh farm. Flashbacks reveal that Tammi's face was horribly burned and scarred in a childhood accident and, in an attempt to be popular, she engaged in sexual relations with a boy at her high school. Ira's sister, Amanda ("Sissie"), also ran away, pregnant, when she was a teenager. Ira and Bea, whose only child, Samuel, died at two, persuade Tammi to return home. Tammi believes she has ruined her father's chances for a better job; the church wants him to stay, but he decides to return to Vermont to a job in which he can love and work for God in a less worldly way. Tammi forgives the youngsters at school who were cruel to her. The Springer family returns to Croughton's Corners in time for Jerome to accompany Ira to the county hospital where Sissie is a patient. The resolution of the novel is filled with redemption and love.

Jay Kendall

In *The Secret Keepers* (1999), Walt and Ira Holden live in Duncansboro on Lake Champlain near the Canadian border. Their son, Clay, fathered two babies, Alder and Janine, with Arlette Luce before he married Angela Surprenant and Arlette married Mark Handy. Clay is now serving in the Pacific. He and his wife, Angela, have a six-year-old son, Michael, five years younger than Alder. Arlette's husband and daughter died within a few months of each other. When the story opens, Arlette has just had twins, Nathaniel and Nadine. The family secret is disclosed from various points of view. When Clay returns from overseas, he faces a significant decision.

Louise Andrews Kent

Mrs. Appleyard's Year (1941) introduces delightful, cultivated Susan Markham Appleyard, who lives happily with serene, fond Mr. Appleyard in a big house on Overbrook Hill in Boston. The children are all grown: Standish is a painter in Texas; Hugh is a schoolteacher in Arizona; Cicely is married; and Sally goes to college. In calendar format, the story follows Mrs. Appleyard's busy life in Boston until May, when they go to Appleyard Center for five months. In front of the house there is a "lady elm," which stands alone, "shaped like a perfect wineglass." Mrs. A. gushes about the elm to a farmer neighbor. "In some places silence means consent. Vermont is not one of them:" the farmer does not like elms. When the children are little, the first week in Vermont goes slowly: they have to check up on everything—new calves, the diving raft at the pond. They are happy in Vermont. "Were there better people anywhere? The answer is no." Mrs. A. has an Emergency Shelf to accommodate all the guests who make their way to Appleyard Center. There are picnics galore. They create a lawn, which, after great labor, serves as a perfect stage for their July Fourth parties. Mrs. A. works in the Corn Barn, restoring Hitchcock chairs, trays, and the table that Old Ebenezer Appleyard, Revolutionary War veteran, made out of his own timber. Mrs. A. loves growing peas; in the sunlight, the pods "hang like pieces of translucent jade." She takes visitors to Jerusalem, where, in 1860, recruiters from the Northern Army took away all the young men. Some died; some went out West. The town never recovered. (Jonathan Evans, an orphan who lived in Jerusalem with Aunt Debby, went with the recruiters, deserted briefly to see her again, and then went back and fought all the way through the war.) September comes, the season for filling the silos. They roast corn and Mrs. A. plays the accordion. Summer people, they start the preparations for closing the house—covering the barn chimney, disconnecting the water, putting away the porch furniture. Neighbors talk about what a shame it is the Appleyards must leave before such-

and-such happens in Vermont. The year is rounded out with Thanksgiving and Christmas family celebrations.

In *Country Mouse* (1945), Mrs. Appleyard is a combination good fairy and cupid. Her friend and neighbor, Ann Spencer ("Nancy") Roland, whose father is "somewhere in France" (it is 1944), needs income to keep up her ancestral property, house, barn, and tavern on Roland Hill. Marcella Carmody, a city girl, and Susan Hunter, whose husband is overseas, need a site for their war work, running an art institute for refugees. Mrs. A. puts them all together. Nancy now works as an assistant at the Roland Hill Institute of Arts and Letters, which explains her presence at the train station to meet boarders, starring Lady Finchfallow, a glamorous and alluring aristocrat. Lady Finchfallow, who is accompanied by her baby, the viscount, and his nanny, is languid and indifferent about Vermont but very interested in her fellow passenger, Captain Owen Thorpe. Captain Thorpe, a forty-three-old widower stationed in Canada, is bringing his twelve-year-old son, John, to stay at Roland Hill. Nancy is smitten with Owen instantly. The staff at Roland Hill—Nancy's cook, Thérèse Le Blanc, who escaped with Nancy from Paris in 1940, and Aaron Sprague, the hired hand—are not impressed with the snobbish Lady Finchfallow's overbearing manners: "There are four freedoms in America and a fifth in Vermont—freedom from patronage." Those boarders who have ration cards bring them, but part of the philanthropic purpose of the institute is to grow its own food. The tradition at Roland Hill is abundant: "Nancy's ancestors had cut down the wilderness, cleared fields, built those red barns, harnessed the stream to grind meal and saw wood, baked the rose-red brick out of which the Tavern was built." Mrs. Appleyard arranges an ideal wedding for Marcella's daughter, Celia (a perfect piece of Alençon lace is fished out of a trunk) and her beau, Myrick, and then sets about helping Nancy and Owen find some private time together. Owen, who is a transport pilot after being wounded in combat, knows Nancy's father, who is working for the underground in France and has

"a Vermont quality of quiet determination." Despite Lady Finchfallow's attempts at disparaging Nancy, Owen falls in love with her and they become engaged before he leaves again for active duty. At the end of this exuberant story, Owen manages to return from Europe with Nancy's father and Lord Finchfallow (who has been missing in action) and suggests that he and Nancy be married that very day. "It couldn't be today, could it?" she wails. "We'll go right down and ask Mrs. Appleyard," says Owen. "I'm sure she will arrange everything."

Brad Kessler

The Woodcutter's Christmas (2001) begins in Manhattan, where a family with two children makes friends with Vars, a man from Dedham's Notch who brings his Christmas trees to their city corner every year. At first the family takes him snacks and drinks and then begins inviting him into the apartment for meals. They are so fond of him that when he ceases to turn up at Christmastime they are disappointed. They exchange cards but don't know why Vars has not returned to Manhattan. Three years pass; the family goes up to Vermont to ski. As they are driving home, one of the children spies a sign pointing to Dedham's Notch. They decide to make a detour and, because it has become dark and snowy, are persuaded by Vars to spend the night. They meet someone he introduces as "Claire." That night, after dinner, Vars tells them why he could not continue his Manhattan trips. Although his parents started out cutting trees, they decided instead to sell Christmas trees and replant their forests. They worked and worked, and, after their death, he continued to sell trees in New York. Because he had no one with whom to spend Christmas Eve in Vermont, he stayed at an inexpensive hotel and explored the city. As he walked around Manhattan on Christmas Day, he found that many trees had been thrown on the sidewalk or dumped behind garbage cans. He was so distressed people did not enjoy their trees for more than a day that he started to fill his truck with abandoned trees to carry them back to Vermont for proper burial. While doing this, he

K

encountered a street-woman so chilled and scrawny that he invited her to a restaurant for a cup of coffee. She told him a little about her sad life. When he returned to Vermont, he discovered her stowed away in his truck. She offered to keep house for him and has been there ever since.

Frances Parkinson Keyes

The Career of David Noble (1921) is situated in Hamstead in the Connecticut River Valley. Hiram and Lizzie Noble, a hardworking farming couple "out back," have five children: David, fourteen, is the eldest; the others are Leon, Sam, Harry, and Susie. Impressed with David's scholarly and industrious ways, Hiram decides to sell his farm, move down to the village, and run the post office so David can attend Hamstead High School. Hal Huntington, a contemporary of Hiram's in a higher social class, moves back to the Big House in Hamstead after the death of his son and daughter-in-law, to raise his granddaughter, Jacqueline Désirée Huntington. David, who needs to earn money for medical school, is hired by the Huntington's foreman, Sheldon, as a chore-boy and, over five years, befriends Jacqueline and eventually loves her. At nineteen, he is the valedictorian of his class and, before leaving for Harvard, asks Mr. Huntington for Jacqueline's hand at a time when he can support her. Her father throws him out of the house, hemming and hawing about why the chore-boy should want to educate himself above his station. Five years later, David has become a first-class surgeon and attends conferences all over the world with his mentor, Dr. Herbert Ross. In London, David calls on Jacqueline to reopen his suit. Finding her immodestly dressed and drinking brandy in the afternoon in the company of indolent men, David is ashamed and disappointed. She thinks he loves his career more than he loves people. They become engaged, although he continues to lecture her on their differences in taste, outlook, and lifestyle. He is entirely self-absorbed. They fight due to a misunderstanding about her being engaged to someone else, and David returns to Boston and the opening of a new hospital, where he is named chief surgeon despite

the fact that no one on the board has ever heard of Hamstead. He knows that, skillful as he is, his patients do not respond to him; it is because he has never suffered. Dr. Ross dies, leaving David his fortune; David heads for Hamstead to rest. His father shows him all the changes, but David feels he has "outgrown" Hamstead. When David learns he misconstrued what happened in London, he begins searching for Jacqueline and finds her in France, where she has gone to live with her grandmother and do charity work in her village. She almost dies, but he saves her life and they decide to marry and return to Hamstead to serve: they want to build a hospital in the village they both underestimated when they were young.

The scene in *Lady Blanche Farm* (1931) is again the village of Hamstead, where the Mannings have lived ever since Colonel Moses Manning, a friend of Lafayette's during the American Revolution, brought home as his bride a countess from France. Lady Blanche died in childbirth, leaving twins. The contemporary Mannings live in three handsome brick houses just outside the village. Violet Manning, a self-absorbed hypochondriac, has two children, Blanche, seventeen, and Paul, twenty. Blanche is an enchanting, elfin young woman; Paul has inherited his mother's inertia and is half-heartedly engaged to his cousin, Mary, also twenty, who runs the household of her widowed father, Seth, and takes care of two small siblings, Moses and Algernon. Cousin Jane, unmarried, lives alone in her house. Philip Starr, a Harvard-educated architect in a distinguished firm in Boston who is just recovering from typhoid fever, comes upon Blanche when he is driving in the direction of Burlington; she persuades him to spend the night at Mary's before he continues his journey. In a few seconds, Philip and Blanche have fallen in love. Violet plans Blanche and Philip's wedding. She thinks it a nuisance they cannot go to Europe because of the "tiresome" war, but she is going to show people from Boston that she knows how to give a wedding, even if she does live in the country. Paul, weakened by his mother's indulgence, takes to drinking and spending time with a flirtatious visitor from New York, Rosalie King; he and

Mary break their engagement. The village considers her jilted, but she continues leading her busy, selfless life, cooking, cleaning, and bringing up her little brothers. "In Hamstead the war was regarded with impatience if it was regarded at all," but, as its young men are called up, the village can no longer remain indifferent. Paul, realizing he has made a terrible mistake, turns over a new leaf, enlists, and asks Mary once more to marry him. She refuses and he goes overseas. Hamstead is now involved in the war—it is not "just foreigners" who are fighting. Philip is the first to die; Blanche, stalwart and brave, has a little boy, Philip. No mail comes from Paul and he is presumed dead. Finally, released from a prison camp, he returns home, thinner, wiser, now a man, and he and Mary marry.

The Safe Bridge (1934) is about Elizabeth Burr, seventeen, banished from Scotland by her parents in 1804 and sent to Ryegate near Newbury to live with the Cameron family as their ward and household-helper. Her "crime" was spending a chaste, chaperoned night with her fiancé, Brian Keith, before he sailed for India with the army; her parents tell everyone that she is dead. James Anderson, the strong, taciturn hired man, falls in love with the tiny, cheerful Scottish lass; she does not love him, but considers him a friend, a "safe bridge" in her turbulent life. She learns to milk, make butter, cook, spin, and sew. Newbury becomes the first capital of Vermont; some heroes of the Revolution live there. The wife of Colonel Thomas Johnson, one of the first founders, befriends Elizabeth, as do priest David Sutherland and his wife, Anna Waters. Because she ministers to a dying, unwed woman and baptizes her dying baby, Elizabeth is tried for heresy. At the trial, she stands up to the judges and defends her actions solemnly and articulately. After two years of courtship, she agrees to marry James and has three little girls, Sue, Jane, and Agnes. He builds them a house and hires a woman to help Elizabeth. Life on the surface is pleasant enough, but she misses "culture and sophistication;" she and James do not share any interests. Her best friend, Mary Dunn, kills herself when her fiancé, Hugh Fowler, goes mad.

Inevitably, Basil Keith discovers after eleven years that Elizabeth is still alive and comes to Vermont to see her: she must choose between the man she has always loved and her loyal and loving husband. Basil has inherited a great estate in England and remained faithful to her, but Elizabeth decides to stay with James Anderson. The epilogue shows the contented family fifteen years later; two of the three girls are married and three little boys have been added to the ménage.

In *Joy Street* (1950), Emily Thayer is a proper Bostonian in the late 1930s: her grandmother is the redoubtable Old Mrs. Forbes, and Emily is surrounded by Boston society. She marries Roger Field because she believes he will give her a dependable life. Her grandmother provides them a house on Joy Street. Roger and his colleagues, David Salomont, Brian Collins, and Pellegrino de Lucca, make their way in their law firm before the outbreak of the war. Roger dies after the war; Emily marries Brian, who has become a politician, and they move to Washington. The counterpoint to life in Boston is the long weekends and vacations Emily and Roger spend in Vermont before the war. Her Aunt Elizabeth, who has never married, teaches chemistry at Bryn Mawr and spends her vacations at Hollyhocks, a brick house in central Vermont reached by train to White River Junction. Emily's grandmother has never visited Vermont though she concedes "there might be a few persons of background and culture in the Vermont village." Emily and Roger and their friends skate and play bridge. Bradford Olcott, one of Roger's classmates from Harvard Law School who practices law in Vergennes, visits with his wife and child. Aunt Elizabeth meets another professor, marries, and has a child, Archie. This is what she says about Vermont: "I love the sort of people who live in those houses. They're sincere and intelligent and kindly. They do more thinking and more reading too, along with their hard physical labor, than almost anyone at Bryn Mawr. And yet they always have time to be neighborly with each other. They're not neighborly with me, but I think they would be if I lived here all the time, if they didn't put me in the class with 'summer people.'

K

Anyhow, I'd be willing to risk loneliness. I love everything about the place so much that I could be happy with very little human companionship. I wish I could stay here all my life."

Roger King

Moving and meaningful with an uncannily appealing first-person narrator, *A Girl from Zanzibar* (2002) is set at small Moore College in southern Vermont near Cavendish ("Solzhenitsyn...lived somewhere up the road") and close enough to Brattleboro to drive there for dinner. While teaching Multicultural Studies at the college, Marcella D'Souza, lonely in her borrowed house in the woods ("It's so cold here the snow squeaks, like walking on mice"), thinks with longing and ambivalence about the two other places she has lived—Zanzibar and London. Marcella's blood embodies every culture—Asian, African, Arab, European—and she is currently doing research on the "modern migrant," partly for her studies but also to find out about herself. Tiny and independent, Marcella is a successful businesswoman—an owner of taxis—in Dar es Salaam. She meets Dr. Geoffrey Sutton, an Englishman, when he comes to Zanzibar for research. He persuades Marcella to accompany him to London. She lives with him in Reading for a while but is unhappy in that stuffy milieu and goes to London, where she meets some similarly illegal immigrants in Bayswater and recommences her life there. She becomes involved with Benji, who does "business deals" and, before she knows it, she is deeply implicated in a money-laundering scheme. That is not what causes her arrest, however; she tries to help a Nigerian friend who is being importuned by the police and finds herself incarcerated in Cookham, sentenced to eight years. Her talents recognized, she is allowed to pursue distance-education courses, which culminate in a Ph.D. Her thesis topic is the migrant community in Bayswater, which she traces back to Zanzibar. When she is released from prison, she is deported to Tanzania, but, through a Tanzanian policeman friend of hers and Geoffrey's in Dar, she is diverted immediately to another plane that takes her to the United States and thus to Vermont. She is able to open the eyes of some of her students to broader issues: "This, I discovered, was the other pleasure in research: not only do all things and people turn out to be connected, but every connection turns out to be unreliable. No one, any more than me, can say exactly where she came from or who she is. I am setting about introducing this subversive concept into my spring courses. They said I could teach anything." Tracked down by one of people from London involved in money laundering, she is forced to commit a violent act. Before the snow melts, she has disappeared into the middle of America, traveling under an assumed name and finding friends among the immigrant populations. She has left Vermont, where "everything is white and strange." She has demonstrated to her students that "nothing is separate, nothing fixed, and that migration is our natural state." Marcella—now Stella Souza and only thirty-four—will surely find that "the world has some use for her."

Stephen King

In *The Shining* (1977), Jack Torrance applies for a job as caretaker at the Overlook Hotel in Colorado, having been fired from his job in Vermont, where he was an English teacher at elite Stovington Preparatory Academy in Stovington (thirty miles west of Barre off I-89). He had a drinking buddy, Al Shockley, there; his wife, Wendy, liked their neat brick house; and his son, Danny, was enrolled in Stovington nursery school and had friends who were children of other faculty members. Jack has an uncontrollable temper: first, he broke his son's arm in a fit of anger; then he beat up a Stovington student, George Hatfield, because George was slashing his tires after Jack kicked him off the debate team for stuttering. Jack believes that he had not done things at Stovington; things were done to him. In Colorado, it is apparent that Danny has occult powers—"the shining"—and can read peoples' minds.

In *The Stand* (1990), the integrity of the Atlanta Plague Center has been breached and the world is almost completely destroyed by a mysterious virus. In Stovington sits a second government plague and communicable diseases center. Ninety-nine percent of the population is dead; the few remaining humans are, for some inexplicable reason, immune to the disease. One of these, Stuart Redman, who used to work at a calculator plant in Arnette, Texas, awakes to find himself in a jail-like hospital in Stovington. He can see the textile mill, the river, the turnpike, and the Green Mountains outside the window. Staff personnel are taking his blood at gunpoint. He escapes and heads east where he meets Frannie Goldsmith and Harold Lauder in Ogunquit, Maine. They decide to pool resources and return to Stovington, leaving a big painted sign telling who they are and where they are going. When Larry Underhill, whose girlfriend Rita Blakemore dies in Bennington, runs into Nadine Cross and her son, Joe, in Ogunquit, they see the sign the others have left and decide to join them. They meet Lucy Swann on the way, take her with them, and make it to Quechee, Randolph, and then Stovington, where they find the place deserted, but Harold has left another sign, instructing them to stay on his route to Nebraska.

In *Firestarter* (1980), students Andrew McKee and Vicky Tomlinson participated in a paranormal experiment at their university. The effects of injected chromosomes show up in their daughter, Charlene ("Charlie"), a mutant with the power to start fires ("pyrokinesis"). The Shop (Department of Scientific Intelligence, based in Longwood, Virginia) has murdered Andy's wife and is now after his daughter. The only place to hide is his grandfather's cottage in Tashmore, Vermont; Tashmore Pond is contiguous with Bradford, New Hampshire. Fortunately, there are a couple of cords of wood and shelves of canned goods in the cottage. They spend the winter there; Andy cuts up blown-down branches for the stove and cross-country skis to the tiny hamlet of Bradford for supplies. The folks in Bradford don't have much use for Vermont and "that fucking Russian laid up in his house like a czar, writing books no one could understand." Unfortunately, the man who runs the local store is an agent for

the Shop and, when the thaw comes, its people arrive to take Andy and Charlie, drugged, to Virginia. Months pass while the Shop tries to make Charlie demonstrate her fire-starter skills and Andy, his mental-domination capability. He uses his powers to trick the headman at the Shop and almost effects their escape. He is killed, but Charlie gets away, and, remembering her father's desire to tell their story to the world, goes to *Rolling Stone Magazine*, the one place that is "honest, nationwide, and not tied to the government or the government's ideas."

Rudyard Kipling

"**A Walking Delegate**" (1898), an amusing political satire, is set on a farm in Dummerston, where Sunday afternoon is salting time. Two men seek out the horses, which are "scattered through the seventy acres of the Back Pasture." "You must go down by the brook that feeds the clicking, bubbling water-ram; up through the sugar-bush, where the young maple undergrowth closes round you like a shallow sea; next follow the faint line of an old county road running past two green hollows fringed with wild rose that mark the cellars of two ruined houses; then by Lost Orchard, where nobody ever comes except in cider-time; then across another brook, and so into the Back Pasture. Half of it is pine and hemlock and spruce, with sumac and little juniper bushes, and the other half is grey rock and boulder and moss, with green streaks of brake and swamp." The two men lie down to rest among the "brown, silky needles" of the pines, while the horses lick salt and talk among themselves. They all belong to the farm save one, a yellow, wall-eyed horse that has been sent up from the livery stable to board. The yellow horse they call "Boney" is a distinct troublemaker. He begins at once with his harangue that the horses are "bowing their heads before the Oppressor." While the other horses continue to lick the salt, Boney pursues his complaints about their not getting their "inalienable rights of unfettered horsehood" and whining about the "degrading servitood" of horses. He thinks they should "uphold the principles of the code wherever pastured." The other horses listen at first, and then take up their points of view against those of the yellow horse. They are angry at his disregard for the humans whom they serve and believe that he is an ingrate. They finally criticize him so severely that he is glad to be returned to the livery stable the next day.

John Knowles

K

In *A Separate Peace* (1959), the class of 1943 at Devon School, "the most beautiful school in New England," is preparing to go to war after graduation. The nub of the story is the complex relationship between Gene Forrester, a conventional young man and excellent student, and Phineas ("Finny"), a superb athlete, a daredevil, and attractive to everyone, who breaks rules, flouts convention, and gets away with everything. Although Gene and Finny become roommates and best friends, Gene sometimes wonders if Finny is jealous of his excellence in scholarship and is trying to subvert his efforts. The terrifyingly tall tree at the river's edge becomes the site of the boys' most daring exploits. Once, when Finny is out on the limb, Gene jounces the tree slightly and Finny falls and fractures his leg. Gene's action was a sudden inexplicable impulse. Finny never blames him for the accident, until the night the older students hold a trial. On that occasion, Finny sweeps out of the room, trips on some steep steps, falls and breaks his leg again, and dies on the operating table. One of their classmates is Elwin ("Leper") Lepellier, the first in their class to enlist. He wants to be in the ski troops: this "cool, clean response to war glided straight into Leper's Vermont heart." During basic training, he breaks down and, threatened with a Section Eight discharge, goes AWOL and heads for his home in northern Vermont. He sends a telegram to Gene, begging him to come. Gene takes a train and a bus to Leper's: "He lived far up in Vermont, where at this season of the year even the paved main highways are bumpy and buckling from the freezing weather, and each house executes a lonely holding action against the cold. The natural state of things is coldness, and houses are fragile havens, holdouts in a death landscape, unforgettably comfortable,

simple though they are, just because of their warmth." At the bus station, Gene finds no taxi to take him to Leper's house. "This was Vermont. But if that meant austerity toward strangers it also meant mornings of glory such as this one, in which the snow, white almost to blueness, lay like a soft comforter over the hills, and birches and pines indestructibly held their ground, rigid lines against the snow and sky, very thin and strong like Vermonters." The Lepers' house has long and narrow windows, like "New England faces." The meal was an "abundant Vermont lunch, more like dinner." Gene and Leper go for a walk and treat each other like criminals and enemies: Leper tells Gene he knows he knocked Finny out of the tree and crippled him for life; Gene tells Leper he doesn't give a damn about his experience in the army.

Joseph Koenig

Smuggler's Notch (1989), about a police lieutenant who feels responsible for his partner's death and an overly self-confident young psychopathic killer, is tightly constructed and embraces the landscape as a main player in the drama. The psychopath, Paul Conklin, picks up a hitchhiker, Becky Beausoleil, whom he rapes and murders. Because Becky's father is Raymond Beausoleil, state's attorney for Cabot County, Lieutenant Lawrence ("Larry") St. Germain is asked by the sheriff in Tremont Center to look for the missing girl. Hunters find her body on the road to Lake Mansfield. Larry is a sympathetic character even with his weaknesses. He is aware of what other people think of him, he cares about his personal appearance, and he hates the coroner, Sajit Singh (some say it is because Singh "hasn't lived in Vermont for five generations"). Larry finally brings in Conklin, after a desperate struggle in Smuggler's Notch, but only after he has first given up his weapon to Conklin, who kills Larry's partner. At the first trial for the deputy's death, Larry is an ineffectual witness and, feeling guilty and dishonored, turns in his gun and his badge. Conklin is sent to the Southern Vermont Correctional facility in East Shaftsbury, from which he makes a dramatic escape. Meanwhile, Larry becomes an ambulance driver. Their paths cross again at Smuggler's Notch, and there, amid a skillful use of terrain and scenery, the drama concludes. "I thought he'd killed you!" exclaims the woman hostage whom Conklin dragged along. "He did," replies Larry, "but I'm over it now."

Kathryn Kramer

Sweet Water (1998) is about secret lives, deceptions, and coincidences in which the past mirrors the present. Lucinda Dearborn and Greta Sayre are parallel heroines. Thrush Hollow ("hill overlapping hill like the soft flakes of a milkweed pod") in West Stilling in northern Vermont is a nineteenth century inn catering to people seeking a water cure. When the owner of Thrush Hollow, Rufus Dearborn, dies in 1870, his daughter, Lucinda, in her twenties, takes over the management of the inn. In the twentieth century, Greta and Ned Dene buy Thrush Hollow. (Stilling is the kind of place where those who live there year round enunciate with disdain the phrase "summah people.") Greta, the daughter of an American diplomat and a mystery writer, was educated abroad, where she fell in love with Lars Crain. Lars married Julia, and Greta married Ned, although she carries on an extramarital affair with Lars and has a fourteen-year-old son, Henry, by him (Ned thinks the boy is his). When the spring at Thrush Hollow dries up, Ned hires Hudson Sleeper, a water witch, who finds not only water but a steel box in the basement, filled with Lucinda's diary and love letters to her from a famous writer—"Let us call him O.," says Ned. Ned is a professor and biographer; the minute he lays eyes on the letters, he knows he has uncovered a gold mine. Although O. is a famous American writer who has been much examined, no one has discovered his unknown lover, whom he visited five times in forty years. He burned all his letters from Lucinda before his death. O.'s novels describe American expatriates in Europe and feature neurasthenic heroines based on Lucinda. The scene returns to 1865 with O.'s arrival at Thrush Hollow, in the company of his younger brother, S., who was in the Civil

War with Rufus. Lucinda has learned to perform water cures and also has a dowsing skill. Lucinda and O. are immediately attracted to one another. After O.'s death, Lucinda falls in love with her married neighbor, Zebulun Snow, and they carry on a life-long affair. Lucinda later drowns herself. The two lives of deception—Lucinda's and Greta's—reflect each other: Lucinda pines for O.; Greta pines for Lars. At one point, Ned says, "Maybe you can't believe that someone could live a whole life without having what she wanted." He knows Greta is unhappy but doesn't know why. Greta invites Julia to visit them, using as an excuse her business relationship with Lars over the ownership of the horse, Ransom. What the confrontation between Greta and Julia reveals is surprising and effective. (The title is from the passage, "and everywhere the character of the land had been shaped by this striving: to go back, sweet water joining to salt, back to where neither knew where one stopped and the other began.")

William Kritlow

Crimson Snow (1995) is set on Lake Champlain's Grand Isle. Widower Bray Sanderson is a detective in Sugar Steeple. When the assistant pastor at Sugar Steeple Church is thrown from the belfry and killed, Sanderson enlists the help of the new assistant pastor, Win Brady, to solve the crime. Win falls in love with policewoman Ginger Glasgow and everyone else, except Sanderson, finds comfort in religion.

Mary Alice Kruesi

In *One Summer's Night* (2000), Laurel Carrington, twenty-one, is applying to graduate school to study biogenetic engineering when she is invited to Fallingstar (between Wallingford and Danby) to apprentice with a famous illustrator of fairy tales, Maybelle Starr. Laurel doesn't know that Maybelle is an actual fairy who fell in love with a mortal (Arthur Carrington) twenty-one years ago, had a baby (Laurel), and was punished by being sent into exile in Vermont. Only if Maybelle can gain Arthur's human love will she be released from the fairy spell. Living next door to Maybelle is Dane Walden, a farmer and her

K

hired man (and also a self-educated expert on the flora of rain forests). After an exchange of barbs between city girl Laurel and country boy Dane, Arthur arrives and the two sets of lovers solve their problems.

Regina P. Krummel

Looking Good (1985) reveals the painful struggle of fifteen-year-old Ariadne ("Ari") with anorexia nervosa, told through a daily journal entry to her Thomas Laird High School English teacher, Ms. Robbins. The father, mother, Ari, and two younger brothers move from Long Island to a college town near Burlington, where both parents have teaching appointments. Ari feels isolated in "the bucolic splendor" of Vermont. In the college town she sees "a sharp distinction between the brainies, the townies or locals, and the old-timers." She notices many immigrants—Germans, Poles, Austrians, and Italians—in "austere, frugal Vermont." Here, she writes, "we live near simple cemeteries—quiet and secluded—places of pure death." Ari, however, is not really interested in anything other than herself. She is self-absorbed, wanting to be petted and cherished. She knows that "women must be slim and youthful to make it." She scorns her parents: she sees her father as "a workaholic drudge;" her mother, a colorless whiner. Inevitably she ends up in a hospital, where she basks in the attention of the lean young interns bending over her bed. When she is better, she starts meeting a motorcyclist she picks up. John is a rough bully (an angry, neglected kid who sees other men beat up their women); she is living on beer, marijuana, and Marlboros. She becomes bulimic; her stomach hurts so much John starts giving her Demerol. By the time she is rushed to the hospital, she is almost dead. Whether or not she survives is shown in the last pages.

Edward Kuhn, Jr.

Ski Week (1975), set at a ski resort at White Ridge in central Vermont "just across the river" from Hanover, contains an unusual collection of characters. The manager of the resort is an athletic widow who is America's first gold medal woman skier. A thief with a phony leg cast is after the massive profits of the resort. A revolutionary Jewish hippie is out for revenge. A former SS Colonel serves as ski instructor. A corrupt senior senator from Vermont is anti-Semitic. The daughter of the big boss is a nymphomaniac. The big boss is a rich man trying to buy a seat as the junior senator from Vermont (he has schemed to have an eight-lane highway built right to the door of his ski resort). The former owner of the land seeks vengeance. And someone has built a dangerous racetrack on too short a slope.

James Kunstler

The eponymous heroine of *Maggie Darling* (2004), who has been married to bond salesman Kenneth for twenty-five years, caricatures a Martha Stewart lifestyle of extravagant parties, recherché menus, glamorous hangers-on, and a garden estate named Kettle Hill in Fairfield County. The plot, which begins with Maggie's throwing the adulterous Kenneth out of the house, follows the witty, irreverent, self-centered heroine as she looks for love in all the wrong places—a youthful English rock star, Frederick Swann; her photographer, Reggie Chang; her editor, Harold Hamish, inter alia. The Vermont interlude is at Harold Hamish's fishing cabin, found by leaving I-91 at Windsor, thence to Catamount Creek on the Otterkill River. Here Harold ties elaborate flies and takes Maggie fishing. She watches the process of casting with fascination: "The leader unrolled like a red carpet and deposited the fly at the head of the pool like a little foreign dignitary landing in a new country." In order to seduce Maggie, Harold tells her that he has pancreatic cancer and, in a few months, will disappear into a hospice run by monks in Montpelier. Seeing through his ruse, she speeds back to Fairfield, where she finally finds true love.

L

Karen Latuchie

Taking place partially in Overton, Pennsylvania, and more extensively near Manchester, *The Honey Wall* (2004) juggles two stories and time frames. The protagonist of the primary story is Nina Webber, now forty-two, a maker of toys and a car mechanic, who has lived with painter Tony for almost twenty years, most of them in Vermont. These years have been fraught with distrust, adultery on both sides, lack of communication, and an obsessive interest in dissecting their relationship. (The character in the secondary story is Bill, who as a young man was seduced by his brother's wife, Eva, in her bedroom, which had a beehive in the wall. Bill lives in a cabin on Eva's farm across the road from Nina and Tony's house in Overton.) Twenty years earlier, Nina and Tony leave Manhattan to live on a college campus in Cannen. They are given a cottage in a cul-de-sac next door to fellow faculty member George Gunter, and his wife, Diane. Nina, who is used to living in Manhattan, has trouble adjusting to small-town Vermont life; she spends a lot of time driving around Cannen in her convertible. Faculty-member Alan Gill asks Tony and Nina to his large, formal house for his annual cocktail party; Nina feels dislocated and unhappy. She can never tell Tony what she is thinking. Three years later they buy a house with a pond fifteen miles from campus. She is working at a garage and sleeping with one of her co-workers, Nick, in retaliation for an affair Tony had with a student. She has become a regular at a bar on the New York border where Nick and her other co-worker, Gary, hang out. Fourteen years after they arrive in Cannen, Nina walks into Tony's studio and finds him with a student, Suzanne Garyle. Nina goes to Alan Gill's home for a drink to recover from her shock. Alan comforts her, saying the girl is a consummate flirt. The climax occurs some weeks later when Nina, who has left the garage and is working at the Greenville Women's Center, discovers that her first interview is with Suzanne about a "possible pregnancy." The resolution is full of questions about ethics, choice, and loyalty.

Wendi W. Lee

In *Habeas Campus* (2002), Angela Matelli, who is almost thirty-three and belongs to a close-knit Italian family living in Boston, is a former-marine private investigator. Professor Cannon at Hartmore College in Bristol has received several weird voodoo warnings. A student, Amy Garrett, engaged to her teaching assistant, Jonathan Sharpe, has died mysteriously. Intrepid Angela goes undercover as a student in forensic anthropology. She meets Jonathan, who was a Peace Corps volunteer in Haiti; teacher Kirsten Sorenson-Andersen, who did research in Haiti; artist-in-residence Simon Lynch, who is from Haiti; Amy's roommate, Savannah Andersen (who resembles Kirsten); and Dr. Francs Rathman, who has also worked in Haiti. Professor Cannon is reeling from the fact that he thinks he has seen Amy; since it hasn't occurred to him to check the morgue, Angela does—Amy's body is gone. Angela meets graduate student Jack Wade, with whom she has an affair and whom she persuades to do background checks of her suspects on his computer. The Haiti connection is that the drug tetrodotoxin can cause a zombie effect; there is an antidote, which Jonathan believes he has discovered, but someone has stolen it. Angela solves the crime and breaks up with Jack.

Peter Lefcourt

The Woody (1998), funny and well done, features fifty-six-year-old Woodrow ("Woody") Wilson White, the junior senator from Vermont and ranking Democrat on the Medicaid and Health Subcommittee. His chief of staff is Ishmael Leibovitz, whose first name enables Woody to leave messages on his voice mail saying, "Call me, Ishmael." Woody lives in an A-frame house in Peru. He is divorced from and not compatible with Daphne, who is having a lesbian affair with a Finnish ice skater. Beverly

Levesque, head of his state reelection committee, warns him that the Vermont Maple Syrup Distributors Association (VMSDA), which has given him five hundred thousand dollars toward his reelection, may be a laundering operation for an extortion-and-loan-sharking organization. Woody is in Vermont to give some speeches ("It's your self-reliance-and-Yankee-integrity speech, Senator"). A vulgar running joke concerns Woody's sexual impotence; another periodic jest is the observation that, no matter how benign the weather, one's interlocutor will say, "Might rain." The Vermont Republicans back a woman candidate against Woody, a state's attorney from Burlington named Rebecca Gatney. Woody does the rounds: a staff meeting in Burlington, a speech at Middlebury College, and a potluck in Vergennes. "In some of the resort areas, Woody would draw crowds of what the Vermonters call disdainfully 'summer folk'—people with $100 haircuts, Porsche Carrera sunglasses, and Banana Republic work shirts. They were, by and large, liberal Democrats, but they didn't vote in Vermont. They came out of their vacation condos and *Architectural Digest* summer homes to hear Woody for the entertainment value, tired of mosquitoes, corn on the cob, and CNN." Woody's campaign receives four hundred thousand dollars from the Tourette's Syndrome Foundation, a front for the Togo government that expects Woody to push for foreign aid for its mining industry. Ishmael is a closet heterosexual in a breakfast club of gay chiefs-of-staff in order to pick up useful gossip. The framework for the book is the authorized biography of Woody by Lee Schumock. He interviews Woody's worldly mother in California, his daughter who has moved to an Amish farm, his son who sells drugs in Florida, and his first wife, Sharon, who left him after she moved from Ohio to Peru and found that it "didn't even have a bowling alley." The VMSDA asks Woody to nominate the state's attorney, Vincent Ruggiero, for a judgeship so that he will discontinue his investigation. The Vermont Citizens for Ethical Government, headquartered in Winooski, files an official complaint of influence peddling against Woody to the Senate

Select Committee on Ethics. It turns out that the VMSDA is responsible for eighty percent of the organized crime in Vermont. Woody challenges Rebecca Gatney to a Debate in the Field, with a Marlboro College professor as moderator. It rains. Woody has numerous other problems, but, as the conclusion demonstrates, his staff has good reason to be loyal to him.

David Leitz

Divorced former New York ad-agency writer Max Addams, in his forties, runs Whitefork Lodge in Loon, sixty-eight miles north of Montpelier on Route 16. The lodge was built in 1908 by the grandson of Daniel Webster. Whitefork River and Sweet Lake are perfect sites for brook trout (strictly "catch and release"); his loyal housekeeper, cook, and reformed alcoholic Stormy Bryant helps run the place for him; and his old dog, Spotter, stand on rocks and points for fish. He has a grown daughter, Samantha; his wife has remarried and lives in Florida with someone at Sea World; and he is forming a relationship with Ruth Pearlman. In *Casting in Dead Water* (1996), a honeymoon couple is staying at the lodge. Red Crosley, his hired hand, reports that Collari International, which owns the local pulp mill, is clear-cut logging on Morning Mountain above the lodge. Max was assured, at the last town meeting, that the logs for the pulp mill would come from Canada. Clear-cutting on his mountain would ruin the Whitefork River for fish. He acknowledges that he is not an environmentalist so much as he is a businessman running his lodge for personal financial gain. Max goes to see Ruth, the woman who took over as mayor from Claremont Taylor. Ruth introduces Max to a lawyer, Wally Murray, who files a restraining order to stop the clear-cutting because of the diesel oil that has seeped into the water and killed a number of fish. The town is instantly divided between environmental protection and jobs. Max's geologist friend, John Pulver, comes from Colorado to take core samples to find out if the aquifer is polluted, doing the job with Max by night. Darren Foley, the sheriff, and his deputy, Mark Edward, arrest John for trespassing and beating up one of the guards at the clear-cut. Red, the hired man, is murdered. John and Stephanie, a guest, begin an affair. Someone steals the wallet with the fingerprint of Red's murderer, trashes the lake, vandalizes the canoe and boat, and sets the lodge afire with a dead body inside. It is not Stephanie, because she turns up murdered in the Charles River. Max joins John in Boston, where they are accosted unexpectedly by the villain. After the crimes are satisfactorily explained, Ruth Pearlman moves in with Max.

In *Dying to Fly-Fish* (1996), Whitefork Lodge has been entirely rebuilt after the fire, strictly from the plans of the original building. Max has added modern accoutrements, such as new bathrooms, and erected a new cabin near the lake. His business is doing fairly well since the release of Robert Redford's movie about fly-fishing. Stormy's brother, Rayleen, who lost a leg in World War II, is now the lodge's handyman. Ruth Pearlman, Max's first serious relationship since his divorce, has decided to "separate" from him because she plans to run for governor. Max's old ad agency, Kempton and Kearsy, which he left ten years ago, wants to shoot a German beer ad at his lodge. They offer him so much money he can't refuse, even though the local Loon Lager-makers are annoyed. The crew arrives: Jane Ornstein, the abrasive executive producer; Sharon Long, the lissome star; Paul Greco, lighting and assistant director, and his partner, Kerry Mahoney, wardrobe and make-up; Bendel Domini, the photographer; and Bernie Sultz, the client's ad manager. The local religious community boycotts the shooting of the beer ad. The days are long and unpleasant under Jane's whip and, when she is found drowned in the river, everyone seems rather relieved. They all had reasons to kill her: she was blackmailing Bernie because of his drinking; she turned down Paul's promotion; she was rude and authoritarian to Bendel, whom she called "old man." The sheriff points out to Max that this event may bring him bad publicity and even a "wrongful death" suit from Jane's family. In the midst of the drama, Bendel asks Stormy to marry him; Sharon succeeds in seducing Max. From the autopsy, the sheriff reports that the pH

of the water in Jane's lungs was high in acid, which could kill the fish. When Max tests the water, he realizes that she could not have drowned in White Fork River. She was drowned elsewhere, probably in her own bathtub, with the simple vinegar solution used for cleaning purposes. The sheriff thinks Max is crazy. The *Loon Sentinel* staff arrives and interviews the movie crew. Two of them lie: Max knows that Bernie was not in his room and Paul was not at the beaver dam. The crew leaves and Max tries to forget Sharon. When his old friend, John, invites him to go fishing in New Zealand, Max realizes he can stop over in Los Angeles to see Sharon but instead has a shocking clash with the killers.

In *Fly-Fishing Can Be Fatal* (1997), Ruth lost her bid for governor the previous fall and has recently been spending weekends with Max to help with a lodge construction project. He is adding four more bedrooms and another bath but has run out of money and can't continue to pay the contractor, Lyle Martin. Stormy is still there, married to Bendel, along with her brother, Rayleen, and Spotter. A Rhode Island Corporation called Dantell proposes reserving the lodge for a week for its CEO, Vincent d'Antella, and associates. The Corporation will pay a lot of money up-front, which will cover Max's construction costs. Mayor Ruth is furious when she hears, because d'Antella happens to head New England's largest organized-crime family and she is in a tight run for reelection against a man who heads the Citizens Committee for a Better Loon and its crime-fighting agenda. Vincent arrives by helicopter with his two bodyguards, Thomas Marchetti and Ralph Garrett, and a glamorous moll named Constance Roth. The bodyguards buy fishing licenses in Loon and their criminal records immediately appear on Ruth's computer. She tells Max he has put her in an untenable position. Someone with a deer rifle murders Lyle Martin in a bowling alley. Ruth insists upon calling the state police, although the acting deputy sheriff, Billy Kendall, objects; brash and badly trained, he sees himself as the new sheriff. The *Loon Sentinel* is writing incendiary stories about Max's guests. Meanwhile, the fishing is going well at the lodge—Vincent turns out to be an expert fisherman and a gentleman, but Bendel is misbehaving with Connie and Stormy is furious. When she disappears with her Winchester rifle, Max is terrified that she will turn to drink in this crisis. While out on Sweet Lake, Bendel and Vincent are both shot and killed; now Max is terrified that Stormy is the murderer. The final violent scene takes place in Stormy's cabin where Rayleen and Max are tied up by the perpetrator, whom Max manages to subdue and kill. After a funeral for Bendel, his friends go to a special spot to scatter his ashes; old Mrs. d'Antella arrives in a limousine with Vincent's ashes, to cast them on the river where he was so happy fishing.

In *Hooked on Death* (2000), Max, having broken his ankle, invites his old friend, Abenaki "Chief" Danny Shortsleeves, to act as a fishing guide until Max's cast is removed. His twenty-eight-year-old daughter, Samantha, makes her first appearance at the lodge, accompanied by two glamorous career women friends from New York. While fishing on the lake, one of Samantha's friends hooks and lands a human skull. This discovery creates a crisis in the community over who is the owner of the skull. Is it the local historical society? Or is it the Abenakis? Or is it, as the new sheriff, Simon Perkins, claims, evidence of an old murder? As the sheriff digs for clues, tensions mount and one of the young women is murdered. The traditional ending finds Max in a deadly confrontation on a mountaintop.

Jeffrey Lent

In *In the Fall* (2001), Norman Pelham's family has owned a farm on the Bethel Road south of Randolph since before the Revolutionary War. Norman is wounded in the Civil War and cared for by Leah, an escaped slave, whom he brings home to Vermont. She had a violent childhood, raped by teen-aged boys when she was twelve and then attacked by her white half-brother, Alexander Mebane, whom she killed. Norman's mother, who claims to be an abolitionist, is shocked by Norman's bringing

home a black woman and moves out of the house, taking his sister, Connie, with her. Leah has two daughters, Prudence and Abigail, followed by a boy, Jamie. Connie moves back into the house to help Leah after the first baby is born. Other than her mother-in-law's reaction, Leah does not suffer racism at the hands of the neighbors. Abigail's courtship with Dan Martin does not lead to marriage, however, because, as Abigail says, "I'm a colored girl." Jamie is beaten up at school. Leah takes the young people to a fair where she meets Ben, billed as the "African Behemoth." He is the first Negro she has seen since 1865, twenty-five years earlier. This chance meeting prompts her to go to North Carolina to see her mother, Helen. When she returns from her trip, Leah hangs herself. In 1909, Jamie, now nineteen, runs away from home to Barre, where he finds work with Victor delivering wine. On a street in his neighborhood, he meets a girl named Joey, an entertainer, whom he takes back to his room after a drunken client beats her. Jamie asks Victor for the money he is owed; when Victor shortchanges him, Jamie savagely plunges a knife through Victor's hand. Jamie and Joey escape to New Hampshire. She gets a job singing and he makes deals. Five years pass. Joey is still an entertainer and Jamie is a bar manager, running a liquor business for White Mountain resorts. Joey leaves him for a rich and married man who tempts her with better prospects, but, when she discovers she is pregnant with Jamie's baby, she comes back. By now Jamie is a bootlegger dealing with many unsavory characters. He dies a horrible death at the hands of one of them, who turns out to be the son of Victor, whom Jamie had treated so viciously many years before. Foster, his son, finds the money that Jamie has hidden, as well as a letter from his Aunt Abigail in Randolph, and takes off for Vermont. When he reaches the Pelham farm, he is astounded to find that his aunts are Negroes; when they tell him his father "passed," he doesn't know what the term means. He determines to go to Sweetboro, North Carolina, to learn the secret of his grandmother's suicide. The explication is shocking and heartbreaking.

Ellen Lesser

The Other Woman (1988), adroit and insightful, features Jennifer Gold, twenty-six, a free-lance writer living in a farmhouse near Middlefield and Deer Mountain ("The white birches were deepest in bud; a halo of iridescent spring green seemed almost to float around their thin, supplicant branches"). Her amusing mother, who calls weekly to check up on her, always implies that Vermont is "a wasteland, a pioneer settlement." Jennifer falls in love with Richard Avery, thirty-eight, an environmental lawyer. Their relationship is nearly perfect. He is married, but he had fallen out of love with his wife before he began the affair with Jennifer and is getting a divorce. Richard can afford to give Ruth Ann a generous settlement for her and the two boys. Before Jennifer knows what has hit her, his two boys, Benjamin, five, and David, eight months, are spending every weekend with her and Richard. She, who has never had occasion to change a diaper, is suddenly getting up in the middle of the night to heat a bottle. Jennifer is smart and sensitive (she is a poet), but she is awkward with the children, resents them, and doesn't think Richard provides proper discipline. Her relationship with Richard deteriorates. She is the outsider; Richard and Ruth Ann amiably discuss the kids over the telephone several times a week. When the divorce papers are final, Richard asks Jennifer to marry him. She must decide whether he really wants her for herself or as a stepmother for his children and, if the latter, whether she deserves better.

Five of the eleven stories in *The Shoplifter's Apprentice* (1990) are situated in Vermont. Sharp and literate, the stories look at young women who are needy, lonely, jealous, searching, and incomplete. The narrator in the title story, "**The Shoplifter's Apprentice**," is a young working girl who has natural yearnings for material goods that she cannot afford. When she sees a shoplifter help himself to a bottle of champagne, she tries to ignore him: the next thing she knows, she has shared the bottle and gone to bed with him. He mesmerizes her, turning her on to shoplifting like a drug. "This rush of chemicals wasn't only fear, it was a terrible freedom. Anything could happen now." The first-person narrator in "**Stinking Benjamin**" has moved from the city up to Vermont to work for the *Valley Tribune* and rents a farmhouse on a back road. At work, she meets Jan Lowe, in her fifties, who does pen-and-ink sketches for the paper. The narrator is in need of a friend and Jan rapidly fills that vacuum. She teaches the narrator the names of wildflowers; she cooks for her. When the narrator wants to buy one of her paintings at a show, Jan suggests exchanging the painting for writing lessons: Jan aspires to be a writer. Shortly, Jan begins to be published; simultaneously, she begins to gripe: there are typos in her piece; she is stuck in the back of the paper. Jan suffocates the narrator with her overtures, which become increasingly sexual. The narrator meets Mark, who soon moves in, and she stops seeing Jan, who has moved to another city and another job. Nevertheless, the narrator is reminded of Jan often, particularly when she thinks about wildflowers. In "**Eating Air**," Rachel, twenty-nine, a roommate of Susan's in college, is flying to Vermont from Miami and looking forward to seeing Susan again and meeting her husband, Hank, and her new baby, Aja. Hank, who is with a company that remodels old farmhouses with skylights and solar collectors, meets Rachel at the airport, explaining in a rather accusatory way that Susan has been up all night with the baby. Rachel looks at their house: "the blue clapboards embedded with cool, faceted jewels of glass; the epidemic of daylilies; the two-seated lawn swing under a mantle of apple trees." Rachel has always compared herself with Susan; perhaps this weekend is a chance to measure Susan's current life against her own. Rachel can't bring herself to tell Susan that she feels "suspended," waiting for the lucky break in love, work, and friendship. At first Susan seems happy and complacent; then Rachel senses that Susan is unhappy with, even afraid of, Hank. There is not enough air in the house for them all to breathe. "**Pressure for Pressure**" describes, in heartbreaking, precise detail, the ordeal of Anna, a twenty-eight-year-old waitress, as she sits in a clinic waiting to undergo her second abortion. A teenager in the room wants to chat. Anna is "seeing someone" whose name is Tom, but she has not told him she is pregnant. She wonders if she has made a mistake not telling him. The teenager, whose boyfriend has abandoned her, goes into the examining room first. When Anna's turn comes, she lies on the table and thinks about her first abortion and the old black nurse who squeezed her hand. Anna had held on tight, but the old woman matched her, "pressure for pressure." When this procedure is over, Anna cries. The cool but sympathetic receptionist asks if she wants to call someone. Anna dials Tom's number and, "whether it was the right thing or not, she would say something." The young woman model in **"Life Drawing"** works at a gallery. When one of the students calls for a private sitting, she goes to his farmhouse. She questions whether it is safe to go, but after she has smoked a joint with him she feels more relaxed. She assumes a pose from which she is able to watch her body take shape under his charcoal: it is a practiced seduction. She wonders if he will give her the picture.

Julius Lester

The Autobiography of God (2004) is both a rich human story and a philosophical examination of the nature of good and evil. Rebecca Nachman, thirty-eight, divorced, lame, a rabbi, and the daughter of Holocaust survivors, is a psychological counselor at John Brown, a small college in Brett. She gave up her former job as a rabbi because she felt she had failed her congregation. Patric Marsh, a popular professor and authority on religion, asks her to lead Shabbat services at her house, through which she meets members of the Jewish community in northern Vermont, many of whom moved there in the late sixties to pursue a "back-to-the-land fantasy." Because they have no Torah scroll, another faculty friend, Saul Greenberg, urges her to send for one of the Torah scrolls recovered by the British after the war. Her scroll, one that was taken from the Czechowa Jews by the Nazis in 1944, arrives. So strong is Rebecca's faith that the scroll brings with it vivid spirits of these Polish Jews, who have

chosen her to be their rabbi. Even more magically, on one visit an angel leaves God's autobiography for her to read. God has chosen her because she has always hated the evil He does. God, in human and unexpected form, begins to visit her to discuss issues that others over the centuries have misunderstood; for example, the paradox that He "makes peace and creates evil." A counseling student, Allison Manchester, confides to Rebecca that she is depressed over an abortion she had the previous summer. In The HangOut, where Rebecca often sees students informally, Allison tells her that all is now well. After Allison is found murdered in Boston, Rebecca is asked to address the student body; one of the other speakers is Evan Green, an African-American and president of the student body. He discloses to Rebecca that he and Allison were lovers and expecting a baby. He says that she went to Boston to meet "Agathon," the father of her aborted baby. Rebecca is able to break into the college computer system to read Allison's e-mails. She finds obsessive notes from "Agathon," and, from the wording and later disclosures, Rebecca knows who the murderer is. The murderer begs not to be identified. Rebecca meets with the police and the college president to propose another student body meeting, which she is again asked to address. The summary of her inspiring and forgiving message with interdependent themes is from a psalm in the Sabbath evening liturgy: "Love God. Hate Evil." The president offers her a position as campus director of religious affairs and as teacher of a course in Judaism.

Jonathan Lethem

Painter Abraham Ebdus, and his wife, Rachel, send their boy, Dylan, to the local public school in Brooklyn in **The Fortress of Solitude* (2003). Then Rachel leaves home. Dylan is one of four white children in the school. He befriends a black boy named Mingus Rude, also motherless, who protects him as well as he can; Dylan is daily head-locked by older black boys who take his money. Dylan and Mingus pour over comic books and fantasize about being superheroes. In 1977,

Dylan, twelve, exiled to the New England countryside, boards a Greyhound bus for Vermont. He is a Fresh Air Kid—"Brooklyn-bereft in Vermont"—staying with his host family, the Windles, who live near Route 9. They have a delinquent teenage son, Buzz, and a daughter, Heather, thirteen. Dylan tries to show Heather his superhero costume, but she runs away. "He didn't need to be known in Vermont, this null area that was only measured in its distance from the city, its use as a restorative, a place to get your act together before returning to the real world. In his case, to prepare to be thirteen in the city, to kiss city girls, to be the flying boy who fights city crime, shit incomprehensible to anyone from Vermont." Back in New York, he endures the eighth grade and is chosen for Stuyvesant High School, after which he will be safe, "scot-free in Vermont," at Camden College. When Dylan shows him a special ring, Mingus teases him: "He's taking it with him to Ver-*mont*, where the girls go swimming without any clothes and niggers work in gas stations." Just before he leaves, Mingus is involved in a shocking experience; for Dylan, "Vermont was my antidote." The "bucolic acres" of the campus are a "trimmed-green sanctuary…high-strung urban children were allowed to play however they liked." Camden College was "one part New England farmland, complete with white clapboard dorms, twisted apple trees bearing inedible fruit, low lichen-covered Frostian stone walls wending nowhere through the woods, and tattered cemetery plots with burial dates in the 1700s; one part experimental arts college, founded in the 1920s by passionate Red-leaning patrons, and legendary for its modern dancers and faculty-student marriages; and one part lunatic preserve for wayward children of privilege, those too familiar with psych counseling and rehab to follow older siblings to Harvard or Yale, and which recapitulated in junior form the tribal rituals of Mediterranean resorts and East Hampton summers and the VIP room of Studio 54." Dylan rooms with another "fresh-faced, short-haired scholarship student." He shows off his inner-city knowledge by turning himself into a cartoon of Mingus, "a splendid

container for his self-loathing and hostility toward his classmates." The remainder of this wonderful novel shows Dylan's attempts to rehabilitate his life.

Pam Lewis

Carole Mason, the plump and insecure narrator of *Speak Softly, She Can Hear* (2005), is graduating from The Spence School in early sixties Manhattan. She and a friend, Naomi Leonard, determined to lose their virginity before going to college, concoct a plan to meet Eddie Lindbaeck, a twenty-six-year-old New York actor, at a motel in Stowe. The plan goes badly awry when another woman, Rita Marie Boudreau, joins them and, after a confused scene of drunken sexual activity and rough use of ropes, dies. Eddie accuses the horrified and confused Carole of breaking Rita's neck. They and Naomi bury Rita's body and swear each other to secrecy. Guilt overwhelms Carole. Eddie, a sociopath, threatens blackmail. She tries to hide in California, but Eddie traces her there, so she returns to Montpelier with Rachel and Morgan Weaver-Lear and their two children to start a new life. Ten years later, attractive and self-confident though burdened by her secret, she is running a successful restaurant, Chacha's, and living with Will Burbank, an intelligent, sympathetic black man, who teaches survival skills at a community college. (He had moved to Adamant with some "purist" hippies who, after they voted to become vegetarians, set their animals free and the animals all died. "It set me thinking about survival.") Carole's nightmare returns when Naomi and Eddie unexpectedly buy a house nearby in Montpelier. The tension builds to a crescendo when, during a life-threatening dénouement on a skiing trip, Carole uncovers the truth concerning Rita's death. The weather begins to change and the May hillsides are "pale chartreuse."

Sinclair Lewis

Martin Arrowsmith, the eponymous hero of *Arrowsmith* (1925), born in 1883, goes to university and medical school in the Midwest, becoming fascinated with the work of bacteriologist Professor Gottlieb. Simple, rustic, and unformed, Martin is dazzled by Madeline Fox, a woman from another world, but meets and marries Leora Tozer. Once graduated with a medical degree, he practices medicine at Zenith General Hospital and then takes a job in public health in Iowa. He is unhappy in his administrative position and gratefully accepts an offer as a pathologist at the Rouncefield Clinic in Chicago. The administrators are more interested in money than research, and Martin accepts an offer from his old mentor, Dr. Gottlieb, to come to New York to the McGurk Institute of Biology. Dr. Gottlieb pledges to protect him from success, and Martin lunges into his work on staphylococcus so single-mindedly that he becomes almost ill with nervous exhaustion. The ambitious partners at the Institute encourage him to publish his results before they are ready. When a plague epidemic consumes the West Indies, he travels there with Dr. Gustaf Sondelius and Leora. Martin does heroic work, but both his friend and his wife die. Back in New York, he is attracted to Joyce Lanyon, a fabulously wealthy woman, whom he marries; soon she has bought him golf clubs and hired a valet. He works well with his friend, Terry Wickett. When, again, the trustees try to force them to publish their work prematurely, Terry resigns and retires to Birdies' Rest, his five acres in the hills of Vermont. Martin visits him there among the oaks and the maples, where Terry wants to create a lab, patent his experiments, and work independently on his quinine derivatives. Martin's life with Joyce—the dinner parties, the posturing—is a painful failure. He travels again to Birdies' Rest, where he and Terry snowshoe, shoot rabbits, and make plans. Joyce is furious with Martin; she has turned into a grande dame, treating him like an impertinent servant. She does not want him to go to "this horrid Vermont place," but he stays with Terry. While there, Martin decides he will not give up his real work. When he turns down the position as head of the institute, he realizes that Joyce has never understood him or his work. After he tells her he is moving to Birdies' Rest, she excoriates him for

thinking that by wearing a "flannel shirt" he will be "pure." He resigns from the institute and takes a train to Vermont. It is "rapture" to be allowed to work twenty-four hours a day in the "ringing winter woods." Terry is an excellent campmate and washes their clothes with "melody and skill." Martin's work progresses splendidly. "It is the first spring he had ever seen or tasted. He learned to dive into the lake, though the first lunge was an agony of fiery cold. They fished before breakfast, they supped at a table under the oaks, they tramped twenty miles on end, they had blue jays and squirrels for interested neighbors; and when they had worked all night they came out to find serene dawn lifting across the sleeping lake. Martin felt sun-soaked and deep of chest, and always he hummed."

In *It Can't Happen Here* (1935), Doremus Jessup is the editor in 1936 of the *Daily Independent*, a newspaper in Fort Beulah north of Rutland in "the provincial hills." The slopes of Mount Terror are three miles away: "They looked through a distant mountain gap to the faint mercury of Lake Champlain, and across it, the bulwark of the Adirondacks." Jessup is driving to a meeting at Isaiah College. Here is what he sees: "An upland hollow and mist beneath the moon— a veil of mist over apple blossoms and the heavy bloom of an ancient lilac bush beside the ruin of a farmhouse burned these sixty years or more." Later, he evokes winter: "It had been cold in Vermont, with early snow, but the white drifts lay on the earth so quietly, in unstained air, that the world seemed a silver-painted carnival, left to silence. Even on a moonless night, a pale radiance came from the snow, from the earth itself, and the stars were drops of quicksilver." Jessup is over sixty, liberal, cynical, tough-minded, fair, a good and loving father to his three children, and loyal to his silly wife, Emma (though in love for some time with Linda Pike). Doremus and Emma were born in Beulah Valley. Linda, the widow of a preacher, owns and runs the Beulah Valley Tavern. Doremus's daughter knows that he and Linda are lovers and is sympathetic to their plight. Doremus watches with concern as a fanatic named Berzelius ("Buzz") Windrip begins to make a successful bid for President with his League of Forgotten Men and the Democratic Party. Buzz's advisor is a man named Lee Sarason. As the situation becomes subtly, quietly worse, Jessup prophesies that Buzz could become a dictator. A friend replies, "Fascism can't happen *here.*" Excerpts from Windrip's book, *Zero Hour,* are epigraphs for each chapter. Windrip's planks discriminate against Jews and Negroes. He is elected president and forms the Corporate State. The universities are closed. Units of uniformed Minute Men are mobilized. The press is silenced. Books are burned. Concentration camps are opened. Doremus's half-witted yardman is made a "Corpo," a worker for the State. Walt Trowbridge, the other presidential candidate, flees to exile in Canada. Doremus ponders all utopias "and their regulation end in scandal, feuds, poverty, grimness, disillusion." Doremus's weak, anti-Semitic son, Peter, thinks they should collaborate. Doremus cannot countenance a dictatorship; he joins the New Underground and is duly arrested. In the camp, one of his closest friends is the Communist Karl Pascal, until the latter turns into a zealot. Doremus hopes that "at worst, the Liberals, the Tolerant, might in the long run preserve some of the arts of civilization, no matter which brand of tyranny should finally dominate the world." Sarason overthrows Windrip and becomes president. His followers resent his Roman-Emperor ways; another tyrant, General Haik, succeeds him. Meanwhile, a rebellion is underway. Trowbridge has emerged from exile and instituted the American Cooperative Commonwealth. Doremus goes underground to work for him: "And still Doremus goes on in the red sunrise, for a Doremus Jessup can never die."

Reeve Lindbergh

In *Moving to the Country* (1983), Nancy King, twenty-nine, moves to the village of Winsom in the north country with her English-teacher husband, Tom, and her two daughters, Annie and Lisa. "Like many couples who move to the country, the Kings fell in love with the house by looking out of its windows." Neither branch of their family believes that "Vermont was a feasible

year-round habitat." Nancy is pregnant; she and her husband are not getting along well. Tom's recently widowed Uncle Les is living with them indefinitely, and soon Henrietta ("Henry") Laramie and her two kids, Lin and Claire, fugitives from a hippie commune, move in, too. Nancy suffers a miscarriage and has a hysterectomy. She is despondent and hopeless about any meaning to her life. May and Frank Willard, who own the country market, don't know what to make of the changes in the village. The summer peoples' children are returning to their parents' summer homes in Winsom as year-round residents. Tom King has bought the farm where May grew up, and her Harvard-educated son, Greg, resents selling the family farm, which his grandfather worked until it killed him. Greg is sick of "missionaries," people with "down country solutions to problems we have handled for two hundred years." They bring "inflated land values, super highways, and housing developments." Nonetheless, after Nancy's hospital stay, May brings a casserole from the Sunshine Club and Greg offers to help bank the foundation of the house for winter. When the Willards sell their store to a young couple from away, Greg is angry that it can't stay in the hands of local people. Tom asks why "the nice couple can't turn into local people after a decent interval—say fifty years?" Tom is trying to bring back the basics of composition, grammar, and arithmetic into the school system and realizes that the parents, under economic pressures, have low expectations for their children. He notices "houses in the lost hayfields, sad to think of the foundation cement poured over the tangled roots." His teaching situation is soon threatened: he learns, to his dismay, that a substitute teacher, Terry Bussette (who grew up in Winsom), is suing the state's attorney because she believes Tom's job is rightly hers and that she is the victim of sexual discrimination. Ironically, Terry and Nancy are brought together through starting the Children's Center and find themselves friends. Ed Yarrow (referred to as a "born-again Rural") has come to Vermont with an arts grant and is writing "Ballads of Old Winsom Town." Martha Yarrow finds living simply "so complicated:" all their friends talk about is "how much wood they've cut, their wood stoves, and how much honey, cracked oats, and lecithin to put in their homemade bread." Ed has told her that moving to the country will help her see the light, but all she sees is "the dark ages."The results of the lawsuit are revealing and important.

In *The Names of the Mountains* (1992), Cressida Linley narrates a touching story of children dominated by their famous and powerful parents. Calvin Linley was a tall, handsome hero aviator, married to a refined, sensitive writer named Alicia, whose baby boy, also named Cal, was tragically abducted and murdered. After that death, the Linleys had three more sons, Matthew, Mark, and Luke, and two daughters, Helen and Cressida. Cressida was married for the first time to Garrett Trainor, with whom she had two daughters, Sarah, now seventeen, and Megan, now thirteen, and a little boy, Jason, who died at two from complications of encephalitis. Their tragedy forced them to divorce; with her second husband, Joe, she is the joyful mother of Nicholas, three. She brought seven chickens, four sheep, and one horse to her second marriage; she needs animals to write her rhyming picture books for young children. Her northern Vermont farmhouse is an early New England cape, about 1830, formerly white, now light grey with white trim and a red roof. "This morning, my own farmhouse nestles down in its valley in a colorful, welcoming squat, looking as comfortable there as a red-capped hen settled on her nest, and as ample as an ark." She has lived in Vermont for twenty years; at the outset, Cal and Alicia came to visit. Alicia is now eighty-two and lives in the old family house on the Sound in Connecticut; her husband has been dead for fifteen years. Her neighbor, Martha Elsen, helps out occasionally. From her vantage point in Vermont, Cressida is concerned about Alicia, whose short-term memory is becoming increasingly faulty. Her mother always knew the names of the mountains wherever they lived; now, Alicia can't remember them. Cressida's sister, Helen, also lives in Vermont, almost next door. She, too, is worried about Alicia. Cressida thinks of her father, an

exhausting talker, of his exuberance and energy. Cressida decides to take her children to Connecticut to assess Alicia's mental status. She drives south on Route 91, looking at the hills as she goes. "The distant ones pass slowly, sleeping beasts with a haze of bare trees for fur, while the ones close to the highway flash past with brief, sharp silhouettes of tree trunks running down their spines like harp strings."When they arrive at Alicia's, they find her sister, Aunt Violet, and Cressida's brother, Luke. As they gather for tea, Alicia behaves normally and then, occasionally, loses interest in the conversation. She is often repetitive, forgetful. Cressida cannot accept her mother's memory loss, believing that something can be done. The two other brothers arrive; they are all together, every one of them aware of the "Linley heritage, the family obsession with itself." As children, they were always celebrities, continually watched. Cal couldn't act like other people because The Press wouldn't allow it. Alicia's children seek and find an accommodation to their mother's new situation.

Gail Link

Modern-day Stowe and New Orleans during the Civil War alternate as settings for Rebecca Gallagher Fraser in *There Never Was a Time* (1995). She is a divorced, successful writer of television soap operas who is taking a break before starting a new series. In her family's old stone farmhouse in Stowe she discovers the journal of her ancestor, Rachel Gallagher Fraser. Reading about Rachel's life in New Orleans, her passionate love affair with Matthew Justin Devereaux, his joining the Union Army and being executed as a spy, and her subsequent marriage to Captain Barrett Fraser of Vermont, kindles the idea for a soap opera. Traveling to New Orleans to absorb local color, Rebecca stays at Belle Chanson, the Devereaux family house, now a bed-and-breakfast. Rebecca meets a descendant of the family, Morgan Devereaux, a well-known historical novelist, and falls hopelessly in love with him. After a passionate week together, she retreats to her Vermont house. It is only when Morgan, beginning a new novel about the Civil War, reads

Matthew Devereaux's journal that he realizes who Rebecca is and why they are made for each other. He traces her to Vermont to continue the love story begun one hundred and fifty years ago.

Elinor Lipman

The Inn at Lake Devine (1998) manages to be light-hearted despite death and anti-Semitism, due to the caustic wit of the heroine, Nathalie Marx. As a child in the 1960s, she obsesses about the Inn at Lake Devine (not far from Rutland) because the management of this resort, family-owned since 1922, once sent her parents a letter saying, "Our guests who feel most comfortable here, and return year after year, are *Gentiles*." Nathalie cannot imagine why Mrs. Berry, the signer of the letter, would dislike Nathalie personally just because she happens to be Jewish. She plots ways to humiliate Mrs. Berry. At camp in the summer of 1964, Nathalie meets a girl named Robin Fife, who seems humorless and not very bright until she mentions that she and her parents summer at the Inn at Lake Devine. Nathalie ingratiates herself with Robin ("I'd be Heidi helping Clara in Dusseldorf: she'd get out of the wheelchair and I'd get to experience a holiday on the other side of the tracks") and soon Robin has persuaded her mother to invite Nathalie to spend a week with them. Nathalie takes a sadistic pleasure in watching Mrs. Berry's face as she is introduced to "Nathalie *Marx*." Nathalie isn't really comfortable with the Fifes, who are an overbearingly decent American family, but she enjoys a mild crush on the older Berry boy, Nelson, who is a lifeguard at the Inn. Ten years later, Nathalie, a professional chef-in-training, is invited to a reunion of her old camp friends. She doesn't want to attend, but the mimeographed list of alumnae shows that Robin Fife is now working a few blocks away from Nathalie in Newton, Massachusetts. She reestablishes contact with Robin in time to be invited to her wedding. She is going to marry Nelson Berry at the Inn at Lake Devine. Nathalie agrees to attend out of a certain relish for personal pain and vindictiveness but is soon embroiled in a family tragedy: Robin is killed in an automobile accident on her way to

the Inn. Nathalie stays at the Inn to help cook (it is out-of-season). While there, she and Kris Berry, the younger brother, fall in love. Nelson slowly emerges from his sorrow and, to help him recover his spirits, Nathalie and Kris persuade him to spend a weekend with them at a carefree Jewish resort in the Catskills. The story concludes in a delightful and ironic way.

Florence Bingham Livingston

In *Under a Thousand Eyes* (1922), Heather Davenway, twenty-three, takes a leave of absence from her editorial job after eight years out West and in New York to return to Hampton Valley in Spinooski County (across Lake Champlain from New York, where her mother was born). She plans to persuade her mother to sell her house and move back to New York with her. Heather's humiliation is keen when she learns that her mother is forced to take in boarders and, in the evenings, a couple of extra "mealers." "Hampton Valley was full of watchful eyes and gifted tongues:" the town believes Heather is putting on airs. Two eligible and contrasting men in Hampton Valley admire her. Clifton Stanleigh works in his depressing family store to support his two brothers, an engineer in school and an as-yet-unpublished playwright, and boards in his family's foreclosed house. Wylie Chamberlain is a lawyer who has a reputation as an up-and-coming citizen-professional (he had learned "studied familiarity," so every one says, "No airs"). Heather is aware that she is back in an old order, stronger than any individual. She wants to "lift" her mother from the "pettiness of existence" in Hampton Valley (even though her mother is serenely contented there). Heather's great-grandmother lives nearby and continues to do her own housework ("Ain't no use in rustin' out"). Heather's mother is holding on to the riverside property where their once prosperous mill stands in ruins. One of the boarders, Booth Ransome, whom Heather distrusts on sight, is eager to buy the land to build, he says, "a little summer colony" (but he is really an agent for a power company that will pay him handsomely if he can procure the property). Miss Cula Clare Leathers, a mealer, lives in a house with four rooms, which "huddle as simply as tea biscuits in a pan." Because Heather is accused of being "stuck up," she agrees to go to the Cemetery Festival Association Dance (a contest between New England Thrift and New England Puritanism takes place over whether the Association should allow dancing at the Cemetery Festival since a free orchestra has been offered—Thrift wins). Heather sees both sides of Hampton Valley, the petty and gossipy one as well as the one generous in money and service. She wonders if the diversions in New York can replace the simple, friendly life her mother leads now. The residents of Hampton Valley are a close-knit community with an avid interest in the smallest details of the lives of its members. They evince no interest in what is going on outside, except to say that "the country is going to the dogs" and "times are not the way they used to be." Heather is distressed at the gloomy setting of Clif's store and the air of tragedy he carries with him; she has no idea that he is supporting his two brothers and about to lose his house. Kitty Judevine, another childhood friend, invites Heather to a party at Tipping Rock Lake, eight miles away. In those pleasant surroundings, Wylie Chamberlain asks her to marry him and she agrees, thinking that this a perfect solution to her dilemma; he is making a good living and can soon afford to take her to a larger city. The town is happy with Heather's engagement and the townsfolk seem to be friendlier toward her. She befriends Cula Clare and helps her "catch" eligible bachelor Zelotes Joselyn. Into this climate comes Henry Nye, whose dead son was the best friend of Clif's brother, Mason. Nye, in his bereavement, is looking for a new purpose in life and is immensely impressed with Clif's talents when he discovers the latter's designs for children's games. Booth, who is frightfully injured in an accident, admits to Mrs. Davenway that her property is worth a lot of money and relinquishes his rights to it. Mr. Nye offers to buy the property at twice what the power company would pay; with her profits, Mrs. Davenway proposes to pay off Clif's mortgage because she and the Stanleighs have been life-long friends. Heather, deciding she wants to help and learning that Wylie holds the

mortgage, goes to him with her savings. Wylie refuses to accept her money and, when she realizes what he is really like and how he makes his money, she breaks her engagement. Mr. Nye, meanwhile, has fallen in love with Mrs. Davenway. Clif and Heather acknowledge their love; she realizes that happiness does not depend on settings but on human relationships.

Bret Lott

In *The Man Who Owned Vermont* (1987), Rick and Paige Wheeler live near Springfield, Massachusetts. She works as a secretary at Mt. Holyoke; he is a salesman for the RC Cola/Schweppes companies. This spare novel begins when the couple has split up. At first, she stays with friends in Colrain, then returns to her family in New Jersey. He recalls the tragedy of her miscarriage and his inability to comfort her. After that event, he has been unable to communicate with her, physically or intellectually. He only learns his mistake—his weakness—in the relationship when, at the end of the novel, he goes on a deer hunting trip just over the border in Vermont with Lonny, a plumber acquaintance, and Rick's friend, Cal. Rick learns from Lonny the secret of interpersonal relations: "You have to share the stories you got or you will die." When Rick is sitting in the deer stand, this is what he sees: "The deer started in on the acorns, its black nose pushing a few around, then taking them up with its tongue. I saw for the first time that there were no antlers, no spikes. And I saw it was a beautiful animal, harmless and hungry. It took in the acorns, then slowly raised its head, turned as though to some sound or smell, the acorns moving around in its mouth like so many marbles. I could see its eye then, large and brown, just the touch of white at the outside corner." At that moment, Cal shoots the doe—twice.

Michael Lowenthal

Twenty-eight-year-old Jeremy Stull, the first-person narrator of *Avoidance* (2002), divides his story among three time periods. The first is the present, when Jeremy, a graduate of Harvard, is at the Divinity School, writing his dissertation on excommunication. He is using, as a case study, the Amish practice of *meidung* or "social avoidance." In the Amish culture, a person who has misbehaved is shunned until he or she apologizes. The second is the near past, when he was the assistant director of a camp called Ironwood, situated in woods on a lake near Killington. The third is the summer he first went to the camp as a boy and teenager. To do research for his dissertation, he lives in an Amish community with the Yoder family and becomes acquainted with Sadie Yoder's sister, Beulah. The Amish church shuns Beulah's husband, Jonas, because he stops attending; the church asks her to shun her own husband in accordance with their notion of "self-denial for the community's sake." Instead, she has a baby and is banished from the church, dead even to her own family. Jeremy's father died when Jeremy was a child, and his character and experience were formed by summers at Ironwood, chiefly through the influence of the headmaster, Ruff Peterson, and his friendship with Charlie Moss, to whom he lost the job as head of the camp. As Jeremy thinks back about Ruff, whom he idolized, he belatedly and intuitively recognizes a sexual interest on the older man's part. As assistant camp director, Jeremy meets fourteen-year-old Max Conner the first day, when the boy breaks his wrist and is taken to the infirmary; the boy captivates Jeremy. The feeling, not exactly of lust, but of delight and interest, terrifies him. Even as he is attracted to Max, Jeremy realizes that the boy is consciously seductive and, perhaps, untruthful. When Max tells Jeremy that Charlie has molested him, Jeremy does not report that incident, as he is obliged to do. He thinks about a time at camp when he and Charlie were taken out into the woods with Ruff, who chooses Charlie to share his tent and "shuns" Jeremy. Jeremy confronts Charlie with Max's accusation and the former takes off, leaving Jeremy as the new director. He fantasizes about becoming Max's guardian and taking him to Cambridge to live with him, but he resists the urge. The end of this fine story is a compelling and believable. Three noteworthy images: "Along the ridge, each single spruce appeared separate

and dimensional, a stand of benedictory totem poles," "Split-open trunks tangled lurid, exposed, as disconcerting as broken bones," and "Dusk dropped its scrim over the valley."

Patricia MacDonald

Britt Anderson, a successful TV producer in Boston in *Suspicious Origin* (2003), is summoned to the town of Coleville near Montpelier after the death in a fire of her sister, Greta. Alienated from her sister and her family for many years, Britt has never met her brother-in-law, Alec, a snowmobile salesman, or her niece, Zoe, eleven, but when the fire turns into an arson homicide she immediately suspects Alec. Everything points in his direction, although he claims to have picked up a hitchhiker at the time of the fire and driven him to Montpelier. The next-door neighbors, Kevin, an attorney, and Caroline Carmichael, have an adolescent girl named Vicky staying with them; she is expecting a baby whom the Carmichaels will adopt at birth. When Alec is arrested, Kevin takes his case. Britt happens upon a young man named Dave, who fits the description of the hitchhiker, Alec's alibi. She traces him to his home and learns that he is the father of Vicky's baby. He promises to go to the police the next day but instead disappears with Vicki. His landlady agrees to talk to the police, and Alec is freed. Britt is on her way to the airport when she discovers Vicky's car in the Carmichael's garage. Before she can act, she is kidnapped by the people responsible for the murder and the fire and finds herself in grave danger.

Bernard Malamud

Center Campobello on the New York-Vermont border is the venue for *Dubin's Lives* (1979). William Dubin is a biographer now embarking on a life of D.H. Lawrence. He walks every day "from the rural to the pastoral." In the late-afternoon warm sunshine, he becomes gloomy. "August was a masked month: it looked like summer and conspired with fall; like February it would attempt to hide what it was about." Dubin once uncovered shoots under dead leaves in February. In the woods today he had seen color in a broad maple. "A sense of short season: Northeast cheat. The days had secretly cast off ballast and were drifting toward autumn. Cold air descended to the roots of trees. The leaves, if you touched, were dying. The noise of bees sucking pale flowers, of crickets rasping, seemed distant. Butterflies, flitting amid trees, flaunted their glad rags a moment before generating and expiring." Dubin cannot bear the changes he feels in the seasons. "He forbade his mind to run to tomorrow. Let winter stay in its white hole." On his walk he notices "a sparse quarter mile of old houses went by as on a rusty turntable, then broad fields with now and then a stark farmhouse, upright and spare to a point of principle—with weather-beaten barns, red or black silos, Angus and Herefords on cow paths in the pasture." Dubin has lived for fifteen years in a black-shuttered, yellow clapboard house with his wife, Kitty; his children have grown up and moved away. One summer Robert Frost was Dubin's neighbor. Near the covered bridge, a young woman stops her car to ask directions of Dubin; he finds her tremendously appealing. She turns out to be Fanny Bick, their new twice-a-week cleaning woman. Roger Foster, the librarian, picks her up after work. Dubin begins to obsess about Fanny and is soon besotted. He invites her to travel to Venice (having made up a story for his wife about seeking Lawrence's essence abroad). The tryst is disastrous: Fanny runs off with a gondolier. Dubin returns home, even less able to work. He realizes that "he has given up life to write lives." Kitty gives dinner parties to bring a semblance of order to their lives (she has flirted with Roger while she is volunteering at the library). Fanny returns to Vermont and moves in with Roger. Dubin is "tired of the house—of living in the country. He'd had his fill of housebound cold Northeast

winters; of short, savage springs; increasingly hot humid summers." He cannot stay away from Fanny. He makes himself miserable; he makes his wife miserable. Fanny matures into someone who is independent and thoughtful. She buys the neighboring farm. The question remains whether she and Kitty can somehow share Dubin's life. The language is luminous: "Early fall had run a cool hand through the air," "bare pewter-trunked silver maples," "In the morning, mist lay like a deep sea on the hills, their tops breaking through like green islands in white water," "An ash tree, slender, virginal…its young leaves were light-green, seed pockets lavender, like a girl's spring dress," and "nature shrouded, playing dead."

David Mamet

"Vermont Sketches" in *Goldberg Street* (1985) are all save one a dialogue between two people. They are brief, understated, and witty, and use silences, expressions like "Mm," "Uh-huh," or "Ayuh," and italicized remarks for emphasis (which, in the case of these stories, is largely a repetition of the same point). In **"Conversations with the Spirit World,"** two men exchange stories about supernatural events. One tells of a boy who saw the exact figure of a hired man dead one hundred years; the other man's wife saw a boy materialize in a place he couldn't have been. **"Pint's a Pound the World Around"** is a one-sided conversation between two men, the owner and a customer, in a hardware store north of Manchester. The customer has come into the store for a minuscule item. The owner, who doesn't have the part, detains him by boasting about investing in a new system to keep stock on hand the way the big chains, his competition, maintain their inventories. The customer never gets a word in edgewise, except for an occasional "Uh-huh." In **"Dowsing,"** two older men in a country store are talking about the conference of dowsers up in Morristown. One tells of someone who found a girl's watch by dowsing. "—Mm? —Yessir. — Ayuh." Another two men in a country store (**"Deer Dogs"**) discuss the law that allows shooting a dog running deer. They are having trouble understanding the logic of the argument that a tame dog might get loose, chase the other dog, and get shot for running deer. A man and a boy are in a mall ("**In the Mall**"), where the boy does all the talking, filled with anti-authority statements. "**Maple Sugaring**" is a vignette about Morris, whose father built the sugarhouse in 1912. Morris is at a sugaring with his wife, Susan, his son, Joe, and his grandson: "In the sugar shack the benches were made of wood. There was a square door on a running track to the woodshed. The sun streamed through the large vent in the roof. The people talked in whispers. The steam rose. Joe's baby was asleep." The title characters in "**Morris and Joe**" remember a bear they saw in the woods. Morris says Joe was so scared he shot himself in the foot. Joe reminds Morris of some drunken disaster with the milk tanker. It is an easy, friendly, relaxed conversation while they are lunching. They are at peace. The bear is in Canada, they think. In "**In Old Vermont**," Roger and Maud are imagining Vermont in olden times, the times of Indian massacres: "We are alone. In a vacation home." Maud envisions them, unprotected, fallen upon by Indians, who abduct them. When people come to the house later, they find a flapping window shade, an upset lamp, a guttering candle, and a spilt bag of salt.

The Village (1994) deals in generic topics: The Village (unnamed, located off the eastern end of Route 4) adjacent to the Town, the Green, the Store, the Trooper, and Summer and Winter. The action takes place almost entirely in the heads of the residents of the Village; the internal monologues are interlaced with terse exchanges in homes and stores around the Village. The tragedy is that no one is able to articulate his/her thoughts aloud. As Marty Breen's daughter, Beth, says: "Nobody knows what I am thinking." Marty's other child is a teenager named John. At the end, John is dead and his girlfriend is fatally wounded at an accident at the old quarry. Henry, who cannot communicate with his wife, spends his days chopping wood. One fateful day, he loses his direction in a storm and drops his com-

pass and his jacket carrying a distinctive patch, which he had recently bought at an auction. Following a slow truck on a mountain road, Henry feels "assaulted" by the truck's slow pace. Dick, at the hardware store/gas pumps, imagines conversations with his banker, who finally forecloses on him. Maris, whom the men watch as she walks down the street and who has an abusive stepfather, is a tramp. Trooper Bill is one of Maris's clients, until his wife finds the motel-room key in his pocket. He sits in a bar with Trooper Tom and Trooper Bobby. Rose is the postmistress; James works at the food store. Lynn is an old man and wise hunter. The only person who talks aloud is the Minister. Henry looks out the window: "The moon had just risen, and the shadows were long. The lawn was striped light blue where the moon shone, and otherwise a black so soft as to be almost brown." Trooper Bill talks to another cop, who, searching for words to describe an illness, "moved his head from one shoulder to the other, like a railroad crossing signal." Maris disappears and Marty reports to the Trooper that he has found a jacket in the snow with a distinctive patch on it...perhaps the killer's? The story ends with old Lynn's telling a cryptic tale of a man crushed to death by a bear. Someone else responds, "But you *know*, I didn't think he should of told that story. How did he know it was a bear? Or, I'll tell you *what*: I'm not sure that it was true. It ought not to've been true, or, if it was true, he shouldn't of told it that way."

Kate Manning

White Girl (2002) analyzes the motivations underlying the interracial marriage between blonde Californian Charlotte Halsey and black North Hampshire-raised Milo Robicheaux, who meet in 1984 at Cabot College in the Green Mountains (near Stowe). Charlotte is under the influence of a possessive, brutal lover named Jack Sutherland; he and Milo are on the Cabot ski team together. After college, in New York, Charlotte becomes a successful model; Milo, after competing for the Olympic ski team, is a sports broadcaster and then iconic film star. They

M

marry, have a child, and are unhappy, especially after Milo sleeps with a young black dancer. Charlotte is attacked and almost killed; the police arrest Milo, but the assailant is someone else.

Rebecca Marsh

In *Summer in Vermont* (1955), Laura Staley's great-great-grandparents established the first farm in Saunder's Bluff (named for Jacob Saunder, who bluffed hostile Indians into surrendering to him). Her father is a wealthy businessman in town, owner of the Staley Hotel. Laura is engaged to Brad Holbrook, a farmer, who keeps putting off their marriage until he can support her. When Ken Albright, a successful New York producer, offers Brad a handsome sum for the use of his barn as a summer theater, he cannot refuse. Brad tries to explain to Laura yet another postponement, at which she returns his ring. Laura persuades the mayor, Rachel Wolfe, and her father, that a summer theater would cause a healthy boom in Saunder's Bluff, bringing tourists to the town. Laura becomes involved with Ken, although she believes he is in love with famous star Julia Trotter, and develops friendships with cast and crew, including Prudence Drane. When Julia tries to remove Prudence from her starring role, Laura intercedes on Prudence's behalf. At the end, Ken must decide whether he wants to live on a farm.

Kirk Martin

In *Shade of the Maple* (2002), David and Anna Collins live in Colchester, a recently developed subdivision of Burlington. Anna grew up in Brandon, where her grandparents ran a small hardware store. David thinks they are living the American Dream; Anna feels deeply disillusioned with her marriage and lives vicariously through romance fiction written by "Morgan Jackson," who turns out to be her former lover, Evan Forrester. He has been writing novels as love letters to her over the years. They meet; they are still in love; they cannot marry; they must part because she is pregnant by her husband. Years later, the couple is reunited through an interesting device.

Steve Martin

In *Shopgirl* (2000), a disarming and tragicomic novella, Mirabelle Buttersfield, twenty-eight, works at the glove counter at Nieman Marcus in Beverly Hills. She takes drugs for depression, "which was first set in the bow in Vermont, where she grew up, and fired as a companion arrow that has traveled with her ever since." She learned ten years ago, living in Dunton, that her father carried on a seven-year affair with a neighbor. When he returned from Vietnam, she heard him sobbing in his bedroom, although he could not speak of his experience. "He is a stoic like a good WASP from Vermont should be." Despite her dead-end job, Mirabelle is "an educated spirit with a sense of irony;" she has a Master of Fine Arts degree from a California institution and occasionally sells a drawing. She meets Jeremy Kraft at a Laundromat and begins an affair; they seem to have nothing in common. Ray Porter, divorced, in his fifties, buys a pair of gloves from her and presents them to her with an invitation to dinner. They enter into an affair. She falls in love with him; he is using her. Her depression deepens as Christmastime arrives, and she flies to Dunton to be with her mother and father, her brother Ken, a policeman, and his wife, Ella. Her parents treat her like a child. Their motto is "Moderation in all things, including success." Her parents believe that she is a virgin. She goes for a walk with her father: "In Vermont, no matter in which direction you go, you end up in the woods." She gives her father a card from Carter Dobbs, who served with him in Vietnam. As he touches the card, he is powerfully distant from his daughter in the Vermont woods. She hears him crying in his room. She moves to San Francisco and rediscovers Jeremy, who has been on the road with a rock band selling amplifiers and has become mature, suave, and polished. She is seeing Jeremy and talks to Ray occasionally. She tells him that she has stored her gloves in her memory box in Vermont.

Caroline Atwater Mason

The setting for *A Woman of Yesterday* (1900) is the "white village" of Haran in northern

Vermont near the Monk River. Anna Mallison is eighteen in 1869, on the brink of being welcomed into the church of her father, Reverend Samuel Mallison, who preaches about "human depravity." Her mother, from a German Moravian family, finds "the tone of the frigid little north New England community more chilling than she dared to own." Anna's older sister, Lucia, is married, has moved deeper into the hills, and works with the "immoderate industry of New England women." Her best friend is Malvina ("Mally") Loveland, who is also joining the church. A Boston minister, head of foreign missions, comes to Haran with a woman missionary who addresses the congregation. No one in the village has ever before heard a woman speak in public. When Anna, moved by the speaker's presentation and presence, expresses her desire to become a missionary, her father's health begins to fail. Anna leaves Haran in its "ice-bound valley" to go to Boston to meet with the missionary board, which accepts her with the proviso that she study for two years before going abroad. Her father dies and the family has to give up the house: her mother moves in with Lucia; Anna and Mally take rooms in Burlington. There, Mally joins an attractive set, but Anna is not sophisticated about social matters. She attracts the attention of Mrs. Senator Ingraham, however, and is invited to speak at a soirée. Anna speaks from her heart, without artifice, and the society ladies are vaguely condescending toward her. The minute Kevin Burgess, who is staying with the Ingrahams, sees Anna he knows that God has brought them together for the purpose of sending them to India as a married couple. She agrees to marry him, although she knows he does not view her with an earthly passion and "she had not awakened to love." Shortly thereafter, he falls ill and sends for her. He will recover but is unable to go to India. He begs her to marry him at once. Anna becomes a prisoner in Keith's snobbish, chilly mother's house. Because Anna's marriage was in advance of the arranged date, her mother and sister send her a simple trousseau, handmade, with some little maple sugar cakes especially for Keith's mother, who patronizes the gifts. Anna is trapped by the

formal daily monotony. In Vermont, she was used "to serious mental work, to much strenuous bodily labor, to the wholesome severity of long walks in all weathers, and more than all to the stimulus of a great, immediate purpose ennobling every homeliest task and smallest service." Professor Ward, a family friend, tells her that her New England Calvinism has blocked out of her life the pleasures of music, art, and literature. Reading the work of John Gregory, a socialist who used to be an evangelist, she believes she has found a philosophy to which she can relate. After Keith's mother's death, Anna visits her mother and sister in northern Vermont. She faces the fact that her original belief, "that God will condemn to everlasting torment all the heathen who do not believe in a means of salvation of which they have never heard," has disappeared from her heart and soul. She goes to Burlington to hear John Gregory speak and, when he tells the audience about Fraternia, his utopia in North Carolina, she is ready to sign up. Keith agrees to give up everything and go with Anna to North Carolina, where Anna becomes a saint among the residents. John and Anna fall in love and studiously avoid one another. The experiment of Fraternia works for a while, but then the mill closes, the food is bad, the winter is freezing, the mortgage payment is due, and the people are unhappy. Keith dies, and Anna reapplies for a missionary job in India. On her way there, she returns to Fraternia to say goodbye to John. He has been paralyzed in an accident, and the community is closed, except for a few faithful hangers-on. She turns her brave and spiritual face to the East.

Charles Mathes

Molly and Nell O'Hara are sisters in their twenties in *The Girl at the End of the Line* (1999) who run an antique shop in North Carolina. Nell has not spoken since she was eight years old, when she witnessed their mother's murder. At a tag sale, Nell finds a playbill featuring their grandmother, Margaret Jellinek, in a show in Manhattan fifty years earlier. To find out about their grandmother's thespian past, they go to her nursing home to discover that she has just died. She leaves the girls an emerald ring. Wishing to discover their roots, they travel to New York for research and meet an older actor, Richard Julian, who knew their grandmother, and a young actor, David Azaria, who falls for Molly. Richard tells them that their grandfather married a titled English lady and that he and their grandmother, whose maiden name was Gale, were born on Gale Island in the Ashalaca River above Montpelier. Molly and Nell travel to Vermont, where they find their grandfather Archibald Gale's second wife, Dora, who is in her nineties. The rest of the Gales have just departed and all been killed in a plane crash. This disaster leaves Molly and Nell heirs to a huge fortune—except that someone is trying to kill them with the same gun that killed their mother seventeen years ago. Once the mystery is solved, Nell regains her voice and becomes an actress; Molly and David marry.

Evelyn Wilde Mayerson

Well and Truly (1990) is about Maggie Hatch, forty, who came to Manchester twenty years ago with her doctor husband, Alan; her mother-in-law, Letitia, has never accepted Maggie because she is an outsider. Letitia does not let her forget that Alan was a sixth-generation Vermonter; his great-great-grandfather fought at Ticonderoga under Ethan Allen. "The town exacted proscribed behavior in exchange for acceptance and, for families who settled prior to Andrew Jackson's defeat of John Quincy Adams, unqualified inclusion." Alan dies, leaving Maggie with his house and a daughter, Kristen, who has just dropped out of Smith College. Maggie's lawyer advises her to economize. Alan's unattractive brother, Owen, pressures her to sell the house; Letitia informs Maggie that she owes Letitia thirty thousand dollars from a loan to Alan. When she receives a summons to jury duty, Maggie assumes she will be dismissed in the voir dire, but she is chosen and assigned to a murder case. Melody Jessica Bean is accused of poisoning her mother, Joyce Hibbert Bean, and then pushing her body into the quarry. Her boyfriend, Kevin Clapp, has turned state's witness. One of

Maggie's fellow jurors is intriguing Amos Stringer, who was never inducted but went to Canada for ten years during and after the Vietnam War. Juror Bill Hogan is "the only black man in his township [and] was used to excessive courtesies." Eunice, another black juror, is unhappy in Vermont because she likes to rock when she sings the Gospel and the other choir members prefer to hold back. A professional widower, Justin Herrick, who represents "outside interests" in "guiding change" in Vermont, invites Maggie to dinner: he is complacent and condescending to widows. Her best friend, Anne Bouchard, will not speak to Maggie because Anne believes Maggie has been flirting with her husband, Peter. Maggie's glamorous, oft-married mother, Sybil, arrives. She likes to refer to Vermont as a "rustic gulag." Maggie learns that Alan and Anne had a notorious affair. Maggie becomes romantically involved with Amos; she also makes friends with a woman juror, LaDonna Dyer, whom Letitia considers not of their "class." When Maggie asserts herself and asks Letitia for proof of the loan, the whole town turns against Maggie: "This town's got a world-class grapevine." Maggie becomes reconciled to Sybil's form of mothering—even though Sybil kept leaving her, she was someone special—just before Sybil dies of heart failure. The finding of the jury is stimulating and the resolution of the plot satisfying. The similes are sophisticated and amusing: "Maggie tucked her anger out of sight, like pinning a bra strap to a shoulder pad;" someone appeared, "trailing a young boyfriend behind her like a life raft;" and Letitia's earrings "had been handed down like chromosomes from her maternal forbears." (The title is from the juror's oath: "I solemnly swear to well and truly try, and true deliverance make, between the state of Vermont and the prisoner at the bar.")

Archer Mayor

Lieutenant Joe Gunther, a middle-aged, long-time police officer based in Brattleboro, is the attractive central character in this addictive series of regional murder mysteries. The sense of place is vivid and detailed. A veteran of the Korean

War, his young wife, Ellen, dead of cancer, Joe is involved in an independent relationship with a former-hippie, wealthy realtor, selectwoman, and lawyer named Gail Zigman. He grew up in Thetford in northeastern Vermont and spent summers with his aunt and uncle in Gannet. He attended college in California. As chief detective, he is an endearing character because he often makes mistakes, such as using the wrong tone to a superior officer, or blundering while bluffing in interviews, and often apologizes. He works and thinks hard to put together the pieces of the puzzle and is always, near the end of the novel, working on the breakthrough, worrying in his head some piece of information that doesn't quite fit. The formula requires Joe to do something that is not quite by the book and worry about losing his job or the trust of his squad. He usually has a near-death confrontation with the killer in the last chapter. Fortunately, he always survives, though often badly hurt. Some of the recurring characters are members of his four-person detective squad. Samantha ("Sammie") Martens is an ex-army ranger and the newest member of the squad. Ron Kleszewski is a documentation and paper-trail expert and J.P. Tyler is a forensics expert. Willy Kunkle is a Vietnam veteran and narcotics specialist, who loses the use of one arm in a shooting spree with the "Ski Mask Avenger." Others are Dr. Beverly Hillstrom, the chief medical examiner for the state; Harriet Fritter, a super-organized secretary in the department; Tony Brandt, the police chief; Billy Manniere, chief of patrol; *Brattleboro Reformer* "cops-and-courts" reporter (later editor) Stanley Katz; James Dunn, state's attorney, and his successor, Jack Derby. In the last five in this series of fifteen novels, Joe has joined the Vermont Bureau of Investigation (VBI), an independent branch of the Department of Public Safety.

Open Season (1988) describes a nightmare for Joe: a ski-masked murderer is manipulating Joe into making mistakes with serious consequences. The chain of events starts when a woman kills a man because she believes he has killed her cat. Both woman and man were members of the jury in the Kimberly Harris murder

case three years earlier that put William Davis in prison. A third juror is sexually assaulted, and a fourth is framed in her assault. Someone is lobbying to reopen the case, which was headed by Willy in 1986. (Joe remembers the long-denied racial prejudice that almost convicted a "Nigger flatlander.") Joe meets Chief Medical Examiner Hillstrom, who becomes his friend, and he and Frank Murphy, the police captain and a mentor of Joe's, take some human remains to West New Haven, Connecticut. On the way back a truck sideswipes their car and Frank is killed. Joe is named acting captain. Joe begins to suspect that Frank may have allowed the wrong man to go to jail "and the realization…spread through my veins like ice water." He interviews the pharmacist for whom Kimberly worked and learns the name of a friend, Susan Lucey. Susan, a hooker, tells him all she knows and asks for protection. Joe assures her she will be all right, but "her last words rattled around in my mind." Susan is beaten up after Joe leaves. He learns Kimberly's real name—Pamela Stark—and the name of the man, Lew Hill, who sold drugs to the person who set up Davis. Once Joe and his team learn the identity of the ski-mask murderer, they track the drug seller through the medication he is taking. Cooperating with the New Hampshire police, Joe and his team plan to intercept the man as he accepts a package of money from New York. The scheme goes awry, the police take off on Sno-Cats to capture him, Willy's arm is shattered by a bullet, and the murderer escapes on skis. The final scene is an encounter between the murderer and Joe.

In *Borderlines* (1990) Joe takes a leave of absence to work as a special investigator for the state's attorney in St. Johnsbury, which gives him the opportunity to stay with his Uncle Buster in Gannet. He learns of the hardships facing this small northern town— the economic and social problems of no jobs, no opportunities, a killing climate, very difficult conditions just to survive—and of the mysterious cult, the Natural Order, a back-to-nature group that has taken over much of the town. Connected events happen almost immediately. A fire breaks out in which Joe plays a heroic role, but five cultists are killed, including the leader, "Fox." Bruce Wingate, the father of Julie (who has joined the cult and suffers from borderline personality disorder) is stabbed. Joe's childhood friend, Rennie Wilson (who once pushed his wife, Nadine, down the stairs in a drunken rage) is killed. A smooth-talking man who runs an organization to deprogram young cultists arrives. The body of the original victim, "Fox" (Ed Sylvester), burned beyond recognition, was not identified correctly, and he lives to kill again. "And then it came to me, like a bolt from the blue." After Joe solves the puzzle, he faces his final confrontation with the killer.

In *Scent of Evil* (1992), when Charlie Jardine, a local businessman, is found murdered, patrolman John Toll is seen at the scene and his smoked cigarette is found in the victim's grave. Jardine and Toll went to high school together and vied for the hand of Rose, whom John married. "A bell went off." Cocaine is found in Jardine's house. Joe uses a stoolie to arrange "a buy" with Milly Crawford, who is killed before the deal comes off. Evidence mounts against Toll, which makes Joe suspect the policeman is being set up. "I put that thought in a mental cubby hole." Every time the detective squad gets a lead or sets up an appointment, the killer knows about it. The squad interviews Tucker Wentworth, with whom Jardine was in business; his glamorous daughter, Blaire; some people at the local bank; and the building inspector, against whom evidence is also piling up. The head selectman, Luman Jackson, is furious at what he perceives to be bad police work. The press is having a field day. Joe is taking it hard, trying to put the pieces together. Toll commits suicide, or is he murdered? "That scenario snagged on something in my mind." The lab in Burlington finds curare in Jardine's body. After Joe discovers his office is bugged, the police are able to trace the murderer. Before they can arrest him, he appears in Joe's office, tapes Joe to a chair, and injects him with curare in a replay of the murder of Jardine.

In *The Skeleton's Knee* (1993), Abraham Fuller dies of a gunshot wound sustained twenty-five years earlier. The hospital turns over the dead man's backpack, which contains moldy money printed nearly twenty-five years earlier. Joe searches the dead man's cabin out on Sunset Lake Road, and photographs an astrological chart over the bed. He steps away to his car to telephone headquarters and, when he returns, the chart is gone. Joe notices that Fuller circled the title of *The Scarlet Letter* with a bloody fingertip. Joe discusses the chart with Billie Lucas, a friend of Gail's, and the money with Richard Shimke, an expert in old currency. He takes the squad out to the Fuller place with metal detectors to search for the missing gun. Instead, they find an artificial knee attached to a skeleton. Accompanying the hearse away from the scene, they come under machine-gun fire. Chief Brandt exhorts the troops with his famous maxim: GOYA and KOD, or, "Get off your asses and knock on doors!" Joe goes to Burlington, where a forensic anthropologist tells Joe about his skeleton, and thence to Chicago to check out the artificial knee. With the help of Norm Runnion of the Chicago Police Department, he traces the doctor who did the operation—Kevin Shilly—and the name of the patient—Robert Shattuck—who came in with a gunshot wound to the knee. Shilly's corpse turns up in Shattuck's apartment. Joe finds a Social Services form at the hospital showing that "Robert Shattuck" gave Angelo Salierno as next of kin. Salierno's son, Timmy, was declared dead twenty-four hours after the knee operation. Joe and Norm research the sixties radical past of Shattuck, which leads them to David Pendergast up in Michigan. Joe is called back to Chicago for a stakeout, a big subway chase, and a confrontation between Shattuck and Joe; Shattuck has a chance to kill Joe but runs out of bullets. Joe is rescued and ends up, briefly, in the hospital. They now know the identities of two of the bodies, Fuller and Pendergast, but don't know who the third man is. This person, whose disclosure comes as a great surprise to Joe, was part of a radical sixties movement. After trying to destroy the evidence, the murderer escapes.

Fruits of the Poisonous Tree (1994) begins with shocking personal news: Gail is raped a few hours after Joe leaves her bed. She is taken to the hospital and then to the home of her friend, Susan Raffner, who runs Women for Women. Because Gail is chair of the select board, she is a high-profile personality; because she is on the board of Women for Women, she cooperates with the *Brattleboro Reformer* on the story instead of keeping her identity secret; because Joe is her lover, he shouldn't be assigned to the case. His desperation to solve it quickly leads him to make some mistakes. "In the back of my mind, however, an unacknowledged bell kept sounding that, despite all my care, I was too tired to be doing such detail work." Through the night, piece by piece, team members put together a formidable case against Robert Vogel, a former rapist on parole. The more they fasten on Vogel, the more physical evidence they accumulate. When they are ready to make the arrest, Vogel has been inadvertently forewarned by his parole officer and takes off for Harriman Reservoir. There, under the dam, he stabs Joe before being taken into custody. Joe almost dies but recovers and, learning that State's Attorney James Dunn, who is running for reelection, has decided to take the case to court, reviews the files of the case and seriously doubts they have the right man. Joe discovers that the man who gave them their rationale for a search warrant was lying. "The tainted pieces of evidence, secured under what amounts to an illegal search, are termed 'fruits of the poisonous tree.'" Joe and Tony Brandt inform the state's attorney right away, and Joe starts over with his team—but not from scratch, because, through the offices of a hypnotist, Gail has remembered more about the attack, and they can narrow down their suspects. They figure out who the rapist is and put him under surveillance, but he evades them and goes to Gail's house. In a confrontation, Joe is put out of action and Gail shoots and wounds the rapist. To deal with her trauma, she decides to enroll in a law school refresher course and proposes that she and Joe live together. He accepts.

In *The Dark Root* (1995), Joe has moved with Gail into a house on Orchard Avenue in Brattleboro, although she spends most of her time in South Royalton studying for the bar

exam. Three events coalesce: three Asians are arrested on their way to Montreal; Thomas Lee, a respected Asian-American restaurant owner and his family are terrorized by three Asians and his daughter, Amy, raped; and Benny Travers, a local hood, dies by torture and traffic accident. Joe uses all resources at his disposal, including Dan Flynn at the Vermont Criminal Information Network (VCIN), to analyze the evidence. He assigns a tail to Travers's second-in-command, Vince Sharkey, but then calls it off. "A small doubt lingered—one I hoped I wouldn't come to regret." He does regret it when he and Ron are almost killed in a shoot-out with Asian youths, four of whom they kill. Ron is so traumatized he has to take administrative leave. The case assumes federal proportions—organized crime, illegal aliens, money laundering, and contraband weapons ("dark root" is the Chinese expression for the underworld), and Joe proposes that the local police and the FBI assign him to the case as U.S. marshal. Gail is more involved in his work now, because she has ambitions to be a prosecutor. Through a new contact (his technique is enhanced by having friends in a range of agencies), Joe learns about the tragic childhood of one of the dead Asians, Henry Lam. As Joe struggles with the various strands of the case, he cautions his squad against any racist attitudes. "I don't want the Asian population in general—such as it is here—tainted by something like this. Vermont is mostly white, rural, and lower-middle-class-to-poor, and racism is always just below the surface." A police car is blown up, killing Dennis DeFlorio, and seriously wounding Chief Brandt. A federal FBI task force is put together, with Joe as liaison from Brattleboro, and representation from the Canadian Mounties. The two warring Asian gangs in Vermont have ties to Canada, and the vengeful figure of Truong Van Lac is pitted against Da Wang. Linked up again with Lester Spinney from Waterbury, Joe goes to Montreal. They enter into a wild chase after Michael Vu, who is murdered by his own people. Ron, who was shaken up by the shooting, does not leave the force but steps down as second in command, replaced by Sammie. A description of the social geography: "It all spoke richly of Brattleboro as a whole, and went far to explain why many people found the town appealingly unique. Neither left to decay in economic depression or totally gutted and replaced by urban renewalists hellbent on the latest architectural kick, Brattleboro had thrashed and battled its way up the food chain like a born survivor, making do with what it had, creating citizens of whoever was willing to stake a claim, and establishing itself as an outspoken, politicized, often contradictory place to live. Old and new, rich and poor, native and flatlander— and, most pointedly, right wing and left—all existed in a jostling, noisy harmony that baffled outsiders and imbued residents with a begrudging sort of pride." And a Vermont custom: "I waved to half the drivers on the road when I was out driving around, as they did to me. It was just something you did, living in Vermont."

The Ragman's Memory (1996) introduces the discovery of body parts belonging to Shawna Davis, a young runaway who was apparently drugged with phenobarbital in the week before her death; then a homeless man is found dead of rabies. Since Gail's traumatic experience with rape, she has taken a law-school refresher course and developed an obsessive drive to see justice done. She is now the state's attorney office liaison with the police department. As Joe and his team investigate people who knew the girl, the path leads them to Mary Wallis, a town character violently opposed to the fifteen-million-dollar convention center being built on Putney Road, a development for which Gail voted while a selectwoman. Wallis is abducted; an old woman in a local nursing home is strangled. The evidence connects the three deaths and the abduction to the building of the convention center. Everyone involved with that project, including Paul Hennessey, head contractor, and Ned Fallows, a former mentor of Gail's who has tucked himself away in a cabin in the Northeast Kingdom, is under suspicion of corruption. Clues suggest the involvement of a Satanist cult. Bernie, one of the patients in the nursing home, is a veteran of the Battle of the Bulge, one of those soldiers called a "ragman"—"wide-eyed, shell-shocked ghosts of

their former selves, walking around like robots." Joe believes that Bernie saw the killer of the old woman patient and, working with the doctor at the facility, arranges for Gail to spend time with Bernie and a borrowed cat, which Bernie readily accepts as his own. Through an enactment, in which Bernie thinks Gail is his daughter, he identifies the killer in a photograph. The detailed descriptions of Brattleboro again reflect the social and economic life of the town, "the staunch conservatives" and the "new liberals."

Emile Latour, the police chief in *Bellows Falls* (1997), calls on Joe to conduct an "internal affairs" investigation of a cop who has been charged with sexual harassment. Because Bellows Falls is only thirty minutes north of Brattleboro, Joe can continue to live at home with Gail, who is now deputy to Jack Derby, recently elected state's attorney over James Dunn. Joe will be able to keep track of his detective squad as well as the escape of youngster Jasper Morgan, who struck an officer and stole his gun. Jasper's disappearance soon ties into the events in Bellows Falls. "It keeps gnawing at me—like I'm supposed to be hearing something I can't make out." Descriptions of towns, the way they sit on the land and their architectural and historical features, are effective. Bellows Falls is a failed manufacturing town with more than its share of social problems—drugs, abuse, and unemployment. Joe works with the attorney general's office on this case, in tandem with Jonathan Michael, a good policeman. Brian Padget is a poster-boy cop who has been accused by Norm Bouch of sexually harassing his wife. Brian tests positive for cocaine. Bouch's wife, Jan, is hardly able to answer a simple question and appears totally dependent upon her husband. Joe senses that Brian is being set up and learns that Bouch is involved with a ring of high school kids who are running drugs for him. Jasper is found dead, after leading them to a man named Lenny, whom they put in jail after he kills one of the boy drug runners. Joe manages to persuade Jan to leave Norm and seek shelter with a woman's group. The scene is set for the final confrontation between Joe and the murderer, this time in a vast old milk and creamery plant during a fireworks exhibition (producing the additional complication of a hostage situation). Joe acknowledges making a mistake here: "Having overlooked the obvious possibility that [the killer], finding his escape blocked, had hidden among the spectators, I'd exposed us all to lethal danger." Bellows Falls may have an identity problem but, by the end, the town is taking a new and positive approach, especially to the problems of its teenagers. Latour, retired from the police department, will help.

At the start of *The Disposable Man* (1998), Joe and a couple of his squad find a body dumped in a quarry with no identification, clothing tags cut out, and Russian tattoos on his toes. Walt Frazier of the local FBI and a CIA man view the body. Joe is summoned to Washington where he is almost knifed to death and then interviewed by a CIA agent who tells him to drop his investigation. J.P. finds a gingko seed in the body's hair sample, which leads Joe to the Windham Hill Inn near Townshend. (An arresting image: "The trip home had been by the sepulchral gleam of a full moon, washing the tree-covered mountains and the undulating road with the colorless light of a hundred-year-old photograph.") He interviews the owner, John Rarig, for names of guests and staff. After a robbery at a jeweler's shop on Main Street in Brattleboro, Joe is found with a valuable brooch in his breast pocket. The case is sent to the attorney general, an arrogant, ambitious man named Fred Coffin; Joe hires lawyer Richard Levay and is put on paid suspension. He is stunned by what has happened to his life: a dead Russian; CIA intervention; an attempt on his life; and planted incriminating evidence. He makes a mistake ("overriding all warning signals") and confronts the jeweler. Joe is arraigned and released with several stipulations, including not speaking to his staff and reporting daily to the state police barracks. "I was feeling as I had a lifetime ago—a teenage warrior in full retreat—empty, alone, beaten, and like the most disposable man on someone else's game board." Though Joe is not allowed any contact with his staff, Willy and Sammie plan to help him but don't want to involve J.P. and Ron. Sammie and

Willy investigate Rarig and find he is not who he says he is; they persuade Joe to meet them at the inn. When Rarig orders Joe to Middlebury to save the life of another defector, Joe thinks it may be the only way to clear his name. Willy and Sam follow armed with police radios. A top Russian, Georgi Padzhev, materializes in Middlebury, captures Joe, Willy, and Sammie, and takes them to a motel on Route 7 where he is also holding Gail (now deputy state's attorney). The drama culminates at a radar station in the Northeast Kingdom. After the action, Joe's name is cleared, but he cannot forget the attorney general's remark in court that Joe is the "frustrated, impotent, older boyfriend of a rich, indulgent woman."

In *Occam's Razor* (1999), Joe is called out on a freezing January night to view a corpse decapitated on the railroad tracks in downtown Brattleboro. The corpse is dressed as a bum, but his underwear is "snowy white." A patrolman finds an abandoned truck smelling of toxic waste ("haz mat"), and Joe gets in touch with Vermont's Agency for Natural Resources (ANR). He and his squad canvass potential witnesses around the crime scene, and Sammie falls for one of them, a young man named Andy Margat, who was playing poker in a flat above the railroad tracks. Joe feels that his relationship with Gail is not working; she, more ambitious and driving than he, is drifting away. Jim Reynolds, former defense attorney now senator, is proposing a bill to streamline the various police agencies in Vermont (based on the principle of Occam's Razor: the simplest of two or more competing theories is preferable). A second homicide in a seedy apartment takes the life of a young woman, Brenda Croteau; her baby dies of hypothermia. Brenda was a welfare person involved in prostitution, drugs, and stolen goods. A name from the poker party arises in interviews related to Brenda's death, and a car registered to Senator Reynolds is reported to be the one seen depositing the body at the train tracks. A fingerprint on the knife that killed Brenda is traced to Owen Tharp, whose name turned up in the interviews, and he confesses to the murder. Gail is assigned lead lawyer in the prosecution. The dead

M

truck driver is identified as Phil Resnick, who is known to have driven trucks in illegal disposal of haz mat. Gail asks Joe to question the medical examiner about the death of Owen's girlfriend, Lisa Wooten. ("The request struck me as wrong. I just couldn't put my finger on it.") Owen was told that Brenda murdered Lisa, but Lisa's death turns out to be a simple overdose. Evidence is uncovered linking Billy Conyer to the railroad death. Conyer is killed in a shoot-out with the police. Connections between the two killings mount up. Five years earlier, Reynolds defended Kathadin Trucking in Maine on illegal shipping of haz mat. The police suspect Reynolds staged the whole thing: the break-in, the abandoned truck, his car at the scene, and the killing. The police believe Walter Freund may have killed Lisa to get control of Owen and then steered Owen to Brenda. Joe collects blood from Freund, who disappears. Finally, a new witness incriminates a political opponent of Reynolds, allowing Reynolds to get his new department, the Vermont Bureau of Investigation (VBI). Joe and Gail decide to live separately although remain friends and lovers. He takes a job with the new VBI, and she goes to Montpelier with an environmental organization; and Sammie breaks up with Andy, who lied to her about what he knew about the killing, and clues point to her becoming closer to Willy. Another illuminating passage: "It is an irony that Vermont is so well known for skiing the locals can't afford, maple sugar they have to sell, and photo-op cows that have all but disappeared. In fact, Vermont is a blue-collar state, only minimally agricultural, marked by marginal incomes, low education investment, small manufacturing, and heavy welfare rolls. Unemployment isn't too bad, but the kinds of jobs those numbers represent are not the stuff of careers. When Vermonters are asked what they do for a living, more often than not they answer, 'Everything.'"

The Marble Mask (2000) takes Joe from southern Vermont to the frozen landscape of the Vermont ski country and Sherbrooke in Canada. He is number-two man in the newly formed VBI. The existing Bureau of Criminal Investigations

(BCI) is made up of state troopers; VBI is composed of the cream of all departments. Joe and Gail remain in love though living apart; she has moved to a condo in Montpelier, where she is currently staff counsel for Vermont's most powerful environmental lobby. She is very ambitious, and Joe has not forgotten the cruel words of the attorney general. Sammie and Willy, in love and on Joe's team, are summoned to the Stowe Ski Resort on Mount Mansfield to investigate the discovery of a frozen body, fifty years dead, whose missing, broken-off parts suggest that it was dropped from a height. They explore the site on snowshoes with the Hazardous Terrain Team and in a whiteout Joe plunges into a hole from which he is later rescued. The body—"the Popsicle," as Willy calls it—is identified as Jean Deschamps. A snapshot of Stowe: "Stowe is tourist-dependent now, to the point where most of its money actually comes in during the summer months, and many of its key decision-makers are originally from out of state, referred to by disgruntled, dispossessed locals as 'flatlanders.' It has become a place gently at odds with itself, where wealth conflicts with poverty, residents with tourists, native-born with newcomer, tradition with trendy." Leaving Sammie and Willy in Stowe, Joe travels with the rest of the team to Sherbrooke in Canada to meet with their counterparts. Captain Gilles Lacombe, head of the police force, informs them that the Deschamps family is famous as a mafia set-up, run by Jean's son, Marcel (the other son, Antoine, died in Italy in World War II). Marcel's son, Michel, will inherit the organization (Marcel is dying of cancer). There are rival gangs in Sherbrooke as well—Hell's Angels and Rock Machine. They trace Deschamps's movements to Stowe fifty years earlier by the "road kill" in his stomach (there was a "Game Night" at a local restaurant) and find a suitcase filled with his possessions, including a letter from his son inviting him to Stowe. All the evidence falls too neatly into place. "Something isn't right about this." Joe goes alone and unarmed at the invitation of a purported member of Hell's Angels, "a fundamental and potentially fatal mistake." He and Willy interview Jean's former secretary, who was in love with both Jean and his son, Antoine. They return to Stowe where they find a restaurant owner with a large freezer. Then he is killed. The trail leads them to the killer, who found a treasure trove outside of Rome and killed Antoine for it. The marble mask over his fireplace is probably a Michelangelo. The dénouement comes as the killer's house is being consumed by fire while Sammie is trapped inside.

The action in **Tucker Peak** (2001) picks up about a month after the Stowe case. Joe is head of VBI Southeast, based in Brattleboro, with Sammie, Willy, and Lester on his team. Gail is working for VermontGreen in Montpelier. A sheriff in neighboring Windsor County asks for VBI's help with a robbery at one of the luxury condos owned by William Manning at Tucker Peak, a case complicated by a lot of "tree huggers" who are fighting the new development there. Like other ski resorts, Tucker Peak is making a big investment in "diversity," developing summer facilities as well as winter. The team finds that Marty Gagnon has stolen some valuables belonging to a rich New York woman, Jorja Duval; she is found dead. Gail introduces Joe to Roger Betts, the courtly head of the Tucker Protection League (TPL). Joe and Sammie go undercover at the resort. With a beard and a hair-color change, Joe gets a job as a carpenter (he has a woodworking shed at home, with his father's tools) and Sammie, in blonde hair and tight clothes, is hired as a ski instructor. Richie Lane, one of the ski instructors who cruises the local bar for women, is having an affair with Manning's wife. Lester and Joe track Richie to the house of Shayla Rossi in Newfane. As they approach the house, an armed Richie releases Shayla's rottweiler, which attacks Joe. He manages to kill the dog, Lester shoots Lane simultaneously. Lane was casing and robbing the condos with Marty. Someone is sabotaging Tucker Peak: ugly yellow dye is leaked on the pond; the generator goes out; a water-main breaks; a woman is almost killed in a chair lift accident (saved by Joe); the pump house is burned up. Sammie is wired and sent off to pick up Kurt Peterson (another of the ski instructors) and to arrest him when he sells her coke. She suc-

ceeds, after a terrifying chase and a near-rape, and Peterson incriminates Andy Goddard, one of the condo owners. TPL's Roger Betts simultaneously identifies Norman Toussaint, a member of the league, as responsible for some of the sabotage. Fingerprints from Jorja's dead body match the person who turns out to be the murderer. The head of Tucker Peak, Phil McNally, is in league with his chief financial officer, Gorenstein, to embezzle huge amounts of money from Tucker Peak and pay Toussaint to sabotage Tucker Peak. "A small flurry of nagging questions kicked up in my head." The final scene is a snowy chase for the killer below the windmills on top of Tucker Peak.

Only the first chapter of *The Sniper's Wife* (2002) takes place in Vermont. In a departure from tradition, the point of view is Willy's. He receives a call from the New York Police Department telling him that his ex-wife has been found dead in her apartment, apparently from an overdose of heroin. He takes off immediately, but Sammie is able to learn the cause of his abrupt departure by making a callback to the NYPD. The rest of this dramatic story, which reveals a great deal about Willy's past, takes place in New York, where Joe and Sammie eventually join him.

In *Gatekeeper* (2003), Joe is head of VBI Southeast, with regulars Sammie, Willy, and Lester on his team. The problem is heroin in Vermont, and Sammie once more goes under cover as blonde Greta Novak to infiltrate the drug gang in Holyoke, Massachusetts. She identifies the Vermont dealer and sets up shop in Rutland with one of the dealer's men, a killer named Manuel Ruiz. Sammie, not altogether stable, is attracted to this man. Meanwhile, her lover, Willy, is secretly following to ensure her safety. Lester is drawn into the web because his teenaged son, David, is mixed up in drugs at his high school. Joe is having problems with Gail, who is still troubled by her rape experience and is considering running for state office. Gail becomes involved in the drug situation because her niece, Laurie Davis, is an addict who robs a store and is shot (but not killed) in the process. Joe's reputation with VBI is on the line in this one.

M

A death after a domestic dispute in *The Surrogate Thief* (2004) catapults Joe back thirty-two years to a death in an unsolved grocery-store robbery: the same gun is used in both cases. Ambivalent about his behavior in the earlier case—his wife, Ellen, was dying of cancer at the time—Joe seeks permission to trace the gun and, perhaps, close the Klaus Olderfeldt case at last. Gail is running for state senate and has less time for him than usual. As Joe digs into the past, he is forced to confront his feelings of inadequacy about the Oberfeldt case and his anguish over his loss of Ellen. He seems more forbearing and gentle now, as he identifies the witness, Peter Shea, and the gun. When Shea is knifed and then Hannah Shriver is killed at the Tunbridge Fair, the deaths collide: the knife-slaying methods are identical. A Putney town constable uncovers Shriver's killer, Gabe Greenberg, who is connected to Tom Bander, the leading supporter of Gail's right-wing opponent for state senator. Bander, under a different name, had apparently killed and robbed Oberfeldt to bankroll his new identify and hired Greenberg to silence the witnesses, Peter Shea, his girlfriend, Katie Clark, and Hannah Shriver, the court reporter on the case. Joe confides to Gail that one of the reasons the Oberfeldt case had so obsessed him was that, after Oberfeldt's death, his widow, frustrated by poor police work, committed suicide; Gail realizes she has been insensitive to what Joe is experiencing. The knife with the thumb print at the mugging site was meant to incriminate Pete Shea, the "surrogate thief," but Joe finds the hard evidence needed—the killer's own blood on the knife—to issue a warrant for the killer's arrest. When they arrive at his mansion, they find him dead, a suicide. Gail wins her election, and Joe goes to a rest home to comfort Hannah Shriver's old mother.

Anne McAllister

In *Imagine* (1990), reality collides with fantasy when author Frances Moon opens her front door to find Jack Neillands, dazzling male model from Manhattan, on her doorstep. Her publisher's art director used Jack's likeness on the cover of her latest novel. A Radcliffe graduate, former English teacher, and injured divorcée, Frances has moved to Boone's Corner to raise goats, write, and enjoy small village life. Her best friend, Annabel Archer, lives next door with her two children. Jack is enchanted with Frances's intelligence and beauty and soon falls in love with her; she is unable to believe he is interested in her and does not want to be hurt again. The question is whether, despite their apparent differences in taste and lifestyle, they will decide to throw in their lots together. In *MacKenzie's Baby* (1992), Carter MacKenzie, looking for time off from running his health-food store in New York, offers to stay at the Boone's Corner house of friends Frances and Jack, who need someone to supervise in their absence the installation of a new roof. Still next door to them is Anabel, thirty-six, and her two children, seventeen-year-old Libby and twelve-year-old Leif Campbell. Anabel has always considered Carter glib and sardonic; he has found her intimidating and opinionated. The Campbell children and he become great pals; a baby, Conan, deposited on his doorstep, is assimilated into his life with no trouble. Conan's own mother finally claims him. Will Carter and Anabel finally acknowledge their love, marry, and have a baby of their own?

Elliott Merrick

After his mother's death, George Frain of Seronia, New Jersey, takes care of his younger brother, Henry, in **Ever the Winds Blow* (1936). Henry is sent away to Haverton School for Boys in New England, suffers the usual terrors and embarrassments, grows up a bit, tries too hard, and begins to have some academic success. He goes to Yale, where he meets and later marries Sally Enfield. They live in a tenement in New Jersey; Sally is pregnant and he is driving a delivery van. Henry is offered a management job, but he quarrels with the owner over the treatment of the workers and is fired. Sally has a baby boy, David. They want to live on a farm in Vermont and, after prowling across long-abandoned farms, find an empty, unpainted house near Arburg. The owner, Calvin White, gives them a favorable price because the bank is about to start foreclosure proceedings. He says that nearby at Claymore Lake a thousand or more summer people are potential buyers for their produce. The idyll of their life—and the constant hard work—is described with appreciation. Collins Larrabee, a neighbor, helps Henry with the rebuilding of the old woodshed and stays on to work regularly for Henry and teach him everything he needs to know. Old Lige Wheelwright, a voice of Vermont, counsels Henry not to be in too much of a hurry: "I been livin' in this place for thirty year and I ain't got it to suit me yet." Sam Pervis, who owns the big apple orchard that used to belong to the summer mansion of a wealthy railroad magnate, hires Henry to help pick. Everywhere Henry looks "goodness and happiness were lying on the ground." The winter is made for reading. Henry labors with the other men on the sugaring, and the families all assemble for the sugaring-off party. To the Frains, Vermont seems a "bountiful" place. The farmers "had not known the stony sterility of crowded places." As the Frains' way of life becomes more satisfying, the prose reflects their state of mind: "small-grained silver birch with thousands of dropping oval dots like a stylized picture of raindrops." The rich Cuthbert Royces, who live at Claymore Lake, are "dilettantes" who feel sorry for Sally because she does not have a modern bathroom but claim themselves "real Vermonters." Many people assume the Frains came to Vermont because of the Depression, but that had nothing to do with their move. They are learning every minute. Sally is expecting another baby. Henry understands that the forces of nature come first in importance and industrialism, second. (The title is from Emerson's essay, "The American Scholar:" "Ever the winds blow; ever the grass grows.")

Don Metz

Vietnam is the backdrop for these two deft and pithy novels. *Catamount Bridge* (1988) is set in 1967 in Catamount in northern Vermont within sight of the Connecticut River. Amos Woodard returned from the Revolutionary War

in 1782 to clear the land and build his house: eight generations have lived there. Leon Woodard served in the First World War; his son, Purdy, was killed in World War II; his twin grandsons, Harmon and Bodeman ("Bodie") have just received their selective service notices. Harmon, married to Darlene, wants to go to Vietnam; Bodie plans to go to Canada. In Catamount, a new bridge replaces the old covered bridge, washed away in the flood of 1938. Bodie likes to climb up into the arches of the bridge, which form an enclosed walkway across the river. He went up there one night with Darlene; Harmon is convinced that the baby she is expecting, after four years' of marriage, is Bodie's. Darlene and Bodie know that it is not, but Darlene has the impression that, if she does not tell Harmon the truth, he will be more motivated to come home to find out. Bodie's grandfather, Leon, is punishing himself because he was not able to tell his son, Purdy, he loved him before the latter went overseas; now, as Harmon leaves from the White River Junction train station, Leon is again unable to express his feelings. Vera, Purdy's widow, is strong and brave. While Harmon is away, Bodie digs the foundation for the doublewide house Harmon and Darlene are building on the property and makes the frame for the cement. The Valley Region Draft Board searches out Bodie, who has never shown up for his hearings. When Harmon is killed by a booby trap in Vietnam, Bodie, his twin, can feel the explosion in his own body. Darlene has her baby, called "Esther" after Leon's wife. Harmon's casket is flown home for a military service at the graveyard where Esther and Purdy are buried. The Reverend Hall, who presided over both Esther's and Purdy's funerals, delivers the eulogy for Harmon in the "terse patois that comes of ninety winters six months long, of flint and granite and early frost." Darlene wishes she had told Harmon the baby was his. At the end, Bodie climbs up into the arches under the bridge and thinks about the future.

In *King of the Mountain* (1990), Junior Audette was a big high school football star and king of the mountain; then he went to Vietnam, stepped on a mine, had both legs amputated

M

above the knees, and lives in a wheelchair. His parents, Wendell ("Snoot") and Francine ("Frouncey") Audette live on the farm Snoot's great-grandfather started and worked. It is in northern Vermont overlooking Dalton Pond and under the sacred Indian spot, Abenaki Ledges. Junior lives with them, having married Claire Tatro shortly after getting out of the hospital. Claire, half-Abenaki and the daughter of Horton Flint, grandson of the famous shaman, Horton Eagle-in-the-Wind, has become a nurse and still takes night classes at a local college. Ten years or so pass. Junior is bitter and cruel. Snoot and Frouncey, sad about their son's life, give him a free title to the farm. Junior sells one-third of the farm to the police chief, Bud Benoit, and one-third to Claire's stepfather, Tot Tatro, with plans to develop the property into a lodge with condos under the aegis of the Abenaki Development Corporation (The Mission Statement reads: "A jewel the whole community can be proud of, conceived in the spirit of our native American heritage, the Abenaki Ledges Lodge and Condominiums will continue the age-old tradition of living quietly with the land"). Snoot, appalled at this betrayal, calls their friend, Walker Owen, who once lived in their cabin (and loved Claire) and is now a lawyer, in the hope that he can stop this development project. After a drunken sexual attack on Claire by jealous Junior, she moves out; she and Walker make plans to rent a house to share with Snoot and Frouncey. Walker, driving back and forth from St. Johnsbury to study the applications for the development, opens a law office in Jordan. While Walker is getting more involved in the legal implications of challenging the development, Claire (who has received a no-contest divorce) is losing her nerve. She wonders if challenging the development is worth all the passion, hatred, and division it will arouse. The logging crews have already started work with their chain saws, and the architect figures ninety acres will be opened up. The point of view turns to Horton Flint, Claire's father, who has become a skilled "dynamite jockey" in Maine. He loved Pearle (who married Benoit) but impregnated Laurie Pippin and married her before taking off. Horton comes back, dropping in briefly to see Claire. The final drama concerns the future of Abenaki Ledges Lodge.

Ruth Tracy Millard

In *Candleflame* (1938), there are two classes of people in Bradley north of Burlington in 1909: those who live "down by the saw mill" and those who don't. Constance Trubee, whose father is superintendent of schools, is one of the latter; Christabel Driggs, who has no father and whose sister, Violet, had an illegitimate child, is one of the former. Constance and Christabel, who meet at school, become best friends, spending most of their time with John and Bill Burnett and Harvey Moore. Their sugaring expedition is a new experience for Christabel. The high school mothers gossip about Christabel: she is seen in compromising circumstances with Harvey. She becomes pregnant; the two marry, but she loses the baby. Harvey is killed overseas in the first months of World War I. Christabel is pretty and intelligent; with top grades, she is valedictorian of her class and goes to college with Constance, where she continues to excel. In their senior year, Christabel develops a crush on their English teacher, Whitney Durant. He boards near their dormitory, and Christabel begins calling on him, taking Constance along to allay gossip. At the end of the year, she tells Whitney that she loves him, but he confides that he loves another: her heart is broken. Constance has always been in love with John, who is now in medical school in New York. The two girls move to New York, Christabel to work in an ad agency and Constance in a publishing house. Christabel is a gallant and forthright person who is a great success in her career but contracts tuberculosis and has a difficult time recovering and then finding work. Constance marries John and has a baby. While Christabel is in a sanatorium, Constance returns to Vermont for their college reunion and discovers that she is the woman whom Whitney loves. All these years, Christabel has supported her mother and the two children of her sister, Violet, who ran off with a "Canuck." When her mother dies, Christabel returns to Bradley to care for Harry, thirteen, and George, ten. The gossips continue to gabble about her, but instead of being insolent to them, as she was in childhood, she is poised and independent. Whitney comes to see her at Constance's urging and finds Christabel serenely engaged in the lives of her nephews. He asks her to marry him and come with him and her nephews to California where he has a new appointment at a university.

Sue Miller

In *The World Below* (2001), Catherine Hubbard, who lives in San Francisco, has just been divorced for the second time when she learns that an alienated aunt has left Catherine her grandmother's house. This house is in West Barstow, fifteen miles from the Connecticut River in southern Vermont with a view of the Green Mountains. Catherine lived here for short periods in her youth after the suicide of her disturbed mother. Catherine remembers Vermont: "This was what I dreamt of: the village, the house itself. Its smell of wood ash and damp and oranges and rosewater. The stillness that fell over it in the afternoons when my grandmother napped, and the yearning I felt in the summers during that stillness, when I could hear, rising and ringing from elsewhere in the village, the sounds of life. I dreamt of the tangled lilacs by the front door. Of the raspberry patch behind the house and the iridescent Japanese beetles that gathered on the fruit. Of the smell of jam boiling after we'd picked the berries, of fireflies glinting in the summer dark, of snow lightening the nighttime winter sky." Since Catherine's children are grown and married, she conceives of starting over in a new, rustic life in West Barstow. Once in the house, Catherine discovers her grandmother's diaries. Reading them casts a whole new light on the way Catherine interprets her grandmother's life and marriage. She learns that her grandmother, Georgia, was sent unnecessarily to a tuberculosis sanatorium by a doctor she later married and at the "san" had an affair with a dying patient. Catherine goes on a fishing expedition with Samuel Eliasson, a retired academic, on Quabbin Reservoir in Massachusetts and remembers a

similar trip as a child with her grandfather. She is certain she saw a submerged village—"a world below." With this image, she evokes both her own suffocation in Vermont and the suppressed mystery of her grandparents' lives. Catherine faces the choice of staying in Vermont or returning to California.

Richard Mindell

Thirty-two years before *Eden Falls* (2000) begins, a shocking event occurred in the town of Eden Falls in northern Vermont, forty-five miles from Williston. A masked teenager, with three accomplices, tortured and hanged a ten-year-old boy because he was a flatlander. The then sheriff, Stanley T. Wohojowski (father of the current sheriff, "Wojo") never investigated the case; the perpetrators' names were not released because of their ages. The town was traumatized by the affair; today, Eden Falls continues torn with strife between flatlanders and natives. A case in point is the Douglas Farm Project. Vesticate Douglas, whose family has farmed the land for two hundred years, is forced to auction his belongings and sell his property for taxes. He wishes to develop his land, but the planning commission, filled with flatlanders (the Eden Falls Citizens for Responsible Land Management, devoted to "preserving the town's rural character"), has rejected his proposal. Thomas Downey, who came with his father and mother to Eden Falls in the sixties, was another victim of the barbarous teenagers: left to hang, he was cut down by a boy his age and rushed to a doctor. Crazed by the incident, he has spent many years planning his precise military operation revenge. His first target is Adrien Bessette, who hated every flatlander on the planning commission. After this killing, Simeon Cotter, lead detective for the Vermont State Police Special Investigations Unit, comes to Eden Falls, much to the displeasure of Wojo. Cotter, born in Washingtonville and now living in Halifax on the Vermont-Massachusetts border, is famous for having little regard for procedure. After Thomas Downey kills Peter Roi, Roi's son, Rick, disappears. Cotter is mystified about the connection between the two murders. Wojo, who is

M

assisted by a mute detective named Dennis Cain, is unsympathetic to Cotter's approach. Cotter finally hears the story of the hanging: Bessette and Roi were two of four boys involved; a second boy was hanged. Cotter looks into Downey's background and learns he was in military intelligence but failed the mental evaluation. After a hearing of the Douglas Project, Douglas is killed. When Wojo reports that Rick Roi is in Canada, Cotter himself picks him up and stashes him with Cotter's wife at their house. Cotter uncovers several important facts about the grisly events, but he overlooks an important clue to the identity of the masked leader before finally capturing him and solving the crimes.

Don Mitchell

Two circumstances underlie *The Nature Notebooks* (2004): the emission of radiation from the TV broadcast towers on Mount Mansfield and the development and expansion of the Stowe Mountain Resort. Erin Furlong, the facilitator of a nature-writing workshop in Burlington, who has published one book some years ago called *Peas in a Pod*, has assigned nature notebooks to her students and, to each, a model nature writer's identity. Lauren Blackwood (Henry David Thoreau) is a divorced woman working her father's farm in Underhill. Marianna Finch (Ralph Waldo Emerson) is a widow, mother of a teen-ager at the Putney School, and former dressage instructor now selling real estate and living in Shelburne. Rachel Katz (John Muir) is a trainer of young delinquents in sports like mountain climbing and lives in a poor neighborhood in Burlington. The first woman, Lauren, has a "pick-your-own" along the highway to earn quick cash and owns seven breeding llamas that generate more money than her one hundred sheep. She looks at nature from a practical angle, dealing with daily problems like stubborn weeds and ailing animals. Her father, realizing that the dairy business was failing, built three cottages for "agri-tourists;" he saw Vermonters as caretakers of a landscape that outsiders paid to see. Lauren wants to fix up the cabins for rent. When Kyle Hess comes unannounced to their writing group,

she recognizes him as a well-known writer and forest activist from California. Erin suggests that Kyle rent one of Lauren's cottages and help with her chores. They are soon in bed together. She writes a letter to the editor about the illegal development of the acres at the top of Mount Mansfield, which has belonged to the University of Vermont since 1859; Kyle criticizes her passive type of activism. A few days later Kyle brings over National Guard Major Cooper and his artist wife, who rent another of Lauren's cottages. Cooper says he is connected with the Ethan Allen Firing Range a few miles down the road. Lauren is not ready for the kind of activism Kyle has in mind. Soon, she is so in love with Kyle she is willing to do anything he wants. The second woman, Marianna, can see that real estate development is ruining "a lost Vermont:" the state is down to less than fourteen hundred dairy farmers. She is angry when Erin brings Kyle to class but is soon under his spell. He uses her contacts to get information about the Stowe development, jeopardizing her career, but she is already sleeping with him. She goes as his wife to a Stowe promotional weekend, where he sabotages the meeting and steals blueprints. The third woman, Rachel, invited to Erin's to meet Kyle before he even comes to class, is sure that he is her love and soul, and goes to bed with him. They spend idyllic days together, whitewater rafting and mountain climbing. He uses her skills to integrate her into the Mansfield project. The epilogue belongs to Erin.

David Morrell

The first section of *The Fraternity of the Stone* (1985) is set in a Carthusian monastery ten miles from Quentin in northern Vermont, where Andrew ("Drew") MacLane has lived as a hermit after going underground to escape Scalpel, the CIA's clandestine unit that conducts strikes against terrorists. Seven years pass before Scalpel traces him to the monastery (Drew thought this organization believed him dead) and poisons all of the other monks (Drew survives only because he fed the poisoned bread to his pet mouse). Drew heads for Boston to see Father

Hafer, who accepted his application into the monastery, and to find Arlene, his former lover, and her brother, Jack, his best friend, who were both Scalpel operatives. Drew learns that the villain is his Uncle Ray, who took him in after his parents were killed in Japan when he was ten. Another priest, Father Stanislaus, who helps Drew in his quest, is a member of the Fraternity of the Stone, founded during the Crusades, which is a group of priests who assassinate terrorists. Uncle Ray is tracked down and killed, but the Fraternity of the Stone is looking for Drew, so he goes into exile in Egypt and becomes a hermit again.

Mary McGarry Morris

Vanished (1988) is a sad and painful tale about two unfortunate people named Aubrey Wallace and Dotty Johnson. The former, who works on a road crew, was put in an orphanage by his father as a child, is almost illiterate, and speaks little. The latter, a disadvantaged, amoral teenager, is abused by her father, whom she kills and burns up in his house. The first chapter takes place "on a narrow mountain road in the Flatts near Atkinson" in the vicinity of Killington. The men on the road crew are referring to a terrible murder in which someone has killed a man and set his house on fire. The "someone" is Dotty, who seduces Aubrey into going on the run with her. Shortly after they take off, she manages to kidnap a child, Canny, from her house. The three flee on their unhappy path together. Five years pass in which they lead a dismal life, selling junk they steal. Dotty is a liar, a prostitute, and a thief. In Massachusetts, they meet some vulgar, brutal people at a motel cabin. The man is an ex-convict and former murderer; he talks them into claiming the reward for Canny. The scheme goes frightfully wrong.

Also set in Atkinson, *A Dangerous Woman* (1991) has as its heroine a psychologically damaged woman named Martha Horgan, thirty-two, who was the victim of an attempted gang rape when she was a teenager. Her father and aunt did not pursue the case against the young men, who were sons of prominent people in the communi-

ty. Martha's father and Aunt Frances grew up poor in the Flatts, but after Frances married elderly Horace Beecham, the wealthiest man in southern Vermont, she moved into his big house, keeping her widowed brother and his daughter, Martha, in the garage apartment. Frances has been a widow for many years, which she has spent in the intimate company of Steve Bell, a local lawyer married to an alcoholic named Anita. Martha was always a strange child, different from others, but since the attack upon her, she has been the butt of teasing and innuendo. She becomes more and more eccentric, asocial, and nervous. Moving to a boarding house in town, she is hired by a dry cleaner because her Aunt Frances pays a dividend to the owner. Her obsessive behavior, particularly her crush on Birdy, one of the women employees, and her accusations against another employee, Getso (which are true), force the manager to let her go. Back at her Aunt Frances's house, she becomes attracted to Colin ("Mack") McKay, the writer manqué whom Frances hires to rebuild her deck and do other chores around the property. He takes Martha to the Flatts one day to meet her relatives and to show her where her father and aunt grew up. Drunk one night, Mack takes advantage of Martha, who becomes seriously dependent upon him (and also pregnant). When Frances's affair with Steve ends, she begins an affair with Mack. Martha witnesses their relationship, which unhinges her even more than usual. She tries to reclaim her room at the boarding house but is treated like "a dangerous woman." She is offered a room at the house of Ben Weilman, a kindly old man who was a friend of her father's and who has developed a pleasant relationship with some of the children on his block. Martha is frighteningly harsh with these children. When she reveals to Mack and Frances that she is pregnant, they try to persuade her to have an abortion. The ending is tragic and convincing.

Songs in Ordinary Time (1995), again set in Atkinson, reveals the secret and sordid horrors of ordinary people in an ordinary town in 1960. The central character is Marie Luseau Fermoyle,

M

daughter of a butcher, who becomes pregnant as a teen-ager by Sam Fermoyle and marries him, even though he is engaged to Nora Cushing, the richest girl in Atkinson. Marie divorces Sam, who becomes a drunkard and, for the last ten years, has lived at the house of his sister, Helen, and her husband, Renie LaChance, owner of a hardware store who makes obscene telephone calls to local women. Helen takes care of Sam's and her dying mother, who lies in a big crib in the dining room. Helen has a helper named Fozia Menka, a black woman in her fifties whose dim-witted twin brother, Howard, works for the Monsignor at the local Catholic Church. For ten lonely, penny-pinching years, Marie has worked a menial job to support her three children, Norm, seventeen, Alice, fifteen, and Benjy, twelve. Into their dismal lives comes confidence man Omar Duvall, whom Benjy has seen from a hiding place in the woods scuffle with two black men, Reverend Pease and Luther, and knife the third (Earlie). Benjy, tortured by this image, keeps it to himself. Omar sweeps Marie off her feet, and soon she has taken out a loan, forging her brother-in-law Renie's signature, so that she can participate in Omar's enterprise, selling soap products from home. As Benjy sees his angry mother melt under the gaze of Omar, he has even stronger reasons not to reveal his secret, even though he discovers the dead body, putrefying in the woods. Alice is going out with Lester Stoner, whose father, the police chief, is sleeping with Eunice Bonifante, owner of the gas station, while his wife lies at home, dying of cancer. Joey Sheldon, a former police chief, runs a popcorn kiosk near the town bandstand and is periodically threatened by the town council for disturbing the peace. Montgomery Ward is opening a catalogue store on Route 4, which will ruin business in town. Mr. Hinds, the bank president, learns about the forged co-signature but suggests to Marie that if she is "good" to him, he can be persuaded to forget it. Grondine Carson, the local pig raiser, loves Jozia. No one has found Earlie's body, and Omar is dining at Marie's every night. He has rented a room that used to be deceased Judge Clay's, which gives him access to all the latter's files, including evidence that Sam's

mother drew up a trust stating that all her property, including the decrepit tenements managed by Helen, go to his children. Despite the abuse and deceit that follow, there is a sense of redemption at the end. In a coda, the neighbors living on Marie's street assemble to paint her house while she is driving Alice to Burlington to attend the University of Vermont.

The Lost Mother (2005) of the title is Irene Jalley Talcott, who abandons her family in Belton near Atkinson in the midst of the Depression and moves to Collerton, Massachusetts. Taciturn, sad Henry Talcott, an itinerant butcher, lives in straitened circumstances in a tent in the woods with his young children, Thomas, twelve, and Margaret, eight. His luck has run out. Even his car, upon which he depends for work, breaks down. Henry's life-long friend, Gladys Bibeau, tries to help, but the longstanding feud between Henry and her father makes her efforts fruitless: her unpleasant farmer father brought up Henry after he was orphaned and expected him to marry Gladys. When Henry is unjustly put in jail for taking something that belonged to him, the children are farmed out, first with Aunt Lena Lessing, a drunk, and her indifferent husband, Max, and then with Fred and Phyllis Farley. Fred, the biggest dairy farmer around, bought the mortgage to Henry's farm from the bank; his wife wants Margaret as a companion for her ailing, crippled sixteen-year-old son, Jessie-boy. This forlorn tale of betrayal, sorrow, and longing is told from the point of view of Thomas, a bewildered and angry loner. Margaret is overly eager to be agreeable and appealing because she fears being rejected again; Thomas is reluctant to make contact with others because he fears being disloyal to his mother, who, he is certain, will return to live with them. The children are so unhappy with the Farleys—Jessie-boy makes improper advances to Margaret—that they run away to Collerton. They find that their mother is the mistress of Louis Dexter, the wealthy head of the mill; she is unable to care for them. The children have always believed she left home because of the death of her third baby, but she lacks the skills to cope on any level. The children are taken into a Catholic orphanage, where Margaret becomes popular and Thomas continues to be as "empty" and "distrustful" as ever. He is learning that "growing up feels like being alone." The dramatic conclusion is powerful and affecting.

Stephen Morris

Beyond Yonder (1987) is the first of two novels about Upper Granville, which is in central Vermont directly east of Middlebury on Route 100. An early settler, Alton Blanchard, wrote a book about Upper Granville called *Over Yonder Hill*, which gives the history of the hamlet and explains the reasons for people's moving away, houses vacant, schools closed, and family farms consolidating. Darwin Hunter, a new resident, decides to update the book in recognition of the revitalization of the town through the "back to the land" movement. His book aims to analyze the balance of power between woodchucks and flatlanders. He organizes his material alphabetically and provides a glossary of Vermont under such headings as "auctions," "beer," "deer hunting," "dogs," "haying," "mud season," and "recipes for potluck suppers." This first book provides useful background, introduction, and explanation for its successor, *The King of Vermont* (1989), which pursues the same characters and, looking at the scene again through Darwin Hunter's eyes, picks up the action about five years later. Darwin wants to move on in life and run for the senate seat from his district. He finds a rock-and-roll musician, Goo-Roo, to act as his campaign manager. His campaign slogan is "Total Disclosure." He knows nothing about the issues, but he is willing to be completely honest with the voters. The plot careens past every traditional Vermont event from the local talk show to the Tunbridge World's Fair, giving the author shots at "the Hip and the Hick." Darwin improbably wins the election; he turns out to be a nice person, a good friend, and a caring neighbor. On moving to Vermont to run a county inn: "It was very romantic: nonstop repairs, wood hauling, sheet changing, and bill paying, interrupted periodically by the whimsical demands of tourists."

Howard Frank Mosher

The following novels and stories are all set in the Northeast Kingdom. Place is paramount: they all reflect the isolation and the sense of community, the harsh climate and the exquisite landscape—blue clay, mountains, lakes, rivers, swamps—of that remote area near the Canadian border. Some of the same characters drift through several of the stories. A member of the large multigenerational Kinneson family always makes an appearance. Characters like Judge Forrest Allen, Sheriff Mason, Frenchy LaMott, Henry Colville, and Armand St. Onge appear several times. There are numerous examples of a young-man, coming-of-age narrator like Ethan (WYSOTT) Allen, Frank Bennett, Wild Bill Bonhomme, James Kinneson, Austen Kittredge, and William in "Alabama Jones." *Disappearances* (1977), extraordinary and eloquent, is told from the point of view of fourteen-year-old Wild Bill Bonhomme. He lives in the Northeast Kingdom with his father, Quebec Bill Bonhomme, his mother, Evangeline, a French woman from Montreal, his Uncle Henry Colville, and his great-aunt Cordelia, ninety. It is 1932. "One by one the farms are disappearing." Quebec Bill has had to cut down and sell the maple trees in his sugarbush and needs hay to feed his wife's herd of cows. He decides to take a whiskey run to Lake Memphremagog with his brother-in-law, Henry Coville, Wild Bill, and the hired man, Muskrat ("Rat") Kinneson. Rat is "the last of a certain tradition of hired men, which in him seemed to have reached its apotheosis: unreliable, malingering, censorious; perpetually disconsolate, infuriatingly dogmatic; prodigiously talented with crops, animals, and machinery." Wild Bill listens to his father's stories about disappearances in the family. (His father's ancestor, René St. Laurent Bonhomme, was a habitant who came to Kingdom County in 1792, built a fine library in the Common, and disappeared in the swamp in the 1850s. His son Calvin, the founder of the village of Kingdom Common, went to Yale, became a minister, and established the first Universalist Church in northern Vermont. His children were Cordelia and

M

William Shakespeare Goodman — he anglicized the name, who cast the bronze statue of Ethan Allen and was killed at Bull Run. Cordelia raised his son, also William, born in 1855. This William, Wild Bill's grandfather, disappeared from Cordelia's care in 1869.) In audacious fashion Wild Bill's group picks up Carcajou's whiskey and burns his barn. On the water, Carcajou, a terrifying figure with his long white hair, is gaining on them. Quebec Bill puts a knife in his teeth and slips into the water to kill one of the men; it is up to Wild Bill to shoot Carcajou. "The launch was starting to turn. I brought up the shotgun as I had brought it up dozens of times before when my father and I walked slowly through the old apple orchard below the maples, cider-fragrant, October-still, waiting for the hard sudden burr of wings, the flash of pastel gray and soft brown, the gun swinging up almost independently, leading, leading, point don't aim, point, lead, the roar — you got him, Bill, you got him." Wild Bill worships his father but now realizes that "he was haunted by disappearances and the possibility of disappearances." His father steals a plane, and Wild Bill looks down on the winds, water, swamp, and mountains with a sense of wonderment. Carcajou catches up with them again. Wild Bill carries his father, struggling across the snow, until he collapses. Suddenly, Cordelia appears with a musket. "William Goodman," she screams as she shoots Carcajou and he disappears. Wild Bill is still not certain what his birthright is, but it takes him a year to recover from his father's death. He becomes a lawyer and then a judge, marries a French woman, and has a son, Henry, who has paranormal experiences. "Everything, it seems, is disappearing." The cedar swamp "is vast and wild and shimmering a little in the heat of the young summer. It is a place of mirages and illusions. A place of horrors and wonders. It is a vestigial corner of the primeval world, waiting patiently for us to disappear." By 1976, Wild Bill realizes that Kingdom County has disappeared. Three farms have been renovated as summer homes. The cedar bog is gone, inundated by an Army Engineers dam—gone, too, are the wild animals, the fish, the flowers, and the white-water river. The lake is lined with camps and resorts. The elms on the Common are gone from disease. Gone as well is a way of life.

Where the Rivers Flow North (1978), the title novella in this collection, begins in 1927, when Noël Anderson Lord is living on the property in the Northeast Kingdom that he inherited from his great-great-grandfather. Twilight Anderson came down from Canada in 1759, having been with Rogers's Rangers at St. Francis. His son, George, joined the state militia with his muzzleloader in the Revolutionary War. His son, Joseph, went to the Civil War at sixty years of age. His son, Gilles Lourdes, was a logger who died running the river drunk in a bateau. Noel makes cedar oil in his cedar still, he has his two-hundred-and-fifty-year-old pine trees (the last stand of virgin pines in Vermont), and he has a housekeeper, Bangor, whom he met years before when she was a slim young Indian whore in Maine. Against the opposition of the governor, the legislature, and every daily newspaper, the court approves the plans of the Northern Vermont Power Company. After July 4, 1927, blasting starts at the foot of the notch. Noël refuses to close the gate to the driving dam, because it would flood his cedar still and he couldn't pay his lease. The company offers him one thousand, then five thousand dollars. The company proposes to move him up to the pine stand, build him a little house, and make him the custodian of a tourist park. He is beginning to feel the cold: "In the early days he had worked in the woods without discomfort when a jet of tobacco juice froze as it hit the snow and shattered on the crust like beads of opaque amber glass." Friends like Armand St. Onge urge him to sell out and come live at the inn. Stubborn, tired, and spiteful, Noël decides to cut down the virgin pines and float them down the river. He makes use of the big flood of 1927 to take out the Kingdom Power Dam being built at the foot of the flume. Tragically, he is killed in the process. Bangor, who cannot live without him, commits suicide. This collection includes six short stories. **"Alabama Jones"** is a young woman hitchhiker whom William picks up. She was treated in the hospital in Burlington for a burst appendix and is making her way back to Kingdom Common to meet her brother and appear in his road show at the fair grounds. As William drives along the country road, he sees "the sugar maples, as polished and yellow as hard butter." Because Alabama is looking ill and tired, William takes her to his house, where his father, Lucien, and he care for her. The two young people establish a lovely friendship, and her brother offers William a job with the fair on the road. He is tempted, but he loves his life in the Kingdom. **"Burl"** is a woman whom her father and brothers mistreat and ill-use. When she is fourteen, after slaving all her life for her family, her father sells her to an older man to take care of his thirteen children. When she is nineteen, he marries her and they have a good life together, although the daily work would kill a normal person. When the bank threatens to foreclose on the farm, she begins making and selling moonshine. Just as they are ready to pay off the mortgage, her husband dies of cancer. Another man comes into her life: an agent who almost arrested her years before and has always remembered her. They have a few good years together in which she experiences the childhood she never had. She is telling this story from the hospital where she plans to thwart being put in the criminal ward by taking pills she saved from her husband's illness. In **"First Snow,"** Walter lives with his wife on property abutting that of his older half-brother, Eben. Walter is out cutting spruce boughs to bank against the house before the bad snows come. He hears the partridges flying up, "burring their wings like a big John Deere starting up." He walks over to Eben's to offer to help him bring his heifers up and finds that Eben has two down country people visiting who want to hunt deer on Walter's side of the mountain. They shoot a doe. Walter waits until they have left before he calls the game warden (named Kinneson) to report that "someone" shot a doe on his property. In **"The Peacock,"** a man, once a basketball player, is dying. His wife runs their single gas pump and takes care of him. She once brought

him from a zoo in Canada a peacock egg, which he hatches and raises as a pet. Then it disappears. Henry Coville visits him, but he is inconsolable. **"High Water"** is told in the vernacular of Waterman's younger sister. They are driving his Chevy to the stock car race, but become stuck on a bridge. Through Waterman's ingenuity, they arrive in Canada on time, but the race has been canceled on account of bad weather. They have to rush home to move the heifers so they won't drown. Although Waterman's father scorns his intellect, Waterman figures out how to cross the roaring river to save the heifers, even though he sacrifices his beloved racing car. **"Kingdom County Come"** is Henry Coville's own story. He and his friend, Fletch, board at the Common Hotel. Henry was an assistant cook and then a logger, who took time out to fight in World War I and was gassed. He lost a lung and returned to the Northeast Kingdom to work as a guide and bootlegger. As his coughing worsens, he goes out alone in his canoe. He sleeps out and shaves every day—"the sun rose, red as a winter apple." He concentrates on the landscape and on the tamarack trees, "evergreens that were not evergreen at all but dropped their needles each winter and leafed out again in May." At the end of this lovely, sad story, Henry cuts his wrists: "The cedar water was too dark to stain, and the translation was not unpleasant, less like departing his life than joining the bog. Like a man going to sleep at night after being on the water all day, he thought he could still feel the motion of the canoe under him. Then he was sure he was in a canoe. It was snowing lightly and his father was pointing at a dark buck watching them from the bank at dawn."

Marie Blythe (1983) portrays the arduous life of Marie Blair, who in 1899 walks with her father, Claude, and her half-Indian mother, Jeanine, from the St. Francis River in Canada to a railroad station. They take a cattle car to Hell's Gate, ten miles from Kingdom Common on Lake Memphremagog ("Beautiful Waters," named by the Abenakis) in the Northeast Kingdom. The other three children having died of smallpox, the Blairs have come to join other Canadians at a mill town, Hell's Gate, a paternalistic company town run by Captain Abraham Benedict. The KKK comes briefly to intimidate Hell's Gate residents because it considers the Canadian workers strike-breakers, but Captain Benedict dispatches them by coolly impaling their leader with a harpoon. Marie's father is killed in a logging accident; after her mother dies of consumption, Marie joins a pack of gypsies (the gypsy mother changes her name to "Marie Blythe"). She returns to Hell's Gate and works as an apprentice to the Benedicts' cook, Wyalia Kinneson, who is a cruel taskmaster. Captain Benedict reassigns Marie as his wife's companion. The son of the family, Abie, is a spoiled and lazy youth who seduces Marie. When she becomes pregnant, the Benedicts propose adopting the child as their own. Refusing, Marie leaves their household, has a miscarriage in the woods, and falls asleep in a boxcar. The tramp who rescues her is John Trinity Kinneson, Wyalia's husband, who invites her to ride the rails to Portland. They end up in a pulp camp on the Allagash. This platonic two-year partnership ceases when John tries to sell Marie to cover his gambling debts. She returns to Pond in the Sky where the foreman, Jigger Johnson, takes her to Pond Number Four on the Nulhegan River to homestead; Jigger has been hired as a tower watcher above Wenlock, in the most northeastern part of Vermont. They are happy for four years, until Jigger goes through the ice with his team. "He could have jumped, but didn't," she reports to the big boss. She works at Bull Francis's Pond House as a dancer, but when she refuses to become a prostitute, he puts her in jail (he is also the justice of the peace). In jail, she gets consumption but is sent to the state sanatorium on the Connecticut River. Here she finds her purpose in life—to become a nurse at the sanatorium. Dr. Philbrook Jamieson arrives at the hospital; they are soon working and sleeping together. She is moved to Ward D, with the sickest patients and the highest mortality rate. In 1917, Ward D is assigned to soldiers who are victims of poison gas. Jamieson realizes he can treat the soldiers more effectively in the field and applies for service in France, where he is gassed and dies. Marie is fired for refusing to segregate a carload of black soldiers. She returns to Hell's Gate to find that the Captain is dead, Rachel has moved, and Abie, wounded in the war, is running the company. She takes a night job at the factory and goes to school during the daytime to learn to read and write. Abie has grand plans for building a hotel on the mountain; Marie meets a local auctioneer, Harlan Smith. By 1921, farms, family lumbering operations, and general stores are starting to go under. Soon Abie is bankrupt and the entire village is auctioned. Marie bids for Indian Island, where she wants to live. She also buys the Captain's diaries and finds out that he has left her—and his putative grandson—all his money. There is a final confrontation with the embittered Abie, after he sets fire to the mountain and the village. Marie survives, badly burned, and lives with Harlan Smith on the island where they run a fishing-guide service.

James Kinneson is the narrator of riveting and meaningful *A Stranger in the Kingdom* (1989). He is thirteen in 1952 when the new preacher, a black man and former Royal Canadian Air Force officer, Walter Andrews, arrives in Kingdom County from Canada with his seventeen-year-old son, Nathan. James is a bright, hard-working boy who helps run the presses for his father, Charles Kinneson, Sr., editor of the *Monitor*, and does chores for his "fine-tuned" mother. His big brother, Charlie, is an unconventional lawyer who defends all the disreputable characters in town but would rather be trout fishing or playing baseball. Charlie lives in a filthy trailer and is half-heartedly courting Athena Allen, daughter of the local judge, Forrest Allen. No one will take Charlie seriously until he stops defending reprobates like his criminal second cousin Resolvèd Kinneson and runs for prosecutor. As a joke, Charlie helps Resolvèd to advertise for a housekeeper. A lovely teenager, Claire Larivière, turns up in answer to the ad, in a bid to escape an abusive parent and get to Hollywood. James befriends Claire, who flees Resolvèd's quarters to stay at the preacher's house until other arrangements can be made. Soon some of the less savory characters in Kingdom County start making racist remarks about the Andrews family.

Andrews learns that after the Civil War a highly educated former slave, Pliny Templeton, founded the Common Academy. Andrews begins researching Pliny's life. Elijah Kinneson, Resolvèd's brother, a religious fanatic and type-setter at the *Monitor*, is angry because, as sexton at the church, he had hoped to be named preach-er. Resolvèd goes to Andrews's house to retrieve Claire and wildly fires several bullets into the porch while Andrews is standing there; Andrews shoots him in the hand to disable him. Concerned by this attack, Andrews takes Nathan back to Canada; when Andrews returns, Claire is miss-ing. Her murdered and mutilated body is found in the quarry, and a search turns up Andrews's RCAF service revolver. Andrews is arrested for the murder and jailed. An autopsy shows Claire was a month pregnant. Charlie is hired to defend Andrews, and the family is united in believing Andrews innocent. Resolvèd, in cahoots with Mason White, the bigot sheriff, states in surprise testimony that through the window of the minis-ter's study he saw Andrews having sexual inter-course with Claire. "Did you see his face?" No, but he saw his legs and his voice, saying, "Turn off the bloody light." When the family is gathered in the newspaper office to rehash the trial, James uses the term "bloody." Charlie, transfixed, asks him where he heard the term. "From Nathan." Charlie sends for Nathan, who testifies that it was he who was having intercourse with Claire. Frenchy LaMott's mother, who works for Reverend Andrews, persuades Frenchy to testify that he saw Elijah in the minister's office, remov-ing documents and a revolver. The jury finds Andrews innocent. Elijah goes berserk in the courtroom and stabs Andrews before turning the knife on himself. Elijah's vengefulness results from knowing that Pliny Templeton did not com-mit suicide as everyone had thought. Elijah's grandfather, Charles Kinneson, murdered him. Elijah knew that Andrews, in his historical research, was close to discovering this fact. In an editorial, Kinneson asks why there was a "con-spiracy of silence." Why didn't more people defend Andrews? "Is it fear? Fear of what, exact-ly? Of Negroes? Of outsiders? Of strangers? Of

change?" James knows that his father has no illu-sions about Kingdom County and that, "for all its flaws, Kingdom County was a basically good place to live and work...He believed that most of its failings were correctible."

Northern Borders (1994) introduces the his-tory of Austen Kittredge's great-great-great-great-great-grandfather, the "fleeing Tory" Sojourner Kittredge, who traveled up to Kingdom County in 1775 and founded Lost Nation Hollow. Sojourner built a school, Lost Hollow Atheneum, and offered ten thousand acres to the state of Vermont if it would build a university there. The state chose to build the uni-versity in Burlington, on the banks of Lake Champlain, but set aside a full scholarship for the university to any graduate of Lost Hollow Atheneum. Austen's widowed father, who is the headmaster of a school at White River, decides in 1948 to send six-year-old Austen to stay with his grandparents, Abiah and Austen, on their hill farm in Lost Hollow so that Austen can attend the Atheneum. Abiah and Austen are engaged in a Forty Years' War, much to the consternation of their four children, Austen (Austen's father), Nefertiti, Cleopatra, and Rob Roy. The young narrator is aglow with decency, loyalty, and intel-ligence. Austen loves his grandparents and describes their life on the farm with zest and nos-talgia. He misses only one day of school, the day that his grandparents face off in court before Judge Forrest Allen in Kittredge v. Kittredge. Austen's grandmother has requested a perma-nent injunction to prevent his grandfather from raising the level of his millpond, which would flood out her apple orchard. Austen attends the March town meeting, helps his grandfather every summer with clearing the "Vista," the border with Canada, hunts deer with his grandfather, goes bird hunting with his young Uncle Rob and the Manchester sharpshooter, and participates in annual family reunions and theatricals. One year they put on *The Tempest*, with young James Kinneson from Kingdom Common in the cast and Editor Kinneson in the audience. In a fren-zied attempt to vacuum the cluster flies in her house, Austen's grandmother has a heart attack

M

and dies. In a moving scene, his grandfather makes her coffin in the shape of a sarcophagus, filled with all her Egyptian relics and sweet tamarack branches. Austen graduates from high school and goes on the long-promised canoe trip to his grandfather's hunting camp. They share a thrilling adventure heightened by his grandfather's revelation of the Indian woman he loved who died in childbirth. His grandfather is determined to move her bones before the lake is flooded. After the trip, his grandfather tells Austen that he will stay on No Name Lake and "go partners" with Danny Snowball on a trap line. He deeds the farm to his four children and his hunting camp, "Labrador," to Austen. Austen doesn't want to leave, but his grandfather urges him to go to college. "But who will run the Farm?" asks Austen. "There isn't any more Farm on Lost Nation Hollow, Austen. There hasn't been since I quit shipping milk. It was just barely a farm for years before that. The sawmill's played out too. There aren't ten acres of usable timber left on the entire place...Lost Nation Hollow is a bygone place. I watched it pass into history and so did you, though at the time you were too young to know what was happening. The farms are all gone. The big woods are gone. The best of the hunting and fishing is gone. The kids, including four of mine, have grown up and gone away and not come back. What is there for them to come back to? What is there for any of us to come back to?" As they part, his grandfather, a voice of Vermont, says, "You did all right this summer. You're a good fella to go down the river with."

The Fall of the Year (1999), subtle and sweet, is told by Frank Bennett, a young man from Kingdom Common. He was three when his parents were killed. Father George Lecoeur, "an unorthodox priest and greatest scholar and third baseman in the history of Kingdom Common," adopts Frank. Each chapter (with an epigraph from Father George's *A Short History of Kingdom Common*) is a discrete story; strung together they describe the way Father George raises Frank and what kind of a man Frank becomes. In the first chapter, **"The Savant of Kingdom Common,"** Frank returns home from college—

it is 1959—and his adoptive father puts him to work helping Foster Boy Dufresne, an idiot savant who is ill-used by the village and finally goes missing. Frank, Foster Boy's only friend, searches for him for weeks. In **"The Journey,"** Frank spends an afternoon with Louvia DeBanville, a clairvoyant who lives in Little Quebec. In the patisserie, she introduces him to Chantal, the most beautiful girl he has ever seen, with "morning glory eyes." Louvia tells Frank that once she was in love, but her lover went for a soldier. He imagines her, "young and beautiful, gliding across the hardwood floor of the pavilion with the colored lanterns shimmering to the trombone runs of the big bands." In **"Enemies,"** Frank learns about the feud between the Lacourse and the Gambini families. Father George plays a significant role in bringing the families together when he marries a son from one family to the daughter of the other. Father George assigns Frank, in **"Daredevil,"** to watch out for seventeen-year-old Molly Murphy, who has been threatening since she was five to run away to join the circus. The Slade Bros. Railway Extravaganza is coming to town. The show is everything anyone could want. As the crowd is leaving, the expensive white-faced Kilimanjaro monkey escapes from the tent and rushes up the face of the town hall to the weather vane; just as quickly, Molly runs after him and, climbing as nimbly as the monkey, rescues the shivering creature. That night, Molly appears high above the ring on a tiny platform. She performs four complete mid-air revolutions off the flying trapeze and is caught—by her ankle—just in time by Young Count Zempenski. She joins the circus and marries Young Count into the bargain. In **"Land of the Free,"** Frank tells about his friendship with Dr. Sam R. Rong, a Chinese gentleman who comes to the Common to start a business from scratch. He does everything from selling food, to exporting ginseng root, to cutting hair, to acting as surgeon. He is so successful that the town fathers deport him as an enemy alien. Frank goes to see him in New York, where he has started a new business on Staten Island in full view of the Statue of Liberty. Frank's next task in **"Night School"** is to take Father Brown's place teaching the citizenship class for immigrants who want to become Americans. Frank, who has no experience in such endeavors, finds Louvia in his class, and Frenchy LaMott, and Abel Feinstein, the tailor, among about twelve participants. The approach may be unorthodox, but the class is free-spirited and hardworking. The selectmen, who come to visit, are dissatisfied with the informality and untraditional aspects; in a word, they do not want these people to succeed. They send an announcement that the class may not use the town hall for its final meeting. This ultimatum only encourages the class to show up at the hall anyway to try for perfect scores on the tests. The selectmen are shamed into letting them use the hall, the students all make one hundred percent, and Abel Feinstein gives the valedictory address. He was born in Poland, he tells them. He escaped, at the behest of his parents. He walked and walked for hundreds of miles and finally arrived in America: "For Abel, no more walking away from." **"The Mind Reader"** is about the illusionist show of Mr. Moriarty Mentality and his "ravishing assistant, the Petrograd Princess." Again, Frank is designated their guide and interpreter; again, Frank sees the town officers try to cheat this hapless couple of their fee. Mr. Mentality gets his revenge, with the help of someone in the village. **"A Short Local History"** brings Chantal back to the village. Father George is becoming more and more frail, and Louvia proposes that he rent his spare room to a housekeeper. Frank is astounded to find Chantal back in his life — and to find her spending all of her time with Father George, having lunch together and driving long distances around the county. After Father George's death, Frank is even more surprised to find that the two hundred and fifty thousand dollars Father George had saved up to give to the Academy, where he had taught, had been bequeathed instead to Chantal. She disappears, telling Frank she has a lover whom she met in Quebec. He learns that she has given the money to the Academy after all. In **"The Fortuneteller's Daughter,"** Frank tells Louvia he wants to find Chantal to thank her for

what she has done. In the last and most beautiful chapter, **"The Fall of the Year,"** Frank takes Father George's ashes up to their cabin, where they fished together, and, by canoe, farther yet, to the spawning pool deep in the bog, where he leaves the ashes in the crook of an old tree. He returns to the cabin to find Chantal waiting for him. She has a letter from Father George, explaining that one time he fell in love, dancing in the pavilion, and later, after the war, he came together once with that person, and the result was his daughter — Chantal. And Chantal is in love with Frank, whom she did meet in Quebec — Little Quebec, where Louvia lived.

"Second Sight" is a short story from *Granite and Cedar* (2001). Subtitled "The Highroad," it concerns Jane Hubbell, who was born in 1887 and lived her entire life on Kingdom Mountain. Rob Hubbell, her nephew, tells the tale. Plans arise to build an interstate highway right through the Northeast Kingdom; worse, from Aunt Jane's point of view, the road intersects the Kingdom Mountain cemetery where her parents are buried. At the town meeting to hear the state exercise its right of eminent domain, Jane knows that protesting would do no good (there is a lovely image about the interstate's unspooling inexorably just the way the glacier did ten thousand years ago when it carved out the hills and valleys). Other citizens protest, but Aunt Jane stands up to pronounce her acceptance of the inevitable; however, she insists upon her right to move her parents' bodies from the cemetery before the state sets foot on her property. Her nephew, Rob, will do the work.

The True Account, A Novel of the Lewis & Clark & Kinneson Expeditions (2003) begins with a first chapter in Vermont in 1804, before the adventure takes off on a trek across country to the Pacific. The narrator, Ticonderoga Kinneson, sixteen, is the son of Charles Kinneson, editor of the *Kingdom County Monitor*. His mother is as beautiful as Kinneson women always are. The language about Vermont is lovely: "Sunrise struck the soaring peaks of the Green Mountains, turning them as pink as one of my mother's sugar-glazed apples." His uncle, Private

M

True Teague Kinneson, was with Ethan Allen and the Green Mountain Regiment, First Continental Army, at the fall of Fort Ticonderoga in 1775. Unfortunately, he struck his head and never quite regained his wits. He is a sort of Don Quixote in his "ways and strays." Ti grows up playing imaginary games with his uncle, who is an adventurer, angler, playwright, gardener (cannabis), and Ti's Greek and Latin tutor. Ti, even at this early age, is an accomplished painter. Uncle True learns that Jefferson is mounting an expedition to discover a route by river to the Pacific and wishes to lead it, but unfortunately Merriwether Lewis and William Clark have already been chosen. Ti follows Uncle True to Boston and together they go on their way to Delaware via New York and thus on a two-year trip. He and Uncle True save the American explorers from the Blackfeet, and Ti falls in love with Yellow Sage Flower Who Tells Wise Stories. Ti becomes the first American painter of Louisiana. His wife, Yellow Sage, dies in 1838, leaving Ti with their daughter, Helen of Troy Kinneson, her husband, Crouching Panther, and their daughter, Sacagewea. True marries Miss Flame Danielle Boone (Daniel's daughter). Ti's great-great-grand-daughter is Cora Soaring Eagle Kinneson.

Waiting for Teddy Williams (2004) is a moving, graceful evocation of Ethan Allen's transformation from an eight-year-old boy to an eighteen-year-old man. Descended from his great-great-great-great-great-grandfather, Colonel Ethan Allen, whose weathered statue stands in the center of Kingdom Common, E.A., as he is called, is a member of the WYSOTT Allens—Wrong Side of the Tracks (the "Y" was added to make it easier to say). E.A. lives in his grandmother's house with his mother, Gypsy Lee, twenty-six, who supports them by writing and singing songs in neighboring taverns on the weekends and running her RFD Escort Service during the week. (Some of Kingdom Common's most worthy citizens like to see Gypsy dress up in period costumes that appeal to their fantasies.) Gran hasn't stirred from her wheelchair since the Red Sox lost the playoffs to the Yankees in 1978. The Common, like the whole Red Sox Nation, is crazy about baseball. The local

team, the Outlaws, always draws a crowd to the rickety bleachers. Judge Charlie Kinneson is now in his seventies but umpires for the team. His younger brother, James, has taken over the editorship of the *Kingdom County Monitor* from their father. Because E.A. is illegitimate, Gypsy homeschools him, fearing the hurtful tongues of the school children. He is already teased, called "woodchuck," because his family eats the animal. Times are hard, and Gypsy has to take wood off the house and barn for the stove. Traditionally, Kingdom Common people pay their taxes with maple syrup; WYSOTT Allens ran whiskey to Canada (Gypsy and Gran now buy in New Hampshire and sell in Kingdom Common to a beau of Gypsy's in the Royal Canadian Mounted Police). E.A.'s principal "friend" is the statue of Colonel Allen, to whom he confides his innermost thoughts; his main desire is to learn the identity of his father. Gypsy will only refer to him as "Gone and Long Forgotten." E.A. shares the town's passion for baseball, and he and Gypsy have built a fine "Fenway Park" on Gran's meadow where he practices tirelessly; Gypsy is equally tireless trying to provide batting practice for him. Bill, the feckless but loyal hired man, often shags balls for E.A. One day, a stranger appears, rumpled, chain-smoking, and sipping from a paper bag in his pocket. Called "Teddy," he begins giving E.A. playing tips; soon E.A. cannot wait for the winter to end and Teddy to arrive. Gypsy tells E.A. a bit about the wild times she had with his father and the shocking automobile accident that killed him just before E.A. was born. When E.A. digs into the archives of Editor Kinneson's newspaper, he discovers that E.W. ("Teddy") Williams went to prison for ten years for the automobile accident that killed his father; E.A. furiously accuses Teddy. Firmly but gently, Teddy explains that he is E.A.'s father and out on parole. Teddy, E.A., and Gypsy go to Cooperstown in Gypsy's car, The Late Great Patsy Cline, with Warden Kinneson's borrowed license plate on the back. Teddy and E.A. work out every day at their own Fenway Park. As each year passes, E.A. becomes a better baseball player and, finally, a wonderful pitcher. Seventeen and almost six feet tall, he starts playing for the Outlaws and working at the bat factory. The thrilling climax comes after E.A. is recruited by the Red Sox and, with one game in the balance, Gypsy and Teddy and the whole Outlaws team are in the Boston stadium to watch E.A. pitch.

Faye Smith Moulton

In *Witch's Child* (1994), after Hannah Spenser developed psychic abilities in high school, people in Sherfield Center began to draw away from her, calling her a "witch." Now fifty-nine, she rarely leaves her hilltop; Ken Jarvis, a thirty-five-year-old logger, brings her groceries and mail. She withdrew from society after her college beau, Andrew Perkins, was killed in a deer hunting accident. In the woods, Hannah finds a little boy who tells her his name is Josh Coughlan, three. She realizes that he is the child of her neighbor, Ken. He and an unknown woman (Annie Coughlan) were burned to death in Ken's trailer the day before. Some premonition about the safety of the child keeps her from telling the game warden, Greg Choquette, part Abenaki, who drops by to deliver her mail on the way to Ken's place on the Stinson land. Greg is trying to figure out why the deer herd is diminishing so rapidly: he finds the answer in a pile of rotting entrails and deer guts and a large pit for storing iced carcasses on Ken's property. He also meets a sympathetic young woman at the schoolhouse, Lisa Jensen, who is staying with her brother, his wife, and seven children. In a tense climax, the killer, who is involved in the poaching business and other illegal activity, comes after Josh, who witnessed his crimes.

Joseph M. Nassise

The premise of **Riverwatch** (2002) is that, long before there were men, the Elders, who were good, and the Nightshades, a race of evil gargoyles, competed for control of the earth. War wiped out all but Gabriel Armadorian, the last Elder, and Moloch, the last Nightshade: both, coincidentally, are in Harrington Falls, where aging Gabriel is in a hospital and Moloch is slumbering in a chamber under Hudson Blake's house. When Jake Caruso, who runs a construction company, uncovers an underground passage at Blake's, he inadvertently awakens Moloch, who flies away on leathery wings. Jake, his friend, Sam Travers, who works at the hospital, and Katelynn Riley, who is writing her doctoral thesis on the Blake family, join forces to defeat Moloch after the latter commits numerous murders too gruesome to describe. They enlist the aid of Sheriff Damon Wilson, who finally believes their unlikely story. Jake and Sam sacrifice their lives to kill Moloch (bullets aren't effective, but fire is), leaving Kate, shaken but alive, to enter into a relationship with Damon.

Daniel A. Neary, Jr.

The stories in *Rage in the Hills* (2002) are concerned with dispossessed Vermont farmers and with the out-of-staters buying up the lost farms as second homes. In "**Plague**," Dewey Morse runs a one-hundred-and-fifty-acre dairy farm with his wife and hired man, Ned, in rural Tinmouth in the 1950s. They cannot afford to switch from using milk cans to bulk tanks. Even though they win the plaque for the cleanest milk in the state, they are forced to sell their farm and auction off their belongings. Clem Grout, who lives in Scampsville on the edge of the Green Mountain National Forest in "**Mountain Justice**," cuts logs for dealers using horse-drawn carts. When someone begins stealing from his woodpile, Clem retaliates by rigging a log with dynamite; the thief's house burns to the ground. Ed "Progress" Blanchard, director of tourism in 1965 in **"The Political Appointee,"** hires an advertising consultant to lure visitors to the state to buy up abandoned farmland as second homes. He claims he wants to move Vermont into the twentieth century; his wife, Edna, does not approve of the kind of progress that puts farmers out of work. Hoss Martin runs the general store in **"The Country Store."** One of the old-timers is rude to a "suntanner" who comes in to buy supplies; Hoss quietly tells the customer that he appreciates his business. Bud Reynolds, a reporter from Boston, takes a TV crew to Topsham in **"An Interview"** to get some footage of auctioneers Doc and Eddie Morton at the Morton Commission Sale of livestock. Bud gets the footage all right, but he doesn't understand why he fails to get any "emotion or expression" in the interview with Doc, who is sweating and subdued. Bucky Cole in **"The Mountain Man"** works for the road commissioner in Plainfield. He plows the roads on farms purchased from failed Vermont families by newly elected selectmen. After work, he goes out bird shooting; he gets one bird and the dog of an out-of-state neighbor. Glenda and Scott Emerson moved to Vermont in **"Belly Up"** to get away from crowds. Now that the four-hundred-and-fifty-acre farm next door is being sold (the original owner, Cliff Hill, went out West and the current owners can't make ends meet), Glenda tries to organize the neighbors to buy up the place to protect their view. In **"The Speech,"** Maud and Sonny Cabot run the last of the thirteen dairy farms in Scampsville; the other farms have been developed into lots for ski cottages for flatlanders. Maud is infuriated that the state is spending millions to study "rural growth." When there is a hearing on Act 200, mandating regional review of town plans, Maud stands up to speak as a native Vermonter watching the state become a "preserve for wealthy out-of-staters." She is applauded, but there is no mention of her intervention in the newspaper coverage the following day.

Carla Neggers

In *Finders Keepers* (1993), Julian Stiles has found buried in the basement of his house in southern Vermont the silver Revere goblets that Holly Paynter desperately wants. He is curious to find out what she is willing to do to reclaim the valuable objects and falls in love with her despite their competing interests. Cozie Hawthorne, the heroine in *Finding You* (1996), is a newspaper editor in Woodstock who experiences sudden fame when her book becomes a bestseller. She wants to remain true to her New England traditions but falls in love unexpectedly with oil-rich Daniel Foxworth, who is hiding out in Vermont after his helicopter is sabotaged. He suspects Cozie's brother, Seth, of trying to kill him. In *The Waterfall* (2000), the Wheaton farm, the yellow farmhouse, and Joshua Falls (very loosely based on Hamilton Falls) are located near Manchester. Granny Wheaton left the property to her grandson, Sebastian Redwing, who wanted to give it to—but finally agreed to sell it to—Lucy Blacker Smith (who has two children, a boy and a girl) when her husband, Colin, died three years earlier. Lucy is still considered an outsider in Vermont, but she is finding peace for herself and her children there. Sebastian, who is in the international security business, once saved Colin's life; Colin told Lucy that if he died she should appeal to Sebastian if she needed help. She does need help: she is being subtly harassed but does not want to consult with the local police because her father-in-law is prominent U.S. Senator Jack Swift from Rhode Island. Lucy and Sebastian work together to terminate a blackmail scheme that is designed to intimidate Senator Swift and discredit Sebastian. *Dark Sky* (2005), set in and around Hartford, tells the story of Juliet Longstreet, a deputy U.S. marshal who teams up with Ethan Brooker, a former Special Forces officer, to thwart an escaped killer threatening her family in Vermont. Juliet's five older brothers include a state trooper and a local police officer; most of the action takes place at the Longstreet family home, where they also run a landscaping business. Juliet and Ethan discover that the killer has joined forces with a group of dangerous vigilantes.

Jack Newcombe

The divorced, nomadic narrator in *In Search of Billy Cole* (1984) is a professional football scout who has for some years been watching the career of brilliant quarterback Billy Cole. Now twenty-two, Cole left a full football scholarship at the University of Michigan to come "in chosen obscurity" to Middlebury College in Vermont: the narrator wants to find out why. He arrives in Middlebury in time for the final game of the season ("Vermont had its own expectant look that comes with the last falling of the leaves") between Middlebury College and Norwich University. Observers have labeled Cole "flaky" and a "loner" and Middlebury too "quaint and neat" to have a good football team; the college appears to the narrator "pro-academic, preppy, and mostly white privileged, middle class." Middlebury's philosophy is that football is not separate and special but part of the whole college experience. Dr. Morey, the president, doesn't want football to get "too big." Middlebury coach Ernie Day invites the narrator to watch the team practice during the week leading up to the big game; he also has a chance to talk to Billy Cole and to dine with him and his girlfriend, skier Holly McKenna. The narrator notices, during practice, that "receiving and accepting contributions [suggestions] from the players was a Middlebury habit." Billy is "an independent," but he is a team player: he doesn't yell at his teammates; he is self-controlled. The climax of the story is the big game, which Middlebury wins, gracefully and sportingly: "It was their moment, and in the years ahead they would realize the game was as good as it ever gets." Billy and Holly are fulfilled and in love; the narrator drives off to "another town and another game."

John Nichols

When *The Wizard of Loneliness* (1966) opens, Wendall Bates Oler, ten, whose mother, Helen, is dead, and whose father, Fred, is a marine serving in the Pacific in World War II, has been pronounced incorrigible by his Aunt Nancy. She ships him off to Stebbinsville in central Vermont (between Montpelier and Barre) to live with his grandfather and grandmother, Dr. William Frederick and Cornelia Oler. Sitting on the train, Wendall, an angry, bewildered, and precocious little boy who wears glasses, is reading *A Farewell to Arms* when a bearded man sits down next to him. The man steals a dollar from Wendall's wallet and also alights in Stebbinsville. In addition to Fred, the Olers have two other children, John T., who couldn't enlist because he broke his leg in four places, and Sybil, who has a four-year-old son, Tom, and whose husband (not Tom's father), David Mathewson, is overseas in the army. The bearded man is Duffy Kahler, high-school hero, presumed dead after his plane was shot down over Morocco. The war is present in the town: the paperboy's older brother is killed, as is Sybil's husband. Wendall is rude, naughty, and unhappy that he cannot fit in. He bosses and bullies little Tom. He befriends ugly Marty Haldenstein, the librarian, organist, photographer, and classmate of Fred Oler, who holds Wendall's hand in the hummingbird blind and then disappears from Wendall's life, just when Wendall feels an affinity towards another human. Small town life proceeds. John T. takes Wendall fishing. Wendall slowly feels closer to the family and, for the first time, thinks of "home" and "my town." As war's end approaches, the crisis in Stebbinsville is jobs: the can factory is losing its war contract. Sybil discovers Duffy down by the pond; Tom's father, he is suffering terrible trauma from the war. When Wendall is naughty he feel bad and tries to behave better. In his imagination he sees himself as the Wizard of Loneliness, capable of smiting the world's evil with his sword. He falls to his knees one night, prays for his father, and cries for the first time. Dr. Oler is becoming sicker and more lethargic, worrying that he has been a friend to everyone but his own family members. "Death, he remembered, was quiet and solid and drameless in this part of the country." In his dreams, Wendall wants to say "I love you" to everyone in the small town. John T. feels everything is useless. After slashing Tom's cheek, Duffy is apprehended and escapes. The Germans surrender and the townsfolk are celebrating when Dr. Oler, in financial difficulties, drives wildly down the main street, hitting another car and killing

Duffy. Dr. Oler dies, and, after the funeral, John T. loses his rancor and marries Ercel Perry. Wendall discovers how vulnerable and mortal he is, because of the way his heart feels; he has changed and mellowed. Fred comes home safely from the war. Cornelia sells the house and she, Sybil, and Tom move to Boston. Wendall finally dares approach Fred ("Is it okay if I call you 'Dad'?") and goes to California with his father. An example of the pure language: "Below them on the right, blueberry bushes and dry yellow grasses covered a slope that ran down to a river. Across the river, green grass rippled, polished in silver streaks where breezes disturbed it. Beyond the meadow, birches flashed whitely and the dull lemon spears of poplars leaned slightly to the east."

Christopher Noël

Hazard and the Five Delights (1988) is a tender, eloquent story about "nice and simple" Baker Samuels, nineteen, who lives with his parents and two younger sisters in Elton, half an hour's drive from Rutland. "In Vermont, you didn't care about getting more money all the time and buying more things because no one was trying to take the things you had." Baker grew up in the constant company of two best friends, Rolly Miller and Anne Hazel ("Hazard") MacIntyre. In clear, intense prose, the ambience of the small town is evoked in their walks past peoples' houses, in the woods, in the village. Hazard, a year older than the boys, invited Baker to her senior prom three years before, then left for Texas with her parents. It is summer and Baker is working in the garden of a neighbor, Frances Cherryhill, in her thirties, who suffered a nervous breakdown and whose husband, Jack, divorced her. Because of her continuing madness (she calls it her "Cheer"), her husband has custody of their eight-year-old daughter, Gwynn. While weeding or working in his father's hardware store, Baker thinks about Hazard. "Whenever she moved, it was a surprise, like a lawn sprinkler suddenly turning on and hitting your bare back." He remembers kissing her (just once) in the Scoop-Out in the woods, going with

her to the prom, watching her climb to the nest of the Hunch (the prehistoric bird they found), and hearing about the Five Delights. Frances's sister, Constance, tells her that Jack has agreed to let Gwynn visit her. Hazard suddenly returns to Elton, both excited and frightened about her new life and her new friends. Baker knows what he must do: he wants to build a house for Hazard and spend the rest of his life with her. Frances goes for a walk and falls; her former husband, Jack, brings Gwynn, Constance, and Frances's mother to the hospital. Hazard and Baker come to see her, too. She makes them promise to take Gwynn on one of their walks in the woods. There in the Scoop-Out, their special place, Hazard tells Gwynn about the Five Delights that make life worth living. The First is quick motion; the Second is stillness; the Third is being near someone even though you are far away; the Fourth is being close even though you are near; and the Fifth is being right in the middle of things, balancing, never knowing what's next. And that's where Hazard leaves Baker.

Jack Noon

The Big Fish of Barston Falls and *Old Sam's Thunder* take place in Barston Falls, situated on the Vermont side of the Connecticut River across from Rattlesnake Hill in New Hampshire. After a fire in 1804 destroyed the wooden houses in the village, Israel Barston rebuilt with brick from his brickyards. In 1810, he raised money from British and Dutch sources to build a dam and canal, charging fees for flatboats passing through the locks. He raised four mills. In 1816, when there was frost and snow every month of the year, many relatives moved out West: "There's no flesh on this land. It's all bone." In a brief introductory scene to *The Big Fish of Barston Falls* (1995), Reuben White, while salmon fishing in 1794, sees a huge, dark shape in the water. In 1822, widower Joe Reckford and his twelve-year-old daughter, Sue, arrive in Barston Falls and move into one of the Barston houses. They are both shy and awkward about meeting people: Joe, who gets a job working for Jared Barston on the canal, misses his wife, Betsey; Sue is embarrassed about her unusual height for her age and her large hands and feet. Tom Barston, Israel's son, has two sons, Seth and Jared, and an uncle, Old Sam. Three mischievous local boys, Benjy Barston (Jared's boy), Foss Richardson, and Tom Beasley, tease Sue and play pranks on an old Abenaki, Malik. Sue finds lonely comfort in fishing for perch and pickerel and meets Malik, who teaches her the most efficient way to clean her fish; soon they are fishing together. He tells her about the olden days, when salmon was plentiful on the Connecticut River and moose and deer were in the valley. Now, he says, dams keep the salmon from ascending the river and all his people are gone. Rum helps him not to think of his own daughter, dead of smallpox. Malik and Sue make a deal: they will fish together, he will teach her, she will cook for him, and he will stay off the rum. Joe likes Mark Hosmer, with whom he works, and George Ballard, the blacksmith, and his wife, Annie, who is very friendly and attractive. In fact, Joe tries to avoid her because he likes her so much. Sue asks Old Sam to take her up to Malik's shelter. Old Sam and Malik are friends; Old Sam and George and Annie are the only villagers who have ever asked Malik to share a meal. Malik bets Sam one silver dollar that Malik can catch a fish longer than ten feet. Sue and Malik devise a rig to catch a big fish, although no one believes it is there. The excitement builds; the town gathers at the point above the big eddy; Joe, who at first didn't believe in the fish's existence, joins in; the boys now appreciate both Sue and Malik and help by taking care of the reserve rope, laying it out in long, parallel lines. Everyone enters into the event, giving Sue and Malik gloves, food, and encouragement while the two struggle for hours with the fish. Joe acknowledges "the feeling that he fit in and belonged where he was." He also finds out, to his delight and relief, that Annie is George's sister. The mammoth fish—a sturgeon—is finally reeled in; it is judged to be about one hundred and fifty years old, fourteen feet long, and between six hundred and a thousand pounds in weight. Malik throws the silver dollar in the river and presents the fish to Old Sam as a gift.

Old Sam's Thunder (1998) concentrates on Old Sam. His parents, his four brothers (Isaac, Caleb, Israel, and James), and his wife, Amanda, are all buried in Barston. His six children have all moved out West. His father died of wounds suffered in the attack with Major Rogers on the Indian village of St. Francis. Old Sam is deeply proud of his heritage and has recommended every year that in 1826 the town buy a cannon to celebrate the fiftieth anniversary of July Fourth. Steve Danforth, whose store is the natural gathering place for the village, is the moderator of the annual town meeting. Unfortunately, thanks to the intervention of the dreadful Deacon Uriah Russell, the motion is voted down again. Because Old Sam is dying, the pro-cannon villagers vow to raise the money privately to buy a cannon in his honor, but they cannot find one anywhere. There are many important players in this drama. Annie and Jo Reckford, now married with twin infant sons, Amos and Aaron, and Sue, now sixteen; Seth and Jared Barston, Old Sam's great-nephews; Jared and Elizabeth's son, Benjie, and his friends, Tom and Foss; George Ballard, Annie's brother and a blacksmith; and George's friends, Charlie Porter and Mark Hosmer. Annie and Sue cook for Old Sam; Benjie sleeps in his one-room house. They are all determined to celebrate Old Sam's life on July Fourth, and each sets out to steal a cannon. Seth and Jared manage to steal an iron cannon from Dartmouth. George, Jo, Charlie, and Mark head for Charlestown and, after many difficulties, especially with rain, take one. Seth and Jared return to Hanover for a second, more elegant, brass cannon. Leaving some clothes on the shore (stolen from Deacon Russell's line) to give the impression that the owners have drowned, they compel the town to drag a cannon to the water's edge to shoot it off and raise the bodies to the surface. The brothers steal the cannon that night. Old Sam, complaining that no one has had the gumption to steal a cannon, makes a plan for Benjie to steal one from Wheelock Village with him. When July Fourth arrives, there are four cannon for the celebration, a happy occasion for everyone, including Sam, who lives on another two years, much beloved by all.

N

Howard Norman

The two short stories from *Kiss in the Hotel Conrad* (1989) set in Vermont are affecting and persuasive. The title **"Catching Heat"** is a phrase used in calling trotting races that means the caller has let his emotions take over his judgment. David, the first person narrator, angers Donny Malick, who rides a winning horse even though David predicted mid-race another horse the winner. Donny and David are also enemies because Donny is now seeing Abigail, the woman with whom David lived for five years on Danville Hill in Cabot. Abby works at Dunn's in Montpelier. David and Abigail discovered together that there was a little stretch of road on the way home where they could get a Canadian station on the radio. It was their secret. At races, Abby would sit up in the elevated announcer's booth with him and Dwight Hatch, a retired caller. David loves his work: pronouncing aloud the horses' names on the race program "struck him as poetry." David and Abby's troubles started when he brought up marriage and she wasn't interested. She began seeing Donny without David's guessing: he was "as ignorant as a field mouse." There was a moment when David and Abby seemed to be all right together: "A kind of patchwork tenderness sprung up between us," but then she left him for Donny and told the latter the secret about the radio. David is calling trotters at the races one day when he spots Donny and Abby standing at the rail where they know he will see them. Losing his place in the race, he feels miserable and betrayed because they laugh at him. In 1912, a tragic accident occurs in **"Milk Train"** on the Bennington-Montpelier run. Second Engineer Corbett Ingham is injured but alive—lying facedown in milk. The wreckage "had the look of dinosaurs in battle." It is October and the drying leaves are "blood-colored." Corbett lives and eats in a hotel. Every week, on his overnight in Burlington, he has dinner with a schoolteacher friend, Rose, ten years his senior, and her sister. Rose has short curls, "cut evenly all around," that reminded Corbett of "window shades that could snap up at any moment." He has never been out of Vermont.

At the site of the wreck, he is in agony: "Pain toured Corbett's body fast, outlining it the way lightning illuminates a coastline at night." He manages to pull himself closer to the train. Jake Charyn is pinned inside the locomotive, alive; Walter Till is dead. Before he dies, Jake advises Corbett that, since his life is unsatisfactory, he should marry Alice Till as soon as she is over her grief. Corbett lies on the ground all night, thinking he is going to die. He sees a fox that has been drinking some of the spilled milk. Finally, help comes; the rescuers climb up to find the dead bodies inside the train. Willlis T. White, the famous catastrophe photographer, is there and poses the men jauntily on the locomotive.

Freya North

In *Polly* (1998), under the auspices of an international academic exchange program, Polly Fenton goes to Hubbardtons Spring near Grafton in southern Vermont to teach Jen Carter's English classes, while Jen is sent to London to take Polly's English classes at Belsize Girls' School. Not surprisingly, Polly soon meets Jen's boyfriend, Chip Jonson, the school's athletic trainer, and Jen meets Polly's five-year beau, Max Fyfield, a graphic designer. Inevitably, long distance romances being what they are, Polly is tempted into a one-night stand with Chip, even as Max spends one night with Jen. Since these interludes were strictly meaningless, Polly and Max forgive each other and move toward a life together.

Craig Nova

In *The Congressman's Daughter* (1986), the narrator lives in a village near the West River next door to former Vermont Congressman Harlow Pearson. Three families dominate the town: the Critchfields, the Keiths, and the Thachers have lived there for generations. Even a wealthy, famous person like Pearson can never compensate for not having been born there. The narrator watches Alexandra Pearson grow up. She learns to fish with her father. Many passages describe these expeditions: "the water was high, the color of hot chocolate." Father and daughter are very competitive. He buys her expensive clothes and takes her places to show her off. She is sent to school in New York. When Alexandra appears at the family homestead confessing that she is pregnant, Pearson fends off the criticism of the community by marrying her off to his assistant, Bryce McCann, whom she does not love. She has already fallen in love with a local boy, Willie Shaw, who leaves town. Pearson dies, leaving Alexandra a great deal of money in his will, with a clause making the inheritance contingent upon her "moral behavior." Since her husband, Bryce, knows about her illegitimate child, he is in a position to blackmail her to stay with him. Bryce takes an apartment in Boston, but spends some loveless weekends in Vermont with Alexandra and, in the fullness of time, with her daughter, Anne, who believes Bryce to be her father. He is occasionally unfaithful. Once Alexandra has to rescue a young woman whom Bryce has abandoned in a motel room and send her back to Manchester, New Hampshire, on a bus. He persuades Alexandra to go to Manhattan from time to time, where he pays a man to pick her up in her hotel and photograph her. Bryce has also taken a part-time job in a prison as a teacher, where he meets Sonny, a killer for hire. Alexandra's daughter, Anne, grows up, and Bryce begins to pay unwarranted attention to her. One day they go to Saratoga to the races and he is flagrant in his advances. When Willie returns to Vermont to see Alexandra, he tells her that her father stole the last election. He arranged so that the Critchfields and Thachers, "snooty and Republican," could not get out of their driveways to vote against him (he was also a Republican, but they would have voted for anyone to get rid of him). Anne goes to Berkeley to college. Alexandra and Willie leave town together, heading north toward the Canadian border, with Bryce and Sonny in pursuit. In a confrontation on the median of a highway, Bryce is killed. After his death, all the old local families, like the Critchfields with their "Groton accents," come to the funeral and make a point of approaching Willie to ask him to log their places. Willie and Alexandra finally marry.

In *Cruisers* (2004), two men move in their separate and seemingly parallel spheres in southern Vermont. Russell Boyd is a state trooper who lives in a mill town on the Connecticut River with his girlfriend, Zofia Wira, a special education teacher. Frank Kohler, thirty, a loner whose hooker mother was murdered when he was a boy, is looking for a mail-order bride. The structure of the novel is taut and the tone, terse. Russell and Frank have childhood experiences that churn in their brains. Russell's grandfather told him about watching exhausted, starving Russian soldiers kill and eat a German guard outside a prisoner-of-war camp where his grandfather was interned; one of Frank's mother's customers gave him twenty dollars and made him hide in a closet while the man coupled with his mother. Russell and Frank both appear on the brink of self-revelation and are both accelerating toward a disastrous intersection. They meet three times. The first is when Russell and Zofia take two of her students fishing on Frank's property. Katryna Kolymov, whom Frank has married by proxy, arrives at the bus station in Brattleboro. Zofia is pregnant, as is Katryna, who has a lover in Moscow; the two women meet at the local health clinic. Russell and another cop, Tony Deutsche, are called to a scene of domestic violence; Tony kills the husband in self-defense. The police find a dead woman near the highway. Katryna's "cousin" Dimitri arrives. Zofia cannot decide whether or not to have an abortion. Although they love each other, Russell and Zofia are unable to communicate. Everywhere Russell notices emblems for his life. the "slow steady attrition from the accumulation of winters in Vermont;" "an air of just hanging on" in some of the older towns; a house looked "in the harsh landscape, like an outpost that was about to be overrun." The second time is when Frank and Katryna have met Dimitri at the bus station, Frank speeds off the exit ramp, hitting another car, and Russell is the trooper at the scene. When Frank discovers Katryna and Dimitri having sexual intercourse, he shoots them both and sets fire to his house. He drives into town (something like Newfane) and is picked up by a young woman probationer who wants to go cruising in his car. Tony is the trooper who stops Frank's speeding car. The girl escapes into the woods while Frank kills the police officer and steals the latter's cruiser. The third and final collision occurs when Frank is staked out on a hill waiting for the cops to find the cruiser; he has left the radio on. Russell and three other men start up the road toward the cruiser. One man is shot in the leg and one in the lung before Russell gets a shot and kills Frank. In the last scene, Russell, again sitting in his cruiser at night, approaches a suspicious couple, all his antennae alert. The man turns in the woman for heroin possession; the woman tells Russell that the man is the murderer of the dead woman found earlier. The color silver infuses the imagery: "he saw balls of moisture on each blade, each one silver and perfectly shaped, as to suggest an essence of grass and light like a handful of diamonds spread on a green cloth."

Jenny Offill

Eight-year-old Grace Davitt lives an unconventional life in Windler on Lake Champlain in *Last Things* (1999). The surface facts are that her mother, Anna, is an ornithologist who works at the raptor center; her father, Jonathan, teaches chemistry at Windler Academy; her babysitter, Edgar, is a sixteen-year-old science prodigy; and her Uncle Peter, her father's twin, is "Mr. Science" on a TV show in New York. Beneath the façade are indications that Grace's charming, if eccentric, mother is balancing precariously on the edge of insanity. Anna immerses Grace in myths, superstitions, and legends of the supernatural. Grace reads endlessly from *The Encyclopedia of the Unexplained*. Anna believes she has seen the Lake Champlain monster. She takes Grace out of school in order to teach her at home from a Cosmic Calendar she creates. Anna is

unpredictable, nervous, odd. She is drawn to the lake. She tells Grace that "stones were last things and would be around long after people were gone. Other last things were oceans, metals, and crows." Grace's father, an atheist who carries on his person a summary of the Constitution, is increasingly angry that Windler Academy is showing signs of conflating barriers between Church and State. He loses his job after telling a boy that "God was a monkey." Their income declines. Uncle Peter runs off with a woman from his show and Jonathan applies for his brother's job as "Mr. Science." While her husband is in New York, Anna, in one of her manic moods, takes Grace on a long trip, first to New Orleans and then to California. Jonathan finds them by tracing their credit card receipts. They return to Vermont, and Anna disappears. They believe she committed suicide but are never actually sure. They do find her coat, which apparently had stones in the pockets (she had been reading Virginia Woolf), although they do not find the stones. Not unsurprisingly, Grace acts out in all sorts of ways: she won't speak to her father, and she locks the little girl next door, who is blind, in the doghouse. It is impossible to imagine what long-term effect her mother's life—or death— will have on young Grace.

John O'Hara

In *The Instrument* (1967), Robert Yancey ("Yank") Lucas, in desperate need of a third act for his first play, falls asleep while heating some coffee in his small Chelsea kitchen in Manhattan. The pilot light goes out, and Yank is almost asphyxiated; fortunately, a neighbor smells the gas, runs in, opens the window, and saves the playwright's life—and his play. He incorporates the gas scene into the third act and the play is a smash success. Feeling oppressed by the interviews, the publicity, and the glamour, he drives north until he runs out of gas in East Hammond, Vermont, nine miles across the New York border. He finds a bed-and-breakfast run by a Vermonter named Anna Phelps. He becomes immersed in village life: Anna Phelps, a widow; Ed Cross, the bus driver and snow plow operator; Matt Lewis, service station manager and town constable. The contrast between the ugly, aggressive people in New York and the kind, friendly people in East Hammond is revealing and refreshing to the jaded New Yorker. Hungry for a New York paper, Yank is sent to the Atterbury farm where Anna's cousin, Adam Phelps, is the superintendent. Seymour Atterbury is a rich gentleman farmer, running a twelve-hundred-acre model dairy farm and raising Ayrshire cows. Through this visit, Yank meets Sheila Graham, Caroline's daughter by her first husband. Sheila, in the midst of a divorce, seduces Yank on the day they are introduced and sets about trying to coerce him into marrying her. Since Yank doesn't love real women, but only the women characters in his plays, she goes off to Reno. Next of the women who fall for Yank is Bessie Thompson from Burlington, whom he meets when she is wheeling the chair of a paralyzed cousin of Anna's who comes to interview him. Their one-night affair ends violently when Bessie, driving home from a tryst with Yank, runs into a tree and is killed. Yank, "emotionally impotent" as Sheila describes him, moves on to the local postmistress, Helen MacDowell, having failed to interest either Anna or Caroline, Sheila's mother, in his bed. Helen takes him to the local hangout in Cooperstown. Later, in his motel room, she gossips about local characters. He learns, for example, how people in East Hammond feel about the Atterburys. Seymour's grandfather was a farmer with two mules. Then the family went to New York and made a lot of money. Now that the Atterburys are back, none of the locals has been invited into the house, not even Adam's wife, whose husband works there, although Adam, his wife, and Anna were Atterbury's intimate childhood friends. Yank finishes his play and, suddenly, the small town becomes stifling. As he says in an exchange with his agent: "The place has served its purpose, and I see no use in hanging around any more." "Then by all means get out. Those small towns can be death, once the novelty's worn off." "Or once you've discovered that there *is* no novelty." When he departs, he thanks Anna for her kindness.

"We believe in manners," she replies. When he wants to tip Ed Cross for his help, Anna, a voice of Vermont, says, "If you gave him something to do to earn it, that'd be an altogether different proposition, but don't offer a man like Ed Cross a tip."

Joseph Olshan

Clara Mayfield is a Jamaican in *In Clara's Hands* (2001) who came to America after her young son committed suicide. She has worked as a nanny for several families, including the Kaplans. Will Kaplan's older brother, Danny, is killed in a skiing accident while he is at the University of Vermont and the family falls apart. Will spends periods of time in mental institutions and finally moves to Burlington, where he works as a cartographer and lives on the shores of Lake Champlain. He is alienated from his lover, Peter Arcenaux, a landscape gardener who lives in Santa Barbara, California, with his sister, Grace, who has Hodgkin's Disease and is undergoing chemotherapy. The novel begins with Clara's leaving Flatbush on the train to visit Will in Burlington and ends with her visit there. (Clara's description of Vermont to her friend Blanche, the beautician, in Flatbush: "Everybody in Vermont white except me.") In the middle are flashbacks from Will, from Clara, from Peter and Grace, and from their mother, Marie Claire, who has become Will's great friend. She moved to Burlington to run a bookshop-cum-café with Will called The Traveler (even though she is travel-phobic). The question that moves the novel forward: was Marie Claire on the plane that crashed off Long Island or has she simply disappeared? She has a history of fading away at crucial moments, as does Will's mother, who had an affair with a Roman Catholic priest and, after his death, moved to a community of nuns in Germany.

P

Dalia Pagani

Mercy Road (1998) is a haunting story about a family living at the back of the beyond—on a ridge in the Northeast Kingdom. Earl Summer, a trapper, and his wife, Darlene Hank, are locked in a desperate, lonesome, hardscrabble life with three children, Butch, Sid (who is mentally retarded or at least mute), and Tina. The winters are beyond description. There appears to be a curse on their road, which is named for a hanged man and a drowned woman. Darlene becomes more and more frantic with her life, cooped up in an isolated, barren place. Her mother's house next door has been for sale for more than four years and finally collapses, buried in the soil. One day, after her husband strikes her, Darlene packs a bag, hitches a ride to Smallford, the nearest town, and takes a bus to New York City where she ekes out a bare existence, enduring humiliating waitress jobs. In her absence, Earl becomes even more primitive and cruel. Tina runs away, imagining herself a fox in the wilderness. Sid kills himself. Butch moves into his friend Suzanne's house. A kind old couple living far up the ridge in the wilderness finds Tina when she is almost frozen to death and saves her life. In the resolution, these tragic characters are given a glimpse of hope and reconciliation despite the almost unendurable setting.

Katherine Hall Page

The Body in the Snowdrift (2005), the fifteenth Faith Fairchild mystery, is set at Pine Slopes Resort near Williston in northern Vermont. Faith Sibley Fairchild, married to Reverend Thomas Fairchild and mother of two young children, Ben and Amy, runs a catering service, Have Faith, in Aleford, Massachusetts. Her indomitable in-laws, Dick and Marion, invite the entire Fairchild clan—four children, their spouses, and four grandchildren—for a week's holiday at the ski resort owned by their great friends, Harold Stafford, and his son, Fred. The rifts in the Fairchild family are obvious (the marriage of one of Tom's brothers is shaky; his sister, Betsey, is rigid with her unhappy teenaged sons, Andy and Scott). Fred Stafford's teenaged stepdaughter, Ophelia, is causing problems, with no intervention by her mother, Naomi. The resort's team includes Boyd Harrison, wealthy lawyer in his late sixties who is the principal investor in the resort; restaurant manager Simon Tanner; Pete Reynolds, head of maintenance; and John Forest, the chef at the resort's French restaurant, Le Sapin. Faith, skiing the first day, comes upon Boyd's dead body in the snow. Then a plastic inflated woman dummy, dripping blood, is found floating in the pool; someone wedges the bull wheel on one of the lifts; and sand is put in the machine that grooms the snow. When John disappears, Faith is asked by Simon to fill in until he can hire a replacement. Indefatigable and sympathetic, Faith enjoys working with the young Latin American staff to create interesting food (recipes in this series are in the backs of the volumes). She is in a position to find out what is behind the unpleasant occurrences at the resort and is trying to sort out family affairs, especially with her nephew Scott, who has befriended Ophelia. Faith learns that the mysterious aging hippie dining at Le Sapin is Gertrude Stafford, Harold's sister, who was Boyd's lover and single heir to his fortune. Gertrude decides to call in Boyd's loans to the resort, which will ruin a number of people, including Tom's brother, Craig, and possibly the resort itself. Following Ophelia, Faith discovers the young woman idolizes Gertrude. When John is found dead (he was pushed into the reservoir in the pump house and chewed up by the machinery), the police are finally called to the scene. In a frightening and near-fatal encounter with one of the villains, Faith realizes who they are and is able to pull together the strands of this entertaining and ingenious plot.

Tom Paine

In "**Unapproved Minutes of the Carthage, Vermont, Zoning Board of Adjustment**" (2000), the Zoning Board has assembled to discuss the status and possible zoning violation of the Montpelier-based radio broadcaster, WIKD. One of the complaints of the residents is appliance interference, hearing music through their telephones, toasters, and electric toothbrushes. The assembly is held at the Carthage Central School cafeteria with the very large crowd, including a substantial legal representation for the radio station, crammed into small chairs. The subheading of the title of this devilish and amusing story is important: "As recorded by Town Secretary Betty Bradley." Betty Bradley takes her responsibilities seriously and writes down every word everyone says and every movement anyone makes. Her run-on style is uproarious: she is unable to distinguish between essential details and trivia. For example, instead of stating that one of the members of the board will be late (which isn't really requisite), the secretary goes into long detail about the fact that Gloria's "husband, Homer, was down with postoperative pain from his recent surgery for appendicitis and son Mike's hockey game had gone into overtime and she was the only one left to do the evening milking." One of the mothers at the meeting is overwrought because her daughter, Stacey, is in the hospital in Boston with leukemia, due, the mother believes, to the radio station. Betty records that Stacey "was sleeping over at the house of this secretary when she vomited and was run home at three in the morning and was seen later that morning by Dr. Skip Hadley at the Carthage Health Clinic and rushed to Boston for a bone marrow transplant for which she is still waiting, brave little thing."

Jay Parini

Bay of Arrows (1992) takes place on a small college campus in Vermont and, simultaneously, in a prior historical period. Christopher ("Geno") Genovese teaches a special seminar on modern poetry at Barrington College in Leicester County. With degrees from Dartmouth and Oxford, he is the author of a well-received book, *Decline of the Modern*, is married to Susan, and is the father of two young boys, James and Milo. Both he and his wife are seeing therapists. In his spare time he is working on a long poem about Christopher Columbus; the contemporary events are interspersed with scenes from Columbus's life. The cast of characters from academe includes a feminist, a deconstructionist, a lesbian couple, and an African-American studies person who happens to be white. The bickering and petty jealousies are a constant motif. Geno falls victim to the attractions of one of his advisees, Lizzy Nash, who is doing her senior thesis on Virginia Woolf. He sleeps with her; he gives her a B-plus on her paper; she sues him for sexual harassment. Meanwhile, Susan is vaguely attracted to Andrew Ridgeway, a hippie who lives with his dog, Sam, in a camp in the woods. Her hopeless brother, Charles, arrives, having left his wife and their father's business. They go to a fair staged by the Rainbow Family of Light, and Geno has a mystical experience with the hippies, dressed like Indians, whom he imagines to be the Taino Indians persecuted by Columbus. He thinks of New Jersey, which he fled as a young man: "The disturbing thing was that Barrington had come to resemble his hometown more than ever, with condos and tracts of prefab houses spreading like cancer cells on the town's periphery." Just when his life couldn't be bleaker, he receives a "genius grant" of half-a-million dollars from the McAlistair Foundation enabling him to resign from his job and his predicament. He takes his family to the Dominican Republic and builds a house. There he again envisions events from his Columbus research—a second episode of Columbus's life merging with his. Susan is unhappy in the D.R., or, at least, unhappy with the way Geno behaves. They meet a racist Scot named Alec Selkirk, who has lived there for years. The country is preparing for a big celebration of the quincentennial of Columbus's arrival. A lighthouse is being built and the Japanese are doing a historical reenactment. The bay where Geno lives—the Bay of Arrows—is the site

P

where the Taino Indians refused to let Columbus come ashore. Susan's radio is stolen and Geno assumes their "houseboy," Augusto, has taken it. The idyll does not materialize. They miss Vermont and return home. Some examples of lovely imagery: "The pond was milky gray now—a weirdly translucent eye—with a foot-high rim of snow ringing it like bleachers," "One bad spot on the ice: the pond's soft fontanel," "trees whose greenness is fragile as the first beard of an adolescent boy," and "Humming birds stitched the air."

Robert Newton Peck

Justice Lion (1981) presents an intractable problem that occurs when Prohibition is four years old in 1923. Widower Jess Bolt is a "down-hiller" and lawyer in the small town of Liberty (roughly in the center of Addison County) who aspires to become a county prosecutor. Justice Lion is an "uproader" who lives on Kipp's Mountain (deeded to his forebear, Kipp Lion, by King George in 1731) and supports his family by running a still. The Lion family members are mountain people: "People in town tend to look down their noses at mountain men." A federal agent arrives, sniffs out Justice Lion's still, and arrests him for moonshining. Almost simultaneously, the current district attorney, promoted to judge, appoints Jess district attorney (Jess is in debt and needs the money), putting Jess in the position of prosecuting his old friend, Justice (years ago, Jess defended Justice's son, Drury, on a homicide charge). Complicating matters further, Jess's fifteen-year-old son, Muncie, is the best friend of Justice's son, Hem, and in love with his daughter, Blessing. The Bolt's beloved housekeeper, Patience Bly, a mother figure to Muncie, has been supplying sugar to the Lions' still. The courtroom scenes are the centerpieces of the drama, with Muncie desperately torn between his loyalty to his father and to the Lions. The town is divided but has suffered many difficulties together: "Vermont barns were akin to Vermont farmers, strong in the beam, built to face up to winter." The young lawyer appointed to defend Justice is brave and bright, but the jury finds Justice guilty and the judge sentences the proud old mountain man to a year in the penitentiary. That evening, a tragic event occurs with serious consequences for the Bolt and Lion families.

Theodora Peck

Hester of the Grants (1905) begins in May 1777, when Ezra Robinson of Bennington is unable to choose between the King and the Continental Congress. He lives in a fine house with his wife, Charlotte, his comely nineteen-year-old daughter, Hester, a dedicated patriot, and his charming niece, Polly Fay, whose uncle, Colonel Stephen Fay, runs the Catamount Tavern. Vermont has been newly named and declared independent by the Congress of the Hampshire Grants. The two young ladies are invited to a dance at the tavern, where many attractive young men are in attendance. One is Mark Ellis, who has been paying court to Polly; another is Neil Barton, who loves Hester (though she does not love him). In the middle of the party, the calamitous news comes that Fort Ticonderoga has fallen, the Americans are defeated at Hubbardton, Seth Warner is retreating, and Burgoyne is marching south. That night, Ezra decides to remain a Loyalist. Bennington is preparing for battle; by August 10, 1777, all the troops are assembled, including General John Stark and his army from New Hampshire. Colonel Samuel Herrick raises "Herrick's Rangers." One of his men is Captain Nathan Bennett, who has fallen in love with Hester; Cochise, half-Indian, half-French, is working for the rebels and also idolizes Hester. Nathan is assigned to test Ezra's loyalty; when his perfidy is discovered, he flees to the British lines in New York. Hessians capture Nathan. A young officer, carrying the news to Bennington about the battle, is wounded and cannot ride. Hester volunteers to take the message herself; afterward, she is escorted home by Lieutenant Ira Allen, who tells her that Ethan is still being held by the British in New York. The Battle of Bennington between General Stark and General Baum is held on August 16, 1777: the Americans win a glorious victory on the heights of the Walloomsac and prove that they are capable of resistance. The treachery of Mark and the heroism of Cochise are revealed. The British surrender at Saratoga. The secret in Nathan's past is that his brother, George, became a thief: he has changed his name to Mark Ellis. In November 1777 the Council sits in session and decides to confiscate Ezra's property. Hester has gone to Arlington to live with her Aunt Jane. Nathan wonders if she can ever forgive him for the part he played in exposing her father. Ethan Allan returns to Bennington amid much jubilation. The Robinsons join the disgraced Ezra in New York, but Hester is captured on the way by Bennett/Ellis and taken to his hideaway. Allan Kinsdale saves her and Cochise, but Bennett/Ellis murders Ezra. Hester marries Nathan, Polly marries Allan Kinsdale, and Ethan Allen restores the Robinsons' property to them.

The heroine of **White Dawn** (1914), Grace Stuart, is as beautiful, brave, and resourceful as Hester of the Grants. The year is 1758 and Grace's father, Alan Stuart, resentful of the British victory at Culloden, has joined the French at Fort St. Frédéric. The Stuarts are at Fort Carillon (later Fort Ticonderoga) to welcome Captain Philip Aubrey, whose release from Prisoner's Island (after the French massacre of the British at Fort William Henry) Grace has obtained from General Montcalm. She and Philip fall in love and return together to Fort St. Frédéric. Grace's childhood friend and Abenaki foster-brother Flying Swallow and his warrior-sachem father, Red Plume, hate the French for the death by suicide of Flying Swallow's sister, Floating Cloud. When Philip asks Alan for Grace's hand in marriage, the father refuses him. Alan knows that Philip's mother, Margaret Campbell, is the sister of the man Alan killed in Scotland. The villainous Duke Rupert de Valois arrives, turns his lascivious attentions toward Grace, and decides to throw Philip in jail; Philip manages to escape. Grace slips away by canoe to warn the British about the French entrenchments. General Abercrombie is in command, but she insists upon seeing Lord George Augustus Howe, the great Englishman revered by his troops. He, too, falls in love with Grace but

knows she is engaged to Philip. In a very short time, Lord Howe and Grace develop a deep friendship and, before they embark, he gives her a family ring as a keepsake. Among the colonials assembled are John Stark, Israel Putnam, Robert Rogers, and Philip Schuyler. Lord Howe is killed in the fearful battle the next day in which the British are defeated. Grace's father gives her permission to marry Philip; shortly after that de Valois kills her father and Red Plume. Meanwhile, Philip is in Albany dallying with Cicely Van Dersen, coquettish daughter of a wealthy Dutch fur trader. Flying Swallow and Grace escape from de Valois and Fort St. Frédéric and travel as fugitives along the Otter and West Rivers to Fort Dummer on the Connecticut River. In the wilderness, Grace notices "the crimson arras of the woodbine, the scarlet banners of the maple, the gold and russet pennons of the sumac." De Valois is in pursuit with a large company of men. Fort Dummer is commanded by Colonel Nehemiah Endicott, also a Puritan minister. The soldiers at Fort Dummer fight bravely, but when their ammunition gives out Grace persuades Endicott to offer up the two fugitives. Grace and Flying Swallow are taken back to Fort St. Frédéric and, from there, to Quebec. Philip, repentant, arrives too late. Grace realizes that Flying Swallow loves her, not as a brother, but as a man. The French priest traveling with de Valois urges Grace to sign a marriage contract; she does so on the understanding that Flying Swallow be freed. Instead, he is given over to the Abenaki with whom he is feuding and they prepare to burn him to death. Grace pleads with General Montcalm to save Flying Swallow; he agrees in exchange for General Wolfe's plans, which are in Grace's possession. Wolfe arrests Philip as the traitor and, just as he is to be shot as a spy, Grace confesses her guilt. She saves Philip's life, Wolfe forgives her, and she shows him the way up the cliffs to take Quebec ("If a girl can climb down, an army can climb up"). In the fierce battle on the Plains of Abraham, Flying Swallow takes his vengeance upon de Valois; both Wolfe and Montcalm are also killed in this decisive battle that ends the French and Indian Wars. Philip and

Grace marry. Flying Swallow saves Grace's life in a fire, but he himself dies of burns. Finally, after seven years of war, the Peace of Paris is signed in 1763. Seventeen years later, in another war, Grace and Philip's son, George Augustus Aubrey, serves in his father's regiment. George Howe's brother, William, captures young George. When Lord Howe recognizes George's ring, he realizes he is the son of Grace Stuart, whom his brother had widely praised.

William Dudley Pelley

The Greater Glory (1919), a paean to "the greater glory of" women and their lot in life, is set in 1896 in Paris near St. Johnsbury, with "solitary farm homes barnacled against the rocky hillsides." The narrator, Bill, is one of two editors of the *Paris Daily Telegraph*. The other editor is Sam Hod, a kind and sympathetic man. Bill's position enables him to look through old files, mentioning an item here, an item there, since the newspaper is "a diary of the town's life." (The name of the heroine is not a coincidence. Bill alludes to Molly Stark Wood, Wister's heroine in *The Virginian,* when he recites the misconceptions that the rest of the country has about Vermont: "chiefly valuable to the union as a producer of turkeys for its Thanksgiving dinners, maple syrup for its breakfast pancakes, or pretty school ma'ams for its western romances.") Mary Wood, almost twenty, has grown up unhappily in the dysfunctional household of her stepfather, Silent ("Si") Wheeler. Her mother, Sarah, exhausted from hard labor and lack of love, counsels Mary to marry a rich man if she can. Si beats her mother (little Artie is crippled "on account of the way Pa Wheeler abused me 'fore he was born"); then he beats Mary and throws her out of the house because she goes to school instead of earning her living. Herb Truman, a young man about town whose father runs a successful blacksmith business, rescues Mary and finds her a room in a boarding house and employment with the local newspaper. Mary learns to set type and works hard, but she is unable "to find herself in the community." She is ostracized socially because "nice girls don't work in back rooms." She is hurt by this "small-town snobbery." A young man named John ("Jack") Purse comes to work at the newspaper. The son of a failed newspaper owner in northern Vermont, Jack is trying to make his way and pay his father's debt of four thousand dollars. He and Mary are chosen leads in the local talent play and are soon in love, much to Herb's dismay, since he too has fallen in love with her. Shortly thereafter, Si murders his wife and hangs himself. Because of this shocking tragedy, Mary and Jack decide to marry right away, even though they have no money and no prospects. The years pass; they have six sons. Herb, who still loves Mary, arranges a bequest from a fictitious source. She uses the money to pay off Jack's debts, even though he wasn't legally responsible for them. Wallowing in loneliness and self-pity, Herb marries Mabel ("Mibb") Henderson, a coarse and vulgar creature who has always been spiteful to Mary. Jack and Mary have a chance to buy up the mortgage for the old Wheeler place on Cobb Hill, where she grew up, believing it will be best for their children. Mary ages rapidly from hard work and childbearing: "The features which had made her once the prettiest girl in Paris took on deep dull lines of work and worry and motherly anxiety. She was growing rapidly into a plain, middle-aged woman with nothing ahead but the successful manhood of her boys, like a million other wives of average men all over America tonight." She wonders whether her mother wasn't right to warn her against a life of drudgery and poverty. Jack is so worn down with worries he can hardly function. He has seen many opportunities for his own business come and go because he lacks start-up capital. Mary conceives of asking E.E. Ezekial, a rich summer person from New York, for help in beginning a business with an ochre field that is for sale. Ezekial is despondent because his son has taken much of his father's money to sink into Mibb's career (she has dumped Herb). Jack is offered a profitable job by Ezekial, but Jack contracts pneumonia and dies before the offer comes to fruition. At thirty-five, Mary is old, face sunken, eyes hollow, and a widow with six sons to support. The chorus in the novel is the Sewing Circle of the Calvary

Church, which comments periodically on the dramas and tragedies of Paris. Mary, whom they proclaim is the "sticking" type, begs Sam for her old job. Even though the paper has long abandoned the equipment that she used, Sam purchases a special machine for her, pays her more than the going rate, and warns everyone in the back room that they had better respect her or else. She works all day, goes home at night to do her chores, her cooking, and her washing, and raises six fine men who all go to college.

The chronicler of the "bucolic narrative" *Drag: A Comedy* (1925), which takes place in 1907 in Paris, is once again Bill, owner and editor with Sam Hod of the *Paris Daily Telegraph*. He sees the young hick, David Haskell, when he makes his entrance, in a tasteless suit and a worse tie, into this "twenty-dollar-a-week, picket-fence-and-hitching-post" town. Coming from his home in Foxboro, David, whose father is still alive but whose mother abandoned the family when he was three, gives a ride in his buggy to Carrie Flint, who is going to act as a companion to an ailing lady in Paris. When David applies for a job at the paper, after being tormented in the local diner by malicious men and a "mopsy," Lill Whalen, Bill gives him a chance and discovers David to be a gifted humorist. He does a brilliant interview with Jim Thorne, an important man in town, who takes an interest in David (his own son had behaved criminally at the bank and committed suicide). The paper makes money on David's stories. David comes upon Lill robbing a drunken man who is down on his luck; David's testimony sends Lill to the reformatory in Vergennes. The proofreader at the paper is pretty Allie Parker, who is kind to David and sews his torn trousers. He thinks he is in love and they marry. The marriage is a disaster: Allie becomes a shrew overnight. Her indolent father "gives" David his jumble shop, which means that David has to leave the paper and become a salesman. He suddenly finds that he is supporting the entire family, including Mrs. Parker, her two other dreadful children, and his own father, who moves in with them. He realizes he has married the wrong girl: Carrie is still taking care of Thorne's invalid wife,

Fanny. When Lill is released from prison, David is kind to her and gives her some money. After the jumble store burns down, Thorne decides to invest in David's future and loans him the money to buy the *Wickford Times*. When Bill visits him in Wickford, he realizes that David has created "a born newspaperman's model weekly." Bill remonstrates with David when the whole family arrives to live with him in his four rooms (he has to sleep at the paper office). "You're under a nonsensical drag," Bill says to David. Lill turns up, now affluent, and wants to help him. She is very seductive, but "he knew Wickford and the moral code of its gossips." Meanwhile, the Parker family is bleeding him for money. Because of the pressures of the family, his paper fails, he cannot repay Thorne, and he takes a job in Springfield, Massachusetts. He is writing a play based on his experiences with the Parkers, a comedy called *How's The Family?* He is half in love with Lill. His play opens in New York and is a success. Allie comes to New York, bringing the whole horrible family with her so that they can continue to sponge off him. They are, he knows, "his drag of nine years standing." He leaves Allie and joins the aviation corps. After a flying accident, he is taken to a hospital where Carrie is a nurse. They finally get together after loving each other from a distance for almost ten years. (In aerodynamics, "drag" is caused by air friction.)

Twenty years before *The Blue Lamp* (1931) begins, a New York banker named John Harmon built a mansion near Paris where he raised a daughter, Mary, and entertained her suitor, Count Josef Briskow, to whom she became engaged. When the father died, Mary inherited five million dollars and then vanished, as did Dr. Euclid Hawkins, the medical student who was treating her for encephalitis. The case was never solved. All these years later, Jacob Gleason, a Paris resident, sees an apparition on the grounds of the Harmon estate on a night when "a vast coral moon" became "cold silver" as it mounted the heavens. It was a woman's figure crying out that she is looking for her child and a blue light inside the house. He rushes to the home of the caretaker, Squire Jabez Butterworth, "a tall, lank, grizzled old Vermonter." They, Sheriff Amos Crumpett, and Paul Lyman, a reporter from the *Paris Daily Telegraph*, return to the house where they find no one, but can make out footprints. The newspapers take up the story of the Harmon mystery, and James ("Jimmy") Bartlett, a Boston newspaper man in his twenties from Vermont and the nephew of the sheriff, is sent to Paris to sleep alone in the Harmon house and write a story about it. He has a terrifying experience, discovers the body of a man, finds a moving staircase (operated by pulleys), and stumbles upon a young woman (the exact image of Mary), alive, who is lying on a cot, an oil lamp with a blue glass chimney beside her. The man disappears, as does the staircase, and the girl is locked in the tower. Jimmy hurries into town to his uncle—"the mountains rolled around like blackened tents of gigantic size"—and is followed by the man he has seen at the Harmon place. The man is Lawyer Ephraim Watts, who has mistaken Jimmy for someone else (Walker Wilson) and who escapes. When they all return to the Harmon house, they discover a murdered body with a blue lamp near it. The coroner, Dr. Ansell Chapin, identifies the dead man as Briskow, Mary's lover. The drama is explained during a fascinating recapitulation.

Bliss Perry

Three of the eight stories in *The Powers at Play* (1899) are set in Vermont. "**His Word of Honor**" illuminates the moment in twenty-two-year-old Dr. Sam Colburn's life when he realizes he has strayed from his rightful path. From a poor family in North Enderby between Wilmington and Brattleboro, Sam attends Dartmouth and Columbia University College for Physicians and Surgeons, where he succeeds dramatically and is favored by the famous surgeon, Dr. Warburton, who encourages Sam's socializing with his only daughter, Elinor. When Elinor asks him to go traveling in Vermont with a party of young people for two days during his vacation, he is flattered into accepting. He knows his absence will be a disappointment to his widowed mother and to Juletta Perkins, to whom he has been engaged for five years. His life is changed when he hap-

pens upon a young woman, a performer in a circus, who is staying with her injured husband and little baby in an abandoned charcoal kiln. She is fishing for her husband's supper and brings Sam back with her. Jake Hunter has a dislocated shoulder that Sam snaps back into place with "a sort of smothered click as from a well-oiled breech-loader." The young mother cooks a fine supper of trout and potatoes for them and turns aside modestly to feed young Reginald Adoniram. Sam is charmed and touched by the brave, forthright, loyal young woman and her little family. He must figure out a way to get them fifteen miles to Huckleville, where her relations live. He spends the night on some straw in front of the stove, brooding about his contact with this young woman's real "anxiety, joy, pain, humor, devotion." He will not desert them now; he is back in Vermont and "they were to him as his own people." He realizes that he had been tempted by the great surgeon to spend time with his daughter, to go to dances and weddings, and was on the verge of treachery. The first selectman arrives the next morning with a wagon to take the Hunters to their relatives, dropping Sam at the Cross Roads. Sam does not keep the rendezvous with Elinor but goes back to Juletta. In "**Madame Annalena**," the narrator has been bicycling on Green Mountain roads and stops off in Slab City (not far from White River Junction), where he stays at Mr. Dakin's—a post office, general store, and tavern rolled into one. There are a dozen story-and-a-half white houses, a blacksmith's, a dam and saw mill, and a fine, square frame house with a Mansard roof on the hill. He learns that the big house belongs to Jabez Dunham, the legal husband of the great opera singer, Annalena. The narrator is astonished to hear that the diva was born here in the heart of the Green Mountains. The loungers at the tavern tell him that she was Ann Ellen Darby, raised in the Hollow, and has been away twenty-two years. Jabez lights the lanterns in all the windows of his house every night, "until Annerlener gets back." "**The Fish-Warden of Madrid**" concerns the death of Beriah Tate, who has just been elected in the March town meeting to such civic functions in

Madrid as first selectman, road-master, overseer of the poor, and constable. His death also leaves open the post of fish-warden, and Tate's hired man, Alonzo Turnham Robbins, twenty-three, is appointed to the task. Widow Tate takes in boarders, and handsome eighteen-year-old Henrietta helps her around the house. Alonzo fancies Henrietta and hopes, with the fines from his job as fish-warden, he will be able to take her to the band concert in neighboring Warwick. Benjamin F. Dupree, a well-dressed youngish broker from New York, arrives at Mrs. Tate's. He and Alonzo discuss horse breeds—"one word of Green Mountain freemasonry"—and soon Alonzo has suggested that he accompany Dupree fishing. After watching Dupree catch scores of tiny fish, Alonzo arrests him in the name of the State of Vermont. Alonzo takes Dupree to the justice of the peace in Warwick, where Dupree is fined twenty dollars. Dupree writes a check, which Alonzo endorses (since he will gain ten dollars from this transaction); unfortunately, the check is worthless and Alonzo is held liable for the twenty (of which he has only ten). Henrietta and one of Mrs. Tate's boarders overhear this exchange and lend Alonzo the money he needs. Further, Henrietta agrees to go to the band concert with him. (The title of the collection is from Robert Browning's poem, "By the Fire-Side:" "The forests had done it; there they stood;/ We caught for a moment the powers at play.")

Kathrin Perutz

The young women at this plush Vermont college for girls in *The Garden* (1962) are rich, spoiled, and shallow, except for the narrator, Kath, who is an intellectual but conforms to the norm—Bermuda shorts with knee socks, Ivy League dates, and endless talks about sex. The college is "five hours by train from New York;" they come "up from Boston" by train in the fall: "Trees were yellow and rust; some leaves were crimson as blood." Kath's best friend, Susie, kills herself at the onset, and Kath begins idolizing a young woman called The Blossom, who is "queen of the debutantes." Kath is desperate to room with The Blossom, but the latter's parents do not want their daughter to room "with a Jew." She works hard for Mr. James, her English professor, who thinks she is too intelligent for this silly college where she has no competition. The Blossom develops a crush on her history teacher, Mario Carelli, and much of the group's energies and emotions are taken up with this fancy. Kath endures a drunken Ivy-League weekend with a nonentity date. Snow comes in November: "only occasional ivy looked mournfully out of its pillow." The ethos of a woman's college—close personal relationships, constant consultation on everyone's problems, heart-to-heart discussions—is evoked in poetic prose. Kath wants to transfer out of this college where everyone dresses alike and thinks alike (mostly about sex) and goes through the ritual fulsome farewells where everyone is a best friend and nothing will ever be the same. The college is a garden where this female culture can bloom behind closed gates.

Judson Philips

In *Thursday's Folly* (1967), the sixth in the Peter Styles series, the hero returns to Barchester in southern Vermont over a mountain from Peru. Ten years earlier, he and his father had been forced off the road by "joy killers:" his father was killed; Peter's leg was amputated below the knee. A Korean War-commando veteran, Peter is a successful magazine writer living in a borrowed house to work on a story. He is pulled into a drama involving a young woman, Linda Grant, who lives in a house on Barchester's main street that has been in her family for five generations. On her own after her fiancé was killed in Vietnam, she has turned the front room into a book-and-gift shop. Suddenly, she is abducted. The village has made Peter feel comfortable and welcome; he joins in the rescue effort. He and the sheriff go to Thursday's Folly, a 1920s-era hotel now owned by an elderly man named Thursday Rule, a painter, and his common-law wife of fifty years and former model, Emily. Peter is captured by a gang of five men who have murdered and burned a family in Brattleboro and are now holding Linda hostage. This maniacal group is made up of Kramer, the leader, Trudy, a camp follower, and four sociopaths, Ben, Jake, Duke, and George. They immediately subdue Peter and tear off his artificial limb. Fortunately, there is an ancient wicker wheelchair available at the former hotel. Peter acknowledges to himself that they are going to die, but he wants to be the one to determine how and when. Peter figures out the moves and manages, with the help of the Rules and Linda, to outwit the torturers. Linda falls in love with Peter.

Jodi Picoult

Second Glance (2003), complex and thought-provoking, is set near Burlington in the hamlet of Comtosook on Lake Champlain, where the paranormal is immediately apparent as rose petals fall like snow in the middle of August and rolling garter snakes cover the ground. There are four central characters. Shelby Wakeman, a librarian in Comtosook, is the single mother of Ethan (who has a rare genetic skin disease and will probably not live beyond his teens). Her brother, Ross Wakeman, full of suicidal rage since the death of his wife in an automobile accident, works as a consultant in the paranormal field. Meredith Oliver, a genetics counselor assigned part-time to Washington, D.C., lives with her grandmother, Ruby Weber, and her daughter, Lucy. Eli Rochert, half-Abenaki, is a detective and police officer in Comtosook. These people are drawn together because of a proposed development project on Otter Creek Pass, where Newton Redhook wants to build a strip mall on property belonging to Spencer Pike, who is now in an old person's home. Local Abenakis, including their one-hundred-and-two-year-old elder, Az Thompson, are demonstrating against the development project, because they claim the property is an Indian burial site. Ross is visiting his sister because he has been hired to exorcise the ghosts in town. He sees and falls in love with a ghost, only to learn that she was Cecilia Beaumont Pike, dead for seventy years. After Eli reopens the investigation of her death, the narrative reverts to 1932 and reveals facts about Cecilia's life—and death. Her father, a professor of biology at the University of Vermont, and her husband, Spencer Pike, a professor of anthropology there, were disciples of Henry Perkins, who introduced genetics to Vermont. They were all complicit in the shameful Vermont Eugenics Project and the passage of the Vermont Sterilization Act of 1931. Woven into this powerful and shocking mystery are scandal, suspense, murder, suicide, coincidence, friendship, and love. Some examples of the stunning imagery: "The moon was beaded and yellow as a hawk's eye," and "Old tombstones listed like tired foot soldiers."

Suzi Pizzuti

Raising Cain...and His Sisters (2000) tells of Olivia Harmon, whose husband and daughter were killed five years previously and who lives in an amiable boarding house in MacLaughlin. She finds new purpose in life when she is able to help three homeless orphans and hopes to find a father for them in charismatic and handsome Zach Springer, contractor and widower.

L. J. Pratt

The Unfortunate Mountain Girl (1854) contains four stories set in Vermont. In "**Emma, the Belle of the Village**," a successful farmer named Hall lives in the village of P____ in 1832 with four sons and an adorable daughter, Emma, eighteen, who is the beloved of Egbert Cornwall, son of a merchant. Mr. Hall vehemently opposes the match because the suitor is not wealthy. Emma's health begins to fail and, before Mrs. Hall can take her to The Springs for a cure, she is on the brink of death. She forgives her parents and tells them that, since she has nothing to live for, she welcomes death. What, asks the doctor who attends her, is wealth in the face of love? In "**The Berry Boy**," Mr. Benson is traveling home to his village from The Springs in the summer of 1838 when he comes upon a boy selling fruit. The boy tells Mr. Benson that he does not go to school but stays home to take care of his blind grandfather. Mr. Benson is so impressed by this youth that he sets up a subscription for him through which Simon Powell, for that is the boy's name, obtains a liberal education. When Mr. Saxe, who adopts Simon at eighteen, dies, Simon inherits a substantial business from him. Reading that Mr. Benson is selling at auction for debt, Simon buys the whole property and informs Mr. Benson that he purchased the stand to give him ample time to redeem it. Simon marries Miss Amelia Benson into the bargain. Also set in the village of P____, **"The Early Graves"** tells of Ella, the only daughter of Mr. Ashland, who has won the heart of James Wilson. Mr. Wilson wonders why his son would want to marry the daughter of a farmer, when he could court and win the aristocratic Imogene Cornwall. When James tells Mr. Ashland that his father has disowned him, Mr. Ashland welcomes James into their family, but it is too late: by the time the wedding day arrives, Ella is on her deathbed. After her death, James studies to become a missionary, but he, too, falls deathly ill. Their two monuments stand side-by-side. In **"Mysterious Strangers,"** a post-chaise arrives in the hamlet of Dresden, and a well-bred lady and exquisite child alight. They take rooms with Mrs. Dustan, who lets her little parlor to lodgers to make ends meet. The people of Dresden are naturally curious about the lady, who some say is Angeline Baker, the widow of a young Revolutionary War general. Angeline dies of tuberculosis, and her daughter, Parthena, adopted by Mrs. Dustan, earns her living by herding sheep in the pastures of the Comstocks of Dresden Hall. Young Arnold Comstock falls in love with Parthena before he must leave for the army. He returns to Dresden, a major, in the company of an older man, who turns out to be Parthena's father, General Baker. The elder Comstock spread the story about General Baker's death so that he could press his duplicitous advances upon the fair Angeline. Arnold and Parthena marry.

John Prendergast

The plot of *Jump* (1995) is confined to a single weekend at a ski chalet in southern Vermont with a group of edgy, stoned people in their twenties, who met five years earlier at the University of Pennsylvania. The narrator, Walter, watches television tracing "themes" for a living

His partner, Nancy, is a saintly manipulator who teaches third grade and thinks she might be pregnant. Dave is the charismatic and dangerous leader and everyone's friend. His cousin, Robin, is a tough-talking, aggressive flirt on permanent leave from Cornell. Patrick is gay and has recently come out. Lois, who is apparently unbalanced, and Rick are an odd couple. The year is 1984: Walter Mondale, Gary Hart, and Jesse Jackson are running for president. In the few flashbacks in this tight narrative, Walter reveals that his mother accosted him sexually, that he was a loner and failure in college, and that the only family he felt he ever had was in the college residence with Nancy and Dave. The pressure-cooker weekend finally explodes.

Francine Prose

In *Blue Angel* (2000), resident novelist Ted Swenson teaches creative writing at Euston College in the Northeast Kingdom. The college is private, expensive, and so remote that the administration is trying to market its isolation in the "moose-ridden wilderness." It was founded by a conservative Puritan named Elijah Euston whose children all came to tragic ends (many suicides) and who has imported an English look—Gothic gray stone cloisters—framed by native two-hundred-year-old maples. Swenson refers sarcastically to "idyllic Euston." He is married to the college nurse, Sherrie, who is attractive, sensible, and funny. They live in an old house: "Installing it [a window] was their second and final attempt to make the old Vermont farmhouse satisfy their needs or just acknowledge their existence. Mostly they've settled in and let the house do what it wants. Although (or perhaps because) they told the hippie carpenter not to make it look like a bay window in a tract home, it looks exactly like a bay window in a tract home." Swenson has published two novels, *Blue Angel* and *Phoenix Time,* which have achieved considerable literary attention. Angela Arko, a student in his composition class, asks for an appointment for him to critique her novel-in-progress, *Eggs.* The college has a new policy on sexual harassment: "Teacher-student attraction is

P

an occupational hazard," as Ted himself has learned, because soon he is in thrall to Angela. He checks her erotic poems out of the library, drives her to Computer Land, carries her new machine to her dorm, and attempts to make love to her, breaking a tooth in the process. Swenson is surprised to find that Angela has borrowed the film, *Blue Angel,* from the local video store. This dark, caustic, witty book looks at every campus foible—the phony British president, transplanted like the British cathedral to northern Vermont, the exaggerated gender studies woman, the fumbling librarian, the gay couple, and the biting deconstructionist. The affair takes a surprising turn: Swenson faces a hearing of his peers on sexual-harassment charges brought by Angela, who seduced him only to force him to send her novel to his editor and taped their last exchange. The climax of the sexual-harassment hearing is cleverly executed and the outcome intriguing. An example of the graceful imagery: "A doe calmly crosses the quad, delicate, flamingo-like, poking her nose in the snow."

E. Annie Proulx

Heart Songs (1988), a collection of strong, evocative stories set in Chopping County in northeastern Vermont, is about infidelity, rage, abuse, and frustration. **"On the Antler"** concerns the feud between Leverd Hawkheel and Bill Stong about hunting on Antler Mountain. In **"Stone City,"** an outsider who has come for the bird hunting teams up with Banger to learn the tricks of the trade. Banger was involved in a feud with the Stones, who burned his house (with his wife and child in it). Banger and a gang tar and feather the Stones and run them out of town. A Stone son kills Banger's dog. On the fall weather: "The sky was an intense enamel blue, but the afternoon light had a dying, year's-end quality, a rich apricot color as though it fell through a cordial glass onto an oak table, the kind of day hunters remember falsely as October." In **"Bedrock,"** when Perley's wife, Netta, dies, he marries Maureen Bobhot, who is younger than his daughter. Maureen turns out to be a slob who neither cooks nor washes dishes. Rainwater is

slowly washing away the "thin mantle of soil" that is his farm. Perley realizes Bobhot and his daughter, Maureen, are trying to take his farm away. There is a hint of incest at the end, which may explain why Perley's own daughter is so angry with him. **"A Run of Bad Luck"** describes a day in the hunting life of Mae and Haylett and their four boys, the younger two, Phil and Clover, and the older two, Amando and Ray. There are detailed and rich descriptions of Mae's cooking dinner the night before and then making up lunches for them to carry the next day. On the way to Hawk Mountain, they drive by the trailer where Julia, Amando's estranged wife, still lives. Brother Ray's car has been there all night. The father tries to save Amando from the knowledge, but he already knows. The title story, **"Heart Songs,"** tells of Snipe, who left his wife for Catherine and the city for Chopping County. Catherine, who is hateful, has been trying to learn Peruvian weaving but cannot make any money at it. She finally explodes, saying that people want Peruvian weaving, not "Vermont Peruvian." They live on a lake with a dock, and in the evenings Snipe starts to play country music with the Twilight family. He thinks he loves the hugely fat Nell, the lead singer, who he assumes to be Eno Twilight's daughter, but she turns out to be his wife. She is, nevertheless, a slut. Snipe thinks he might move "out West," but he never will. In **"The Unclouded Day,"** Earl, a rich man, approaches Santee for lessons in hunting birds. Earl just can't seem to learn how to shoot. Finally, in his anger, he shouts at Noah, Santee's dog. They get caught in lightning, which kills three birds that Earl believes he actually shot. They part company; Santee is sardonically amused to think of Earl's unwrapping the birds at home and finding them already "cooked." **"In the Pit"** follows Blue, who visits his fat old mother and then goes to fix up his family's camp, which has been vandalized. He jumps to the conclusion that the damage was done by old Mr. Fitzroy's friend, Gilbert, who is just out of prison. He steals their toaster only to find out, too late, that he is wrong. In **"Wer-Trout,"** Sauvage and Rivers are neighbors. Rivers's wife leaves him; Sauvage's wife has a nervous break-down. To seek refuge from their lives, they go to Yellow Bogs for trout. Rivers starts to drink again, but Sauvage catches lots of fish. As a last straw, Rivers, who has lost his apple trees, his lawn, and his wife, breaks his favorite fishing rod. "**Electric Arrows**" tells of Mason Clew, who has failed in everything. His father "let the farm drip through his fingers like water until only an anxious dampness was left in our palms." Mason lives in the house his family's hired man used to live in, while a rich doctor and his wife buy the house the narrator was born in. The condescending, rich neighbors think they have found rare Indian carvings on their land; Mason bitterly comforts himself with the fact that the "rare carvings" are pictures his father chiseled in the rock. In "**A Country Killing**," Rose Noury, fat and lecherous, moves into Warren's trailer. Albro and Simone run the store and the garage. Someone murders Rose and Warren by setting their trailer on fire. Albro was infatuated with Rose. "**Negatives**" describes the experience of Buck B., a former TV star, who builds a fabulous glass house in the mountains. His friend, the photographer Walter Weller, comes to live with him. Walter befriends a dirty, semi-homeless woman named Albina Muth, whom he wants to photograph. Albina starts sleeping in Buck B.'s Mercedes. Buck announces that he is throwing Walter out and selling the house; there are strong hints that Buck murders Walter.

Postcards (1992) relates the downfall of a New England farming family named Blood, living during World War II in Cream Hill: Jewell and Minkton M. ("Mink") Blood and their three children, two of whom are grown men: Loyal, Dub, and Mernelle. In the first chapter, Loyal buries the body of his girlfriend, Billy, whom he has unintentionally killed, in a stone wall. He tells his parents that he and Billy are leaving together and that she does not want to say good-bye to her parents. His departure leaves his father, Mink, with inadequate help, since Dub lost an arm jumping off a train and cannot milk cows. Mink muses about the times — and the past. As he strips a cow, he thinks that in some

mysterious way the cow is going to be the death of him. He is exhausted from lying awake at night worrying about his sick pig and trying to figure out how to break out of his bad luck. Every year he is poorer, the work harder, the prices higher, and his chances of getting away fewer. Even though everyone had been poor when he was a child, it was different now. In those days, people kept going because relatives and neighbors came unasked to help out. "Where the hell were they now when he was sinking under the black water? Ott moved, Ronnie out of farming, Clyde Darter sold out and disappeared into Maine. The bank had changed hands, bought out by some big outfit over in Burlington, mean sons. The Dovers were storing hay in the old Batchelder house, the bales filling the kitchen and front room, packed on the staircase, pushing the banister spindles out. He remembered Jim Batchelder as if he'd seen him last night, the chapped face and parsnip nose, could hear him talk to his horses in his spare voice. And the past swelled out at him with its smell of horses, oats, and hot linseed poultices. When the horses went the people went." After his cows develop Mad Itch, Mink kills them and, with the help of his son, Dub, burns down the barn. They are arrested and put in jail. Dub serves his time; Mink hangs himself. Jewell, unable to make a go of it, falls prey to Ronnie, a contemporary of her son Loyal's, who is in real estate. He sells off most of her land for a trailer park. She feels absolutely alone and she, too, wonders what has become of the past. She remembers that when she was a girl she was surrounded with relatives. When the big family got together, "The men would put the plank tables together. Every woman would bring something, I don't care, biscuits, fried chicken, pies. Potato salad, berry pies. They'd bring these things if it was a get-together or a church picnic or times of trouble. The kids go runnin' around, laughin,' I can remember the mothers trying to hush them up at my brother Marvin's funeral, but they'd just slow down for a little bit and then start up again."

P

Bernadette Pruitt

When her brother and sister-in-law are killed in *The Man Next Door* (1998), Erin March is given guardianship of their daughter, Lily, after a court battle in which Lily's financially stable and childless aunt and uncle, Yale and Mallory Holbrooke, sue for custody of Lily. Erin lives in her brother's house in Maple Springs in central Vermont, with his potter's kiln in the back. She is defensive and fearful when the civil lawyer from Boston, Wyatt Keegan, who represented the other side in the custody case, moves into the house next door. She and Lily are happy and congenial, but Lily is sometimes undisciplined, and Erin's home business, Dream House Imports, Inc., has not taken off as she had hoped. As adversaries, Erin and Wyatt keep their distance, but daughter Lily falls for him instantly. Erin grudgingly admits that his eyes are "strikingly handsome," but she finds him arrogant and he finds her arch. At issue is whether they will fall in love.

Diana Ramsay

Northvale College near Rutland in *Killing Words* (1994) exhibits two syndromes of a college town: internal academic politics and town-versus-gown rivalry, with gossip about the college characters on the part of the locals. ("Gossip can nail you to the wall in this town, even if the college does its usual sweeping under the rug.") Also present is the conflict between Vermont natives and flatlanders. Amelia Cunningham is a faculty wife, married to handsome Gabriel in the English department and, as a faculty wife, must endure the petty gossip that goes on in her knitting class with other faculty wives. Once, when she is fed up with the talk about tenure, she jokingly suggests sending threatening anonymous letters to upset the dull, campus routine. Her women friends are stunned at her outrageous remark, even though she quickly apologizes, say-ing she was just teasing. Unfortunately for Amelia, someone acts on her suggestion and sends out over a dozen anonymous letters on computer print-outs, saying, "You think nobody knows what you've been up to but you're wrong. Pretty soon everybody will know. Nothing you can do about it except repent." Amelia is ashamed and embarrassed that everyone thinks she is the perpetrator, but she is even more horrified when Katherine Ellsworth, dowdy and eccentric wife of William Ellsworth, the flamboyant head of the English department, kills herself. Feeling responsible, Amelia vows to find out who actually sent the letters and what secret problem would lead Katherine to kill herself. Amateur sleuths often cause more problems than they solve, and Amelia becomes deeply embroiled in unfolding developments. She learns that her best friend, Suzanne, is the one who sent the letters, that the one sent to the Ellsworth household was addressed to "William Ellsworth, Esq.," and that Ellsworth, a renowned seducer of young coeds, had in fact seduced Suzanne's own daughter and nearly ruined her life. Amelia and Suzanne, certain that William murdered his wife for her money, make a plan to blackmail him and, during the transfer of payments, photograph him. Unfortunately, their plan goes awry in a serious way and Amelia realizes that it was not William who murdered his wife. Amelia does get to the bottom of the case, but in the process she discovers that her husband has been having affairs with his students (a note in feminine handwriting is thrust indiscreetly into one of Gabriel's pockets). She leaves Northvale forever.

Franklin D. Reeve

David ("Davy") Eames Spencer is the first-person narrator of *The Brother* (1971), about a family living in the suburbs of Middlebury in the 1950s. The father, William Anthony Spencer, is a judge; the mother, who was Louise Eames Winthrop, is a strict believer in well-regulated, moral lives, and a proud member of the DAR. She pronounces some of the girls in town "lower class." The Spencers have four sons, Will, Rod, Davy, and Alec. Davy idolizes his brother, Will, who is eight years older than he. Will is hand-some, athletic, successful, and popular. He writes stories that are published in the school magazine; he has a sense of justice and fair play; and he falls in love with an exquisite ballet dancer named Edie Clark, who, from Davy's point of view, is everything a man could want in a woman. (Davy understands the ironical point of one of Will's stories, saying, "You can see through it clearly, as through a Vermont stream.") Rob, the second son, is unsuccessful, never pleases his parents, and dies young in a car crash. Will and Edie are socialists; Davy thinks of his parents, strict Episcopalians, who talk about "troublemakers" and "Communist agitators." On a trip home to visit his parents, Will tries to talk about Rob's death. His mother, as always, walks out of the room, which is her way of avoiding confrontation. Davy is aware, as he looks at his parents through Will's eyes, of how staid and perfunctory they are. His mother always criticizes rather than enjoying life. Davy thinks, "In spring I suppose the ice always breaks up the way we did. One big chunk is cut off and, half sinking, rushes downstream on the swollen torrents until, battered against rocks and melted in the slower waters of the plain, it vanishes forever." Edie and Will are married in Waltham, Massachusetts. As Davy is taking his little brother, Alec, to the refreshment table for some ginger ale, his mother calls, "But no champagne, Davy." "That went through me like a bullet through a squirrel, leaving hardly a mark outside but zipping the guts apart." As Edie becomes more successful in New York, Will fails and is "morose, bitter." In Davy's senior year, Will and Edie split up. Will, who has lost his job at a newspaper, comes home and, to Davy's horror, turns on him. After his divorce, Will marries Dorothy Underwood from Scarsdale. The Spencers, who shut out their own children, embrace the notion of middle class, respectable Dorothy. Davy sees Will's life "unwinding." When Davy, now at Williams College, acknowledges he is serious about Susan Schwarz, his mother says, "Susan doesn't belong, David. Dad knows her people in his law work, and they aren't like us. They're a different sort, darling, and you're only going to

ruin your career if you let yourself..." Davy is aware that Will has completely failed. "His life had been full of feeling, but never aimed anywhere. He had gotten stuck in his own feelings, like Br'er Rabbit in Tar Baby." Will is drinking steadily and, as Davy can see, "Will was passing through locks to the sea, lower and lower, devising ever more intricate means of letting himself down." The conclusion is tragic and meaningful.

Helen Reilly

The murders in *Murder on Angler's Island* (1945) occur off the coast of New England, but the heart of the story is an exclusive conclave near the village of Bangall in the mountains southwest of St. Johnsbury. There the summer people reside: "best people, bon ton, cream of the crop, backbone of the nation, social register." Elizabeth Spires, a private first class in the WAC, is reunit-ed with her childhood friends from Bangall when they all meet on Angler's Island. Jeffrey Crale, a major in the American Rangers, is also stationed at Fort Johnson. Elizabeth's heart was broken when Jeffrey married Faith Ann Blake, three years earlier; when Faith Ann is murdered Elizabeth is the obvious suspect. Because of the high profile of the families involved in the case, Inspector Christopher McKee is sent from New York's Manhattan Homicide Squad to investigate. Underneath their well-dressed exteriors lurk bigamy, blackmail, and intrigue. It is apparent that all of these socialites are short of cash. It is also apparent that one of these old acquaintances is a murderer and a thief. Elizabeth thinks linger-ingly of the long-ago days in Vermont, when they were all young and there was no tomorrow. She sees "sheep fields, tawny with autumn." Each one of those gathered might have a motive. Was Compton Yarrow in love with Faith Ann? Is Jeffrey in love with Compton's wife, Cicely? Who was blackmailing Faith Ann? Who stole her jewelry? Who killed the insurance adjuster, Mr. Manxman? Who stands to inherit Faith Ann's fortune? Who tried to murder Compton? After the villain is revealed, Jeffrey and Elizabeth are free to marry at last.

R

Herbert Resnicow

Windham College in Rockfield is full of the petty grievances and jealousies of academia in *The Seventh Crossword* (1985). The president is seeking higher office in Washington, and there is an undignified scramble to fill his shoes. Untenured assistant professors will do anything to achieve security. Six of these assistant professors have been working for three years for the Teutonic and rigid Professor Fabian Humboldt in his Crossword Project. Three times a week they receive and solve six crosswords as part of an effort, on the surface anyway, to stimulate reading among school children. A seventh crossword is mysteriously inserted into the Project mailbox. The format and style are perfect: who constructed it? Three times this happens. Professor Humboldt threatens withholding tenure if they do not discover the perpetrator. Meanwhile, Dean of Students Isabel MacIntosh welcomes as her visitor Giles Sullivan, famous criminal attorney and cruciverbalist, and his servant, Oliver. When Humboldt is murdered with one of his collection of ancient arms, Giles and Oliver are caught up with Isabel in trying to solve the mystery: who killed Humboldt and are there any clues to his/her identity in the three seventh crosswords? They interview each of the six professors: Karen Kares, English; Dag Norstad, statistics; Carl Richer, education; Evelyn Tinguely, sociology; Bruce Yablonski, psychology; and Jennifer Zapata, Third World studies. Then they study the puzzles, trying to analyze words for some clue or message. They finally figure out that the words must be pronounced aloud to extract the meaning and thus discover the identity of the murderer.

Stanley Reynolds

Better Dead Than Red (1964), fiercely satirical, features Franklin Lear, who lives on Spruce Street in Milltown River Junction with his wife and daughter. Lear has just stepped down as head of Top Name Pharmaceuticals, forced to sell out to an internationally financed corporation, Entey Inc. In his retirement, Lear, who has "the blood of Vermont grocery clerks in his veins, but also the blood of Ethan Allen's Green Mountain Boys," stops being a "shrewd, practical Vermont Yankee" and takes on the Communists. To express his antipathy to the Red Menace and International Bolshevism, he sends letters to newspapers around the country. Clairmont Whiteside, the editor of the Milltown River Junction *The Chameleon*, suggests that Lear should find a free enterprise corporation under whose banner to fight the International Communist Cartel and urges him to go to Washington to talk to Democratic Senator T.K. ("Citrus") Slardy. Lear names his organization John Henry Drake, Inc., after a Milltown River Junction boy executed by Chinese Communists when his plane was shot down. Joined by his cynical and womanizing Vermont nephew, Nicholas Drummer, Lear sets off on his picaresque caravan across America. He makes speeches at meetings of local DAR branches; he is interviewed on talk shows; he utters phony jargon at dinners. A two-time Pulitzer Prize-winning journalist, Elmer Hueckner, publishes a piece on Lear who, he says, seems a harmless quack who could, under unusual circumstances, constitute a real danger to the Republic. When Hueckner dies of a heart attack, the story goes to page one and the article makes the neo-fascist "man from Vermont" the target of every liberal thinker in America. *The Conservative's Advocate* takes up Lear as its hero. Only two papers, *The New York City Grey* and *The Chameleon,* defend Lear's right to speak. Lear's bizarre pilgrimage continues through America, picking up eccentric, rightwing characters at every stop. Lear is receiving letters and money for his crusade from grassroots America. His success is based on saying what people want to hear. Chapters of John Henry Drake, Inc., shoot up at colleges across the country. *The New York City Grey* is now questioning why competent businessmen encourage the "economic bilge water" of this Vermonter. Back in Vermont, Clairmont Whiteside, archconservative Yankee, criticizes Lear's empty rhetoric. His hometown calls that "sour grapes." A brick is thrown through Whiteside's office window. Ironically, Whiteside has forgotten it was he who sent Lear on his present "path of self-destruction." The state's attorney shuts down Whiteside's paper. Citrus Slardy is nominated by the Democratic Convention; the Republican Convention throws its nomination to Lear. Just at that moment, John Henry ("Big Hank") Drake returns from China, where he has been living as a movie actor. The press loves him, talking about "the blessedness of an All-American boyhood among the green hills of Vermont." Hollywood is doing the "Henry Drake Story" with Jimmy Stewart as the "Vermont yokel." Big Hank thinks everyone should help one's neighbors and support the United Nations: "the big fellers got to keep an eye out for the little fellers." Lear loses the election, and he and his hangers-on end up in an insane asylum.

Claudia Ricci

Three generations of women inhabit *Dreaming Maples* (2002). Widow Audrey Burdett lives with her lover, Marjory Leibowitz, and three other women—Francine, Martha, and Pit—on a farm in Wilmont near Snowstack in southern Vermont. Audrey's daughter, Eileen, abandoned her baby, Candace, when a young woman but is now reunited with her in North Adams, Massachusetts. Candace is pregnant by her boyfriend, Mark Sarazian, a musician. Candace's father, Rusty, also lives in Vermont with his second wife and two sons. The commune women support themselves sugaring and devote themselves to sculpture and painting, photography, and fiction writing. They are having a more and more difficult time as each year passes and, when Snowstack offers them a lot of money for their property, they must face facts. Candace has a share in the property and will inherit Audrey's. Candace moves back to North Adams, where she starts using drugs until her mother puts her in rehab to await the birth of her baby, Gretchen. Candace is unable to cope with a crying baby and is put back in a hospital, leaving Eileen to care for Gretchen. Ultimately, the women design a satisfactory solution to suit all their futures.

Eric Rickstad

The bleak setting for the stricken and violent lives of the characters in *Reap* (2000) is Ivers, a mill town on the Lamoille River in northern Vermont. Reg Cumber served time in Fairland for selling marijuana and now lives in a cabin at Unknown Pond, while his brother, Hal, crippled and in a wheel chair from a freak accident, lives at "Ma's house." Their sister, Marigold, lives in a trailer on a tiny patch of land, all that is left of acres of sheepherding and then dairy land owned by four generations of her family. Her husband, Hess, was in a severe accident at the mill and has lost his nerve—and his livelihood—with a saw. Lamar, the Cumbers' cousin, who is in the marijuana business with them, is killed in a horrifying way. Reg is illiterate. None of these people has two living parents; all are dead except the Cumbers' mother, who has remarried and lives in Florida, and Hess's mother, Clare, who lives with his unpleasant stepfather, Max. Early in the action, the rich French-Canadian couple who have bought a ski house near Marigold run into a ditch, and she pulls them out with her pickup for an agreed upon twenty dollars. He passes her a bill when he shakes hands; it turns out to be five dollars Canadian. Into this lost and desperate mix comes Jessup Burke, a sixteen-year-old with a bike whose father is dead and who lives with his mother, Anna, and pines for a "summer girl," Emily, who, with the coming of fall, has moved back home. They spent time at the Barker place, an abandoned farm. Hitchhiking one day, Jessup is picked up by Reg, introduced to marijuana, meets the family, and becomes embroiled in Marigold's charms ("fingers soft as sumac's twigs") and Reg's schemes. Reg tempts Jessup, by taking him to bars and giving him pot and booze, to head for Caratunk, Jessup driving, where Reg breaks into the cabin—marijuana is growing indoors—to find his cousin, Lamar, dying of gunshot wounds. Reg, badly wounded in a shoot-out, puts Lamar out of his misery, just as he did his father when the latter was dying years earlier. Meanwhile, Hess beats up Marigold because she has been seeing Jessup. The resolution of the story is partially violent, but an act of generosity sows seeds of hope.

R

John Rickards

In *The Touch of Ghosts* (2004), Alex Rourke, thirty-seven, is a private investigator in Boston who left the FBI's office of violent crimes after a nervous breakdown caused by the deaths of his parents. He enjoys an amiable relationship with Dr. Gemma Larson, a Regional Medical Examiner in Bleakwater near Newport in northern Vermont. He is hired to trace the whereabouts of Adam Webb, who has been missing since he called his mother from Burlington several months previously. Before Alex reaches Vermont to see Gemma and investigate Adam's disappearance, she is shot and killed while driving her car. Once he has talked to Detective Sergeant Karl Flint of the Vermont State Police and started his research, he learns that a woman hiker and a tourist couple have recently disappeared and a prostitute has been murdered. He concludes the solution to the mystery lies in the ruins of the old ghost town, North Bleakwater, which used to be a resort for summer people called Echo Springs before the Great Flood of 1927. Alex consults with a reporter at the *Burlington Free Press*, interviews relevant people, and finds a stash of smuggled heroin at the old Echo Springs Hotel. (Alex muses on the fact that President Jefferson encouraged drug smuggling to and from Canada by prohibiting trade with Canada after the War of 1812.) Evidence points to two individuals—a "Mr. Delaney" and a cop. Alex succeeds in tracing the identity of "Mr. Delaney," the murderer of the prostitute, but realizes in the nick of time that someone else is responsible for the murders of Adam and Gemma.

Kenneth Roberts

Captain Peter Merrill, whose father runs a successful shipping business in Arundel, Maine, narrates *Rabble in Arms* (1933). After returning from London, he and his brother, Nathaniel, volunteer as scouts with Benedict Arnold in Canada. After smallpox inoculations, they head to Allen's Landing, where the Winooski River flows into Lake Champlain, and then north. The Northern Army retreats with eight thousand men, many suffering from smallpox. The soldiers have no shoes, medicine, food, or blankets. In Canada Peter sees Marie De Sabrevois, whom he and his brother had met in England, and her ward, Ellen Phipps, just released from Indian captivity, with whom Peter falls in love; he believes Marie to be a spy, but Nathaniel fancies himself in love with her. Arnold sends Peter to Crown Point (and the "swelling blue hills of the New Hampshire Grants") and thence to the sawmill in Skenesboro to build a fleet of ships to stop the British. He sees Ellen again and meets her "Indian" brother, Joseph, who has stayed with the Indian tribe. Peter, with the help of shipwrights from New England, builds and has fitted fourteen armed vessels. A bloody fight near Valcour Island on October 11, 1776, saves Lake Champlain and wins the delay that gives the Americans a chance to fight at Saratoga. Exhausted beyond measure, beating against the wind, Arnold's remaining ships manage to slip though the British fleet at night in the fog. Arnold gets the *Congress* to Buttonmould Bay to take the wounded ashore. Everyone escapes except Peter, Nathaniel, and two friends who are captured by Indians and taken first to Grand Isle, where Peter finds Marie's "uncle," Lanaudiere, an officer in charge of the Indians, and sees Ellen for a minute. They are held in captivity all through the winter. Disguised as Indians, they make their way back to Buttonmould Bay, where they find Marie, Ellen, and Nathaniel, a captive-cum-guest of General Burgoyne's. Nathaniel, persuaded that the war is lost, cites the fact that twenty-five thousand Loyalists are under arms against the Americans. St. Clair has evacuated Fort Ticonderoga. Burgoyne and his troops are twenty-three miles behind them, but Peter is able to get a ship to Skenesboro and on to Fort Ann and Fort Edward, taking women and wounded along. They have neither food nor powder, but Colonel van Rensselaer finally arrives with supplies, followed by General Philip Schuyler, then the Commander of the Northern Army, accompanied by Continentals to stop the victorious advance of the British. Morale is at an all-time low. The Congress has let the troops down badly.

Unfavorable rumors have been circulating about both Arnold and Schuyler. Peter is sent to recruit New England men by telling the story of "Jennie" McCrae (Jane McRae), scalped and murdered by Indians. When he returns to Bennington, General Stark has already beaten the Germans and Indians there. Congress replaces General Schuyler with General Gates, who behaves objectionably to Arnold. Peter and his friends are with Morgan near Freeman's Farm; all Morgan's men are hunters and woodsmen and, therefore, dangerous to the British. Arnold rides up and down the line exhorting the troops. Again they are victorious at Bemis Heights and Stillwater just north of Bennington. Burgoyne's army under Baum retreats to the Heights of Saratoga, where it is surrounded and defeated. Peter sets off to look for Nathaniel and Ellen and to apprehend Marie, the spy. Arnold pardons Nathaniel, and the Arundel Company brothers head for home with Ellen.

The narrator of *Northwest Passage* (1937), Langdon Towne, born in Kittery, Maine, is a painter. After being expelled from Harvard for joining a student demonstration, his father ships him off to an uncle's farm. Langdon hates farming but loves Elizabeth Browne, the daughter of a frowning-browed minister. In 1759 the British capture Fort Ticonderoga and Crown Point and Langdon's father summons him home. Elizabeth's family is hostile to his "effeminate" plans to become a professional painter. Langdon is overheard making derogatory remarks about Wyseman Clagett and Governor Wentworth and escapes arrest with his friend, Hunk, carrying a letter of introduction to British officers in the French and Indian War. "The sky was the color of skimmed milk, and the sun no brighter or warmer than a pewter button." After a stop at Fort Number Four, where Langdon's ancestors were raided and captured by St. Francis Indians, they cross the Green Mountains to Crown Point. There they meet Major Robert Rogers, the famed Indian fighter and head of Rogers's Rangers. Langdon feels he is in the presence of an unusual man, an "indomitable figure, in whose brain was stored a fund of knowledge

possessed by no other living man." Langdon recognizes later "his astounding fortitude, which held us up and helped us up, long after we had lost the power to stand." The mission of Rogers's Rangers is to wipe out the St. Francis Indians, who had been committing atrocities against the people of the Hampshire Grants. They are successful in their siege, although it is a deadly battle. The trip home to Memphremagog to the Connecticut River to the Ammonoosuc Valley is frightful—no food, no fire (Indians and French officers are pursuing them), sleeping in their ragged, freezing clothing, making their way over mountains and through swamps. It is a grueling and riveting tale, and the leadership of Major Rogers is the reason they survive. When they finally arrive at the rough fort in Ammonoosuc Valley, they can "see smoke lying against crowded spruces like a veil upon a bride's hair," but the officer sent with the supplies and food ordered by General Amherst has just fled. He feared the Rangers' musket shots were Indian fire and is later arrested for negligence. Rogers and Langdon, another officer, and an Indian captive boy, Billy, fashion a raft to go downstream for supplies. They are wrecked at White River Falls but make another raft (they are so weak from starvation that they have to fell the trees with fire) and finally succeed in getting to Number Four. Rogers sends back food to the rest of his men and talks of a utopia he will build in the wilderness on Lake George. The rest of the story describes Robert Rogers's marriage to Elizabeth, Langdon's going to London to paint and his meeting with Ann Potter, and Rogers's plans to discover the Northwest Passage. Ann travels as Elizabeth's servant and Langdon is sent to search out the possible routes to the great "River Oregon." Ann and Langdon marry and are living a happy, productive life in London when they hear talk about "those louts" who have declared America a free and independent nation. Rogers and his Rangers have joined with Lord Howe to fight against New England troops. Langdon and Ann know that their place is with the rebels and return home.

R

Nora Roberts

In *From This Day* (1983), B.J. Clark, twenty-four, is the youthful and enterprising manager of the Lakeside Inn in Lakeside, with a view of Lake Champlain. Guests return regularly to the inn because of the old-fashioned atmosphere and the friendly staff. B.J. fears the new owner, hotel-tycoon Taylor Reynolds, who is thirty-two, will spoil her lovely inn by modernizing it. "Domineering and sophisticated," he pronounces the inn perfect for a resort and brings in his svelte decorator, Darla Trainor, and his architect to assess the possibilities. In the process of quarreling about the future of the inn, B.J. and Taylor fall in love: will he decide to move his corporate headquarters to Lakeside? *Cordina's Crown Jewel* (2002) is part of a series about the royal family of Cordina (a bit like Monaco). Camilla, unmarried and the oldest daughter of the family, is the crown jewel of Cordina, but being a princess is not always agreeable: the press will not leave her alone and she has many commitments at bazaars and charities. One day, when the family is on display in Washington, D.C., she rents a car and takes off alone, telephoning periodically to let her parents know that she is all right. She drives for some distance and ends up in the Northeast Kingdom. She is a good driver, but a deer runs across the road forcing her into a ditch. A young man who is passing grudgingly agrees to take her to his house to call the local garage, but the electricity and telephone are out and she has to bunk there for the night. Delaney Caine has dislocated his shoulder and has his arm in a sling. Camilla cooks his meals, tidies up the cabin, types his notes (he is an Oxford-educated paleontologist), and fills old bottles with wildflowers. They are mutually attracted; however, he overhears a telephone conversation she carries on in French and realizes who she is. He is not prepared for Delaney's true identity when he arrives with his parents for the Cordina annual fall ball.

Sherry Roberts

In *Maud's House* (1994), Round Corners near Burlington has been home to generations of Calhouns. Maud Calhoun is a thirty-five-year-old recent widow, a painter who adorns her entire house inside and out, and a waitress at the Round Corners restaurant. Maud drinks a fair amount of Rolling Rock and talks angrily to her dead husband, while being importuned by the sheriff and chief selectman, Obie Dorfman, to paint a mural in the town hall. Obie wishes to be reelected on a platform of bringing leadership and culture to Round Corners. Maud finally paints the mural and realizes she loves her shy, handsome farmer neighbor, "T-Bone." A series of comic portraits are painted of a Small Vermont Town: Wynn Winchester, the knitting beautician; Freda Lee, love-smitten fellow waitress; Ella Snowden, the poet postmistress; Frank Snowden, General Store owner; and Obie, who goes out of his way to help neighbors. Here is Round Corners in a nutshell: "If Round Corners has a dream, it is one of balance, of not letting the government push it one way and the outsiders push it another. The countryside is speckled with New York stockbrokers raising sheep, corporate vice presidents running businesses by modem, and best-selling authors hunched over wood stoves. They come to Vermont to get away. They want out of the rat race and into nature. They want to live off the land in L.L. Bean boots and cashmere sweaters. They seek self-sufficiency…They come to escape and end up trying to turn the town into the one they left. They have all kinds of ideas for streetlights and road maintenance. They grow impatient when voters turn down a bond issue to renovate the seventy-four-year-old school but support an initiative declaring the town 'nuclear free.'" A chapter on town meetings illustrates their purpose, which was "not only to put the town's business in order, but to restore and renew friendships frozen in place by the long winter."

Margaret A. Robinson

The site of the first quarter of *Courting Emma Howe* (1987) is Warwick near St. Johnsbury in 1905, where Emma Howe, twenty-five, "tidy, bright, and buck-toothed," lives with her parents and her two Civil War-widow aunts; her two younger sisters, who live nearby, are both married. She has been corresponding with Arthur Smollett, a homesteader in North Falls, Washington State, who has read and admired one of her published poems. When he proposes marriage to her, she presents the idea to her clan. Her mother, Frances Walker Howe, is against the idea of Emma's marrying a stranger: Frances's family had known her husband's family for three generations before they were married. Emma has been brought up to think that the Howes and Walkers were the best and that "outsiders"— people from "away"— were to be feared and distrusted. Her aunts and sisters assume Arthur cannot be a serious suitor because Emma is not a beauty. Her father, Ezra, who once persecuted her for loving Paul Goddard, a Canadian man ("a Canuck," in Ezra's words), does not want her to leave her familial duties. Emma realizes that in the Howe/Walker household, "thrift and self-denial earned the highest esteem." There are outside pressures on her father as well. He is involved in a creamery union with other Vermont farmers who are forced to compete with Canadian dairy farmers selling their products in Boston. Knowing that she can always support herself through her seamstress work, Emma decides to go to Washington State without her family's approval. The long trip by train exhausts her, and Arthur, delayed, is not at the station to meet her. After a few false starts, however, they do marry and soon it isn't "Arthur's ranch" but "her place."

Rowland E. Robinson

Danvis (based on Ferrisburgh) is west of the Green Mountains in the valley bordering Lake Champlain. This new edition of *Danvis Tales: Selected Stories* (1995), with an introduction by Hayden Carruth, contains selections by David Budbill, who pared down the collection from seven hundred pages to two hundred and fifty. Robinson, a Quaker, had been an engraver, farmer, naturalist, and essayist before writing these stories about "the genius of the folk." The stories take place "fifty years ago" in the pre-Civil War 1830s. The dialect in the dialogue is difficult at first, but the lustrous and elegant prose, full of glorious sights and sounds of nature, is well worth the effort. Sam Lovel, master woodsman, is an engaging hero—tall, wiry, good-humored, and kind to both neighbors and animals. The first selection is from *Uncle Lisha's Shop*. "**In Uncle Lisha's Shop**" describes the store of Lisha Chase, the shoemaker, where locals like Canadian Antoine Bassette, Solon Briggs, Joseph Hill, and Sam Lovel gather in the evenings to smoke their pipes and "swap lies." They all have stories to tell about bears, panthers, and an owl whose noise was taken for a sawmill saw. In "**A Rainy Day in the Shop**," Aunt Jerusha, Lisha's wife, is always there in the next room. Lisha asks Sam to get him some partridges for Thanksgiving dinner. "The sodden dun fields bounded by the grey wall of mountain with its drifting coping of mist—all dun and grey but for one poplar that shone like a pale flame among the ashy trunks and branches of its burned-out companions, and when a gust fanned it, showered down its yellow leaves like sparks from a flaring torch." "**The Turkey Shoot at Hamner's**" evokes the joking and kidding among the men who come to Hamner's hostelry to shoot a turkey for Thanksgiving Dinner. They tease Hamner about the size of the turkeys and the distance the birds are from the shooters. Sam, who has been off in the woods shooting partridges for Lisha, goes to the turkey shoot and, seeing that Joseph Palatiah is having trouble hitting the target, hurries back into the woods and from there shoots Palatiah's turkey for him. In "**Sam Lovel's Thanksgiving**," he leaves his father and stepmother's house in the morning to go foxhunting with his dog, Drive. While in the woods, he thinks he sees fire coming from the Puringtons' house. He hurries down to find Huldah (whom he loves but hasn't told) at home. She makes him lunch, but then he hears his hound and rushes off after the fox. Huldah tells Jerusha her grievance; Jerusha in turn tells Lisha. Huldah is watching Polly, her six-year-old sister in "**Little Sis**," when her mother comes home and Huldah realizes she hasn't seen Polly in over an hour. She goes out looking for her and, when she can't find her, hurries to the various neighboring farms to ask for help. Soon at least twenty-five neighbors have volunteered to look

R

R

for Polly, although Huldah can't find Sam, the best and bravest woodsman of the lot. He is off hunting bees. In **"Sam Lovel's Bee Hunting,"** he hears a cry and soon discovers Polly's berrying basket and then the little girl. He returns Polly to her mother's arms and finds himself in Huldah's arms—at last. In **"In the Shop Again,"** Sam tells the group that he saw a deer track. Most of the deer have been wiped out by men who go out on snowshoes, force the deer into deep snow, and club them to death (this hideous "sport" is called "crusting"). **"Noah Chase's Deer Hunting"** describes Noah's killing with a club a lot of deer, including a pregnant doe. As retribution, he suffers a broken leg, has all kinds of bad luck, and dies of tuberculosis. Sam says he hates partridge snares, too, and always unsets them. "Give all God's creatures a fair chance," he says. The following passage comes at the end of **"In the Sugar Camp:"** "Then they filed out of the sugar camp on their homeward way, while far above them in the black growth of the mountain-side the hoot of an owl and the gasping bark of a fox voiced the solemnity and wildness of the ancient woods." In **"Indians in Danvis,"** Sam tells about coming across some Indians who could talk English, "clever, candid fellows," whose language, he feels, is "perfect for the woods"—"doesn't make any more noise than a little brook running." He persuades the Indians to make him a canoe. There's a rumor in **"The Boy Out West"** that Lisha is going to sell out and move to Wisconsin, where his boy lives. Sam wants to know how Lisha can live without trees. In **"Breaking Up,"** everyone is dismal, as at a funeral, and Lisha wishes his boy hadn't moved away. Their little daughter had died in Danvis. At an auction of their goods, each of their friends buys something to take care of for them. **"The Departure"** sees them off. In **"There they go,"** Sam says they are "just like two old trees torn up by the roots and drifting downstream." When Sam visits the Chases' former house a year later, in **"The Wild Bees' Swarm,"** he can see the "fog of old stories" hanging around the room where they used to gather. The second selection is from *Sam Lovel's Camps*, headed "The Camp on the Slang." In

"Under the Hemlocks," Sam has gone into the trapping business with Antoine. He again shows his soft heart by setting free a wood duck. Here are some of the sounds they hear from their camp near the Little Otter: "Along the winter roadway of ice, now made the most of by teamsters while it lasted, frequent loads of logs and wood or empty returning sleds came and went, crunching in and out of sight and hearing. To the eastward beyond the wide fields, from where the smoke of farmhouse chimneys drifted upward, came sounds of busy life: the 'jingjong' of old-fashioned Boston sleigh bells faring to and fro on the highway, the steady thud of flails in barns, the lowing of cows and bawling of calves, the cackle of hens and the challenge of chanticleer; at noon the shouts of schoolboys and the mellow blasts of the conch-shells sounding for dinner." In **"News from Danvis,"** their friend, Palatiah, comes to visit them with Sam's dog. They feed their friend muskrat meat but pretend it is rabbit. In **"Shooting Pickerel,"** Sam and Antoine catch many fish, which Antoine cleans and fries up for them to eat. Palatiah shoots his three fish rather than catching them. "Any proposition to protect fish and game of any kind, to prescribe any method of taking, to limit the season of killing, would have been thought an attempt to introduce hated Old World laws and customs." In **"Antoine's Redoubtable Victory,"** they regale themselves with their adventures of the day before. The author sums up his feelings for the characters in this delightful book: "I feel myself forgetful of the lapse of fifty years, thinking of my old friends as yet alive, preserving the quaintness of speech, the homely pastimes, the simplicity of dress and manners, and above all the neighborly kindness that belonged to their day and generation untouched by the strife and ambitions and changes of the busy world that chafes and beats around them, and without a desire for a part therein."

James Robison

In *The Illustrator* (1988), Ash, an angry and cynical painter, forty years old and ten years divorced, comforts himself with Pauline, a promiscuous high school girl who calls herself "Q." Living in Boston, Ash becomes a commercial artist, then takes a job with a big sugar company that sends him to Brazil, then fires him. He returns to painting and Boston, where his former wife, Lucia, reenters his life. He is painting in his loft; Lucia arranges for a one-man show for Ash, and then takes him and Q to a cabin in an academic community in Shellington: "O.K., Vermont: a bowl of painted green mountains, a basin filled with flinty lake water. Streamlets the colors of coins sewn through masses of birch, moss, fern clouds, jack pine. Barn-red barns, tumbling hills hemmed by jumbled rock walls. Hot days, chilled nights. Vermont, high summer." Ash remains icy and nihilistic. He is injured in a bike accident and loses a leg. His friends fade away: Q returns to high school and Lucia to Boston. Ash stays in Vermont with his wheelchair and a girl he picks up in a bar, who is recovering from trying to kill herself by drinking drain cleaner.

Judith Rossner

In *Any Minute I Can Split* (1972), Margaret Adams, twenty-nine, pregnant with twins, borrows the motorcycle of her husband, Roger, in Hartsdale, New York, and heads for Boston. There she visits her father briefly, stops to pick up a nineteen-year-old hitchhiker named David, and heads for a commune he knows about in southern Vermont (his stepfather, Mitchell Kastle, owns the property). A man named De Witt is in charge of the farm, which is north of Brattleboro near Putney. He has practiced psychiatry, chiropractic, law, teaching, and other professions without a license around the country before settling in Vermont with his wife, Mira (currently a celibate vegetarian), their two children, Lorna and Baba, and a house full of communards. Carol and Jordan are potters with two children; Paul, an artist, and Starr, a batik maker and seamstress, have a baby; Dolores, a weaver, was once married to De Witt; and Butterscotch is single. Also there are some young people who were forced by the police to leave a commune in Canada. De Witt maintains a schedule for the

many chores: feeding animals, picking and preserving vegetables, storing potatoes in sand, preparing meals and baking bread, building and insulating the barn, and chopping wood. He wants to look into licensing for a free school. Myra delivers her twins the night she arrives with the competent assistance of the serene De Witt. Hannah Berkson, poised and assured, arrives in her own trailer with two poised and assured kids, Daisy and Mario. The farm is a refuge from the communards' previous lives in which they felt pressured to produce. As the winter comes on, they become testy. They change partners (De Witt has slept with all the women). One of them starts an affair with a Putney School student. Margaret realizes that "their life style was both the subject and object of their lives...they didn't just eat and farm organically, but worried over it so much of the time." "They were conscious of their haloes growing shinier with each whole-wheat loaf baked, each tidbit of garbage plowed back into the earth, each Kleenex not used." Jordan is now sleeping with Butterscotch; Dolores has a lesbian lover. In a place like this, with all the coming and going, "you feel the whole thing could split up any minute." Roger suddenly arrives to take a look at his twins. "Making fun of her was something Roger did instead of working," but he can't provoke Margaret anymore: she has changed and matured. When Roger proposes buying the farm from Mitchell, who claims he is broke, Margaret panics at the thought of giving up the Other Life. Roger wants to borrow money from his rich parents in Ardmore; his mother assumes the communards are "dirty sex fiends who take drugs." Roger sells his parents on the scheme: "it is a model organic farm, not a hippie commune." After his parents give them the money, they wonder if they really want to live in a house with all those other people.

Cyrus D. Roys

Captain Jack (1909) romanticizes a situation after the Revolutionary War in 1783 when encroachments from New York continue to keep the Green Mountain Boys in a state of conflict.

The property of Alonzo Chase and Colonel Stetson, who have built two houses on Valley Farm at the base of Waits Mountain, is usurped by the outlaw, Captain Jack, who leads a band of mountain marauders. The Green Mountain Boys evict the villains on behalf of the Stetson and Chase families; Lieutenant Bill escapes. The next year, troops led by Major Martin call on Valley Farm looking for Captain Jack. The major is in love with Ruth Stetson, who is in love with Henry Chase. Henry and Robert Stetson, Ruth's brother, volunteer to go with Martin to seek Captain Jack. Robert is taken captive in the encounter. Henry continues on the quest with Colonel Upton's men and finds Captain Jack and his gang, who are hiding in the rocky recesses of Devil's Den. Captain Jack is captured and all his men killed. Captain Jack is held in the hospital, under the care of Dr. Claudius, but escapes due to the negligence of a man named David Brandt. Lieutenant Bill frames Henry for murder and robbery; Henry and Brandt are both arrested. Henry is cleared and helps Brandt escape because there is something appealing and familiar about him. He is actually Robert, mesmerized by Captain Jack. Robert explains to Henry that he has been in Canada, a captive of Captain Jack's, where he fell in love with Vida, Captain Jack's ward. Vida turns out to be Dr. Claudius's daughter. The novel ends with a double wedding for Robert and Vida and Henry and Ruth, and no one knows positively whether Captain Jack is alive or dead.

Philip Russell

In *Body and Blood: A Novel of Linked Stories* (1998), Matt and Alice each had a dysfunctional childhood, evoked in vivid vignettes. As a young boy, Matt lives in Vermont with his mother, Susan, and her boyfriend, John. A neighbor boy kills the beaver that Matt and his mother have raised as a pet. He goes after the boy with a bow and arrow and keeps on running. He grows up and marries much too young, then divorces, a woman named Leslie. Alice Bourne from the hills of Vermont is haunted by her father's disappearance and by her mother's death in a car accident with her drunken Uncle Louis. She continuously recalls her Uncle Louis's sexual advances and abuse. Back in Vermont from Boston, Matt meets Alice when she is looking for a room to rent near Lemon Fair River and they soon fall in love and marry. Although Alice has a daughter, their marriage is doomed because Matt cannot forget Leslie and Alice cannot rid herself of the "dark woman" she became when Uncle Louis forced himself upon her. Jake, Patti, and baby Brittany are neighbors who flaunt a sauna. Alice is tempted into an adulterous affair with Jake. At one point Mona, another friend, takes them to Karme-Choling, a Buddhist study group three hours up the Connecticut River in a nineteenth-century village "fusing New England and Tibet." Even as their marriage is failing, Matt is building them a house. He bonds with their daughter at the end.

Henry Barnard Safford

Samuel Safford was a real officer with the Green Mountain Boys; his younger brother, Joel, an invention of the author's, narrates in *That Bennington Mob* (1935) the events leading up to the Battle of Bennington in 1777. In 1762, Samuel Safford comes with his mother and brothers to Bennington in the New Hampshire Grants, erects a stockade against the Abenaki, and five years later is building a mill. Indians capture Joel and four other white men. Forced to watch as his friends are tortured and killed, Joel develops a deep hatred of Indians. They take him over the Green Mountains past Winooskie-Took ("onion land") and northward to an Algonquin village. He meets another captive, Ruth Tamblyn, and they escape to Memphremagog and walk three hundred miles to the Connecticut River, where they come upon Ethan and Ira Allen's campsite. Ruth goes home to Albany; Joel in Bennington is swept up in the plans at Fay's Catamount Tavern to oppose the Yorkers. The Green Mountain Boys are formed, "that Bennington mob" to a scornful Governor Tyron. The colonials move from opposing the impingement of a colonial governor to resisting the King's authority. In 1773, Joel is sent to Albany as a scout to discover whether the British plan to destroy the Green Mountain Boys. Invited to a party at Colonel Schuyler's mansion, he recognizes the belle of the ball as Ruth Tamblyn and comes to blows with Lucius Corning, who is courting her. Joel calls on Ruth at her house and is spurned by her Tory father, Squire Thomas Tamblyn. John Brown from Massachusetts comes to Bennington to ask the Green Mountain Boys' help in recruiting Indians to the American cause. Joel refuses to negotiate with Indians, but agrees to go independently to Montreal. Traveling through Westminster at the time of the massacre, Joel hurriedly returns to Bennington to summon the Green Mountain Boys. Brown sends Joel to Boston to warn Samuel Adams against trusting the Indians, especially St. Luc La Corne. Joel participates in the capture of Fort Ticonderoga, is made a first-class scout, and is assigned a pass from the Continental Congress to escort some people to Canada, one of whom is the infamous La Corne—Lucius Corning. Joel heads for Isle La Motte to warn Ruth and her father, whom he takes to safety at Crown Point. Joel accompanies Ethan Allen in his quest to capture Montreal with less than eighty men. The Americans are taken prisoner and sent, in horrifying conditions, on a transport ship to England. The men all contract lice and scurvy. Allen tries to keep up their spirits with songs and stories and, when they arrive in Falmouth, he marches at their head to Pendennis Castle. Joel is finally sent home on the *Mercury* and released in New York. The Americans have retreated from Canada and, under General Benedict Arnold, are building boats to hold back the British fleet. Joel heads to Crown Point and engages in the Battle of Valcour Island, which results technically in a British win but cripples their fleet and sends them back to Canada. The Green Mountain Boys have one more fight ahead at the Battle of Bennington against three thousand German mercenaries and St. Luc La Corne with five hundred

Indians. Seth Warner and Samuel Safford are marching once again with the Green Mountain Boys. At Hubbardton, under fierce attack, Joel watches his friends and neighbors "wilt in windrows, like the tall hay in the meadows before the scythe." The gallant band of farmers and woodsmen wins the day at Bennington, and Ruth and Joel can return home.

Ajay Sahgal

Pool (1994) showcases Emery Roberts, a famous movie star who, with only a few weeks left of shooting a forty-million-dollar production in Hollywood called *Sun City*, hurries off to Suzanna between Dorset and Bennington. He is staying with Jeremiah and Anne Factor, the children of Monty Factor, the producer of Emery's film. "Why Vermont?" someone asks. "It's as far from L.A. as Emery could get and still know people." Danny, who carries his camcorder with him, accompanies Emery. Also at the house are Louis, an agent, and Nathan, a screenwriter, who is digging a pool with his bare hands. He won't swim in nearby Turtle Lake because of the biting turtles. The locals are not pleased to have this group as neighbors: "I don't think they like the fact that we took over," says Louis. The house had not been lived in for fifty years before Jeremiah bought it. Word leaks out of Emery's whereabouts and reporters start calling; an article about him runs in *The Suzanna Star*. The group is constantly drunk and stoned. At one point Danny goes out for food: "No one delivers in this burg. This is *not* civilization." They celebrate the town of Suzanna's two hundredth anniversary. Monty Factor himself arrives with Danielle, Emery's agent. They cannot persuade the vacuous and passive Emery to return to the set. Monty goes back to Hollywood and returns with the entire cast and crew—two hundred people—to finish the remaining twenty pages of script. One morning before shooting Emery has already taken six Valium. The set people build a Spanish adobe hacienda on the lake. By the end of shooting, Monty has offered Emery a three-picture, multi-million-dollar deal. Turtles have found their way into Nathan's pool.

Anna C. Salter

Dr. Michael Stone, the serial heroine of *Shiny Water, Fault Lines, White Lies,* and *Prison Blues,* is a forensic psychologist living alone in an A-frame house in the woods, fifteen minutes from Jefferson University near Middlebury. She is blonde, smart, sassy, frequently quotes Wallace Stevens, and has a gift for seeing into the minds of psychopaths. In *Shiny Water* (1996), Michael reveals a bit about "Mama," her no-nonsense mother in North Carolina, and Michael's life before Vermont. She was married to a man named Doug, a university teacher; their little girl, Jordan, died of Sudden Infant Death Syndrome at three months. Michael simplified her life by moving to Vermont and stripping her possessions to two hundred and fifty items. There is a stream by her house—"I always did love shiny water." She works several days a week at Jefferson University Hospital, a tertiary care institution, and carries on a private practice in an old Victorian house she used to share with her best friend, Carlotta, a prosecutor. Michael is called in on a case of child abuse. Sharon (who has that "Vermont-back-to-earth-style") and Nathan Southwick, a glamorous surgeon, have two children, Andrew, six, and Adrienne, three. The Southwicks are getting a divorce, and Andrew has accused their father of abusing him and his little sister. After interviewing the children and their mother, Michael testifies in the custody trial that she believes the children's accusations. Arthur Morrison, a "sweet and conscientious" retired lawyer who works as a guardian ad litem in the court system, assists Michael. Sharon is given custody of the children, the children are murdered in their beds, and their mother is arrested for their murder. A page of a book belonging to Michael (Toni Morrison's *Beloved*) turns up. Michael realizes that someone has access to her house and to her sessions with her private patients, whose psychological states are all deteriorating. She goes to the local prison to interview a sex offender, Alex B. Willy, to ascertain what kind of person the perpetrator might be. She meets a friend at the basketball court who turns out to be the killer. The person attacks and

almost strangles her to death before Adam Bowman, her friend the police chief, rescues her. Still suffering post-traumatic stress from that incident, she begins an affair with Adam.

In *Fault Lines* (1998), Michael sees a new patient, Camille, who is suffering flashbacks from a ferocious attack upon her. She comes to Michael's office with Jeeter, a fierce-looking rottweiler that Camille introduces as her "seizure dog." Michael learns from her friend, Carlotta, that Alex B. Willy is out of jail awaiting a new trial, because the reliability and suggestibility of the testimony of the children whom he molested is in question. Michael interviewed and taped him in jail with his permission and is now in a dangerous position. When Adam comes over to warn her and hurts her feelings by referring to the death of her daughter, she throws him out. Camille turns up in bad shape at the hospital, which refuses to admit her with her dog. Michael hires a private investigator, but his debugging equipment turns up nothing. She deals with other cases—a college rape, a mother's problem with a child—but becomes more and more concerned about Camille, because Camille's flashbacks to her five-year-old abduction and torture are getting worse; Michael can relate to them because of her own post-traumatic stress. Adam assigns a policeman to Camille's house, yet she claims that the perpetrator has found his way inside. Michael enters the house and discovers a tape: the killer has been terrorizing the woman, repeating details of her ordeal that only Michael knows. Michael discovers the way he has been eavesdropping on her therapy sessions and, accompanied by Jeeter, confronts the killer in his hiding place. He is about to seize and torture Michael when Jeeter attacks him. Since Camille is convinced that this person is the one who tortured and raped her, Michael does not interfere to try to save him. She and Adam make up.

In *White Lies* (2000), anesthesiologist Reginald Larsen, on the verge of a major discovery in his field, comes to Michael for an evaluation because he has been suspended from Boston Harbor View Hospital, charged with sexual misconduct. Michael knew his father, a late beloved professor of pediatrics at Jefferson University, and has met his mother. Michael orders him to write his "sexual autobiography," listing anything "inappropriate or deviant." Michael's friend, psychiatrist Marv Gliesen, seeks her help with a patient, Jody Carlson, twenty-seven, who has recovered memories of sexual abuse by her father and wants to confront him. Michael warns Marv of the dangers of a lawsuit from falsely accused parents but agrees to sit in on the meeting at which Jody's father is dominant and aggressive and her mother, weak and passive. Meanwhile, a polygraph shows Larsen is lying about his behavior; Michael must recommend against his practicing medicine. She meets his former lover, Zania, a drug-dependent nurse who witnessed his rape of a comatose patient but fears telling the truth. When Michael is almost killed by a lethal dose of anesthetic, she believes Larsen to be her attacker, but she is wrong: the killer is someone else. Adam is still in Michael's life, but she cannot commit to a full-time relationship. Since she is over forty, she decides to stop taking birth-control pills.

In **Prison Blues** (2002), Michael is eight months pregnant with Adam's baby. She lives alone and is trying to adjust to the idea of Adam's moving in with her. She continues to work at Jefferson University Hospital and conducts group therapy at Nelson's Point Correctional Center, about thirty minutes away. Gary Raines, the warden at Nelson's Point, asks her to take the place of a woman therapist, Eileen Steelwater, whose job has been terminated for having sex with an inmate. Michael has met the inmates in her group only a few times before a new inmate, Clarence, is murdered. There seems to be no weapon and no means, and the warden is under great pressure by the press and the legislature. Then the social worker at the facility, Stacy James, is badly beaten and almost killed. This is a further blow for the warden, who, Michael learns, has serious personal problems: his daughter, Aspasia, eleven, is a diabetic who is not taking care of herself. Gary and Susan, his wife, at their wits' end, ask Michael to talk to her. Michael learns from Eileen that Jim Walker, one

of the members of her group, has been obsessing about Michael. Eileen is in love with Jim and believes he is innocent; Michael knows him to be a psychopath. She believes there is something sinister about the print shop in the prison. Without checking with anyone, she visits a print shop in Berlin, New Hampshire, which has been shipping parts to the prison. The killer comes to her house at night, lays a stranglehold on her, and slices her belly. She and the baby are not hurt, but she is seriously frightened. She realizes that he will come after Gary next, so she goes to his house to warn him. She is too late: the killer is already on the property, so she, Susan, and Aspasia devise a way to prevent Gary's entering the driveway. After Gary manages to kill the villain, they face the problem of the troublesome inmates. Michael figures out a plan. The case ends successfully, but Adam takes Michael into hiding so that she can spend her last weeks of pregnancy out of harm's way. Some of Michael's refreshing insights about Vermont: "The promise of a Vermont summer was definitely in the air, like the undercurrent running through children right before Christmas. Heaven, after all, was a moveable feast and every summer it set up a brief camp in Vermont." "It's those damned Puritans, I thought, as we moved from rocks to dairy farms. Even the silos looked forbidding against the sky." "Dodging deer on the highway was such an essential skill in Vermont; they really ought to put it on the driving test."

Edwin Webster Sanborn

People at Pisgah (1892) concerns the Reverend Dr. Theodore Van Nuynthlee, who lives in Manhattan and seeks a refuge in which to prepare a speech for an Interdenominational Ecumenical Conference in Saratoga. Patience Winthrop of Boston, who is currently in New York, has set her cap for the doctor, who, in turn, is in love with a comely widow named Mrs. Suydam. A friend recommends North Pisgah in northern Vermont, to which he entrains and takes a room in the household of Deacon Meiggs, where he is unable to rest or find any leisure in which to write his speech. He is carrying the famous and valuable Cortwright diamond brooch, placed in his possession until Mrs. Cortwright returns from a trip. Bathing in the pond one day, he hears people coming and hides behind a tree. One of them is Mrs. Suydam, who is also summering in North Pisgah. She passes on and he is about to retrieve his possessions when a cow ambles up and begins to eat the doctor's clothes, including the diamond brooch. The chain of events that follows includes butchering the wrong cow to find the brooch and buying another cow, before learning that a little boy had found the brooch. The boy reveals that he has swapped the brooch for something belonging to Sammy Gookin. Found "raking after" the hay, Gookin, in turn, has lent the brooch to his sister, Lorissa, who is wearing it at the circus the next day. The doctor makes his way to the circus in Dohan Mills. En route, they meet with a hopeless tangle: Elder Bawker's wagon has blocked the road. (Elder Bawker has a difficult time walking and often takes the whole of the church service to make it to his pew. Once he fell from his pew, causing "a long and demoralizing delay in the devotional exercises.") "News of the obstruction, and of progress toward its removal, was passed up the line from time to time like water at a fire, to cool the fevered anxiety of the late comers." The doctor finds Lorissa, but not before he is mistaken for the proprietor of the circus and then for a clown, as he tries to snatch his hat from under the hooves of the circus animals. It is at this moment that he looks up and meets the "stony gaze" of Mrs. Suydam. Gentle vignettes illustrate the people at Pisgah, a colorful and voluble group, not taciturn as the stereotype suggests. Bill Blood talks nonstop except when he is fiddling with his pipe or expectorating. His mother carries on her style of conversation, which consists of non sequiturs like, "There's nothing like yarrer tea for the liver" and "Pie is good, but you must be keerful about eating it mor'n three times a day." Grandfather ("Gappy") Meiggs is also quite a conversationalist. "Throughout the doctor's stay in the house, it [Gappy's monologue] has been an unbroken accompaniment to his literary labors." Frightful doings—noises of all kinds—throughout the night keep the doctor awake. In delight-

fully ornate prose, this story burlesques not the people at Pisgah but the doctor himself. Finding Pisgah "fertile in mishaps," the doctor is self-important and narrow-minded, and, on the train going to Saratoga, tries to avoid any passengers of "bucolic aspect." He is late for his conference in Saratoga and, after his speech, falls into a chair in an anteroom. There he discovers that kind Mrs. Meiggs has packed him a lunch with some cold tea in an old whiskey flask of Gappy's. He is asleep when the ladies of the Women's Christian Temperance Union find him obviously—to them—drunk. Patience, leading the pack, decides this is just the sort of information she can filter to Mrs. Suydam, thus making the doctor safe for Patience.

Herbert Ravenel Sass

"Affair at St. Albans" (1948) casts light on a little-known historical event. In 1864, the Confederate Cause is flagging: Sherman has taken Atlanta, Sheridan is sweeping through the Shenandoah Valley, and the Confederate Treasury is diminished. In the town of St. Albans, near the Canadian border, strangers begin arriving in twos or threes; they describe themselves as members of a Canadian sporting club assembling for a fishing trip on Lake Champlain. If they are noticed, at the railroad station or one of the three hotels, it is because some are carrying odd-looking leather valises hanging by straps from their shoulders. Their leader, Lieutenant Bennett Young of the Confederate Army, had ridden with Morgan's troopers into Ohio; many were captured, but he slipped across the line into Canada and is now in charge of a Confederate Army of twenty men, escaped prisoners like himself. Their mission— to invade the most "rock-ribbed Yankee" state in the Union—is to create a diversion, a panic about an invasion from the north. Young was advised by the Confederate Commission in Canada to have his men wear haversacks, their regular field equipment, so they wouldn't be considered spies. They also all register in the hotels under their own names. The priest in the hotel room next to Young is actually a woman secret agent, sent ahead by Senator Clay of the

Confederate Commission to give him advance information. She advises Young to act at once. Donning their gray Confederate uniforms, the men swing into action: one squad commandeers horses, a second takes on the banks, a third herds citizens onto the town green. Word of the invasion goes out on the telegraph: Secretary of War Stanton hears that Confederates have invaded Vermont. By chance, Captain George Conger, First Vermont Cavalry, on leave from the front in Virginia, rides into town, escapes the raiders, and begins to assemble the opposition. "Time to go!" shouts Confederate Tom Collins, "Here come Ethan Allen and his Green Mountain Boys!" The Vermont men, "granite-jawed" and angry, chase the raiders, who escape to Canada carrying two hundred thousand dollars for the Confederate Treasury in Richmond. Young's men are all safe, but the Canadian Government arrests and brings him to trial. Papers are brought from the South (some say by a woman) proving that the Confederate force was authorized and just in time to save him from execution.

Susan Fromberg Schaeffer

Time in its Flight (1978) is a family saga, starting in the early nineteenth century, documenting life, death, and continuity. Edna Dickinson, born in 1829, lives in Boston with her very proper mother, Edith, and father, Edmund, who commits suicide. Edith's best friend, Teniel Richardson, resides in Williamsville with her widower brother, Dr. John Ashbel Steele, a country doctor whom Edna marries when she is not yet seventeen. She is a good horseback rider and is able to accompany her husband on his difficult rounds, thus learning basic nursing. Kind and helpful to a man whose wife dies of puerperal fever, her actions are known by everyone the next day: "News travels faster than lightning here." They have five children: Martin, Ella, Anna, Letitia, and John. Dr. Steele undergoes the travails and strenuous rounds of a country doctor and a family man. "Every family [he] knew had a dead child in it." His family survives two epidemics—diphtheria and yellow fever. Dr. Steele's hobby is the daguerreotype. Noah

Webster comes to preach at the Old Stone Church. *The Reformer* is their newspaper. One of Edna's best friends is Alice Moffatt, the wife of a farmer, Howard. A voice of Vermont, she is full of good advice about life: "Get ready for the storm. Bank up your house." "Don't torture yourself. All you did was embroider the wrong fabric." Martin marries Minnie Moffatt; Ella marries Minnie's brother, William, who goes to medical school with the help of the Steele family. The young Moffatt and Steele couples return from Boston in 1869; both men are doctors. A young minister, Matthew Hewitt, asks Anna to marry him. A new generation begins. After losing one baby, Ella has four children over the next eight years. Dr. Steele becomes interested in—and testifies at—the famous Florence Gilman trial, which involved a fifteen-year-old girl, three months' pregnant, whose boyfriend, Griffin, is charged with her murder. Anna has been living with her husband, Matthew, in New Bedford. When he and their daughter, little Millie, die of diphtheria, she comes home, mad with grief, to Williamsville. She has religious revelations and finally kills herself by lying down in the snow and going to sleep. Dr. Steele contracts pneumonia and is dying, but hangs onto life by a thread for Edna's sake. The children beg her to let him go. He dies after she promises she will be all right. She leaves home to see her mother in Boston, but stops first at the Massachusetts Infirmary to have a lump taken from her left breast. She tells only her son-in-law, Richard, who is married to her estranged daughter, Letitia.

In *The Madness of a Seduced Woman* (1983), Agnes Dempster, the narrator, recounts the story of her life in a letter to someone named Margaret, sent from Highbury Asylum for the Insane. Agnes's parents and grandparents were farmers. Eurydice Druitt, her grandmother, married Edward Saltonstall, a wealthy man in North Chittenden with four hundred acres, two hundred of them cultivated, a herd of Holstein cows, ten goats, chickens, vegetable gardens, and a house with ten bedrooms. They had a number of children, only one of whom, Helen, survived. Helen moved to Montpelier to Bea Brown's boarding house to escape the life her mother led, trapped on a farm, and there she met Amon Dempster, a lawyer, who had decided to become a farmer. He bought Agnes's grandmother's property (Eurydice saves fifty acres for a log cabin for herself), and he and Helen married in 1869. They, too, had many babies, but only one, Agnes, born in 1880, survives. Agnes describes her childhood, especially the fearsome death by scalding of her sister, Majella, before Agnes's birth, and her psychological development during which her mother appears to hate her. When she is sixteen, Agnes goes to Montpelier to live in Iris Trowbridge's boarding house and work for her living (although when twenty-one she will inherit quite a bit of money from her grandmother). She makes friends at the boarding house with Polly Southcote and with two young stone-carvers in Barre, Frank Holt and Charlie Mondell. Agnes works as a seamstress in the house of Mrs. James. Agnes begins "walking out" with Charlie, but it is soon to clear to everyone that she is attracted to Frank. She has heard at work that Frank often goes to church with a young woman named Jane Holt (no relation), but Agnes throws herself at Frank and into his bed: she is his seducer. When she becomes pregnant, Frank finds—and pays for—a doctor to perform an abortion. She is very sick from this traumatic event and goes home to visit her father (her mother has since died), taking Frank, whom she introduces as her fiancé. Agnes is possessive and obsessive about Frank, who finally tires of her, breaks off their relationship, and becomes engaged to Jane. Agnes seeks out Jane and shoots her, then herself. Jane dies, but Agnes survives an operation to remove the bullet from her brain and is soon well enough to stand trial for murder. The prosecutor, Frederick Parsons, wants the best defense attorney in town to give Agnes every opportunity because he believes she will be hanged. There were three or four witnesses to the shooting. Parsons persuades Charles Kingsley to take the case, who decides to offer a plea of insanity because Agnes has a history of mental illness in her family. Dr. Paley Train, from Highbury, questions her and becomes the main

expert witness at the trial, which takes place in Washington County, testifying that she suffers from the "madness of a seduced woman." The audience becomes first obsessed with and then sympathetic to Agnes's cause. The trial is masterfully depicted and the aftermath gripping.

The Golden Rope (1996) is also about obsession, this time the preoccupation of Doris Meek with her twin sister, Florence, who disappeared twenty years earlier and whose body was never found. The action takes place in New York, London, Provence, and Vermont, but it is to the sisters' lives in Peru that the narrative reverts, both in contemporary references and in flashbacks. Florence and Doris had a difficult relationship, both dependent and contentious. Their mother, who could not tell the sisters apart, thought they had one soul. Doris was a painter first but believes Florence stole her painting from her. Florence, a successful painter, married Jack Pine, a famous playwright, and lived in Goult, Provence; Doris, a fabricator of expensive jewelry, married John James, a psychoanalyst. They are all very rich. When Florence first disappears, it is apparent from newspaper accounts that she told everyone she was an orphan. This dismays Doris so much she is forced into a mental hospital. Many years later, determined to look into Florence's disappearance, she gets in touch with a reporter named Dennis Cage, who grew up in Athens, Vermont, and has written extensively on the Meek sisters, interviewing a family friend, Dr. Steiner, in Peru. Doris meets Dennis in London, who tells her a great deal about his research into Florence's work, especially her famous painting "The Golden Rope," and the other so-called "White Paintings," which remind Dennis of Vermont. While in London, Doris receives calls from and finally meets a young man named Antonio Mercado, who introduces himself as her son (he means he is Florence's son). Doris travels to Provence to meet Jack Pine, who does not know of her existence but is thrown into upheaval, because she looks exactly like Florence. It is inevitable that they have an affair, just as it is inevitable that Doris will take Antonio to Vermont with her. Doris thinks about Peru and the old Vermont houses, "porches loaded down and sagging, the yards overflowing with wrecked cars, mattress springs that once had looked so promising as trellises for morning glories, old headless dressmakers' forms, some still wearing their wire hoop skirts, rotten wicker rockers, rockers made of willow wood left out so long they'd taken root and turned back into trees, houses that announced, We've kept everything we ever had, and this is what it's like." When Doris visited Florence in Provence (Jack was away): "On her arms and hands were smudges of blue paint, a grayish blue, the color of the skies over our house in Peru before the snow came." She remembers "Peru itself, and the countryside, and the snow in winter and the blazing leaves in the fall and the muddy roads in spring and, in the summer, the river running over its speckled stones, and the gold light through the trees splashing the high grass waving in the soft winds, and the tasseled rows of corn, and the raccoons who picked up the chain-link mat in front of the door and dropped it down, and the porcupine hanging upside down from the aspen boughs." Hints surface that Florence is alive. Doris misses her sister and her childhood in Peru. She remembers autumn leaves "beginning to burn behind the houses as the mists clear and the sun rises" and winter, "with the trees standing encased in ice, and when the light hits them, the glass trees sparkle and shine against the pale-blue sky."

Deborah Schupack

The Boy on the Bus (2003) is about a dysfunctional family living in a big white farmhouse with charcoal shutters and an old vertical-board barn in Birchwood in central Vermont. Meg Landry and Jeff Carroll, who have never married, have two children, thirteen-year-old Katie, and eight-year-old Charlie ("Chappy"). They came to Vermont seven years earlier to raise the children "free from commerce and competition." Jeff, an architect, finds jobs farther and farther away; he now lives in Montreal and is seldom home. Katie, thinking her mother spends all of her time and attention on Charlie, who has a serious asthma condition, has succeeded in being sent away to boarding school, Green Mountain Academy, where she concentrates on being popular. Meg, a painter manqué, considers herself a bad mother because "she does not deserve this child." She thinks she is a bad daughter because she wasn't actually in the room when her father died after Meg cared for him for five years. She believes herself a failure because she is not a famous painter. She feels unrequited because she dreams about the school bus-driver, Sandy Tadaveski. One afternoon when the school bus stops at her driveway, her son doesn't climb off as is his wont. Meg boards the bus to find a sole boy, seated at the very back, who, while he looks like her son, isn't quite. He is much more assertive, eats better, and has no asthma. Is he the son she wishes she had? Certainly Katie, who is summoned home, likes him better. There are hints that Sandy has done away with the original Charlie, but that cannot be right. Who is he?

Karl Schwenke

The narrator of *In a Pig's Eye* (1985) is a newcomer ("downcountry") to Vermont, who settled in Newbury near Chelsea in a quest to understand "the rural idiom and myself." He arrives regarding Vermonters as "insensitive rustics" but soon changes his mind. Vermonters, he learns, have a "rock-hard sense of proportion and a sense of humor." The experiences he describes center around pigs. For example, he inappropriately tries to sell for slaughter pigs that the owner's children have already named. A Bicentennial Committee meeting, organized for tourists in the way it would have been held in 1776, entertains nominations for Hog Reeve (town negotiator in pig-related matters). Schwenke wins because the group votes not to allow the other nominee, a woman, to run. A parson asks the author's help writing letters to the Personals column in *The New York Review of Books* (which he never sends). The pigs enter the MacIndoes' garden and start eating the flowers alphabetically. Numerous permutations of the pig theme embroider the prose: "independent as a hog on ice," "hog heaven," "if pigs could fly," "room at the trough," "eating too high on the hog," "to pig out," and "in a pig's eye." Here is the author's epiphany: "It was, I decided, good to be here in this place, to be beginning again, to be alive. For whatever reason we are put here to suffer or to savor, this is *it*, and we need to prize it, nourish it, pig out on it, for unlike spring, it will not come round again. This place, right here and now, is hog heaven, and those who believe will sprout wings and fly."

Lucy Jameson Scott

The townsfolk of Gilead in *The Gilead Guards* (1893) gather somberly in the year 1862 to hear Elder Putnam preach Gilead's first wartime sermon. The congregation is divided: some fervently believe the preacher's burden that slavery is the special sin of the nation; others, copperheads, just as fervently disagree. Few men have gone to war from Gilead, but on this day many, including handsome, solid Abram Steele (who has read *Uncle Tom's Cabin*), are inspired to enlist. Ruby Fletcher, the Squire's only daughter, who enjoys an "understanding" with Abram, believes he should go ("The rough beard of war is arousing many slumbering princesses"), though she knows that some brave young men will never come back; Abram's little brother, Benjie, wishes he were old enough to go, too. Abram has been trying to pay off the mortgage on the Steele farm and to make needed improvements. One volunteer is Joe Armstrong, whose young wife, Victoria, new mother of Nell, begs him not to enlist. Abram's sister, Esther, who loves intelligent, polite Don Stanley (resembling the men she has read about in novels), tenderly promises she will visit his mother regularly. Esther's mother thinks Don is "too elegant" compared to country-bred young men. When work is "done up," the Steele farmhouse is ready for a quiet afternoon. As Mrs. Steele is braiding rags to be coiled and sewed "round and round" into a rug, Reverend G. Harmon Phelps and his wife come to call. He believes the war is a mistake: would Elder Putnam love his "colored brother" as well if he were a little nearer? Mr. Steele, who has helped slaves escape through the Underground Railroad, flushes red with anger. In a letter addressed to his

father (who has the same name), Abram learns that his brother Austin's employers in Boston accused him of stealing one thousand dollars. Instead of enlisting, Abram will have to raise the money to repay the firm without letting anyone know. Ruby cannot understand his not enlisting and refuses to see him; brother Benjie is ashamed of him. The only person to whom he can turn is the hired man, lean, wiry, shrewd, good-natured Hiel Saunders, who lends him the money (he had saved up for a speculation scheme) and swears not to tell anyone. Gilead's paper, the *Standard*, takes for its motto: "No compromise with slavery." Company F is known as the "Gilead Guards," every young man a member except Abram. All his friends turn against him except Don Stanley and Joe Armstrong. Blue uniforms arrive for the new recruits; Judge Plumley and a large crowd see the men off at the station. This moment is the apex of Abram's loneliness and suffering, but he has a strong, well-balanced character and his integrity and high sense of duty inform him that he is saving the family honor by remaining silent. No one knows the way he is suffering (Ruby returns his letter), except Esther, who suspects something is wrong. Austin writes his parents that he has enlisted and is in Virginia. Abram continues to manage the farm. In 1863, the Emancipation Proclamation is issued. The first to enlist, Captain Charlie Plumley, is the first fatality; Abram almost envies his martyrdom. Esther starts work as a schoolteacher. The county is full of "strange contradictions:" while men are dying in hospitals, in rural districts of the North "pleasure-seekers are invading" and speculation is rife. The loyal women of Gilead organize a Soldier's Aid Society to send boxes to their "boys." They receive a letter from Marian Hargit, a slave who is raising a subscription for the "colard solgers," and are impressed by her appeal. Abram is still trying to pay off his debt. A terrible battle occurs at Cold Harbor and many of their boys, including Don, are killed. Hiel breaks the news to Esther, who "belonged to a race of strong-nerved men and women, and the habit of self-control and self-repression was as forceful within her as life itself. To conceal her pain—this was her first thought." When Mrs. Stanley hears of her son's death, she has a heart attack and dies. "But Gilead had not yet paid her full share of the national debt:" Joe is reported killed; Captain Bartlett, John Henry Hickey, and Victoria's brother, Chester, are taken prisoner. Fortunately, Joe is not dead but at the Andersonville Confederate prison. Southern raiders clean out the St. Albans banks; Benjie and Abram guard the roads. The Steeles mourn over their son, Austin, as though he were a hero and a saint; suddenly he reappears, having lost one arm, and explains to Abram that he was unjustly accused of stealing the money. When Ruby learns the truth, she is ashamed and apologizes to Abram. They marry and inherit the Fletcher estate; Abram becomes a writer. Esther never marries but works to help the colored women of the South.

The four stories with Vermont settings in *Compound Interest and other Stories* (1896) embrace the theme of neighborliness, assisting friend and stranger alike and thereby increasing the benefits accruing to all parties. In **"Judson's Tramp,"** young Judson Parsons is sugaring when he finds a tramp in the sugarhouse near Brockway. Ralph Whitney, a nice-looking young man, is in a scrape: drinking and playing cards, he fell into a quarrel with his best friend and shot (but didn't kill) him. Judson shares his sandwiches and coffee with Ralph and talks a bit about his life working for his Uncle Seth and his hope to better himself one day. Judson receives a gratifying letter from his "tramp," saying that Judson has helped him on a better path and sending him money for his education fund. In **"Polly Moulton's Wild Geese,"** the whole family, which is in straitened circumstances, is going to church in Dumstead save little Polly, who stays home because she doesn't have proper shoes. A flock of wild geese flies over Roundtop Mountain and settles in her father's barnyard. She has a good Puritan ancestry, of whose "courage and coolness in emergencies" she has often heard, but she is quite frightened of the large birds. She puts on her brother's boots, fetches a whip, and manages to herd all the geese into the big barn. Polly's father sells the geese for money to buy winter cloaks for Polly and her

sister, Phebe. In **"How Three Girls Helped,"** some of the boys in Byville are drinking and getting into trouble. To give them something constructive to do, young Willie Bailey wants to start a public library with a reading room and free lectures. Temperance is not a popular topic among the aristocrats ("the seal-skins") of the town, and Willie wonders how to raise a subscription for the cause. He calls on singer Christine Thorpe to ask her to sing for his project's first entertainment. Her father disapproves, but Christine not only agrees to help but also offers to ask Jennie Stacy (an aristocrat) to recite. Jennie is snobbish and uninterested in the cause, but Christine explains about "lending a hand" to help others, and Mildred Ross, a young lady visiting with Jennie, volunteers her help in selling tickets. The evening is a great success: once the aristocrats discover who the other patrons are, each stands up and pledges subscriptions, too. In **"The Stronger Tie: A Story of '63,"** the desperate war situation in the country has reached even the "sleepy little towns along the border of northern Vermont" like Glover Hills District, set in a charming valley sheltered by the Green Mountains. Seventeen-year-old Elsie Wyman, a teacher, is already involved: her brother, Will, is at Vicksburg; Joe Royce, the brother of the man she loves, is also away at war. Crippled John Royce cannot help on the farm or go to war, but is firmly patriotic. When she enters her schoolhouse, Elsie is frightened because she sees a man's boot rising into the chimney and is certain it belongs to a deserter. Receiving word from Isr'el Hopkins that John is dying, she hurries to his side. John had dragged himself to the schoolhouse to warn his brother, Joe, who is the deserter whom Elsie saw. When Joe hears that John died from his effort to help his brother, this sacrifice persuades Joe to reenlist.

Catharine Maria Sedgwick

In **"A Reminiscence of Federalism"** (1835), the village of Carrington in 1798 (Vermont is still referred to as "the *new* state") is divided both physically and ideologically. The main street traverses a hill and a plain: the democrats occupy the hill and the federalists, the vale. Nine-year-old Fanny Atwood lives happily with her devoted clergyman father, Dr. Atwood, an aristocratic gentleman and devout federalist. Dr. Atwood was forced to move to Vermont from Connecticut, where he scandalized his congregation by remarrying, after his wife's death, a young and very pretty girl instead of one of the "quite mature candidates." Squire Silas Hayford, a rich man and an equally fervent democrat, has not been so fortunate in his domestic life: daughter Mary married a southerner (a "slave driver," according to the squire) named Gordon and was disinherited by her father. After a tragic life, in which she was widowed and reduced to penury, she is brought home to the squire's home with her son, Randolph, thirteen. On her deathbed, her father promises to raise Randolph providing he takes the Hayford name; the boy refuses but his mother insists. Randolph is a paragon of respectfulness, generosity, and intelligence; he and Fanny become favorite playmates. Eight years pass, and their friendship blossoms into love. Their guardians, however, refuse to sanction their children's marriage because of their longstanding political enmity. The weekly journal in Carrington, a democratic organ, begins to carry articles by a writer calling himself "Hamden." They are articulate and lauded. When the old squire discovers that Randolph is "Hamden," he is delirious with pride. He proposes a deal: if Randolph will break the tie in the coming election by voting for the democratic candidate, his grandfather will buy him a law library and allow him to marry Fanny Atwood. Knowing that the democratic candidate is corrupt and undeserving, Randolph discusses his dilemma with Fanny: she agrees that he must vote his conscience and not be blackmailed by his grandfather. He votes for the republican candidate, but, surprisingly, the democrat wins anyway by one vote. Squire Hayford celebrates so obstreperously that he has a stroke and dies; Randolph, his sole heir, gives away his inheritance to his great-aunt, Martha Hunt, marries Fanny, moves with her to another town, and supports them through his own brains and enterprise. Old Dr. Atwood lives with them until his death.

John Sedgwick

Edward Arnold Rollins, the protagonist in *The Dark House* (2000), is a neurotic survivor of an unhappy childhood, the death by drowning of an infant sister for which he feels responsible, the divorce of his parents, and the disappearance of his favorite cousin, Cornelia Blanchard. On one of his voyeuristic expeditions in Boston, following in his automobile an unknown person and dictating observations into a tape recorder, the threads of his past converge into a series of frightening revelations that culminate at the family farmhouse in Townshend. There, in the town where the family spent their vacations in a "frosty white world," he finds out from his father that the latter seduced his niece, Cornelia, while he was still married. His father then entered into a scheme with realtor Jerry Sloane to appropriate Cornelia's inheritance and to murder Cornelia with Sloane as his accomplice. Edward is freed from his guilt when he realizes that his baby sister, Stephanie, died because his father and Cornelia had been otherwise engaged when they were supposed to be watching the baby. The dénouement is violent and inevitable.

Maggie Shayne

Eighteen years before *Colder Than Ice* (2004) begins, Elizabeth Marcum, a teenager in thrall to cult leader Mordecai Young, father of her baby, was seriously injured when the compound was attacked by agents from the ATF (Bureau of Alcohol, Tobacco, and Firearms). Presumed dead by everyone, including the young agent, Joshua Kendall, who shot her, she survived, entrusted her daughter, Dawn, to a friend, entered the Federal Witness Protection Program, and is hiding out as Beth Slocum in Blackberry. Beth's whereabouts are discovered by the psychopathic Mordecai, who moves to the town under an assumed name. Now a private security consultant and widower, Joshua is chosen by the government to protect Beth; she has no idea that Joshua is the agent. Bryan, Joshua's seventeen-year-old, accompanies his father and believes Joshua should tell Beth the truth about his identity. Dawn comes secretly to Blackberry and befriends

Bryan, with whom she determines to find her father, Mordecai, before he can harm Beth. A number of tense situations result in a final clash and satisfying resolution.

Irwin Shaw

One chapter in *The Young Lions* (1948) takes place in Vermont. Noah Ackerman (one of the three central characters whose army life carries them inexorably toward the Black Forest of Germany) falls in love with Hope Plowman and travels to Vermont to ask her father, a Presbyterian elder, for her hand in marriage. Hope has promised to warn her father that Noah is a Jew. The train "rattles along between the drifts and white hills of Vermont." The car is unheated and looks out at the "forbidding scenery." He gets off the train and has "a glimpse of one of those tightly-put-together, unpromising white streets with steeples rising at both ends." Noah, tortured and low in self-esteem, is not surprised when he arrives to press his suit to find that Hope has been unable to break it to her family that he is Jewish. She meant to but "my brother came in, he's over from Rutland with his wife and their children, for the holidays. They started to talk about the war, and my brother, he's an idiot anyway, my brother began to say that there were no Jews fighting in the war and they were making all the money, and my father just sat there nodding. I don't know whether he was agreeing or just getting sleepy." Noah sees himself as unlovable: "no family, no accomplishments, no friends, with a face that must seem harsh and foreign to this man, and a voice that nearly stuttered and was stained with the common accents of bad schools and low company." The father, in his cozy family town in Vermont, has never known any Jews: "A man goes a good deal of his life living more or less automatically. But every once in a while, he has to make a real decision. He has to say to himself, now, what do I really believe, and is it good or is it bad? The last forty-five minutes you've had me doing that, and I'm not fond of you for it. Don't know any Jews, never had any dealings with them. I had to look at you and try to decide whether I thought Jews

were wild, howling heathen, or congenital felons, or whatever." Hope's father invites Noah to Sunday lunch.

Nightwork (1975) begins in Burlington, where the hero, Douglas Grimes, works as a pilot for a private airline and is mildly in love with a decent, dedicated young woman, Pat, who works as a high school history teacher. Outside the big public school where Pat teaches, "There was a peculiar muted hum coming from the big red-brick building with the Latin inscription on the façade and the flag flying above it. The hum of learning, I thought, a small decent music that made me remember my childhood." When Douglas develops a problem with his retina that makes it impossible for him to fly, he decides to leave Vermont. Unmanned by his loss of job as a romantic pilot, he drifts around, gambling in Florida for a while, and then takes a dead-end job as night clerk in a seedy hotel in Manhattan. His life begins, in a sense, when a man is murdered in the hotel and, before calling the police, Douglas finds in his room—and helps himself to—one hundred thousand dollars in hundred-dollar bills. He heads for Europe on an adventure that turns unexpectedly wild and dangerous—and not without romantic interest. When he returns to Burlington at the end, he finds that he has outgrown Pat and leaves town without speaking to her.

Harry Sholk

In *Drumbeats in the Valley* (2004), protagonist Ben Walker, an eighteen-year-old from New Jersey, enters in 1838 the institution founded in 1819 by Captain Alden Partridge, a West Point graduate, as the American Literary, Scientific, and Military Academy (Norwich University). Ben's father, Reverend Mr. Aaron Walker, is warmly acquainted with a lawyer named Jonathan Bennett, who acts as Ben's in loco parentis in Norwich and has a lovely, intelligent daughter, Kate. Ben is fortunate to meet outstanding classmates right away: his roommates, Tom Harrison from Lebanon, New Hampshire, Billy Stanton from Charleston, South Carolina, and Gordon Chandler from New York, a gifted leader and excellent student. The unwritten law is that the students help each other according to their strengths: Gordon tutors Ben when the latter falls behind in mathematics; Ben is a mentor to Henry Crane, whose father informs Ben that Henry has suffered from being bullied. Sam Dennison, a troublemaker and a fanatic on states' rights (his family has been slaveholders for generations and he sees the northern clergy as the most vocal opponents of slavery), tries to divide the friends on this issue; he is later dismissed for beating up Billy. As Ben spends more time with Kate, he realizes they are falling in love; she plans to attend the recently founded Mount Holyoke Female Seminary in Massachusetts to become a teacher. Instruction in the classroom and in the field progresses: Ben does well and is attracted to the artillery field piece, which reminds him of Ethan Allen and Benedict Arnold when the British garrison surrendered at Fort Ticonderoga. The cadets make an excursion on foot to Fort Ticonderoga, river-bathing and sleeping on the ground. Another troublemaker, Fred Turell, informs Henry that Ben was hired for pay to take care of him. Ben is able to explain the real circumstances to Henry, but when Turell is dismissed for drinking, Gordon holds Ben responsible for reporting Turell (which he did not). Their fine friendship is over. Ben graduates, takes a job with the Baltimore & Ohio Railroad, marries Kate, and has two children. It is not until 1847 that Gordon, having heard the true story about Turell's dismissal, writes to Ben to apologize. Ben travels to New York where Gordon is in a hospital, having been wounded in the Mexican War. Gordon, divorced, depressed, is unable to perform the required physical therapy. The end of the drama is redemptive and fulfilling.

Philip Singerman

In *Proof Positive* (2001), super sleuth Roland Troy, mourning the recent death of his wife, is in seclusion in a cabin in rural northern Vermont, which he bought sight unseen from a friend who worked with him as a government operative. Troy's former partner lures him out of his retirement by offering a challenging assignment—to search for the truth in a young woman's past. Angela Becker, an undercover police officer, joins Troy in this task; their action-packed quest takes them from the swamps of Florida to the border between Austria and Italy, where their thrilling discoveries include secrets about Nazi concentration camps and torture.

Susan Snow Sirois

In *Sawyer's Crossing* (2002), Officer Kelly Douglas, best sharpshooter in her graduating class at the Vermont Police Academy, has spent twenty years repressing the murder of her parents, which she witnessed. A series of robberies of tourists in covered bridges in the town of Sawyer's Crossing in southern Vermont releases a memory: the man who killed her parents was named Pitman. Now engaged to the new police chief, Mark Mitchell, Kelly and he find and kill Pitman, leaving his three sons to seek revenge. Kelly and Mark bring two of them to justice; they adopt the third, an innocent boy of fourteen. To his graduation from police academy nine years later Kelly brings four Mitchell children of her own. Their Christian faith has buttressed Kelly and Mark's lives.

Robert C. Sloane

In *The Vengeance* (1983), Nick and Christine Marino, forced into violent acts in Long Island when victimized by trolls (who assume human form at will), flee with their son, Joey, to Torchester, where they live in a condominium at Mad Mountain ski resort. They become embroiled in a conflict with suave developer Dexter Cabot, who wants to build a luxurious Cabot Inn at the foot of the mountain, even though engineers have questioned the availability of water for such a vast scheme. Having followed the Marinos to Vermont, the trolls embody the physical presence of a local psychiatrist, who is treating Joey, and of his wife, Joey's babysitter. Nick gives his life to save his family by falling over a cliff while grappling with the head troll; Joey, now a troll, defects to Norway, and Christine marries Turk Brandon, Cabot's reformed henchman.

Alison Smith

The serial sleuth in *Someone Else's Grave* and *Rising* is Judd Springfield, in his fifties, chief of police for twelve years in Coolidge Corners on the Mill River in southeastern Vermont near the New Hampshire border. He has a good team of men, woodsmen since grade school, who know how to hunt, fish, trap, and trail. *Someone Else's Grave* (1984) begins when Miss Adams goes to the cemetery on Memorial Day to leave flowers and finds a freshly dug grave. Before she can report to Judd, she is savagely hit on the back of her head. Judd sequesters her at home with a woman caretaker and has the corpse unearthed: it is Diana Scott, who worked for State Senator Bill Carson. During the course of Judd's investigation, two more women are murdered, Barbara Thibodeau, whose husband, Paul, has a nervous condition, and Linda Drazel, wife of the local cab driver. A range of suspects is presented. Frank Hatch, the nephew of Diana's landlady, has a police record. Paul Thibodeau, though married, has developed a crush on Diana. Bill Carson may be cooking the office books. Stanley drove a mysterious fare to another town the night of his wife's murder. Judd sets a trap for the killer. The ominous title of *Rising* (1987) suggests the theme: the reservoir for the new Mill River Dam is rising rapidly—too rapidly—and three murders by drowning in rapid succession, all victims connected to the dam, tell Judd something is amiss. He and his partner, Ray Stone, a quick-witted African-American from New York, start investigating the circumstances of the building of the dam; several firms thought the site unsuitable. Oldsters Charlie Boone and Ishmael Brown, whose property was condemned by the state, tip off Judd, confirming his worries about the condition of the rock, the seepage, and the dam's situation over a populated area. He insists, against everyone's recommendations, on installing an emergency alarm system with the cooperation of the fire department. The evacuation is carried out when the dam goes, taking the life of the perpetrator, whose wife and children were drowned in a dam accident ten years ago. He killed the three people connected with the dam construction because they had been siphoning off funds intended for safety measures. During this process, Judd falls in love with the new librarian, Nancy Hanks.

Annie Smith

Sally Forster, a kindergarten teacher who lives in Hartley, Ohio, is summoned to Brattleboro in *Home Again* (2002) after a devastating automobile accident kills her oldest friend, Deborah, and her husband, Kevin Fennessy. Sally is the legal guardian of their son, Micah, a fourteen-year-old hockey star, who sustained serious spinal cord injuries in the car crash. After the funerals and a long period of hospitalization in Brattleboro for Micah and reading and consultation with neurologists for Sally, she sends Micah to a rehab clinic in Cleveland and returns home to Hartley with Micah's dog, Sophie. Micah's Aunt Mary is strongly opposed to his leaving Vermont and undermines Sally's efforts to rebuild Micah's life. When Micah is finally installed in Sally's house, he is depressed, indifferent, and passive. The intervention that saves Micah—and Sally—is that of Tanner Dodge, a local dog trainer, who teaches Micah to train Sophie to enter an obedience competition. The remaining question is whether Tanner will also become Micah's father.

Edward H. Smith

In "**The Vermont Raffles Who Transcended the Tomb**" (1921), Clarence A. Adams is a farmer and leading resident of the village of Chester in Windsor County. He is involved in community affairs, occasionally runs up to Montpelier to look in on the state legislators, and spends a great deal of time at the library, where he is chief trustee. His interest in books spills over into his house, where he has a large collection of mystery and detective fiction, featuring masters like Chesterton, Gaboriau, Poe, Sue, Stevenson, and Conan Doyle. Beginning in about 1885, a series of burglaries occurs in Windsor County; the whole community is in ferment. The burglaries, sometimes perpetrated by more than one person, appear to be inside jobs. In 1902, by use of a trap, Adams is identified as the burglar, arrested, and confesses. Adams rationalizes that he was actually investigating the theories of the police after each of his burglaries, testing out different techniques from his collection of detective fiction. He is sentenced to ten years in the Windsor penitentiary and becomes a model prisoner. Almost at once he begins to plan his escape. He draws inspiration from Stevenson's *The Master of Ballantrae*, in which a man is able to put himself to sleep by hypnosis. Using his former accomplices on the outside and a convict doctor on the inside, he plans to die and be born again. He complains to the outside physician of certain influenza-like symptoms and is sent to the prison infirmary. Three days later he is pronounced dead by the convict doctor. He is examined, placed in a coffin, taken to a cemetery, and there spirited away by his accomplices. He is sighted on a number of occasions in Canada. (The Raffles of the title is the gentleman-burglar hero of the Ernest William Hornung nineteenth-century novels.)

Elinor Spielberg

The setting of charming *Uninvited Daughters* (1993) is Downsboro near Chelsea in central Vermont. From Russian-Jewish peasant stock, Odessa finds it hard to make friends with the Yankee residents of Downsboro, especially Sam, a woman of patrician heritage and eccentric tastes. Odessa lives in an "unpainted house the color of thorn [that] was surrounded by the cunning, surviving shoots of a vine as old and half-alive as the town itself." Odessa befriends Sam's stepdaughter, Megan Vasquez, who is woefully in need of the kind of love that Odessa believes she is unable to give. Odessa has just extricated herself from a dead-end relationship with the odious Malcolm, a married Electrolux salesman. Megan's father, Gil, is Mexican; Megan feels as unwelcome as Odessa; in fact, Odessa comments about them both, "And here's where we wound up, two uninvited daughters wandering around lost in the north country." By the end of the novel, Odessa, who is an amusing and appealing narrator, begins to love Megan and, slowly, Megan's father.

Danielle Steel

A rural Vermont setting provides the bookends for *Granny Dan* (1999) about a ballerina, Danina Petroskova, who was born in St. Petersburg and danced *Swan Lake* for the Czar. The narrator only knew her as Granny Dan, who arrived in Vermont in 1917 and has just died at ninety. Her granddaughter learns of Granny Dan's pre-Vermont life by finding letters and mementos. Because her lover, Nikolai Obrajensky, was sent to Siberia during the revolution, Danina escaped to Vermont to live with the family of his older cousin, Viktor, whom she later marries.

Lynn Stegner

The three novellas in poetic, powerful *Pipers at the Gates of Dawn: A Triptych* (2000) share a continuity of place—Harrow in northern Vermont, set upon Crescent Lake, bordered on one side with cottages of summer people and mountains on the other. "Hired Man" is about native Vermonters; "Pipers at the Gates of Dawn" is about summer people; and "Indian Summer" is about a summer person who becomes a native. Sam Chase and Heidi Greenfield appear in all three. In *Hired Man*, in the nineteenth century a man named Coulter built the tall, white farmhouse up a long steep drive on the ridgeline, which can be seen from the village road. Sheep grew on the land until the wool market collapsed, when Coulter turned to dairy farming. The family managed until there were only girls in the family, who married and went off, and then gave up. Some summer people bought the house after a while, but they too are defeated. (Stegner refers, at one point, to the "summer houses of Vermont's absentee landlords.") A man named Rinaldi, a stonecutter from the marble quarries in Dorset, buys the house. Mysteriously, he disappears one day, and his brother, Champ, comes with a wife and children to run the place. When Champ becomes a drunk, Ray, the seventeen-year-old son, takes over. There are seven children in the family, and his mother is expecting another. Swamped with milking cows and other chores, he only goes to high school once a week, but is talented enough to stay at the head of his class. One of the incentives for going to school is to see Heidi Greenfield, the girl he loves. The hired man leaves and, knowing he needs help, Ray finds a new helper, Sam Chase, who says he is good at fixing machinery. Chase is very good-looking, as Luisa, the next oldest child observes, "like a glossy poster of someone you would never meet and who could not really exist." Something unpleasant is in the air this spring. "And yet there was a more than usual desperate quality to spring that year, the snow so late leaving, and as it left, exposing not only last year's life long gone—the pale tufts of grass, and blackened lumps of half-moldered vegetation, the cinereous vertebra of ferns lying across one another, the raw dirt—but this year's promise so late made, and so far from being fulfilled, foliage and flowers and hidden lives waiting, waiting and straining. Spring's hold seemed unconvincing. Even the moles who had begun and left off their tunneling so many times had retreated to the stone walls to wait and see. The black flies were out, though not in confident numbers; the deer flies hovered about the spruce woods, ventured no further; mosquitoes hatched as they could. And a vague anxiety infected the people of Harrow: knowing that it could not, they were nevertheless afraid that winter would return." Sam Chase fixes machines, but he "doesn't get his pants dirty," as Ray's mother points out. He is also seen in the local bar drinking with Champ, something no one else would dream of doing with a man who has a drinking problem. Champ finally goes on such a drinking spree that when he comes home, he passes out on the kitchen steps. Ray drags him into the house and props him up in a chair. The result of this act is tragic.

In **Pipers at the Gates of Dawn**, Dru Hammond is a summer person at Crescent Lake whose husband, Fletcher Hammond III, and his family have been coming to this house for three generations. Fletcher's past "waded into the future: even his future, the food he ate in his future, was shaped in part by family history, for each summer they came to Harrow, anticipating in ripening turn the strawberries, wild raspber-

ries, garden lettuce, followed by beefsteak tomatoes, and best of all, the sweetness of August corn; and randomly throughout, maple syrup, Maine lobsters and blueberries, local goat cheese, Vermont lamb, cob-smoked hams from Barton, Ben and Jerry's ice cream from down in Waterbury." Dru's parents were killed in a fire when she was ten; she was brought up in various institutions. As a result, she has no history; she does not feel that she belongs anywhere. She is a mother, but her older boy, Miles, doesn't seem to need her any more and her younger boy, Ian, has retreated into using the third person for himself. Worst of all, she and Fletcher are not getting along. He is sarcastic and critical; she is angry and unresponsive sexually. She wants to be alone, but she is lonely. Outside, "The surface of the lake was pleasingly flawed, like nineteenth-century glass, bubbling here and there, inexplicable lines, swirls that did not finish themselves." In the house, Dru notes that "There was a heavy work table between the kitchen and dining area, with a slab of worn, hollowed maple on top, and hooks underneath from which a colander, cheese grater, ladle, and other items of cookery hung, most of it dented or stained in ways that were attractive to visitors from the cities downcountry where perfection was a burden not unlike a second job. In Harrow it was the plain flawed thing that charmed, and perfection a tactless error of judgment." Because Fletcher likes to potter around in the summers and fix things, he hires a man, Sam Chase, to help him repair the dock. Dru finds herself shy about swimming from the dock when Sam Chase is there and wonders if he is flirting with her. She sees him around town, at parties, on the street helping a woman put a package in a car, driving with Heidi Greenfield and one of her friends. The day of the orchid hunt, she sleeps with Sam Chase in the morning. That afternoon, Ian is lost for an entire night but is finally returned to them, safe and speaking of himself in the first person. Fletcher analyzes the community: "That was the trouble with being a summer person, you always felt that you were crowding into someone else's picnic spot. Winter had earned it for them." At a party, Fletcher spells out his six-tier caste system. Natives ("Brahmins with chain saws") are people like John Abbot, who runs the local gift shop and descends from six generations of Vermonters. Nonnative natives, more native than natives, are like Harry Young, who bought a big piece of the lake at age twenty-two, is "in" everywhere, and has started the local land trust. Old-time summer people are like the Hammonds. Permanent summer people are like the Bettencourts, not especially long-time summer people, retired now and here year-round, but, in the eyes of Vermont, everlastingly summer people. And, finally, Fletcher explains, there are newcomer summer people and two-week-a-year tourist leaf peepers.

Indian Summer is a story within a story. Kimball ("Kim") Sayers Dodge, a young man who spent some summers in Harrow, returns to the northeast to attend Dartmouth College. He gets in touch with his Uncle Jack (Jackson Sayers), his mother's brother, to visit him in Harrow. Uncle Jack lives in a sod house without a telephone, so Kim calls Uncle Jack's closest neighbors, Norman and Gladys Courchaine, to ask them to pass along a message. Kim remembers all too clearly the summer he broke Norman's new hay mower. When he gives his name, all Norman says is, "I remember." "It was really kind of him," thinks Kim, "and so like a Vermonter—quiet, not showy, not asking to be noticed." The instant Kim sees his uncle, he knows that the latter is not well. Uncle Jack confesses that he has prostate cancer for which he is not seeking treatment. Kim spends two or three days with Uncle Jack, in which they work, take walks, and cook meals (including a masterpiece of an apple pie). Uncle Jack tries to explain about his life, where he started out, why he came back to Vermont, and "the accident." Uncle Jack felt burdened by his advantaged background and wanted to serve humanity: "Your parents, your family name, your wealth, they're all just up the beach, keeping an eye on you from their wide, sandless mats. And there you are, walking about under a big soft yellow sun; no depths threaten you, no sea serpents or storm clouds, no experience is required." He loved a Harrow woman, Lara, but he couldn't

commit to a wife and children. He took odd jobs, gave away all his money to the American Field Service Committee, and finally carved his sod house up above the Courchaines. The suspense is excruciating as Uncle Jack leads up to the accident, punctuated by the need to eat or sleep or do chores. Meanwhile, gossip reports that Heidi Greenfield is pregnant. The dénouement revealing the motive behind the accident and the accident itself is brilliantly told. Kim is shocked and saddened. The imagery is exquisite, whether in a single phrase like "fields gathering about it like quilting squares" and "another pause lit between us like a hawk on a high wire," or in a paragraph: "The air was so clear and sharp that the blue of the sky and the white of the clapboards seemed to enter my eyes physically in slices and shards of color, and then the maple leaves piled in, orange, yellow, red, and the whole scene was impossible to look at, impossibly brilliant and beautiful and pure...the purity of the white houses, the white church and steeple, the white posts and pickets, the intensity of the violating color." (The title of the triptych is a chapter heading in Kenneth Grahame's *The Wind in the Willows*.)

Wallace Stegner

Second Growth (1944) is a montage of three stories taking place in Westwick, New Hampshire (a fictional Greensboro, Vermont). The linked characters are Helen Barlow, Abe Kaplan and Ruth Liebowitz, and Andy Mount. Helen Barlow, a schoolteacher, has always lived in Westwick, except for four years at college. Helen is lonely and afraid because "she was neither village folks nor summer folks; she had been successfully educated away from her own life but not into the other." Flo Barnes, exotic with short blonde hair and bronzed limbs, works for Mrs. Weld, a rich summer person who tries to buy her acceptance in the village by starting a music festival. When Flo Barnes begins to court Helen, inviting her to go swimming, Helen's response so terrifies her that she drowns herself. Abe Kaplan is a Russian-Jewish emigrant who supports himself as a tailor and lives in a tent. He meets Ruth Liebowitz, a Jew from New York who is staying at the

Westwick Inn where the owners, who have "restricted clientele" rules, tolerate Ruth but ask her to sit at a table by herself. Relieved and grateful to meet each other, Abe and Ruth marry and plan to build a house together. She feels as isolated and different as before. When Helen kills herself, Abe and Ruth, out on the lake, hear the splash and Abe tries to rescue her. Chilled, he is rushed to the hospital. The neighbors put together a "sick basket" for him and Ruth, each person contributing a home-made pie or a preserve. They belong at last. Andy Mount is a village boy whose stepfather took off and whose mother died in prison. Andy is apprenticed to Allan Richie, who teaches him farming and other trades, and he graduates at the top of his high school class. Peter Dow, a distinguished summer resident, specialist in American history, and headmaster at the Dryden School, offers Andy a scholarship. Andy wants to be educated so that he can return and be useful but, fearing he will not measure up, he does not accept. Peter Dow argues that "if you had any intelligence, you had an obligation to develop it to the limit, not let it rust like unused machinery in a leaky shed." Andy looks at the village, which is no different from what it was in the years after the Revolution when the first houses went up along Broken Musket Brook. It is still colonial, with houses clustered around its square. On the hills are abandoned farms that were too far off the roads for farmers to make a living, too remote for farm women to endure, and too distant for the school bus or the snowplow to reach in bad weather. There, in the wilderness, "houses and barns the color of tarnished silver rotted slowly in the quiet, and every summer the golden glow sprang up tall and yellow around their untrodden doors, and little by little the spruce marched in from the woods and engulfed the meadows, took them back. Every year the banks gave up on some of those farms, tired of the struggle to find a tenant; and every year the hedgehogs found new sheds to nest and gnaw in undisturbed. Every spring the hazel brush was closer to screening off the blind openings of what had once been roads." Allan attributes Andy's opportunity to spending too much time with

"summer folks," who are "gettin' to stick their noses too much into how this village runs." Andy works in the shop of old John Mills, a voice of Vermont whom Andy respects. A group often gossips in John's shop and Andy feels ashamed: "Some people made one sort of shift and some made another against the stony acres and the mortgage and the loneliness and the endless labor without profit." After a shocking accident in the shop, Andy decides to take John's advice: "I'd go, Andrew. There isn't much else we can teach you around here. You'd stay the same size all your life." Here are two more examples of the author's superb imagery. He describes "an axe stuck in the block, its new handle white as china." He pictures Mrs. Emma, whom her husband, George, had traded in for a blonde from the South: "The hussy had died of pneumonia the first winter, but Mrs. Emma remained in the village, a scarred trunk in the burned-over forest of George's matrimony." On summer people: "Village people went [to the dances] because they liked the music and crowds and the sense of frolic. Many summer people — professors and economists and prep school masters and Hartford lawyers and writers and whatnot — went because they thought the dances quaint survivals of a simpler and more wholesome past."

In *Crossing to Safety* (1987), Larry and Sally Morgan are summoned to a retreat at Battell Pond in northern Vermont by Sid and Charity Lang, long-time friends also in their sixties. The Morgans have spent time ("the best time of our lives") at the Lang compound over the years, but this time they have come to celebrate Charity's birthday, even as she is dying of metastasized cancer. In a single day in 1972, Larry looks back on their lives. Coming to Madison, Wisconsin, from California in 1937, Larry and Sally meet Sid and Charity almost immediately. They become an inseparable foursome: Sid is also in the English department; Charity is also expecting a baby the same month; they react the same way to everything. A writer, Larry publishes a short story in *The Atlantic* and then, after only two months of work, writes a novel that is accepted by an A-level publisher. He is on his way; jealousy and competition in the English department abound. Sid broods about promotion and his need—and inability—to publish. The night after their arrival in Vermont, Charity plans a picnic for the entire family. Larry takes a walk alone on the property: "Dew has soaked everything. I could wash my hands in the ferns, and when I pick a leaf off a maple branch I get a shower on my head and shoulders. Through the hardwoods along the foot of the hill, through the belt of cedars where the ground is swampy with springs, through the spruce and balsam of the steep pitch, I go alertly, feasting my eyes. I see coon tracks, an adult and two young, in the mud, and maturing grasses bent like croquet wickets with wet, and spotted orange Amanitas, at this season flattened or even concave and holding water, and miniature forests of club moss and ground pine and ground cedar. There are brown caves of shelter, mouse and hare country, under the wide skirts of spruce. I watch the sun climb powerfully and confidently and see below me the unchanged village, the lake like a pool of mercury, the varying greens of hayfields and meadows and sugarbush and black spruce woods, all of it lifting and warming as the stretched shadows shorten." Charity's plan is to slip away to the hospital while the family is celebrating, there to starve to death. This has all been arranged in advance with the doctor. Sid is desolate that she doesn't want him to go with her. They have another, final, fight for control.

In his introduction to *Collected Stories* (1990), the author explains that he only wrote short stories as a young man, some of which later became part of a longer work. This is true for **"Hostage,"** which tells of Andy Mount's being arrested for burning down his stepfather's barn for the insurance money. Richie, the insurance inspector from his village, and Rufe, the detective from Montpelier, visit him in jail every day to ask him how the fire started. He claims he dropped the lantern by accident because swallows flying down from the rafters of the barn frightened him. Richie knows that it is a matter of time before the boy's mother will confess. Martha Mount appears on the fourth day and says it was Willard Branch's idea, but she helped

him. They needed the money. She is put in jail and dies there; her husband has run off. Mr. Richie takes Andy in, to go to school and earn his keep. **"The Berry Patch"** describes the end of Perley Hill's army furlough. He and Alma, his wife, drive up Stannard Mountain, with Elmore Mountain, Mount Mansfield, and Camel's Hump all visible in the distance. "The lake was like a mirror leaned on edge against the hills, with the white houses of the village propped against its lower edge to keep it from sliding down into the river valley." They pass farms that are failing because men are away in the service. They pass Donald Swain's place, which is for sale. He is in the hospital and his son is in the navy. Alma has been running the farm for the year Perley has been away. She has been fussing over him since he came home, eager to do anything he wanted, and trying to give him a good time. He doesn't want to do anything but be in the berry patch with her: "Funny about a berry patch," he said. "Nobody every plowed it, or planted it, or cultivated it, or limed it, but there it is. You couldn't grub it out if you tried. More you plow it up, the more berries there is next year. Burn it over, it's up again before anything else. Blow everything down, that's just what it likes." **"Saw Gang"** is a day in the life of Ernie, fifteen, who accompanies some of the older men (including Donald Swain) to George Pembroke's house. They are going as friends, not employees, to help him out as he has helped them out. They work all day without stopping and get in enough wood for two years. The description of the process of cutting, sawing, and splitting is detailed and loving. Ernie knows they have "done a day's work that amounted to something." He is sore at the end of the day but full of respect for his companions. He left the woods "feeling good, feeling tired and full of October smell and the smell of fresh-sawed wood and hot oil." In **"The Sweetness of the Twisted Apples,"** Ross, a painter, and Margaret are out driving near Harrow in the fullness of fall. He calls her "Vermont-autumn crazy." They pass many abandoned farms and realize that twenty or thirty years ago "this was a carriage road with farms all along it, and now it's just a dead-end ghost road in the wilderness." They pull into a farmyard where "there were tin patches on the barn's roof like bright metal teeth in a mouth." While Ross paints, Margaret walks through the village, seeing the blind-windowed houses, the shed doors sagging open. She passes a cemetery. "She imagined how it might have seemed to some old grandmother who had lived in the village for eighty years, watching the hill farms go dead like lights going out, watching the decay spread inward from the remote farms to the near ones, to the place next door." She walks back to where Ross is working. "On every house and building she passed, failure and death were posted like contagion warnings." They meet and speak with a mother and a child, who, at closer range, is not a child but a pinched and starving-faced young woman. They learn that she "was 'going out' for a year," but then "she had a disappointment." The young man married someone else and now lives next door. Ross shows them his painting of the apple orchard. Margaret wonders aloud how long an orchard can go on living and bearing. "Years and years," the girl said. "It's wonderful how apple trees hang on sometimes." In **"Traveler,"** a salesman of pharmaceuticals becomes stranded when his car breaks down on a mountain road in the middle of winter. It is a freezing night and he waits, at first, for someone to pass by, making a small fire, but he soon realizes that he has to walk out into the darkness to look for help. He finally finds a house and barn, with a young boy there whose grandfather is sick. The boy is frightened and dares not leave his grandfather, so the traveler takes the cutter and horse to drive to the next village to telephone for the doctor. The traveler is also an orphan. He looks at the little boy and remembers how "he himself, thirty years ago, had searched the faces of passing strangers for something he could not name, how he had listened to their steps and seen their shadows lengthen ahead of them down roads that led to unimaginable places, and how he had ached with the desire to know them, who they were. But none of them had looked back at him as he tried now to look at the boy."

Aaron Marc Stein

A skiing weekend in Vermont turns sour in *Chill Factor* (1978) when Matt Erridge's Porsche digs into a snow bank during a blizzard and he attempts to ski to the nearest habitation. En route, he finds an abandoned car with a dead body inside. Stan Sobieski, a friendly local man on a snowmobile, rescues Matt by taking him to his house where Matt finds Stan's wife, Sally, her charming baby, and two other orphans of the storm, unpleasant and whiney Michael and Irene Moore. They cannot be separated from their briefcase, with "M.K." embossed on the cover. Neighbor Bert Dawson also comes over, uneasy about being stranded in his own lonely cabin. The storm is fierce: the electricity goes out; the vehicles are snowed in; the cold is unendurable. By the next morning, tensions have mounted: Stan has decided that Matt has murdered and robbed Hoffman (the dead man in the car who was known to trade in diamonds), and Stan points a gun at Matt. By the time the electricity is back on, a newscast reveals that a missing bank manager, Melvin King, has absconded with considerable assets. The tension in the claustrophobic cabin builds. No one believes anyone else. The situation, filled with murder and deception, is finally resolved.

John Steinbeck

*To a God Unknown (1933) describes the life journey of Joseph Wayne, who has lived on the family farm in Pittsford his whole thirty-three years. He has a large nose, high hard cheekbones, a silky black beard, and blue eyes. His brothers, Burton and Thomas, have brought wives to the land, and now that Benjamin is courting Jenny Ramsey there will not be enough land for all. Joseph hungers for land of his own, and good cheap land can be had out West, where people are homesteading in this year 1903. His father, disappointed, wants to accompany Joseph. "The winter came soon, with deep snow, and the air was frozen to needles." Joseph heads alone for California and settles in the San Antonio Valley. When he sees the land, he feels that he "had been asleep and was awakened," but

he also feels a traitor to his past and his home. He thinks of "the strength and eternal rightness of his father" and believes that "his father and this new land were one." There is a noble oak on the property to which he talks as though to his father. After his father's death, he invites his brothers to come out West with their families. The soil is rich, he writes, and there are "no rocks or ledges." Joseph is the undisputed head of the clan: "On the old farm in Vermont his father had merged with the farm until he became the living symbol of the unit, land, and its inhabitants." In Monterey lives a saddler who has a daughter, Elizabeth, seventeen, a teacher. Joseph seeks her out as he would a prime animal. They marry and Elizabeth has a baby, John. There are disasters of various kinds. Joseph continues to speak to the oak tree. His brother, Burton, a religious extremist, believes Joseph is worshiping the tree like a pagan and girdles the tree, killing it. The drought comes. Elizabeth falls and breaks her neck. All the members of the family, except Joseph, leave with the herd of cows (his sister-in-law takes the baby) to try to save the animals. The rain finally comes, but it is too late.

Barbara B. Stevens

In *Walk Humbly* (1935), West Waterford has a West End and an East End. In the West End live Ashleys, Churchills, Pringriolays, Crockers, and Tuttles. Ashleys have lived there since Bildad Ashley hacked and hewed his way into the settlement behind his yoke of steer. Their descendants ran town meetings, encouraged schools, and built the Congregational Church. Reuben Ashley died in the Civil War; Ethan Ashley survived and, at age sixty, married Elspeth and had two daughters, Drusilla, now seventeen, and Emily, sixteen. An orphaned colored girl named Leah takes care of their household; Sykes is the hired man. Beyond the timothy meadow at their dairy farm "the Green Mountains piled, checkered with bare, far-away pastures." Ethan's brother, Robert, also has two children; they are so snobbish they do not speak to Leah. Drusilla begins to recognize the division of social classes in the village when she starts high school. She forms a

friendship with Joe Gordon, whose father runs a livery stable in the East End. Joe, who wants to be a doctor, comes to her house to do homework. He goes to medical school and Drusilla to Wellesley. In the summer vacation, she feels "trapped by the circle of the Green Mountains." When she finds that Joe has left school to work at the depot, she feels scornful until she learns that Joe's father, intoxicated, was kicked by a horse and died and his mother, Honora, is left with the mortgage and taxes. Members of the community (mostly her father) arrange for Joe to return to school. Emily's engagement to Stephen Churchill is broken and she marries a socialite named Pieter Van Braam. Joe finishes medical school, and he and Drusilla are married. She thought he would take her away to Boston, but he settles in West Waterford and the residents embrace him. Now forty, her children grown, she is still vaguely dissatisfied with West Waterford. Unexpectedly she becomes pregnant again. The little boy lives five days and dies, but she is too ill to know. While she is in the hospital, her daughter dies of meningitis. The neighbors pour into the house to comfort the family. Joe works night and day but is not invited to join the staff of the hospital. Drusilla's cousin, Bobbie Ashley, chairman of the hospital board, will not appoint Joe because, years before, when Bobbie impregnated a young East End woman, Joe performed an abortion. Emily divorces her husband and goes to live in Europe with her old lover, the married Stephen Churchill. The town gossips lick their chops over this scandal in one of their first families. Drusilla's cousin, Bildad Ashley, is giving up the ancestral farm for taxes to move out West; Drusilla buys the farm for her son, Ethan, and his wife. She had wanted Ethan to get way from West Waterford, as she had hoped to, but here he is on the family farm. Though the head of the bank, Eddie Pringriolay, continues to claim, "It's our kind against the others," Joe is one of the most respected people in town. He has worked hard all his life and "hard work was their creed." Now the gossips say, "Dr. Gordon's family is one of the oldest." The Ashleys are gone from their ancient place of prominence. (The title is from *The Bible*, Micah 6:8: "...to do justly, and to love mercy, and to walk humbly with thy God.")

Abigail Stone

The first-person narrator in *Recipes from the Dump* (1995), Gabby Fulbriten, is a funny, smart, courageous single mother raising three kids in Leadbelly off Route 7. She is also, by her own admission, an inadequate housekeeper, overweight, and desperate for a man. She interlaces her narrative with amusing recipes, not for food but for life ("Good Mother Recipe"). She works at the Hurry Up Grocery, keeping the books, and is always behind on her own bills. The children, preteen Shelley, and the seven-year-old twins, J.D. and Grace, are normal, bratty kids. Her best friend and neighbor, Hester, is a wonderful Vermont character—kind, hardworking, long-suffering, keeping house, "putting up your winter's food." The life Gabby is describing is tough and lonely; the Gulf War is on the radio; recycling is a losing battle. Gabby's house—the old Watts place—is right next to the dump. When she has her yard turned over for a garden, the soil is full of broken glass. She agonizes over the community of condominiums going up on the neighboring hill: "I could just cry when I see the bulldozers plowing up the earth and knocking down the dead elms. The thing about those dead elms is, we have these pileated woodpeckers that love to peck on the dead trees and the blackbirds love to rest there in the spring. I hate to see them get bulldozed to make a better view for the condos." She drives up to her house one night and sees six raccoons in the garbage: "When they saw the headlights of our car, they trundled like a six-piece band, in file, up our popple tree."

Mira Stout

Anna, the narrator of *One Thousand Chestnut Trees* (1998), remembers that it was winter when her Uncle Hung-Do came from Seoul to stay with her and her mother near Starksboro: "The pines would have bristled sparsely against the hushed white snow. The gray, swelling sky would have been as vast and lonely as a northern sea." Anna, half-Korean and half-Boston Irish, considers the place where she lives in Vermont a "red-neck town." When her mother and uncle speak Korean together, Anna finds the sound ugly. They take the uncle to the Timberline Restaurant on Route 9, with its famous view of Massachusetts. The "creamy blue" of the mountains beckoned "like a majestic frozen dessert." People stare at them: "Orientals were rarely seen then in the Vermont hills." School bullies tease Anna because of her Oriental blood. Her uncle's "Oriental vibrato sounded surreal and faintly sinister" in the Puritan Vermont woods. Uncle Hung-do returns to Korea; prior to her decision to go to Korea, Anna lives in Manhattan for a while and then returns to Starksboro: "I had never felt a sense of belonging to this landscape." She looks out the dining room window: "The horizon returned my stare with peaceful blankness. There was no doubting that New England, with its stone walls, woods, and red barns, was an utterly different world. The Yankee landscape had its own past to digest. Murdered colonial settlers lay beneath the foundations of the ruined mill behind our house. The summer camp nearby, Camp Winnepesaukee, had a quaint Native American name, but no Native Americans remained in the county. Ghosts of unknown soldiers, Ethan Allen's Green Mountain Boys, were said to haunt the overgrown woods nearby. A Mississippi-born Vietnam veteran turned motel owner had shot himself in the head on our road in 1974. I felt little connection to any of it." The bulk of the novel concerns Anna's experiences discovering her family and her culture in Korea.

Harriet Beecher Stowe

Uncle Tom's Cabin (1852) takes place in Vermont marginally but is imbued with and informed by Vermont sensibility and morality. Augustine St. Clare, the son of a wealthy planter, lives in Louisiana. His father's brother settled in Vermont and established a successful farm there. Because Augustine was never robust, he spent many of his boyhood years with his uncle in Vermont, where the family hoped he would become more vigorous in the cold climate. His only daughter, Little Eva, has inherited his delicate constitution. Because her mother is "inefficient," her father worries about Little Eva's health and takes her on a visit to Vermont, where he persuades his cousin, Miss Ophelia St. Clare, to come to the South with him to take care of Eva. Miss Ophelia is a strong-minded and independent Yankee woman, who is used to carrying her own luggage. Her Cousin Augustine, who teasingly refers to her as "My dear Vermont," tells her that "positively you mustn't come the Green Mountains over us that way. You must adopt at least a piece of a southern principle, and not walk out under all that load." She finds it difficult to accustom herself to servants and is an abolitionist in soul and mind. "I think you slaveholders have an awful responsibility upon you," she tells her cousin. "I wouldn't have it, for a thousand worlds. You ought to educate your slaves, and treat them like reasonable creatures." The more time Miss Ophelia spends in the South, the more indignant she is with her cousin's "shiftless ways." "My dear Vermont," he replies, "You natives up by the North Pole set an extravagant value on time! What on earth is the use of time to a fellow who has twice as much of it as he knows what to do with?" They have many discussions and disagreements, such as the following (Augustine speaks first): "Look at the high and the low, all the world over, and it's the same story—the lower class used up, body, soul and spirit, for the good of the upper. It is so in England; it is so everywhere; and yet all Christendom stands aghast, with virtuous indignation, because we do the thing in a little different shape from the way they do it." "It isn't so in Vermont." "Ah, well, in New England, and in the free States, you have the better of us, I grant. But there's the bell; so, Cousin, let us for a while lay aside our sectional prejudices, and come out to dinner." Augustine muses about the differences and similarities between his Cousin Ophelia's father and his. They are the same aristocrats, but fate has set them down in different parts of the country: "What poor, mean trash this whole business of human virtue is! A mere matter, for the most part, of latitude and longitude, and geographical position, acting with natural temperament. The greater part is nothing but an accident! Your father, for example, settles in Vermont, in a town where all are, in fact, free and equal; becomes a regular church member and deacon, and in due time joins an Abolition Society, and thinks us all little better than heathens. Yet he is, for all the world, in constitution and habit, a duplicate of my father. I can see it leaking out in fifty different ways,—just the same strong, overbearing, dominant spirit. You know very well how impossible it is to persuade some of the folks in your village that Squire St. Clare does not feel above them. The fact is, though he has fallen on democratic times, and embraced a democratic theory, he is to the heart an aristocrat, as much as my father, who ruled over five or six hundred slaves." During her stay, her cousin buys for Miss Ophelia a slave girl named Topsy, who learns about love from the saintly Little Eva. Miss Ophelia takes Topsy home to Vermont with her, much to the surprise of the local "grave deliberative body." "Our folks, at first, think it an odd and unnecessary addition to their well-trained domestic establishment; but, so thoroughly efficient was Miss Ophelia in her conscientious endeavor to do her duty by her élève, that the child rapidly grew in grace and in favor with the family and neighborhood. At the age of womanhood, she was, by her own request, baptized, and became a member of the Christian church in the place; and showed so much intelligence, activity and zeal, and desire to do good in the world, that she was at last recommended and approved as a missionary to one of the stations in Africa."

John Stephen Strange

In *Reasonable Doubt* (1951), Ruth Ney, an artist and illustrator of books, grew up in and inherited a white clapboard cottage in Burnham (fifteen miles from Copland on the New York border), where she spends a great deal of her time. When her husband, George Purdy, is poisoned at their house in Manhattan, she is arrested and tried for his murder. Her sister-in-law, the disagreeable Jane Purdy Grant, is introduced.

Ruth is acquitted on "reasonable doubt," but many, including police Lieutenant Forbes, are not convinced of her innocence. Shortly after the trial, she marries Arnold Bricker, the family lawyer who has been in love with her for several years, and they spend the summer in Burnham. Ruth's neighbor and caretaker, Jud Staple, has a woodworking shop in his barn and issues warnings about the dangerous equipment therein. Arnold is attracted to Jud's Yankee character, the "caustic ribbing which is a countryman's form of humor." Arnold also meets Ben White, the seductive painter who is building a house next door. Lieutenant Forbes comes up from New York to discuss the case. He has new evidence that George was planning to divorce Ruth because she was Ben's mistress and had been supporting him for years. The seeds of doubt are sown: Arnold begins to see hints of Ruth's faithlessness and guilt. He has to return to New York to work, and she does not accompany him. Finally, on a visit, he is almost fatally wounded in an accident in the woodworking shop because of Ruth's "carelessness." He forces Ruth to tell him, as though on the witness stand, what happened on the day of the murder. He believes her story, finally, and is able to prove, when back in New York, who the real killer is.

Peter Straub

The narrator, a writer, hears the story of *Shadowland* (1980) twenty years after the fact, when he runs into Tom Flanagan, with whom he went to Carson School in Arizona. Tom Flanagan, an aspiring magician, makes friends with Del Nightingale, a younger classmate who is already an accomplished magician. They mount a magic show that ends in a tragic shambles when the auditorium burns down. That summer, Tom travels to Hilly Vale (about fifty miles north of Putney) to spend the summer with Del and his Uncle Coleman Collins at Shadowland. This huge Victorian summer house, renovated by generations of owners, sits on a remote compound with big iron gates and a wall and is surrounded by a fathomless lake in the woods. A number of parallels exist between the

Carson School and Shadowland and between the satanic headmaster and Uncle Coleman. Uncle Coleman, a famous magician and a drunk, subjects Tom to a series of magic tricks, illusions, hallucinations, and dreams. Tom falls in love with Rose Armstrong, whose trustworthiness is in doubt. Life becomes so mysterious and scary at Shadowland that Tom pledges to escape with Rose. The fantasy becomes "lurid and fantastic," two modifiers the narrator ascribes to Tom's narrative twenty years later, and the ending is terrifying.

Anne Stuart

In *Banish Misfortune* (1985), Jessica Hawkes is a neurotic executive in New York with a tormented past. Her friend, Springer McDowell, rescues her from making a personal mistake, and she reluctantly starts an affair with him. When she becomes pregnant, she flees to northern Vermont to start a new life and conceals from Springer that he is the father of her baby. She befriends an appealing single mother next door, who has a pleasant relationship with a Scotsman. Springer, who understands that Jessica is in pain, forces her to confront her past. She is finally able to tell him what happened to her and how much she loves him. *Still Lake* (2002) is located in Colby near the Northeast Kingdom. Sophie Davis buys Stonegate Farm and moves there with her senile mother, Grace, and her promiscuous stepsister, Marthe, to run the farm as a bed-and-breakfast. Sophie is unfazed by the fact that a triple murder took place on and around this property twenty years previously. Thomas Griffin, who was arrested for the crime and released on a technicality after serving five years, moves back to the area under the name "John Smith" to rent the Whitten cottage next door and to try to discover if he did in fact commit the crimes. He is melancholy and handsome, and Sophie is attracted to him despite her attempts to discourage any friendship between them. The real killer, who is motivated by Old Testament imperatives, is the last person in town anyone would suspect.

Dorothy Sucher

In *Dead Men Don't Give Seminars* (1988), Vic Newman, thirty, a former psychiatric aide at a state hospital in Washington, D.C., is now a private investigator working for detective Sabina Swift. Sabina, married to physicist Bruno Hershel, invites Vic to Burlington for the twentieth anniversary celebration of the Champlain Valley Physics Institute. Two Nobel co-Laureates, Herve Moore-Gann (né Harvey Morgan) and Saul Sachs, are to meet there for the first time in twenty years. Just as he greets his old rival, Moore-Gann is poisoned with digitalis at the cocktail party and dies in the hospital hours later. Florian Gawthrop, head of the institute, hires Sabina and Vic to solve the murder. This adroit and delightful tale presents an array of suspects among whom Vic and Sabina must choose. Judith Wiley, assistant to Gawthrop, had an affair with Moore-Gann that produced a baby, Jordan. Jordan, now a handsome, though half-witted, young man, works as a gardener at the Institute. Theresa Moore-Gann, the widow, has semi-adopted a young Polish physicist, Magda Tenofska (whose mother, an activist in the Solidarity struggle, is in prison in Warsaw). Magda has just broken off an affair with an introspective Corsican physicist with a Defense Department contract. Vita Sachs, Saul's wife, is a provocative flirt. Judith is found dead, apparently a suicide. Someone tampers with Magda's car brakes, almost killing her. One of the items Vic finds in his various searches is a quotation written on distinctive notepaper. Literate Sabina discerns the source to be Ford Madox Ford's *The Good Soldier*, enabling her to identify the murderer and solve the crimes.

Mark T. Sullivan

Patrick ("Pat") Gallagher, with a Ph.D. in anthropology and several documentary films about religion and culture under his belt, is having a mid-life crisis in *Ghost Dance* (1999): he is forty and his wife is divorcing him. He comes to Lawton in central Vermont to investigate a canonization process involving a local priest, Father D'Angelo, and rents a cabin on the Bluekill River. His landlady is a policewoman named Andromeda ("Andie") Nightingale with the Vermont Bureau of Criminal Investigation. Lawton thinks idly that he would like to know Andie better. He has his chance when, his first day fishing on the river, he discovers the dead — and raped and mutilated — body of the local dentist. A death note and drawing, illuminated in blood, are found at the crime scene, and Pat is able to interpret them through his knowledge of mythology: "Charon," the River Styx boatman, is the symbol the murderer has chosen. A second rape-and-murder victim, an old lady who was Andie's late mother's best friend, is found, with another note and drawing. Meanwhile, Pat, the child of drunken parents, learns that Andie has a drinking problem of her own. She also kept some evidence from the authorities — a golden chain and pages of the diary of a Sioux woman named Sarah Many Horses. Other members of the police department are not sympathetic toward Andie (except for Lieutenant Bowman, a woman from an "old Yankee family in Plymouth"); the mayor, who is pushing for a hotel-and-condominium development, is downright hostile. The third victim is a librarian, who had been doing research on the Indian woman and was perhaps getting too close. The emerging drama involves a deeply held secret in the town of Lawton, dating back to the forefathers of the present mayor and police chief and relating to the murder of the Sioux woman. How did she get to Vermont and who murdered her? A crazed serial murderer is picking off all the characters in the town owning pieces of the woman's diary. There is an enactment of the ancient Ghost Dance. Andie and Pat are almost killed before they solve the mystery. A year later, recovering from their wounds, Andie is pregnant; Pat has decided to stay in Lawton after all.

Thomas Sullivan

Two hundred years ago, Erasmus Moon of Gloucester, England, sent his four sons—a thief, a social degenerate, a manic-depressive, and a drunkard—to the colonies. These same characteristics reappear in *The Phases of Harry*

Moon (1988) in the Moons' American descendants, Harry, Stu, Stanley, and Nicki, sons of Edward Winslow and Alice Vila Stenner Moon. Alice is from Chewbagin— "Vermont was regular and self-assured"—and takes her eccentric sons home to see her family (two sets of grandparents, two uncles, one great uncle, and five cousins) because "The Vermont human being in her memory was God's archetype for the species." She finds the whole Stenner clan eccentric. Seeking solidity, Alice perceives that "Vermont was teetering as though its great granite mountains were as honeycombed as the rest of the world." Seeking "substance," Alice finds instead "caricature." The rest of the novel takes Harry through marriage, a daughter, adopting a "junior felon," and winning the lottery. He can make no meaningful contact with the "supporting cast of his life" and goes to England to swim the English Channel. He inadvertently saves some swimmers from drowning and becomes a national figure.

Mark Sumner

In *News from the Edge: Vampires of Vermont* (1999), lighthearted in tone, ace-reporter Savannah McKinnon—"Savvy Skye" is her pen name—works for a tabloid in St. Louis, where she is doing a series on vampires. She comes to Williams Crossing (based on the town of Chester) to verify the existence of Count Yorga, an alleged nosferatu (vampire). He turns out to suffer from a metabolic disorder called porphyria, which an evil laboratory transmitted to him. Yorga bites Savvy, infecting her with the disease. He, though suspect, turns out to be a good CIA agent; the handsome Cooper Armistead, who pays court to Savvy, is actually bad. Her beau, Jimmy, also a reporter in St. Louis, puts in an appearance at the last minute to help her out of her difficulties.

Donna Tartt

A glimpse of Hamden College is given at the start of *The Secret History* (1992): "Trees creaking with apples, fallen apples red on the grass beneath, the heavy sweet smell of them rotting on the ground and the steady thrumming of wasps around them. Commons clock tower: ivied brick, white spire, spellbound in the hazy distance. The shock of first seeing a birch tree at night, rising up in the dark as cool and slim as a ghost. And the night, bigger than imagining: black and gusty and enormous, disordered and wild with stars." A sect of students worships a cult teacher, Julian Morrow, who is handsome, urbane, and eccentric. Students signing up for his classics course (if he accepts them) must also be his advisees. Richard Papen, the first-person narrator, comes from a dysfunctional working class family in California to attend the college. When he sees the five rich, well-dressed preppies in Julian's coven, he yearns to be one of them. Fortunately, he has taken a couple of years of classical Greek in his inadequate high school and is invited to participate. He is fascinated with his colleagues: Camilla and Charles Macaulay, spellbinding twins; the two rich members, Francis Abernathy and Henry Winter; and Edmond "Bunny" Corcoran, an incorrigible sponger. Bunny's humor and unattractive behavior are beginning to pall. Richard is not above lying about his past to be acceptable to his new classmates. After Richard has befriended them and spent time with them in Francis's aunt's fancy country house an hour from Bennington, Henry reveals to him that four of them (excluding Bunny) had staged a "Bacchanal" in the country in which, inadvertently, a farmer was killed. They did not go to the police because they were dressed in blood-soaked bed sheets, and they believed that a jury of "poverty-level Vermonters would [not] have the remotest bit of pity for four college students on trial for murdering one of their neighbors." Bunny, learning of the murder, is blackmailing them. In addition to the blackmail, his thousands of "religious slurs, temper tantrums, insults, coercions, debts" are offensive to the group. The only recourse, according to this sick quartet, but especially Henry, is to murder Bunny. Henry works on various poisons and dosages, practicing on a dog, and finally decides to waylay Bunny where he walks on the mountain. The events that follow are violent and tragic, transforming the lives of all the characters.

Sarah Stewart Taylor

In nimble and literate *O' Artful Death* (2003), Sweeney St. George is the daughter of a famous painter and a professor of art history in Boston. A specialist in funerary art, Sweeney becomes fascinated by a sculpture of a young woman, Mary Denholm, with a figure of Death leering over her shoulder, from a cemetery in Byzantium. When her best friend and colleague, Toby Di Marco, invites her to spend Christmas in Vermont, she cannot resist the researcher's urge. Toby's great-grandparents built the house on Birch Lane currently lived in by other relatives. Before she leaves Boston, Sweeney makes one telephone call to a woman in Byzantium named Ruth Kimball, who may know something about Mary's death. The call is cut off unexpectedly, but Sweeney suspects that Ruth knows something. When she tries to reach Ruth the next day, Sweeney finds that Ruth has committed suicide. What do the two deaths—in 1890 and 1990—have in common? It seems that Ruth was planning to sell her property (which has been in her family for one-hundred-and-fifty years) to a developer, much against the wishes of the old-timers at the Byzantium Artist's Colony, who are very attached to their past. According to Vermont's Act 250, the select board must examine each major development. This conflict only exacerbates the social and cultural differences between the colonists and the "natives" (as the artists call them). "It's funny about these people up here. You're either from here or you aren't. It really matters to them. They don't like to tell

you things if you're not a native." Excerpts from a history of the artist's colony serve as epigraphs for each chapter; each epigraph introduces an aspect of former Byzantium life that is paralleled in the modern scene. The "small townness" is illustrated in "Everybody knows everybody's business." Sweeney finds in a Boston library a copy of the journal of a contemporary of Mary's. Sweeney is torn between her sense that her platonic feelings for Toby are turning to something else, as she jealously watches him with Rosemary Burgess, and her attraction to (or is it revulsion from?) Ian Ball, a handsome young Englishman who makes Sweeney very nervous. What is his connection to the scene? Why was he following her in Boston? The resolution is charming and leaves the door open for Sweeney to choose between Toby and Ian in a sequel. One of a number of lovely images: "the red barns and white farmhouses like exotic holly berries, nestled amongst the green."

Douglas Terman

In **Free Flight* (1980), Gregory Mallon, an airforce officer, was on leave when, a year-and-a-half previously, the Soviets mounted a nuclear attack upon the United States, thereby starting World War III. Greg was stranded in his cabin in northern Vermont but managed to avoid radiation; his wife died. He discovers that there is no transportation, no industry, and no organized resistance to the new government; a system is in place to turn in to the authorities anyone who is hostile to the new regime. Greg is captured by one of the new leaders but escapes with an African-American prisoner named Wyatt. Greg steals a sailplane, and he and Wyatt, despite heavy enemy helicopter fire, make it to French-speaking Canada where they meet a brave and appealing woman, her aphoristic grandfather who is dying of cancer, and her son, who has been brainwashed by the Soviets and their collaborators. After the son slips away to inform upon them and Wyatt dies of his wounds, Greg and the woman, who have fallen in love, plan to escape, with the grandfather's blessing, to western Canada and freedom.

Nancy Tesler

At the start of *Slippery Slopes & Other Deadly Things* (2003), Carrie Carlin has returned to Snowridge, a ski resort in the village of Sunnyvale near Stowe, where she used to ski with former husband Rich Burnham, and her two children, Allie, fourteen, and Mark, twelve. The current man in her life, homicide Lieutenant Ted Brodsky, is bringing her children up from New Jersey after Carrie finishes with her biofeedback conference. Carrie, a professional in the biofeedback field, uses electroencephalogram brain waves on Attention Deficit Disorder children, for example, and is eager to hear Dr. Hubert Freundlich, acknowledged leader in the field, speak on his exciting new research. Assembled conferees, in addition to Dr. Freundlich's wife, Gerta, are Flo Zimmer, president of Doctors Against Holistic Medicine; Joe Golden, a psychiatrist who once treated Carrie; Charlie Anders and Kate Donovan, two research assistants to Dr. Freundlich; and Dr. Nadine Claughton, a psychologist. When Charlie is murdered, Carrie arranges for her children to stay with their father; Ted comes up alone, just in time for more murders to occur. The couple solves the mystery, but not before Carrie volunteers to act as bait for the murderer and almost dies herself.

Nancy Thayer

Although Westhampton College, where Daphne Miller, forty-six, works as a secretary in *My Dearest Friend* (1989), is just over the border in Massachusetts, she buys a cottage in Plover on a dead-end road in the woods. When she first came to Westhampton, she was married to Professor Joe Miller and seeking her doctoral degree in medieval literature. After having her daughter, Cynthia, Daphne stayed home. Now, fourteen years later, Cynthia has gone to live with her father in California. Daphne's dearest friend at the college is elegant, gentle Hudson Jennings, head of the English Department; their friendship would have blossomed into something more if Hudson had not been married to aristocratic, self-possessed Claire. Daphne's dearest friend used to be Laura Kraft, married to Otto.

After Otto began an affair with another woman, Laura started an affair with Daphne's husband, Joe. He divorced Daphne to marry Laura and took her to California. Since then, Daphne has had one affair with an alcoholic lawyer named David, who died of cirrhosis of the liver. Into this scene comes English professor Jack Hamilton, thirty-one, who buys an A-frame house just down the road from Daphne for his wife, Carey Ann, and his two-year-old daughter, Alexandra. Joe and Carey Ann's marriage is in difficulty. He and Daphne begin to spend time together—just friends. He often stops at her house for a drink after jogging; she often keeps him company in the evening while tiresome, shallow Carey Ann is off at one of her support groups. Daphne and Joe, who are attracted to each other, agree that they like leaving the college civility daily to go to the wilderness in Vermont (a different state, both literally and figuratively). Daphne, Jack, and Hudson must each make decisions about the future.

Daniel Pierce Thompson

Three novels, *The Green Mountain Boys: A Historical Tale of the Early Settlement of Vermont, Locke Amsden, or, The Schoolmaster*, and *The Rangers, or, The Tory's Daughter* are discussed, followed by descriptions of two collections of stories, *May Martin, or, The Money Diggers and Other Green Mountain Tales*, and *Centeola and Other Tales*. The period of *The Green Mountain Boys* (1839) is just prior to the Revolutionary War. Yorkers are threatening the settlers in the New Hampshire Grants and forcibly taking away their farms and property. The action near Otter Creek on Lake Dunmore starts when a sheriff from Albany named Munroe, with ten men and a spy named Jacob Sherwood, try to overtake a small band of Green Mountain Boys, Captain Charles Warrington, Lieutenant Edward Selden, and Pete Jones. Neshobee, a friendly Indian, has brought Warrington a message from the widow Ann Story on Otter Creek, warning him about Munroe's approach. Sherwood leads the Yorkers to the cave where the Green Mountain Boys are camped, but the Green Mountain Boys outwit the Yorkers and

Sherwood is taken prisoner and given a beech-branch beating (the "beech seal") before being released. The Green Mountain Boys then travel to Ann Story's house, carrying fish and venison to her and her family. For their safety, she and her children spend the nights in a secret cave that she has fashioned near the house. At midnight, Charles hears a familiar woman's voice singing, but Ann Story will not explain this mystery. They continue to the compound seized by Colonel Reed and his Highlanders. Reed, who was largely responsible for turning over Montreal and Canada to the British, secured a huge tract of land near Lake Champlain, drove out the inhabitants forcibly, and took possession of the sawmills. Donald McIntosh runs the fort as a military operation. Charles and his men peacefully assume command of the fort, held by Reed's daughter, Jessy. In a charming scene, Warrington takes McIntosh's surrender and then invites him and his men into the house to spend the night. The fort and property are restored to their rightful owners; McIntosh returns to the area and lives on a farm in Panton until his death in 1813. Edward volunteers to escort Jessy and her maid to Skenesboro. Charles then leaves his men to go to his own property near Snake Mountain, granted him by New Hampshire. Charles finds his land inhabited, and much improved, by a Yorker, Captain Hendee, who is living there with his beautiful daughter, Alma, whose singing Charles heard at Ann Story's. Charles first met the Hendees and fell in love with Alma when he was traveling incognito as Mr. Howard on Green Mountain Boys business. He reveals his true identity and explains to her the plight of the settlers. Her suitor is Sherwood, whom she does not love but to whom her father is greatly indebted. While Charles is at the Hendees, a very large gentleman named "Smith" (Colonel Ethan Allen) arrives, tells them about the Battle of Lexington, pretends to get drunk, and is billeted with Charles in the barn. Munroe's men come to arrest them, but they escape with the help of Neshobee, who works for the Hendees. Meanwhile, Edward has accompanied the "volatile but not ungifted" Jessy to Skenesboro, and they have fallen in love. Jessy,

in a letter to her good friend, Alma, describes Edward as "a handsome, quizzical, audacious rogue." Mr. Prouty, an inhabitant of the Grants, carried away with his own importance, accepts the office of Justice of Peace of New York against the rules of the Green Mountain Boys, who capture and punish him. Edward and Charles are at the encampment with Captain Remember Baker and Colonel Allen. In Middlebury on May 4, 1775, the Green Mountain Boys meet to discuss the quarrel between the colonies and England. (The author sings the praises of the "high-minded and worthy" early settlers of Middlebury and their "enterprise, firmness, and intelligence" in building a college almost immediately.) Allen proposes capturing the British forts at Ticonderoga and Crown Point. They agree to meet at Castleton on May eighth. Jessy receives a letter from Alma, telling her that Alma is now engaged to Charles, but her father still wants her to marry Sherwood. The men are assembling to make the trip across the lake when Colonel Benedict Arnold arrives, expecting to lead the troops. Charles explains that the men have volunteered to serve under Colonel Allen, and Arnold, understanding, offers to volunteer as a common soldier. The Green Mountain Boys take Ticonderoga without loss of life, and Crown Point, and Major Skene's fort, and Edward leads the ladies to safety at Alma's house. Alma learns from a traveling tinker that Charles is already married (this is a trick of the execrable Sherwood) and breaks off her engagement to him. (The author then passes rapidly over two years and several campaigns, including the attempt on Montreal, during which Ethan Allen is captured and taken to Britain.) Alma finds out that Charles is not married; Edward's Tory father dies, but not before changing his will, acknowledging that he has cheated the Hendees and making restitution. Through the narrative hints are dropped that Hendee's son, who disappeared as a child, may yet be alive. Burgoyne's army is on the march. Sherwood and a group of Indians capture the Hendees as they start for Castleton. Neshobee seeks help and Charles sends Edward to the rescue. The party escapes and hides at Ann

Story's, with great damage to her property. The Battle of Hubbardton takes place. Although they receive the mistaken word that Charles is slain, they are all reunited and find out that Edward is Hendee's son. The two couples are married.

The eponymous hero of **Locke Amsden** (1847) is one of two children of a successful, reputable farmer: Benjamin, twelve, works well with horses and in the fields; Locke, sixteen, is constantly reading and figuring. A chance visit by a stranger, whose carriage horse has lost a shoe, brings Locke in contact with a gentleman who recommends public education for farmers so that agriculture does not remain less honorable than other professions. "Knowledge is power," he states. He believes that "those who think and those who toil should be one and the same class." Locke is astounded that this stranger is articulating thoughts that he himself has had. The visitor, whose name the Amsdens never learn (although his lovely daughter is called Mary) sends Locke a box of books on science and mathematics. The local schoolmaster is not pleased with Locke's superior learning, so Locke works away on his own. A well-qualified teacher, Mr. Seaver, takes a post at Locke's school and recognizes the latter's talents. Mr. Amsden gives permission for Locke to spend a year at an Academy, where he again finds Seaver employed. Locke finds his first job at a school in the vicinity of Horn of the Moon, north of his parents' village. Captain Bill Bunker, a fine man who can neither read nor write, is head of the school committee and delighted with Locke. The school's students have a reputation for being rough, but Locke treats them as "men and women" and they respond well. He is put to the test by a couple of bullies, but Locke uses such consideration and tact that the boys all rally around. When the students begin to look pale and sickly—one little boy becomes seriously ill— some in the community, including Deacon Gilchrist, accuse Locke of black magic. Bill Bunker points out to the committee, which is on the verge of firing Locke, that the problem is poor ventilation in the classroom. From then on, the school prospers and the intellectual and moral tone of the whole district improves; Locke

also sponsors physical education activities. Locke leaves the school to pursue his studies and to attend college at the urging of Mr. Seaver. Locke wants to continue teaching at the common schools, because he believes deeply that it is the young children who are most in need of a qualified teacher. After finishing college with high credentials, he passes through thriving Mill Town Emporium and decides to apply for a job. He loses to Mr. Blake, a patent ignoramus who dazzles the school committee, and rides away, meeting Dr. Lincoln from his last school. Dr. Lincoln appreciates Locke's fine qualities and invites him to be the schoolmaster at the common school in Cartersville, an interior village in the general vicinity of Montpelier dominated by the Carter family, son of the founder. The current Mr. Carter is a rich man who lives in a vulgar house with an affected wife, three vain and empty-headed daughters, and a niece. The Carters have started a private school to provide a "genteel" education for the children of a few "distinguished" families and hired Manlius C.W. Tilden, Professor of Elegant Literature, to guide them. Because the common school is run down and the children without ambition, Dr. Lincoln hopes Locke can elevate the morale. Dr. Lincoln proposes to the Carters that their niece, Mary Maverick, attend the common school. Her father, who was a great friend of Dr. Lincoln's, lost his fortune and his health, went off to South America, and is presumed dead. The Carters are horrified at the idea of her going to a "vulgar district school" with a "rustic" for a teacher. Mary comes to Locke's school to discover they are old acquaintances. Locke finds that the children have endured bad teachers but, worse, the inhabitants have totally neglected the school. He tries to interest the parents and guardians in the school but does not succeed. He is ignored socially, which is hurtful, but what injures him more is the low estimation in which the teaching profession is held. Tilden tries to sully Locke's reputation and ends up exposing himself (and Mr. Blake) as frauds. After Tilden's departure, Locke's accomplishments are finally appreciated. He is able to save Mary from a terrible fire just as Colonel

Maverick returns unexpectedly. Mary and Locke declare their love.

The Rangers (1851) begins in March 1775 as a carriage of Tories travels from Bennington to Westminster to take part in a session of the Westminster Court. Inside are Squire Haviland, his daughter, Sabrey, with her fiancé, John Peters; and Jane McRae with her fiancé, Mr. Jones. The vindictive character of Peters is defined when he runs the rig of Henry ("Harry") Woodburn off the road in Brattleboro and kills the latter's horse because Harry is suing Peters over the deed to Harry's rightful farm in Guilford. Instead of challenging Peters, Harry bides his time, since the opportunity is coming for the Americans to choose their own leaders and rid themselves of foreign oppression. Demonstrating the class distinctions of the time, Jane McRae says she "would not have expected such magnanimity from one of his class." The chief business of the courts is disputed land titles; the judges, all Yorkers, favor their brother speculators and Loyalists. On the way to Westminster, Harry saves Sabrey's life in a flooded river and falls in love with her. A Tory's daughter, she is pure, guileless, and noble-minded, with a lively sense of right and wrong. Alas, she is engaged to the repellent Peters. The haughty and aristocratic Loyalists underestimate the intelligence and spirit of the "common people." The night before the meeting, Colonel Carpenter cautions the Americans to be prudent and not shed the first blood. The next day, the unarmed rebels take control of the courtroom; many of them are shot and, with Harry, thrown into prison. Sabrey sends a note of thanks to Harry in prison. Peters wins his case by default. The rebels take over the courtroom and release their friends. So, with this resistance, the British authority in these parts is subverted, leading to Lexington, Ticonderoga, and Bunker Hill. Harry's farm is in Guilford, where a minion of Peters has turned Harry's widowed, educated, sick, and destitute mother out of her house and into a deserted and dilapidated log cabin. The minion has also thrown all her possessions into the snow and sold off her stock. A week later Harry finds her. Vermont now exists as a state and

the Guilford residents choose a Whig moderator for the first time in several years. Colonel Carpenter offers a resolution to shake off York rule forever. As she dies, Harry's mother recommends that he look up Uncle Charles Woodburn who, though he was "improvident and profligate in living," swore that he would make it up to the family. Harry sees Sabrey but tries to dampen his feelings for her; he knows his love for her could only end in "disappointment and mortification." He finds his buried deed and seeks out Peters, who raises a loaded whip to strike Harry; Harry parries with his cane and fears he has killed Peters. Harry makes his way to the house of Father Heriot, who has just been cleared of a crime he did not commit. Two years later, the story focuses on the "gloomy and portentous" summer of 1777. The long dispute between New York and New Hampshire has produced a crop of "hardy, determined, liberty-loving men" who resolve to declare themselves independent and produce a constitution. Fort Ticonderoga falls, the colonial troops are scattered, and the British army is sweeping along the western border of the state, "flanked by merciless savages." The Old Council of Safety is established in Manchester, with Thomas Chittenden as head and people like the Fay brothers and Ira Allen as members. Daily, people defect to the Loyalists. The Council moves to raise a full regiment, to be called The Rangers, and to be paid for by confiscating Tory property. Harry has been in the Continental Army with Arnold, captured, and imprisoned. Now a captain in Herrick's Rangers, Harry and Sabrey meet again. He tells her that he loves her, even though she is the daughter of wealth and prosperity and he, the son of poverty and misfortune. He learns that Sabrey is secretly on the side of the rebels but is bound in a marriage contract to the malevolent Peters, who is a colonel in the British army; her father also joins the British. Sabrey's father is furious that Sabrey won't marry Peters because she has been "allowed to mingle with an ignorant, rebellious populace." She announces that she has no sympathies for those who come "to oppress and enslave my country." The Council, which has determined to confiscate the Haviland property, hears her words and allows her to stay with the Risdons, her neighbors, until she can return to relatives in Guilford. All of the main characters meet again in Cavendish, on the old military road, where Captain John Coffin runs a house of public entertainment. About one hundred Loyalists and Indians are making their way across the mountains to the Connecticut River. Sabrey is also en route, escorted by Bart and accompanied by her friend, Vine Howard. The Tories, led by the fell Peters, take the two young ladies prisoner. Harry is at Coffin's when he hears the distressing news; a small band sets out to rescue the captives. They find Vine, but Sabrey has escaped on her own and is wandering in the dark forest. She comes upon an Indian encampment and watches in horror as wolves eat the Indians. Finding a gun, she shoots into the pack of wolves, scaring them off, only to be tricked by the treacherous David Redding, who recaptures her and takes her to Albany. Stark and Herrick arrive at Coffin's and are met by Ira Allen, who has a letter from Sabrey (smuggled to Ira by Bart, who is spying among the British troops) to report that something important is stirring at Bennington. In Albany, poor Sabrey is forced to meet with British officers and Loyalists, who all assume she is engaged to Peters. Lady Reidsel helps her escape with Bart, and they turn toward Fort Edward. Passing the house of the McRaes, they see Jane, dressed for her wedding with Jones and about to set out with an Indian escort provided by the ill-advised bridegroom. In fact, he has offered rewards to two bands of Indians; they fight over the unfortunate girl and murder and scalp her. Sabrey and Bart head for Bennington and are dangerously snaking their way through enemy ranks when she is once again captured by the ubiquitous minions of the "vindictive" Peters (Bart gets away). Sabrey joins her friend Vine in captivity. Their log cabin looks out on the field where Baum and Stark are encamped. Baum finds himself in an unexpectedly perilous position. He had been told that "large bodies of friendly inhabitants would rise up in arms to join his standard as he advanced to the interior." Colonel Stark and his men go to the rear of Baum's army and

surround him. Stark perseveres, ably aided by Seth Warner and the Green Mountain Boys. After fighting gallantly, Harry goes to see Father Herriot, who gives Sabrey back the deed to her house and a deed to a house for Bart—and Vine. He then confesses that he is Harry's long-lost, indiscreet Uncle Charlie and Bart's father. Ethan Allen returns from captivity and presides at the hanging of David Redding, traitor and spy. Harry is in New Jersey, fighting with Washington.

May Martin, or, The Money Diggers and Other Green Mountain Tales (1835) contains three stories about Vermont, including the title tale, "**May Martin, or, The Money Diggers.**" May, who lives in Harwood Settlement in western Vermont in the early years of the nineteenth century, is of uncertain birth but has been brought up as the adopted daughter of a couple named Martin. Her beauty and breeding attest to her superior background. She is engaged to handsome, manly William Ashley, who goes down to Massachusetts to make a payment on his pitch in this beautiful Vermont valley. She reveals that the Martins are not her real parents and that they are excessively cruel to her. While he is away, the villainous counterfeiter and con man, Gow, conspires with Mr. Martin to dupe local people into investing in the hunt for a mythical treasure buried somewhere nearby. He is also privy to some secret about May's birth. By forging a letter from William to May, breaking their engagement, the heinous Gow and Mr. Martin trick his daughter, May, into agreeing to marry Gow. She finds out that her real grandfather has left her a fortune, which is the reason that Gow wants to marry her. Meanwhile, he is pretending to dig for buried treasure and duping the diggers into giving him money. May enlists help from Shrewd David Butler, a teenager, to act as her messenger. Her father is Frank Harwood, after whom the settlement is named. Shamed and ruined, Martin commits suicide. Gow is jailed, released, becomes a minister, and seven years after the event asks forgiveness of May and William, now happily married. "**Ethan Allen and the Lost Children**" tells the dramatic story of Colonel's Allen's helping to find two young children who have wandered off into the woods. Allen enlists the aid of local farmers to search for the children. When they fail, after several nights' search, and are ready to quit, he exhorts them by telling them that he will not rest until the children are found. They do find them that night, but not before the children are almost devoured by wolves. The hunters quickly dispatch the ravening beasts. **"The Guardian and the Ghost"** concerns Old Jude Hosmer, whose brother, Colonel James Hosmer, died and left his brother the guardian of his daughter, Lucy. She loves Lot Fisher, who has been befriended and raised by Squire Stacy, the town lawyer. Lot has every conceivable sterling quality except that he was, in the words of the village gossips, "kinder unfortunate about his birth." When Old Jude refuses to accept Lot's suit, Squire Stacy tells Lot about Old Jude's rapacious wrongdoings. An eavesdropper overhears their conversation, giving Old Jude an advantage in this negotiation. In his "flagitious" plot to rob Lucy of her inheritance, Old Jude pays a woman who has been "misfortunit" to tell people her baby's name is "Lot Fisher." Soon the village gossips start dropping in at Lucy's, full of scandalous hints. Meanwhile, Shadrack "Shack" Rogers, Old Jude's "deaf" servant, who is loyal to Lucy, pretends to be Colonel James Hosmer's ghost and terrorizes Old Jude at night. Old Jude, frightened—and chastened—becomes a changed man. Seven years later, Shack goes out West to start a new life.

Centeola and Other Tales (1864) contains four stories with a Vermont locale. **"The Starving Settlers"** is about a man who, mustered out after the Revolutionary War, goes to Vermont, builds a log cabin on the east bank of the Onion River, and there installs his wife and two children, Minnie, sixteen, and a younger boy. Running short of supplies, he travels to the settlement of Burlington, where Gideon King is in charge. Gideon has sent a sloop for supplies but finds the narrator work while he is waiting. Uneasy, the narrator dreams one night that his family is in great difficulty: the children fish and lose their rod and tackle; a bear family eats their store of meal. The next night he dreams that because the

family is starving Minnie sets out for the southern settlement where she has a beau, Constant Martin. The narrator is so worried he decides to return home, experiencing great difficulties on the way. He finds the mother and son starving; Minnie is away. He gives them each a tiny sip of spirits, with which Gideon had supplied him, sets water to boiling, and goes into the forest where he shoots a moose and drags back a joint to put in the water. He feeds them a little broth until they regain their strength. Minnie and Constant return with provisions, flour and meal. They enjoy "more truly a Thanksgiving supper than anyone has ever partaken in the Green Mountains." **"The Unfathomable Mystery: A Tale of Circumstantial Evidence"** is narrated by Mr. Bradley to a supper club in New Orleans. Mr. Bradley is involved in this case in the town of B_____ in central Vermont. His sister, Mrs. Nymore, has a boarder, Mr. C. Craney, who suddenly appears to have a great deal of money. Craney confesses to Mr. Bradley that he is in possession of a dreadful secret. He has seen two men with a dead body and is being bribed not to tell anyone. After Craney leaves town, he writes the details of the incident to Mr. Bradley, who informs the sheriff. Upon his arrest, Craney denies the whole story. An inquiry is held; the body cannot be found. An agent is hired to investigate two related events—the disappearance of a Scottish peddler and an Irishman purported to have a trunk filled with silk and jewels. Craney is offered immunity from prosecution if he will return to B_____ to locate the body, but it has been removed. **"The Rustic Financiers"** is set in Cozy Corner, where three scoundrels, Riah Cutefight, Bill Versute, and Eph Equivoke devise a money-making scheme in the tavern barroom ("that standing Elysium of small, country village loungers"). Riah and Bill go off in a wagon and, on their return, ask the landlord to store some flour, which they make a show of locking up. Everyone is suspicious. Eph, playing his part as objective observer, reports to the village that his friends know where there is a lot of money but lack operating capital and are looking for subscribers. He enlists thirty men (including the deacon) at one hundred dollars each. They are duped, but none of them wants to confess his gullibility. Riah and Bill take off immediately out West and Eph follows. **"The Counterfeiter"** is notorious Stephen Burroughs, who, after a career in Vermont, flees to Canada to run a counterfeiting training school. In central Vermont in the Green Mountains lives an avaricious farmer, Joseph Bidwell, with his wife, son, Tom, and daughter, Kate, who is engaged to John Perley but cannot marry him because he has no money. In the village, Tom hears that some men returning from the French wars buried some silver coins in nearby mountains; Kate overhears Tom telling their father. Shortly thereafter, a young traveler, John Gale, seeks lodgings with them. The next day, he describes a wondrous dream to Bidwell in which he dug up some gold coins. Bidwell persuades Gale to take him to the site he visualized in the dream, and they find a cache of coins. They stow it in a cellar hole Bidwell had built, and he agrees to change the specie for paper, which will be easier for Gale to carry. Kate Bidwell sees and hears everything and, when she examines the coins, discovers they are counterfeit and goes immediately to the sheriff. He sends Tom and John Perley after Gale, and a Court of Inquiry is held with the state's attorney. It turns out Gale is the man Tom had heard talking in the village. Gale, however, doesn't have any of the counterfeit money on him and Bidwell *does*. Bidwell is granted immunity if he will testify against Gale and pledges to give his one thousand dollars to his daughter, Kate, for her dowry. Gale is sentenced to ten years in prison.

Mari Tomasi

The quarry in *Like Lesser Gods* (1949) in Granitetown (a fictional Barre) opened after the War of 1812, making first doorsills and later memorials and stone blocks for buildings. Scottish, German, and Italian immigrant cutters came in droves to work the quarries on the hill. In 1924, Michelle ("Tiff") Tiffone, a well-educated teacher in a Piedmont village school, travels to America to join a bachelor nephew in Rich Haven, whom he finds dying and his store

in debt. A former student from Italy now living in Granitetown, Pietro Dalli, sends word that his home is open to Tiff, who finds the town in an uproar. The workers are on strike. Pietro's wife, Maria, who is expecting their fourth child, expresses her fears to Tiff about the silica dust that is poisoning the workers' lungs (the sheds have to be closed against the bad winters). A friend named Italo Tosti dies of lung disease. The priest and Tiff go next door to the town tramp, Josie Blaine, to ask her to stay with the widow, Lucia, while Pietro and another friend work in Massachusetts for a few weeks. As he enters Josie's house, Tiff notices the escaping figure of her customer, Asa Conway, the local storekeeper. All the children, especially Petra and Vetch Dalli, adore Tiff. Like a guardian angel, he intervenes when affairs go awry. He convinces Italo's widow to stop selling bootleg liquor and to start a sewing business; he persuades Asa to let the children play on his field; and he saves the life of a boy in the abandoned quarry. The Douglas family, which lives in the yellow brick mansion on Douglas Hill, owns the quarry. There is resentment on the part of the workers against the "moneyed social order." The workers raise a purse to send Tiff back to Italy (where he does not want to go). He stops off in Maple Junction to visit Josie, who steals his money, and works as a handyman there until he can return to Granitetown, repay the workers' money, and pay rent to the Dallis. Seventeen years pass and war is being waged in Europe, although no hostility has been shown to the German and Italian immigrants in Granitetown. Vermont has enacted a law requiring granite sheds and quarries to install suction hoses and dust-removing equipment. Petra Dalli is now a nurse; her brother, Vetch, is a quarryman, married to an Irish girl; Gino Tosti is a doctor; and Danny Douglas wants to be a stone-carver against his parents' wishes. A tuberculosis sanatorium has been built on the old Vitleau pasture (they moved away after their son, Leo, was killed in the quarry). Tiff dresses in a suit once a week to teach Italian to the workers' grandchildren. Pietro, who contracts tuberculosis-silicosis, tries a few weeks of sunshine at a camp at Chisel Point Pond, fifteen miles away, but finally has to go to the sanatorium. At the camp, Americo Dalli meets Aster Mitcham, who is the daughter of Josie by Asa. Josie has moved back to Granitetown to run a hotdog stand. Tiff gets Aster a job at Asa's store so that she can earn money for college. A romantic triangle arises: Petra must choose between Gino and Danny.

U

John Updike

Seek My Face (2002), which takes place in 2001, consists of a day-long conversation between seventy-nine-year-old painter Hope Oudekirk Chafetz, living in seclusion northeast of Montpelier, and a chic young interviewer from New York named Kathryn D'Angelo. This dialogue allows Hope the opportunity to review her life. She grew up in Pennsylvania in a Quaker family and led a wild life in an artist community in East Hampton, Long Island, with her first husband, Zack McCoy. McCoy was a drunken brute who discouraged her attempts at painting, treating her "as a painter upstairs like the mad Mrs. Rochester." He was driving with a "groupie" and another woman friend when he overturned the convertible, killing one of the women and hurtling himself into a tree. She married her second husband, Guy Holloway, and lived in Connecticut with him and her family. Holloway painted junk food, did silkscreens, made experimental films, took drugs, and was responsible for suicidal actresses. He is still alive with Alzheimer's. She retired to Vermont with her third husband, Jerome Chafetz, a successful businessman and art collector. Her two Holloway sons, Piet and Paul, went to the Putney School and became financial wizards. Her daughter, Dorothy, a lesbian, has not found a career. As the interviewer seeks Hope's views on the post-War American art scene, Hope responds with sentiment, with resentment, and with alacrity. While she is thinking about her life throughout the day,

she looks out the window periodically at her Vermont view, which provides many examples of delightful language: "the big Andersen windows that provide a wide view of the old apple orchard staggering up the slope to the north." Some of the images are from a painter's eye: "The far mountains overlap in waves like viscid, studiously continuous blue brush-strokes on glass," and "A sickly wash of white light lies low over the horizon of the mountains." Others are dazzling similes: "sitting on a warm flat rock in the wall, he [the squirrel] holds it [a nut] in two paws corn-on-the-cob style and chitters at it like a tiny electric typewriter," "pieces of snow visible in the woods like scattered laundry," and "the [window] glass itself, the bubbled, faintly wavy, faintly violet-tinged panes, had seemed thinned, like the skin of an old person." (The title is from Psalm 27: "You speak in my heart and say, 'Seek my face.' Your face, Lord, will I seek.")

William Hazlett Upson

Alexander Botts in "**Botts Runs for his Life**" (1952), ingenious, comic, diligent, and vulnerable employee of the Earthworm Tractor Company based in Illinois, was a favorite character of readers of the *Saturday Evening Post*. Here, he is asked by his boss to go to Middlebury to call upon James Jorgensen, who is engaged in a big logging project there. Jorgensen has been experiencing technical difficulties with his Earthworm tractors and has threatened to transfer his business to the Superba Tractor Company. On the New York-Vermont train, Botts arranges to meet Harold Quincy, the Superba rep, and, under an assumed name, to worm out of him Quincy's sales secrets. Quincy commandeered the services of a young man named Oswald, a dissatisfied tractor operator at Jorgensen's operation, by offering Oswald a job with Superba (and a house and other perquisites) in exchange for sabotaging Jorgensen's fifteen-year-old Earthworm tractors. (Quincy cautioned against too much sabotage: he plans to sell the perfectly good Earthworm tractors later). Botts turns up at the Earthworm Company disguised as a Superba representative. He arranges to make

Oswald confess to him while Jorgensen is within earshot; this is possible because there are army surplus interphones in every office. Botts contrives to lock Jorgensen in one room, turn the machine to "talk," and prevail upon Oswald in another room to describe what he has been doing to the tractors. The trick works, even though Botts, as usual, ends up in the hospital with wounds sustained in the line of duty.

V

Frederic Franklyn Van de Water

In addition to the four historical novels described below, Van de Water wrote three contemporary novels: *Mrs. Applegate's Affair, Fool's Errand,* and *The Sooner to Sleep.* In **Mrs. Applegate's Affair** (1944), Lucy Applegate, thirty-four, is staying at her summer home in Walden with her twelve-year-old son, Ashley, and her younger sister, Muriel. Her husband, Harrison, is serving a four-month tour with the Ordnance Corps in Washington. Lucy has suggested to Harrison a "trial divorce" in which, unfettered, they experiment with other companionship. Lieutenant Richard ("Dick") Banning, a marine, and Bailey Ward, head of the Walden Defense Council, are both courting Muriel. Lucy's hired man, Cyril Handrow, who is married to her cook, Rena, pronounces Bailey's name in the "dry special voice Yankees use for the mention of the wealthy." The most prestigious member of the summer colony, Mrs. Eliphat Starkweather (daughter of a governor, widow of a senator) arrives in Walden with her granddaughter, Mehitabel, and the latter's husband, Larry Moncure. Larry, tall, lean, and attractive, is soon flirting with Lucy and proposing a dalliance; she is seriously tempted but realizes, in time, that he is a cad. Dick returns home in civilian clothes on a secret mission that he is unable to reveal to Muriel; she misunderstands, thinking he has been dishonorably discharged. A romantic con-

fection in picture-perfect weather, the novel ends happily when Muriel becomes engaged to Dick and Harrison returns home from temporary duty to Lucy's eager arms.

In the more somber **Fool's Errand** (1945), the idyll that Martin Brent, forty, imagined his Vermont life would be does not materialize. He left Manhattan with his daughter, Molly, thirteen, at the urging of his wife, Anne, whose Aunt Hattie Sawyer left her a farm in Appledore near Walden. Martin feels "uncomfortably alien" among these "brown, solemn men, grave and composed." He feels more at home when he and Anne are introduced into a society of people with "equivalent background and speech," but he soon learns that their idea of simple living is several uniformed servants, gleaming silver, and napery on the table. These people, also "outlanders," turn out to be conservative Republicans against the New Deal. Anne is worried because Molly likes Seth Hathaway, the son of the hired man, who is not "her class." The cynosure of their crowd is writer Luke Cloud, who has abandoned fiction to enter his "Vermont book" period ("This is the best thing I've done yet"). His house has a "carefully contrived air of antiquity" and his wife, Phyllida, is a sultry flirt. Martin falls under her spell and, with her encouragement, has a brief affair with her. He becomes more and more disillusioned with Vermont, which is not the "clean, bright Arcady" that Anne sees or the "Currier & Ives serenity" extolled in Cloud's books. When Martin almost despairs of making any money, Cloud's agent, Rappaport, commissions him to do some illustrations and jacket designs for Cloud's work. Martin's fortunes go from bad to worse: his potatoes develop blight; he learns that Phyllida is having an affair with Meredith Bishop; Cloud learns of Martin's involvement with Phyllida; and Bishop buys up his mortgage and announces he is going to foreclose. Seth suffers a mysterious illness; meanwhile, his father has been working with Ora Spangler at his still. Seth moves in with Dan Henry, the game warden. Martin learns that Ora is drunkenly spreading stories about Martin and Phyllida. He goes into the woods with Dan's gun (lent to him when Dan hurt himself) and fires a warning shot at Ora. The shot kills Ora and, eventually, Martin is arrested. Desperate, he skis over a cliff and kills himself. Of Martin's inability to assimilate, Dan, a voice of Vermont, points out, "Tain't easy to transplant full-grown trees." Seth, whom Anne spurned for her daughter's company, plans to attend college to become a lawyer; after all, his great-grandfather Holcomb was attorney general of Vermont.

The Sooner to Sleep (1946) concerns the Carroll family of Grantchester in southern Andros County near the Indian River, ruled by the melodramatic and self-absorbed matriarch, Agatha Fife Carroll. Her husband's family has lived in Grantchester for generations. It is wartime. All the Carroll men are overseas: husband John is on a mission in South America, son Roger is a lieutenant in the navy, daughter May Atherton's husband, Bill, is in the South Pacific (May's daughter, Melissa, nine, is also in Grantchester), and brother Colonel Greg Fife is in Burma. Agatha, a former actress, is playing to the hilt the role of keeping the homefires burning for her men, no matter what the cost to her personally. Into the household comes Roger's fiancée, Juanita Peble (her Grandfather Peble was born in Vermont but ran off to California and married Grandmother Diaz); Roger had planned to marry Juanita before being called back to active duty. Their next-door neighbor is famous and glamorous poet Vera Thorne Isherwood, mother of the obnoxious, tubby Roscoe. Vera cannot control her unscrupulous, seductress self and has soon taken in thrall local carpenter and housepainter David Howells. (Vera is reassured when she learns Howells is married. A wife is "like a library to which you, in your own time, could return a borrowed book.") Then Greg comes home on leave and he, too, falls prey to Vera's charms. There are several frivolous subplots—training Melissa to compete in the annual poetry contest; trying to keep Greg from seeing Vera—but the main theme is Juanita's victory over Agatha's attempts to subjugate her as she has everyone else in the household. At the end Juanita declares her independence from Agatha and goes to New York to spend a twenty-four-hour leave with Roger. (The title comes from Charles Kingsley's poem, "The Three Fishers:" "For men must work, and women must weep/And the sooner it's over, the sooner to sleep.")

The four novels discussed below, *Reluctant Rebel*, *Catch a Falling Star*, *Wings of the Morning*, and *Day of Battle*, are concerned with early Vermont's struggle for self-ownership. The four young heroes from different backgrounds face the same ambiguities, conflicting loyalties, and the complexity and confusion of the first years of the War of Independence. In **Reluctant Rebel** (1948), on his way to Canada, Adam Corlaer, who grew up in Albany but has been at Oxford University, stops in Bennington to visit property he owns in Panton. The year is 1771, and the tavern he chooses is full of men rebelling against the governor of New York's claims on the New Hampshire Grants. Colonel Ethan Allen is having a meeting upstairs with his Green Mountain Boys. Adam initiates a fight with a British officer who is bothering a young lady. Learning that she, Felicity Sherwood, and her brother, Justus, are headed north, he pursues them, befriends them, and stays with them at the house of widow Mindwell Royden, her son, Olin, and her daughter, Delight. Mindwell has made a home in the wilderness and has a clear New Hampshire title (ironically, it emerges later that Adam's York title, inherited from his deceased father, is to the Royden land). Adam finds that he rejects references to what he still considers "treason," but he concedes that the Grants rebels have "abiding fortitude…but no reverence for established order or decency." He returns to Albany and becomes a land agent for James Duane. Later, he joins a raid with the Green Mountain Boys and changes his first impression to respect for Allen's men: "The dingy riders were alertly obedient and competent, quick to execute…orders, swift in making and breaking camp, tireless and uncomplaining." He helps to negotiate a truce that stipulates no more settlements or disturbances on either side until the King makes a decision. Adam no longer dislikes the countryside or the people— "earnest, willing, hopeful"— and imagines living here—"this rough Arcady, in this empty land that gave to the questing its own spacious liberty"—with Felicity. Nevertheless, he has doubts and wonders whether he shouldn't go on to Canada, "as befits his station." The truce does not endure, and Adam is "proscribed," along with Ethan Allen, with a price upon his head. The effect of this ban is that Felicity is no longer interested in him. Adam is now ready to dedicate himself to the cause of liberty and equality and he wants to protect Mindwell and Delight, to whom he has given his deed. He becomes Ethan Allen's aide-de-camp. They set up their office in Salisbury, Connecticut, for over a year. The price on their heads has been increased. After William Tyron in Albany publishes restrictive orders, Ethan and Adam return to Bennington and the Fays' tavern. Adam is now thoroughly engaged in the cause. He sends a letter to Delight assuring her of his love, which is intercepted by Felicity. Delight goes to Fort Ticonderoga with a British couple to care for their children. Felicity elopes with a British officer. Ethan Allen brings news that the Continental Congress will reconvene in Philadelphia in May. Adam arranges through Duane for a "safe conduct" to go to Fort Ticonderoga. Ethan gives him the task of assessing the strength of the British garrison at the fort. Meanwhile, news has come that there has been fighting with the regulars at a place called Lexington in Massachusetts. The finale at Fort Ticonderoga is thrilling, and Adam and Delight, a charming and believable couple, escape together.

The narrator in **Catch a Falling Star** (1949) is Olin Royden, the brother of Delight who has married Adam. The action begins in 1780, another complex period in Vermont history, in which Vermont, with few resources, is being denied statehood by the Continental Congress, stripped of troops, and compelled to make an allegiance with Britain (General Clinton in Albany) or with Canada (General Haldimand). No one knows who is on which side; British agents are everywhere. When Royalton is burned, Olin, now a lieutenant, tries to help the starchy and unpleasant Faith Marshall. Captured by Indians led by a British officer, who comments on the "resistance

and endurance" of the Vermont troops, Olin escapes and heads for Ethan Allen's headquarters at Fort Warren in Castleton. He meets old friends like Justus Sherwood and realizes that once they faced a common enemy in New York and now the choice is between King and Congress. Ethan Allen quotes some John Donne to Olin, which starts, "Go and catch a falling star," and ends, "And find what wind serves to advance an honest mind." The theme of the novel is playing a game of dishonesty with the enemy while staying honest to the cause. Major Ira Allen is trying to string out a truce with General Haldimand, but troops are deserting in droves to go back to their farms. Major Allen puts out word that the truce has been violated. Has it? "Wal, I don't know that it ain't." Olin and his old sergeant, Archelaus Tupper, undertake a secret mission to find out what Colonel Ira Allen, Major Joseph Fay, and Captain Sherwood are up to. A mysterious cloaked stranger, who twice tries to do them damage, is Roger Lorrimer, engaged to marry Faith and in the land business (Olin jealously takes him for a British agent). Lorrimer disappears the day before his wedding, and Faith, shamed, flees for Boston. Her uncle, Seth Warner, sends Olin after her. Warner has learned that "conspirators" have been meeting at the Arlington house of Thomas Chittenden and sends Olin to infiltrate the meeting. Word of treason spreads on the heels of Benedict Arnold's treachery and escape to England in 1781. Olin overhears the "conspirators" say that if Vermont withdraws from the war it could signal the end and decides to join this audacious band, including Ira Allen and Jonas Fay, who are trying to postpone any action so that they don't have to join Canada. Olin's decision means that he is countermanding what Seth Warner asked him to do. Olin, sent north on a mission, views all of the wreckage and burned homes of northern Vermont. He goes on another mission, purportedly about an exchange of prisoners, this time to Isle aux Noix, where Justus Sherwood is working for General Haldimand. Ira Allen wants an armistice between Canada and Vermont and an exchange of prisoners "before reunion" (although

V

this group has no plan for reunion but is trying to keep the truce alive). They achieve another two-month postponement—it is clear that Canada wants Vermont as protection against the Indians. Olin joins the Rangers as a captain, knowing that when there is renewed war—a certainty unless a miracle occurs—he will be in the thick of it. Haldimand's patience is finally at an end. The Continental Congress has embargoed Vermont, leaving it with no military supplies: it is Vermont versus the United States. Meanwhile, Olin becomes engaged to Faith. There is another postponement until October; Ira Allen has fought for and held this truce for a year, enabling soldiers to go home to bring in their harvests. The miracle occurs at a place called Yorktown, where Cornwallis is taken prisoner. The gamble has paid off. Lorrimer and a band of Indians abduct Faith, but Olin and his good friend, Tupper, save her. Tupper is killed, but he dies taking Lorrimer with him, a promise he made to Olin months before.

The Wings of the Morning (1955) is set mainly in Dummerston and Westminister. When his brother Amos dies in 1774, Job Aldrich comes from Massachusetts to the Grants to take over his pitch in Dummerston. A Quaker, Job has no interest in politics or violence. He finds trouble almost immediately, is arrested by Yorkers, and put in jail in Westminster because he will not inform against another man. The Yorkers offer to release him if he would spy on the Dummerston folk. Job refuses, is finally released, tries to make his way home, and collapses in the Houghtons' barn. Melissa Sprague finds Job, and he instantly falls in love with her. Job's good neighbors are Nat and Betty French; William French is currently courting Melissa. When Job collapses again, this time with a serious fever, Zurvilla Alvord, who was captured by Indians and is a bit crazy, cares for him. Discouraged and humiliated, he finally returns home, where the neighbors have banded together to finish the outside of his house, led by the man he refused to betray. The Dummerston residents plan to rid themselves of the York courts in Westminster. Job finds himself at a meeting opposing a proposal to set up a Committee of Safety (which turns into

a Committee for Detecting Conspiracies). The question of loyalties is real and complex: Job realizes that he cannot remain neutral; he certainly cannot side with the Yorkers; he does not want to be perceived as a "trimmer." Job learns that Melissa and William's banns are to be announced. When he goes to the Westminster meeting, a bunch of roughnecks put him back in a cell. In the Westminster Massacre, William is killed, and Job is badly beaten up by the sheriff. He is taken, almost dead, to the nearby house of Silence Thayer, a young widow with a little boy, Parmenas. Job's friend, Alvah Reynolds, explains that Job should stay on in Dummerston to help make the land free, not beholden to Yorkers or aristocrats from Bay Province. News comes that Ethan Allen has taken Fort Ticonderoga; there is fighting in Massachusetts. Alvah informs Job that he, too, plans to woo Melissa; Silence has fallen in love with Job. There is a change in Job's attitude: he is now the first to sign a petition to summon a special meeting on the insidious Committee for Detecting Conspiracies. The terror that this Committee has sown is responsible for Zurvilla's suicide. Job speaks eloquently at the meeting and also realizes he is in love with Silence. Meanwhile, Parmenas tells his mother (mistakenly) that Job plans to marry Melissa. The Grants is voted free of York, named Vermont, and becomes an independent state. When Melissa finds she is pregnant by Alvah, her sister, Beulah Houghton, asks Job to go after Alvah, who is with Seth Warner's Vermonters. Job signs up with Warner's Regiment to find his friend and kills a number of mercenaries in the Battle of Hubbardton, before being shot and taken to the house of Silence's relatives. He and Silence reaffirm their love and are married the day after Alvah and Melissa.

Day of Battle (1958) reintroduces Adam, his wife, Delight, her brother, Olin, Alvah Reynolds, and Justus Sherwood. The action begins in July 1777 with the retreat of the Northern Army after the fall of Fort Ticonderoga. Having served his two years, Lieutenant Jeremy Shaw, in command of the *Trumbull*, is ready to give up the "so-called cause of liberty" if he can evade the British fleet. He escapes in the company of Abner Holloway, a private in Warner's Regiment, to Abner's sister's house. Even though it looks as if the war is lost, Jeremy begins to feel guilty about leaving the cause of "worth, not birth." Jeremy, though well educated, is the son of a humble shipwright; he is a Yorker because he lives on the Hudson, but he does not love the gentry. This tale brings out the social class aspect of the struggle. While making his way home, he is run over by a young woman racing her horse. She is entrancing Cynthia Warren, ward of Loyalist Colonel Pfister of White House Manor in Hoosick. Cynthia has been taught that "Vermonters are little better than bandits." Her guardian returns, recognizes Jeremy, and imprisons him. Jeremy escapes with Cynthia's help and is then captured by rebels and taken to Bennington. Ira Allen is interrogating Jeremy when Adam, now a captain, arrives and identifies Jeremy. Adam persuades Jeremy to fight for Vermont, which has swept away social divisions; Vermonters respect learning but not lineage; people are judged by worth alone. Vermont is denied entrance to the Union. Vermonters are facing serious issues. Jonas Holloway (Abner's brother) wants to stay home and farm. Yorkers threaten to confiscate his property and hang him if he does not sign a paper taking protection from them. He signs. Alvah appears with his pregnant wife, Melissa, who is a whiner and a bad housekeeper. Even though some in the group still think Jeremy is a spy, he is made secretary of Ira Allen's Council of Safety. Elon Whittaker, with whom Jeremy is staying, is a spy who sends messages to Colonel Pfister through the unwitting Jeremy, who is visiting Cynthia clandestinely. Burgoyne is poised to strike; Vermont stands alone, because no neighboring states will help. Can it raise an army of rangers in its impecunious situation? Jeremy suggests sequestering all abandoned Tory property and auctioning it. He is offered a lieutenancy in Colonel Herrick's Rangers in the Army of Vermont; they wear green cockades. Word comes that New Hampshire is sending General John Stark to help. Jeremy finds Justus, a captain in Queen's Loyal Rangers, at Cynthia's. Jeremy and Cynthia have now acknowledged their love for

one another. Jeremy is captured again by Colonel Pfister and realizes that Cynthia's guardian wants his ward for himself. Jeremy spends much of the Battle of Bennington bound hand and foot, until Justus, a gentleman, frees him. The rebels finally win the day and Jeremy, his girl.

Hendrik Willem van Loon

Invasion (1940), a fictional memoir about the Nazi invasion of America, is a cautionary tale for Americans to alert them to the fact that fascism can happen in their land. Van Loon had tried to warn people, but the attitude he met was indifference or isolationism ("Keep America out of the war!"). Van Loon is in Connecticut visiting friends when the Nazis bomb and invade New York, while simultaneously destroying other cities and shelling various ports. In this emergency, he sends his wife, Jimmie, to the house of their daughter-in-law, Janice, in Vermont: "Drive until you get to Dorset." He and his son Hansel ("Hank"), who has spent most of his life in Vermont, start off in their car. (Jimmie's ancestors were Vermonters and Hansel has inherited their "hard practicality.") A car full of Nazis tries to assassinate them as they are leaving for Vermont. They stop off in Stamford to consult a journalist friend and there learn that the Germans have bombed sites all around the country, destroyed ships and civilians, and flown planes as far as Detroit and Akron. New York was the center of the attack and Nazi troops are actually in the city. Van Loon hastens to Norwalk to pick up some friends ("You are right—it can happen here") and they take the road for Bennington and press on to Dorset. As they arrive, they can make out parachutists in the sky. Seeing where the parachutists are heading, van Loon and his friends, plus farmers they have been able to mobilize, make their way creeping and crawling to the targeted building. "At last we were joined by a few men who had arrived from the village. I had always accepted the average Vermont farmer as a somewhat slow-moving and slow-thinking creature, but now I saw him as the English must have known him in the days of Ethan Allen. Without anyone telling them, they not only seemed to know exactly what to do, but—still better—what not to do."Van Loon and his friends are able to intercept some important orders found on the body of a dead parachutist and appreciate that the "prompt and unexpected action of the people of Vermont" has kept the enemy from disrupting all communications in the state. They learn from these orders that a large number of parachutists is expected in Mattawee Valley en route through Vermont to Albany. Van Loon conceives the idea of hoisting a Swastika so that the reconnoitering parachutists will think that their forward guard has been successful. He and his friends then activate the Vermont militia through orders from Montpelier, where a man named Walter Harrington is in charge. Van Loon thinks to himself, "They [the enemy] don't know these Vermonters and they will probably have the surprise of their lives." The Vermonters wage a successful campaign against the parachutists and kill them all. Despite what happened in the rest of America, "here in Vermont, everything was still as it had been in the days when Ethan Allen and his mob of nondescript volunteers had tied a few uncomfortable knots in the tail of the mighty British lion." He goes on to reassert how "magnificent" the Vermont men and women were with their "sudden and absolutely natural acceptance of that discipline upon which all successful efforts in our world must ever depend."

Lilian Van Ness

Henry Calhoun, a famous sculptor in *The Indifferent Blade* (1947), lives in Derby-Four-Corners near Bellows Falls on property that includes a pond, a waterfall, and a view of Mount Olney. He and Charlotte have two daughters, Catherine and Michele, who love the same man: white Russian architect Andrew Suvaroff. Catherine and Andrew marry in Derby in 1938. Prudence and Abel Tracy work for the Calhouns; Prudence was a Swedish immigrant abused by the man who brought her to America. Her teenaged daughter, Molly, is promiscuous. Catherine and Andrew live in New York, where he is successfully employed in an architectural firm. He travels to Derby one weekend and,

finding the Calhouns gone, stays at the Derby Inn, run by Fern and Herman Hulda. They are abortionists whom Molly frequented when she became pregnant. Andrew finds her ill in the inn and helps her into his room. He gives her brandy, asks what is wrong, and, when she tells him, escorts her to her parents' house and calls the local doctor. Back in New York the next week, he reads in the paper that Molly is dead, the Huldas have been arrested, and he is implicated. Because of an act of generosity that is misunderstood (Prudence, quite crazy, accuses him of being the father of Molly's baby), he meets injustice, is regarded with suspicion and loathing, and loses his job and his self-respect. Andrew begins to drink. Everyone is affected: Henry cannot work; Catherine is unhappy. Andrew decides to join the Royal Canadian Air Force. Before he can do so, a shocking accident happens while they are staying in Derby.

Kurt Vonnegut, Jr.

In *Slaughterhouse-Five* (1969), it isn't cracking his skull in an airplane crash in 1968 on Sugarbush Mountain that causes Billy Pilgrim to be "unstuck in time;" that happens in 1944, when he finds he can remember the future as well as the past. Billy, a chaplain's assistant in the army, was captured by Germans after the Battle of the Bulge and sent to an extermination camp for Russian prisoners on the Czech border where he was put in the English compound ("It's the Children's Crusade," gasps a British infantry colonel captured four years previously at Dunkirk, when he sees the ragtag young American prisoners). From there, Billy was shipped to Dresden, an open city, undefended, with no war industries or troop concentrations, as contract labor and housed in a former slaughterhouse. He survived the Allied bombing, which killed one hundred and thirty-five thousand civilians, was repatriated, became an optometrist, and married ugly, rich Veronica Merble. He had two children, Barbara and Robert, who is a Green Beret in Vietnam. Billy broke down (he found life meaningless because of what he saw in the war and often weeps for no apparent reason) and was taken to a veteran's hospital for nonviolent mental patients near Lake Placid. He believed that he was kidnapped by a flying saucer and taken to Tralfamadore. At the time of the crash in Vermont, Billy is flying to an optometrist's conference in Montreal. Everyone on the plane is killed but Billy and the co-pilot. Austrian ski instructors, speaking German among themselves, are the first on the scene. When one of the ski instructors asks where Billy is from, he answers, "*Schlachthof-fünf*." Brought down the hill on a toboggan, Billy looks up at all the young skiers swinging in yellow chairs and thinks it is an amazing new phase of World War II. A famous brain surgeon from Boston comes to Vermont to operate for three hours on Billy's fractured skull. Billy is sharing a hospital room with a Harvard history professor, Bertram Copeland Rumfoord, who is writing a history of U.S. American Air Force bombing in World War II. Billy tries to tell the professor that he was there in Dresden, but the professor thinks Billy is brain-damaged. The professor finally believes Billy and defends the bombing; Billy reassures him with words he learned on Tralfamadore: "Everything is all right and everybody has to do exactly what he does." "And so it goes."

Chuck Wachtel

In "**The Eye**"(1996), Jeff and Andy, brothers, and their friend, Mack, grew up in the same neighborhood in Brooklyn and have known each other for twenty years. After high school, Jeff enlisted in the navy, married and divorced, is the father of two, and lives with a girlfriend in Hoboken where he is a telephone installer. Andy went to college and now teaches at the high school they all attended. Mack went to prison on a drug charge for eighteen months, was detoxified, and spent two years in a halfway house and

five years on parole. Jeff and Andy are visiting Mack on Memorial Day weekend at his half-finished house in central Vermont near Lincoln, where he has lived for twelve years. The house is a metaphor for his failed relationship with Ginny Salerno, his former girlfriend, who was supposed to move in with him, bringing her six-year-old son, Lee. Instead, she has become pregnant by another man, who is married. Mack has stopped working on the house. The three of them are sitting around outside, drinking tea, talking cursorily, futilely, looking up at the sky as it gets dark and the stars come out: "The last of the sun spreads a belt of copper light just over the mountain that faces Mack's house." Their pasts disappoint them. "Nothing holds still long enough to be ours in that way [understanding it]," says Mack. As they look at the stars, each sees different shapes. Their laconic dialogue speaks volumes. It is a moment in time. "To the future," they say, toasting each other in tea.

Dan Wakefield

In **Selling Out* (1995), Perry Moss, a writer of literary short stories (one published collection; two O'Henry awards), has taught for seventeen years in the English Department at Haviland College in southern Vermont and is happily married to his second wife, Jane, a photographer. Unexpectedly, he is invited to Hollywood to write a pilot film based on one of his short stories. He is forty-three, and life in the old farmhouse on the rutted road with the "blue-green hills" in the background strikes him as too ordered and tranquil. Life in Hollywood is, at first, heady. His old Vermont existence seems like a dream. The studio, Paragon, is going to create the "New England ambience" of his story by shooting the pilot at a San Jose community college. The two-hour film is a huge success. Perry has changed: he is unresponsive to the suggestion of his best friend, Al Cohen, that he come out from Vermont to visit Perry, reneges on a promise to a colleague, forgets to ask about life in Vermont when Jane calls, and finally forfeits his tenure at Haviland. The quality work Perry was promised turns to dust and, discouraged and disillusioned, he heads back to Vermont where his Robert Frost-quoting friends, the Cohens, and his wife are waiting to forgive him ("Home is the place where, when you have to go there, they have to take you in").

Mildred Walker

The Quarry (1947) begins in 1857 in Plainsville where the Converse family—Orville and Abigail, and their three sons, Jonathan Ridgeway, Daniel Peabody, and Lyman Webster—live in a brick house on a farm on a hill above their soapstone quarry. The town also has a cheese factory, a cashmere mill, and a churn manufacturer. The Converse family is deeply religious and, like their neighbors, zealously abolitionist. An eleven-year-old run-away slave, Ezekiel ("Easy") Williams, is brought to town by Deacon Bangert, the principal agent of the Underground Railroad, and is living with the Converses (even though Abigail would have zpreferred to have him continue on to Canada— "We don't want a Negro here!"). Easy meets with the congregation, whose members have listened to talks by Frederick Douglass and Wendell Phillips but never by an actual slave. They are slightly disappointed by Easy's story: he was a house slave and never beaten. By June 1862, John (engaged to Louisa Tucker) and Daniel have gone off to war. Daniel writes that he has married Virginian Willie Delaney and is sending her to Vermont to await the birth of their baby. When Willie, a professional stage actress with blonde corkscrew curls, sees Easy sitting with the family, she announces, "I don't sit down to eat with niggers." Used to parties and the theater, she feels cold and lonely during the winter and rather scornful of "grown-up Vermonters" who consider a spelling bee entertainment. She has a little girl, Juliet. John is killed in the Battle of the Wilderness (on his tomb is carved, "Killed in the slaveholders' rebellion"). The war ends and Lincoln is assassinated. Daniel comes home from the war and prison with a limp and takes Willie and Juliet out West. An 1869 newspaper editorial comments, "Our farms are becoming tenantless." Lyman, the third son, goes to Brown University and falls in love with his first cousin, Isabel, though they cannot marry and have children. Lyman takes up with a rich older crowd (especially the vaunted Chauncey Westcott III), gambles and drinks, and is brought home in disgrace. Before Lyman can escape Vermont, his father dies in an accident leaving Lyman in charge of the quarry. Isabel has married Chauncey and moved to France. Easy returns to the South, marries Jewel, and brings her to the hill. Louisa, deceased John's fiancée, is clearly interested in Lyman and he finally marries her and moves into her house in town. Weeks later, Isabel comes back to Vermont. She is divorcing Chauncey, from whom she contracted syphilis, and is unable to have children. She and Lyman love each other their entire lives and never see each other again. Lyman and Louisa have a son, Jonathan Tucker Converse. Lyman urges him to play with Easy's children, but Jonathan says his mother doesn't want him up there "with the darkies running all over." Louisa, jealous and intolerant, opens a bed-and-breakfast at their house. One of her summer guests observes: "Most of these Vermont towns that are back from the railroads have declined almost to the vanishing point, though of course that is perhaps the secret of their charm for the urban visitor." She has a second son, Holbrook, who is more like Lyman. Son Jonathan becomes a minister, orthodox in his views of a jealous God. Holbrook goes to France, where he befriends Isabel. He marries Susan and has a baby, Lyman. When war is declared in 1914, Holbrook joins the French army and sends Susan and the baby home to Vermont—just in time, because Lyman was seriously considering throwing himself into the quarry.

The Southwest Corner (1951) is about Marcia Elder, eighty-three, who lives all alone in her family's 1802 three-story brick house on Ryder Hill near Rutland. Orville Greenstead, who sees to her shoveling and to her woodpile, is concerned about her living so far away from the village. As she begins to feel her age and the cold, she decides to advertise for a companion, someone to whom she will leave the house when she dies; her sister, two brothers, and husband are all dead. The most promising applicant, Bea Cannon, comes for an interview and seems so reliable and pleasant that Marcia settles on her. Soon, Bea has taken over the housekeeping and the cooking, making large meals with too much meat and having Orville over for supper every night. Bea is sensible and kind but bossy, and Marcia is uncomfortable having her around. Before Marcia can even imagine such a turn of events, Bea and Orville marry, Bea organizes an auction of all Marcia's old family furniture, and they drive to Dedham to live in Bea's small house there. She feels old and sad, sitting in her chair all day missing her house, meadow, and mountains. Suddenly, Bea dies of a heart attack, and Marcia, after the funeral, persuades Orville to drive her home to Vermont. It has begun to snow, and Orville, not sure his car can make it up the hill, stops at the store to find out if the road is open. In the store is a young woman in ski pants, Claire Stellwagon, warming her boots by the fire. She is looking for a farmhouse to turn into an inn for skiers. Marcia offers her house for sale, except for "the southwest corner." When her grandfather built the house, he added a one-story addition to the southwest corner for him and his wife to live in when the children were married and had their own children. Claire agrees to look at the house, and Marcia realizes that this is the perfect solution to her problem: the southwest corner had been waiting for her all along, her "New England social security." They climb the hill, with Claire driving, and after dinner Marcia goes outside. "Against the white, unbroken field of snow that stretched to the hill, she saw a body arch itself and disappear again into the darker shadows." She runs inside like a child. "I saw a deer," she cries, "as close to the house as that row of currant bushes!"

In *The Body of a Young Man* (1960), James and Phyllis Cutler and their twelve-year-old son, Harp, leave Illinois to spend the summer in a "real New England village" near Manchester with James's great friends, Josh and Lucy, their sixteen-year-old son, Rich, and twelve-year-old daughter, Ella. James is distraught over the suicide of a boy, Leonard, whom James had tutored

and whom he had encouraged to take an examination for an important scholarship. Phyllis believes his depression can be cured through spending extended time at a country farm with friends. The visit is at first idyllic and then strained. A summer turns out to be too long a period to sustain the intimacy of this friendship, in which Phyllis has always felt herself an outsider. Josh, a college teacher who believes he is attuned to the needs of others, is impatient with James's continual brooding and harking back to what is past and irreparable. Josh tells James that he is punishing himself by feeling guilty. Josh believes that a change of job will do the trick and introduces James to the head of an important lab in the nearby city where Josh himself teaches. Josh also tells Phyllis that she is too anxious and wrapped up in James and that her constant hovering makes him feel trapped. James reads drafts of Josh's advice book for teenagers and criticizes the entire premise. This quiet novel poses some realistic human questions about offering and accepting advice between friends.

Maggie Wall

One darn thing after another (1970) describes with good humor the obstacles and the pleasures of simplifying life. Margaret buys a "deserted lonely little schoolhouse" ("Vermont's early spring was flecking the drab gray paint with a lovely silver") with Ellen ("Aunt Nell") Rebecca and has it moved ("skidded") to a bluff on Lake Champlain for use as a camp. At an old cemetery, Margaret finds an unused flagstone to serve as a front step. Relaxed and full of good will, she calls her camp "Blarney Castle." They have visitors galore. They experience rapid changes in the weather: Margaret quotes Mark Twain, "If you don't like the weather—wait a minute." The man they think is a night prowler is catching frogs to sell for research purposes. Bees swarm onto their stump fence and keep them captives in their own house. "Knock-knock-knock"—a raccoon has his head caught in a mayonnaise jar. When someone is in trouble in a rowboat on the lake, she drives down the main street collecting neighbors to help rescue him. She drives a neighbor's pregnant wife to the hospital in Burlington. They are warned that an escaped murderer is crossing by boat from New York: she follows the wrong man. She decides to sell her neighbors on the idea of sponsoring a Fresh Air kid. The seasonal transition has come; a hostile neighbor informs her that the title to her land is not sound. A lawyer checks and assures her the title is just fine.

Mary Ella Waller

At the start of *The Woodcarver of 'Lympus* (1904), Philip Venever, a gentleman from New York traveling on the Alderbury stage driven by Uncle Jo Cheatle, passes the butternut tree where a young girl sits, watching the coach go by. The driver explains that she lives up the Mountain at 'Lympus Bethel with the Lewis family. Uncle Jo explains the family's circumstances. Lize Prindle, daughter of old Si, married Shim Lewis. Their family consists of Theodora ("Twiddie"), thirteen, who is the illegitimate daughter of Shim's deceased half-sister, and Hugh Armstrong, twenty-three, who is a nephew of Shim's deceased sister. Hugh has been flat on his back for a year-and-a-half, crushed by a huge log that fell across his legs. Philip spends the night nearby and visits the Lewis family the next day. The narrative is taken up from Hugh's point of view, as told to his journal. He has spent the time since the injury cursing his fate and despising God. A cot-bed with pulleys to raise him to a half-sitting position has arrived on the coach. He realizes that Shim and Lize have scrimped and saved—gone without sugar, coffee, tobacco, and the newspaper—to buy him this contraption, which changes his whole state of mind: he is able to sit up. Realizing that he can't help in the fields, he offers to knit stockings for the family. Philip sends Hugh some information from the Society of Woodcarving in St. Louis. Soon, his friend procures for Hugh a seventy-five dollar commission carving panels for a mantelpiece. He sends Hugh a flood of books. Hugh, who had received an education at the Academy before his accident, absorbs all the new information avidly and enjoys his new job. His days, which were once empty and meaningless, are now "full to the brim,

sometimes overflowing, with springtime, work, reading, studying, and just living." Philip comes for another visit, together with Dick Mallory, about Hugh's age. The Society orders sixteen panels, depicting the four seasons. Twiddie is miserable at school, where she is teased about being illegitimate. Dick visits again, bringing his cousin, Madeline Cope. It is clear that Dick is interested in Twiddie, who is growing more enchanting each year, and Hugh believes himself in love with Madeline. "She carries her head in a free, glad, uplifted way, like a red deer breaking from cover at sunrise." Two years pass. Hugh makes no journal entries but records some letters he has received from his friends in Europe. Those from Madeline suggest their friendship has deepened into love, though hint at one serious difficulty. The drama is resolved when Philip learns that he is Twiddie's father from an affair that he had as a very young man, much against his father's will, with a young woman who disappeared before he knew she was pregnant. He has been unable to engage himself to Madeline until the mystery of the young woman's whereabouts is solved. Now Philip and Madeline can marry and invite Twiddie to live a life of luxury with them. Twiddie rejects this plan because she loves Hugh; he realizes that he has always loved her as well. This lovely story of a resurrected man is written in language that does justice to its subject: "The forest belts lay on the mountain's flank like the tarnished bosses of a huge shield," and "The bare poles of white and yellow birch are set as thick on the face of the hillside as a hedgehog's quills."

Beverly C. Warren

Dr. Nicole Winters, a veterinarian from New York in *That Gentle Touch* (1984), comes to live in Essex Junction to assist Dr. John Carey in his burgeoning practice. Nicole, pretty and competent, is received in a friendly way. Like everyone else in town, she is curious about black-haired, brooding Jason McBride, a computer genius and inventor who is connected to the big local computer company, Bitron, and has a mysterious past—perhaps a wife. Nicole is popular and is soon being courted by Dr. Stephan Baker, but she is not interested in him. She falls ill near McBride's estate where he finds her and carries her off to be tended by his warm, loving housekeeper, Mrs. Beaton. When Nicole recovers, he takes her riding on one of his thoroughbred horses and flies her to Montreal for a day of sightseeing. She loves him, but she wonders about the identity of the forbidding woman calling herself "Mrs. Jason McBride."

Larry Watson

In *Laura (2000), Robert Finley, an editor at a publishing concern in Boston, and his wife, Doreen, a college teacher, spend summers in Garrett in southern Vermont with their two children, Paul, eleven, and Janie, eight. They stay in a large Victorian house "with a huge front porch that tilted toward New Hampshire." There are always many visitors and much drinking; in the summer of 1955 Paul meets Laura Coe Pettit, twenty-two, when she comes to his room seeking refuge from the other adults. The meeting instills in Paul a lifelong obsession with Laura. The following summer the Finleys do not go to Vermont: the parents divorce. Robert keeps the house in Boston, and Doreen and the children go to Fairmont, Minnesota. Paul dreams about Laura constantly. Robert comes to Minnesota to visit his children and takes Paul to a conference in Minneapolis, where Laura is interviewing for a job at the university. Paul discovers she is having an affair with his father. She takes a teaching job instead at Dorson College in southern Vermont, near the Finleys' old summer home. As the years pass he sees Laura twice; he goes to medical school, marries, and has twins; he continues to yearn for her. He reads an interview with her in Esquire: she remains at Dorson College, living in a tiny stone cottage in rural Vermont with two cats and a dog. When he learns that she will be speaking at a writer's conference in Warren, New Hampshire, he leaves his family and drives there to see her. He wants to live with her in Vermont; she presses him to leave. About ten years later he reads that she has Alzheimer's and is in a private nursing home.

Taking his family with him this time, he flies to Burlington and drives to The Pines near his old house. The ending is sad yet liberating.

Patrick Wayland

The first chapter of *The Waiting Game (1965) takes place at the Green Mountain Ski Resort near Adamsville in central Vermont. Lloyd Nicholson, West Point graduate, army captain, language expert, and native of Putney, has been seconded to Counterstroke, a privately funded cold-war operation. Having lost a leg from a car bomb in Mexico, he feels awkward on skis on the Vermont slopes, especially since a joker named Gene Waldrop has taken a roll of pictures of Lloyd's falling into a drift. Since Lloyd's identity is his profession, he is forced to take the film away from Waldrop. Lloyd learns from Cramer, his acid-tongued control at the International Trade Research Bureau in New York, that "Maria Boleslawski," whom Lloyd met at the ski resort, is ballet dancer Tamara Kuprinskaya, daughter of a Soviet boss, and has either defected or been abducted. When Waldrop leaves the resort in his car with Maria, Lloyd follows them to New York. The chase takes him to Chicago, where he finds and falls in love with Tamara. The rest of the plot concerns the machinations of Morgan Gilchrist IV, who is testing new methods of brainwashing ("reorientation"). Lloyd and Tamara escape his clutches with the help of another Counterstroke agent, and Lloyd escorts her safely back to the Russian Embassy in New York, where they must decide whether to part.

Charles Richard Webb

New Cardiff (2001) is told almost entirely in dialogue. Englishman and artist Colin Wares drops into New Cardiff randomly (he gets off the bus because he admires the Revolutionary War monument), where he falls in love with Mandy, an attendant at the Shining Shores nursing home He has left home because he has been jilted by his fiancée, Vera Edwards. Suddenly, Vera appears in New Cardiff. She was only joking when she told Colin that she had married someone else. Colin returns to England with Mandy—he gets her a job taking care of pensioners—and Vera stays in Vermont with a Chamber of Commerce executive who makes her Queen of New Cardiff.

Carolyn Wells

In *Spooky Hollow* (1923), a millionaire named Lamont built in the 1880s in Hilldale in northern Vermont a remarkable gentleman's country house designed as an exact reproduction of a French Renaissance chateau. After his wife was murdered, the house stood empty for many years. The villagers call the gloomy, swampy spot behind the Mausoleum "Spooky Hollow" and claim to have heard a ghost playing a harp there. Homer Vincent of Burlington buys the mansion, Greatlarch, and establishes a perfect, self-indulgent routine, with his every eccentric need catered for by his sister, Anne, his niece, Rosemary, twenty-one, and his many servants. A man comes by train and taxi to the house, introduces himself to the butler, Mellish, as Henry Johnson, does business with Vincent and his sister, and retires for the night. The next morning, Anne is found murdered in her bed (in her room locked from the inside), and Henry Johnson has disappeared. The county medical examiner, Archer, the county sheriff from Burlington, Lane, and his two detectives, Brewster and Brown, are summoned. Everyone assumes Henry Johnson is the murderer. Rosemary begs her uncle to allow her to see her beau, Bryce Collins, twenty-six, who belongs to a local aristocratic family. Homer Vincent refuses, informing Rosemary that she is not the daughter of his brother, Carl, but adopted; she is penniless, but he will give her an allowance if she stays and takes her aunt's place in his household. Naturally, he assures her, she can never marry anyone respectable. Bryce, however, still loves her and vows to discover the secret of her birth for better or worse. Rosemary fears she is the "lowborn" child of "the scum of the earth." Bryce hires Fleming Stone, a famous detective, and his young sidekick, Terence ("Fibsy") McGuire. They quickly learn that someone has rigged up a device to send recorded harp music into the air and

that Henry Johnson is John Haydock of Chicago, mysteriously missing, who recently paid suit to Rosemary. The villain, the secret of Rosemary's birth, and the explanation of the locked room are all revealed in gratifying fashion.

Tobias Wells

In *How to Kill a Man* (1972), Boston Police Department Detective Knute Severson and his new wife, Brenda Purdue, receive a call from her cousin, Antoinette Evers, a sixty-five-year-old spinster poet who lives in Vale near the Canadian border. She is in Boston at a conference where writer Arthur Glenn Pendleton is poisoned. Knute helps the police look into the death: the poison that killed Pendleton, arsphenamine, is a specific for syphilis, but the medical examiner finds no sign of syphilis in the body. Pendleton leaves a suicide note, saying he feared syphilis because his father died of it, and bequeaths his fortune to a couple he has never met, who have adopted a baby with a birth defect. Knute reads some of Pendleton's novels, does research on syphilis, interviews some adoption agencies in New York, and travels to Vale in the Valley of Eden to see if he can unravel the mystery. People there (a bartender, a fishing guide, a pharmacist, the postmistress) are all amenable to gossip from which he discovers that Pendleton spent some time fishing in Vale two years ago. Knute figures out that the natural mother of the baby must live in Vale, since the timing fits. After more digging, Knute tracks Antoinette's niece, Doreen, to the local mental hospital, where their encounter enables him to unravel the mystery.

Nathanael West

A Cool Million (1934) is a trenchant account of "the dismantling of Lemuel Pitkin" (which is the subtitle). Lem grows up in Ottsville on Rat River near Bennington in southern Vermont. Raised by his kindly mother on the family farm, Lem fishes for bullheads in Rat River as a child and attends Ottsville High School, where he participates in amateur theatricals and stars on several athletic teams. When Lem is about sixteen, Joshua Bird announces that he is going to foreclose the mortgage on the Pitkin family house (spurred by the fact that the decorator, Asa Goldstein, has offered to buy the house and reassemble it as a colonial exhibit in his store front on Park Avenue). Lem seeks help from Nathan ("Shagpoke") Whipple, former President of the United States and current head of Rat River National Bank. Shagpoke urges Lem to go forth into the world to seek his fortune through "honesty and industry." A parody of a Horatio Alger rags-to-riches hero, the gullible rube is enlisted into Whipple's National Revolutionary Army, a fascist movement (with storm troopers in coonskin caps carrying squirrel rifles) fighting "international Jewish bankers and Communists." Throughout the course of the novel, Lem is tricked, robbed, abducted, arrested, and tortured, losing an eye, his teeth, his scalp, a thumb, a leg, and, finally, his life. The Vermont boy becomes a martyr with his own national holiday and, in his honor, "The Lemuel Pitkin Song."

Donald Westlake

Middleville ("south of Rutland, north of Bennington, in the general vicinity of Mount Tabor and Weston and Peru") is the hideout for the villains in *Don't Ask* (1993). John Dortmunder is once more at the center of the plot, which involves the United Nations-membership aspirations of two small eastern European countries (Tsergovia and Votskpjek) and a holy relic. Dortmunder is masterminding several activities simultaneously, with a larger team than usual, but he is responsible for the heist in Vermont. Chief villain Hadck Kralowc's friend, hotel owner Harry Hochman, has created Happy Hour Inn ski center at Mount Kinohaha ("Ogonquit for *broken ankle*"), which has a summer theater, arts fair, and other distractions for out-of-season guests. Twelve miles away he maintains a chateau with a climate-controlled dungeon housing his art collection worth six million dollars. Dortmunder finds that everyone in Vermont goes to sleep very early; in fact, the restaurant in which he dines is through serving by eight-thirty in the evening. He observes that "Vermont, it's full of cute little bed-and-breakfast

places with interesting histories and authentic architectural details and amiable current owners and fairly solid antique furnishings and Laura Ashley *everywhere*, check it out." The story ends with a newspaper report about the robbery caper with comments from the Vermont State Police and the Windham County Sheriff's Department.

Blythe White, Jr.

The period for *Green Mountain Girls* (1856) is the War of 1812; the setting is Brandon Valley near the Canadian border, where a robust smuggling business is carried out between the mountain folk of northern Vermont and the British Army on the other side. The past master at smuggling in these parts is Dr. Field. His main traffic is in liquor, but one of his most amusing stunts is to concoct a sleigh ride of young people to cross the border; every other bonnet smothered in furs is a pork carcass. It is a point of honor among the Green Mountain boys and girls to outwit the customs officers. Alida Blythe, twenty-one, lives in Brandon Valley with her mother; her father, Theron, died of drink in Deacon Brandon's distillery. Alida becomes engaged to the Deacon's son, Nat Brandon, a popular young man-about-town. Another young man, not so fortunate, is Michael Granly, sixteen, an orphan, scapegoat, and outcast. Alida has befriended him and taught him to read and write; he has always worshiped her. He reveals to Alida astonishing news: Nat plans to take her over the border for a mock marriage ceremony in Canada, after which her one thousand-dollar bequest from her grandmother will be his. After passing on this shocking message, Michael kisses her and leaves. Thereupon, Dr. Field confirms the news about Nat, with the further information that Nat owes Dr. Field, among other creditors, a large sum of money. Dr. Field plans to clothe and equip young Michael and send him for employment in New York. Believing that drinking is the downfall of all the young men of Brandon ("Drinking destroys humanity and makes man a brute"), Dr. Field and Alida swear to promote temperance. Alida reveals herself to her mother as a feminist: "I hope the time will come when woman will think she has some rights in the world, and not be afraid to speak what she thinks." Nat returns from Canada, where he has married his Canadian girlfriend, marries Alida in Vermont, and takes her money. Michael, meanwhile, is working for Dr. Field's brother on Lake Champlain and has become a successful and competent scribe, clerk, bookkeeper, cashier, and salesman, and converts everyone in his ambit to the temperance cause. Alida has a little girl, Celestine, but has been robbed and forsaken by Nat. Seven years pass, but, not being a widow, she cannot remarry. Learning that Nat is in New York, she decides to beg for his assistance. The friendly stage driver (who calls Alida a "perfect specimen of a Green Mountain girl") tells her that Nat, head of a gang of criminals, is married with three children. She faints at this news and the driver leaves her at the house of the other Mrs. Brandon. Nat is sent to the penitentiary and dies in prison. Lafale, a Frenchman, offers to drive Alida and Celestine back to Brandon Valley. Nervous about Lafale's intentions, Alida flees into the woods, where she is chased by wolves, is rescued, and then dies. Her last words are of Michael. The repellent landlady keeps Celestine as a menial servant. Nat's family goes to the poorhouse. Celestine and her stepsister, Luthella Brandon, finally meet. Lafale wants to marry Celestine, but she too dies. Luthella marries Celestine's cousin, Blythe White.

Homer White

Norwich Cadets (1873), set at Norwich University on the Connecticut River in 1859, stars two heroes: Tom Lyon ("honorable, high-minded, patriotic, and true"), son of a Vermont farmer, and Bill Wolfe ("strong and recklessly brave"), son of a Georgia planter. Best friends, they engage in various feuding activities with the Dartmouth youth across the River. After the election of 1860, there are threats of secession in the land. The two friends cannot agree politically: "The Vermonter was a staunch republican and anti-slavery man, a firm supporter of Lincoln, while the Georgian was a Breckinridge democrat and a pro-slavery man." When Georgia secedes

from the Union in January 1861, Bill returns home to serve with the Confederate Army. Lincoln becomes president, Fort Sumter is fired upon in April 1861, and the First Vermont Regiment is on its way under Colonel Phelps. Tom is commissioned captain and goes to the Army of the Potomac under General McClellan. When his friends march him to White River Junction, their Dartmouth "foes" turn up to give three cheers. Their regiment enjoys equality between men and officers unlike the regular army. One night in camp someone sings the Vermont Volunteers song, "I sing of Vermonters, the bold and the free," which includes the lines: "Their sprigs of green hemlock—the badge of their State—/Wherever they wave are the gods' nod of fate,/O, the Green Mountain Boys, the bold mountaineers—The pride of their State are Vermont's volunteers." In the Battle for Richmond in April 1862, Tom and his former "Dartmouth foe," Captain Staples, from a New Hampshire regiment, are captured and taken to Libby Prison. Tom's best friend, Bill, now a colonel in the Confederate Army, comes to see them in prison to ensure they receive improved rations and cigars. He also brings his eighteen-year-old sister, Heloise, who defies her family by believing in the Union and immediately falls in love with Tom and he with her. Tom and Staples dig their way out of their cell to find Heloise's slave, Caesar, waiting for them with a carriage, provisions, and civilian clothes. Tom is involved in more fighting and becomes a major. General Burnside leads the Army of the Potomac, followed by General Hooker. Tom is promoted colonel for his gallantry. In June 1863, General Meade in command, they meet Lee at Gettysburg. The second brigade of Vermonters, five regiments under General Stannard, fights gallantly. Tom's regiment is ordered to the front on the second day to relieve a regiment; Bill receives the same orders. The two friends are both wounded and taken to a hospital in Washington where Caesar nurses them. They both go back to their regiments. Grant is now in charge of the U.S. Armies. The Vermont brigade engages in the Battle of the Wilderness, May

1864. Tom is presumed dead. Bill finds Tom gravely wounded on the battlefield and, knowing he would die in Andersonville, has him conveyed to his aunt's house, where Heloise, incidentally, is staying. After the war, Tom and Heloise marry and move back to Vermont, where Bill (who regrets his "secession fever") joins them to establish a law practice: **Lyon and Wolfe**.

Tom Wicker

"A Novel of the South Today" is the subtitle of *Easter Lilly* (1998), a novel about murder, race, and justice. The first chapter, set in Rutland, introduces a lawyer who becomes involved in the trial of Easter Lilly Odum in Chattanooga, Tennessee. W. Shepherd ("Shep") Riley, a cum laude graduate of the Harvard Law School, left his New York law firm to practice law in Rutland. He uses an old dining table bought second-hand as a desk. His backyard runs down to Otter Creek and sometimes in snowmelt season the water rises to Shep's rear steps. He seldom goes upstairs, where there is no furniture and no heat. He bought his office equipment, such as it is, from the Otter Creek Credit Union, when it was run out of business and auctioned off its remains. He prefers this life to his prestigious law firm in Manhattan, where he can fish in the summer and ski in the winter. He can read the books for which he once had no time and feel accepted in a community he likes. He had been one of those who, in the sixties, really thought the Age of Aquarius would arrive in America. He now experiences a "dull contentment" in a town where "little was likely to cause a man to stir himself." He had wanted not only to "cause justice to be done," but to "help *define* justice." When he reads about Easter Lilly Odum, he decides to intervene and begins to construct her defense.

Kevin Wignall

William Hoffman, known as JJ, is a contract killer in *People Die* (2002): he kills people for money not ideology or politics. He is paid to kill David Bostridge in Russia, which he does as neatly and quickly as possible. He allows the young woman with Bostridge to leave, carrying a package. Two years and several killings later, in Paris, an American colleague named Ed Holden tells JJ that Philip Berg plans to kill JJ and that he should head for a guesthouse in Vermont and await further instructions. Susan Bostridge, the widow of the man JJ killed, runs The Copley Inn in a picturesque village along the lines of Newfane or Grafton. She is an attractive, sensitive woman with two appealing teenaged children, Jack and Jem. Holden is not there, so JJ heads for Holden's house in New Haven, where he kills a Russian on Holden's trail. An address scrawled on a scrap of paper in the Russian's pocket sends JJ back to Vermont to the Fallen Pine Inn, a few miles from The Copley Inn, where he kills another Russian on Holden's trail. By this point, he likes the Bostridges so much that he is trying to protect them from further disruption. Returning to the Copley Inn, he finds Holden; they spend a few warm, happy days with the Bostridge family. JJ is particularly drawn to young Jem. When they spend a day together skiing, she reveals to him a secret.

Alix Wilber

The Dufore farming family in *The Wives' Tale* (1991) has lived in Esperance between Bennington and Searsburg for generations and is generally respected in the community, though many of the family members have been known for self-destructive tendencies (quite a few commit suicide). The novel weaves together four generations of this tragic and eccentric family. One of the men ties up his jaws because he tends to spew locusts out of his mouth. Another goes literally soft in the head and rots away, while a third puts stones in his pockets for fear of being carried away by wind. One spontaneously combusts and throws himself into Crockett's Creek, drowning in the process, and another builds an underground bunker and lives in it with his family for fifteen years because he fears being struck by a meteor. The last, brooding about sin and punishment, decides to escape the Flood by becoming a fish (taking his small son under water with him). A dark and desperate picture is painted of these hapless people. Two of the wives have affairs with members of the LaStrange family, which lives next door in a trailer situated on the town dump; another wife goes off with a LaStrange girl and the tattooed man from the circus (both the LaStrange men had tattoos, too). This ethereal novel begins and ends with the great-grandmother, Marie, whose husband turned into a trout and who hasn't slept for forty years. The final scene presages the future for the Dufores.

Paul Wilkes

In *Temptations* (1993), Joseph, a Catholic child of Eastern-European parents, becomes a successful writer, long-time analysand, and celebrity guest in Manhattan. Leaving this glamorous life, he goes on a spiritual quest, stopping for a night at a Trappist monastery called Our Lady of New Citeaux situated in Falmouth near Vernon in southern Vermont. After his visit, he decides he wants to do a story about monastery life and persuades the vocational director, Father Columban Mellary, to let him stay in a cottage next door, meet regularly with him, and allow him to soak up as much of the monastic atmosphere as possible. As he begins this process, he is aware of the hostility of Father Polycarp, one of the residents. When he begins receiving cryptic notes, he suspects Polycarp. The notes lead him to four men, three of whom tried, and failed, to enter the monastery. Robert Trumbull is in a mental hospital, recovering from a nervous breakdown; Peter Vanik is practicing law, trying to challenge the Catholic Church on every doctrine; Trevor Haskins is dead, a suicide; and Octavius Kiernan is investigating a homicide. Joseph enters into a chaste relationship with Margery Fowler, another Catholic, who is trying to find the meaning of her life in Vermont through involvement in town affairs and volunteering in the local fire department. Joseph is becoming more devout, more attuned, reading, working, meditating, but still doesn't know whether he is researching a story or a possible way of life. When the abbot accepts him for a month

of observation, Father Columban seems to ignore and discourage him, calling him an "arrogant poseur." The climax and its aftermath reveal the identity of the homicidal maniac, the explanation of the notes Joseph received, and whether Joseph recognizes his vocation.

Edward Williams

Philip Mintern, the narrator in *Black Forest* (1975), discovers the papers of his ancestor, poet Lloyd Mintern of Ferrisburgh, and refashions them into the story of the Mintern family, including *The Notebook Poems: Black Mirrors*, Lloyd's narrative poem. Philip concedes that the material is "impenetrable;" that is, ambiguous, repetitive, and layered. Joseph Mintern arrived in Ferrisburgh in 1789. The family line then becomes indistinct until 1893, except for a few facts. Oscar F. Mintern was shot in the face and killed by a comrade's defective firearm in 1825. Rachel Mintern described the family house in 1840. Great-aunts Rita and Faith Mintern kept elaborate accounts of daily life at the farm—the vast orchards, the Merino sheep, "the corn shackled in the shade." For two hundred years the family has been "turning the same earth." Lloyd was married to Amalia (daughter of Joe and Maria); his brother, Philip, married a Miss Parker in 1893, and had three sons: Edward, Oliver, and George. Edward and his wife, Julie Keese, had a daughter, Julie, who married and had three children: Molly, Julia (married), and Robert. Philip (Robert's cousin) formulates the idea that Edward shunned the poetry of his uncle, Lloyd; Edward, who is very elderly, has written an autobiography called *The Mysterious Citizen*. Edward looks out and sees the "white pencilled moon" coming up over the neighboring farm. Molly, pale and tired, manages the old homestead, tidying and dusting. Robert walks around the farm and on Fuller Mountain; he comes upon the ruins of the hired man's house, which burned one hundred years ago. A black walnut forest surrounds the house on three sides. Phillip thinks the title of Lloyd's poem represents the black picture windows at night in any of the rooms of the house.

William Carlos Williams

The central event in *White Mule* (1937) is the first year in the life of Frieda Florence ("Flossie") Stecher, born to Gurlie Torlund, twenty-four, daughter of Norwegian immigrants, and Joe Stecher, who came from Germany when he was nineteen. On arrival, he was shocked by the conditions in the printing trade, started the Typographers' Union, and made a good record as a labor leader until he quit the unions because he thought they were dishonest and wanted "too much." The year is 1893, and Joe and Gurlie live in New York, where Joe is working for Wynnewood-Crossman Co., who bid for the big post-office form contracts (unbeknownst to Joe, the bidding is "fixed" by an influential friend). Joe works tirelessly and is always worried about money: "America without money is nothing." The baby, Flossie, does not flourish: she is weak and scrawny and almost dies of whooping cough. The Pressman's Union threatens to call a strike the night before Joe has to produce a big job. This action is precisely what angers Joe about the unions: he does not think it is "manly" or "honest" to call a general strike when he is facing an emergency job. Mr. Lemon offers to lend Joe the money to start his own business. Joe, decent and intelligent, wants to run an open shop with good pay. Gurlie, unpleasant and dissatisfied, never misses an opportunity to needle Joe. She talks constantly about money and what she would do "if I were a man." Gurlie is insulted when a pediatrician examines the ailing Flossie and tells Gurlie it is essential for the baby to spend a whole summer in the country, in the mountains. Through arrangements with Scandinavian friends in Vermont, Gurlie takes Flossie and the older girl, Lottie, by Hudson River boat ("the shudder of the boat") to Troy, New York. From there they travel by narrow-gauge train ("the unrelenting clatter and shivering of the train"), the Hoosack Tunnel & Westminster Railroad (HT&W stands for "Hoot, Toot, and Whistle," joke the locals) to Westminster. Gurlie finds a young man with a carriage to take them to the Payson farm past Ray Pond. Gurlie, curious about how people make money here, learns a good deal about Vermont from the carriage driver. Most people work in the pulp mill: "No money in farming these days." She sees one fine house, but the owner did not make his money here: he is a lawyer from Boston who fixed up this house as a summer place. When she arrives at Emil Payson's farm, she sees "a wide panorama of down-sloping fields, undulating wooded eminences, the corner of a glinting lake and, beyond that, hill after hill and mountain after mountain as far as the eye would take her. The sky was blue, clouds hung in white patches." The Paysons are an old couple who are happy to see the children; Gurlie, feeling tied down by them, is glad to turn the baby over to the deaf old woman (Gurlie feels the "closeness, the intimacy" of life in the country). A land development company had bought up some of the abandoned farms as people moved out West and many Scandinavians moved to Vermont. Gurlie and her children meet the Ferry family, poor, with many children, but happy. Flossie improves immeasurably during the summer months. "The grass everywhere was brilliant green and soft as it always seems to be in Vermont." At the end, the girls go berrying with the Ferry children. Mr. Ferry returns from hunting with some friends. "The children were standing back in a fascinated circle, the baby's face smeared with berry juice, her hands sooty, quite a part of it all." (The title is a term for moonshine whiskey.)

In the Money (1940), the sequel to *White Mule*, starts in Vermont where the first novel ends. The idyllic, happy, peaceful life of Vermont ("with the taste of fall in the air") is contrasted with the harsh, stressful, competitive life in Manhattan (with its "blistering city streets and breathless rooms"). At the start, someone at Topping's store says Flossie is "a little mule, like her father." Gurlie and the children are again staying with Emil Payson. Gurlie's sister, Olga, lives nearby, as do the Ferry children. Gurlie is a whiner and complainer; Joe is educated and eager to get ahead. One of the Ferry boys "waded the shallow stream — cold almost as ice-water now — went up the road walking in the soft reddish, shale speckled dust, home." Joe, who has been working for W. Wynnewood of Mohawk Press, decides to resign, set up his own printing business, and bid against his firm on a contract for post-office forms. Wynnewood is furious ("that German bastard") and hires lawyers to see if he can stop Joe. United Printing Associates claims Joe's action encourages treachery among employees ("God damned talk about a full dinner pail and square deal to labor and all that crap"). The labor organizations are also protesting against giving a contract to a nonunion person. Joe goes to Washington to meet President Grover Cleveland and Postmaster General Payne, who determine him a qualified bidder. After he wins the contract, he is boycotted by his enemies and cannot get the presses he ordered or buy ink, but he overcomes these obstacles. Some of his former employees come to work for Joe; he is able to set up shop by the legal deadline. He is now "in the money." Gurlie, unfeeling and abrupt with her children, sends them off to Vermont without her for the summer. Aunt Hilda and Uncle Gunnar have bought a farm there; Gurlie's sisters, Olga and Mangna, live there with their children. Lottie and Flossie have a blissful time. Out of the window they "could see far, far away over bright green fields, with a high hill in the distance and walls and stone fences going off at an angle." Uncle Gunnar nicknamed the buildings "the opera:" "the separate units all in a row as Vermont houses are constructed so that even in deepest snow all parts of the establishment can be reached under the same roof." There is a lawn for croquet—"the miraculous grass of Vermont"—and animals ("a beautiful Jersey heifer…with her eyes of a wild deer and delicate legs and shaded coloring") and a spring to fetch the water. "You could lie on your back on the grass without care, the phlox was in flower over the top of the east wall and a luxuriant silence filled the whole little valley." Summer was "wearing away," and they have a party on the lawn—a perfect day with homemade ice cream. Joe comes to fetch the children, and Olga travels with them on the boat back to the New York suburbs. Gurlie never once visited them in four months. Olga thinks Gurlie

is selfish and spoiled, always wanting "more" instead of living contentedly in Vermont the way the rest of the family does. Joe has planted a dwarf plum tree in the backyard: "the children are impressed and satisfied."

Owen Wister

Although only two scenes of *The Virginian* (1902) take place in Vermont, this fine Western drama is very much about Vermont. The Virginian is a young cowpoke (about twenty-seven at the start), who has been on his own since he was fourteen and never had any formal education. He is tall and "irresistibly handsome," with naturally "gentle" and "civil" manners. When people say rude or provocative things to him, nothing shows but a "certain change of light" in his eyes. He works for Judge Henry in Sunk Creek, Wyoming. Molly Stark Wood grew up in Bennington and decides—perhaps to get away from Sam, the man she does not want to marry—to go out West to become a schoolteacher. On her way to Bear Creek, Wyoming, her drunken stage driver plunges the coach into a flooding river. Fortunately, the Virginian rescues Molly and falls in love with her the minute they meet. She spends almost the entire novel trying not to fall in love with him because her "Vermont heart" thinks that there is too great a gap between them in background and culture. As the couple begins to go riding together and talk, Molly lends him books from her library. Her reactions to the books are filtered through other peoples' opinions; his are natural and untutored. She writes home to "the circle at Bennington" about her new life and new acquaintances; there is no possible way they can appreciate someone like the Virginian. They perceive her as living in a "community of roughs." The Virginian is promoted to foreman at Judge Henry's ranch. Easterners named Ogden appear at Sunk Creek Ranch. Molly and they have many places and ideas in common: "They bring the East and its memories powerfully back to her." When they travel to the East, she accompanies them to Bennington for her vacation. Trouble has been brewing between the Virginian and his nemesis, Trampas (it is to

Trampas that the Virginian utters the line, "When you say that—smile!"). The Virginian tells Molly he loves her; she responds that because of the differences in their cultures and customs she can never marry him and begs him to let them continue to see each other as friends. She is unable to think independently of her relatives in Bennington, who continuously put pressure on her by writing letters saying, "How exciting to have you bring a live cowboy to Bennington!" and, "Would he wear his pistol at table?" These arch remarks make her very unhappy. The Virginian is unable to see her for a spell because, under orders from the judge, he must apprehend and hang some cattle thieves. Molly hears of this event and cannot appreciate the way he suffered in carrying out his responsibilities, especially since one of the men he hanged was his best friend, Steve. Molly's kind next-door neighbors, the Taylors, realize they cannot help her understand the "justice" of this hanging, since she expects this territory to "be like Vermont." Finally, she submits to her love for the cowboy and agrees to marry him, although there is still some vestige of fear in her heart. When she looks at the "harmonious" yet "tremendous" landscape of Wyoming, the "vast beauty" has in it "something almost of dread...The small, comfortable, green hills of home rose before her. She closed her eyes and saw Vermont: a village street, and the post-office, and ivy covering an old front door, and her mother picking some yellow roses from a bush." Trampas continues to threaten the Virginian, who knows Trampas is a thief and a murderer. As the Virginian and Molly ride together he tells her the whole story of his relationship with Trampas. "Vermont sank away from her thoughts." The showdown finally comes: Trampas shoots first and the Virginian kills him. Finally, Molly can take her cowboy home to Bennington—not in his cowboy duds but "in a straw hat and Scotch homespun suit of a rather better cut than most in Bennington." Bennington finds that "Molly's cowboy could be invited anywhere and hold his own." They return to Wyoming, where the Virginian becomes an important man in the coal business.

Suzi Wizowaty

In *The Round Barn* (2002), a rare round barn built in 1901 by Thomas Fletcher, with the help of Hoke Smith, stands on East Hill in Eustis, which is in northern Vermont just south of Troy. In the mid-eighties, the round barn is dismantled and moved to the outdoor folk-art museum, a collection of historic buildings such as a sawyer's cabin, stone cottage, old schoolhouse, jail, railroad station, and circus building with carved figures and animals. The intersecting characters, which are sympathetically and successfully portrayed, are all in some way associated with the museum. Tuesday Bailey, in charge of the plant, has always been in love with his cousin, Mary Bailey Daly, who lives with her husband, Jimmy, at the store, and though a talented dowser was unable to discover her own inoperable ovarian cancer. Didi Jamison works at the museum as public relations officer and has lived for twenty years with her lesbian partner, Maude Dodge Lake, an artist. Didi, who loved to draw as a child but was squelched by her painter father, is beginning to wonder whether her friendship with Adrian, a newspaper reporter, is turning into something more than friendship. Didi's gay eighteen-year-old nephew, David Michaels, who comes to spend the summer, wants to be an architect and spends his time making small houses out of twigs and grasses. Dean Allen, an unappreciated employee at the museum, stares out the window of his office and writes letters to Cynthia, the sister with whom he had an incestuous affair. David meets Lucy, who is spending the summer in Eustis with her widowed mother, Freida Maxwell, an art collector and museum board member, who is having a summer affair with David Hopper, the head of the museum. The museum has decided to sell a few of its old masters to pay the bills. Dean becomes crazier and crazier as he watches his receptionist, Ella Lee Domenico, paint her fingernails every day. David Hopper (and Mary, independently) feel that there is something wrong about the round barn. The resolution to the tale relieves some of the pent-up feelings about the barn.

W

Ted Wood

Reid Bennett and his German Shepherd police dog, Sam, are serial sleuths in mysteries set in Canada, where Bennett is the police chief of a one-man department. In *Snowjob* (1993), Bennett comes to the Vermont ski resort of Chambers (a combination of "community people and ski lodge owners") because a marine buddy from Vietnam, Doug Ford, a black police detective, has been charged with the murder of Cindy Laver, a local employee. When Bennett visits Doug in prison, the latter insists that he was not, contrary to local opinion, having an affair with Laver but was working with her on activities related to the mob and money-laundering. Bennett experiences the usual hostility of a local police force toward an outsider and eventually helps to solve the mystery, but not before Wendy Tate, Jack Grant, and a hood named Manatelli are killed. One of the suspects is former U.S. Olympic ski-team member, Walter Huckmeyer, who manages the ski resort, Cat's Cradle. Bennett is hired by Paul Grant to investigate his son's death; Jack was involved in gambling and other illegal activities. Paul claims he doesn't want a "snowjob"—doesn't want Bennett to whitewash his son's name. Bennett solves the murder and returns to his wife, Fred, and baby, Louisa, in Canada.

Elvirton Wright

Craig Sternhold, ready to start his first year at the University of Vermont in *Freshman and Senior* (1889), has settled into the Carvers' boarding house in Burlington with gun, fishing rod, and books, when he learns that his widowed mother is dying. What will happen to his five-year-old brother, Fitz-James Jamison ("Jamie") Sternhold? Craig's stiff and prosperous aunt and uncle, the Talbots, assume they will take care of Jamie, but Craig decides he and Jamie cannot be separated: he takes Jamie to college with him. Most of the big men on campus (Garrison Colfax, prominent family; Jack Kirk, football hero; Ed Hastings, class clown) would shudder at the idea of a little boy to look after. Craig relishes the role of caring for the enchanting child, who becomes

a mascot at the college and a great favorite with President Graham. Audrey Brooks, the only girl in a class of forty boys, is soon enamored of both Sternhold brothers (Craig is the "handsomest" in the class). Craig, who is cordially treated by all the young men, especially likes Tracy Clifford, a sensible, serious senior, whom he accompanies to a prayer meeting. He is flattered to be invited by popular Bullstrode and Allen to Lush's, a tavern, but is shocked to find that they are being served intoxicating liquor. Craig politely leaves; the "gentlemen" are offended by his stance but are later expelled. In the "cane rush," a freshman ritual, Craig wins the cane; in a football match, Craig kicks the last goal. Audrey and Craig become friends with President Graham's daughter, Nan, and her beau, Severn. Clifford supports Craig for membership in the Nu fraternity. When Craig offers to help Mrs. Carver, his landlady who is not very strong, with the Coffee House, her Sunday school program for unruly boys, Audrey comes along to help. Soon they start a reading room for the boys and invite them to tea and treat them as friends. In a serious talk with his friends, Craig questions why all the "home business" should be "shelved" on women. During the Christmas break, Jamie takes a fall from his toboggan and cuts his head badly; everyone, even President Graham, comes over to see how the "little man" is. As the first year ends, Craig and Audrey stand very high in their class. The second section finds them—and Jamie, now eight—seniors. Craig and Jamie are invited to a party to welcome students to the campus. Jamie thinks it a grand party and says to his hostess on leaving: "Thank you, Mrs. Derby. If I ever have a party, I would want you and Mr. Derby to come, but I don't think I am likely to have one." Cogswell, with a group of the least respectable students, waylays and bullies Jamie. Instead of cringing, Jamie stands his ground, calling the group "sneaks and cowards." The bully, holding Jamie's arm tightly, blows cigar smoke in his face. Jamie tells them his brother "is clean inside and out." When Craig finds Jamie crying, Jamie tells him what happened but makes Craig promise not to seek revenge. Audrey, who leaves college for a week to represent the Coffee

House at a convention in Indiana, takes Jamie with her: the "little delegate" is a great success. The senior year draws to a close. Craig comes in first in academic achievement and gives the class oration. Jamie, dressed in black velvet and sitting on the stage with the dignitaries, has the last word as he thanks the president for their college experience. Audrey and Craig become engaged, their names "bracketed" in the college Bible.

Nancy Means Wright

Branbury is a college town just east of Salisbury and within sight of Breadloaf Mountain. The heroine of this series of four novels and a novella is Ruth Willmarth, in her forties, separated (then divorced) from her husband, Pete. She runs, with the help of hired-man Tim Jenkins, a working dairy farm that belonged to Pete's great-grandparents (his ancestors rafted along the Otter in the 1700s to make their pitch in Branbury). Her former high school beau, Colm Hanna, son of a mortician and a practicing realtor and part-time cop, is usually in the picture. She has a young son, Vic, a teen-aged daughter, Emily, and a married daughter, Sharon. In *Mad Season* (1996), an elderly neighbor couple, Lucien Larocque and his half-Indian wife, Belle, are found savagely beaten. Ruth swears to find the culprits and enlists Colm to help her. Among the suspects is Wilder Unsworth, Emily's boyfriend. Wilder's younger brother, Garth, torments Vic at school because he lives on a farm. Another suspect is Joey Godineaux, Tim's retarded foster son. After Belle dies, the charge is murder. The Unsworths moved from New York to Branbury because their oldest son, Kurt, had been in trouble with drugs. Ruth sympathizes with Vic's problems at school because she suffers from the social divisions herself ("I see how it is in town meetings. They sit together, the flatlanders...asking questions, criticizing"), and she worries about keeping her farm. A woman broker from New York, Esther Dolley, who may be in Pete's pay, is handling land in the area and wants to sell Ruth's farm. Pete's sister, Bertha, has always been in love with Colm and is acting very strangely. Vic has seen something incrimi-

nating at the Unsworths and is kidnapped. Several barns burn down. Vic is restored to his family: justice is served and greed punished. (The explanation for the title is that "the world goes wacky now and then. Mad season.")

In *Harvest of Bones* (1998), Fay Hubbard, in her fifties, divorced from a husband who still lives in the Northeast Kingdom, is renting Glenna Flint's house and trying to run a bed-and-breakfast. Fay has bought a cow to make her B&B look authentic, and she hooks rugs with cows in the design. The Healing Place is a commune full of strange-looking women. The men in the picture include Kevin Crowningshild, whose wife, Agnes, may be a prisoner at the Healing Place; Willard Boomer, who makes house and business signs by hand; Alwyn Bagshaw, a crazy, aging neighbor; and Mac McGinniss, Glenna's former husband. Ruth is still friends with Colm, who has a bumper sticker on his truck: "Moonlight in Vermont—or starve." Ruth finds a finger bone with a ring on it, and soon the whole body is uncovered at the Flint place. There was a fight, a grave was dug, someone was buried in it, and Glenna has thought, all these years, that it was she who had killed Mac and that it was his body in the grave. The ending is suitable and satisfying.

In *Poison Apples* (2000), Ruth becomes involved in the lives of Stan and Moira Earthrowl, who have moved to Branbury to manage an apple orchard after their teen-aged daughter, Carol, was killed in an automobile accident in Connecticut. Stan especially has been depressed since her death and has started drinking heavily. The first spring, many of the apple trees are poisoned, and Stan believes that someone "knew he was a flatlander and wanted him to fail." He feels very much an outsider because Vermont is "so WASP." His orchard manager, Rufus Barrow, has an ancestor who fought at Fort Ticonderoga; Stan's Jewish ancestors came to America in steerage. There is a crew of Jamaicans picking the apples, but other locals are helping, including Ruth's daughter, Emily. Other disasters start befalling the apple trees, and Moira calls in Ruth to help solve the crimes. Stan is embroiled in a fight with Cassandra Wickham, a member of the school board who is persecuting a young Jewish teacher. When she is knocked down and killed by a car, Stan is the prime suspect. He has a stroke. There are multiple suspects for the crimes in the apple orchard and then at Ruth's farm. Is it Ruth's ex-husband, Pete, who is working with two developers to buy up land for building? Or Rufus Barrow, whose family once lived on this farm and who turns out to be one of Pete's development partners? Or the minister, Reverend Turnbull (actually Cassandra's husband, Arnold Wickham), who heads a sect of local women called Messengers of Saint Dorothea, whose perspective is racist and anti-Semitic (it has formed a White Citizen's Council to "keep Vermont pure")? Or Pete's sister, Bertha, who is part of the sect and jealous of Ruth? Or Adam Golding (who turns out to be the brother of Trevor, who was driving the car in which Carol was killed and committed suicide after feeling persecuted by Stan), the handsome young man for whom Emily falls? Or Opal, Stan's visiting niece, whose father is a gynecologist and performs abortions? Or is it a surprise suspect, Pete's current girlfriend, Violet Jones, who wants Ruth to sell her property?

Stolen Honey (2002) deals with intolerance toward both Abenakis and farmers and tackles the ugly and disturbing story of the Eugenics Project in Vermont. Donna Woodleaf-LeBlanc, who goes to Branbury College with Ruth's daughter, Emily, lives with her mother, Gwen Woodleaf, a bee-keeper; father Russell, of Abenaki and French-Canadian ancestry, who does Revolutionary War reenactments; and grandfather Mert, who weaves baskets in the traditional Abenaki way. Donna goes to a fraternity dance with Emily, but decides to ride home on the back of the motorcycle of Shep Noble, who, drunk, tries to attack her. Leroy Boulanger, who helps Gwen with the bees and idolizes Donna, intervenes and sends Donna into the house. The next day, Shep is found dead. Donna receives hateful messages: "Go back to your teepee. You don't belong." Donna and Emily are both taking a sociology course from Camille Wimmet, a young woman eager for tenure and disturbed over the death of her lesbian partner who, she feels, was driven out of Branbury.

Camille plans to come out as soon as she gains tenure. She is very interested in Donna's proposal for her term paper to research her mother's ancestor, Elizabeth Jackson, who was captured in Massachusetts in an Abenaki raid and taken to Canada. Her daughter married an Abenaki and refused to leave him when she had an opportunity to return home. Ruth also experienced not belonging to the "cocktail crowd" when she first arrived, and Emily is having troubles with her snobbish roommate, Alyce Worthington. Pete insists that she buy her share of the house from him. Harvey Ball, Gwen and Russell's neighbor, is trying to force them to sell him their land to enlarge his farm, which they cannot because it is sacred property—a young Indian "princess" is buried there. Camille's research is on the Perkeys, the people who ran the Vermont Eugenics Project in the thirties, which detained people whom they considered "degenerate" and in some cases steril-ized them. Mert's aunt was one of its victims. Ruth believes that Joey, Tim's foster son, may be a descendant of one of the families Camille is study-ing. When Camille is murdered, Ruth begins to investigate. She discovers that Leroy Boulanger, Camille's cousin, stands to profit from her death. Someone has dug up the Indian's grave; someone else tries to run down Donna when she is riding her bicycle. Tilden Ball abducts Donna, who escapes into the woods. All the skeins are gathered together at the end and Ruth and Colm are one step closer to a more formal relationship.

In **"Fire and Ice"** (2002), Pete is back in town, staying with his paramour, Violet, at the house of Pete and Ruth's daughter, Sharon. Before Pete and Ruth were married, Pete had a fling with enticing Crystal Hiland, so when she is murdered on an icy evening, he is a suspect. Ernie, Crystal's lineman husband, was very jeal-ous of her flirtatious behavior, especially since she was pregnant with Gracie when she married him, so he is a suspect, too. The electricity is out all over Branbury ("maple limbs hunched over like old men in wheelchairs"), and Ruth takes into her house teacher Noah Hemphill, and his wife, Dawn, who has just discovered she is pregnant. Violet is a suspect because she had a public row with Crystal, drove off in Pete's car, but was brought back by the police. Ruth herself, Colm tells her, could be a suspect in the murder because of potential jealousy over Crystal's affair with Pete. Ernie falls during the ice storm and, taken to the hospital, confesses while delirious to the murder of his wife in a "crime of passion," but the real killer is someone else.

Y

Dana Yeaton

Mad River Rising (1999) is a two-act play dramatizing scenes in the life of Angus Michael Stewart, seventy-seven, who lived through two floods—the literal flood of November 3, 1927, when he was a seven-year-old boy in Moretown, and the figurative flood of machines, new faces, and progress today. His great-great-grandfather came over from Scotland with two heifers and a bull calf, with which he slept on the ship. Sam, one of Angus's sons, is in California. Charlie, in his thirties, is a management consultant with a cell phone attached to his ear. He is divorcing Karen and has a son, Nick, seven. Marie Cousino Stewart was married to one of Angus's sons; her daughter, Cindy, is engaged to marry Spencer Eddy. Marie's mother Mae, half-Abenaki and half-French-Canadian, is the Voice of the Past in the play. When the play begins, Angus has just escaped from the retirement home where he has been staying (after a cancer operation). He thinks that all his possessions are to be auctioned off, but Marie has arranged for him to keep the farm and sell the development rights; he refuses to sign the documents. Mae intervenes from time to time, providing a panoramic view of the flood. When the Stewart house is cut off from the village, Angus's grandfather, Hopley, tries to rescue the stranded family members by ox cart but is swept away (first managing to pull the pin and free the animals), and the house slips into the river.

"When the waters finally recede, the valley will be a carpet of stones, great boulders that a team of six can barely move. Down along the intervale, covering the crow-black soil, there will be a bed of sand, up-to-nine feet thick in some places." By the end of the play, Charlie has decided to stay to help his grandfather, to act as his legal guardian, and to bring his son, Nick, to Vermont where he belongs. Angus dies at the end of the play, but before doing so he signs his name to the land trust agreement. (His son Sam is the anonymous donor of one hundred and twenty-eight thousand dollars to the trust.) Mae sums up: "What we care for truly will truly care for us, whether water or sand or children or land."

Christy Yorke

Since 1794, Graham Payton's family in *Magic Spells* (1999) has had a house in Pendleton north of Rutland. Jane Gregory's mother, Salvation, and her grandmother, Esther, a magic healer, have also lived in Pendleton for generations. Jane has inherited her grandmother's magic gifts. Graham, a doctor, has been in love with Jane since he was a little boy; she loved his brother, Ned (whom Graham hated), and was engaged to and pregnant by him when he was killed in an automobile crash. She moved away to Middlebury with her son, Alex, for seven years but has now returned to Pendleton to the house she inherited from her mother and in which she lives with Esther. Alex has not spoken a word since he was born. Graham, despairing of Jane, marries his high school sweetheart, Ginny, but he still loves Jane and harbors a jealous hatred for his brother, Ned, who was insouciant, reckless, and selfish. Graham and Ginny have no children. A stranger comes to town named Devon Zeke, who bears an uncanny resemblance to Ned. All the women in town fall in love with him, but he sets his sights on Jane. Graham, wildly jealous, competes with Devon in athletic feats as he once did with his brother. Ginny is fed up and moves out. Graham pledges to cure Alex's speech problem. The resolution involves decisions, changes, and improvements in all the characters' lives.

Z

Edra Ziesk

In *A Cold Spring* (2002), the village of Amity is located off Route 22, twenty minutes across the Vermont border from New York near a "state forest." The road "up the mountain" from Amity has on it three houses and three sets of occupants. Lenny Bingham is a young widow who works in a plant nursery and takes care of her grandson, Jody, who is mute. James Easter teaches history at the local high school. Nell and Billy Maye have recently arrived to live in her grandparents' house. Lenny is attracted to the local fuel salesman, widower Eli Root, who has five children. James Easter, who grew up in an orphanage, is immediately attracted to Nell, who has a job teaching music (she plays the cello) at the high school. Billy, who is unreliable (he lost his job in New York), volatile, and jealous of Nell, plans to run a restaurant. He disappears in the middle of the night to drive to New York to bring back a Mexican immigrant, Fernando, to be the cook at his new restaurant. Nell is paralyzed by the prospect of going through, and discarding, many of the old, moldy possessions in her grandparents' house. Events, some violent, begin to happen, although no one acknowledges them. The terse and poetic writing and the brief, finely drawn vignettes, switching from one set of characters to another, bode friction and, possibly, disaster.

Resources

Bibliography

Appendixes

Indexes

BIBLIOGRAPHY,
alphabetically by author

This list gives author, title, city, publisher, date of publication, setting, with quotation marks to indicate fictitious names, and author's residence, with dates if deceased, and connection with Vermont. It includes 334 authors of 484 novels, short stories, and plays set in Vermont. Titles marked with asterisks, or 80, take place partially in Vermont. Some works are available in bookstores; some can· be found in libraries or through the interlibrary loan system; some can be ordered secondhand by a bookstore or online; and some early ones can be read on websites like Project Gutenberg. Forty-six percent of the authors, or 153, lives or lived full-time or part-time in Vermont.

A

Peter Abrahams, *Hard Rain* (New York: E.P. Dutton, 1988), Bennington
(Abrahams lives in Cape Cod, Massachusetts.)

Glenda Adams, *The Tempest of Clemenza* (Winchester: Faber & Faber, 1996), Ludlow
(Adams lives in New York.)

Dean Albarelli, "Passengers," "O Sole Mio," "Cheaters," from *Cheaters and Other Stories* (New York: St. Martin's Press, 1996), Burlington
(Albarelli grew up in Burlington, Vermont, and lives with his wife, writer Sara London, in Northampton, Massachusetts.)

Laurie Alberts, "Dealing," from *Goodnight Silky Sullivan* (Columbia: University of Missouri Press, 1995), "Shelby"
The Price of Land in Shelby: A Novel (Hanover: University Press of New England, 1996), "Shelby"
(Alberts, a faculty member at Vermont College in Montpelier, lives in Westminster, Vermont.)

Clifford Lindsey Alderman, *The Arch of Stars* (New York: Appleton-Century-Crofts, 1950), Arlington
(Alderman, 1902-1988, who commanded an officer training school at Middlebury College in Vermont in World War II, lived in Massachusetts and New York.)

Charlotte Vale Allen, *Promises* (New York: E.P. Dutton, 1979), Echo Lake
Grace Notes (New York: Myra Books, 2002), Brattleboro
(Allen lives in Norwalk, Connecticut.)

Horatio Alger, *Madeline, the Temptress: the tale of two continents,* Philadelphia: Polygot Press, 2005
(Alger, 1832-1899, lived in Massachusetts. The novel, a first edition of an 1857 serialized tale set in Vermont, was not available in time to include in the text.)

Marguerite Allis, *Not Without Peril* (New York: G.P. Putnam's Sons, 1941), New Hampshire Grants
(Allis, 1887-1958, lived in New Haven, Connecticut.)

Lisa Alther, *Kinflicks* (New York: Alfred A. Knopf, 1976), "Stark's Bog"
Bedrock (New York: Alfred A. Knopf, 1990), "Roches Ridge"
(Alther lives in Burlington, Vermont, and Jonesborough, Tennessee.)

Harriette Ashbrook, *The Murder of Sigurd Sharon* (New York: Coward-McGann, Inc. 1933), "Colville"
(Ashbrook, 1898-1946, whose pseudonym was Susannah Shane, lived in New York City and Nebraska.)

Paul Auster, *The Book of Illusions* (New York: Henry Holt, 2002), "Hampton," "West T_____"
(Auster lives with his wife, writer Siri Hustvedt, in Brooklyn, New York, and West Townshend, Vermont.)

Phil Austin, *On Bethel Ridge: A Christmas Fable* (Santa Fe: Sherman Aster, 1998), "Bethel Ridge"
(Austin lives on Nantucket Island, Massachusetts.)

B

Irving (Addison) Bacheller, *Eben Holden: A Tale of the North Country* (Boston: Lothrop, 1900, the first best-seller of the twentieth century, selling more than one million copies), Vergennes
(Bacheller, 1859-1950, was for a time the children's tutor at Shard Villa in Salisbury, Vermont, according to *Green Mountain Ghosts, Ghouls & Unsolved Mysteries*, Joseph A. Citro, Houghton Mifflin, 1994. He received a Ph.D. from Middlebury College in 1892 and lived in White Plains, New York.)

Abbey Pen Baker, *In the Dead of Winter* (New York: St. Martin's Press, 1994), Brattleboro
(Baker, the pseudonym of Rebecca Morean, lived in Putney and Saxtons River, Vermont, and now lives in Yellow Springs, Ohio.)

Harry Barba, *For the Grape Season* (New York: Macmillan, 1960), "Barstowe"
(Barba lives in Ballston Spa, New York.)

Elaine Barbieri, "Winter Moon," from *Seasons of Love*
(New York: HarperCollins, 1995), "Benton Falls"
(Barbieri lives in northern New Jersey.)

Philip (Edward) Baruth, *The Dream of the White Village*
(Winooski: RNM, Inc., 1998), Burlington
(Baruth, a professor at the University of Vermont, lives in
Burlington, Vermont.)

Mary Beth Bass, *Follow Me* (New York: Dorchester
Publishing, 2005)
(The setting is a fictitious town based on certain ele-
ments of Dorset and Manchester. The novel was not
available in time to include in the text. Bass lives in
Ridgefield, Connecticut.)

Tricia Bauer, *Hollywood & Hardwood* (New York: St.
Martin's Press, 1999), "Greene"
(Bauer lives with her husband, playwright Bill Bozzone,
in Redding, Connecticut.)

Ann Beattie, "Vermont," "Wally Whistles Dixie," from
Distortions (Garden City: Doubleday, 1976)
Love Always: A Novel (New York: Alfred A. Knopf, 1985),
"Lake Venue"
"Summer People," from *Where You'll Find Me* (New York:
Charles Scribner's Sons, 1986)
(Beattie, a visiting writer at Goddard Collage in
Plainfield, Vermont, in 1977 and at Middlebury College
in Middlebury, Vermont, in 1997, lives with her husband,
artist Lincoln Perry, in Charlottesville, Virginia.)

Geoffrey Becker, *Bluestown* (New York: St. Martin's
Press, 1996), "Denton"
(Becker lives in Iowa City, Iowa.)

Madison Smartt Bell, *Anything Goes* (New York:
Pantheon Books, 2002), Vergennes
(Bell, a faculty member in 1997 at the Middlebury
College Bread Loaf Writers' Conference in Ripton,
Vermont, lives with his wife, poet Elizabeth Spires, in
Baltimore, Maryland.)

Jason Berger, *Forested Moments* (Chesterfield, Mo.:
BeachHouse Books, 2002), "Fall Hill"
(Berger lives in Colchester, Vermont.)

Ambrose (Gwinett) Bierce, "At Old Man Eckert's,"
from *The Collected Works of Ambrose Bierce, I* (Washington,
DC: Walter Neale, 1909), "Marion"
(Bierce, 1842-1914, was born in Ohio, lived in San
Francisco, and disappeared in Mexico.)

Robert Bingham, "Marriage is Murder," from *Pure
Slaughter Value* (New York: Doubleday, 1997), Killington
(Bingham, 1966-1999, lived in New York.)

Chris (Christopher A.) Bohjalian, *Hangman* (New
York: Carroll & Graf, 1991), "Deering"
Past the Bleachers: A Novel (New York: Carroll & Graf,
1992), "Havington"
Water Witches (Hanover: University Press of New England,
1995), "Landaff"
Midwives: A Novel (New York: Alfred A. Knopf, 1998),
"Reddington"
The Law of Similars (New York: Harmony Books, 1999),
"East Bartlett," Middlebury
The Trans-Sister Radio (New York: Harmony Books, 2000),
"East Bartlett," Middlebury
The Buffalo Soldier: A Novel (New York: Shaye Areheart
Books, 2002), "Cornish"
Before You Know Kindness (New York: Shaye Areheart
Books, 2004), Hinesburg
(Bohjalian lives with his wife, artist and photographer
Victoria Blewer, in Lincoln, Vermont.)

Jon Boorstin, *Pay or Play* (New York: Carroll & Graf,
1997), "Mucklinburg"
(Boorstin, documentary filmmaker and son of historian
Daniel Boorstin, lives in California.)

Miriam Borgenicht, *Booked for Death* (New York:
Worldwide, 1987), "Cedar Springs"
(Borgenicht lives in New York City.)

Gerald Warner Brace, *The Wayward Pilgrims* (New York:
G.P. Putnam, 1938), Windham County
Light on a Mountain (New York: G.P. Putnam, 1941),
"Stafford Mountain"
(Brace, 1901-1978, who often hiked in the mountains of
Vermont, lived in Belmont, Massachusetts, and Deer Isle,
Maine.)

Ned and **Yanna Brandt**, *Land Kills: A Mitch Stevens
Mystery* (Woodstock: Countryman Press, 1991),
"Southborough"
(The Brandts live in New York City and Brattleboro,
Vermont.)

Don (Donald Gerard) Bredes, *Cold Comfort: A Novel*
(New York: Harmony Books, 2001), "Tipton"
The Fifth Season: A Novel of Suspense (New York: Shaye
Areheart Books, 2005), "Tipton"
(Bredes, a fellow in 1976 at the Middlebury College
Bread Loaf Writers' Conference in Ripton, Vermont,
lives in Wheelock, Vermont.)

Thomas Brennan, *The Debt* (Waterville: Five Star,
2005), "Eastham"
(Brennan lives on the west coast of England.)

Howard Breslin, *The Tamarack Tree* (New York: Whittlesey House, 1947), Stratton
(Breslin, 1913-1964, whose pseudonym was Michael Niall, lived in New York City.)

T. (Thomas) Alan Broughton, *Hob's Daughter* (New York: William Morrow, 1984), Charlotte
"Bill's Women," "My Other Life," from *Suicidal Tendencies* (Fort Collins, Colo.: Center for Literary Publishing, 2003), Orleans County, Burlington
(Broughton, a poet and professor emeritus at the University of Vermont, lives in Burlington, Vermont.)

Joseph Bruchac, III, *Dawn Land* (Golden, Colo.: Fulcrum Publishing, 1993), Lake Champlain
Long River (Golden, Colo.: Fulcrum Publishing, 1995), Connecticut River
The Waters Between: A Novel of the Dawn Land (Hanover: University Press of New England, 1998), Lake Champlain
(Bruchac, an Abenaki, is a poet, storyteller, and publisher living in Greenfield Center, New York.)

Frank M. Bryan and **Bill J. Mares**, *Out! The Vermont Secession Book* (Shelburne: New England Press, 1987, illustrated by Jeff Danziger), Brownington
(Bryan, a professor at the University of Vermont, lives in Starksboro, Vermont; Mares, a teacher at Champlain Valley Union High School in Hinesburg, lives in Burlington, Vermont.)

Perdita Buchan, *Called Away* (Boston: Little Brown, 1980), "Circe"
(Buchan, who lived in Wilmington, Vermont, from 1967 to 1968 and Marlboro, Vermont, from 1968 to 1972, lives in Ocean Grove, New Jersey.)

Pearl (Sydenstricker) Buck, *Voices in the House* (New York: John Day, 1953, under the pseudonym John Sedges), Manchester
Letter from Peking: A Novel (New York: John Day Company, 1957), "Raleigh"
(Buck, 1892-1973, lived in Virginia, China, and Danby, Vermont.)

David Budbill, *A Pulp Cutter's Nativity*, with drawings by Lois Eby (Woodstock: Countryman Press, 1981), "Judevine"
Judevine: A Play in Two Acts, from *New American Plays 2* (Portsmouth, N.H.: Heinemann, 1992), "Judevine"
(Budbill, a poet and the editor of Rowland E. Robinson's *Danvis Tales*, lives in Wolcott, Vermont.)

(Carl) Frederick Buechner, *The Entrance to Porlock* (New York: Atheneum, 1970), "Langdon," Tinmouth Mountain
(Buechner lives in Rupert, Vermont.)

Pamela Burford, *His Secret Side* (Toronto: Harlequin Books, 1996), "Pratte"
(Burford Loeser lives in Baldwin, New York.)

Herbert Burkholz, **Sister Bear* (New York: Simon & Schuster, 1969), "Copperjack Mountain"
(Burkholz lives in New York.)

Michael Burns, *Gemini* (Morrison, Colo.: Poncha Press, 2001), "Groveton"
(Burns was born in St. Johnsbury, Vermont, and now lives in Concord, New Hampshire.)

C

Carl M. (Mattison) Chapin, *Three Died beside the Marble Pool* (Garden City: Doubleday, 1936), "Tremont Valley"
(Chapin, 1879-1938, author of *Manchester in Vermont History*, 1932, lived in Manchester, Vermont.)

Joan Chase, "The Harrier," from *Bonneville Blue* (New York: Farrar, Straus, 1991), near Lincoln
(Chase lives in Brattleboro, Vermont.)

Ruth Chatterton, *Homeward Borne* (New York: Simon & Schuster, 1950), "Mapleton"
(Chatterton, 1893-1961, an actress and novelist, lived in New York City.)

Steve Chontos, *The Death of Dover, Vermont* (New York: Vantage Press, 1974), Dover
(Chontos, who lived in West Dover, Vermont, now lives in Prescott, Arizona.)

Joseph A. Citro, *Deus-X: The Reality Conspiracy* (Hanover: University Press of New England, 1994), Burlington, "Hobston"
Shadow Child (Hanover: University Press of New England, 1998), "Antrim"
Guardian Angels (Hanover: University Press of New England, 1999), "Antrim"
The Gore: A Novel (Hanover: University Press of New England, 2000, originally published by Warner Books in 1990 as *The Unseen*), "Eureka"
Lake Monsters: A Novel (Hanover: University Press of New England, 2001, originally published by Warner Books in 1991 as *Dark Twilight*), "Friar's Island"
(Citro, a native of Vermont, lives in Burlington, Vermont.)

Eleanor Clark, *Gloria Mundi* (New York: Pantheon, 1979), "Boonton"
Camping Out (New York: G.P. Putnam, 1986), near Ascutney
(Clark, 1913-1996, lived with her husband, writer Robert Penn Warren, 1905-1989, in Fairfield, Connecticut, and Stratton, Vermont.)

Felicia Buttz Clark, *Hester of Pepper Tree Ranch* (London: The Epworth Press, 1931), "Stanton" (Clark, 1862-1931, lived in Rome, Italy, and Madison, New Jersey.)

Mary Higgins Clark and **Carol Higgins Clark**, *The Christmas Thief* (New York: Simon & Schuster/Scribner, 2004), Stowe (Clark lives in Saddle River, New Jersey; her daughter lives in New York City.)

Sarah N. (Norcliffe) Cleghorn, *A Turnpike Lady: Beartown, Vermont, 1768-1796* (New York: Henry Holt, 1907), Beartown
The Spinster: A novel where a nineteenth century girl finds her place in the twentieth (New York: Henry Holt, 1916), "Tory Hill"
(Cleghorn, 1876-1959, a poet and novelist whose autobiography, *Threescore*, New York: Harrison Smith and Robert Haas, 1936, has an introduction by Robert Frost, lived in Manchester, Vermont.)

Judith Beth Cohen, *Seasons* (Sag Harbor: The Permanent Press, 1984), "Leech Pond" (Cohen, who taught at Goddard College in Plainfield, Vermont, from 1970-1977, lives in Allston, Massachusetts.)

Merle Estes Colby, *All Ye People* (New York: Viking Press, 1931), "Billymead"
(Colby, 1902-1969, lived in Boston, Massachusetts, and died in São Paulo, Brazil.)

Linda Collins, "When the Pipes Froze," "Going to See the Leaves," from *Going to See the Leaves* (New York: Viking Press, 1986), "Ashfield," southern Vermont (Collins lives in New York.)

Peter Collinson, *The Northeast Kingdom* (New York: Jove, 2002), "Gilchrist"
(Collinson, a pseudonym of Chuck Hogan, lives in Brookline, Massachusetts.)

B. (Barbara) Comfort, *The Vermont Village Murder* (Landgrove: Landgrove Press, 1982), "Bellsville"
Green Mountain Murder (Landgrove: Landgrove Press, 1984), "Lofton"
Phoebe's Knee: A Tish McWhinny Mystery (Landgrove: Landgrove Press, 1986), "Lofton"
Grave Consequences: A Tish McWhinny Mystery (Landgrove: Landgrove Press, 1989) "Lofton"
The Cashmere Kid: A Tish McWhinny Mystery (Landgrove: Landgrove Press, 1993), "Lofton"
Elusive Quarry: A Tish McWhinny Mystery (Woodstock: The Countryman Press, 1995), "Lofton"
A Pair for the Queen: A Tish McWhinny Mystery (New York: W.W. Norton, 1998), "Lofton"
(Comfort lives in New York and Londonderry, Vermont.)

Richard S. Conde, *Shelburne, Vermont: A Novel* (Utica: Pine Tree Press, 1998), Shelburne (Conde lives in Manchester, Vermont.)

Edward J. (James) Connolly, *Deer Run* (New York: Charles Scribner's Sons, 1971), "Heartwell" (Connolly graduated from Marlboro College, lived in Wilmington and Halifax, Vermont, and lives in Amherst, Massachusetts. His play, *Misery for Breakfast*, about a lesbian couple running a café in Brattleboro, Vermont, was produced in May 2005 in Northampton, Massachusetts.)

Joan Connor, "Here on Old Route 7," "Camp," "The Attic," "Aaron's Rod," from *Here on Old Route 7* (Columbia: University of Missouri Press, 1997), Historic Route 7A
"October," "And I Isolde," "Ursa Major in Vermont," "Second Nature," from *We Who Live Apart* (Columbia: University of Missouri Press, 2000), Barre, Healdville, Rutland, "Tannerville"
(Connor, who has degrees from Middlebury College and Vermont College in Montpelier, is a professor at Ohio University and lives in Athens, Ohio, and Belmont, Vermont.)

Robin Cook, *Fatal Cure* (New York: Putnam, 1994), "Bartlet"
(Dr. Cook, physician and novelist, lives in Florida.)

Ellen (Josephine) Hodges Cooley, *Boom of a Western City* (Boston: Lee & Shepard, 1897), "Blankridge" (Hodges was born in 1834 in Medway, Massachusetts, and married Benjamin Franklin Cooley in 1867.)

Arnaldo Correa, *Spy's Fate* (New York: Akashic Books, 2002), Burlington
(Correa, who lived in Burlington, Vermont, while researching this novel, lives in Havana, Cuba.)

Art Corriveau, *Housewrights* (New York: Viking Press, 2002), "Cabot Fields"
(Corriveau, raised in East Barre, Vermont, lives in Boston, Massachusetts.)

Gail Crease, *The Dream Spinner* (New York: Jove Books, 2000), Barre
(Crease, the pseudonym of Gail Whitiker, lives on Vancouver Island, Canada.)

Jay Cronley, *Funny Farm: A Sweeping Epic of the Sticks* (New York: Atheneum, 1985), "Redbud"
(Cronley lives in Tulsa, Oklahoma.)

Willis T. (Tete) Crossman, *Willis T. Crossman's Vermont*, from *Told in Vermont* and *Heard in Vermont* (North Montpelier: The Driftwind Press, 1938, 1939; Tampa: University of Tampa Press, 2005, edited by Sean Donnelly and Leland M. Hawes, Jr., with an Afterword by Welford D. Taylor), Worcester, Morgan, Charleston, North Montpelier, Barnard, Hanskville, Eden, Newfane, Bristol, Belvidere Center
(Crossman, 1880-1948, was the pseudonym of William Paul Cook, born Arthur Garfield Cook in Mount Tabor, Vermont, who lived among other places in North Montpelier, Vermont.)

D

Janet Ann Dailey, *Green Mountain Man* (Toronto: Harlequin Books, 1979), Randolph
(Dailey lives in Branson, Missouri.)

Gloria (Rand) Dank, *As the Sparks Fly Upward: A Bernard and Snooky Mystery* (New York: Doubleday, 1992), "Lyle"
(Dank lives in Wyncote, Pennsylvania.)

Jeff Danziger, *Teed Stories* (Shelburne: New England Press, 1988), Plainfield
(Danziger, a fellow in 1992 at the Middlebury College Bread Loaf Writers' Conference in Ripton, Vermont, is an artist and writer who lives in New York.)

Deane C. (Chandler) Davis, *Justice in the Mountains: Stories & Tales by a Vermont Country Lawyer* (Shelburne: New England Press, 1980) Montpelier jurisdiction
(Davis, 1900-1990, former Vermont governor, lived in Barre, Vermont.)

Eugene N. (Norman) Davis, *The Axe with Three Nicks: A Vermont Novel* (Boston: The Christopher Publishing House, 1929), Bridgewater
(Davis, 1877-ca 1950, was born in Plymouth, Vermont, and moved to Bridgewater, Vermont.)

Thomas C. Davis, *The Duval Conspiracy* (Manchester Center: Marshall Jones Company, 1995), Burlington
(Davis, son of Governor Davis, lives in Barre, Vermont.)

Nicholas (Franklin) Delbanco, *Possession* (New York: William Morrow, 1977), North Bennington
Sherbrookes (New York: William Morrow, 1978), North Bennington
Stillness (New York: William Morrow, 1979), North Bennington
Old Scores (New York: Warner Books, 1997), "Catamount"
(Delbanco, a faculty member in 1984, 1986-1989, 1991, and 1993 at the Middlebury College Bread Loaf Writers' Conference in Ripton, Vermont, and at Bennington College, is a professor at the University of Michigan and lives in Ann Arbor, Michigan, and Bennington, Vermont.)

Barbara Delinsky, *An Irresistible Impulse* (New York: Silhouette Books, 1983), near Woodstock
Suddenly (New York: HarperCollins, 1993), "Tucker"
Three Wishes: A Novel (New York: Simon & Schuster, 1997), "Panama"
(Delinsky, whose pseudonym is Billie Douglass, lives near Boston, Massachusetts.)

Barbara Dimmick, *Heart-Side Up* (Saint Paul: Graywolf Press, 2002), "Shroveton"
(Dimmick, who lived in South Reading and Weathersfield, Vermont, for a total of sixteen to seventeen years and later in Norwich for a year, lives in West Lebanon, New Hampshire.)

Edwin Asa (Augustus) Dix, *Deacon Bradbury: A Novel* (New York: Century Press, 1900), "Felton"
Old Bowen's Legacy (New York: Century Press, 1901), "Felton"
(Dix, 1860-1911, lived in Newark, New Jersey.)

Susan M. Dodd, "What I Remember Now," from *O Careless Love: Stories and a Novella* (New York: William Morrow, 1999), near Burlington
(Dodd, who taught at Vermont College in Montpelier from 1983-1984, lives in Ocracoke, North Carolina.)

Julia (Caroline Ripley) Dorr, *Farmingdale* (New York: D. Appleton & Co., 1854, under the pseudonym Caroline Thomas), "Farmingdale"
Sybil Huntington: A Novel (New York: C. W. Carleton, 1869), "Valleythorpe"
Expiation (New York: J.B. Lippincott, 1872), "Altona"
(Dorr, 1825-1913, lived in Rutland, Vermont.)

Basil S. Douros, *The Roots of the Blackthorn Tree* (Rancho Murieta, Calif.: Five and Dot Publishing, 2002), Underhill
(Douros lives in Sacramento, California.)

Anne Miller Downes, *So Stands the Rock* (New York: Frederick A. Stokes Company, 1939), "Winston"
Heartwood (Philadelphia/New York: J.B. Lippincott Company, 1945), "Matlin Mountain"
(Downes, 1879-1964, lived in New York.)

Elizabeth Doyle, *A Country Christmas* (New York: Kensington Publishing, 2002), Peacham
(Doyle lives in Austin, Texas.)

David (Allen) Drake, *Patriots* (New York: Tor Fantasy, 1996), "Greenwood"
(Drake lives in Chapel Hill, North Carolina.)

Robert Luther Duffus, *Roads Going South* (New York: Macmillan, 1921), "Middleton"
That Was Alderbury (New York: Macmillan, 1941), "Alderbury"
Victory on West Hill (New York: Macmillan, 1942), "Alderbury"
(Duffus, 1888-1972, was born in Waterbury, Vermont, received an LL.B. from Middlebury College, and lived in New York.)

E

Dikkon Eberhart, *On the Verge* (Owings Mills, M.D.: Stemmer House, 1979), near New Haven
(Eberhart, son of poet Richard G. Eberhart, 1904-2005, taught in Thetford, Vermont, from 1968-1969, and in East Burke, Vermont, from 1972-1975, and lives in Phippsburg, Maine.)

Bret Easton Ellis, *The Rules of Attraction* (New York: Simon & Schuster, 1987), "Camden"
(Ellis, who graduated from Bennington College, lives in New York City.)

Margaret Erhart, *Old Love* (South Royalton, Vt.: Steerforth Press, 1996), near Barre
(Erhart lives in Flagstaff, Arizona.)

F

Earl Faine, *Green Mountain Man: The Odyssey of Ethan Allen* (New York: Tom Doherty Associates, 1997), New Hampshire Grants
(Faine lives in Stanford, Connecticut.)

John Farris, *Son of the Endless Night* (New York: St. Martin's Press, 1985), "Chadbury"
(Farris lives in Atlanta, Georgia.)

Sebastian Faulks, *A Fool's Alphabet* (Boston: Little Brown, 1992), Lyndonville
(Faulks, who spent a week in 1991 with his friend, *New Yorker* film critic Anthony Lane, on the Vermont-New Hampshire border with journalist Mark Steyn, lives in London, England.)

J. (James) E. Fender, *On the Spur of Speed* (Hanover: University Press of New England, 2005)
(This historical novel, Volume Four of the Frost Saga, describes the battle of Valcour Island and the adventures of Geoffrey Frost's brother in Vermont and New York. The book was not available in time to include in the text. Fender lives in Portsmouth, Maine.)

Frederick Fenn, *Journey to Common Ground* (Avon, Conn.: Publishing Directions, 2002), New Hampshire Grants
(Fenn, born in Springfield, Vermont, lives in New Hartford, Connecticut.)

Dorothy (Frances) Canfield Fisher, *Hillsboro People* (New York: Henry Holt, 1915, with Occasional Vermont Verses by Sarah N. Cleghorn), "Hillsboro"
The Bent Twig (New York: Henry Holt, 1915), "Lydford"
The Brimming Cup (New York: Harcourt, Brace, 1921), "Ashley," Arlington
Raw Material (New York: Harcourt, Brace, 1923), around Arlington
The Home-Maker (New York: Harcourt, Brace, 1924), near Brandville
Her Son's Wife (New York: Harcourt, Brace, 1926), "Gilmanville"
Tourists Accommodated (New York: Harcourt, Brace, 1932), Arlington
Bonfire (New York: Harcourt, Brace, 1933), "Clifford"
Seasoned Timber (New York: Harcourt, Brace, 1939), "Clifford"
Four-Square (New York: Harcourt, Brace, 1949), around Arlington
(Fisher, 1879-1958, who received a Litt.D. from Middlebury College, lived in Arlington, Vermont, where her ancestors settled in 1763.)

Ian (Lancaster) Fleming, *For Your Eyes Only* (London: Jonathan Cape, 1960), "Echo Lake"
(Fleming, 1908-1964, who paid visits to his friend, Ivar Bryce, at Black Hole Hollow Farm in Vermont, lived in London, England.)

Christine Flynn, *Going Home Trilogy: Trading Secrets, The Sugar House, Confessions of a Small Town Girl* (New York: Silhouette Books, April, June, August 2005)
(Maple Mountain, the setting for the trilogy, was inspired by St. Johnsbury. The novels were not available in time to include in the text. Flynn, who has spent time in Vermont, lives in Arizona.)

Edith Forbes, *Nowle's Passing: A Novel* (New York: Avalon, 1996), "Worthing"
(Forbes lives in East Thetford, Vermont.)

Frederick Forsyth, *The Negotiator* (New York: Bantam, 1989), Northeast Kingdom
(Forsyth lives in London, England.)

Catherine Anne Fought, *Rabble's Curse* (New York: New American Library, 1980), "Rowe"
(Fought lives in Keene, New Hampshire.)

Valerie Frankel, *The Girlfriend Curse,* New York: Avon Books, 2005, "Manshire"
(Frankel lives in Brooklyn, New York. The novel was not available in time to include in the text.)

Castle (William) Freeman, Jr., *The Bride of Ambrose and Other Stories* (New York: Soho Press, 1987), "Ambrose"
Judgment Hill: A Novel (Hanover: University Press of New England, 1997), "Ambrose"
My Life and Adventures: A Novel (New York: St. Martin's Press, 2002), "Ambrose"
(Freeman lives in Newfane, Vermont. The next Ambrose novel is based on Malory's "The Tale of Sir Gareth of Orkney.")

Mary E. (Eleanor) Wilkins Freeman, "Symphony in Lavender," "A Taste of Honey," "A Modern Dragon," from *A Humble Romance and Other Stories* (New York: Harper and Brothers, 1887), "Ware," Bolton, Dover
"A Village Singer," "A Wayfaring Couple," from *A New England Nun and Other Stories* (New York: Harper & Brothers, 1891), Derby, "Bassets"
Madelon (New York: Harper & Brothers, 1896), "Ware Center"
(Wilkins Freeman, 1852-1930, lived in Brattleboro, Vermont, and Randolph, Massachusetts.)

Frances (Mary) Frost, *Innocent Summer* (New York: Farrar & Rinehart, 1936), northern Vermont
Yoke of Stars (New York: Farrar & Rinehart, 1939), central Vermont
Kate Trimingham (New York: Farrar & Rinehart, 1940), "Weather-Glass Mountain"
Village of Glass (New York: Farrar & Rinehart, 1942), "Young-Mountain"
(Frost, 1905-1959, mother of poet Paul Blackburn, 1926-1971, lived in St. Albans, Vermont, and New York City.)

Len Fulton, *Dark Other Adam Dreaming* (Paradise: Dustbooks, 1975), "Essexville"
(Fulton, who was raised on a farm from 1947 to 1950 in Jeffersonville, Vermont, lives in Paradise, California.)

G

John (Champlin) Gardner, *October Light* (New York: Alfred A. Knopf, 1976), Prospect Mountain
(Gardner, 1933-1982, a faculty member from 1974-1975, 1977-1979, and 1981-1982 at the Middlebury College Bread Loaf Writers' Conference in Ripton, Vermont, lived in Bennington, Vermont.)

David Gates, **Preston Falls* (New York: Alfred A. Knopf, 1998), Brandon
(Gates lives in New York.)

Rebecca (Clair) Gilman, *Spinning into Butter: A Play* (London: Faber & Faber, 2000), Belmont
(Gilman lives in Columbus, Ohio.)

Gerald Jay Goldberg, *The Lynching of Orin Newfield* (New York: Dial Books, 1970), "Farnum"
(Goldberg lives in Los Angeles, California.)

Christopher Golden, **The Gathering Dark* (New York: Ace Books, 2003), "Wickham"
(Golden lives in New York City.)

Lee Dana Goodman, *Dunster Revealed: Echoes from a Vermont Town* (Shelburne: New England Press, 1997), "Dunster"
(Goodman, 1920-1996, lived in Windsor, Vermont.)

James Gordon, *Escape from Vermont* (New York: Henry Holt, 1948), south of Manchester
(Gordon, a pseudonym of James Stewart-Gordon, 1917-1977, lived on the eastern end of Long Island.)

Peter (L.) Gould, *Burnt Toast* (New York: Alfred A. Knopf, 1971), near "Adam's Ear"
(Gould, a performer and director who lived at Total Loss Farm in Guilford, Vermont, now lives in Brattleboro, Vermont.)

Anna Katharine Green, *A Strange Disappearance* (New York: G. P. Putnam's Sons, 1879), Panton
(Green, 1846-1935, "the mother of the detective story," graduated in 1867 from Ripley Female College in Poultney, Vermont, and lived in Buffalo, New York.)

Michael (Jonathan) Green, *Dry Skull Dreams* (New York: Simon & Schuster, 1995), Brattleboro
(Green lives in Vermont.)

Jennifer Greene, *Wild in the Moment* (New York: Silhouette, 2004), "White Hills"
(Greene lives in Benton Harbor, Michigan.)

Thomas Christopher Greene, *Mirror Lake: A Novel* (New York: Simon & Schuster, 2003), "Eden"
(Greene, who has a Master of Fine Arts from Vermont College in Montpelier, lives in Montpelier, Vermont. *I'll Never Be Long Gone,* New York: William Morrow, 2005, is also set in the fictional town of Eden, Vermont.)

T. (Tammy) Greenwood, *Breathing Water* (New York: St. Martin's Press, 1999), "Lake Gormlaith"
(Greenwood, who grew up in St. Johnsbury, Vermont, lives in Flagstaff, Arizona.)

H

Jane Haddam, *A Stillness in Bethlehem: A Gregor Demarkian Mystery* (New York: Bantam, 1993), "Bethlehem"
(Haddam, a pseudonym of Orania Papazoglou, lives in Milford, Connecticut.)

Sue (M.) Halpern, *The Book of Hard Things* (New York: Farrar, Straus, 2003), "Poverty"
(Halpern lives with her husband, writer Bill McKibben, in New York and Ripton, Vermont.)

Robert P. Hansen, *Back to the Wall* (New York: Mill-Morrow, 1957), "Waynesbury"
(Hansen, a native of Freeport, Long Island, lives in Arroyo Grande, California. In *Mark Three for Murder*, Mill-Morrow, 1957, Ethan Dwyer's hunting trip to Turkey Hill, Vermont, turns into a hunt for a murderer.)

Rosemary (Jeanne) Harris, *Three Candles for the Dark* (London: Faber & Faber, 1976), "Cabb Town"
(Harris lives in London, England.)

Richard Warren Hatch, *This Bright Summer* (New York: Covici, Friede, Inc., 1933, reprinted in Vintage paperback in 1952 as *Go Down to Glory*), "Lobe's End"
(Hatch, 1898-1988, lived at North River Farms in Marshfield, Massachusetts.)

Nathaniel Hawthorne, *"The Ambitious Guest,"* from *Twice-Told Tales*, Volume II, "Legends of the Province House" (Boston: Houghton Mifflin, 1837), en route to Burlington
(Hawthorne, 1804-1864, lived in Massachusetts.)

Joseph Hayes, *The Ways of Darkness* (New York: William Morrow, 1985), "Shepperton"
(Hayes lives in Sarasota, Florida.)

Emory James Haynes, *A Farmhouse Cobweb: A Novel* (New York: Harper & Brother Publishers, 1895), "Northbrook"
(Reverend Haynes, 1846-1914, who was born in Cabot, Vermont, where his father, Zadoc Seymour Haynes, was a Methodist preacher, lived in Brooklyn, New York, and Boston, Massachusetts.)

Mary Hays, *Learning to Drive: A Novel* (New York: Shaye Areheart Books, 2003), "Beede"
(Hays, who went to Bennington College, lives with her husband, Stephen Long, publisher of *Northern Woodlands*, in Corinth, Vermont.)

Daniel Hecht, *Skull Session* (New York: Viking Press, 1998), Norwich
(Hecht lives in East Montpelier, Vermont.)

William Heffernan, *Blood Rose* (New York: E.P. Dutton, 1991), "Blake"
Beulah Hill (New York: Simon & Schuster, 2000), "Beulah Hill"
(Heffernan lives in Huntington, Vermont.)

Ursula Hegi, *Salt Dancers* (New York: Simon & Schuster, 1995), Proctor
(Hegi, a faculty member in 1998, 2002, and 2004 at the Middlebury College Bread Loaf Writers' Conference in Ripton, Vermont, lives near Spokane, Washington.)

Mark Helprin, "A Vermont Tale," from *Ellis Island and Other Stories* (New York: Dell, 1976), Addison County
(Helprin lives in New York.)

George V. (Vincent) Higgins, *Victories* (New York: Henry Holt, 1990), "Canterbury," "Occident"
(Higgins, 1939-1999, lived in Milton, Massachusetts.)

Grace Livingston Hill (Lutz), *The Prodigal Girl* (New York: Grosset, 1929), "Briardale"
(Hill, 1865-1947, whose pseudonym was Marcia Macdonald Duskin, lived in New York.)

Gerald A. Hinckley, *The Great Green Mountain Horn Hunt* (New York: Carlton Press, 1988), "Dunbar"
(Hinckley lives in Williamstown, Vermont.)

Tami Hoag, *Mismatch* (New York: Bantam, 1989), rural Vermont
(Hoag lives in Virginia.)

Douglas Hobbie, *This Time Last Year* (New York: Henry Holt, 1997), "Speedwell"
(Hobbie lives in Conway, Massachusetts.)

Emma Holly, *The Night Owl*, from the anthology *Hot Blooded* (New York: Jove, 2004), "Maple Notch"
(Holly lives in Minneapolis, Minnesota.)

Ann Hood, *Three-Legged Horse* (New York: Bantam, 1989), near Mount Snow
(Hood, a faculty member in 1994 at the Middlebury College Bread Loaf Writers' Conference in Ripton, Vermont, lives with her husband, writer Bob Reiss, in Providence, Rhode Island.)

Lester Eugene Hood, *You Must Love the Enemy* (New York: Carlton Press, 1974), Bradford
(Hood, 1905-1999, lived in West Hartford, Vermont.)

William Dean Howells, *The Rise of Silas Lapham* (Boston: Houghton Mifflin, 1885), "Lapham"
The Landlord at Lion's Head (New York: Harper & Brothers, 1897), "Lion's Head"
(Howells, 1837-1920, was born in Ohio, married Elinor Gertrude Mead of Brattleboro, Vermont, and lived in Boston, Massachusetts, and New York City.)

Barbara Howes, "The Road Commissioner," from *The Road Commissioner and Other Stories* (Lunenburg: The Stinehour Press, 1983, with block prints by her son, Vermont artist Gregory Smith), southern Vermont (Howes, 1914-1996, a poet and essayist, graduated from Bennington College, was married to poet, critic, and translator William Jay Smith, and lived in North Pownal, Vermont.)

David (R.) Huddle, "In the Mean Mud Season," "The Gorge," "The Crossing," "The Beautiful Gesture," from *The High Spirits: Stories of Men and Women* (Boston: David Godine, 1989), Burlington
"The Hearing," "Henry Lagoon," from *Intimates* (Boston: David Godine, 1993), Burlington, Barre
"The Village," "Wherever I am not," "Not," from *Not: A Trio* (Notre Dame: University of Notre Dame Press, 2000), Bennington, Lincoln
*La Tour Dreams of the Wolf Girl (Boston: Houghton Mifflin, 2002), Burlington
(Huddle, a faculty member from 1989-1994 and in 2000 at the Middlebury College Bread Loaf Writers' Conference in Ripton, Vermont, is a professor at the University of Vermont and poet who lives in Burlington, Vermont.)

Richard E. (Edward) Hughes, *Unholy Communion* (Garden City: Doubleday, 1982), "Pineville" (Hughes lives in Duxbury, Massachusetts.)

Maria Hummel, *Wilderness Run: A Novel* (New York: St. Martin's Press, 2002), "Allenton" (Hummel, born in Underhill, Vermont, is a poet and novelist living in Los Angeles, California.)

Zephine Humphrey (Fahnestock), *Over Against Green Peak* (New York: Henry Holt, 1908), Dorset
The Homestead (New York: E.P. Dutton, 1919), "Marshall Hollow"
Mountain Verities (New York: E.P. Dutton, 1923), Dorset
Winterwise (New York: E.P. Dutton, 1927), Dorset
Chrysalis (New York: E.P. Dutton, 1929), Dorset
(Humphrey, 1874-1956, lived with her husband, landscape painter Wallace Weir Fahnestock, 1877-1962, in Dorset, Vermont.)

Siri Hustvedt, **What I Loved: A Novel* (New York: Henry Holt, 2003), near Newfane
(Hustvedt lives with her husband, writer Paul Auster, in Brooklyn, New York, and West Townshend, Vermont.)

Elisabeth Hyde, *Her Native Colors* (New York: Delacorte Press, 1986), "East Winslow"
(Hyde, a graduate of the University of Vermont, lives in Seattle, Washington.)

I

Elizabeth (Ann) Inness-Brown, *Burning Marguerite* (New York: Alfred A. Knopf, 2002), "Grain Island" (Inness-Brown, whose pseudonym is Liz Monley, is on the faculty of St. Michael's College in Colchester, Vermont, and lives on the island of South Hero in Lake Champlain, Vermont.)

J

Samuel Alexander Jackson, *Among the Maples* (Pittsburgh: United Presbyterian Board of Publication, 1908), "Renwicktown"
(Reverend Jackson, 1863-1940, lived in South Ryegate, Vermont.)

Shirley Jackson, "The Lottery" (*New Yorker Magazine*, 1948, collected in *The Magic of Shirley Jackson*, New York: Farrar, Straus, 1966), near Bennington
Life among the Savages (New York: Farrar, Straus, 1953), North Bennington
Raising Demons (New York: Farrar, Straus, 1957), North Bennington
The Haunting of Hill House (Cutchogue, NY: Buccaneer Books, Inc., 1959), "Hillsdale"
"Maybe It Was the Car," "Fame," "Home," "The Possibility of Evil," from *Just an Ordinary Day: The Uncollected Stories of Shirley Jackson* (New York: Bantam, 1996), North Bennington
(Jackson, 1919-1965, a faculty member in 1964 at the Middlebury College Bread Loaf Writers' Conference in Ripton, Vermont, lived with her husband, literary critic Stanley Edgar Hyman, 1919-1970, in North Bennington, Vermont.)

William Jaspersohn, *Native Angels: A Peter Boone Novel* (New York: Bantam, 1995), "Earlsville"
Lake Effect: A Peter Boone Novel (New York: Bantam, 1996), "Gatwick Lake"
(Jaspersohn lives in Johnson, Vermont.)

(Theodora) Sarah Orne Jewett, **"Fame's Little Day,"* from *The Life of Nancy* (Boston: Houghton Mifflin, 1895), "Wetherford"
(Jewett, 1849-1909, lived in South Berwick, Maine.)

Arthur F. Joy, *Vermont Adventure: Turn Left to East Wallingford* (South Wellfleet: Saturescent Publishers, 1985), East Wallingford
(Joy, 1910-1988, stayed for a time in East Wallingford, Vermont, and lived in South Wellfleet, Massachusetts.)

Margaret H. (Haddican) Judd, *Murder is a Best Seller* (New York: Arcadia House, 1959), "Loomisville"
(Judd, 1906-1995, who was born in East Barre, Vermont, lived in Springfield, Massachusetts.)

Ward (Swift) Just, *The American Blues* (New York: Viking Press, 1984), Northeast Kingdom
"A Guide to the Geography of Vermont," "Maintenance," from *Twenty-One Selected Stories* (New York: Ivy Books, 1990), Northeast Kingdom, Lyndonville
(Just, who spent from 1973 to 1979 in Warren, Vermont, lives in Vineyard Haven, Massachusetts.)

K

Garrison Keillor, "Christmas in Vermont," from *The Book of Guys* (New York: Viking Press, 1993), "Redford"
(Keillor lives in Wisconsin and New York.)

Clarence Budington Kelland, *Scattergood Baines* (New York: Harper, 1921), "Coldriver"
Scattergood Baines Returns (New York: Grosset & Dunlap, 1939), "Coldriver"
(Kelland, 1881-1964, lived in Detroit, Michigan, and Wilmington, Vermont.)

Victor J. Kelly, *MacIntosh Mountain* (Grand Rapids: Zondervan Publishing, 1983), "Croughton's Corners"
(Kelly lives in Phoenix, Arizona.)

Judith (Ann) Kelman, *The House on the Hill* (New York: Random House, 1992), "Dove's Landing"
(Kelman lives in Stamford, Connecticut.)

Jay Kendall, *The Secret Keepers* (Athol: Haley's, 1999), "Duncansboro"
(Kendall, born in Newport, Vermont, lives in Orange, Massachusetts.)

Louise Andrews Kent, *Mrs. Appleyard's Year* (Boston: Houghton Mifflin, 1941), "Appleyard Center"
Country Mouse (Boston: Houghton Mifflin, 1945), "Appleyard Center"
(Kent, 1886-1969, lived in Berlin, Vermont.)

Brad Kessler, *The Woodcutter's Christmas* (San Francisco: Council Oak Books, 2001, with photographs by Dona Ann McAdams), "Dedham's Notch"
(Kessler lives in Sandgate, Vermont.)

Frances Parkinson (Wheeler) Keyes, *The Career of David Noble* (New York: The Sun Dial Press, 1921), "Hamstead"
Lady Blanche Farm: A Romance of the Commonplace (New York: Liveright, 1931), "Hamstead"
The Safe Bridge (New York: Julian Messner, 1934), Ryegate, Newbury
Joy Street (New York: Julian Messner, 1950), "Hollyhocks"
(Keyes, 1885-1970, lived in Newbury, Vermont.)

Roger (Frank Graham) King, *A Girl from Zanzibar* (New York: Books & Co., 2002), near Cavendish
(King, a fellow in 1990 at the Middlebury College Bread Loaf Writers' Conference in Ripton, Vermont, lives in Leverett, Massachusetts.)

Stephen (Edwin) King, *The Shining* (Garden City: Doubleday, 1977), "Stovington"
The Stand (Garden City: Doubleday, 1978), "Stovington"
Firestarter (New York: Viking Press, 1980), "Tashmore"
(King, one of whose pseudonyms is Richard Bachman, lives in Bangor, Maine.)

Rudyard Kipling, "A Walking Delegate," from *The Day's Work* (New York: Doubleday & McClure, 1898), Dummerston
(Kipling, 1865-1936, married an American, Caroline Starr Balestier, 1862-1939, with whom he lived at Naulakha in Dummerston, Vermont, from 1892-1896. They returned to Bateman's in Sussex, England.)

John Knowles, *A Separate Peace* (New York: Macmillan, 1959), northern Vermont
(Knowles, 1926-2001, lived in Connecticut and Florida.)

Joseph Koenig, *Smuggler's Notch* (New York: Viking Press, 1989), Smuggler's Notch
(Koenig lives in New York City and San Francisco, California.)

Kathryn Kramer, *Sweet Water* (New York: Alfred A. Knopf, 1998), "West Stilling"
(Kramer, a faculty member at Middlebury College, lives in Middlebury, Vermont.)

William Kritlow, *Crimson Snow: A Lake Champlain Mystery* (Nashville: Nelson, 1995), "Sugar Steeple"
(Kritlow lives in southern California.)

Mary Alice Kruesi, *One Summer's Night* (New York: HarperCollins, 2000), "Fallingstar"
(Kruesi lives outside Chicago, Illinois.)

Regina P. Krummel, *Looking Good* (New York: Michael Kesend Publishing, 1985), near Burlington
(Krummel lives in Norwalk, Connecticut.)

Edward Kuhn, Jr., *Ski Week* (Garden City: Doubleday, 1975), "White Ridge"
(Kuhn lives in Chappaqua, New York.)

James Howard Kunstler, *Maggie Darling* (New York: Atlantic Monthly Press, 2004), "Catamount Creek"
(Kunstler lives in Saratoga Springs, New York. *A Clown in the Moonlight*, St. Martin's Press, 1981, is a marriage farce set on the campus of a progressive Vermont college.)

L

Karen Latuchie, *The Honey Wall* (New York: W.W. Norton, 2004), "Cannen"
(Latuchie lives in Jersey City, New Jersey.)

Wendi W. Lee, *Habeas Campus: An Angela Matelli Mystery* (New York: St. Martin's Press, 2002), Bristol
(Lee lives in Muscatine, Iowa.)

Peter Lefcourt, *The Woody* (New York: Simon & Schuster, 1998), Peru
(Lefcourt lives in Los Angeles, California.)

David (E.) Leitz, *Casting in Dead Water: A Max Addams Mystery* (New York: St. Martin's Press, 1996), "Loon"
Dying to Fly-Fish: A Max Addams Mystery (New York: St. Martin's Press, 1996, originally published as *The Fish-Flying Corpse*, Grand Junction, Colo.: Centennial Publications, 1994), "Loon"
Fly-Fishing Can be Fatal: A Max Addams Mystery (New York: St. Martin's Press, 1997), "Loon"
Hooked on Death: A Max Addams Mystery (New York: St. Martin's Press, 2000), "Loon"
(Leitz, 1940-2001, lived in New York and in Brattleboro and Guilford, Vermont.)

Jeffrey Lent, *In the Fall* (New York: Random House, 2001), Randolph
(Lent lives in Tunbridge, Vermont.)

Ellen Lesser, *The Other Woman* (New York: Simon & Schuster, 1988), near "Middlefield"
"The Shoplifter's Apprentice," "Stinking Benjamin," "Eating Air," "Pressure for Pressure," "Life Drawing," from *The Shoplifter's Apprentice* (New York: Simon & Schuster, 1990)
(Lesser, a faculty member at Vermont College in Montpelier, lives with her husband, poet Roger Weingarten, in East Montpelier, Vermont.)

Julius (Bernard) Lester, *The Autobiography of God* (New York: St Martin's Press, 2004), "Brett"
(Lester, who was a lay reader for nine years at a synagogue in St. Johnsbury, Vermont, lives in Belchertown, Massachusetts.)

Jonathan (Allen) Lethem, *The Fortress of Solitude* (Garden City: Doubleday, 2003), "Camden"
(Lethem, son of artist Richard Brown Lethem, went to Bennington College and lives in Brooklyn, New York.)

(Harry) Sinclair Lewis, *Arrowsmith* (New York: Harcourt Brace, 1925), "Birdies' Rest"
It Can't Happen Here (Garden City: Doubleday, 1935), "Fort Beulah"
(Lewis, 1885-1951, lived with his wife, journalist Dorothy Thompson, 1894-1961, in New York and Barnard, Vermont.)

Pam (Pamela) Lewis, *Speak Softly, She Can Hear* (New York: Simon & Schuster, 2005), Stowe, Montpelier
(Lewis, who has lived in Montpelier and Middlesex, Vermont, lives in Storrs, Connecticut.)

Reeve Lindbergh, *Moving to the Country* (Garden City: Doubleday, 1983), "Winsom"
The Names of the Mountains (New York: Simon & Schuster, 1992), northern Vermont
(Lindbergh, daughter of Charles Augustus and Anne Morrow Lindbergh, lives with her husband, writer Nathaniel Tripp, in Passumpsic, Vermont.)

Gail Link, *There Never Was a Time* (New York: Dorchester Publishing, 1995), Stowe
(Link lives in Concordville, Pennsylvania.)

Elinor Lipman, *The Inn at Lake Devine* (New York: Random House, 1998), "Lake Devine"
(Lipman lives in Northampton, Massachusetts.)

Florence Bingham Livingston, *Under a Thousand Eyes* (New York: Cosmopolitan Book Corporation, 1923), "Hampton Valley"
(Livingston, 1887-1966, was born in Burlington, Vermont, and lived in Berkeley, California.)

Bret Lott, *The Man Who Owned Vermont* (New York: Viking Press, 1987), Readsboro
(Lott, a fellow in 1991 at the Middlebury College Bread Loaf Writers' Conference in Ripton, Vermont, lives in Charleston, South Carolina.)

Michael (Francis) Lowenthal, *Avoidance* (St. Paul: Graywolf Press, 2002), near Killington
(Lowenthal, a fellow in 1999 at the Middlebury College Bread Loaf Writers' Conference in Ripton, Vermont, lives in Boston, Massachusetts.)

M

Patricia J. MacDonald, *Suspicious Origin* (New York: Atria Books, 2003), "Coleville"
(MacDonald, a pseudonym of Patricia Bourgeau, lives in Cape May, New Jersey.)

Bernard Malamud, *Dubin's Lives* (New York: Farrar, Straus, 1979), "Center Campobello"
(Malamud, 1914-1986, a faculty member at Bennington College from 1961-1986, lived in Oregon and then Bennington, Vermont.)

David (Alan) Mamet, "Conversations with the Spirit World," "Pint's a Pound," "Dowsing," "Deer Dog," "In the Mall," "Maple Sugaring" "Morris and Joe," "In Old Vermont," from "Vermont Sketches," from *Goldberg Street: Short Plays and Monologues* (New York: Grove Press, 1985), near Cabot
The Village (Boston: Little Brown, 1994) central Vermont
(Mamet, a graduate of Goddard College in Plainfield, Vermont, and later an artist in residence there, lives with his wife, actress Rebecca Pidgeon, in Cambridge, Massachusetts, and Cabot, Vermont.)

Kate Manning, *White Girl* (New York: Dial Press, 2002), near Stowe
(Manning lives in New York City.)

Rebecca Marsh, *Summer in Vermont* (Charleston: Arcadia Publishing, 1955), "Saunder's Bluff"
(Marsh, the pseudonym of William Arthur Neubauer, 1916-1982, lived in Santa Cruz, California.)

Kirk Martin, *Shade of the Maple* (Highpoint, N.C.: Cantwell-Hamilton, 2002), Burlington
(Martin lives in Northfield, Vermont.)

Steve Martin, *Shopgirl* (New York: Hyperion, 2000), "Dunton"
(Martin, an actor and writer, lives in Los Angeles, California.)

Caroline Atwater Mason, *A Woman of Yesterday* (Garden City: Doubleday, Page, 1900), "Haran," Burlington
(Mason, 1853-1939, lived in New York City and Greenwich, Connecticut.)

Charles Mathes, *The Girl at the End of the Line* (New York: St. Martin's Press, 1999), "Gale Island"
(Mathes lives with his wife, writer and artist Arlene Graston, in New York City.)

Evelyn Wilde Mayerson, *Well and Truly* (New York: NAL Books, 1990), Manchester
(Mayerson lives in Miami, Florida, and Manchester, Vermont.)

Archer (Huntington) Mayor, *Open Season* (New York: Warner Books, 1988), Brattleboro
Borderlines (New York: Warner Books, 1990), "Gannet"
Scent of Evil (New York: Warner Books, 1992), Brattleboro
The Skeleton's Knee (New York: Warner Books, 1993), Brattleboro
Fruits of the Poisonous Tree (New York: Warner Books, 1994), Brattleboro
The Dark Root (New York: Warner Books, 1995), Brattleboro

The Ragman's Memory (New York: Warner Books, 1996), Brattleboro
Bellows Falls (New York: Warner Books, 1997), Bellows Falls
The Disposable Man (New York: Warner Books, 1998), Brattleboro, Middlebury, Northeast Kingdom
Occam's Razor (New York: Warner Books, 1999), Brattleboro
The Marble Mask (New York: Warner Books, 2000), Stowe
Tucker Peak (New York: Warner Books, 2001), Tucker Mountain
The Sniper's Wife (New York: Warner Books, 2002), Brattleboro
Gatekeeper (New York: Warner Books, 2003), Brattleboro
The Surrogate Thief (New York: Warner Books, 2004), Brattleboro
(Mayor, a novelist and police officer, lives in Newfane, Vermont. The sixteenth in the series is *St. Albans Fire*, 2005.)

Anne McAllister, *Imagine* (Ontario: Harlequin, 1990), "Boone's Corner"
MacKenzie's Baby (Ontario: Harlequin, 1992), "Boone's Corner"
(McAllister, a pseudonym of Barbara Schenk, lives in Iowa and Montana. Her novella, "Never Say Never," also set in Vermont and loosely connected to the other two novels, was collected in *New Year's Resolution: Family*, Harlequin Books, 1998.)

Elliott Tucker Merrick, III, *Ever the Winds Blow* (New York: Charles Scribner's Sons, 1936), "Arburg"
(Merrick, 1906-1997, lived in New Jersey, Labrador, and Craftsbury, Vermont.)

Don Metz, *Catamount Bridge* (New York: Harper, 1988), "Catamount"
King of the Mountain (New York: Harper, 1990), "Dalton Pond"
(Metz, a fellow in 1988 at the Middlebury College Bread Loaf Writers' Conference in Ripton, Vermont, lives in Lyme, New Hampshire.)

Ruth Tracy Millard, *Candleflame* (Philadelphia: Penn Publishing, 1938), "Bradley"
(Millard, 1905-1988, born in Turkey of missionary parents, was brought up in Strafford, Vermont, and lived in New York City.)

Sue Miller, *The World Below: A Novel* (New York: Alfred A. Knopf, 2001), "West Barstow"
(Miller lives in Boston, Massachusetts, and Strafford, Vermont.)

Bibliography

Richard Mindell, *Eden Falls* (Stoughton, MA: Reginald vanFenwick Press, 2000), "Eden Falls" (Mindell lives in Jericho, Vermont.)

Don (Donald Earl) Mitchell, *The Nature Notebooks: A Novel* (Hanover: University Press of New England, 2004), Mount Mansfield (Mitchell, a fellow in 1986 at the Middlebury College Bread Loaf Writers' Conference in Ripton, Vermont, is a faculty member at Middlebury College and lives in Vergennes, Vermont.)

David Morrell, *The Fraternity of the Stone* (New York: St. Martin's Press, 1985), "Quentin" (Morrell lives in Iowa City, Iowa.)

Mary (Joan) McGarry Morris, *Vanished* (New York: Viking Press, 1988), "The Flatts"
A Dangerous Woman (New York: Viking Press, 1991), "Atkinson"
Songs in Ordinary Time (New York: Viking Press, 1995), "Atkinson"
The Lost Mother (New York: Viking Press, 2005), "Belton" (Morris, who grew up in Rutland, Vermont, lives in Andover, Massachusetts.)

Stephen Morris, *Beyond Yonder* (Lexington: The Stephen Greene Press, 1987), "Upper Granville"
The King of Vermont (New York: William Morrow, 1989), "Upper Granville" (Morris lives in Randolph, Vermont.)

Howard Frank Mosher, *Disappearances* (New York: Viking Press, 1977), near "Kingdom Common"
Where the Rivers Flow North (New York: Viking Press, 1978), near "Kingdom Common"
Marie Blythe (New York: Viking Press, 1983) "Hell's Gate"
A Stranger in the Kingdom (Garden City: Doubleday, 1989), "Kingdom Common"
Northern Borders (Boston: Houghton Mifflin, 1994), "Lost Nation"
The Fall of the Year (Boston: Houghton Mifflin, 1999), "Kingdom Common"
"Second Sight," from John M. Miller, *Granite and Cedar: The People and the Land of Vermont's Northeast Kingdom* (Hanover: University Press of New England, 2001), Kingdom Mountain
The True Account (Boston: Houghton Mifflin, 2003), "Kingdom Common"
Waiting for Teddy Williams (Boston: Houghton Mifflin, 2004), "Kingdom Common" (Mosher, who did postgraduate work at the University of Vermont, lives in Irasburg, Vermont.)

Faye Smith Moulton, *Witch's Child* (Rutland: Academy Books, 1994), "Sherfield Center" (Moulton lives in Rutland, Vermont.)

N

Joseph (M.) Nassise, *Riverwatch* (New York: Simon & Schuster, 2002), "Harrington Falls" (Nassise lives in Phoenix, Arizona.)

Daniel A. Neary, Jr., *Rage in the Hills: A Collection of Short Stories* (Montpelier: Plateau Press, 2000), Tinmouth, Plainfield, "Scampsville" (Neary lives in East Montpelier, Vermont.)

Carla (Amalia) Neggers, *Finders Keepers* (Ontario: Harlequin, 1993), southern Vermont
Finding You (New York: Pocket Books, 1996), Woodstock
The Waterfall (Ontario: MIRA, 2000), "Joshua Falls"
Dark Sky (Ontario: MIRA, 2005), Hartford (Neggers lives in Quechee, Vermont.)

Jack (Eugene A.) Newcombe, *In Search of Billy Cole* (New York: Arbor House, 1984), Middlebury (Newcombe, 1923-1990, born in Burlington, Vermont, lived mainly in New York and Washington, D.C.)

John (Treadwell) Nichols, *The Wizard of Loneliness* (New York: W. W. Norton & Company, 1966), "Stebbinsville" (Nichols grew up in Montpelier, Vermont, and lives in Taos, New Mexico.)

Christopher Noël, *Hazard and the Five Delights* (New York: Alfred A. Knopf, 1988), "Elton" (Noël, a faculty member at Vermont College in Montpelier, lives in East Calais, Vermont. His collection, *A Frail House: Stories*, Lincoln, Neb.: IUniverse, 2005, contains two stories set in Vermont: "Timing" and "Emergency Preparedness.")

Jack Noon, *The Big Fish of Barston Falls* (Warner, N.H.: Moose Country Press, 1995), "Barston Falls"
Old Sam's Thunder (Warner, N.H.: Moose Country Press, 1998), "Barston Falls" (Noon lives in Sutton, New Hampshire.)

Howard A. Norman, "Milk Train," "Catching the Heat," from *Kiss in the Hotel Joseph Conrad and Other Stories* (New York: Summit Books, 1989), Burlington, Cabot (Norman, a faculty member in 1999 at the Middlebury College Bread Loaf Writers' Conference in Ripton, Vermont, lives with his wife, poet Jane Shore, in New York City and Calais, Vermont.)

Freya North, *Polly* (United Kingdom: Heineman, 1998), "Hubbardtons Spring" (North lives in London, England.)

Craig Nova, *The Congressman's Daughter* (New York: Delacorte Press, 1986), southern Vermont
Cruisers (New York: Shaye Areheart Books, 2004), southern Vermont
(Nova, a fellow in 1978 at the Middlebury College Bread Loaf Writers' Conference in Ripton, Vermont, lives in Hillsborough, North Carolina, and Putney, Vermont.)

O

Jenny Offill, *Last Things* (New York: Farrar, Straus, 1999), "Windler"
(Offill lives in Brooklyn, New York.)

John (Henry) O'Hara, *The Instrument* (New York: Random House, 1967), "East Hammond"
(O'Hara, 1895-1970, lived in Pennsylvania.)

Joseph Olshan, *In Clara's Hands* (London: Bloomsbury Publishing, 2001), Burlington
(Olshan, who attended the University of Vermont from 1974-1976, lives in New York City and Barnard, Vermont.)

P

Dalia Pagani, *Mercy Road* (New York: Dell, 1998), "Smallford," "The Ridge"
(Pagani lives in Thetford, Vermont.)

Katherine Hall Page, *The Body in the Snowdrift: A Faith Fairchild Mystery* (New York: William Morrow, 2005), "Pine Slopes"
(Page lives in Lincoln, Massachusetts.)

Tom Paine, "Unapproved Minutes of the Carthage, Vermont, Zoning Board of Adjustment," from *Scar Vegas and Other Stories* (New York: Harcourt, 2000), "Carthage"
(Paine, a faculty member at Middlebury College, lives in Middlebury, Vermont.)

Jay (Lee) Parini, *Bay of Arrows* (New York: Henry Holt, 1992), "Barrington"
(Parini, a faculty member in 1992, 1997, 2000, and 2005 at the Middlebury College Bread Loaf Writers' Conference in Ripton, Vermont, is a faculty member at Middlebury College and lives with his wife, writer Devon Jersild, in Weybridge, Vermont. He is the author of *Robert Frost: A Life*, Henry Holt, 1999; Frost lived at the Stone House, now a museum, in Shaftsbury, Vermont, from 1920-1929, and in Ripton, Vermont, from 1938-1963.)

Robert Newton Peck, *Justice Lion* (Boston: Little Brown, 1981), "Liberty"
(Peck, born in Vermont, lives in Longwood, Florida.)

Theodora Agnes Peck, *Hester of the Grants: A Romance of Old Bennington* (New York: Fox, Duffield, 1905), Bennington
White Dawn: A Legend of Ticonderoga (New York: Fleming H. Revell, 1914), Lake Champlain
(Peck, 1882-1964, lived in Burlington, Vermont.)

William Dudley Pelley, *The Greater Glory* (Boston: A.L. Burt, 1919), "Paris"
Drag: A Comedy (Boston: Little Brown, 1925), "Paris"
The Blue Lamp (New York: The Fiction League, 1931), near "Paris"
(Pelley, 1890-1965, an American fascist who was the prototype for Buzz Windrip in Sinclair Lewis's *It Can't Happen Here*, lived in California, Indiana, and St. Johnsbury, Vermont.)

Bliss Perry, "His Word of Honor," "Madame Annalena," "The Fish-Warden of Madrid," from *The Powers at Play* (New York: Charles Scribner's Sons, 1899), "North Enderby," "Slab City," "Madrid"
(Perry, 1860-1954, professor of American literature and model for Peter Dow in Wallace Stegner's *Second Growth*, began summering in Greensboro, Vermont, in 1896 and lived in Massachusetts.)

Kathrin Perutz, *The Garden* (New York: Atheneum, 1962), near Lake Champlain
(Perutz lives in New York City.)

Judson Philips, *Thursday's Folly: A Peter Styles Mystery* (New York: Dodd, Mead, 1967), "Barchester"
(Philips, 1903-1989, lived in Sharon, Connecticut. As Hugh Pentecost, he wrote *Where the Snow Was Red*, New York: Dodd, Mead, 1949, a murder mystery in a tiny Vermont village starring psychologist Dr. Smith.)

Jodi Picoult, *Second Glance: A Novel* (New York: Simon & Schuster, 2003), "Comtosook"
(Picoult lives in Hanover, New Hampshire.)

Suzi (Carolyn Suzanne) Pizzuti, *Raising Cain...and His Sisters* (New York: Waterbrook Press, 2000), "McLaughlin"
(Pizzuti lives in Canada.)

L. (Luthera) J. Pratt, "Emma the Belle of the Village," "The Berry Boy," "Early Graves," "Mysterious Strangers," from *The Unfortunate Mountain Girl: A Collection of Miscellanies in Prose and Verse* (Middlebury: The Register Book and Job Office, 1854), "village of P____," "Dresden"
(Pratt, a blind woman who married James Rider in 1849, lived in West Berkshire, Vermont.)

John Prendergast, *Jump* (Minneapolis: Mid-List Press, 1995), ski resort
(Prendergast lives with his wife, poet Carole Bernstein, in Philadelphia, Pennsylvania.)

Francine Prose, *Blue Angel* (New York: HarperCollins, 2000), "Euston"
(Prose, a faculty member from 1984-1988 and in 1991, 1993, and 1995 at the Middlebury College Bread Loaf Writers' Conference in Ripton, Vermont, lives in New York City.)

E. (Edna) Annie Proulx, *Heart Songs* (New York: Charles Scribner's & Sons, 1988), "Chopping County"
Postcards (New York: Charles Scribner's & Sons, 1992), Cream Hill
(Proulx, who graduated from the University of Vermont in 1969, lived in many towns in Vermont including Canaan and Vershire, and now lives in Wyoming. She no longer uses the initial "E" in her name.)

Bernadette Pruitt, *The Man Next Door* (New York: Avalon Books, 1998)
(Pruitt lives in Tulsa, Oklahoma.)

R

Diana Ramsay, *Killing Words* (New York: Tom Doherty Associates, 1994), "Northvale"
(Ramsay, a pseudonym of Rhoda Brandes, lives in Middlebury, Vermont.)

Franklin D. (Dolier) Reeve, *The Brother* (New York: Farrar, Straus, 1971), Middlebury
(Reeve lives with his wife, novelist Laura C. Stevenson, in Wilmington, Vermont. A literature professor, poet, and translator, Reeve accompanied Robert Frost to Russia in 1962. His book, *Robert Frost in Russia*, Little Brown, 1964, was reissued by Zephyr Press in 2005. He is the father of the late actor Christopher Reeve.)

Helen Reilly, *Murder on Angler's Island: An Inspector Christopher McKee Mystery* (New York: Random House, 1945), "Bangall"
(Reilly, 1891-1962, lived in New York and New Mexico.)

Herbert Resnicow, *The Seventh Crossword: A Giles Sullivan and Isabel MacIntosh Crossword Puzzle Mystery* (New York: Balantine, 1985), "Rockfield"
(Resnicow lives in New York.)

Stanley Reynolds, *Better Dead Than Red: A Novel of the Extreme Right* (London: Elek Books Ltd., 1964), "Milltown River Junction"
(Reynolds, a journalist with The Guardian, lives in Liverpool, England.)

Claudia Ricci, *Dreaming Maples* (Austerlitz: Star Root Press, 2002), "Wilmont"
(Ricci lives in Spencertown, New York.)

John Rickards, *The Touch of Ghosts* (London: Michael Joseph, 2004), "North Bleakwater"
(Rickards lives in England.)

Eric Rickstad, *Reap* (New York: Viking Penguin, 2000), "Ivers"
(Rickstad, a graduate of the University of Vermont in 1994, lives in Shelburne, Vermont.)

Kenneth (Lewis) Roberts, *Rabble in Arms: A Chronicle of Arundel and the Burgoyne Invasion* (Garden City: Doubleday, Doran, 1933), Lake Champlain
Northwest Passage (Garden City: Doubleday, Doran, 1937), New Hampshire Grants
(Roberts, 1885-1957, lived in Kennebunkport, Maine.)

Nora Roberts, *From This Day* (New York: Silhouette, 1983), "Lakeside"
Cordina's Crown Jewel (Ontario: Harlequin, 2002), Northeast Kingdom
(Roberts, whose pseudonym is J.D. Robb, lives in Maryland.)

Sherry Roberts, *Maud's House* (Watsonville, Calif.: Papier-Maché Press, 1994), "Round Corners"
(Roberts lives in Eagan, Minnesota.)

Margaret A. (Atwood) Robinson, *Courting Emma Howe* (Bethesda: Adler & Adler, 1987), "Warwick"
(Robinson, a University of Vermont graduate, lives in Swarthmore, Pennsylvania.)

Rowland E. (Evans) Robinson, *Danvis Tales: Selected Stories*, edited by David Budbill, with an introduction by Hayden Carruth (Hanover: University Press of New England, 1995, first published as *Danvis Folks*, Houghton Mifflin, 1894), "Danvis"
(Robinson, 1833-1900, lived in Ferrisburgh, Vermont; poet David Budbill lives in Wolcott, Vermont; poet Hayden Carruth lived in Johnson, Vermont, and now lives in New York.)

James Robison, *The Illustrator* (New York: Summit Books, 1988), "Shellington"
(Robison lives in Boston, Massachusetts, and in Houston, Texas.)

Judith (Perelman) Rossner, *Any Minute I Can Split* (New York: McGraw-Hill, 1972), north of Brattleboro
(Rossner lives in New York City.)

Cyrus D. (Dustian) Roys, *Captain Jack: A Story of Vermont, Illustrating the Struggles of the Green Mountain Boys during the Most Romantic Period of Their History* (Chicago: Lakeside Press, 1909), near "Waits Mountain"
(Roys, 1841-1915, was born in Vermont, lived in Chicago, and died in Indiana.)

Philip Russell, *Body and Blood: A Novel of Linked Stories* (Columbia: University of Missouri Press, 1998), near Lemon Fair River
(Dr. Russell, who has a Master of Fine Arts from Vermont College in Montpelier, lives in Wells, Vermont.)

S

Henry Barnard Safford, *That Bennington Mob* (New York: Julian Messner, 1935), Bennington
(Safford, 1883-1953, a descendant of Major Samuel Safford, lived in New York City.)

Ajay Sahgal, *Pool* (New York: Grove/Atlantic, 1994), "Suzanna"
(Sahgal lives in Los Angeles, California.)

Anna C. Salter, *Shiny Water: A Dr. Michael Stone Book* (New York: Pocket Books, 1996), near Middlebury
Fault Lines: A Dr. Michael Stone Book (New York: Pocket Books, 1998), near Middlebury
White Lies: A Dr. Michael Stone Book (New York: Pocket Books, 2000), near Middlebury
Prison Blues: A Dr. Michael Stone Book (New York: Pocket Books, 2002), near Middlebury
(Salter spent twenty years as a forensic psychologist in Middlebury, Vermont, and lives in Madison, Wisconsin.)

Edwin Webster Sanborn, *People at Pisgah* (New York: D. Appleton, 1892), "North Pisgah"
(Sanborn, 1857-1928, lived in Hanover, New Hampshire.)

Herbert (Ravenel) Sass, "Affair at St. Albans" (*The Saturday Evening Post*, 1948, collected in *New Confederate Short Stories*, edited by Katharine M. Jones, Columbia: University of South Carolina Press, 1954), St. Albans
(Sass, 1884-1958, lived in Charleston, South Carolina.)

Susan Fromberg Schaeffer, *Time in Its Flight* (Garden City: Doubleday, 1978), Williamsville
The Madness of a Seduced Woman (New York: E.P. Dutton, 1983), Montpelier
The Golden Rope (New York: Alfred A. Knopf, 1996), Peru
(Schaeffer, a professor at the University of Chicago, lives in Chicago, Illinois, and South Newfane, Vermont.)

Deborah Schupack, *The Boy on the Bus* (New York: Free Press, 2003), central Vermont
(Schupack was a faculty member at Vermont College in Montpelier and lives in New York City.)

Karl Schwenke, *In a Pig's Eye* (White River Junction: Chelsea Green Publishing Company, 1985), Newbury
(Schwenke lives in Newbury, Vermont.)

Lucy A. Jameson (Mrs. O.W.) Scott, *The Gilead Guards: A Story of War-Times in a New England Town* (New York: Hunt & Eaton, 1893), "Gilead"
"Judson's Tramp," "Polly Moulton's Wild Geese," "How Three Girls Helped," "The Stronger Tie: A Story of '63," from *Compound Interest and Other Stories* (New York: Eaton and Mains, 1896), "Brockway," "Dumstead," "Byville," "Glover Hills"
(Jameson, 1844-1920, was born in Irasburg, Vermont, and married Reverend O.W. Scott in 1867. The town of Brighton in northern Vermont was originally chartered as Gilead in 1780.)

Catharine Maria Sedgwick, "A Reminiscence of Federalism," from *Tales and Sketches* (Philadelphia: Carey, Lea, and Blanchard, 1835), "Carrington"
(Sedgwick, 1789-1867, lived in Stockbridge, Massachusetts.)

John Sedgwick, **The Dark House* (New York: HarperCollins, 2000), Townshend
(Sedgwick, a descendant of Catharine Maria Sedgwick, lives in Newton, Massachusetts.)

Irwin Shaw, **The Young Lions* (New York: Random House, 1948), "small Vermont town"
*Nightwork (New York: Delacorte, 1975), Burlington
(Shaw, 1913-1984, lived in New York City and Klosters, Switzerland.)

Maggie Shayne, *Colder Than Ice* (Ontario: MIRA, 2004), "Blackberry"
(Shayne, the pseudonym of Margaret Benson, lives in New York.)

Harry Sholk, *Drumbeats in the Valley: A Story of Life at Norwich University in the Early Nineteenth Century* (Haverford: Infinity Publishing Company, 2004), Norwich
(Sholk, who graduated from Norwich University in 1952, lives in Florham Park, New Jersey.)

Philip Singerman, **Proof Positive* (New York: Tom Doherty Associates, 2001), northern Vermont
(Singerman, a Vermont native, lives in Longwood, Florida.)

Sharon Snow Sirois, *Sawyer's Crossing* (North Haven: Lighthouse Publishing, 2002), "Sawyer's Crossing" (Sirois lives in Waterbury, Connecticut.)

Robert C. Sloane, *The Vengeance* (New York: Crown, 1983), "Torchester" (Sloane lives in Baldwin, Long Island.)

Alison Smith, *Someone Else's Grave* (New York: St. Martin's Press, 1984), "Coolidge Corners" *Rising* (New York: St. Martin's Press, 1987), "Coolidge Corners" (Smith lives in Harmony, Rhode Island.)

Annie Smith, *Home Again* (New York: Kensington Publishing, 2002), Brattleboro (Smith lives in Gahanna, Ohio.)

Edward H. (Henry) Smith, "The Vermont Raffles Who Transcended the Tomb," from *You Can Escape* (New York: Macmillan, 1929, in the short-fiction collection, *Some Things Fierce and Fatal*, edited by Joan Kahn, New York: Harper & Row, 1971), Chester (Smith, 1881-1927, was born in Ohio.)

Elinor Spielberg, *Uninvited Daughters* (New York: St. Martin's Press, 1993), "Downsboro" (Spielberg, who lived in the Chelsea, Vermont, area for seventeen years, now lives in Brooklyn, New York.)

Danielle Steele, *Granny Dan* (New York: Dell, 1999), rural Vermont (Steele lives in San Francisco, California.)

Lynn (Marie) Stegner, *Pipers at the Gates of Dawn: A Triptych* (Hanover: University Press of New England, 2000), "Harrow" (Stegner lives in Santa Cruz, California, and Greensboro, Vermont, with her husband, Professor S. Page Stegner, son of Wallace Stegner.)

Wallace (Earle) Stegner, *Second Growth* (Boston: Houghton Mifflin, 1947), "Westwick" *Crossing to Safety* (New York: Random House, 1987), "Battell Pond" "Hostage," "The Berry Patch," "Saw Gang," "The Sweetness of the Twisted Apples," "Traveler," from *Collected Stories of Wallace Stegner* (New York: Random House, 1990) (Stegner, 1909-1993, a faculty member in 1938, 1940, 1942, 1944, and 1946 at the Middlebury College Bread Loaf Writers' Conference in Ripton, Vermont, lived in Los Altos, California, and Greensboro, Vermont.)

Aaron Marc Stein, *Chill Factor: A Matt Erridge Mystery* (Boston: Atheneum, 1978), northern Vermont (Stein, 1906-1985, who wrote the Inspector Schmidt series under the pseudonym George Bagby, lived in New York and Washington, D.C.)

John (Ernst) Steinbeck, *To a God Unknown* (New York: Viking, 1933), Pittsford (Steinbeck, 1902-1968, who included Vermont in his itinerary in *Travels with Charley: In Search of America*, 1960, republished by Penguin in 1997 with an introduction by Jay Parini, lived in Salinas, California.)

Barbara B. Stevens, *Walk Humbly* (Boston: Houghton Mifflin, 1935), West Waterford (Stevens, 1901-1996, lived in Massachusetts.)

Abigail Stone, *Recipes from the Dump* (New York: W. W. Norton, 1995), "Leadbelly" (Stone, daughter of poet Ruth Stone, lives in Middlebury, Vermont.)

Mira Stout, *One Thousand Chestnut Trees: A Novel of Korea* (New York: Riverhead Books, 1998), near Starksboro (Stout lives in Italy and London, England.)

Harriet (Elizabeth) Beecher Stowe, *Uncle Tom's Cabin, or, Life Among the Lowly* (Boston: J.P. Jewett, 1852), southern Vermont (Stowe, 1811-1896, who spent fifteen months from 1846 to 1847 at a water cure in Brattleboro, Vermont, lived in Hartford, Connecticut.)

John Stephen Strange, *Reasonable Doubt* (Garden City: Doubleday, 1951), "Burnham" (Strange is the pseudonym of Dorothy Stockbridge Tillett, 1896-1983, who lived in New York.)

Peter (Francis) Straub, *Shadowland* (New York: Coward, 1980), north of Putney (Straub lives in New York City.)

Anne Stuart, *Banish Misfortune* (Ontario: Harlequin, 1985), northern Vermont *Still Lake* (Ontario: Harlequin, 2002), "Colby" (Stuart, a pseudonym of Christine Ohlrogge, lives in Greensboro, Vermont.)

Dorothy Sucher, *Dead Men Don't Give Seminars* (New York: St. Martin's Press, 1988), Burlington (Sucher lives in Silver Spring, Maryland, and Cabot, Vermont.)

Mark T. Sullivan, *Ghost Dance: A Novel of Suspense* (New York: Avon Books, 1999), "Lawton" (Sullivan lived in Rutland, Vermont, before moving to Bozeman, Montana.)

Thomas (William) Sullivan, *The Phases of Harry Moon* (New York: E.P. Dutton, 1988), "Chewbagin" (Sullivan lives in Lathrup Village, Michigan.)

Mark Sumner, *News from the Edge: Vampires of Vermont* (New York: Ace Books, 1999), "Williams Crossing" (Sumner lives in St. Louis, Missouri.)

T

Donna Tartt, *The Secret History* (New York: Alfred A. Knopf, 1992), "Hamden" (Tartt, who went to Bennington College, lives in New York.)

Sarah Stewart Taylor, *O'Artful Death* (New York: St. Martin's Press, 2003), "Byzantium" (Taylor, a Middlebury College graduate, lives in Hartland, Vermont.)

Douglas C. Terman, *Free Flight* (New York: Charles Scribner's Sons, 1980), Northeast Kingdom (Terman, 1933-1999, lived in East Warren, Vermont.)

Nancy Tesler, *Slippery Slopes & Other Deadly Things: A Carrie Carlin Biofeedback Mystery* (Santa Barbara: Perseverance Press, 2003), "Sunnyvale" (Tesler lives in Tenafly, New Jersey.)

Nancy Thayer, *My Dearest Friend* (New York: Charles Scribner's Sons, 1989), "Plover" (Thayer, a fellow in 1980 at the Middlebury College Bread Loaf Writers' Conference in Ripton, Vermont, lives on Nantucket Island, Massachusetts.)

Daniel Pierce Thompson, *May Martin, or, The Money Diggers and Other Green Mountain Tales* (Montpelier: 1835; Boston: Sanborn, Carter, Bazin & Co., 1852), "Harwood Settlement"
The Green Mountain Boys: A Historical Tale of the Early Settlement of Vermont (Montpelier: 1839; T. Nelson & Sons, 1840, went into fifty printings by 1860), New Hampshire Grants
Locke Amsden, or, The Schoolmaster: A Tale (first published 1847; Boston: Sanborn, Carter, Bazin & Co., 1856), "Cartersville"
The Rangers, or, The Tory's Daughter, A Tale Illustrative of the Revolutionary History of Vermont and the Northern Campaign, two volumes (Montpelier: 1851; Boston: Lee and Shepard, 1890,), Westminster, Guilford, Bennington
"The Starving Settlers," "The Unfathomable Mystery: A Tale of Circumstantial Evidence," "The Rustic Financiers," "The Counterfeiter," from *Centeola and Other Tales* (New York: Carleton, 1864), Onion River, Cozy Corner (Judge Thompson, 1795-1868, a graduate of Middlebury College, lived in Montpelier, Vermont.)

Mari Tomasi, *Like Lesser Gods* (Shelburne: New England Press, 1949), "Granitetown" (Tomasi, 1909-1965, a native of Vermont, lived in Montpelier, Vermont.)

U

John (Hoyer) Updike, *Seek My Face* (New York: Alfred A. Knopf, 2002), northeast of Montpelier (Updike lives in Beverly Farms, Massachusetts.)

William Hazlett Upson, "Botts Runs for His Life" (*Saturday Evening Post*, 1952) from *The Best of Botts* (New York: David McKay Company, 1961), Middlebury (Upson, 1891-1975, a faculty member in 1946 and 1949 at the Middlebury College Bread Loaf Writers' Conference in Ripton, Vermont, received a Litt. D. from Middlebury College and lived in Ripton, Vermont.)

V

Frederic F. (Franklyn) Van de Water, *Mrs. Applegate's Affair* (Duell, Sloan & Pearce, 1944), Walden
Fool's Errand (Duell, Sloan & Pearce, 1945), "Appledore"
The Sooner to Sleep (Duell, Sloan & Pearce, 1946), "Grantchester"
Reluctant Rebel (Duell, Sloan & Pearce, 1948, republished abridged as *Rebel's Progress*, 1952), Bennington
Catch a Falling Star (Duell, Sloan & Pearce, 1949, republished abridged as *The Green Cockade,* 1956), Bennington, New Hampshire Grants
Wings of the Morning (New York: Ives Washburn, 1955), Dummerston
Day of Battle (New York: Ives Washburn, 1958), Bennington (Van de Water, 1890-1968, lived in Dummerston, Vermont.)

Hendrik Willem van Loon, *Invasion: Being an Eyewitness Account of the Nazi Invasion of America* (New York: Harcourt, Brace, 1940), Dorset (Van Loon, 1882-1972, lived in New York and Boston, among other places, and in Greenwich, Connecticut.)

Lilian Van Ness, *The Indifferent Blade* (Garden City: Doubleday, 1947), "Derby-Four-Corners" (Van Ness, 1911-1983, lived in Kearney, New Jersey.)

Victoria Vinton, *The Jungle Law* (San Francisco: MacAdam/Cage, 2005) (This historical novel describes Rudyard Kipling's stay in Dummerston, Vermont, during the period he wrote *The Jungle Book.* The novel was not available in time to include in the text. Vinton lives in Brooklyn, New York.)

Bibliography

Kurt Vonnegut, Jr., *Slaughterhouse-Five, or, The Children's Crusade: A Duty Dance with Death* (New York: Delacorte Press, 1969), near Sugarbush Mountain (Vonnegut lives with his wife, writer Jill Krementz, in Northampton, Massachusetts.)

W

Chuck Wachtel, "The Eye," from *Because We Are Here: Stories and Novellas* (New York: Viking, 1996), near Lincoln (Wachtel lives in Lafayette, Indiana, and New York City.)

Dan Wakefield, *Selling Out* (Boston: Little Brown, 1995), "Haviland" (Wakefield stayed with poet Richard Moore in Vermont while writing "Waiting for Reality: Death of a Small Town" (1965) about Huntington, Vermont. A faculty member in 1964, 1966, 1968, 1970, and 1986 at the Middlebury College Bread Loaf Writers' Conference in Ripton, Vermont, he lives in Bar Harbor Islands, Florida.)

Mildred Walker (Schemm), *The Quarry* (New York: Harcourt, Brace, 1947), "Plainsville"
The Southwest Corner (New York: Harcourt, Brace, 1951), near Rutland
The Body of a Young Man (New York: Harcourt, Brace, 1960), near Manchester
(Walker, 1905-1998, a faculty member in 1957 at the Middlebury College Bread Loaf Writers' Conference in Ripton, Vermont, and mother of poet Ripley S. Hugo, lived in Great Falls, Montana, and Grafton, Vermont.)

Maggie (Margaret) Wall, *One darn thing after another* (Enosburg Falls: O'Shea Publishing, 1970), Lake Champlain (Wall lives in Farmington, Connecticut.)

Mary Ella Waller, *The Wood-Carver of 'Lympus* (Boston: Little Brown, 1904), 'Lympus Bethel (Waller, 1855-1938, lived in Bethel, Vermont.)

Beverly C. Warren, *That Gentle Touch* (Garden City: Doubleday, 1984), Essex Junction (Warren lives in Newington, Connecticut.)

Larry Watson, *Laura* (New York: Simon & Schuster, 2000), "Garrett" (Watson lives in Stevens Point, Wisconsin.)

Patrick Wayland, *The Waiting Game* (Garden City: Doubleday, 1965), "Adamsville" (Wayland, the pseudonym of Richard O'Connor, 1915-1975, lived in California and New York.)

Charles (Richard) Webb, *New Cardiff* (London: Little Brown, 2001), "New Cardiff" (Webb lives near Brighton, England.)

Carolyn Wells, *Spooky Hollow: A Fleming Stone Mystery* (New York: A.L. Burt, 1923), "Hilldale" (Wells, 1869-1942, lived in Rahway, New Jersey.)

Tobias Wells, *How to Kill a Man: A Knute Severson Mystery* (Garden City: Doubleday, 1972), "Vale" (Wells is the pseudonym of Deloris/Florine Stanton Forbes, who lives in St. Martin, French West Indies.)

Nathanael West, *A Cool Million: The Dismantling of Lemuel Pitkin* (New York: Covici, Friede, 1934), "Ottsville" (West, 1903-1940, lived in New York and California.)

Donald E. (Edwin) Westlake, *Don't Ask* (New York: Warner Books, 1993), "Middleville" (Westlake lives in New York.)

Blythe White, Jr., *The Green Mountain Girls: A Tale of Vermont* (New York: Derby & Jackson, 1856), northern Vermont (White, a pseudonym of Solon Robinson, 1803-1880, was born in Connecticut and lived in Indiana.)

Homer White, *Norwich Cadets: A Tale of the Rebellion* (St. Albans: A. Clarke, 1873), Norwich (Reverend White, 1837-1926, was born in Weathersfield, made pastor of St. Mary's parish in Northfield in 1886, and died in Enosburg, Vermont.)

Tom (Thomas Grey) Wicker, *Easter Lilly: A Novel of the South Today* (New York: William Morrow, 1998), Rutland (Wicker, political reporter and novelist, lives in New York and Rochester, Vermont.)

Kevin Wignall, *People Die* (New York: Simon & Schuster, 2002), between Newfane and Grafton (Wignall lives in the west of England.)

Alix Wilber, *The Wives' Tale* (New York: W.W. Norton, 1991), "Esperance" (Wilber lives in Seattle, Washington.)

Paul Wilkes, *Temptations: A Novel* (New York: Random House, 1993), "Falmouth" (Wilkes lives in Gilbertville, Massachusetts.)

Edward Williams, *Black Forest* (Ferrisburgh: Buckwheat Street Publishers, 1975), Ferrisburgh (Williams was the caretaker at Rokeby Homestead, the Ferrisburgh, Vermont, home of abolitionist Rowland Thomas Robinson, father of author Rowland E. Robinson.)

William Carlos Williams, *White Mule* (New York: A New Directions Book, 1937), near Westminster
In the Money (Norfolk: A New Directions Book, 1940), near Westminster
(Dr. Williams, 1883-1963, pediatrician, poet, and novelist, who was a guest speaker in 1941 at the Middlebury College Bread Loaf Writers' Conference in Ripton, Vermont, lived in Rutherford, New Jersey. In the third novel in this trilogy, *The Build-Up*, Random House, 1952, the Stecher family again spends summers at a farm modeled on Hilldale in Wilmington, Vermont, belonging to Williams's wife's Uncle Elinar.)

Owen Wister, *The Virginian: A Horseman of the Plains* (New York: Macmillan, 1902), Bennington
(Wister, 1860-1938, lived in Philadelphia, Pennsylvania.)

Suzi Wizowaty, *The Round Barn* (Hanover: University Press of New England, 2002), "Eustis"
(Wizowaty lives in Burlington, Vermont.)

Scott Wolven, *Controlled Burn: Stories of prison, crime, and men* (New York: Scribner, Simon & Schuster, 2005)
(The first section of this collection, called "The Northeast Kingdom," includes "Ball Lightning Reported," set in Newport, Vermont. The book was not available in time to include in the text. Wolven lives in New York.)

Ted (Edward John) Wood, *Snowjob: A Reid Bennett Mystery* (New York: Charles Scribner's Sons, 1993), "Chambers"
(Wood lives in Ontario, Canada.)

Elvirton Wright, *Freshman and Senior* (Boston: Congregational Sunday School and Publishing Society, 1889), Burlington
(Elvirton Wright, 1864-1930, was the pseudonym of Jessie Elvira Wright–later Mrs. George H. Whitcomb, who graduated from the University of Vermont in 1884 and lived in Topeka, Kansas.)

Nancy Means Wright, *Mad Season: A Ruth Willmarth Mystery* (New York: St. Martin's Press, 1996), "Branbury"
Harvest of Bones: A Ruth Willmarth Mystery (New York: St. Martin's Press, 1998), "Branbury"
Poison Apples: A Ruth Willmarth Mystery (New York: St. Martin's Press, 2000), "Branbury"
Stolen Honey: A Ruth Willmarth Mystery (New York: St. Martin's Press, 2002), "Branbury"
"Fire and Ice," from *Crimes of Passion* (New York: Worldwide, 2002), "Branbury"
(Wright, a scholar in 1959 at Middlebury College Bread Loaf Writers' Conference in Ripton, Vermont, lives in Cornwall, Vermont. *Mad Cow Nightmare*, 2005, continues the Ruth Willmarth series.)

Y

Dana Yeaton, *Mad River Rising* (Rochester, Vt.: PenStroke Press, 1999), Moretown
(Yeaton, a faculty member at Middlebury College, lives in Middlebury, Vermont.)

Christy Yorke, *Magic Spells* (New York: Bantam, 1999), "Pendleton"
(Yorke lives in Boise, Idaho.)

Z

Edra Ziesk, *A Cold Spring* (Chapel Hill: Algonquin Books, 2002), "Amity"
(Ziesk, who spent summer vacations as a child in the West Dover/Wilmington area, lives in New York City.)

APPENDIX A:
Genres,
alphabetically by category

CAMPUS FICTION

Paul Auster, *The Book of Illusions* (see also Dramatic)

Miriam Borgenicht, *Booked for Death* (see also Mystery)

Nicholas Delbanco, *Old Scores*

Bret Easton Ellis, *The Rules of Attraction* (see also Coming-of-Age)

Rebecca Gilman, *Spinning into Butter* (see also Plays)

Roger King, *A Girl from Zanzibar* (see also Dramatic)

Karen Latuchie, *The Honey Wall*

Wendi W. Lee, *Habeas Campus* (see also Mystery)

Julius Lester, *The Autobiography of God* (see also Fantasy and Magic Realism)

Kate Manning, *White Girl*

Jack Newcombe, *In Search of Billy Cole*

Kathrin Perutz, *The Garden* (see also Coming-of-Age)

Francine Prose, *Blue Angel*

Diana Ramsey, *Killing Words* (see also Mystery)

Herbert Resnicow, *The Seventh Crossword* (see also Mystery)

Dorothy Sucher, *Dead Men Don't Give Seminars* (see also Mystery)

Nancy Thayer, *My Dearest Friend*

Donna Tartt, *The Secret History*

Dan Wakefield, *Selling Out* (see also Comic Fiction)

COMIC FICTION

Lisa Alther, *Bedrock, Kinflicks*

Ann Beattie, *Love Always*

Geoffrey Becker, *Bluestown*

Jon Boorstin, *Pay or Play*

Mary Higgins Clark and **Carol Higgins Clark**, *The Christmas Thief*

Ellen Hodges Cooley, *Boom of a Western City*

Jay Cronley, *Funny Farm*

Deane Chandler Davis, *Justice in the Mountains*

Castle Freeman, Jr., *My Life and Adventures*

David Gates, *Preston Falls*

Shirley Jackson, *Life among the Savages, Raising Demons*

Clarence Budington Kelland, *Scattergood Baines, Scattergood Baines Returns*

Louise Andrews Kent, *Mrs. Appleyard's Year, Country Mouse*

James Howard Kunstler, *Maggie Darling*

Elinor Lipman, *The Inn at Lake Devine*

Steve Martin, *Shopgirl*

Charles Mathes, *The Girl at the End of the Line*

Stephen Morris, *Beyond Yonder*

William Dudley Pelley, *Drag: A Comedy*

Stanley Reynolds, *Better Dead Than Red*

Sherry Roberts, *Maud's House*

Rowland E. Robinson, *Danvis Tales*

Judith Rossner, *Any Minute I Can Split*

Ajay Sahgal, *Pool*

Edwin Webster Sanborn, *People at Pisgah*

Karl Schwenke, *In a Pig's Eye*

Elinor Spielberg, *Uninvited Daughters*

Abigail Stone, *Recipes from the Dump*

Thomas Sullivan, *The Phases of Harry Moon*

Frederic Van de Water, *Mrs. Applegate's Affair, The Sooner to Sleep*

Kurt Vonnegut, Jr., *Slaughterhouse-Five*

Dan Wakefield, *Selling Out*

Margaret Wall, *One darn thing after another*

Charles Richard Webb, *New Cardiff*

Nathanael West, *A Cool Million*

COMING-OF-AGE FICTION

Madison Smartt Bell, *Anything Goes*

Jason Berger, *Forested Moments*

Robert Luther Duffus, *Roads Going South, That Was Alderbury*

Dikkon Eberhart, *On the Verge*

Bret Easton Ellis, *The Rules of Attraction*

Sebastian Faulks, *A Fool's Alphabet*

Frances Frost, *Innocent Summer*

Len Fulton, *Dark Other Adam Dreaming*

James Gordon, *Escape from Vermont*

Peter Gould, *Burnt Toast*

John Knowles, *A Separate Peace*

Regina P. Krummel, *Looking Good*

Jonathan Lethem, *The Fortress of Solitude*
Sinclair Lewis, *Arrowsmith*
Elliott Merrick, *Ever the Winds Blow*
Howard Frank Mosher, *Northern Borders*,
     Waiting for Teddy Williams
Christopher Noël, *Hazard and the Five Delights*
John Nichols, *The Wizard of Loneliness*
Robert Newton Peck, *Justice Lion*
Kathrin Perutz, *The Garden*
Eric Rickstad, *Reap*
John Steinbeck, *To a God Unknown*

DRAMATIC & TRAGIC FICTION

Glenda Adams, *The Tempest of Clemenza*
Laurie Alberts, *The Price of Land in Shelby*
Paul Auster, *The Book of Illusions*
Harry Barba, *For the Grape Season*
Philip Baruth, *The Dream of the White Village*
Tricia Bauer, *Hollywood & Hardwood*
Frederick Buechner, *The Entrance to Porlock*
Chris Bohjalian, *Past the Bleachers*, *The Trans-Sister Radio*,
     The Law of Similars, *Midwives*, *Water Witches*,
     The Buffalo Soldier, *Before You Know Kindness*
Gerald Warner Brace, *The Wayward Pilgrims*,
     Light on a Mountain
T. Alan Broughton, *Hob's Daughter*
Pearl Buck, *Letter from Peking*, *Voices in the House*
Michael Burns, *Gemini*
Ruth Chatterton, *Homeward Borne*
Eleanor Clark, *Camping Out*, *Gloria Mundi*
Felicia B. Clark, *Hester of Pepper Tree Ranch*
Sarah N. Cleghorn, *The Spinster*
Judith Beth Cohen, *Seasons*
Edward J. Connolly, *Deer Run*
Art Corriveau, *Housewrights*
Nicholas Delbanco, *Possession, Sherbrookes, Stillness*
Barbara Dimmick, *Heart-Side Up*
Edwin Asa Dix, *Deacon Bradbury*, *Old Bowen's Legacy*
Julia Dorr, *Farmingdale, Sybil Huntington, Expiation*
Anne Miller Downes, *So Stands the Rock, Heartwood*
Robert Luther Duffus, *Victory on West Hill*
Margaret Erhart, *Old Love*
Dorothy Canfield Fisher, *The Bent Twig*,
     The Brimming Cup, The Home-Maker, Seasoned Timber,
     Her Son's Wife, Bonfire

Edith Forbes, *Nowle's Passing*
Castle Freeman, Jr., *Judgment Hill*
Mary E. Wilkins Freeman, *Madelon*
Frances Frost, *Yoke of Stars, Kate Trimingham,*
     Village of Glass
John Gardner, *October Light*
Gerald Jay Goldberg, *The Lynching of Orin Newfield*
Thomas Christopher Greene, *Mirror Lake*
T. Greenwood, *Breathing Water*
Sue Halpern, *The Book of Hard Things*
Richard Warren Hatch, *This Bright Summer*
Emory James Haynes, *A Farmhouse Cobweb*
Mary Hays, *Learning to Drive*
Ursula Hegi, *Salt Dancers*
Douglas Hobbie, *This Time Last Year*
Ann Hood, *Three-Legged Horse*
William Dean Howells, *The Rise of Silas Lapham,*
     The Landlord at Lion's Head
David Huddle, *Not: A Trio*
Zephine Humphrey, *The Homestead, Over Against Green*
     Peak, Mountain Verities, Winterwise, Chrysalis
Siri Hustvedt, *What I Loved*
Elisabeth Hyde, *Her Native Colors*
Elizabeth Inness-Brown, *Burning Marguerite*
S.A. Jackson, *Among the Maples*
Arthur F. Joy, *Vermont Adventure*
Ward Just, *The American Blues*
Jay Kendall, *The Secret Keepers*
Frances Parkinson Keyes, *The Career of David Noble,*
     Lady Blanche Farm, Joy Street
Kathryn Kramer, *Sweet Water*
Ellen Lesser, *The Other Woman*
Reeve Lindbergh, *Moving to the Country, The Names of*
     the Mountains
Florence Bingham Livingston, *Under a Thousand Eyes*
Bret Lott, *The Man Who Owned Vermont*
Michael Lowenthal, *Avoidance*
Bernard Malamud, *Dubin's Lives*
David Mamet, *The Village*
Caroline Atwater Mason, *A Woman of Yesterday*
Evelyn Wilde Mayerson, *Well and Truly*
Don Metz, *Catamount Bridge, King of the Mountain*
Ruth Tracy Millard, *Candleflame*
Sue Miller, *The World Below*
Don Mitchell, *The Nature Notebooks*
Mary McGarry Morris, *Songs in Ordinary Time,*
     Vanished, A Dangerous Woman, The Lost Mother

Howard Frank Mosher, *The Fall of the Year,*
   A Stranger in the Kingdom
John O'Hara, *The Instrument*
Joseph Olshan, *In Clara's Hands*
William Dudley Pelley, *The Greater Glory*
John Prendergast, *Jump*
E. Annie Proulx, *Postcards*
Franklin D. Reeve, *The Brother*
James Robison, *The Illustrator*
Philip Russell, *Body and Blood*
Susan Fromberg Schaeffer, *The Madness of a Seduced*
   Woman, The Golden Rope
Irwin Shaw, *The Young Lions*
Lynn Stegner, *Pipers at the Gates of Dawn*
Wallace Stegner, *Crossing to Safety, Second Growth*
Mira Stout, *One Thousand Chestnut Trees*
Harriet Beecher Stowe, *Uncle Tom's Cabin*
Mari Tomasi, *Like Lesser Gods*
John Updike, *Seek My Face*
Frederic Van de Water, *Fool's Errand*
Lilian Van Ness, *The Indifferent Blade*
Mildred Walker, *The Southwest Corner, The Body of a*
   Young Man
Mary Ella Waller, *The Wood-Carver of 'Lympus*
Larry Watson, *Laura*
Edward Williams, *Black Forest*
William Carlos Williams, *White Mule, In the Money*
Paul Wilkes, *Temptations*
Owen Wister, *The Virginian*
Suzi Wizowaty, *The Round Barn*
Edra Ziesk, *A Cold Spring*

FANTASY & MAGIC REALISM FICTION

Phil Austin, *On Bethel Ridge*
Perdita Buchan, *Called Away*
Richard S. Conde, *Shelburne, Vermont*
Gail Crease, *The Dream Spinner*
Barbara Delinksy, *Three Wishes*
David Drake, *Patriots*
David Huddle, *La Tour Dreams of the Wolf Girl*
Judith Kelman, *The House on the Hill*
Brad Kessler, *The Woodcutter's Christmas*
Mary Alice Kruesi, *One Summer's Night*
Julius Lester, *The Autobiography of God*
Kirk Martin, *Shade of the Maple*

Howard Frank Mosher, *Disappearances*
Dalia Pagani, *Mercy Road*
Jodi Picoult, *Second Glance*
Jenny Offill, *Last Things*
Jay Parini, *Bay of Arrows*
Deborah Schupack, *The Boy on the Bus*
Douglas Terman, *Free Flight*
Christy Yorke, *Magic Spells*

HISTORICAL FICTION

Clifford Lindsey Alderman, *The Arch of Stars*
Marguerite Allis, *Not Without Peril*
Irving Bacheller, *Eben Holden*
Howard Breslin, *The Tamarack Tree*
Joseph Bruchac, *Dawn Land, Long River, The Waters*
   Between
Sarah N. Cleghorn, *A Turnpike Lady*
Merle Estes Colby, *All Ye People*
Julia Dorr, *Sybil Huntington*
Basil Douros, *The Roots of the Blackthorn Tree*
Earl Faine, *Green Mountain Man: The Odyssey of Ethan Allen*
Frederick Fenn, *Journey to Common Ground*
Lester Eugene Hood, *You Must Love the Enemy*
Maria Hummel, *Wilderness Run*
Frances Parkinson Keyes, *The Safe Bridge*
Jeffrey Lent, *In the Fall*
Howard Frank Mosher, *The True Account, Marie Blythe*
Jack Noon, *The Big Fish of Barston Falls, Old Sam's Thunder*
Theodora Peck, *Hester of the Grants, White Dawn: A*
   Legend of Ticonderoga
Kenneth Roberts, *Northwest Passage, Rabble in Arms*
Margaret A. Robinson, *Courting Emma Howe*
Cyrus D. Roys, *Captain Jack*
Henry Barnard Safford, *That Bennington Mob*
Susan Fromberg Schaeffer, *Time in Its Flight*
Lucy Jameson Scott, *The Gilead Guards*
Harry Sholk, *Drumbeats in the Valley*
Daniel Pierce Thompson, *The Green Mountain Boys,*
   The Rangers, Locke Amsden
Frederic Van de Water, *Reluctant Rebel, Catch a Falling*
   Star, Wings of the Morning, Day of Battle
Mildred Walker, *The Quarry*
Blythe White, Jr., *The Green Mountain Girls*
Homer White, *Norwich Cadets*
Elvirton Wright, *Freshman and Senior*

HORROR FICTION

Chris Bohjalian, *Hangman*

Joseph A. Citro, *Deus-X, Shadow Child, Guardian Angels, The Gore, Lake Monsters*

John Farris, *Son of the Endless Night*

Catharine Anne Fought, *Rabble's Curse*

Christopher Golden, *The Gathering Dark*

Michael Green, *Dry Skull Dreams*

Shirley Jackson, *The Haunting of Hill House*

Stephen King, *The Stand, The Shining, Firestarter*

Joseph M. Nassise, *Riverwatch*

Robert C. Sloane, *The Vengeance*

Peter Straub, *Shadowland*

Mark T. Sullivan, *Ghost Dance*

Mark Sumner, *News from the Edge*

Alix Wilber, *The Wives' Tale*

MYSTERY FICTION

Peter Abrahams, *Hard Rain*

Harriette Ashbrook, *The Murder of Sigurd Sharon*

Abbey Pen Baker, *In the Dead of Winter*

Miriam Borgenicht, *Booked for Death*

Ned and Yanna Brandt, *Land Kills*

Don Bredes, *Cold Comfort, The Fifth Season*

Thomas Brennan, *The Debt*

Carl M. Chapin, *Three Died beside the Marble Pool*

Peter Collinson, *The Northeast Kingdom*

B. Comfort, *The Vermont Village Murder, Green Mountain Murder, Phoebe's Knee, Grave Consequences, The Cashmere Kid, Elusive Quarry, A Pair for the Queen*

Robin Cook, *Fatal Cure*

Arnaldo Correa, *Spy's Fate*

Gloria Dank, *As the Sparks Fly Upward*

Eugene N. Davis, *The Axe with Three Nicks*

Ian Fleming, *For Your Eyes Only*

Frederick Forsyth, *The Negotiator*

Anna Katharine Green, *A Strange Disappearance*

Jane Haddam, *Stillness in Bethlehem*

Robert P. Hansen, *Back to the Wall*

Rosemary Harris, *Three Candles for the Dark*

James Hayes, *The Ways of Darkness*

Daniel Hecht, *Skull Session*

William Heffernan, *Beulah Hill, Blood Rose*

Richard E. Hughes, *Unholy Communion*

William Jaspersohn, *Native Angels, Lake Effect*

Margaret H. Judd, *Murder is a Best Seller*

William Kritlow, *Crimson Snow*

Joseph Koenig, *Smuggler's Notch*

Edward Kuhn, Jr., *Ski Week*

Wendi W. Lee, *Habeas Campus*

David Leitz, *Casting in Dead Water, Dying to Fly-Fish, Fly-Fishing Can Be Fatal, Hooked on Death*

Pam Lewis, *Speak Softly, She Can Hear*

Patricia MacDonald, *Suspicious Origin*

Archer Mayor, *Open Season, Borderlines, Scent of Evil, The Skeleton's Knee, Fruits of the Poisonous Tree, The Dark Root, The Ragman's Memory, Bellows Falls, The Disposable Man, Occam's Razor, The Marble Mask, Tucker Peak, The Sniper's Wife, Gatekeeper, The Surrogate Thief*

Richard Mindell, *Eden Falls*

David Morrell, *The Fraternity of the Stone*

Faye Smith Moulton, *Witch's Child*

Craig Nova, *Cruisers*

Katherine Hall Page, *The Body in the Snowdrift*

William Dudley Perry, *The Blue Lamp*

Judson Philips, *Thursday's Folly*

Diana Ramsay, *Killing Words*

Helen Reilly, *Murder on Angler's Island*

Herbert Resnicow, *The Seventh Crossword*

John Rickards, *The Touch of Ghosts*

Anna Salter, *Prison Blues, Fault Lines, White Lies, Shiny Water*

John Sedgwick, *The Dark House*

Irwin Shaw, *Nightwork*

Philip Singerman, *Proof Positive*

Alison Smith, *Someone Else's Grave, Rising*

Aaron Marc Stein, *Chill Factor*

John Stephen Strange, *Reasonable Doubt*

Dorothy Sucher, *Dead Men Don't Give Seminars*

Sarah Stewart Taylor, *O'Artful Death*

Nancy Tesler, *Slippery Slopes & Other Deadly Things*

Patrick Wayland, *The Waiting Game*

Carolyn Wells, *Spooky Hollow*

Tobias Wells, *How to Kill a Man*

Donald E. Westlake, *Don't Ask*

Tom Wicker, *Easter Lilly*

Kevin Wignall, *People Die*

Ted Wood, *Snowjob*

Nancy Means Wright, *Mad Season, Harvest of Bones, Poison Apples, Stolen Honey*

PLAYS

David Budbill, *A Pulp Cutter's Nativity*, *Judevine*
Dorothy Canfield Fisher, *Tourists Accommodated*
Rebecca Gilman, *Spinning into Butter*
Dana Yeaton, *Mad River Rising*

POLITICAL FICTION

Frank Bryan and **Bill Mares**, *Out! The Vermont Secession Book*
Steve Chontos, *The Death of Dover, Vermont*
Thomas C. Davis, *The Duval Conspiracy*
George V. Higgins, *Victories*
Gerald A. Hinckley, *The Great Green Mountain Horn Hunt*
Peter Lefcourt, *The Woody*
Sinclair Lewis, *It Can't Happen Here*
Stephen Morris, *The King of Vermont*
Craig Nova, *The Congressman's Daughter*
Hendrik Willem van Loon, *Invasion*

ROMANCE FICTION

Charlotte Vale Allen, *Promises, Grace Notes*
Elaine Barbieri, "Winter Moon"
Pamela Burford, *His Secret Side*
Herbert Burkholz, *Sister Bear*
Janet Ann Dailey, *Green Mountain Man*
Barbara Delinsky, *Suddenly, An Irresistible Impulse*
Elizabeth Doyle, *A Country Christmas*
Jennifer Greene, *Wild in the Moment*
Grace Livingston Hill, *The Prodigal Girl*
Tami Hoag, *Mismatch*
Emma Holly, *The Night Owl*
Victor J. Kelly, *MacIntosh Mountain*
Gail Link, *There Never Was a Time*
Rebecca Marsh, *Summer in Vermont*
Anne McAllister, *Imagine, MacKenzie's Baby*
Carla Neggers, *Finders Keepers, Finding You, The Waterfall, Dark Sky*
Freya North, *Polly*
Suzi Pizzuti, *Raising Cain…and His Sisters*
Bernadette Pruitt, *The Man Next Door*
Claudia Ricci, *Dreaming Maples*

Nora Roberts, *From This Day*, *Cordina's Crown Jewel*
Maggie Shayne, *Colder Than Ice*
Sharon Snow Sirois, *Sawyer's Crossing*
Annie Smith, *Home Again*
Danielle Steele, *Granny Dan*
Barbara B. Stevens, *Walk Humbly*
Anne Stuart, *Banish Misfortune, Still Lake*
Beverly C. Warren, *That Gentle Touch*

SHORT STORIES

Dean Albarelli, "Passengers," "O Sole Mio," "Cheaters" (from *Cheaters and Other Stories*)
Laurie Alberts, "Dealing" (from *Goodnight Silky Sullivan*)
Ann Beattie, "Vermont," "Wally Whistles Dixie" (from *Distortions*); "Summer People" from *Where You'll Find Me*)
Robert Bingham, "Marriage is Murder"
Ambrose Bierce, "At Old Man Eckert's"
T. Alan Broughton, "Bill's Women," "My Other Life" (from *Suicidal Tendencies*)
Joan Chase, "The Harrier"
Linda Collins, "When the Pipes Froze," "Going to See the Leaves" (from *Going to See the Leaves*)
Joan Connor, *Here on Old Route 7, We Who Live Apart*
Willis T. Crossman, *Willis T. Crossman's Vermont*
Jeff Danziger, *Teed Stories*
Susan M. Dodd, "What I Remember Now"
Dorothy Canfield Fisher, *Hillsboro People, Four-Square, Raw Material*
Ian Fleming, *For Your Eyes Only*
Castle Freeman, Jr., *The Bride of Ambrose and Other Stories*
Mary E. Wilkins Freeman, "Symphony in Lavender," "A Taste of Honey," "A Modern Dragon" (from *A Humble Romance and Other Stories*); "Ware," "A Village Singer," "A Wayfaring Couple" (from *A New England Nun and Other Stories*)
Lee Dana Goodman, *Dunster Revealed*
Nathaniel Hawthorne, "The Ambitious Guest"
Mark Helprin, "A Vermont Tale"
Barbara Howes, "The Road Commissioner"
David Huddle, "In the Mean Mud Season," "The Gorge," "The Crossing," "The Beautiful Gesture" (from *The High Spirits*); "The Hearing," "Henry Lagoon" (from *Intimates*)

Shirley Jackson, "Maybe It Was the Car,"
"Fame," "Home," "The Possibility of Evil"
(from *Just an Ordinary Day*); "The Lottery"

Sarah Orne Jewett, "Fame's Little Day"

Ward Just, "A Guide to the Geography of Vermont,"
"Maintenance" (from *Twenty-One Selected Stories*)

Garrison Keillor, "Christmas in Vermont"

Rudyard Kipling, "A Walking Delegate"

Ellen Lesser, "The Shoplifter's Apprentice," "Stinking
Benjamin," "Eating Air," "Pressure for Pressure,"
"Life Drawing" (from *The Shoplifter's Apprentice*)

David Mamet, "Conversations with the Spirit World,"
"Pint's a Pound," "Dowsing," "Deer Dog," "In the
Mall," "Maple Sugaring," "Morris and Joe," "In Old
Vermont" (from *Goldberg Street*)

Howard Frank Mosher, *Where the Rivers Flow North*,
"Second Sight"

Daniel A. Neary, Jr., *Rage in the Hills*

Howard A. Norman, "Milk Train," "Catching the Heat"
(from *Kiss in the Hotel Conrad*)

Tom Paine, "Unapproved Minutes of the Carthage,
Vermont, Zoning Board of Adjustment"

Bliss Perry, "His Word of Honor," "Madame Annalena,"
"The Fish-Warden of Madrid" (from *The Powers
at Play*)

L. J. Pratt, "Emma, The Belle of the Village,"
"The Berry Boy," "The Early Graves,"
"Mysterious Strangers" (from *The Unfortunate
Mountain Girl*)

E. Annie Proulx, *Heart Songs*

Herbert Ravenel Sass, "Affair at St. Albans"

Lucy Jameson Scott, "Judson's Tramp," "Polly
Moulton's Wild Geese," "How Three Girls Helped,"
"The Stronger Tie: A Story of '63" (from *Compound
Interest and Other Stories*)

Catharine Maria Sedgwick, "A Reminiscence
of Federalism"

Edward H. Smith, "The Vermont Raffles Who
Transcended the Tomb"

Wallace Stegner, "Hostage," "The Berry Patch,"
"Saw Gang," "The Sweetness of the Twisted Apples,"
"Traveler" (from *Collected Stories of Wallace Stegner*)

Daniel Pierce Thompson, "May Martin, or, The
Money Diggers," "Ethan Allen and the Lost Children,"
"The Guardian and the Ghost (from *May Martin, or,
The Money Diggers and Other Green Mountain Tales*);
"The Starving Settlers," "The Unfathomable Mystery,"

"The Rustic Financiers," "The Counterfeiter,"
"Ethan Allen and the Lost Children," "The Guardian
and the Ghost" (from *Centeola and Other Tales*)

William Hazlett Upson, "Botts Runs for His Life"

Chuck Wachtel, "The Eye"

Nancy Means Wright, "Fire and Ice"

Appendix A

APPENDIX B:
Authors and titles,
by publication date

1835

1835 Catharine Maria Sedgwick, "A Reminiscence of Federalism"

1835 Daniel Pierce Thompson, *May Martin, or, The Money Diggers and Other Green Mountain Tales*

1837

1837 Nathaniel Hawthorne, "The Ambitious Guest"

1839

1839 Daniel Pierce Thompson, *The Green Mountain Boys*

1847

1847 Daniel Pierce Thompson, *Locke Amsden*

1851

1851 Daniel Pierce Thompson, *The Rangers*

1852

1852 Harriet Beecher Stowe, *Uncle Tom's Cabin*

1854

1854 Julia Dorr, *Farmingdale*

1854 L. J. Pratt, *The Unfortunate Mountain Girl*

1856

1856 Blythe White, Jr., *The Green Mountain Girls*

1862

1862 Lucy J. Scott, *The Gilead Guards*

1864

1864 Daniel Pierce Thompson, *Centeola and Other Tales*

1869

1869 Julia Dorr, *Sybil Huntington*

1872

1872 Julia Dorr, *Expiation*

1873

1873 Homer White, *Norwich Cadets*

1879

1879 Anna Katharine Green, *A Strange Disappearance*

1885

1885 William Dean Howells, *The Rise of Silas Lapham*

1887

1887 Mary E. Wilkins Freeman, *A Humble Romance and Other Stories*

1889

1889 Elvirton Wright, *Freshman and Senior*

1891

1891 Mary E. Wilkins Freeman, *A New England Nun and Other Stories*

1892

1892 Edwin Webster Sanborn, *People at Pisgah*

1894

1894 Rowland E. Robinson, *Danvis Folks*

1895

1895 Emory J. Haynes, *A Farmhouse Cobweb*

1895 Sarah Orne Jewett, "Fame's Little Day"

1896

1896 Mary E. Wilkins Freeman, *Madelon*

1896 Lucy J. Scott, *Compound Interest and Other Stories*

1897

1897 Ellen Hodges Cooley, *Boom of a Western City*

1897 William Dean Howells, *The Landlord at Lion's Head*

1898

1898 Rudyard Kipling, "A Walking Delegate"

1899

1899 Bliss Perry, *The Powers at Play*

1900

1900 Irving Bacheller, *Eben Holden*

1900 Edwin Asa Dix, *Deacon Bradbury*

1900 Caroline Atwater Mason, *A Woman of Yesterday*

1901

1901 Edwin Asa Dix, *Old Bowen's Legacy*

1902

1902 Owen Wister, *The Virginian*

1904

1904 Mary Ella Waller, *The Wood-Carver of 'Lympus*

1905

1905 Theodora Peck, *Hester of the Grants*

1907

1907 Sarah N. Cleghorn, *A Turnpike Lady*

1908

1908 Zephine Humphrey, *Over Against Green Peak*

1908 S. A. Jackson, *Among the Maples*

1909

1909 Ambrose Bierce, "At Old Man Eckert's"

1909 Cyrus D. Roys, *Captain Jack*

1913

1913 Dorothy Canfield Fisher, *Hillsboro People*

1914

1914 Theodora Peck, *White Dawn*

1915

1915 **Dorothy Canfield Fisher**, *The Bent Twig*

1916

1916 **Sarah N. Cleghorn**, *The Spinster*

1919

1919 **Zephine Humphrey**, *The Homestead*

1919 **William Dudley Pelley**, *The Greater Glory*

1921

1921 **Robert Luther Duffus**, *Roads Going South*

1921 **Dorothy Canfield Fisher**, *The Brimming Cup*

1921 **Clarence Budington Kelland**, *Scattergood Baines*

1921 **Frances Parkinson Keyes**, *The Career of David Noble*

1922

1922 **Florence Bingham Livingston**, *Under a Thousand Eyes*

1923

1923 **Dorothy Canfield Fisher**, *Raw Material*

1923 **Zephine Humphrey**, *Mountain Verities*

1923 **Carolyn Wells**, *Spooky Hollow*

1924

1924 **Dorothy Canfield Fisher**, *The Home-Maker*

1925

1925 **Sinclair Lewis**, *Arrowsmith*

1925 **William Dudley Pelley**, *Drag: A Comedy*

1926

1926 **Dorothy Canfield Fisher**, *Her Son's Wife*

1927

1927 **Zephine Humphrey**, *Winterwise*

1929

1929 **Eugene N. Davis**, *The Axe with Three Nicks*

1929 **Grace Livingston Hill**, *The Prodigal Girl*

1929 **Zephine Humphrey**, *Chrysalis*

1929 **Edward H. Smith**, "The Vermont Raffles Who Transcended the Tomb"

1931

1931 **Felicia Buttz Clark**, *Hester of Pepper Tree Ranch*

1931 **Merle Estes Colby**, *All Ye People*

1931 **Frances Parkinson Keyes**, *Lady Blanche Farm*

1931 **William Dudley Perry**, *The Blue Lamp*

1932

1932 **Dorothy Canfield Fisher**, *Tourists Accommodated*

1933

1933 **Harriette Ashbrook**, *The Murder of Sigurd Sharon*

1933 **Dorothy Canfield Fisher**, *Bonfire*

1933 **Richard Warren Hatch**, *This Bright Summer*

1933 **Kenneth Roberts**, *Rabble in Arms*

1933 **John Steinbeck**, *To a God Unknown*

1934

1934 **Frances Parkinson Keyes**, *The Safe Bridge*

1934 **Nathanael West**, *A Cool Million*

1935

1935 **Sinclair Lewis**, *It Can't Happen Here*

1935 **Henry Barnard Safford**, *That Bennington Mob*

1935 **Barbara B. Stevens**, *Walk Humbly*

1936

1936 **Carl M. Chapin**, *Three Died beside the Marble Pool*

1936 **Frances Frost**, *Innocent Summer*

1936 **Elliott Merrick,** *Ever the Winds Blow*

1937

1937 **Kenneth Roberts**, *Northwest Passage*

1937 **William Carlos Williams**, *White Mule*

1938

1938 **Gerald Warner Brace**, *The Wayward Pilgrims*

1938 **Willis T. Crossman**, *Told in Vermont*

1938 **Ruth Tracy Millard**, *Candleflame*

1939

1939 **Willis T. Crossman**, *Heard in Vermont*

1939 **Anne Miller Downes**, *So Stands the Rock*

1939 **Dorothy Canfield Fisher**, *Seasoned Timber*

1939 **Frances Frost**, *Yoke of Stars*

1939 **Clarence Budington Kelland**, *Scattergood Baines Returns*

1940

1940 **Frances Frost**, *Kate Trimingham*

1940 **Hendrik Willem van Loon**, *Invasion*

1940 **William Carlos Williams**, *In the Money*

1941

1941 **Marguerite Allis**, *Not Without Peril*

1941 **Gerald Warner Brace**, *Light on a Mountain*

1941 **Robert Luther Duffus**, *That Was Alderbury*

1941 **Louise Andrews Kent**, *Mrs. Appleyard's Year*

1942

1942 **Robert Luther Duffus**, *Victory on West Hill*

1942 **Frances Frost**, *Village of Glass*

1944

1944 **Kenneth Roberts**, *Rabble in Arms*

1944 **Frederic Van de Water**, *Mrs. Applegate's Affair*

1945

1945 **Anne Miller Downes**, *Heartwood*

1945 **Louise Andrews Kent**, *Country Mouse*

1945 **Helen Reilly**, *Murder on Angler's Island*

1945 **Frederic Van de Water**, *Fool's Errand*

Appendix B

1946

1946   Frederic Van de Water, *The Sooner to Sleep*

1947

1947   Howard Breslin, *The Tamarack Tree*

1947   Wallace Stegner, *Second Growth*

1947   Lilian Van Ness, *The Indifferent Blade*

1947   Mildred Walker, *The Quarry*

1948

1948   James Gordon, *Escape from Vermont*

1948   Shirley Jackson, *The Lottery*

1948   Herbert Ravenel Sass, "Affair at St. Albans"

1948   Irwin Shaw, *The Young Lions*

1948   Frederic Van de Water, *Reluctant Rebel*

1949

1949   Dorothy Canfield Fisher, *Four-Square*

1949   Mari Tomasi, *Like Lesser Gods*

1949   Frederic Van de Water, *Catch a Falling Star*

1950

1950   Clifford Lindsey Alderman, *The Arch of Stars*

1950   Ruth Chatterton, *Homeward Borne*

1950   Frances Parkinson Keyes, *Joy Street*

1951

1951   John Stephen Strange, *Reasonable Doubt*

1951   Mildred Walker, *The Southwest Corner*

1952

1952   William Hazlett Upson, "Botts Runs for His Life"

1953

1953   Shirley Jackson, *Life among the Savages*

1953   Pearl Buck, *Voices in the House*

1955

1955   Rebecca Marsh, *Summer in Vermont*

1955   Frederick Van de Water, *Wings of the Morning*

1957

1957   Pearl Buck, *Letter from Peking*

1957   Robert P. Hansen, *Back to the Wall*

1957   Shirley Jackson, *Raising Demons*

1958

1958   Frederic Van de Water, *Day of Battle*

1959

1959   Shirley Jackson, *The Haunting of Hill House*

1959   Margaret H. Judd, *Murder is a Best Seller*

1959   John Knowles, *A Separate Peace*

1960

1960   Harry Barba, *For the Grape Season*

1960   Ian Fleming, *For Your Eyes Only*

1960   Mildred Walker, *The Body of a Young Man*

1962

1962   Kathrin Perutz, *The Garden*

1964

1964   Stanley Reynolds, *Better Dead Than Red*

1965

1965   Patrick Wayland, *The Waiting Game*

1966

1966   John Nichols, *The Wizard of Loneliness*

1967

1967   John O'Hara, *The Instrument*

1967   Judson Philips, *Thursday's Folly*

1969

1969   Herbert Burkholz, *Sister Bear*

1969   Kurt Vonnegut, Jr., *Slaughterhouse-Five*

1970

1970   Frederick Buechner, *The Entrance to Porlock*

1970   Gerald Jay Goldberg, *The Lynching of Orin Newfield*

1970   Margaret Wall, *One darn thing after another*

1971

1971   Edward J. Connolly, *Deer Run*

1971   Peter Gould, *Burnt Toast*

1971   Franklin D. Reeve, *The Brother*

1972

1972   Judith Rossner, *Any Minute I Can Split*

1972   Tobias Wells, *How to Kill a Man*

1974

1974   Steve Chontos, *The Death of Dover, Vermont*

1974   Lester Eugene Hood, *You Must Love the Enemy*

1975

1975   Len Fulton, *Dark Other Adam Dreaming*

1975   Edward Kuhn, Jr., *Ski Week*

1975   Irwin Shaw, *Nightwork*

1975   Edward Williams, *Black Forest*

1976

1976   Lisa Alther, *Kinflicks*

1976   Ann Beattie, *Distortions*

1976   John Gardner, *October Light*

1976   Rosemary Harris, *Three Candles for the Dark*

1976   Mark Helprin, "A Vermont Tale"

1977

1977   Nicholas Delbanco, *Possession*

1977   Stephen King, *The Shining*

1977   Howard Frank Mosher, *Disappearances*

1978

1978   Nicholas Delbanco, *Sherbrookes*

1978   Susan Fromberg Schaeffer, *Time in Its Flight*

1978   Aaron Marc Stein, *Chill Factor*

1979

1979 Charlotte Vale Allen, *Promises*

1979 Eleanor Clark, *Gloria Mundi*

1979 Janet Ann Dailey, *Green Mountain Man*

1979 Dikkon Eberhart, *On the Verge*

1979 Bernard Malamud, *Dubin's Lives*

1980

1980 Perdita Buchan, *Called Away*

1980 Deane C. Davis, *Justice in the Mountains*

1980 Catherine Anne Fought, *Rabble's Curse*

1980 Stephen King, *Firestarter*

1980 Peter Straub, *Shadowland*

1980 Douglas Terman, *Free Flight*

1981

1981 David Budbill, *A Pulp Cutter's Nativity*

1981 Robert Newton Peck, *Justice Lion*

1982

1982 B. Comfort, *The Vermont Village Murder*

1982 Richard E. Hughes, *Unholy Communion*

1983

1983 Barbara Delinsky, *An Irresistible Impulse*

1983 Barbara Howes, "The Road Commissioner"

1983 Victor J. Kelly, *MacIntosh Mountain*

1983 Howard Frank Mosher, *Marie Blythe*

1983 Susan Fromberg Schaeffer, *The Madness of a Seduced Woman*

1983 Reeve Lindbergh, *Moving to the Country*

1983 Nora Roberts, *From This Day*

1983 Robert C. Sloane, *The Vengeance*

1984

1984 T. Alan Broughton, *Hob's Daughter*

1984 Judith Beth Cohen, *Seasons*

1984 Ward Just, *The American Blues*

1984 B. Comfort, *Green Mountain Murder*

1984 Jack Newcombe, *In Search of Billy Cole*

1984 Alison Smith, *Someone Else's Grave*

1984 Beverly C. Warren, *That Gentle Touch*

1985

1985 Ann Beattie, *Love Always*

1985 Jay Cronley, *Funny Farm*

1985 John Farris, *Son of the Endless Night*

1985 James Hayes, *The Ways of Darkness*

1985 Arthur F. Joy, *Vermont Adventure*

1985 Regina P. Krummel, *Looking Good*

1985 David Mamet, *Goldberg Street*

1985 David Morrell, *The Fraternity of the Stone*

1985 Herbert Resnicow, *The Seventh Crossword*

1985 Karl Schwenke, *In a Pig's Eye*

1985 Anne Stuart, *Banish Misfortune*

1985 Dan Wakefield, *Selling Out*

1986

1986 Ann Beattie, "Summer People"

1986 Eleanor Clark, *Camping Out*

1986 Linda Collins, *Going to See the Leaves*

1986 B. Comfort, *Phoebe's Knee*

1986 Elisabeth Hyde, *Her Native Colors*

1986 Craig Nova, *The Congressman's Daughter*

1987

1987 Miriam Borgenicht, *Booked for Death*

1987 Bret Easton Ellis, *The Rules of Attraction*

1987 Frank Bryan and Bill Mares, *Out! The Vermont Secession Book*

1987 Castle Freeman, Jr., *The Bride of Ambrose and Other Stories*

1987 Bret Lott, *The Man Who Owned Vermont*

1987 Stephen Morris, *Beyond Yonder*

1987 Margaret A. Robinson, *Courting Emma Howe*

1987 Alison Smith, *Rising*

1987 Wallace Stegner, *Crossing to Safety*

1988

1988 Peter Abrahams, *Hard Rain*

1988 Jeff Danziger, *Teed Stories*

1988 Gerald A. Hinckley, *The Great Green Mountain Horn Hunt*

1988 Ellen Lesser, *The Other Woman*

1988 Archer Mayor, *Open Season*

1988 Don Metz, *Catamount Bridge*

1988 Mary McGarry Morris, *Vanished*

1988 Christopher Noël, *Hazard and the Five Delights*

1988 E. Annie Proulx, *Heart Songs*

1988 James Robison, *The Illustrator*

1988 Dorothy Sucher, *Dead Men Don't Give Seminars*

1988 Thomas Sullivan, *The Phases of Harry Moon*

1989

1989 B. Comfort, *Grave Consequences*

1989 Frederick Forsyth, *The Negotiator*

1989 Nancy Thayer, *My Dearest Friend*

1989 Tami Hoag, *Mismatch*

1989 Ann Hood, *Three-Legged Horse*

1989 David Huddle, *The High Spirits: Stories of Men and Women*

1989 Joseph Koenig, *Smuggler's Notch*

1989 Ellen Lesser, *The Shoplifter's Apprentice*

1989 Stephen Morris, *The King of Vermont*

1989 Howard Frank Mosher, A Stranger in the Kingdom
1989 Howard A. Norman, Kiss in the Hotel Joseph
      Conrad and Other Stories
1990
1990 Lisa Alther, Bedrock
1990 George V. Higgins, Victories
1990 Ward Just, Twenty-One Selected Stories
1990 Stephen King, The Stand
1990 Anne McAllister, Imagine
1990 Evelyn Wilde Mayerson, Well and Truly
1990 Archer Mayor, Borderlines
1990 Don Metz, King of the Mountain
1990 Wallace Stegner, Collected Stories
1991
1991 Chris Bohjalian, Hangman
1991 Ned and Yanna Brandt, Land Kills
1991 Joan Chase, "The Harrier"
1991 William Heffernan, Blood Rose
1991 Mary McGarry Morris, A Dangerous Woman
1991 Alix Wilber, The Wives' Tale
1992
1992 Chris Bohjalian, Past the Bleachers
1992 David Budbill, Judevine: A Play
1992 Gloria Dank, As the Sparks Fly Upward
1992 Sebastian Faulks, A Fool's Alphabet
1992 Judith Kelman, The House on the Hill
1992 Reeve Lindbergh, The Names of the Mountains
1992 Archer Mayor, Scent of Evil
1992 Anne McAllister, MacKenzie's Baby
1992 Jay Parini, Bay of Arrows
1992 E. Annie Proulx, Postcards
1992 Donna Tartt, The Secret History
1993
1993 Joseph Bruchac, Dawn Land
1993 B. Comfort, The Cashmere Kid
1993 Barbara Delinsky, Suddenly
1993 Jane Haddam, Stillness in Bethlehem
1993 David Huddle, Intimates
1993 Garrison Keillor, "Christmas in Vermont"
1993 Archer Mayor, The Skeleton's Knee
1993 Howard Frank Mosher, Where the Rivers
      Flow North
1993 Carla Neggers, Finders Keepers
1993 Elinor Spielberg, Uninvited Daughters
1993 Donald E. Westlake, Don't Ask
1993 Paul Wilkes, Temptations
1993 Ted Wood, Snowjob

1994
1994 Abbey Pen Baker, In the Dead of Winter
1994 Joseph A. Citro, Deus-X: The Reality Conspiracy
1994 Robin Cook, Fatal Cure
1994 David Mamet, The Village
1994 Archer Mayor, Fruits of the Poisonous Tree
1994 Howard Frank Mosher, Northern Borders
1994 Faye Smith Moulton, Witch's Child
1994 Diana Ramsay, Killing Words
1994 Sherry Roberts, Maud's House
1994 Ajay Sahgal, Pool
1995
1995 Laurie Alberts, "Dealing"
1995 Elaine Barbieri, "Winter Moon"
1995 Chris Bohjalian, Water Witches
1995 Joseph Bruchac, Long River
1995 B. Comfort, Elusive Quarry
1995 Thomas C. Davis, The Duval Conspiracy
1995 Michael Green, Dry Skull Dreams
1995 Ursula Hegi, Salt Dancers
1995 William Jaspersohn, Native Angels
1995 William Kritlow, Crimson Snow
1995 Gail Link, There Never Was a Time
1995 Archer Mayor, The Dark Root
1995 Mary McGarry Morris, Songs in
      Ordinary Time
1995 Jack Noon, The Big Fish of Barston Falls
1995 John Prendergast, Jump
1995 Rowland E. Robinson, Danvis Tales
1995 Abigail Stone, Recipes from the Dump
1996
1996 Glenda Adams, The Tempest of Clemenza
1996 Dean Albarelli, Cheaters and Other Stories
1996 Laurie Alberts, The Price of Land in Shelby
1996 Geoffrey Becker, Bluestown
1996 Pamela Burford, His Secret Side
1996 David Drake, Patriots
1996 Margaret Erhart, Old Love
1996 Edith Forbes, Nowle's Passing
1996 Shirley Jackson, Just an Ordinary Day
1996 William Jaspersohn, Lake Effect
1996 David Leitz, Casting in Dead Water,
      Dying to Fly-Fish
1996 Archer Mayor, The Ragman's Memory
1996 Carla Neggers, Finding You
1996 Anna Salter, Shiny Water
1996 Susan Fromberg Schaeffer, The Golden Rope

1996   Chuck Wachtel, "The Eye"

1996   Nancy Means Wright, *Mad Season*

1997

1997   Robert Bingham, "Marriage is Murder"

1997   Jon Boorstin, *Pay or Play*

1997   Joan Connor, *Here on Old Route 7*

1997   Nicholas Delbanco, *Old Scores*

1997   Barbara Delinsky, *Three Wishes*

1997   Earl Faine, *Green Mountain Man: The Odyssey of Ethan Allen*

1997   Castle Freeman, Jr., *Judgment Hill*

1997   Lee Dana Goodman, *Dunster Revealed*

1997   Douglas Hobbie, *This Time Last Year*

1997   David Leitz, *Fly-Fishing Can Be Fatal*

1997   Archer Mayor, *Bellows Falls*

1998

1998   Phil Austin, *On Bethel Ridge*

1998   Philip Baruth, *The Dream of the White Village*

1998   Chris Bohjalian, *Midwives*

1998   Joseph Bruchac, *The Waters Between*

1998   Joseph A. Citro, *Shadow Child*

1998   B. Comfort, *A Pair for the Queen*

1998   Richard S. Conde, *Shelburne, Vermont*

1998   David Gates, *Preston Falls*

1998   Daniel Hecht, *Skull Session*

1998   Kathryn Kramer, *Sweet Water*

1998   Peter Lefcourt, *The Woody*

1998   Elinor Lipman, *The Inn at Lake Devine*

1998   Archer Mayor, *The Disposable Man*

1998   Jack Noon, *Old Sam's Thunder*

1998   Freya North, *Polly*

1998   Dalia Pagani, *Mercy Road*

1998   Bernadette Pruitt, *The Man Next Door*

1998   Philip Russell, *Body and Blood*

1998   Anna Salter, *Fault Lines*

1998   Mira Stout, *One Thousand Chestnut Trees*

1998   Tom Wicker, *Easter Lilly*

1998   Nancy Means Wright, *Harvest of Bones*

1999

1999   Tricia Bauer, *Hollywood & Hardwood*

1999   Chris Bohjalian, *The Law of Similars*

1999   Joseph A. Citro, *Guardian Angels*

1999   Susan M. Dodd, "What I Remember Now"

1999   T. Greenwood, *Breathing Water*

1999   Jay Kendall, *The Secret Keepers*

1999   Charles Mathes, *The Girl at the End of the Line*

1999   Archer Mayor, *Occam's Razor*

1999   Howard Frank Mosher, *The Fall of the Year*

1999   Jenny Offill, *Last Things*

1999   Danielle Steele, *Granny Dan*

1999   Mark T. Sullivan, *Ghost Dance*

1999   Mark Sumner, *News from the Edge*

1999   Dana Yeaton, *Mad River Rising*

1999   Christy Yorke, *Magic Spells*

2000

2000   Chris Bohjalian, *The Trans-Sister Radio*

2000   Joseph A. Citro, *The Gore*

2000   Joan Connor, *We Who Live Apart*

2000   Gail Crease, *The Dream Spinner*

2000   Rebecca Gilman, *Spinning into Butter*

2000   William Heffernan, *Beulah Hill*

2000   David Huddle, *Not: A Trio*

2000   Mary Alice Kruesi, *One Summer's Night*

2000   David Leitz, *Hooked on Death*

2000   Steve Martin, *Shopgirl*

2000   Archer Mayor, *The Marble Mask*

2000   Daniel A. Neary, Jr., *Rage in the Hills*

2000   Carla Neggers, *The Waterfall*

2000   Tom Paine, "Unapproved Minutes of the Carthage, Vermont, Zoning Board of Adjustment"

2000   Suzi Pizzuti, *Raising Cain...and His Sisters*

2000   Eric Rickstad, *Reap*

2000   Anna Salter, *White Lies*

2000   John Sedgwick, *The Dark House*

2000   Lynn Stegner, *Pipers at the Gates of Dawn*

2000   Larry Watson, *Laura*

2000   Nancy Means Wright, *Poison Apples*

2001

2001   Don Bredes, *Cold Comfort*

2001   Michael Burns, *Gemini*

2001   Joseph A. Citro, *Lake Monsters*

2001   Brad Kessler, *The Woodcutter's Christmas*

2001   Jeffrey Lent, *In the Fall*

2001   Archer Mayor, *Tucker Peak*

2001   Sue Miller, *The World Below*

2001   Howard Frank Mosher, "Second Sight"

2001   Joseph Olshan, *In Clara's Hands*

2001   Philip Singerman, *Proof Positive*

2001   Charles Richard Webb, *New Cardiff*

2002

2002   Charlotte Vale Allen, *Grace Notes*

2002   Paul Auster, *The Book of Illusions*

2002   Madison Smartt Bell, *Anything Goes*

2002   **Jason Berger,** *Forested Moments*
2002   **Chris Bohjalian,** *The Buffalo Soldier*
2002   **Peter Collinson,** *The Northeast Kingdom*
2002   **Arnaldo Correa,** *Spy's Fate*
2002   **Art Corriveau,** *Housewrights*
2002   **Barbara Dimmick,** *Heart-Side Up*
2002   **Basil Douros,** *The Roots of the Blackthorn Tree*
2002   **Elizabeth Doyle,** *A Country Christmas*
2002   **Frederick Fenn,** *Journey to Common Ground*
2002   **Castle Freeman, Jr.,** *My Life and Adventures*
2002   **David Huddle,** *La Tour Dreams of the Wolf Girl*
2002   **Maria Hummel,** *Wilderness Run*
2002   **Elizabeth Inness-Brown,** *Burning Marguerite*
2002   **Roger King,** *A Girl from Zanzibar*
2002   **Wendi W. Lee,** *Habeas Campus*
2002   **Michael Lowenthal,** *Avoidance*
2002   **Kate Manning,** *White Girl*
2002   **Kirk Martin,** *Shade of the Maple*
2002   **Archer Mayor,** *The Sniper's Wife*
2002   **Joseph M. Nassise,** *Riverwatch*
2002   **Francine Prose,** *Blue Angel*
2002   **Claudia Ricci,** *Dreaming Maples*
2002   **Nora Roberts,** *Cordina's Crown Jewel*
2002   **Anna Salter,** *Prison Blues*
2002   **Sharon Snow Sirois,** *Sawyer's Crossing*
2002   **Annie Smith,** *Home Again*
2002   **Anne Stuart,** *Still Lake*
2002   **John Updike,** *Seek My Face*
2002   **Kevin Wignall,** *People Die*
2002   **Suzi Wizowaty,** *The Round Barn*
2002   **Nancy Means Wright,** *Stolen Honey,* "Fire and Ice"
2002   **Edra Ziesk,** *A Cold Spring*

2003

2003   **T. Alan Broughton,** *Suicidal Tendencies*
2003   **Christopher Golden,** *The Gathering Dark*
2003   **Thomas Christopher Greene,** *Mirror Lake*
2003   **Sue Halpern,** *The Book of Hard Things*
2003   **Mary Hays,** *Learning to Drive*
2003   **Siri Hustvedt,** *What I Loved*
2003   **Jonathan Lethem,** *The Fortress of Solitude*
2003   **Patricia MacDonald,** *Suspicious Origin*
2003   **Archer Mayor,** *Gatekeeper*
2003   **Richard Mindell,** *Eden Falls*
2003   **Howard Frank Mosher,** *The True Account*
2003   **Jodi Picoult,** *Second Glance*
2003   **Deborah Schupack,** *The Boy on the Bus*

2003   **Sarah Stewart Taylor,** *O'Artful Death*
2003   **Nancy Tesler,** *Slippery Slopes & Other Deadly Things*

2004

2004   **Chris Bohjalian,** *Before You Know Kindness*
2004   **Mary Higgins Clark** and **Carol Higgins Clark,** *The Christmas Thief*
2004   **Jennifer Greene,** *Wild in the Moment*
2004   **Emma Holly,** *The Night Owl*
2004   **James Howard Kunstler,** *Maggie Darling*
2004   **Karen Latuchie,** *The Honey Wall*
2004   **Julius Lester,** *The Autobiography of God*
2004   **Archer Mayor,** *The Surrogate Thief*
2004   **Don Mitchell,** *The Nature Notebooks*
2004   **Howard Frank Mosher,** *Waiting for Teddy Williams*
2004   **Craig Nova,** *Cruisers*
2004   **John Rickards,** *The Touch of Ghosts*
2004   **Maggie Shayne,** *Colder Than Ice*
2004   **Harry Sholk,** *Drumbeats in the Valley*

2005

2005   **Horatio Alger,** *Madeline, the Temptress*
2005   **Mary Beth Bass,** *Follow Me*
2005   **Don Bredes,** *The Fifth Season*
2005   **Thomas Brennan,** *The Debt*
2005   **Willis T. Crossman,** *Willis T. Crossman's Vermont*
2005   **J.E. Fender,** *On the Spur of Speed*
2005   **Christine Flynn,** *Going Home Trilogy*
2005   **Valerie Frankel,** *The Girlfriend Curse*
2005   **Thomas Christopher Greene,** *I'll Never Be Gone Long*
2005   **Pam Lewis,** *Speak Softly, She Can Hear*
2005   **Archer Mayor,** *St. Albans Fire*
2005   **Mary McGarry Morris,** *The Lost Mother*
2005   **Carla Neggers,** *Dark Sky*
2005   **Christopher Noël,** *A Frail House*
2005   **Katherine Hall Page,** *The Body in the Snowdrift*
2005   **Victoria Vinton,** *The Jungle Law*
2005   **Scott Wolven,** *Controlled Burn*
2005   **Nancy Means Wright,** *Mad Cow Nightmare*

APPENDIX C:
Authors Living in Vermont, part-time or full-time

A

Laurie Alberts, Westminster
Clifford Lindsey Alderman, Middlebury
Lisa Alther, Burlington
Paul Auster, West Townshend

B

Irving Bacheller, Salisbury
Abbey Pen Baker, Putney and Saxtons River
Philip Baruth, Burlington
Ann Beattie, Plainfield and Middlebury
Jason Berger, Colchester
Chris Bohjalian, Lincoln
Ned and Yanna Brandt, Brattleboro
Don Bredes, Wheelock
T. Alan Broughton, Burlington
Frank Bryan, Starksboro
Perdita Buchan, Wilmington, Marlboro
Pearl Buck, Danby
David Budbill, Wolcott
Frederick Buechner, West Rupert
Michael Burns, St. Johnsbury

C

Carl M. Chapin, Manchester
Joan Chase, Brattleboro
Steve Chontos, West Dover
Joseph A. Citro, Burlington
Eleanor Clark, Stratton
Sarah N. Cleghorn, Manchester
Judith Beth Cohen, Plainfield
Barbara Comfort, Londonderry
Richard S. Conde, Manchester
Edward J. Connolly, Wilmington and Halifax
Joan Connor, Belmont
Art Corriveau, East Barre
Willis T. Crossman, North Montpelier

D

Jeff Danziger, Plainfield
Deane C. Davis, Barre
Thomas C. Davis, Barre

Nicholas Delbanco, Bennington
Barbara Dimmick, South reading, Weathersfield, and Norwich
Julia Dorr, Rutland
Robert Luther Duffus, Waterbury

E

Dikkon Eberhart, Thetford and East Burke

F

Frederick Fenn, Springfield
Dorothy Canfield Fisher, Arlington
Edith Forbes, East Thetford
Castle Freeman, Jr., Newfane
Mary E. Wilkins Freeman, Brattleboro
Frances Frost, St. Albans
Len Fulton, Jeffersonville

G

John Gardner, Bennington
Lee Dana Goodman, Windsor
Peter Gould, Brattleboro
Michael Green
Anne Katharine Greene, Poultney
Thomas Christopher Greene, Montpelier
T. Greenwood, St. Johnsbury

H

Sue Halpern, Ripton
Emory James Haynes, Cabot
Mary Hays, Corinth
Daniel Hecht, East Montpelier
William Heffernan, Huntington
Gerald A. Hinckley, Williamstown
Lester Eugene Hood, West Hartford
Barbara Howes, North Pownal
David Huddle, Burlington
Maria Hummel, Underhill
Zephine Humphrey, Dorset
Siri Hustvedt, West Townshend

I

Elizabeth Inness-Brown, South Hero

J

Samuel Alexander Jackson, South Ryegate
Shirley Jackson, North Bennington
William Jaspersohn, Johnson
Arthur F. Joy, East Wallingford
Margaret H. Judd, East Barre
Ward Just, Warren

K

Clarence Budington Kelland, Wilmington
Jay Kendall, Newport
Louise Andrews Kent, Berlin
Brad Kessler, Sandgate
Francis Parkinson Keyes, Newbury
Rudyard Kipling, Dummerston
Kathryn Kramer, Middlebury

L

David Leitz, Guilford
Jeffrey Lent, Tunbridge
Ellen Lesser, Brookfield
Pam Lewis, Montpelier, Middlesex
Sinclair Lewis, Barnard
Reeve Lindbergh, Passumpsic
Florence Bingham Livingston, Burlington

M

Bernard Malamud, Bennington
David Mamet, Cabot
Bill Mares, Burlington
Kirk Martin, Northfield
Evelyn Wilde Mayerson, Manchester
Archer Mayor, Newfane
Elliott Merrick, Craftsbury
Ruth Tracy Millard, Strafford
Sue Miller, Strafford
Richard Mindell, Jericho
Don Mitchell, Vergennes
Mary McGarry Morris, Rutland
Stephen Morris, Randolph
Howard Frank Mosher, Irasburg
Faye Smith Moulton, Rutland

N

Daniel A. Neary, Jr., East Montpelier
Carla A. Neggers, Quechee
Jack Newcombe, Burlington
John Nichols, Montpelier
Christopher Noël, East Calais
Howard A. Norman, Calais
Craig Nova, Putney

O

Joseph Olshan, Barnard

P

Dalia Pagani, Thetford
Tom Paine, Middlebury
Jay Parini, Weybridge
Robert Newton Peck

Theodora Peck, Burlington
William Dudley Pelley, St. Johnsbury
Bliss Perry, Greensboro
J.L Pratt, West Berkshire
E. Annie Proulx, Vershire

R

Diana Ramsay, Middlebury
Franklin D. Reeve, Wilmington
Eric Rickstad, Shelburne
Sherry Roberts, South Burlington
Rowland E. Robinson, Ferrisburgh
Cyrus Dustian Roys
Philip Russell, Wells

S

Anna Salter, Middlebury
Susan Fromberg Schaeffer, South Newfane
Karl Schwenke, Newbury
Lucy Jameson Scott, Irasburg
Philip Singerman, northern Vermont
Elinor Spielberg, Chelsea
Lynn Stegner, Greensboro
Wallace Stegner, Greensboro
Abigail Stone, Goshen and Middlebury
Anne Stuart, Greensboro
Dorothy Sucher, Cabot
Mark T. Sullivan, Rutland

T

Sarah Stewart Taylor, Hartland
Douglas Terman, East Warren
Daniel Pierce Thompson, Montpelier
Mari Tomasi, Montpelier

U

William Hazlett Upson, Ripton

V

Frederic Van de Water, Dummerston

W

Mildred Walker, Grafton
Maggie Wall, northern Vermont
Mary Ella Waller, Bethel
Homer White, Weathersfield
Tom Wicker, Rochester
Edward Williams, Ferrisburgh
Suzi Wizowaty, Burlington
Nancy Means Wright, Cornwall

Y

Dana Yeaton, Middlebury

INDEX 1:
Real Places, alphabetically

Index 1

INDEX 2:
Fictitious Places,
alphabetically by region

Index 2

Central Vermont

(Addison, Orange, Washington counties)

Southern Vermont

(Bennington, Rutland, Windham, Windsor counties)

Index 2

INDEX 3:
Titles, alphabetically

Index 3

Index 3

Index 4